# Romans

*Deliverance from Wrath*

# Romans

## Deliverance from Wrath

Zane C. Hodges

Edited by Robert N. Wilkin
Introduction and Selected Notes by John H. Niemelä

Grace Evangelical Society
Denton, Texas 76202

Copyright © 2013, 2022 by Grace Evangelical Society

4851 S I-35 E, Suite 203
Corinth, TX 76210
www.faithalone.org
ges@faithalone.org
940-270-8827

**Library of Congress Cataloging in Publication Data**

Hodges, Zane Clark (1932-2008).
*Romans: Deliverance from Wrath*
Bibliography: p.
1. Salvation. 2. Faith. 3. Romans.
I. Bible. II. Romans

ISBN: 978-1-943399-45-1

Editor: Robert N. Wilkin

Introduction and Selected Notes: John H. Niemelä

Design: Shawn Lazar

Translation of Romans by Zane C. Hodges.

*Printed in the United States of America.*

*For I am not ashamed of the gospel of Christ, since it is the power of God for deliverance for everyone who believes, both for the Jew first and for the Greek (Romans 1:16).*

# Contents

# Abbreviations

| | |
|---|---|
| AB | Anchor Bible |
| BDAG | Bauer, Danker, Arndt, and Gingrich. *A Greek-English Lexicon of the New Testament and Other Early Christian Literature* |
| BDF | Blass, Debrunner, Funk. *A Greek Grammar of the New Testament and Other Early Christian Literature* |
| BECNT | The Baker Exegetical Commentary on the New Testament |
| DTS | Dallas Theological Seminary |
| ESV | English Standard Version |
| Gk. | Greek |
| GWT | Great White Throne |
| HALAT | Walter Baumgartner, Ludwig Koehler, and Johan Jacob Stamm, eds., *Hebräisches und aramäisches Lexicon zum Alten Testament* |
| HCSB | Holman Christian Standard Bible |
| Heb | Hebrew |
| ICC | International Critical Commentary |
| JB | Jerusalem Bible |
| *JETS* | *Journal of the Evangelical Theological Society* |
| JHN | John H. Niemelä |
| *JOTGES* | *Journal of the Grace Evangelical Society* |

| | |
|---|---|
| KJV | The Authorized King James Version |
| LXX | The Septuagint |
| MajT | Majority Text of the Greek NT |
| MT | Masoretic Text |
| NA/UBS | Nestle-Aland/United Bible Societies Greek NT |
| NACE | New Advent Catholic Encyclopedia |
| NASB | New American Standard Bible |
| NET | New English Translation |
| NICNT | New International Commentary on the New Testament |
| NIDNTT | New International Dictionary of New Testament Theology |
| NIV | New International Version |
| NKJV | New King James Version |
| NRSV | New Revised Standard Version |
| NT | New Testament |
| OT | Old Testament |
| OTQNT | Old Testament Quotations in the New Testament: A Complete Survey |
| OxD | Oxford Dictionary of English |
| PNTC | Pillar New Testament Commentary |
| REB | Revised English Bible |
| RNW | Robert N. Wilkin |
| TDNT | Theological Dictionary of the New Testament |
| WBC | Word Biblical Commentary |
| ZCH | Zane C. Hodges |

# Foreword

## About the Author

Z ane C. Hodges went to be with the Lord in November of 2008, after suffering a major heart attack. He was seventy-six.

As a young boy of around ten, living in Pennsylvania, Zane came to faith in Christ through the witness of his parents. He showed a zeal for the Word of God that led him to Wheaton College and Dallas Theological Seminary, where he majored in New Testament Greek.

A few months after graduating from DTS, in the summer of 1958, Zane was hired to work in the DTS library. Less than a year later, he was hired to teach Greek, which he did for twenty-seven years. For a short time he was the Department Chairman, but he decided that it demanded too much of his time and so he gave up that position to Dr. Harold Hoehner.

While teaching at DTS, Zane wrote and published three books: *The Hungry Inherit*, *The Gospel under Siege*, and *Grace in Eclipse*. During those twenty-seven years he also released his work on textual criticism, *The Greek New Testament According to the Majority Text*, which he co-edited with the late Dr. Art Farstad. He was also the author of the commentaries on Hebrews and 1-3 John in DTS's *The Bible Knowledge Commentary*, published in 1983.

After leaving DTS in 1986, Zane lived for another twenty-two years. During that time he wrote many more books, including *Absolutely Free! A Biblical Reply to Lordship Salvation*, and commentaries on James, Second Peter, and the Johannine Epistles. By the time of his death, he had nearly completed this commentary on Romans.

Zane ministered for fifty years at a small Hispanic Plymouth Brethren assembly in East Dallas, Victor Street Bible Chapel. There he honed his skills as a communicator and as a shepherd. Those skills are evident in this commentary.

## About the Commentary

This commentary is the product of several years of daily labor. Zane spent four hours each weekday morning working on it. He rarely took phone calls during those hours. And every few weeks we would eat a late lunch together because he would work until nearly 1 p.m. each day.

Before he died, he had completed the commentary through to Rom 14:15. Despite it being a first draft, it was largely free from errors. Consequently, very little editing has been done on what Zane wrote except for correcting occasional typos and inadvertent variations in his translation and outline. The outline, the translation, and the commentary itself are all outstanding.

First, Zane's outline of Romans is remarkable. While it has similar divisions of other commentaries, his explanation of the sections is unique. His outline makes it much easier to follow the flow of the book. Zane had a gift for discerning the structure of an author's argument.

Second, Zane's translation of Romans alone makes the commentary invaluable. His translation choices are insightful and thought-provoking even without the associated commentary. As an example, consider his rendering of the Greek word *katakrima* in Rom 5:18. It is normally translated as *condemnation*: "through one man's offense *judgment* came to all men resulting in condemnation." By contrast, Zane translates it as *servitude to sin*: "through one offense *judgment came* to all men to produce *servitude to sin*."

The same word occurs in Rom 8:1, which Zane translates as: "Therefore there is now no *servitude to sin* for those who are in Christ Jesus, who do not walk in relation to the flesh but in relation to the Spirit." That leads to a significantly different understanding than one gets from "There is therefore no *condemnation* to those who are in Christ Jesus, who do not walk according to the flesh, but according to the Spirit."

Along with these subtle, but important, insights I should also mention Zane's understanding of the words *save* and *salvation* (*sōzō* and *sōtēria*). Most commentators understand references to salvation soteriologically, as deliverance from eternal condemnation in the lake of fire. But Zane understood those words to refer to *temporal deliverance* from God's wrath *in this life*. This impacts the way one understands practically everything in the letter. Rather than being an evangelistic tract, Zane believed that Romans was better understood as instruction given to Christians showing them how to have abundant fellowship with God.

Third, Zane's exposition is both deeply pastoral and expositional. He does not, as many commentators do, treat each verse or paragraph in an isolated way, but instead links the discussion of verses, paragraphs, and sections to the flow of the entire letter.

## Completing the Legacy

I was chosen to complete the commentary from Rom 14:16 to the end of the book. The reason why was simply because Zane was my mentor both in seminary (1980–85) and to the end of his life (1985–2008). He convinced me that his understanding of Romans was correct. And I am convinced that he would be in basic agreement with all I have written.

In terms of footnotes, Zane had only written a handful before he died. Those notes have the initials ZCH after them. He had planned to add additional scholarly notes after he completed the first draft, so we enlisted John Niemelä (Ph.D. in NT from DTS), whom Zane also mentored, to write them. All of John's notes have his initials (JHN) after them. As Zane had not completed an introduction before his death, we asked John to write that as well. He also assisted in the proofing of the entire manuscript.

Footnotes which carry the initials RNW were written by me.

The author is routinely called *Hodges* in the footnotes. Everyone who knew him outside of seminary called him *Zane*. They did not call him *Professor Hodges, Dr. Hodges* (he intentionally avoided getting a doctorate, in great part due to his Brethren convictions), *Pastor Hodges*, or the like. Everyone knew him as Zane. While we toyed with simply referring to him as *Zane* in the notes, we decided on the more formal designation since many readers will be unaware of Zane's preference and they might think it disrespectful if we regularly used his first name.

Abbreviations have been kept to a minimum. Zane repeatedly cited the leading lexicon on the NT, which is called BDAG after its four authors and editors, Bauer, Danker, Arndt, and Gingrich. A list of abbreviations used is included (see above).

The first time any work is cited, we give full bibliographic information. After the first citation, we simply give the author's last name, an abbreviated title, and the page number(s) cited.

There is a bibliography at the end of the work that lists all the works he cited. The list is not as long as it would have been had Zane not died prematurely because he had planned to do additional research after he completed the first draft. His writing style was to exegete a book on his own and only after that consult the views of a few key authors. He would then write the commentary. Once completed, he would add in additional references that he deemed helpful.

In this commentary we put Zane's translation of the verse(s) to be discussed in bold before his discussion. Then in his discussion any words from the verse(s) in question are bolded the first time he cites them. In this way the reader can easily see when he is discussing words from the text. Second references to the same phrase are italicized to aid the reader. Of course, italics are also used for emphasis, so the reader should be aware that italics may signal either words from the material under discussion or something Zane is emphasizing.

If Zane's translation has something italicized, as when he supplies a word or words for clarity, then it will appear as bold and italics the first time it is mentioned. If something in his translation is in quotation marks, then the quotation marks will also appear in the first mention.

Any time Zane quotes material from Romans outside of the verse(s) under immediate discussion, it is put within quotation marks and is not bolded or italicized (unless Zane italicized it in his translation). All quotations of Scripture within Romans are from Zane's translation unless he is comparing his translation with other versions. Quotations of verses outside of Romans are from the NKJV unless otherwise noted.

It is my opinion that anyone who reads this commentary carefully and prayerfully will be greatly edified in his or her personal life. This is not merely some academic tome. It is a very practical work. As I edited this work I found myself being deeply moved by what I was reading. I have never read a more powerful, scholarly, or practical commentary.

—Bob Wilkin
December 2012

# Introduction[1]

## Authorship

The evidence that Paul wrote Romans is so compelling that even liberal scholars acknowledge him to be its author. Indeed, not only does Paul name himself as the author in the first verse of Romans, just as he does in each of his other NT epistles, but 2 Thess 3:17 says that he signs his name in every letter. Moreover, the various ancient lists of canonical NT books all affirm the epistle's Pauline origins. And while Rom 16:22 says the epistle was *written* by Tertius, given the evidence that Paul suffered from poor eyesight (Gal 6:11), Tertius was most likely a secretary who inscribed a papyrus scroll as Paul dictated the book to him.

## Destination and Recipients

### The Readership Were Roman Believers

Romans 1:7 identifies its recipients as believers living in Rome. Paul speaks of them as already summoned by God to be saints, whose faith is proclaimed throughout the whole world (v 8). Hence, this book focuses on issues concerning *believers*, a fact overlooked by those who use the

---

[1] Editor's note: Zane Hodges had not yet written an introduction to this commentary before he died. The outline of Romans (appended to the Introduction) is that of Zane Hodges. The rest of this introduction was written by Dr. John H. Niemelä, a former student and friend of Hodges. All footnotes in the Introduction are by John Niemelä, except for those that begin with *Editor's note*. A more detailed consideration of much that appears in this Introduction is available in John H. Niemelä, "Evidence for a First Century 'Tenement Church," *JOTGES* 24 (Spring 2011): 99-116.

so-called *Romans Road* to inform unbelievers of the importance of believing in Christ.[2] Paul would be shocked to learn that his message for believers would be construed as a message for unbelievers. John's Gospel, not Romans, is the book God designed for unbelievers (cf. John 20:30-31).

Much interpretive confusion will be avoided if we understand that the term *gospel* should not be viewed as a technical term that is interchangeable with the message of life to unbelievers.[3] Neither should *salvation* be seen in Romans as a technical term for sparing someone from the lake of fire. And while Paul sought to proclaim good news (*to preach the gospel*) to the Roman believers (Rom 1:15), this was not the message of everlasting life, which they had already believed. Rather, this good news concerned how the application of God's Word in their daily lives would deliver them from God's temporal wrath (Rom 1:16). The commentary develops this good news for believers in detail.

## The Readership Included Jewish Believers

Besides specifying that the readers were Roman believers, the book also speaks of their ethnic diversity.

Some named recipients were Jewish, as was Aquila (Rom 16:3; cf. Acts 18:2). Verses 7 and 11 of Romans 16 identify Andronicus, Junius, and Herodion as Paul's *kinsmen*, which suggests they too were Jewish.

The letter itself directly addresses Jews in Rom 2:17*ff.* Furthermore, unless the use of *our* in 4:1, 12 was purely editorial (referring to Paul alone),[4] the natural implication of Paul speaking of Abraham as *our father* is that Jews were among the original readership.

---

[2] Steve Elkins, *The Roman Road Revisited: New Vistas on the Road to Resurrection Living* (Dallas, TX: Allie Grace, 2005) shows that the proper use of the Romans Road is for putting believers on the path of progressive sanctification.

[3] A most cursory reading of Romans demonstrates this. In Rom 1:15 Paul announces his intention "to preach the gospel to you who are in Rome," but in v 7 he called them *saints*. Clearly, *gospel* cannot be restricted narrowly to the message of life for unbelievers.

[4] As the section (on this page) "The Readership Included Jewish Believers," argues, Paul uses first person plural pronouns (*we, our, us*) for Jews, but *you* and *your* for Gentiles. The idea of an editorial *we* would be that Paul did not intend anyone besides himself, which is contrary to established usage in Romans that *we* refers to other Jews as well. Oddly enough, in Romans 7, many scholars imagine that Paul does not include himself when he repeatedly says "I."

### The Readership Included Gentile Believers

But as Paul used first person plural pronouns (*we, our, us*) in Romans to associate himself with those readers who were Jewish (e.g., Rom 4:1, 12), Paul uses second person plural pronouns (*you* and *your*) to refer to Gentile readers. In essence, he said *we* (*Jews*), but *you* (*Gentiles*). Specifically, Rom 11:13 says, "For I speak to you Gentiles; inasmuch as I am an apostle to the Gentiles, I magnify my ministry." Romans 9–11 presents Paul as a Jewish apostle to the Gentiles, with deep concerns for his fellow countrymen (cf. Rom 9:1*ff.*; 10:1*ff.*; 11:14). In expressing this, he urged any Gentile readers to share God's heart for the Jews (Rom 11:20-25).

### The Readers Attended Fifteen or More Separate Congregations

Zane Hodges especially appreciated Robert Jewett for his work on the Roman tenement church.[5] Jewett helped conceptualize the multiplicity of congregations in Rome as a blend of tenement churches and house churches, with the tenement church predominating in Rome. These two issues challenge common assumptions about the constituency and size of the original audience for Romans.

Paul greets fifteen distinct groups of believers in Rom 16:3-15. Each use of *aspazomai* ("greet") distinguishes an autonomous assembly.[6]

The first church mentioned met in a home: "Greet Pricilla and Aquila...[and] the church that is in their house" (Rom 16:3-5). None of the others listed are specifically said to meet in a house. Probably most or all of the other fourteen listed churches met in tiny tenement rooms (about 10 feet by 10 feet). Hence, these are referred to as *tenement churches* (in contrast with larger *house churches*).[7]

Though Paul had not been to Rome, he was acquainted with a host of people there, having met (during his various missionary journeys) many of those he mentions. For example, Acts 18:2, 18, and 26 document Priscilla and Aquila's prior association with Paul in Corinth and Ephesus (March to September AD 52). They traveled extensively[8] and remained

---

[5] Robert Jewett, assisted by Roy D. Kotansky, *Romans: A Commentary*, ed. Eldon Jay Epp, Hermeneia (Minneapolis, MN: Fortress, 2007), 55-88.

[6] The fifteen uses are Rom 16:3, 5, 6, 7, 8, 9, 10 (2×), 11 (2×), 12 (2×), 13, 14, 15.

[7] Cf. Jewett, *Romans*, 64-66.

[8] Aquila was born in Pontus (Acts 18:2); he and his wife Priscilla lived in Rome until the

associated with him whether when accompanying Paul or when separated from him.

Comments Paul made about various individuals show or imply that he had met them. Concerning Mary (Gk. *Mariam*) he says that "she labored much for us" (Rom 16:6). About Tryphena, Tryphosa, and the beloved Persis he says they "labored [much] in the Lord" (Rom 16:12).

He calls Andronicus and Junia his "fellow prisoners," which may mean that they and he were imprisoned together. The Apostles regarded these (who believed before Paul did) as noteworthy (Rom 16:7).

Paul calls Amplias "my beloved in the Lord" (Rom 16:8) and Stachys "my beloved" (Rom 16:9). These appellations suggest that they traveled outside of Rome and spent time with Paul.

Urbanus is called by Paul his "fellow worker in Christ" (Rom 16:9), a term reserved for outstanding partnership with Paul in ministry. Such a commendation would require close association with Paul.

Scholars have sought to calculate the size of the Roman Christian population at the time,[9] using the greetings section of Romans 16 as the basis for their estimates. Paul greets more people by name here than in any other epistle, but the mention of only twenty-six congregants does not immediately suggest a large Christian community. Hence, scholarly estimates of the original audience of the epistle tend to be low—probably too low.

In AD 64, only seven years after Paul's epistle, Nero charged Christians with torching Rome. In the aftermath, Tacitus reports the condemnation of "a huge crowd" (*multitudo ingens*) of Christians.[10] If he is right, the church at Rome could hardly have been small. There is every reason to accept Tacitus' report that the church community in Rome was large by AD 64. Politicians (like Nero) needing a scapegoat do not persecute friends or small, innocuous groups, but attack perceived enemies. Although believers were not revolutionaries (cf. Rom 13:1-7), something must account for Nero blaming them, not others.

---

Claudian edict of AD 49 (Acts 18:2). He was at Corinth (Acts 18:2 and 18) and Ephesus in AD 51 (Acts 18:24-26), at Ephesus in AD 56 (1 Cor 16:19), at Rome in AD 56-57 (Rom 16:3-4), and at Ephesus again in AD 67 when 2 Timothy was written (2 Tim 4:19). The NT probably only records a fraction of this couple's extensive travels.

[9] See studies to which Jewett, *Romans*, 61, refers.

[10] Tacitus *Annals* 15.44 reports the charge against the Christians.

If Rom 16:3-15 greeted twenty-six rank-and-file members, who were key members of at least fifteen congregations, the minimum number (assuming that those with no named spouse were married) could be as small as seventy-five adults. However, four factors could expand this to a much larger community:

1. Paul seems only to greet leaders and sponsors (not congregants) of fifteen assemblies known to him.
2. Each leader (and sponsors) would meet with small congregations weekly.
3. Leaders may meet at different times and places with multiple groups a week.
4. The named leaders might not be exhaustive, but only those known to Paul.

The total number of believers in all the churches in Rome could easily have been over one thousand when Paul wrote in AD 57. Thus while traditional thinking has yielded a small original audience for Paul's letter (i.e., under one hundred), the presence of large numbers of Christians in AD 64 suggests the need to significantly increase the existing Christian population prior to Paul's letter. Certainly, the number of Christians expanded after Paul wrote Romans, but contrary to what advocates of the so-called Romans Road would say, his epistle was not designed as an evangelistic tool.

## Theme: Deliverance from Temporal Wrath

The great theme of Romans is deliverance. Romans 1:16-17 deftly summarizes this thought: "For I am not ashamed of the gospel of Christ, for it is the power of God to salvation [available] for everyone who believes, for the Jew first and also for the Greek. For in it the righteousness of God is revealed from faith to faith; as it is written, 'The just shall live by faith.'"

Unfortunately, this passage has been widely misinterpreted as if it discussed how one can be saved from the lake of fire. But the Roman believers already possessed everlasting life, and were guaranteed never to go to the lake of fire. As a book written to believers, Romans aims to present the truth that believers need to live appropriately before the Lord.

As the commentary argues, Rom 1:16-17 speaks of a temporal salvation, one that makes God's power available to believers in order to deliver them from *temporal wrath*. True, this presentation of deliverance builds on the foundation of Christ's work on the cross, and how the atonement resolved man's sin and death problem. But most treatments of Romans fail to distinguish the theme of Romans (temporal deliverance) from the foundation for the theme (everlasting life). This creates a whole host of interpretive problems.

## Date and Place of Writing

Romans 15:25-26 narrows down both the date and locale of writing: "But now I am going to Jerusalem to minister to the saints. For it pleased those from Macedonia and Achaia to make a certain contribution for the poor among the saints who are in Jerusalem."

Specifically, Paul was in Macedonia or in Achaia (Northern and Southern Greece respectively) on his way to Jerusalem with financial aid for needy believers there. Acts 20:2-4 speaks of Paul being in Greece for three months, specifically distinguishing Greece from Macedonia. Later on that same trip (Acts 20:16), Paul trimmed his itinerary in an effort to reach Jerusalem by Pentecost (May 28, AD 57). A reconstructed chronology of the third missionary journey dates his stay in Greece from late November, AD 56, to late February, AD 57. Second Corinthians 13:1 speaks of Paul planning his third trip to Corinth, while 2 Cor 9:4 warns them that he might come there with some Macedonians, people who knew that the Corinthians offered financial support for the Jerusalem saints a year earlier (2 Cor 9:2). He warns the Corinthians that embarrassment would result, if (after boasting of their generosity) they did not follow through. Paul's planned visit to Corinth would allow him to carry their sizable gift for the suffering Jerusalem saints. While there, Paul would address the many problems confronting that church. Thus, Paul probably spent the entire three months of Acts 20:3 around Corinth.

Romans 16:1-2 instructs the Roman readers to receive Phoebe, the courier who delivered the letter. She lived in Cenchrea, Corinth's eastern port. Paul wrote the epistle to the Romans from Corinth during the winter of AD 56-57. Phoebe carried it to Rome from Cenchrea. In all probability, she delivered it to Aquila and Priscilla, who had stayed in Corinth in AD 51 and who embarked for Ephesus from Phoebe's hometown, Cenchrea (Acts 18:1-19).

## Outline of Romans[11]

I. Introduction: Paul Connects with the Roman Christians (1:1-15)

  A. Doctrinal Salutation (1:1-7)

  B. Paul's Desire to Visit Rome (1:8-15)

II. Thematic Statement: The Gospel Contains
God's Power for Deliverance (1:16-17)

III. Body of the Epistle: Spiritual Deliverance Arises from
the Righteousness God Grants to Faith (1:18–15:13)

  A. God's Displeasure with Humanity Is Manifest (1:18–3:20)

    1. Humanity Stands under God's Wrath (1:18–2:5)

      a. The Declaration of This Manifestation (1:18)

      b. The Cause of This Manifestation (1:19-23)

      c. The Results of This Manifestation (1:24-32)

      d. The Universality of This Manifestation (2:1-5)

    2. Humanity Faces God's Impartial Judgment (2:6–3:20)

      a. The Nature of God's Judgment (2:6-16)

      b. The Vulnerability of the Jews (2:17-29)

      c. The Decisive Witness of Scripture
against Humanity (3:1-20)

  B. The Unrighteous Can Obtain Righteousness
Through Jesus Christ (3:21–5:11)

    1. God's Righteousness Has Been Revealed to Men (3:21-31)

      a. God's Righteousness Is Available by Faith (3:21-22a)

      b. Christ Is the Mercy Seat for All Men (3:22b-26)

      c. Faith-Righteousness Vindicates the Law (3:27-31)

    2. God's Righteousness Is Attested in the OT (4:1-25)

    3. God's Righteousness Makes Spiritual Victory Possible (5:1-11)

---

[11] Editor's note: This outline was done by Zane Hodges.

# Romans 1

I. Introduction: Paul Connects with the Roman Christians (1:1-15)

  A. Doctrinal Salutation (1:1-7)

### 1:1. Paul, a bondservant of Jesus Christ, called to be an apostle who is set apart for the gospel of God

The salutation reveals Paul's sense both of his position and of his purpose before God. Two phrases denote his position: **a bondservant of Jesus Christ** (*doulos Iēsou Christou*) and a **called... apostle** (*klētos apostolos*). The first title stresses subjection; the second stresses privilege. The word *called* (or *selected*) in particular highlights the privileged status of being an apostle. The sequence of the titles is also significant. Paul's apostolic prerogatives were always exercised in the spirit of bond service to Jesus Christ. Indeed, all true authority and privilege in the church operates only within the sphere of subjection to Christ. When carried beyond this sphere, they are mere expressions of the flesh.

A sense of position is naturally accompanied by a sense of purpose. The words **set apart** (*aphōrismenos*) indicate the special orientation of Paul's bond service and apostleship. As an apostle, his special focus was on **the gospel of God** (i.e., God the Father). The Greek verb here for *set apart* is the same one used by the Holy Spirit to call Barnabas and Saul to a new work for the gospel (Acts 13:2). On that occasion they were both separated from the rest of the company (Acts 13:1), among whom they had been laboring, for a special task that called for their full energy. As he writes now to the Roman Christians, Paul probably thinks of his being *set apart for the gospel* as a work of God's Holy Spirit. If so, the implicit reference to the Spirit makes Paul's initial self-identification in Romans Trinitarian.

**1:2. (which He promised beforehand through His prophets in the Holy Scriptures),**

The gospel for which Paul had been separated was not his own invention, nor was it even a revelation made especially for him. Instead, the gospel was **promised beforehand through** God's **prophets** of old **in the Holy Scriptures**. This is precisely the perspective taken in the book of Acts (see, for example, Acts 17:2-3; 24:14-15; 26:22-23; 28:23). In Acts, Paul persistently appealed to the OT Scriptures as giving authority to his gospel. But this viewpoint goes back to our Lord Himself (see Luke 24:25-27, 44-47). The gospel is rooted in the OT.

**1:3-4. which is about His Son, the One who came from David's seed as regards the flesh, the One who was designated as the Son of God with power, as regards the Spirit of holiness, by means of the resurrection of the dead, *namely*, Jesus Christ our Lord—**

The subject of the gospel is God's Son. But the Son whom Paul preached was a specific Person, with a specific identity. This identity is expressed here by two parallel Greek constructions that are indicated in the translation by the repeated words *the One who*. The first phrase, **the One who came from David's seed** (*tou genomenou ek spermatos Dabid*), identifies His human origin in David's royal line. The second phrase, **the One who was designated as the Son of God with power** (*tou horisthentos Huiou Theou en dunamei*), identifies Him as a divine Person who possesses mighty power.

In this twofold identification, Paul begins with a reference to the incarnation. The words *the One who came* (*tou genomenou*) might equally well be rendered "the One who *became*." This divine Person had *become* a descendant of David just as OT prophecy had specified (see Mic 5:2). But this was His human status (**as regards the flesh**). His resurrection, however, clearly disclosed a higher status that was related to God's Holy Spirit (**as regards the Spirit of holiness**).

It is striking that Paul refers to *the Spirit of holiness*, rather than simply to the Holy Spirit. (The phrase *Spirit of holiness* here is unique to Biblical

Greek.) In Romans the Holy Spirit plays a prominent role in the dynamics of Christian living (see chap. 8). He is the divine Agent, both in the resurrection of Jesus Christ and also in the "spiritual resurrection" which *enables* the Christian life (see especially Rom 8:11-13). Thus He is indeed *the Spirit of holiness* since it is He who produces holiness in Christian experience.[1] In so referring to Him here, Paul implicitly articulates a fundamental truth of this book. The Spirit who raised Jesus from the dead is the divine Source of true holiness.

**The resurrection**, Paul affirms, was the *means* by which Jesus was *designated as the Son of God with power*. The Greek verb rendered *designated* (or *appointed*) ought not to be taken in the sense of "declared" (i.e., "shown to be"), since this sense for the Greek word cannot be adequately supported. On the other hand, the text should not be read as though it simply stated that Jesus was *designated as the Son of God*, period. Instead its full force is felt only if the words *with power* are treated as part of the designation.

It is not conceivable (as some interpreters have thought) that Paul believed that Jesus was only *designated as the Son of God* at His resurrection. In fact, Jesus was so "designated" at His *baptism* (Matt 3:16-17) and at the Mount of Transfiguration (Matt 17:5). On the contrary, *the resurrection* was the means by which He was *designated as the Son of God* who now possesses *power*. What does this mean?

It is critical to observe that Paul's reference to resurrection is expressed not as a single event in the life of Jesus Christ, but as a sweeping reality: *the resurrection **of the dead**.* Here, of course, we can detect Paul's well known theology about the resurrection, in which Christ is "the first fruits of those who have fallen asleep" (1 Cor 15:20). In fact, "as in Adam all die, even so in Christ all shall be made alive" (1 Cor 15:22). The reality of *the resurrection of the dead* is manifested in the raising of God's Son back to physical life. Where there are first fruits, there will also be a harvest, and that harvest will include everyone who has ever died.

*The resurrection of the dead*, therefore, has *already begun* in the resurrection of Jesus Christ. The commencement of this eschatological

---

[1] Of course, Hodges does not mean to imply that experiential holiness is a guaranteed result in the life of all born-again people. He makes this clear in his discussion of Romans 5–8. What he means is that the Spirit is moving all believers toward holiness, and those who receive the Word and the work of the Spirit in their lives will indeed become holy in their experience. – RNW

event is the way that God has designated Jesus as *the Son of God with power*. The reference to *power* is obviously connected with the idea of *resurrection*. However, God's Son *already had* divine powers both in His preincarnate and incarnate existence. On earth, His powers were quite evident in the mighty miracles that He performed. So what power is this?

The NT plainly shows us that the risen Christ obtains *special* power in consequence of His resurrection. This is memorably expressed in Rev 1:18: "I am He who lives, and was dead, and behold, I am alive forevermore. Amen. And I have *the keys of Hades and of Death*" (emphasis added). The authority to resurrect is now His so that, as He Himself said, "the hour is coming in which all who are in the graves [both saved and lost] will hear His voice and come forth" (John 5:28-29a). His voice (His Word) has the *power* to accomplish this.

For Paul, of course, this *power* is nothing less than the power to vanquish death itself. "For," Paul declares, Christ "must reign till He has put all enemies under His feet. The last enemy that will be destroyed is death" (1 Cor 15:25-26). But this is not the work of One who is divine, and *only* divine. Instead, "since by man came death, by Man also came the resurrection of the dead" (1 Cor 15:21). God Himself *could*, of course, abolish death. But He has determined to do so only in and through His Son who comes from *the seed of David*. It is as a *resurrected Man* that God's Son acquires the prerogative, and hence the power, to abolish death in all its forms. He has "the keys of Hades and of Death," and He will completely empty them both! This is the fundamental power that His resurrection bestows upon Him.

It should also be observed that this *power* is inseparably related to His right to judge all men. As Jesus personally declared, "…the Father judges no one, but has committed all judgment to the Son" (John 5:22). Moreover, the Father "has given Him authority to execute judgment… because He is *the Son of Man*" (John 5:27, emphasis added). The "keys of Hades and of Death" are a symbol of this authority which He possesses as a *Man (from David's seed)* now risen triumphantly from the dead. The destiny of every human being is in the hands of Jesus Christ. His mighty voice will call all people from their graves in either the first or the second resurrection, and *all* will stand before *Him* (see Rom 14:10-11). Thus He is truly the powerful *Son of God*.

Finally, we should note that here too Paul implicitly lays the foundation for the truth he will more fully expound in this epistle. The gospel, he will soon tell us, "is *the power of God* for deliverance" (1:16, emphasis added). But this power for deliverance is nothing less than the resurrecting power of "the Spirit of Christ" (8:9-11), and so it is also an expression of the power that God has designated His Son as possessing.

The meaty, allusive language of Rom 1:3-4 is a rich mine from which the apostle will draw the superb doctrinal ore of this epistle.

In the English verse divisions, the phrase **Jesus Christ our Lord** concludes v 4. The Greek of this phrase is grammatically in apposition to the words *His Son* of v 3. The intervening material that we have just looked at elaborates the Son's identity in terms of His relationship to David and to God. Climactically, this impressive Person is now named by Paul. He is none other than *Jesus Christ our Lord.*

> **1:5. through Him we have received grace and apostleship to bring about obedience by faith for His name's sake among all the Gentiles,**

Paul acknowledges himself as the recipient both of grace (*charin*) and of apostleship (*apostolēn*) **through Him**, that is, through "Jesus Christ our Lord." [As often in Paul's writings, *we* is the equivalent of "I"—a kind of "modest" plural.] The phrase **grace and apostleship** *could be* construed as a hendiadys ("the grace of apostleship"), but probably is not. More likely, grace is the broad principle of which apostleship is a particular and preeminently significant expression. No doubt Paul thinks of grace as involving the whole scope of his conversion, but apostleship was that conversion's chief earthly goal and a supreme grace (see 1 Cor 15:10).

The grace of God expressed by Paul's appointment to the apostolic office has a specific goal. This goal is **to bring about obedience by faith...** **among all the Gentiles** (*eis hupakoēn pisteōs en pasi tois ethnesin*). This interesting phrase repays close attention. Of course, the Greek noun for *faith* (*pisteōs*) is an important Pauline word in Romans. Here it is grammatically connected to *obedience* (literally, "faith's obedience"). What does this expression mean?

We may dismiss out of hand the view that the phrase refers to the obedience that *inevitably* flows from true faith. No such Pauline doctrine is to be found in Romans or anywhere else in Paul's epistles, and in fact this idea is contradicted by true Pauline theology. It is possible, however, that the phrase might mean "the obedience which is faith" in the sense that faith is a form of obedience. That is certainly a correct doctrine (see

John 3:36 in Greek, *hōapeithōn*). But this idea is also not found in Romans and is questionable in the Pauline literature.

This leads to the observation that the easiest sense for this phrase is that it refers to the obedience that can and should be produced *by faith* in God's Son. The apostle was obviously interested in bringing about a response of faith to the gospel message he proclaimed (vv 1-4). But he was interested in more than that. He was also profoundly concerned with the obedience to God that ought to result from that faith.

In fact here we encounter the basic thrust of Romans. In the expository section beginning with chap. 3, there are numerous references (i.e., twenty) to "faith" until we reach 5:2. Then, from 5:2 through 8:31, also known as the "Christian Life" section, there are no further uses of the word *faith*. But between 5:2 and 8:31 the word *obedience* occurs twice and the word *obey* occurs three times. Neither word occurs from 3:1–5:2. Naturally this distribution is due to Paul's subject matter. The argument of Romans proceeds from the subject of justifying faith to the subject of Christian obedience. In Romans obedience and faith are separate, but related, concepts.

Therefore, in the translation above, the words *by faith* do *not* mean *by means of faith*. In Romans, faith is not explicitly presented as *the means* of Christian obedience. On the contrary, faith in God's Son is the *starting point* from which obedience proceeds. Thus Christian living is obedience stimulated by, and caused by, the original justifying faith. Obedience is the *product* of such faith. Or, as the literal rendering indicates, this is *faith's obedience*! This truth will become more evident when Romans 6–8 are considered in detail.

Paul's apostolic ministry was aimed at producing faith's obedience *among all the Gentiles*. And this obedience was intended to glorify "Jesus Christ our Lord," that is, it was to be done **for His name's sake** (the words *huper tou onomatos autou* actually *follow* the reference to *the Gentiles* in the Greek). Consequently, the present epistle lay fully within the scope of Paul's apostleship and the epistle's effect on its largely Gentile audience was a legitimate expression of his apostolic purpose. The next verse essentially says this.

### 1:6. among whom you too are called by Jesus Christ—

Paul now clearly affirms that the Gentile readership of Romans is part of the larger circle of Gentile believers (**among whom**) who are the object of his purpose to "bring about [an] obedience" that proceeds from their faith (see v 5). Thus this letter to the Roman Christians is fully harmonious with Paul's apostolic goal for Gentile believers in general. His readers are among those **called by Jesus Christ** and thus they possess a faith that should lead them to obey the One who called them.

> **1:7. to all who are in Rome, beloved by God, called *to be* saints: Grace to you and peace from God our Father and the Lord Jesus Christ.**

Paul concludes the formal salutation of his letter by explicitly identifying his audience and by wishing a benediction on them. Specifically he is writing **to all who are in Rome** who have become the recipients of God's gracious love and now have the status of saints,[2] to which status He had summoned (called) them. Paul's hope and expectation for such privileged people was that they might have an ongoing experience of God's abundant **grace and peace**. As Christians they would know that these blessings were sourced in **God the Father and the Lord Jesus Christ.**

## B. Paul's Desire to Visit Rome (1:8-15)

After concluding his formal greetings to the Roman Christians (vv 1-7), Paul proceeds to communicate to them his high regard for their Christian faith as well as his desire to enhance that faith.

> **1:8. First, I thank my God through Jesus Christ for all of you because your faith is proclaimed throughout the whole world.**

The very first thing (*Prōton men*) Paul wishes to do is to assure his readers of his appreciation for their Christian faith, news of which is widely published **throughout the whole** Roman **world**. Though they are not his converts, he rejoices, nonetheless, in the fact that their faith has impacted people in countless places. It must have been no insignificant

---

[2] The Greek of the last phrase of the first half of this verse literally reads *called saints*. It is quite permissible to add (as both the NKJV and this commentary do) the words *to be* (*called to be saints*). Bear in mind, though, that the addressees already were believers. Verse 7 calls them *beloved of God*, while v 8 speaks of their faith being *spoken of throughout the whole world*, and v 13 calls them *brethren*. Thus, not only was the calling of these Romans to be saints a past event, but their response (believing Christ for His promise of life) was also prior history. The epistle to the Romans addresses believers and instructs them; we dare not misconstrue it into a tract for unbelievers. –JHN

matter for the early Christians that their confidence in Jesus Christ was shared by people in no less a place than the capital of the empire. We can well believe that the report of the gospel's fruitfulness there must have spread rapidly from congregation to congregation.

> **1:9-10. In fact, God, whom I serve in my spirit with the gospel of His Son, is my witness that I mention you constantly, requesting always in my prayers that perhaps now at last I might succeed by the will of God in coming to you.**

Paul's interest in the Romans, however, goes beyond merely rejoicing in their faith. As a matter of fact, that interest finds significant expression in his prayer life. God Himself can witness to the fact that Paul has a constant remembrance of them in his prayers. After all, those prayers were made *to Him.* But this prayer activity, Paul suggests, is part of his service to God **in my spirit** on behalf of **the gospel of His Son.** Since Paul knew the value of intercession, he understood that **the gospel** could be truly served not only with our lips, but also with our spirits through the medium of prayer.

But not only did Paul mention the Roman Christians constantly before God, he also was regularly **requesting…in** [his] **prayers** the opportunity to come and visit them in Rome. This had not been possible up to now (see v 13) and Paul realizes that the success of any effort he makes to come depends on **the will of God.** Paul had learned through many experiences that the sovereign hand of the Lord determined where he went and when.[3]

> **1:11-12. For I long to see you so that I may impart some spiritual benefit to you in order that you may be strengthened—that is *to say*, that we might be encouraged together among you through the faith that is in each other, both your *faith* and mine.**

The desire for personal fellowship (*Epipothō gar idein humas*) with the objects of his prayer and the desire to be of **benefit** to them (*hina ti metadō charisma humin pneumatikon*) are merged in Paul's heart as one desire. The man who asks God's gifts for men wishes naturally to be able to give some gift himself. To be attuned to God's generosity is to become

---

[3] Hodges did not believe that God guided Paul or anyone else *via impressions.* He believed and taught that Paul was led by special revelation (visions, dreams, messages from NT prophets). Paul's Macedonian vision (Acts 16:9-10) is a case in point. –RNW

generous; to wish with such an attitude to see individuals is to wish to share with them for their good.

The words **some spiritual benefit** ("some spiritual gift," NKJV) take the Greek word *charisma* in a non-technical sense. Paul's doctrine about spiritual gifts was that every Christian already had one (see Rom 12:6; 1 Cor 12:12-31). There is no persuasive evidence that Paul believed a Christian could change his gift or add one he did not previously possess.[4]

Paul is not so proud, however, as to imagine that only the Romans will benefit from mutual interaction with him. On the contrary he anticipated that he and they would **be encouraged together** by means of their mutually shared **faith**. The Christian teacher who thinks that other believers can no longer bring him spiritual enhancement is a teacher in urgent need of additional wisdom.[5]

> **1:13. Now I don't want you to be uninformed, brothers, that many times I have planned to come to you (and have been prevented until now) so that I might have some fruit among you also, just as *I have had* among the rest of the Gentiles.**

The depth of Paul's desire to see them and serve them is demonstrated by the fact that **many times** (*pollakis* is emphatically placed in the Greek phrase) he had actually decided to come to them but was **prevented** from doing so. Given the multiplicity of his spiritual responsibilities, plus the frequency with which he was persecuted, the delay was fully understandable. But the intention was there and this attested to his desire to come.

The fruit of which he speaks, the aim of his coming, need not be construed as an explicit reference to converts to be won by him. In fact, Paul never uses the term *fruit* in this way. The immediately preceding verse suggests that he is thinking in terms of the "spiritual benefit" his visit would bring. A similar concept of *fruit* seems to be present in Phil 1:21-25 where Paul feels that to remain alive will mean fruitful labor, and

---

[4] Hodges believed that each believer has *only one* spiritual gift, though we are called to do all the non-sign gifts (give, teach, evangelize, help, etc.). He based this on Paul's discussion of the hand and foot and eye and ear in 1 Cor 12:15-17. If a believer cannot be both a hand and a foot or an eye and an ear, then believers do not have more than one spiritual gift. –RNW

[5] I was in the same church with Hodges for fifteen years. He repeatedly not only encouraged the rest of us in the assembly, but he also was encouraged regularly by the rest of us. Though he knew the Bible much better than anyone else in our church, he never felt that encouragement was one way. –RNW

he is thinking particularly of the Philippians' progress in joy and faith. Elsewhere, Paul uses *fruit* of the holy and beneficial results of Christian experience (see Rom 6:21-22; 15:28; Gal 5:22; Eph 5:9; Phil 1:11, 22; 4:17), and somewhat differently in 2 Tim 2:6. No other uses of *fruit* occur in his epistles except 1 Cor 9:7 as a discussion of material remuneration.

It is probable, therefore, that Paul was thinking of the general spiritual results of his ministry in Rome and not only, or even primarily, of prospective conversions. Rome is seen as a necessary complement to Paul's ministry. By a delicate transition of thought, Paul moves from the concept of his burden for the Romans to his obligation to them. He wants **fruit among** them, just as he had elsewhere **among the rest of the Gentiles**. (The words *I have had* are supplied for clarity.) He will now tell the Romans that this desire grows out of his sweeping responsibility to the Gentile world.

> **1:14-15. I am a debtor both to the Greeks and to barbarians, both to the wise and to the unwise. So there is a readiness on my part to preach the gospel also to you who are in Rome.**

Paul's desire for fruit among the Roman Christians is an expression of his sense of being **a debtor** to the Gentile world. But why this debt? No doubt the answer is to be found in the fact (stated earlier) that he had "received grace and apostleship to bring about obedience by faith for His name's sake among all the Gentiles" (1:5). It is not that the Gentiles have some claim on Paul in their own right, but rather that the Lord Jesus Christ has a claim on him because of the "grace and apostleship" that He had bestowed on Paul.

Thus he is a debtor to every kind of Gentile—**to Greeks** (those within Greek culture) and **to barbarians** (those outside the Greek culture). The *Greeks* were those with earthly wisdom. The *barbarians* were those who lacked it. That being the case, he had **a readiness...to preach the gospel also** in Rome. His debt extends to those in that city as well. As the capital of the empire, of course, Rome would be a locale unthinkable to pass by in a ministry designed to reach all types of Gentiles. To pass by Rome in a Roman world would be inconceivable.

It is no wonder, then, that Rome loomed large in his evangelistic and missionary plans. Paul undoubtedly felt that this city was a necessary capstone to his Gentile apostleship. Note that Paul's desire *to preach the gospel* is personalized as directed **to you who are in Rome** (*humin tois en*

*Rhōmē*). No doubt the *you* (*humin*) is broad enough to embrace the idea of "you people" who are in Rome.[6] Naturally this includes the unconverted whom Paul would certainly try to reach. Yet the *you* also implies that he will "gospelize" his readers as well when he comes. No preacher worth his salt would fail to spell out the gospel he preached to a new group of Christian hearers, since the apostle knew quite well how readily genuine believers could be diverted from the simple truths of God's saving grace. If we doubt this, we ought to read Galatians again—more carefully!

Paul's gospel, therefore, will be proclaimed when he comes to Rome.

## II. Thematic statement: The Gospel Contains God's Power for Deliverance (1:16-17)

**1:16-17. For I am not ashamed of the gospel of Christ, since it is the power of God for deliverance for everyone who believes, both for the Jew first and for the Greek. For in it is revealed the righteousness of God by faith, granted to faith, just as it is written, *"Now the one who is righteous by faith shall live."***

Paul now states the fundamental theme that he wishes to discuss in this epistle. It was very much consistent with rhetorical practice in the Greco-Roman world for a statement of this general nature to precede the detailed discussion which a speech or treatise is designed to present. The hearer or reader thus learns right up front the basic subject matter that the speaker or author intends to consider.

Paul has just stated his "readiness to preach the gospel" to the Romans (v 15). And why should he not be ready to do this? The gospel was a proclamation about which he was justly proud. In fact, the words **I am not ashamed of** are an understatement (a figure of speech called litotes) for "I am quite proud of" [**the gospel of Christ**]. The reason for his pride in Jesus' gospel is found in the simple fact that this gospel **is the power**

---

[6] This statement by Hodges seems out of place. The most natural reading of the expression *you who are in Rome* is to the readers, that is, to *the believers who are in Rome*. In Romans 15 Paul explains that a major reason why he had not yet come to Rome was because there were already believers there, but God had called him to take the gospel "where Christ was not named, so that [he] might not build on another person's foundation" (Rom 15:20). See discussion there. It also seems at odds with the way that Hodges takes 1:13 (see his comments there) and 1:16-17, the immediately following verses. –RNW

**of God for deliverance for everyone who believes.** Paul preaches it, therefore, without the slightest embarrassment.

In the translation I give here, the word *deliverance* replaces the more familiar word *salvation* that is found in the English versions. The word *salvation* prejudices interpreters right from the start since it is traditionally understood as "salvation from hell." But this is a presupposition which ought not to be made here on the basis of traditional understanding alone. The word *deliverance* properly leaves the issue open and almost automatically elicits the question, "deliverance from *what*?" No expositor ought to fail to address this question.

An examination of the Epistle to the Romans turns up the surprising fact that after Rom 1:16 the Greek word for deliverance or salvation (*sōtēria*) does not occur again until Rom 10:1 and the verbal form of this word (*sōzō*) occurs next at Rom 5:9-10. Thus the noun and verb are totally absent from Paul's discussion of justification in chaps. 2–4, even though, on the traditional view, this is where they would most naturally appear.

In addition, in Rom 5:9-10, the experience from which we are saved or delivered is specified as "wrath" (5:9). Although this word, too, has a traditional meaning (i.e., the wrath associated with hell), Paul's epistle does not support this. In Romans *wrath* is a manifestation of God's *temporal* displeasure. This is clear from 1:18ff. and 2:5-8. Given the close proximity of 1:16 to 1:18, and in the light of 5:9-10, we may conclude that in Rom 1:16 *deliverance* refers to being rescued, or "saved," from the divine temporal anger that is so vividly described in Rom 1:18-32.

Of course, the final verification of this interpretation will depend on the degree to which it illuminates and clarifies the epistle as a whole. One purpose of this commentary is to show that this approach reveals the cohesiveness of Paul's argument in this epistle. For now, therefore, we shall assume this meaning. Thus v 16 states that the gospel Paul preaches is the vehicle for *the power of God* by which men can be delivered from His *temporal* wrath.

And since this powerful message originated in the Jewish faith, the deliverance is **for the Jew first** while at the same time it is also **for the Greek**. ("Greek" is an obvious synecdoche for "Gentile.") Thus the Roman recipients of this letter can embrace its message, whether they happen to be Jewish or Gentile.

But how, we might ask, can it be true of *the gospel of Christ* that it contains such *power* as this? The answer is given in v 17 (note the *for*). *The gospel of Christ* is a message that reveals **the righteousness of God**. Here, then, Paul correlates God's power and His righteousness. Inherent in this correlation is the basic fact that God's power never operates contrary to, or inconsistently with, His righteousness. For *the gospel of Christ* to be a source of *deliverance* for men, it must also be manifestly consistent with God's righteous character.

There has been much contemporary discussion about the meaning of God's righteousness in Romans. But this discussion seems misguided. There is no reason not to see in the term *righteousness* simply a reference to the "rightness" of God's character and actions. The effort to find more than that in this word can be regarded as a typical case of "illegitimate totality transfer." This mistake occurs when it is believed that the contextual ramifications of a term are constitutive of its basic meaning. Language, however, is improperly handled when this kind of an assumption is in play.

As Paul's words here show, he is thinking principally of *the righteousness of God* that is imputed to those who believe (note especially, 3:21-22). This is made clear by the words **by faith, granted to faith**. The most familiar English translation of these words is the one found in the KJV and the NKJV, "from faith to faith." But this translation is obscure at best, and requires extensive elaboration in order to be meaningful. The Greek expression here (*ek pisteōs eis pistin*) may be very simply rendered by the words "by faith for faith." The point will then be that *the righteousness of God* is attained *by means of faith* and that it is *bestowed on*, or *granted to*, faith. (For this sense of *eis* see especially Rom 3:22.)

Paul's meaning here embraces two major conceptions of the role of faith as it pertains to *the righteousness of God*. On the one hand it is the means, or medium, through which this righteousness is attained. But on the other hand, God's righteousness is not His imprimatur on the otherwise flawed life of the believer. On the contrary, God's righteousness is given directly to faith itself. This concept is expressed by Paul whenever he states that one's "faith is accounted to him for righteousness" (note 4:5, and see 4:3, 22-24). Thus, as chap. 4 discloses, when Paul refers to Gen 15:6, he understands it as meaning that Abraham's *faith* is precisely what is accounted as righteousness.

This is a feature of Paul's theology of justification that is frequently ignored. Contrary to much Jewish thought in his day, in which significant good works might accrue to a person's account to "cancel out" his failures,

Paul holds that *the righteousness of God* is not connected with works *at all* (it is "apart from works" [4:6] and "apart from the law" [3:21]). It has nothing whatsoever to do with "law-keeping." Instead it is not only attained *by means of* faith but it is also *granted to faith.* Faith, then, is the beginning and the end of this divine righteousness.

But where does this take us? The following words express the connection Paul finds between justifying faith and the *deliverance* he has just mentioned. Thus, according to Scripture (Hab 2:4), *"Now the one who is righteous by faith shall live."*[7] The righteous man, therefore, is the one who can *live* in precisely the sense Paul elaborates in Romans 6–8. In fact he states, "if by the Spirit you put to death the deeds of the body, you will *live*" (8:13). Life in the truly Christian sense of that term can only be "lived" by *the one who is righteous by faith*!

As all expositors know, the words *by faith* can be grammatically connected with either *the righteous* or with *shall live.* The latter connection has dominated the English versions (e.g., KJV, NKJV, NASB, NIV). But modern commentators seem to be moving in the direction of a connection with *the righteous* (so Nygren, Cranfield, Dunn, Moo). The Hebrew text of Habakkuk can also be understood in the same way, of course. Paul is not here inventing a meaning that suits his theology. On the contrary Hab 2:4 is a *proof text* for the point he is making. It is not to be doubted that he was well able to defend this meaning in the many synagogues where he had preached.

Although it is quite true that the Christian life can be said to be lived "by faith" (see Gal 2:20), in Romans *faith* plays no role in Paul's discussion of Christian living. Given the approach Paul takes in this epistle, he obviously desired that the word *faith* should be the crucial term only in his discussion of justification. Therefore, from Rom 3:22–5:2, the word

---

[7] Habakkuk 2:4 (as well as Paul's citation of the verse) means "one-who-is-righteous-by-faith will live," not "one-who-is-righteous will-live-by-faith." Compare Anders Nygren, *Commentary on Romans* (Philadelphia, PA: Fortress Press, 1988), 84; Douglas J. Moo, *The Epistle to the Romans*, NICNT, Gordon D. Fee, gen. ed. (Grand Rapids: Eerdmans, 1996), 78; C. E. B. Cranfield, *A Critical and Exegetical Commentary on the Epistle to the Romans*, ICC, J. A. Emerton and C. E. B. Cranfield, gen. eds. (Edinburgh: Clark, 1975- 79), 1:99f; and James D. G. Dunn, *Romans 1-8*, ed. Ralph P Martin, WBC, vol. 38A, Bruce M. Metzger, David A. Hubbard, and Glenn W. Barker, gen. eds. (Nashville: Nelson, 1988), 48f. However, these commentators fail to see it foreshadowing the offer of deliverance to Christians in Romans 6–8. Consider Rom 8:13, which contrasts believers (note the word *you*) under wrath with those who are freed from wrath: "if you [believers] live according to the flesh you [believers] will die; but if by the Spirit you [believers] put to death the deeds of the body, you [believers] will live." –JHN

*faith* occurs a total of twenty times. But from Rom 5:3–8:39 there is *not even one occurrence!* It is in no sense legitimate to say that in Romans the justified person is presented as living "by faith."

Accordingly, in Rom 1:16-17, the apostle has set forth his theme succinctly and effectively. He is proud of the gospel precisely because it makes available *the power of God* that accomplishes *deliverance* in the lives of believers.[8] This *deliverance* of sinful creatures is in full harmony with God's own righteousness. That righteousness is revealed in the gospel as a righteousness actually attained *prior to* deliverance on the sole basis of faith. Thus the gospel leads to the realization of the profoundly important truth stated in Habakkuk: if a person *is righteous by faith* he can *live*. For the NT person, that is nothing less than victorious Christian experience.[9]

## III. Body of the Epistle: Spiritual Deliverance Arises from the Righteousness God Grants to Faith (1:18–15:13)

---

[8] Would not unbelievers benefit from learning this message, even though they would not yet be justified and would not yet be in line to receive this deliverance? Possibly this is what Hodges meant in his comments on v 15 when he indicated that Paul wished to proclaim the gospel to both believers and unbelievers in Rome. –RNW

[9] Romans 1:16-17 is the book's thematic statement. Unfortunately, even though salvation (*sōtēria*) does not again appear until 11:11 (*sōzō* in 5:9-10), the literature uncritically treats its use here as resulting from believing Christ's promise of everlasting life. Paul's discussion of justification by faith (Romans 2–4) uses neither *sōtēria* nor *sōzō* (save). In addition, Rom 5:9 distinguishes salvation from justification: "having now been justified [already] by His blood, we shall be saved [in the future] from wrath."

Those taking the common view—that salvation is deliverance from the lake of fire—struggle with the *gar* linking v 18 with vv 16-17. Consider Moo, *Romans*, 100: "If, then, Paul presents God's wrath as a present reality, how are we to understand that the wrath is now being manifested [since the lake of fire is yet future]? And what is the relationship between the two 'revelations'—of the righteousness of God in v. 17 and of the wrath in v. 18?" Moo's discussion (pp. 100-103) fails to show how a present revelation of wrath (v 18) clarifies an eschatological salvation as good news for unbelievers (vv 16-17). The literature as a whole struggles here. Some weaken the *gar*; others massage the present nature of wrath. Such manipulation red-flags the real problem: contortion of vv 15-17 into a message for unbelievers, when Paul intended it as a message for believers.

A slightly amplified rendering of a portion of v 16 should clarify: *The good news is the power of God for deliverance [available] for everyone who believes.*

Paul does not say the gospel *delivers* all believers. Rather, he says that God makes deliverance from present wrath *available* to all believers. All believers possess "justification unto [everlasting] life" (Rom 5:18), but not all experience deliverance from present wrath. –JHN

Paul now launches into the body of his great epistle. Here he will elaborate in considerable detail the proposition he has stated thematically in vv 16-17.

## A. God's Displeasure with Humanity Is Manifest (1:18–3:20)

### 1. Humanity Stands under God's Wrath (1:18–2:5)

The first step in the development of Paul's theme is to state clearly the fundamental problem that this epistle addresses. What emerges from the opening section of this unit (namely, 1:18-32) is that Paul's concern is focused on the moral and spiritual condition of humanity in this world. Although the theme of final judgment[10] emerges in chap. 2, in this first subunit it has no explicit place at all. What is under review is the widespread and obvious depravity of the human race.

#### a. The Declaration of This Manifestation (1:18)

**1:18. For the wrath of God is revealed from heaven against all the ungodliness and unrighteousness of men who suppress the truth by unrighteousness.**

The first word of this verse in Greek is the one rendered **is revealed** (*Apokaluptetai*). The word carries emphasis because of its position at the front of the Greek sentence (the subject would normally be first if there were no particular emphasis). The gospel, Paul has just said in v 17, is a message wherein God's *righteousness* is revealed (*apokaluptetai* is used there, too). Now he speaks of the revelation of God's **wrath**. The repetition of *apokaluptetai* highlights the contrast.

It is precisely because man is so clearly under divine *wrath* that he stands in need of a gospel of divine *righteousness*. Indeed, the *wrath* of which Paul speaks is directed against man as a response to his character and conduct, which are the direct opposite of the *righteousness* revealed in the gospel. Specifically, this *wrath* is directed **against all the ungodliness**

---

[10] By *final judgment* Hodges means *the Great White Throne Judgment*, not a general judgment of the regenerate and unregenerate. Hodges taught that Church-Age believers will be judged at the Bema, before the Millennium, and that all unbelievers will be judged at the Great White Throne Judgment. He taught that the purpose of these judgments was not to determine eternal destiny, but to determine degree of reward in the kingdom or degree of suffering in the lake of fire. –RNW

**and unrighteousness of men**. Mankind should not think that its perverse behavior escapes God's notice. (In Aristotelian thinking, the supreme deity would be too transcendent and remote even to notice!) On the contrary, the true and living God manifests, i.e., *reveals*, His displeasure with man's ways.

The terms used here for *ungodliness* and *unrighteousness* (*asebeian* and *adikian*) are close to each other in meaning, judging by general NT usage. Besides the obvious rhetorical advantage of this double assertion of man's wickedness, however, there may also be a subtle shade of difference between the two words. In that case, *ungodliness* (*asebeian*), which could also be rendered "impiety," focuses a bit more on the irreligious spirit of man. *Unrighteousness* (*adikian*), on the other hand, would stress the "wrongness" of his conduct. The former, of course, produces the latter, as the development of Paul's thought here shows (see vv 19-23 and following).

Man thus stands far distant from the basic character of God who possesses a perfect *righteousness*. The Creator has every right to be "angered" by the behavior of His creatures, and that is essentially what *wrath* (*orgē*) really is: divine *anger*! But, in addition to this, unrighteous man is also hostile to the truth of God. Hence, the revelation of God's wrath is said to be against the sinfulness **of men who suppress** (*katechontōn*) **the truth by unrighteousness**. It is serious enough for man to deviate from God's holy standards. It is even more serious for him to seek to hold back God's truth.

This tendency is everywhere on display in our own day and time. The person who rejects God's holiness in his own experience can scarcely bear to face God's truth. Hence, he seeks to *suppress* it in his own consciousness and in the consciousness of others. There are many ways in which this is done, but Paul has especially in mind man's headlong descent into idolatrous religion (see vv 21-23). Idolatry is a way of turning one's back on the one true God and ignoring His laws of morality and justice. In idolatry the truth is *suppressed*.

Thus, taken as a whole, this verse declares that God is *angry* with men because of their sin and suppression of His truth. The fashion in which that anger finds expression (that is, the way in which it is *revealed*) will be detailed by Paul very shortly (vv 24-32), but more immediately he must point out that man is, indeed, suppressing self-evident truth.

### b. The Cause of This Manifestation (1:19-23)

**1:19-20. Because what is knowable about God is evident among them, because God has made it evident to them. For His invisible *attributes* are seen clearly by means of the creation of the world since they are discerned from the things that have been made, *namely,* both His eternal power and Deity, so that they are without excuse.**

That mankind really is restraining God's truth is proved by the consideration (*Dioti*) that there is a clear witness to God in the visible world. The words **what is knowable** translate the Greek expression *to gnōston*, which is approximately equal to "the known thing." What mankind can know **about God**, says Paul, is perfectly plain, that is, **evident** (*phaneron*) **among them**. In fact, **God** Himself **has made it evident** (*ephanerōse*) **to them**. Paul does not imply by this, that all the information humanity might need about God falls under the category of self-evident truth. The phrase *to gnōston*, in fact, may be taken to imply the reverse. There is something to be known about God that is *available* to all men, though by so much we might deduce that there is also a *to agnōston* (= "what is unknown") as well. (See the discussion below.)

What Paul has in mind by *to gnōston* is defined in v 20 as **His invisible *attributes*,** specifically, **His eternal power and Deity.** These *attributes* ("attributes" is supplied in my translation) **are seen clearly by means of the creation of the world.** That is to say, the visible creation testifies to the awesome *power*, and hence the undoubted *Deity*, of the Creator.

The Greek phrase rendered *by means of the creation of the world* (*apo ktiseōs kosmou*) construes the Greek preposition in a causal sense, as when we say, "I conclude *from* what you say that…" God has made the invisible realities that pertain to God (*Ta…aorata autou*), that is, the ones Paul is speaking of, a transparent datum that lies on the very face of the created order. Thus they are clearly visible to the rational faculties of mankind, that is, they *are seen clearly* (*kathoratai*), and this perception arises directly **from the things that have been made** (*tois poiēmasi nooumena*). Paul does not entertain the notion here, or anywhere else, that the evidence of creation is somehow insufficient if not buttressed by sophisticated argumentation. Those who reject the testimony of nature **are without excuse.**

Despite many centuries in which the intellectual elite of Western civilization have played down this simple form of argumentation, it remains as valid as ever. The view that the cosmos as we know it could have developed without the activity of a creating Agent is, in the final analysis, an absurdity. It defies all rationality and common sense. The greater the complexity of a system, the more emphatically that system testifies to a Designer. Only with regard to the cosmos, the most complex system of all, is this self-evident truth denied.

We must also be careful to observe here that the apostle does not take a negative view of man's capacity to reason from the creation to the Creator. Indeed, the very essence of the whole process by which God has manifested His "known thing" to men entails that men should have the capacity to see what is revealed. If they did not, no true manifestation would have taken place and no real grounds would exist on which to hold men responsible. But the responsibility of men is precisely Paul's point. Since God's *eternal power and Deity* can be *seen clearly*, humanity has no defense for its ignorance of these realities, **so that they** [mankind] *are without excuse* (*eis to einai autous anapologētous*). If there is ignorance, it is willful ignorance and hence, suppression of the truth (v 18).

It should be stated that man can go only so far in his perception of God as he rationally considers the creation around him. The terms *eternal power and Deity* suggest the limits of the discovery he can make. Even the simplest of men is capable of considering the creation in which he lives in such a way as to draw the inescapable conclusion that it must have been made by Someone whose powers span the ages and whose essence is of a higher order than anything in the world around. *Eternal power* and *Deity* are amply attested by nature, but other realities are not.

Indeed, the gospel Paul proclaims is itself a special divine revelation and in no way deducible from the natural world. But if men were willing to recognize the manifestation of the Creator which creation itself affords them, they would then be in a position to search out the further will of their Maker.[11] However, as long as they suppress, with their idolatry, the true

---

[11] Hodges held the view that God is seeking all men (John 12:32; 16:7-11). In other words, if someone who had never heard of Jesus cried out to the Creator for knowledge of the truth, God would send him more information via a messenger or missionary. Hodges believed that if a person was open, then God would ultimately communicate to him the message of eternal life through faith in Jesus Christ, thereby giving him the chance to believe. If a pagan died without ever hearing about Jesus, he would still be culpable for his unbelief, because had he cried out, God would have communicated with him. Hodges cited Paul's Macedonian vision

witness of nature, no such progress is possible. In fact, this suppression of truth occurs "by [means of] unrighteousness" (v 18). Precisely because man clings to his unrighteousness, he refuses to acknowledge "the truth." To acknowledge the existence of a Creator is implicitly to acknowledge human accountability for unrighteous behavior. Unrighteous man does not want to do that.

> **1:21. Because when they knew God, they did not glorify Him as God, nor were they thankful, but engaged in their empty reasonings and so their senseless heart was darkened.**

The final words of v 20 ("so that they are without excuse") clearly suggest that mankind has not responded properly to the evidence of God in nature. But *how* has mankind come to be in this "inexcusable" condition? Verse 21 makes clear what Paul deems to be the fundamental failure of humanity in this regard.

As is clear from the entirety of vv 21-23, Paul is succinctly tracing man's catastrophic disregard for the testimony of nature to its Creator. Man is "without excuse" (v 20) precisely because (*Dioti*) of his rejection of this unmistakable witness to God. There was indeed a time when the God of creation was known as such. But **when they knew God** (*gnontes ton Theon*) humanity failed to render to Him the appropriate glory and gratitude.

In all probability Paul is thinking here of the period covered in the early chapters of Genesis, after the fall of man, when there was still an awareness of the God who had made all things. Even Lamech, the second murderer in human history, implicitly acknowledges the God who had promised vengeance on anyone who hurt Cain (see Gen 4:23-24). Shortly after, we are told that "then men began to call on the name of the Lord" (Gen 4:26). Neither in this chapter nor in the flood narrative that follows (Genesis 6) is there any evidence of a movement toward idolatry. Yet at the same time, man's failure to honor his Maker and to appreciate His gifts is transparent (Gen 6:5-7).

So mankind's response to the God they knew was dramatically insufficient. Three facets of this response are expressed by Paul here in a series of statements, all of them using the aorist tense (*edoxasan,*

---

(Acts 16:9- 10) as well as his comments to the Athenians (Acts 17:30) to support this view. – RNW

*eucharistēsan, emataiōthēsan*). As simple statements of fact, they recapitulate a historical process of deterioration. Mankind first **did not glorify** God **as God**. His manifest "power" and "Deity" were not acknowledged with the reverence and honor that was fitting. It followed, then, that neither **were they thankful** for His innumerable gifts, starting with physical life itself. This, in turn, caused them to be **engaged in their empty reasonings**. The net result was that **their senseless heart was darkened**.

The assertion that men *engaged in their empty reasonings* (*emataiōthēsan en tois dialogismois autōn*) suggests the ineffectualness—the vacuity—of the reasoning processes of ungrateful humanity. The resulting blindness is conveyed by the words *their senseless heart was darkened* (*eskotisthē hē asunetos autōn kardia*), which point to the utter loss of comprehension and discernment into which these vacuous reasoning processes led. Out of this inward darkness arose the hideous distortion of Deity found in idolatry.

> **1:22-23. Claiming to be wise, they became fools and exchanged the glory of the immortal God for an image made in the likeness of mortal man, and of birds, and of four-footed creatures, and of reptiles.**

Yet, strangely, benighted man is never as self-confident as when his ignorance is most deep. Thus, following the assertion that "their senseless heart was darkened" (v 20), is a further indictment: **claiming to be wise, they became fools**. So far was mankind from recognizing their own darkness that they actually confused it with light! The consequent descent into idolatry was a powerful testimony to this utter lack of true perception.

Something like this darkening process has repeated itself in our present time. Although the scientific evidence for a Creator mounts steadily as the cosmos is studied ever more intensively, still the intellectual leaders of our day profess to find no adequate basis for a belief in divine creation.[12] Although the concept of an "eternal world" (with which the 20th century began) has been exploded by the advances in physics and astronomy, most of academia holds tenaciously to the view that natural processes

---

[12] The September 2, 2010 edition of *The London Times* quoted from a new book by physicist Stephen Hawkins entitled *The Grand Design*. Hawkins is cited as saying that the evidence from the cosmos now conclusively shows that God did not create the universe. –RNW

explain everything, when in fact they explain nothing. What caused the "big bang" remains a mystery.[13] The delicate balance of elements in our universe that permits the existence of life is thought to be a fortuitous accident. Scientists frequently offer improbable explanations (like a multiverse, for which there is no objective evidence at all). For many physicists, an infinite regress[14] is preferable to the concept of a Creator. The folly and perversity of this attitude should be manifest.

The supreme Intelligence that is so obvious in our cosmos, and becomes more and more obvious as new discoveries are made, is excluded from human calculations. Thus, even today, *claiming to be wise*, the wise have become fools.

In Paul's day, this folly was transparent in the degradation to which the image of the Creator-God was subjected by idolatry. **The glory of the immortal God** is exchanged by the idolater **for an image made in the likeness of mortal man** first of all. Thereupon the idolatrous images descend to the lower orders of creation as representations are made **of birds, and of four-footed creatures, and** finally **of reptiles**. The rhetorical arrangement of these elements of idolatry underlines the abject decay of the concept of the living God whom mankind refuses to see in the evidentiary character of the creation itself.

### c. The Results of This Manifestation (1:24-32)

**1:24-25. Therefore God also turned them over, in the lusts of their hearts, to uncleanness so that they dishonored their bodies with each other, because they had exchanged the truth**

---

[13] Hodges believed in a form of the big bang theory. In his view, when God created the heavens and the earth, as reported in Gen 1:1, He did so by setting off a huge explosion. Hodges believed both in six literal days of creation and the big bang. To the best of my knowledge he also believed in a young earth. I believe his position was that the universe is 14 billion years old, but the earth and all life on it is less than 10,000 years old. This is explained by some creationists as being due to the big bang spreading matter and energy at the speed of light. Since the earth is near the center of the universe where the big bang is said to have occurred, it would age much slower than everything outside it according to the theory of relativity. –RNW

[14] Infinite regress, when applied to the origin of the universe, is the idea that there is an endless chain of causes and effects that go back forever. In this view there is no *first cause* of the universe. If the laws of physics caused the original big bang of matter and energy, what caused the laws of physics and what caused matter and energy? And what caused whatever caused the laws of physics and matter and energy? And what caused that? Unless there is a first cause, one is trapped in an impossible situation, infinite regress. –RNW

**of God for a lie and worshipped and served the creature rather than the Creator who is blessed forever. Amen.**

Man's inexcusable descent into idolatry has led to a dreadful consequence. Precisely because of this idolatry (**therefore**), God has **turned them over** to their own iniquity. It is evident that the section encompassing vv 24-32 is unified by a threefold use of the phrase *turned them over* (*paredōken autous*) found in vv 24, 26, and 28. It is here that we meet Paul's fundamental thought about the wrath of God (*orgē Theou*) which the apostle has already declared to be revealed from heaven (v 18). This divine anger (*orgē*), Paul has said, is directed against men who restrain (*katechontōn*) the truth, and that restraint has been detailed in vv 19-23. It is now appropriate that God's wrath should be spelled out specifically.

The first of the three assertions that God has *turned them over* indicates a particularly fitting result of the failure described in vv 21-23. Since men have dishonored the Creator God by misrepresenting Him with creature-like images, they are given over to the outworking of their corrupt inward desires (**the lusts of their hearts**) and are dragged into a moral uncleanness (*eis akatharsian*) that dishonors their own physical bodies (*tou atimazesthai ta sōmata autōn en heautois*). Those who have degraded God with "bodily" representations of Him are allowed to experience their own "bodily" degradation!

There is obvious irony in the fact that when man represents God in corporeal form, then his own corporeal existence is marred. But this is inevitable since physical existence has no real meaning apart from a transcendent reality that gives it that meaning. When man loses his sense of a God who transcends all physical representation, man cannot avoid reducing his own physical experience to the shameful level of immorality. The sanctity of physical life is only maintained by means of the perception of a God who transcends physical life and who thus gives it its ultimate significance and value.

The Greek word rendered **because** (*hoitines*) that begins v 25, although a pronoun, may be used in a causal sense.[15] Here it further elaborates the reason for the "wrath" specified in v 24. The idolatry described in vv 21-23 was nothing less than an exchange of **the truth of God for a lie**

---

[15] See A. T. Robertson, *A Grammar of the Greek New Testament in the Light of Historical Research* (Nashville, TN: Broadman Press, 1934), 728. –ZCH

that resulted in worshipping **the creature rather than the Creator**. This additional analysis is worthy of attention.

In idolatry, Paul says, men have exchanged (*metallassō*, only here and in v 26 in the NT) reality for a falsehood. **The truth** of God's transcendence over His creation is replaced by the implicit lowering of God to the level of a creature of whatever form the idolater chooses. But this in fact is creature worship. Man's reverence and love for the transcendent *Creator* vanishes and is replaced by worship and service directed toward created things. (The word rendered *served* expresses the idea of religious ritual or duty.) In the wake of this wrongly focused religion, the experiences of desire and love no longer draw their meaning from *the Creator*. Thus *the creature* becomes the focus of everything.

Paul of course is here meditating on the appropriateness of man's moral condition in the light of his spiritual departure from the living *Creator*. In a creature-centered world, where the purposes and restraints of *the Creator* are forgotten, immorality is the tragically predictable result. Yet, as Paul affirms in the final words of the verse, *the Creator* whom men have forgotten **is blessed forever**. Man's inexcusable defection in no way touches or diminishes the blessedness of the transcendent God. Though God can be grieved by man's sin and unbelief, His glorious being is not affected by these things at all.

> **1:26-27. For this reason, God turned them over to dishonorable passions. For on the one hand, their females exchanged their natural practice for an unnatural one; and on the other hand, in a similar way the males also left their natural practice with a female and burned in their desire one for another, males with males doing what is shameful and receiving back in themselves for their error the recompense which was due them.**

Following this second condemnation of idolatry (v 25), there is a second description of God's wrath. Verse 25 not only adheres closely to the judgment stated in v 24, it also forms a bridge to the judgment described in vv 26-27. In fact, it provides the reason (*Dia touto*) for the action of God in vv 26-27.

The staircase character of Paul's thought in this passage begins to emerge here. Man's idolatry (vv 21-23) leads to the debasing of his physical experience (v 24). But this debasing is founded on the exchange of truth for a lie (v 25), leading to a similar exchange of truth for a lie in perverted sexual practice (vv 26-27). Thus man descends the staircase of moral corruptness. In lesbian/homosexual behavior, mankind embraces the lie that this form of sexual encounter is an experience equivalent to God-ordained sex.

The **dishonorable passions** to which God has also **turned them over**, therefore, are nothing less than distortions of reality in the sexual sphere. The key phrase here is that **females exchanged** (v 26) and **males also left** (v 27) *their natural practice* (*tēn phusikēn chrēsin*, emphasis added ["the natural use"], found in both vv 26 and 27).

The connection with v 25 is quite evident since the term *exchanged* (*metelassō*) of v 26 recalls the same verb in v 25 and thus stresses the correspondence between the sin and its penalty.

The sexual experiences of vv 26, 27 are described as *dishonorable passions* (*pathē atimias*), so that once again, as in v 24, man's failure to honor God properly leads to his own dishonor. It is noteworthy that Paul's description of homosexuality between males is fuller than his treatment of lesbian activity. In reference to the male activity, Paul explicitly refers to the improper sexual desire for other men that leads to **doing what is** sexually **shameful**. In addition, it is pertaining to males that he speaks specifically of physical consequences. As in Pauline thought generally, men have a more responsible role before God (see 1 Cor 11:7-9; 1 Tim 2:12-14), and thus their failures are to be viewed in a more serious light. A culture is inevitably led by its men.

The first words in vv 24-32 to refer to a direct physical judgment are surely those at the end of v 27. Homosexual males are described as **receiving back in themselves for their error the recompense which was due them**. It is quite improbable that the words *receiving back in themselves* refer to some intangible result like "guilt" or "distress," much less to eternal punishment. Even in Roman times, the connection had been made between sexual promiscuity and certain diseases. Only this adequately explains the words *in themselves*.

No doubt Paul is thinking here of sexually transmitted diseases (STDs), but the arrival of AIDS in our day gives his words special point. Of course, the same penalty may accompany the other sexual sins as well (vv 24, 26), but Paul stresses here the retribution deserved by male deviants.

**1:28. And just as they did not see fit to retain God in *their* knowledge, God turned them over to a debased mind so that they did unseemly things,**

For a third time we are told that **God turned** men **over to** something. This time it is to **a debased mind**. The reason now given is that **they did not see fit to retain God in *their* knowledge**. The sexual perversions just described (vv 26-27) cannot be comfortably engaged in when the human mind is thinking about God. Common sense alone makes clear that male and female are suited for sexual union and childbearing, while same-sex sexual activity requires ignoring or discounting the very structure of nature itself.

But a refusal to keep God before the mind is not confined to this type of sinner alone. Human beings are often at great pains to do away with the idea of God. So they frequently deny, distort, or explain away His existence precisely because the thought of accountability to Him is painful. But when this banishing of God from the mind occurs, God simply allows them to possess the natural result—*a debased mind.*

Deprived of the ennobling concept of the Creator God, people suffer from the depraved and defective mental life to which God has *turned them over.*

The Greek verb translated by *see fit* (*edokimasan*) is related to the term *debased* in the phrase *a debased mind* (*adokimon noun*), so it is clear once again that the punishment corresponds to man's sin. This is especially evident here because the word *mind* (*nous*) picks up the cognitive element expressed by the words in their knowledge (*en epignōsei* [*their* is supplied in English]). Hence, man's banishment of God from his mental processes leads to a mind-set that is both undiscerning and unworthy. The result of this base mindset in humanity is that **they did unseemly things** (*poiein ta mē kathēkonta*). These *unseemly things* are now detailed in the graphic verses that follow.

**1:29-31. *becoming people* filled with all unrighteousness, immorality, wickedness, greed, malice; full of envy, murder, strife, deceit, malignity. *They are* whisperers, slanderers, God-haters, insolent, arrogant, boastful, inventors of evil things, disobedient to parents, undiscerning, unfaithful, unloving, irreconcilable, unmerciful.**

The list of vices contained in these verses falls into four groups that are indicated by the way Paul structures his list. We will look at each of these groupings in turn. (The words *becoming people* are not found in the original text and are added in the interest of clarity.)

The opening series consists of five terms connected with the words **filled with all** (*peplērōmenous pasē*). The adjective *all* (*pasē*) is doubtless intended to apply to all five feminine nouns that immediately follow it. Mankind's character and behavior reflect a surfeit of all kinds of **unrighteousness** (perhaps more specifically, "injustice"), **immorality**, **wickedness**, **greed**, and **malice**. Human beings who "[do] not see fit to retain God in their knowledge" (v 28) are unjust, sexually corrupt, wicked, greedy, and malicious. The middle term of the five (*wickedness*) is the most general in the series and is placed for assonance between *immorality* and *greed*, since these three words begin with the same Greek letter (*pi*). (In fact, of the seven Greek words in this initial chain, beginning with *filled*, five start with *pi*!)

The second series begins with the words **full of** (*mestous*). Five additional characteristics of depraved humanity are now listed: **envy, murder, strife, deceit, malignity** (each of these five are in the Greek genitive case and grammatically dependent on *mestous*). The stress in this series falls on the harsh hostility that so often characterizes human beings' relations with one another. The idea elaborated here was already suggested by the last word of the previous series, *malice*. Man's hostility toward his fellow man finds ugly expression in envy that can lead to *murder* (see Jas 4:2), and if not actually to that, it can lead to its precursors, *strife, deceit*, and *malignity*. This last word, *malignity* (*kakoētheias*), cannot be sharply distinguished from *malice* (*kakia*), which concluded the first chain of words. Thus each series is rounded off by a similar idea, namely, the spiteful spirit that manifests itself in mankind's interpersonal relations.

The third series in Paul's list is marked off by the fact that the qualities enumerated are not grammatically dependent on a leading word (like *filled with* or *full of* earlier in this verse). But it is likely we should split this further enumeration of characteristics into two subgroups. The first subgroup (the third series) contains six words, the last of which has a dependent genitive (**inventors of evil things** [*epheuretas kakōn*]). In the second subgroup (the fourth series) the *first* term is *preceded by* a dependent dative form (**disobedient to parents** [*goneusin apeitheis*]). This juxtaposing of dependent forms (*kakōn* and *goneusin*) suggests a break that is confirmed by the fact that all five of the Greek words that follow *goneusin apeitheis* (i.e., the five words that follow the words *to parents*) begin with the Greek letter *alpha* and thus form a climax to the whole list that has a pleasing alliteration.

In the third series, therefore, the new listing of evil qualities proceeds from the term **whisperers** (again the words *they are* have been supplied) to the charge that men are *inventors of evil things*. While Paul does not seem to be concerned in the larger list with any "progression" in evil, something akin to that appears in this particular unit. As *whisperers* people often convey negative information subtly, or behind the scenes. But no such restraints are suggested by the general word **slanderers**, who may convey their negativity either quietly or very openly.

The next word, **God-haters**, appears a little out of place. Why would such a characteristic be placed *here* in the sequence, rather than first, for example? In fact the rendering *God-haters* is retained in our translation only because it is the traditional interpretation of the Greek word (*theostugeis*) in this passage. Though that could be correct here, this meaning is doubtful. In extrabiblical materials the word is only found in the sense of "hated by God." Given the tendency of compound words in Greek to lose some of their derivational force and grade down to a more stereotyped meaning, it seems quite likely that by Paul's day the Greek term had come to mean something like *repugnant*. This meaning aptly fits the flow of the immediate series.

Taken in this sense, the word would suitably describe the ugly character of *slanderers*, while at the same time it broadens the description of sinful men as generally *repugnant* and disgusting. This repugnance is heightened when men are also **arrogant** and **boastful**. The latter of these two words, *boastful* (*alazonas*), particularly conveyed the sense of empty self-display, which is parodied by the Greek writer Theophrastus. The two terms thus move from the general haughtiness of arrogance to the shameless display of the self-promoter. Finally, they become *inventors* ("devisers") *of evil things*. Nothing evil is beyond the range of their corrupt inventiveness, even if no one has thought of it before!

Finally, the fourth series, beginning with *disobedient to parents*, contains six terms (including the one for *disobedient*) that round off Paul's withering analysis of humanity's condition under God's wrath. The loss of respect for parental authority brings in its wake a lack of discernment (**undiscerning**), a lack of fidelity (**unfaithful**) whether to commitments or to established standards, a lack of concern and affection (**unloving**), a lack in the ability to accommodate or make peace (**irreconcilable**), and a lack of elementary compassion (**unmerciful**). All six of the words begin with the Greek alpha privative, i.e., a negative prefix.[16] Sin is much more than what people do. It is also what people *do not* do!

Thus Paul's sweeping description of man's moral state effectively articulates the broad dimensions of God's displeasure with sin. Man's very own condition proclaims loudly that "the wrath of God is revealed from heaven" (v 18). Here, in Paul's elaborate exposure of the depths of human depravity, the discerning eye can see how God has "turned [humanity] over" to the depraving effects of their own "unrighteousness and ungodliness" (see v 18). One final charge against mankind remains to be stated.

> **1:32. Although they know God's righteous standard, that people who do such things are deserving of death, they not only do them, but they even approve of those who do them.**

This verse offers a grim finale to Paul's depiction of humanity under divine wrath. Although God is no longer held in recognition (v 28), a consciousness of **God's righteous standard** (*to dikaiōma tou Theou*) remains. The verb rendered here by **although they know** (*epignontes*) suggests that man's perception of what is right and just has not been totally effaced. Mankind is not really able to escape a moral consciousness and is always able to sense what the appropriate retribution for real wickedness is. However much he may thrust the thought of God behind him, the realization that sin cries out for punishment can never be wholly eradicated.

Yet tragically men ignore this perception and not only perpetuate their own sin (**they not only do them**), but they even go so far as to **approve of those who do them**. Some have wondered how this last point can be climactic and seemingly worse than the actual doing of such things. But this misses Paul's point. It is bad enough to *do* these things, but instead of expressing chagrin and shame that such things occur, men actually

---

[16] English words use alpha privatives to reverse the meanings of words as well. Consider, for example, theist vs. atheist, moral vs. amoral, political vs. apolitical, symmetrical vs. asymmetrical, and typical vs. atypical. –RNW

extend acceptance and commendation to the doers! The evil of men's actions is deepened by the evil of their attitudes!

In short, man commends and approves what he himself is doing. The result is an elevation of sin to a level of respectability among sinners, with the consequent ignoring of divine sanctions against it. This awful state is exemplified in many ways in our own time as well. Witness, for example, the elevation of gay sin to the level of an approvable lifestyle choice!

The final verse of chap. 1 is therefore an appropriate, but appalling, climax to this passage. Paul's indictment of humanity culminates in mankind's tragic effort to make evil a virtue. The depth to which mankind has fallen under the wrath of its Creator painfully discloses the nature and extent of God's displeasure.

# Romans 2

### d. The Universality of This Manifestation (2:1-5)

Despite the sweeping character of Paul's indictment, the human race has never lacked for moralists whose particular arrogance is to pass unreserved censure on the behavior of their fellow man while excusing themselves. What about such people? Are their explicit or implicit claims to moral superiority to be respected? Are they exceptions to the condemnation Paul has expressed against mankind, and therefore are they exempt from God's wrath? The apostle now wishes to address this obvious issue.

Paul begins this section by addressing anyone at all who might claim moral superiority. There are no sufficient grounds for narrowing the reference of this passage to the Jews, or even to a primary focus on the Jews, as some interpreters have done. The Jews are not specifically in view until v 17.

> **2:1. Therefore you are without a defense, O man (anyone who judges). In fact, in the matters for which you judge someone else, you condemn yourself, since you who pass judgment do the same things.**

The **therefore** (*Dio*) that opens this chapter is surprising at first glance. There seems to be nothing in the preceding passage that suggests guilt on the person who condemns, or deplores, human sin. But a person who *condemns* sin is not the same as a person who *judges* it. Obviously the role of a "judge" does not belong to one who is himself guilty of the very things on which he passes judgment. It is therefore to a person who adopts the morally superior stance of a *judge* that Paul now addresses himself.

As the apostle well knows, an attitude of moral superiority was to be found in all the races and cultures of his time. Accordingly, here he does not have either Jew or Gentile particularly in mind, but rather **anyone who judges** (*pas ho krinōn*). It seems best to punctuate with a period after the parenthetical words *anyone who judges*, as the suggested translation does. The following statement contains the Greek conjunction *gar*, which normally introduces independent statements (here translated **in fact**). The initial sentence states the basic premise of the unit that begins with 2:1.

The words **without a defense** (NKJV = "inexcusable") translate a Greek form that carried overtones of a legal proceeding (i.e., *anapologētos*, which is cognate to the regular word for a legal defense: *apologia*). In his assumed role as the "judge" of others the self-assured moralist actually has no viable defense for himself. So to speak, in the arena of judgment he himself has no case. The reason for this is now stated.

The fact of the matter is that this would-be judge (**you who pass judgment**) does the same things. (The Greek *gar* [= *in fact*] introduces the reason why the moralist is *without a defense*.) From Paul's perspective there is no exception to this simple reality. The would-be judge is as guilty as those he condemns.

We need to remember, however, that Paul is drawing on the extended catalogue of vices found in 1:24-32. He certainly does not mean that the would-be judge does every sin in that catalogue or that he necessarily chooses to condemn only things of which he is specifically guilty (though, of course, that often occurs). Rather, no matter what he condemns in terms of the vices listed, he himself inevitably participates in the sins that are enumerated, whether or not he specifically condemns those he does or those he does not do. The relevant principle here is "He who is without sin among you, let him throw a stone at her first" (John 8:7b, in the general sense usually given to this statement).

This is the basic sense. However, on closer inspection, it is possible to see an additional link between Rom 2:1 and the preceding chapter. The apostle has stated in 1:32 that though men are aware of God's judgment about such things, they both practice them and are pleased with those who practice them. The verb *suneudokousi* (1:32) contains an important ambiguity. Although my translation ("they approve of those who do them") renders an obvious surface meaning, the Greek might also be translated *they take pleasure in those who do them* (KJV = "have pleasure in them that..."). With such a rendering, the nature of this "pleasure" remains unspecified.

Precisely this more general meaning is apparently required for this verb in Luke 11:48. There the Lord Jesus Christ asserts that "you bear witness that you *take pleasure in* [NKJV = "approve"] the deeds of your fathers; for they indeed killed them [the prophets], and you build their tombs." The NKJV's "approve" hardly fits here since the Jews obviously professed otherwise (see Matt 23:29-31). The point is rather that while censuring the deeds of their fathers by adorning the tombs of their victims, the Pharisees in fact were *taking pleasure in* what their fathers had done since it gave them occasion to vaunt their own superior "holiness." This is exactly what can motivate a proud, censorious judge of others, of the type Paul is discussing.

Consequently, although 1:32 surely points to the way in which men often defend and admire those who do evil and even seek their company, it may just as well also refer to the satisfaction men derive from the fact that other sinners exist. Sadly, human beings often derive a perverse gratification from the failures of others precisely because when someone condemns these failures he often wishes to appear superior to those he has condemned. This attitude of superiority is precisely the spirit of the moralist as he is now described by Paul. He may **judge someone else** but, *contrary to his obvious intention*, Paul insists, he condemns himself, since he **who pass[es] judgment do[es] the same things**.

It is important to Paul's overall argument that the description in 1:18-32 not be perceived as merely a denunciation of those who are regarded as deeply depraved. On the contrary, Paul will not allow any claim to spiritual superiority no matter from whom it comes. The pagans or Jewish moralists, whoever they may be, cannot effectively separate themselves from the general condemnation Paul has expressed in chap. 1. Paul was not describing *unique cases* of depravity, but the *universal condition* of mankind. As he will later say, "There is none righteous, not even one" (Rom 3:10).

> **2:2. And we know that God's judgment against people who do such things corresponds to the truth.**

In fact, the only thing a man really demonstrates by his self-righteous judgment of others is that he has an awareness of God's standards. Paul has already affirmed this awareness in humanity (1:32) and takes it for granted here by the use of *we* (that is, "you who judge" and Paul). The knowledge of **God's judgment** is not confined to Israel at all. The moralist in every race attests mankind's awareness of this solemn reality.

It needs to be carefully observed that when Paul confidently declares that **we know** [*Oidamen*] **that God's judgment against people who do such things corresponds to truth**, he does not employ the word *ginōskō*, but its synonym *oida*. This latter verb is capable of suggesting an instinctive/intuitive knowledge or recognition of God's judgment (*krima*). Paul, therefore, is saying, "You who condemn others—you as well as I, that is, we—do indeed have an awareness of God's judgment against such sins and this judgment conforms to reality—that is, it *corresponds to truth*." The point is not that the moralist consciously links his critique with God. Rather, it is that his critique exposes an awareness of the divine standard; however deeply buried it may be in the moralistic conscience. If the moralist finds the doers of these evils "deserving of death" (1:32), his conclusion simply confirms that *God's judgment...corresponds to truth*, i.e., it is truly deserved.

The apostle is not talking here about what we call "final judgment." The traditional division of the material implicitly suggested by the chapter break should be ignored. Paul is continuing to discuss the theme of "the wrath of God...revealed from heaven" (1:18). Indeed, the words "although they know God's righteous standard, that people who do such things are worthy of death" (1:32) make clear that Paul's focus on God's temporal displeasure with sin (that can lead to death) continues from chap. 1 into chap. 2. Moralists can see the temporal judgments that God visits on sinners and can acknowledge their justness (*judgment...corresponds to truth*), whether or not such judgments are explicitly ascribed to God at all. Thus 1:32 prepares for 2:1.

> **2:3-4. So do you suppose, O man—you who judge people who do such things and you do them too—that you yourself will escape God's judgment? Or do you despise the wealth of His kindness and tolerance and longsuffering, not realizing that God's kind *behavior* is drawing you to repentance?**

The moralist is trapped in a "catch-22." Since he condemns the sin around him and justifies the "wrath" inflicted on it, how can he himself hope to **escape God's judgment**? After all, Paul's list of vices (1:24-32, esp. vv 28-32) include the failures of the moralist himself. If he justifies, explicitly or implicitly, *God's judgment* on others, should he not anticipate *God's judgment* on himself?

What is his problem, Paul asks? Just because judgment has not reached *him* as yet, does he in fact despise this delay in experiencing consequences as unworthy of his respect? Rather does not this display of God's **kindness and tolerance and longsuffering** reveal God's desire that the moralist himself should come **to repentance**? Doesn't he realize that **God's kind *behavior*** toward him is His way of drawing the moralist *to repentance*? (The verb rendered **is drawing** [*agei*] could also be translated "is leading," in the sense of "showing you your proper path.") How sad it is when man is so self-righteously proud that God's kindly patience to him is regarded as unworthy of his attention or response. By persisting in his sins, even the moralist endangers his own well-being.

The idea of repentance here, of course, refers to the need the moralist has to turn away from his own sins to avoid the "wrath" that God exercises against such things (1:18). It has nothing to do with Paul's doctrine of justification. Indeed this reference to repentance is the only one in the entire book of Romans.[1] Moo (pp. 134-35) writes: "Repentance plays a surprisingly small part in Paul's teaching, considering its importance in contemporary Judaism." But Paul cannot be correctly understood when he is read, as many do today, as though he reflected the thinking of "contemporary Judaism." On the contrary, his gospel came directly "through the revelation of Jesus Christ" (Gal 1:12).

> **2:5. And by means of your hardness and your unrepentant heart are you storing up wrath against yourself in a day of wrath, and of revelation, and of the righteous judgment of God?**

The sentence of which this verse consists might be either a statement or a question. My translation punctuates it as a question in light of the questions in the two previous verses. On the other hand, the sense is not greatly affected if the verse is understood as a statement. In either case,

---

[1] Since this is the sole use of repentance (*metanoia*) in Romans, it is clear that it is not found in the justification section of the letter, 3:21–4:25. The only condition of justification is faith in Christ. Of course repentance might well result in a person coming to faith in Christ, since it can lead God to send someone with the message of life, or since the repentant person might now actually seek out someone to tell him that message (e.g., Cornelius). But it is also possible to come to Christ without prior repentance (e.g., the woman at the well and the Philippian jailer). The sole condition of justification is faith in Christ. –RNW

Paul obviously believes that the unrepentant (*ametanoēton*) moralist is doing this very thing.

What is most striking about Paul's words is that they obviously pick up the key concepts of 1:18. In 1:18, and here, the theme is God's wrath as "revealed" (1:18 = revealed in the here and now) by His **righteous judgment** against man's sin (= "against all the ungodliness and unrighteousness of men" in 1:18). These conceptual ties make it transparent that here Paul explicitly reverts to the basic idea that introduced his subject in 1:18.

A minor textual problem is significant for the clarification of this verse. The "and" (*kai*) found in the suggested translation of v 5 is omitted by the modern critical editions of the Greek NT, just as it was also omitted in the edition of the Textus Receptus, from which the KJV was translated. Hence it does not appear in the NKJV either. But a substantial majority of the surviving manuscripts of Romans, so far as they are known, read this *kai* and support its inclusion. Stylistically we probably have here a "double" hendiadys, that is to say, three nouns are joined by "and" and two of them function like adjuncts. (As when we might say, "he stepped into the noise and clamor and confusion," which equals, "he stepped into the noisy, clamorous confusion.") Thus we could render this noun series as follows: *the wrathfully manifested* **righteous judgment of God**.

"What you are doing," Paul is saying to the hardhearted moralist, "is simply **storing up** retribution for yourself in this *day of the wrathfully manifested righteous judgment of God*." On this understanding of the text, the phrase **in a day of wrath** (*en hēmera orgēs*) does not refer to some future day of eschatological wrath. Instead it refers to the very day in which the moralist now lives since *this is the day* when "the wrath of God is revealed from heaven" (1:18).

Thus the moralist refuses to come to repentance at the very time when God's *wrathfully manifested judgment* is evident all around him. His hardness and his *unrepentant heart* leave him woefully exposed to *the righteous judgment of God*, which the moralist not only ignores, but which he is actually **storing up...against** himself.[2]

---

[2] For an extended discussion of Rom 2:1-5, the reader should see Zane C. Hodges, "The Moralistic Wrath-Dodger: Romans 2:1-5," *Journal of the Grace Evangelical Society* 18 (Spring 2005): 15-21. There Hodges goes into more detail than the commentary's space limits allow. The commentary is a slightly updated treatment of these verses, although the article has unique features, such as critique of the new perspective on Paul (see p. 19). Also the article emphasizes textual features of the *inclusio* between 1:18 and 2:5. The following sets forth those details in a way that makes a chiastic inclusion apparent:

With the words of 2:5, the unit of thought covered by 1:18–2:5 is concluded. The fundamental truth expressed in this unit is that all men, the moralist included, are subject to God's wrath as a result of their sinful behavior. This wrath is not eschatological, but a distressing present reality.

## 2. Humanity Faces God's Impartial Judgment (2:6–3:20)

What follows now is a theme closely related to the preceding discussion, yet at the same time it is a new consideration. The elaborate description in 1:18–2:5, portraying the sinfulness that has called forth the "wrath of God," leads on to the issue of the fundamental way in which God relates to mankind as its Judge (note 3:5, 6). It goes without saying that if God administers wrath, He does so because He is mankind's Judge. That the Creator God does judge humanity is a truth taken for granted here by Paul and was a basic datum of Jewish thought. The fundamental principles on which the divine judgeship operates are now to be considered. This train of thought will occupy Paul through the balance of chap. 2.

### a. The Nature of God's Judgment (2:6-16)

**2:6. He will repay each person according to his works:**

The Greek text of this verse begins with the relative pronoun *hos*, normally translated *who*. The grammatical structure here, at a formal level, is consistent with the common relative function of *hos*, but this pronoun was originally demonstrative in force (cf. Robertson, 695-96) and "unlike the English, includes in itself the demonstrative idea" (Moulton and Milligan, 324). In Romans it is used as a virtual independent pronoun

---

A   *Apokaluptetai orgē Theou* "God's wrath [and righteous judgment] is revealed" (1:18)

  B   Details regarding the revelation of God's wrath against immoralists (1:19-32)

  B'   Details regarding the revelation of God's wrath against moralists (2:1-4)

A'   *Orgēs kai apokalupseōs kai dikaiokrisias tou Theou* "wrath and revelation of God's righteous judgment" (2:5)

It is crucial to observe that Rom 1:18, which introduces this inclusio, does not narrowly say that God's wrath is revealed *against unbelievers*. Rather, it says, "the wrath of God is revealed from heaven against all ungodliness and unrighteousness of men [in general], who suppress the truth." Since Paul is writing to believers in Rome, he is warning believers of the danger of living in opposition to God. –JHN

at 8:32; 14:2, 5; and esp. at 2:23 (where it is the grammatical equivalent of the articular participles in vv 21-22). Stylistically it serves Paul well here as formally connected with the preceding *Theou*, while functioning as a word marking a new departure. It might almost be rendered "This One" (i.e., God), but I opted for the more straightforward **He** (so JB; NIV = "God").

The fundamental principle stated here is simple: God gives man what he deserves. He deals fairly with humanity. The following verses elaborate this basic concept. If **works** are at issue, mankind can expect to receive whatever those *works* may merit.

### 2:7. to those who seek glory and honor and immortality by persisting in good work, eternal life,

For the first time, Paul refers to eternal realities by the use of the phrase **eternal life**. If God judges men here and now by means of His wrath, He obviously also determines man's future destiny. In line with the teaching of the Gospel of John, as well as with Jewish thought in general, this future destiny is identified in terms of *eternal life*. God will certainly give it to any who deserve it **by persisting in good work**.

Unfortunately, however, no one does this. As Paul later makes quite clear, "There is none righteous, not even one...There is no one doing good, there is not even so much as one" (Rom 3:10, 12). Yet the principle remains true that, if there were someone who *did* do good persistently and who *was* indeed righteous, God would give him eternal life because of that.

The Lord Jesus Christ Himself taught this basic truth. When a specialist in the Jewish law (NKJV = "lawyer") asked Him, "Teacher what shall I do to inherit eternal life?" Jesus asked the counter question, "What is written in the law? What is your reading of it?" (Luke 10:25-26). The lawyer then proceeded to quote the two foremost commandments of the law, the commands to love God and neighbor. To this Jesus replied simply, "You have answered rightly; do this and you will live" (Luke 10:27-28). The problem was, of course, that neither the lawyer himself nor anyone else (other than the Lord Jesus) has ever, or will ever, fulfill these two supreme commandments.

Needless to say, the words of Paul in this verse have been absurdly misunderstood as stating a real possibility if not an actual reality. This is done despite Paul's emphatic statements to the contrary in 3:19-20.

To so interpret Paul here, as if he conceived of this as a possibility, is to totally misunderstand him. What we have here is a statement of *principle*, not of *fact*. As Paul elsewhere states, "For if there had been a law given which could have given life, truly righteousness would have been by the law" (Gal 3:21). In principle, God rewards true obedience to His law with *eternal life*, but in practice no one ever acquires it that way.

Human beings often claim that they do **seek** the **glory and honor** that are inherent in immortality, but this pursuit is continually marred by turning aside to sin. Thus the words *by persisting in good work* express something that no human person ever really does.

> **2:8-9. but to those who are selfish and disobey the truth, but obey unrighteousness *instead*, anger and wrath—tribulation and distress for every human soul who does what is evil, for the Jew first and for the Greek;**

But suppose human beings *do not do* what Paul has described in v 7? (It is already clear from 1:18–2:6 that they do not, but Paul is now discussing the *principles* on which the divine Judge deals with His creatures.) The answer is the same as Paul has stated already, but is now repeated to put it in proper contrast with v 7. If "eternal life" awaits those who persist in "good work," **anger and wrath** (*thumos kai orgē*) are the portion of those whose character is different.

Paul now describes such people as **those who are selfish and disobey the truth, but obey unrighteousness *instead*** [this last word is supplied for clarity]. This description clearly echoes 1:18-32. In 1:19-23 Paul has set forth *the truth* about God that is revealed in nature, as well as the way humanity has turned away from that truth. Mankind in fact *disobeys* this truth when he turns to idolatry. The result is a disastrous descent into a life in which men *obey unrighteousness instead*. The lurid portrayal of this depraved human conduct in 1:24-32 is neatly captured here by the leading word *selfish*.[3] Man thinks of himself rather than of God.

Furthermore, Paul wants to make it clear here (for the first time in the epistle) that God's wrath is directed toward such people whether they are Jew or Greek (= Gentile). Indeed, even in the matter of wrath (contrast

---

[3] The Greek behind the word *selfish* (*ex eritheias*) has been much discussed. The literal sense "of selfishness" seems easily the best option, and the adjectival nuance of the prepositional phrase is expressed in my simple rendering *selfish* (NKJV, NIV = "self-seeking"). –ZCH

1:16), the Jew has priority so that God's manifested displeasure is **for the Jew first**. Here Paul no doubt thinks of his own race in its present condition of servitude and recognizes in them the selfish character that invites divine judgment. In their own way (as vv 17-23 will show) the Jews are among *those who...disobey the truth and obey unrighteousness instead.* As Paul has stated in 1 Thess 2:16, "wrath has come upon them to the uttermost" (see vv 15-16 there).

With good rhetorical effect, Paul here accumulates terms that serve to elaborate and underline his original word *wrath* (see 1:18). In v 8 the additional word is the synonym *anger* (*thumos*). In v 9, the phrase *anger and wrath* is replaced by the explicative phrase **tribulation and distress** (*Thlipsis kai stenochōria*). All these words, of course, are expressive of the present experience of mankind as it lives sinfully under the cloud of divine displeasure.

### 2:10. but glory and honor and peace to everyone who does what is good, both to the Jew first and to the Greek.

Paul has already stated the final destiny of those who persist in doing good (of which there are no cases), but now he wants to contrast the *present* experience that God would award (in contrast to vv 8-9) **to everyone who does what is good**. The "anger and wrath" (v 8) and the "tribulation and distress" (v 9) which afflict sinful man here and now could be otherwise if man did what was right. In that case men could expect God to give them **glory and honor and peace**. As before, this applies **both to the Jew first and to the Greek**.

Of course human beings do indeed at times experience glory, or honor, or peace, but never in the full and consistent measure in which God would give these things if man *does what is good*. (Paul's statement is comprehensive, and not to be taken as though it could be fulfilled partially.) Whether we think of powerful men like Julius Caesar, or like the President of the United States, none of them enjoy undiluted *glory and honor and peace*. From the assassination of Caesar to the political vilification of presidents, there is a wide gamut of unpleasant experiences for powerful people that point to the deep personal imperfections in all of them. The so-called "lifestyles of the rich and famous" are anything but trouble free, as our tabloids continually remind us.

Once again, as in v 7, Paul is discussing a *principle*, not an actual *reality*. The words of 3:12 are his pointed assessment of reality: "There is no one doing good, there is not even so much as one."

**2:11. For there is no partiality with God.**

The bottom line of Paul's discussion from vv 6-10 is simple. God is absolutely impartial. The twice repeated reminder that the Jew stands first in humanity's exposure to divine wrath (vv 8-9) was designed to underline this basic fact. Whatever the privileges of the Jews (Paul will discuss them shortly), his race does not as a result receive an "exemption" from the wrath God manifests toward the Gentile world. In fact, when it comes to wrath, the Jew even has priority, in line of course with the truth that "to whom much has been committed, of him they will ask the more" (Luke 12:48c).

From what has just been said about the impartiality of God's present dealings with mankind, it follows that final judgment will be fair as well. Initially Paul had stated (without elaboration) that if man perseveres in doing good, God will award him eternal life (v 7). But this statement was followed by a careful consideration of how God deals with man's behavior right now (vv 8-11). However, God's present dealings with humanity obviously presage His standards in the final judgment. To this theme Paul now turns for a treatment that is fuller than the allusion in v 7.

**2:12. In fact as many as have sinned without the law shall also perish without the law; and as many as have sinned under the law shall be judged by means of the law.**

The Greek conjunction translated **in fact** (*gar*) draws an inference from the statement of v 11, but the translation given here more effectively marks off the slight change in subject matter. Since the Jew/Gentile distinction has been mentioned in vv 8-9, Paul again picks up on that distinction. As surely as both Jew and Gentile are subject to divine wrath here and now, so also both will someday face the final judgment of God. Yet in dealing with them, God will impartially take account of their differing responsibilities.

The outcome of that judgment for the Gentiles is already envisaged in the statement that since they **have sinned without the law**, they **shall also perish without the law**. (For the term *perish* [*apolountai*]) as a reference to eternal damnation, see Matt 18:14; John 3:15, 16; 10:28; 1 Cor 1:18; 2 Cor 2:15; 4:3; 2 Thess 2:10.[4]) But Paul's main point is that the Mosaic law will not be an issue in the final judgment of those who have not lived under it. Instead their judgment will be *without the law* in the sense that they will not be held to account for it. How God will in fact judge them will be stated in vv 14-16.

By contrast, the Jew who has **sinned under the law shall be judged by means of the law**. The Mosaic law will be the standard by which the Jew who lives under it will have his life assessed. God holds men accountable in accordance with the responsibilities they actually have, not those which they don't have. Thus Jew and Gentile will both be fairly assessed in the last judgment by a God who shows no "partiality."

One must keep in mind throughout Rom 2:12-16 that Paul is using what may be called *neutral courtroom language*. This is particularly obvious in the present verse. The words *as many as have sinned under the law* certainly do not imply that *some* who are *under the law* may *not* have sinned (see 3:23). On the contrary Paul's statement refers to all who fit this description whether none, many, or all. The point of the words *as many as* (used twice in this verse) is that God will deal differently with sinners inside His law and those outside of it, however few or many they may be.

### 2:13. Because it is not the hearers of the law who are righteous before God, but *it is* the doers of the law who will be justified.

Since people who sin under the law are destined to be judged by that very law, it follows that no one is accounted righteous merely because he *has* it in his possession. Thus mere **hearers of the law** will not be accounted **righteous before God** (as Jewish pride sometimes seemed to suppose). On the contrary, in the Day of Judgment *it is* only **the doers of the law who will be justified**.

---

[4] *Apollumi* (perish) occurs ninety-two times in the NT. It is unlikely that Hodges is listing *all* of the places in which he thinks it refers to eternal condemnation since he leaves off John 6:39; 17:12; and 18:9. Hodges seems to be listing here *most* of the times in which he thinks it refers to eternal condemnation. He lists nine verses, once in Rom 2:12 and eight times outside of Romans. My own count is that twelve of the ninety-two occurrences refer to eternal condemnation. While we don't know the exact total Hodges would have listed if he was being exhaustive, it is clear he believed that most of the time this word referred to *temporal* destruction and physical death. He felt that only about 10-20% of the time it referred to eternal condemnation. –RNW

It is a bizarre fact that numerous modern expositors have taken this verse to affirm that there will *actually be* people *who will be justified* because they are *doers of the law*. But this view is completely impossible in the face of the plain declarations of Rom 3:19-20. Such a perspective may even be fairly labeled "anti-Pauline" theology.

The error involved in the view just mentioned is an error about what semanticists call *the illocutionary force* of a statement. Such an error occurs, for example, when a scornful statement (like, "you're a fine person") is mistaken for a straightforward statement of praise. Here the true illocutionary force (a statement of principle) is mistaken for a false one (a statement of fact).

As he does throughout these verses, Paul is simply stating the basic principles of the last judgment. As the account in Rev 20:11-15 makes plain, at the Great White Throne men are indeed "judged according to their works, by the things which were written in the books" (Rev 20:12). If anyone were to merit acceptance before God on the basis of those books, he would *be justified*. But that acceptance will be granted only to those who have *not* sinned under the law (cf. v 12), but are instead truly *doers of the law*. James himself tells us, in fact, that, "Whoever shall keep the whole law, and yet stumble in one point, he is guilty of all" (Jas 2:10).

Paul, therefore, knows perfectly well that "by the deeds of the law no flesh will be justified in His sight" (3:20), but he also knows that everyone at the final judgment will have his day in court. Innocence or guilt will be held in judicial abeyance until the evidence of the heavenly books is presented. But then only *the doers of the law will be justified*. Of these, however, there will be none.[5]

---

[5] Romans 2:7 and 2:13 do not speak about people who have *actually* received everlasting life and justification, but discuss a *hypothetical* possibility of unbelievers at the Great White Throne being so righteous that the righteous Judge would render everlasting life and justification to them according to their deeds (cf. Rom 2:5-7 and 2:13). Unfortunately, many interpreters (oblivious to the hypothetical nature of this passage) are in a collision course against Paul.

What shows that the theoretical interpretation is the correct approach? Consider a portion of this commentary's outline of Romans.

A. God's Displeasure with Humanity Is Manifest (1:18–3:20).

B. The Unrighteous Can Obtain Righteousness Through Jesus Christ (3:21–5:11).

Romans 2:7 and 13 are within section A, not section B. Paul's articulation of justification by faith will not begin until 3:21. Furthermore, vv 7 and 13 lie much closer to the beginning of 1:18–3:20 than to its end. That is, Paul is still in the early stages of constructing an argument that is capsulated well by 3:10 and 12: "There is none righteous, no, not one...There is none who does good, no, not one." In other words, Rom 2:7 says that the righteous judge at the Great White

**2:14-15. However, whenever the Gentiles, who do not have the law, instinctively do the things that are in the law, *then*, though they do not have the law, they constitute a law for themselves. They show the work of the law inscribed on their hearts, because their conscience will be a witness, *as will* also their discussions with each other condemning or even defending *one another*,**

The initial conjunction in v 14 (*gar*) is rendered in my translation by **however**. To render it "for" (as in KJV, NKJV) produces a somewhat misleading sense, as though it connected directly to the previous verse. But v 13 is almost (though not quite) parenthetical, and Paul now returns in vv 14-15 to the idea of judgment "without the law" for Gentiles, which he had set over against judgment "under the law" for Jews, as stated in v 12.

Some modern translators show an awareness of the problem just mentioned. NACE (1961) omits the conjunction altogether; JB (1968) translates it "for instance;" while, strangely, the NIV (1985) turns vv 14-15 themselves into a parenthesis, translating the conjunction by "indeed." How then, one might ask, can God fairly judge the Gentile world if they have no law to be judged by and, furthermore, if only "the doers of the law shall be justified"? How is Gentile judgment possible at all? The present verses answer that question in service of Paul's theme that God is a fair and impartial Judge of His creatures.

Paul's basic idea in the present verses is that Gentile behavior, coupled with their own discussion of that behavior, shows that **the work (= standards) of the law is inscribed on their hearts**. Here of course Paul has in mind the fact that in pagan cultures there is an instinctive sense of right and wrong that often reflects the demands of God's law. Even pagans generally saw evil in actions like murder, theft, extortion, adultery, and lying. Thus when Paul states that **whenever the Gentiles, who do not have the law, instinctively do the things that are in the law**, he is referring to the many manifestations of morality that could easily be found in non-Jewish societies such as that of the Greco-Roman world in which he lived. Paul did not hold a view of total depravity that precluded him from seeing

---

Throne (GWT) will render eternal life to those who patiently continue in doing good, but not one unbeliever at the GWT will merit life, since only 100% consistent doers of good would merit life. Similarly, for Rom 2:13, any unbeliever at the GWT who is a consistent doer of the [whole] law would be justified. Even though Gentiles without the law may do things of the law (Rom 2:14), keeping *part* of the law is insufficient for (hypothetically) meriting life at the GWT. –JHN

any morality at all outside the explicit observance of the law. Instead he acknowledges such morality as an evidence of the work of the Creator God. In fact, the law which God had revealed to Moses fundamentally expressed an innate sense of right and wrong that the Creator had already *inscribed on* all human *hearts*. For Paul, therefore, the image of God was not totally defaced or expunged by human sin.

The Greek word translated as *instinctively* (*phusei*, lit., "by nature") points to the inner being of man where his consciousness of right and wrong resides. (Some commentators construe *phusei* with *do not have the law*, but the sense produced is obscure given Paul's usual use of *phusei*.) Since, as Paul will shortly say, this is something *given* (*inscribed*) to man, these *things that are in the law* that the Gentiles do **constitute** (*eisi*) **a law for** the Gentiles **themselves**. That is to say, there is a sense in which the Gentiles *do* have a law that springs from their inward *nature*, which is where God put it.

Thus, although the revealed law of Moses will not be used against the Gentiles in the Day of Judgment, nevertheless **their conscience will be a witness** against them. This is surely the intent of Paul's words which, in Greek, are a construction known as a genitive absolute. This kind of construction is inherently timeless but draws its temporal reference from the context. Here Paul is obviously referring to the Day of Judgment (he actually says so in v 16) and this is manifested also by the expression *will be a witness*, which reflects the language of the courtroom.

But how, we might ask, will *their conscience* actually render its *witness*? The answer is to be found in the following phrase that grammatically continues the genitive absolute construction. The Greek conjunction that joins the two parts of this construction (*kai*) is rendered in my translation, *as will* **also** (with *as will* supplied for clarity). In fact, this *kai* actually joins the two subjects of the Greek participle rendered *will be a witness* (*summarturousēs*). (As is common in NT Greek, when the verb stands first it may agree grammatically with the first member of a compound subject.) Both *their conscience* and *their discussions* fall under the governance of the participle that begins the absolute construction. The two participles that follow the phrase **their discussions with each other** are then intended to clarify the nature of the *discussions* referred to in this verse. Thus these participles (*katēgorountōn ē kai apologoumenōn* = **condemning or even defending**) are circumstantial adjuncts to *logismōn* (*discussions*). The structure as we analyze it makes it quite unnecessary to puzzle over the connection of v 16 with v 15, as many have done. The large, complex genitive absolute construction, pointed out above, describes what takes place "in the day when God will judge men's secrets" (v 16). Their conscience displayed in their mutual *discussions* will furnish a decisive witness in that day.

The sense is much clearer from the Greek word order than from the English. An awkwardly literal rendering might be: *bearing witness together (sum-) their conscience and (also) their discussions with each other that either condemn or defend.* Thus the *conscience* and the *discussions* that express it will be like co-witnesses in the divine courtroom. Let us look at this interesting statement more closely.

The doctrine of the Apostle Paul in this text may be traced directly to the teaching of the Lord Jesus Christ. According to Matt 12:36-37 Jesus said, "But I say to you that for every idle word men may speak, they will give account of it in the Day of Judgment. For by your words you will be justified, and by your words you will be condemned."

Needless to say, our Lord's statement has a much broader reference than Paul's does in Romans 2. Yet if all of man's words are accessible on the Judgment Day, this obviously includes the kind of communication Paul has in mind here.

Thus in the judgment of Gentiles, the moralizing *discussions* they have had *with each other* (*metaxu allēlōn*) will come into play. Those discussions may have been either *condemning* of one another's conduct *or even defending* **one another**, by justifying this form of behavior or that. Such discussions will reveal at the judgment precisely what aspects of God's law have remained upon these pagan hearts. In that way the standards they have used to evaluate the conduct of their fellow man will become the standards by which they themselves will be judged.

If, for example, a pagan has said to his contemporary, "I think it is wrong of you to deceive others like that," yet he himself in other circumstances has employed the same kind of deception, the very words of this pagan will condemn him in the Day of Judgment, precisely as Jesus said they would! Thus the law inwardly *inscribed on their hearts* will be made manifest by the displays of *conscience* that *their discussions with each other* so clearly reveal. Their own words will provide evidence against them.

**2:16. in the day when God will judge men's secrets through Jesus Christ according to my gospel.**

What Paul has been describing will take place **in the day when God will judge men's secrets.** This has been evident, of course, from v 12 onward, since in v 12 he specifically referred to people being judged. But since an extended sentence began in v 14, where present actions are in view, it is clarifying to be told that the statements just made (contained in the genitive absolute construction) refer to *the day when God will judge.* (Thus the words *in the day when* are to be grammatically connected with the participle rendered "will be a witness.")

The phrase *men's secrets* (*ta krupta tōn anthrōpōn*) stresses what is already implied in v 15. If all of the words men have spoken on moral matters will be made known at the judgment—no matter how much the speakers might wish these words to be unknown or undisclosed—then clearly God knows all about every man. *Men's secrets,* however embarrassing or shameful, will be under scrutiny at the final judgment, precisely as Jesus also declared when He said, "For nothing is secret that will not be revealed, nor anything hidden that will not be known and come to light" (Luke 8:17).

But not only did Jesus say this, He will actually be God's Agent for this total exposure of *secrets* since the judgment Paul describes will be accomplished **through Jesus Christ** in accordance with his **gospel** (= the *gospel* Paul preached). In fact, it was a distinctive part of the Christian proclamation that Jesus Christ would be the Judge before whom men would stand in the final judgment. Thus Paul declared on Mars Hill that God "has appointed a day on which He will judge the world in righteousness by the Man whom He has ordained" (Acts 17:31). Yet, of course, it was not Paul alone who declared this truth (it was not Paul's *gospel* in *that* sense). Instead this fact was another datum in the Christian proclamation that went back to the teachings of our Lord Himself. Jesus clearly stated: "For the Father judges no one, but has committed all judgment to the Son" (John 5:22).

With the climaxing words of this verse, Paul concludes the subunit found in 2:12-16. Though Paul had earlier declared in this passage (see v 7) that God would give eternal life to those "persisting in good work," there is nothing in his detailed treatment of the final judgment in vv 12-16 to suggest that human beings could anticipate such an outcome on that day.

On the contrary, the jarring declaration that *God will judge men's secrets* should function like a convicting arrow aimed at every heart. For what human being does not have *secrets* that he or she hopes will never see the light of day? Of course, Paul has not yet explicitly stated man's universal sinfulness (as he will in 3:9-18) or man's hopeless estate if his hopes rest in God's law (3:19-20). But the perceptive unconverted hearer or reader of Rom 2:7-16 must necessarily be disquieted by Paul's emphatic insistence that in the judgment a person will be awarded whatever he deserves. Anyone who finds hope in that simple fact has not read this passage with sufficient care. Sinners "without the law" and sinners "under the law" are in the same condition. They are subject to judgment. As Paul will shortly say, "both Jews and Greeks are *all* under sin" (3:9, italics added).[6]

But for now, Paul is satisfied to assert that both God's present dealings with humanity (2:7-11) and His future judgment of humanity (2:12-16) are and will be totally impartial for Jew and Gentile alike. Yet this concept was not at all how the contemporary Jew thought of things, even if he agreed with Paul in principle that God was impartial. Was there not, after all, a distinct advantage for the Jew that came from his possession of Torah, God's law? To this question, the apostle now turns.

### b. The Vulnerability of the Jews (2:17-29)

Wherever the gospel went in the Greco-Roman world, opposition to it could be expected from the synagogue. Paul's own experience in Acts demonstrates this fact clearly. In writing a letter to the Christians at Rome, Paul had to assume similar opposition to Christianity there as well. Indeed he probably already had information that confirmed this. What then should the Roman Christians say to Jewish people who might claim that they merited special treatment from God?

Part of the answer lay in the truth already discussed in 2:7-16 where Paul has insisted on God's impartiality toward all. In fact, the Jew stood first in his vulnerability to divine wrath (vv 9-10) and could only expect

---

[6] Romans 2:14-16 is one sentence in Greek. Its context is the Great White Throne (GWT). Observe the phrase "in the day when God will judge men's secrets" (v 16) and "bearing witness" (v 15). This passage does not focus on the function of the conscience *during the present life*, even though the commentary tradition as a whole has followed that rabbit trail. Instead, this passage speaks of the righteous Judge calling for testimony from the consciences of Gentile unbelievers *at the GWT Judgment*. In light of all of the honest accusations by the conscience at such a judgment, it is clear that no one will be acquitted. All of this fits well with what Paul proclaims. –JHN

justification at the final judgment if he were a "doer" rather than a mere "hearer" of the law (2:13). But the vulnerability of his race to divine displeasure and judgment needs somewhat fuller treatment for the benefit of Paul's Christian readers. How would Paul himself address the special claims of his own race? The discussion in 2:17-29 answers this question unambiguously.

**2:17. Look! You bear the name "Jew," and you rest in the law and boast in God.**

Adopting here (as he did in 2:1-5) the popular Greco-Roman diatribe style, Paul hypothesizes an imaginary Jewish interlocutor who represents the quintessential Jewish perspective about the Jewish position vis-à-vis his God. Such a person would in fact be quite proud to **bear the name "Jew"** and precisely because he possessed God's special revelation, **the law,** he could rest his religious hopes on that very law. In fact, he could quite openly **boast in God,** since it was to his racial group that God had given Torah.

**2:18-20. And you know His will and you discern the things that really matter, because you are instructed out of the law and you have confidence that you yourself are a guide for the blind, a light for those in darkness, an instructor of the ignorant, a teacher of babes, since you have the formulation of knowledge and of truth in the law.**

Paul knew his own people. His own personal career as a Pharisee had taught him precisely the religious pretensions that marked this strictest of all Jewish sects. His words in this verse not only state those pretensions plainly but are, in the very statement of them, a withering condemnation of Jewish religious pride.

In contrast, therefore, to the benighted Gentiles, this quintessential Jew would claim to **know** God's **will** (revealed in Torah) and therefore to be able to **discern the things that really matter.** (The Greek word rendered *discern* [*dokimazeis*] implies the ability to sift and test with a view to approving something.) In the phrase *the things that really matter* (*ta diapheronta*), Paul implies the disdain in which a Jew would hold not only the standards but also the aspirations of a non-Jew.

The phrase **because you are instructed** (*katēchoumenos*) and the words **and you have confidence** (*pepoithas te*) are tied rather closely together by the enclitic particle *te* (and), even though the participle (rendered *instructed*) is grammatically linked with *you discern*. The *te* might in fact be rendered *and so*. Since this typical Jew can *discern the things that really matter* as a result of being *instructed* **out of the law**, he has confidence in his own capacity to help others to escape their ignorant blindness.

In the words that follow *you have confidence* **that you yourself are**, Paul heaps up with superb rhetorical effect a series of self-designations that lay bare the Jew's sense of superiority to his Gentile counterparts. He himself, he thinks, is **a guide, a light, an instructor**, and **a teacher**. By way of demeaning contrast, the Gentiles to whom he brings his wisdom are **blind, in darkness, ignorant**, and **babes**.

Paul has no need to point out specifically the vanity latent in such condescending contrasts.

For the third time in these three verses Paul refers to the knowledge this Jew claimed on the basis of the law: (1) *you know His will* ("from the law" is implicit); (2) *you are instructed out of the law*; (3) **you have the formulation of knowledge and of truth in the law**. Indeed each reference to the law is more fulsomely stated than the previous one. The effect of this rhetorical technique is to increasingly highlight how such a person builds his prideful self-esteem through the *information* he has acquired out of the law. But that is only *hearing* and is not the same as *doing* the law (cf. v 13).

The Greek word translated *formulation* (*morphōsin*, also *embodiment*) refers to the fact that God's will was *embodied* or *formulated* in the Scriptures that contained the law. In the Scriptures were found the specific content *of knowledge and of truth* (a hendiadys = *true knowledge*) that God had revealed to the Jewish people. Thus even the sacred writings were a source of pride to the Jew, despite the fact that those very writings condemned him (3:19-20).

> **2:21-23. So, you who teach another person, don't you teach yourself? You who preach not to steal, do you steal? You who say not to commit adultery, do you commit adultery? You who despise idols, do you rob temples? You who boast in the law, do you dishonor God by transgressing the law?**

So (*oun*), says Paul, what about *your performance*? Does your performance match up well with your confident self-assessment? Of course it did not, as the following series of interrogations makes clear. Here Paul does not need to directly charge his hypothetical interlocutor with any of the things he mentions. Instead the probing questions are rhetorically more effective. The sins that are listed are obviously those everyone knew quite well that Jews were guilty of, just as the Gentiles were. The vaunted superiority the Jew imagined that he had turns out to be a mere façade behind which lay the same sins that other men committed.

Has the Jew really learned anything from his own law? You might **teach another person**, Paul says, but **don't you teach yourself?** Have the commands that forbid you **to steal** and **to commit adultery** taught you not to do these things? In the third question of the series, however, Paul gives his interrogation a special slant. True, the Jew who claimed to **despise idols** may never have bowed down to one, but what about gaining financial profit from the false worship of the Gentiles?

The words **rob temples** translate the single Greek word *hierosuleis* and no doubt refer to the willingness to receive property stolen from temples for the purpose of reselling such items for a profit. It is quite doubtful that a typical Jew would enter a pagan temple with the intent of stealing from it (and doubtful Paul would accuse them of this even if it occasionally happened). On the other hand if the actual thief sought to sell the fruits of his theft to a Jewish merchant, it would be all too easy to turn a blind eye to the idol-related object and to acquire it for resale. An observant Jew might even rationalize that in this fashion he was helping to "deconstruct" some pagan practice. In so doing, of course, the Jew in question participated in a theft.

The bottom line was clear. Despite his inclination to **boast in the law**, by his behavior in disobeying the law the Jew was engaged in conduct that disgraced God. The final question in the series furnishes a biting climax: **Do you dishonor God by transgressing the law?** What could be more disgraceful than to claim special privilege and standing before God while at the same time bringing Him grave dishonor?

### 2:24. For *"the name of God is blasphemed among the Gentiles because of you, just as it is written."*

Paul does not leave this last question (v 23) unanswered, however. Thinking no doubt of Scriptures like Isa 52:5 and Ezek 36:22 (but paraphrasing their idea), Paul emphatically affirms that Jewish conduct has led the Gentiles to blaspheme *"the name of God."* This observation is a *coup de grâce* to Jewish pride in possessing God's law and was confirmed by their own Scriptures (referred to by *"just as it is written"*). In so stating Paul prepares the way for the climaxing assertion found in 3:19-20.

Paul for the first time in this subunit refers explicitly to circumcision. From one standpoint, the term *circumcision* could stand for the Jews' commitment to the entire law (cf. Gal 5:3). This inherent connection between circumcision and law-keeping seems implicit in these verses. But from another point of view, mere circumcision was sometimes thought of as virtually sufficient in itself to win the approval of God. This idea, however, Paul wishes to emphatically deny.

> **2:25. After all, circumcision is profitable if you do the law. But if you are a transgressor of the law, your circumcision becomes uncircumcision.**

Paul means exactly what he says in this verse, of course. If someone regards circumcision as the basis for his relationship to the God who "will repay each person according to his works" (v 6) and with whom "there is no partiality" (v 11), then the profitability of circumcision accrues only **if you do the law**. But suppose **you are a transgressor of the law**, that is to say, you "have sinned under the law" (v 12)? In that case, circumcision's profitability before God vanishes and the Jew is reduced to the level of the Gentiles who "have sinned without the law" (v 12). Or to put it another way: **your circumcision becomes uncircumcision**.

Much of the contemporary literature on Romans is hopelessly confused in its treatment of chap. 2. Commentators quickly forget, or completely ignore, the Biblical principle stated by James: "For whoever shall keep the whole law, and yet stumble in one point, he is guilty of all" (Jas 2:10). Indeed, Paul himself quoted the curse of Deut 27:26: "Cursed is everyone who does not continue in *all things* which are written in the book of the law, to do them" (Gal 3:10, italics added). Neither Paul nor James would have tolerated the claim that a "general obedience" to the law of Moses actually met its demands. One was either a law-keeper or a law-breaker. There was no middle ground. It is precisely this truth that underlies the argument of Romans 2. *If you do the law*, Paul says, **circumcision is profitable**. But if you don't, it isn't. That is why he can conclude that the law stops "every mouth" so that "all the world" may "become accountable to God" (3:19). Unless this principle is clearly understood, Romans 2 will be *misunderstood* as it actually is in most modern scholarly literature.

**2:26-27. So if an uncircumcised person should keep the righteous standards of the law, will not his uncircumcision be credited as circumcision? And will not the physically uncircumcised person who fulfills the law judge you, a transgressor of the law who *has its* written *form* and circumcision?**

The converse is true as well. If disobedience to the law nullifies the advantage of circumcision, obedience to the law by a Gentile would make him as acceptable before God as if he had been circumcised. As Paul had earlier stated, "it is not the hearers of the law who are righteous before God, but it is the doers of the law who will be justified" (v 13). Thus **if an uncircumcised person should keep the righteous standards of the law**, he could expect to be justified before God. In that case, obviously, **his uncircumcision** would **be credited as circumcision**.

But as before there are *no such people*. It should be carefully noted that Paul's statement is hypothetical. The rendering *if* [a Gentile] *should keep...the law* is a third class condition in Greek. Third class conditions are employed when the hypothetical character of an assumption is in the foreground.

Paul is saying that *on this hypothesis* the obedient Gentile's uncircumcision would *be credited as circumcision* and that in the Day of Judgment **the physically** [or perhaps, "naturally," *ek phuseōs*] **uncircumcised person who fulfills the law** [will] **judge you** [the Jewish legalist]. That is to say, such a person would be a kind of "witness for the prosecution," just as the Queen of Sheba and the Ninevites will someday be (see Luke 11:31-32).

Paul's supposition here furnishes the ultimate irony for any Jew who thought himself superior to the Gentiles by the mere fact of circumcision, or by the mere fact of possessing God's law. Let not such a Jew imagine that he is automatically invulnerable to righteous condemnation from the Gentiles themselves. For if one can think of a Gentile *who fulfills* (or, completes; *telousa*) *the law*, one could also conceive of that person expressing condemnation of a Jewish person who is **a transgressor of the law**. Thus *the physically uncircumcised person* would judge the *circumcised* person. Certainly this was a role reversal that most religious Jews probably had never conceived of before. But its logic is obvious.

With the words *you, a transgressor of the law* **who *has its* written *form* and circumcision**, Paul heightens the role reversal he has hypothetically suggested. The "judge" in Paul's scenario was *physically uncircumcised* while the object of his condemnation was not just *a transgressor of the law* but one who had its *written form* [i.e., the Scriptures] and also had *circumcision*. His advantages over his Gentile judge had been enormous, but those advantages would be to no avail in the Day of Judgment.

The translation *who has its written form and circumcision* renders the briefer Greek words *dia grammatos kai peritomēs* [lit., "with letter and circumcision"] and, in accordance with one usage of *dia*, describes the "circumstances" under which this Jewish person has become *a transgressor of the law*. The advantages of Scripture and circumcision were his, but his condemnation by an obedient Gentile would still be fully deserved. It remained true that "as many as have sinned under the law will be judged by the law" (v 12). If there were a fully observant Gentile there in that day, he would join in condemning the sinning Jew.

The point of Paul's hypothetical proposition is obvious. The self-confident Jew should consider the reality that once he is *a transgressor of the law*, he not only has no advantage over a Gentile, but he would actually be worthy of condemnation by any Gentile who was not *a transgressor of the law*, even though the Gentile was uncircumcised. This is another way of affirming the utter impartiality of God (cf. v 11), however much a Jew might imagine that God would be partial to him in the judgment.

> **2:28-29. For a person is not a Jew who is outwardly *so*, nor is circumcision something outward in the flesh. But he is a Jew who is inwardly *so*, and circumcision *is* of the heart in the spirit, not in the letter *of the law*, and its praise *comes* not from men but from God.**

Paul now concludes this unit of material with an observation drawn directly from OT revelation. Indeed, Moses himself had exhorted the children of Israel to "circumcise the foreskin of your heart, and be stiff-necked no longer" (Deut 10:16); and he had foreseen the day when "the Lord your God will circumcise your heart and the heart of your descendants, to love the Lord your God *with all your heart and with all your soul*, that you may live" (Deut 30:6, italics added). But Israel's abysmal failure to do this was conspicuous. So Jeremiah declares, "For all these nations are uncircumcised, and all the house of Israel are uncircumcised in the heart" (Jer 9:26; see also 4:4; 6:10).

Jeremiah's point is precisely Paul's point. Israel is no better than the uncircumcised Gentiles, since Israel is "uncircumcised in the heart." Thus Paul is simply pointing out that what it really means to be **a Jew** is not determined by what is **outward in the flesh** nor **is circumcision** a mere matter of **the letter** *of the law* (the words *of the law* are added for clarity). On the contrary, a true Jew is one **who is inwardly** *so* and true **circumcision** *is* **of the heart in the spirit**. In the final analysis, says Paul, Judaism in its spiritual reality is an *inward* religion and not an *outward* one.

It follows therefore that the source of one's praise is crucial. The zealous practitioner of Judaism might well revel in the praise he drew **from men** (see Matt 23:5-7; Luke 11:43), but this was nothing more than empty human glory. True praise could not come *from men*, **but** only **from God** Himself, since God alone knew the heart. This thought, then, is like a final arrow from Paul's quiver aimed at the very soul of any Jew. If the Jew knew his own heart at all, he would have reason to fear a God who knew it perfectly. If he was honest, he would realize that his own heart, like those of his ancestors, was after all truly uncircumcised.

Here ends Paul's direct address (in diatribe style) to the proud, self-confident Jew of v 17. In this unit (vv 17-29) Paul sweeps away all pretext that the Jew somehow will have special advantages in the Day of Judgment. He will not. In his own way he is as uncircumcised as any Gentile.

Thus the bottom line of the entire subunit (2:6-29) has been established. God is indeed utterly impartial in regard to His dealings with, and His future judgment of, humanity. Even the Jew has no special claim on Him by virtue of knowing the law or because of circumcision.

# Romans 3

c. The Decisive Witness of Scripture against Humanity (3:1-20)

The fact that God will give no special status to the Jew in the Day of Judgment runs directly against the grain of general Jewish thought. Is there then no advantage to being among God's chosen people? Paul's answer to this is emphatic: "Yes there is!" But in addressing this question, Paul touches on a consideration that furnishes a suitable transition into the final subunit of the discussion he had begun in 1:18. This consideration is the Jewish possession of God's written revelation.

Thus far in the argument of Romans, beginning in 1:18, Paul has made no direct use of Scripture. Of course, Scripture has certainly furnished the background of his thought, but until now he has not appealed to its explicit testimony. (He refers to it in 2:24, but he simply states the idea involved and does not directly quote.) He does not, for example, appeal to Genesis for the truth of God's creative activity, but instead appeals to the evidence of nature. In the same way, Paul's assertion that God is expressing wrath against the sinfulness of humanity is taken as virtually self-evident from mankind's depraved condition. Even in his description of final judgment (taken for granted as a reality to come) Paul's discussion has been essentially a logical one. No Scriptural testimony (i.e., no quotation from it) has appeared from 1:18–2:29. Most of what Paul has said so far can be deduced from the testimony of nature or from the simple fact that "there is no partiality with God" (v 11). In the present section, Scripture will be pivotal.

**3:1-2. What then is the advantage of the Jew, or what is the benefit of circumcision? Much in every way. For first *is the fact* that they were entrusted with the declarations of God.**

Let it not be thought, Paul now wishes to say, that his comments about **the Jew** and about circumcision lead to the conclusion that there is no advantage in belonging to that community of people. On the contrary, there is much advantage from every point of view (**in every way**). But Paul is not interested in pursuing all the advantages that are alluded to by the words *much in every way* (*Polu kata panta*). The primary (first) advantage, and the one he intends to dwell on, *is the fact* (italicized words added for clarity) **that they were entrusted with the declarations of God.**

The words translated by **the declarations** is the Greek phrase *ta logia*. *Logia* in Greek usage frequently referred to divine utterances (for example, in Plutarch *logia* refers to the words of the Sibylline books). In this context the word would be so understood by Greek hearers/readers of this epistle. (Elsewhere in the NT it is only found in Acts 7:38; Heb 5:12; 1 Pet 4:11.) The more usual NT expression *the Scriptures* is not found in the body of this letter until we reach 4:3 (but it does occur in the introduction at 1:2).

Thus the surpassing importance of Biblical revelation is highlighted by Paul. The chosen race was uniquely privileged to have entrusted to them what God had been pleased to reveal. Paul will now go on to make the point that this entrustment was valuable quite irrespective of Jewish response to these *declarations of God.*

**3:3-4. For what if some did not believe? Their unbelief can't annul the faithfulness of God, can it? Far from it! Let God, then, be true and every man a liar, just as it is written: "That You might be justified in Your words, And might conquer when You are condemned."**

Paul does not raise the question here of Jewish *misunderstanding* of their Scriptures, as we might have expected him to do. On the contrary, in line with general NT thought, he raises the issue of *belief.* He asks, **For what if some did not believe?** From the NT vantage point, the problem of Jewish unbelief in the Lord Jesus Christ was finally a problem of unbelief in their own Scriptures.

This concept goes back to Jesus Himself. After observing that the Jews who did not believe in Him actually "search the Scriptures, for in them you think you have eternal life," He added, "these are they which testify of Me" (John 5:39). Subsequently He stated, "For if you believed Moses, you would believe Me; for he wrote about Me" (John 5:46). Thus if the Jews had really believed what Moses wrote, they would not have failed to believe in our Lord when He came.

Paul, of course, has not yet specifically referred to faith in Christ in his argument (from 1:18 onward). Neither does he do so here explicitly. But his Christian hearers/readers would pick up the idea readily in view of the fierce Jewish opposition to the Christian faith. Paul is reserving explicit reference to faith in Christ until the next major unit (beginning at 3:21), but for the moment he is addressing an obvious question. What about the blatant Jewish disbelief in Christ, which Christians held to be disbelief in the Jewish Scriptures themselves? Does such unbelief **annul the faithfulness of God?**

With the words *the faithfulness of God* Paul alludes to an important issue that he will discuss later in this very epistle. In view of Israel's unbelief, is God through with that nation? Will He abandon His many promises to them as a national entity? Or as Paul here frames the question, **Their unbelief can't annul the faithfulness of God, can it?** The Greek form of this question normally anticipated a negative answer, and this is conveyed in my English translation. But Paul does not leave the question in the air. His answer is a strong Greek phrase that we render: **Far from it!** (The Greek of this is a favorite expression of Paul's, *Mē genoito*; see also 3:6; 6:2, 15; 7:7, 13; 9:14; 11:1, 11.)

It is inconceivable, Paul affirms, that human unbelief could *annul the faithfulness of God*. Indeed, even if **every man** [is] **a liar**, still **God** will **be true**; that is, He will keep His Word and be faithful to His commitments. That truth, in brief, is Paul's conviction about Israel. God will be true to them. As the apostle will later write, "So I say, God hasn't cast away His people, has He? Far from it!" (11:1; the Greek structure is the same as it is in vv 3b and 4a here). This important fact is now confirmed by the first direct Scripture citation in Romans and is introduced by the formula, **just as it is written.**

The words of Scripture here are taken from Ps 51:4, a Psalm which expresses King David's contrition after his sin with Bathsheba. In all likelihood, Paul saw in this Psalm an eschatological dimension in which the "king" personified the nation (much as "Uncle Sam" personifies the USA) and in which he expressed a contrition which the nation felt as a whole. Such a time of repentant remorse does in fact lie ahead of national Israel as Zech 12:10-14 makes plain. Nevertheless the quoted words express a timeless truth.

Jewish unbelief had led them away from God's purpose and blessing. But, by being true to His commitments, God would *be justified*[1] *in* [His] *words* since He would fulfill them. Thereby also He would *conquer when* [He was] *condemned.* Had the Gentiles blasphemed His name because of Jewish sin (2:24)? Yes, but God would ultimately be glorified in His ancient people. As Paul would later also write, "And thus all Israel shall be delivered, just as it is written, *'The Deliverer shall come from Zion, and shall turn away ungodliness from Jacob; and this is My covenant with them, when I take away their sins'*" (11:26-27).

Thus despite the present situation, God's ultimate triumph and vindication were assured. In asserting this Paul has underlined the advantage of the Jewish possession of Scripture (cf. v 2): the declarations of God that were entrusted to them were in fact the "title deeds" for their future blessing. God would be faithful to His people and eschatologically He would be magnified in them.

> **3:5-6. Now if our unrighteousness demonstrates the righteousness of God, what shall we say? God who brings wrath to bear isn't unrighteous, is He? (I am talking in a human manner.) Far from it! Otherwise how will God judge the world?**

Paul's answer to the question of v 3 raises yet another question. If God's truthfulness and fidelity (that is, His righteousness [= His right behavior]) stands out as a result of man's own unrighteousness, is God really justified if He **brings wrath to bear**? Isn't this unfair, and thus unrighteous, on His part? If He is glorified by man's failure, why does He punish that failure?

The Greek word translated *demonstrates* (*sunistēsi*) might also be rendered *recommends.* Man's failure is so acute that it is like a glowing recommendation for God's contrasting righteousness, very much as an exquisite jewel appears more beautiful against a background of dark fabric. But is this not an obvious reason why God should forgo the wrath

---

[1] Hodges understands *justified* (*dikaiōthēs*) in Rom 3:4 to mean *vindicated.* Note that in the next paragraph he says that, speaking of God's *vindication.* Of course God's vindication is also a demonstration of His righteousness, as Hodges points out in his discussion of the next two verses (Rom 3:5-6). –RNW

He everywhere displays against "all the ungodliness and unrighteousness of men" (1:18ff.)?

The precise question, "Is God unfair?" is never expressed here by Paul, however. Instead he writes that if indeed man's failure does recommend **the righteousness of God** (the Greek conditional clause presents something assumed to be true, at least for the sake of argument), in that case **what shall we say?** The question that follows, like the one in v 3, assumes a negative response. We surely would *not* say, would we, that *God who brings wrath to bear* is **unrighteous**? Such an idea is a purely human one (**I am talking in a human manner**) and it is also unthinkable (**Far from it!**).

Paul trumps this idea with yet another question: **Otherwise how will God judge the world?** The idea seems to be that if we claim that it is unfair for God to bring His present *wrath to bear* against manifest human sin, we would also be denying His right to *judge the world*. If the fact that *our unrighteousness demonstrates the righteousness of God* undercuts *contemporary* wrath, it also undercuts *future* judgment.

> **3:7-8. For if God's truth excels to His glory by means of my lie, why am I myself still judged a sinner? And why not (as we are slandered and as some claim that we say), "Let us do wicked things so that good things may happen"? The judgment *passed on* such people is deserved.**

The argument Paul is refuting would be to the effect that **if God's truth** is magnified by my untruth (i.e., **my lie** in denying *His* revealed truth), then why would *my lie* constitute me as **a sinner** in the judgment? Paul is still thinking here of the unbelief referred to in v 2, so that when the Jew expressed a belief contrary to his own Scriptures, that false belief would be a lie. The word rendered *excels* (*eperisseusen*) often carries the connotation of "multiplying" or of "abounding" and it may do so here. Yet the basic thought seems to be that God's truth is *enhanced* by my untruth **to His glory**, and Paul is not concerned with the details of how that occurs.

So, clearly, if one took the approach Paul is referring to, he would be denying God's right to judge a person as a sinner if the sinful actions had somehow redounded to God's glory. But this premise could lead to yet a further (ludicrous) distortion, in which one might say, **"Let us do wicked things [*ta kaka*] so that good things [*ta agatha*] may happen."** In point of fact, as Paul notes parenthetically, he himself had been charged by some as teaching this very thing. This claim he regards as slanderous (*slandered* here translates the normal word for "to blaspheme," *blasphēmoumetha*).

This whole line of thought does not bear detailed refutation. It is obviously wrong on its face, and Paul simply states that those who make such claims deserve **the judgment** *passed on* them. (The italicized words *passed on* are intended to convey the nuance contained in the Greek word *krima* [judgment]. In contrast to the word *krisis* [= the action or process of judgment], *krima* can—and no doubt here does—suggest the sentence, or the punishment, itself.) In Paul's view, such people are already under sentence of judgment because of the manifest untruth of such claims. God's right to "judge the world" (v 6) cannot be denied. To Paul, the whole argument is not only flawed, but perverse.

It is obvious that when he sweeps away the line of argument he is refuting, Paul is also sweeping away the charge that he himself was one of its proponents.

> **3:9. What then? Are we offering a defense? Not at all! For we have previously charged that both Jews and Greeks are all under sin,**

This verse has been much discussed, especially the meaning of the Greek word *Proechometha* (translated here by **Are we offering a defense?**). We may leave aside the poorly attested textual variants on this word, since the standard critical editions of the Greek NT agree with the Majority Text in the form of the word itself. More significant are some of the proposed meanings for the word, such as (1) "Am I protecting myself?" or "Am I making excuses?"; (2) "Are we excelled?" or "Are we in a worse position?"; and (3) "Have we an advantage?" Since the usual meaning of the middle form found here is "to hold something before oneself as protection," some variation of the first idea is to be preferred. The suggested translation includes the legal nuance called for in the context.

It is this legal meaning that correctly ties this new paragraph to the material in 3:1-8. Paul has affirmed that there are advantages to being a circumcised Jew, chief among which is the possession by that nation of the written revelation of God, including of course the law, or Torah. That advantage is not annulled by the fact that the Jews fail to believe their own Scriptures, since their unbelief only enhances the perfect truthfulness of God. Yet this enhancement of "His glory" in no way nullifies God's right to be man's Judge. Therefore it may be asked, could the Jew argue that this "advantage" (having the revealed Scriptures, or having Torah) constitutes a defense against divine condemnation at the final judgment? In short, is possessing the law an argument for the acquittal of a Jew (cf. v 13)?

Taken in this sense, *Proechometha* (*Are we offering a defense?*) is followed swiftly by a sharp negative, **Not at all!** (*Ou pantōs*). By no means are Paul's words designed to temper what he has already said, **for we have previously charged that both Jews and Greeks are all under sin.** The previous material, stretching all the way back to 1:18, was in fact an indictment of the sinfulness of all mankind (*both Jews and Greeks*). Indeed, in God's exercise of present wrath, the Jews even have a kind of priority (cf. 2:9-10). Paul's words in 3:1-8 are in no sense *a defense* for the Jews. On this understanding, the first personal plurals in this verse (both contained in the verbal forms, without separate pronouns provided) are literary plurals and are equal to the first person singular (I, i.e., Paul).

As a matter of fact, the Scriptures ("the declarations of God," 3:2) that the Jews are so privileged to have are the very instrument by which they and the Gentiles are emphatically condemned. Paul will now, *for the first time*, offer Scriptural evidence for this by quoting a withering Biblical indictment of mankind.

> **3:10-18. just as it is written: "There is none righteous, not even one, There is none who understands, There is none who seeks God. They have all turned aside, Together they have become useless; There is no one doing good, There is not even so much as one!" "Their throat is an opened tomb, They have spoken deceit with their tongues." "The poison of asps is under their lips." "Their mouth is full of a curse and bitterness." "Their feet are swift to shed blood, ruin and misery are in their paths, and the path of peace they have not known." "There is no fear of God before their eyes."**

To drive home, once and for all, the truth of universal human guilt before God, Paul now adduces the ultimate proof—the Word of God. His accusations against all mankind, in the final analysis, are confirmed by divine testimony, a testimony the Jews especially must respect. No single Scripture is referenced here, but rather Paul draws up a catena[2] of

---

[2] The word *catena* means *a closely linked series, especially of writings.* A Scriptural catena is

Scriptural statements. (For references, consult Pss 5:9; 10:7; 14:1-3; 53:1-3; 140:3; Eccl 7:20; Isa 59:7-8; Prov 1:16.) Thus we hear the agreed voice of the OT about the sinfulness of the world.

It should be pointed out that Paul apparently made no attempt to use a Greek codex in constructing this catena of quotations. His aim was not exact, verbatim quotation, but an accurate representation of the Biblical testimony he cites. Paul probably quoted from memory.[3]

It should also be noted that verses like Pss 14:2 and 53:2, while not specifically quoted in Paul's catena, are obviously present to his mind. For example, Ps 53:2 states, "God looks down from heaven upon the children of men, to see if there are any who understand, who seek God." That statement is followed by words like those quoted in v 12 above (similarly Psalm 14). Thus Paul's sweeping application of this negative judgment on man accords with the perspective of both of these Psalms whose words come through so clearly in the catena. Paul's condemnation of humanity in 1:18–2:29 was really no broader than that of "the declarations of God," which Israel possessed (3:2) and to which he now appeals.

The collection of OT citations in vv 10-18 constitutes a portrait of man as he really is. The catena has two major subdivisions—namely, vv 10-12 and vv 13-17. In the former verses, the stress is largely on what man does *not* do, thus exposing man's *deficiencies*. In the latter verses, the statements are mainly descriptions of sinful words and deeds that he *does* do, exposing man's *depravities*. One thinks of the familiar classification of sins as *sins of omission* and *sins of commission*, which is analogous. Then the catena is rounded off by v 18.

Thus the manner in which man falls short of what he ought to be is presented first (vv 10-12). He is deficient in terms of basic character, that is, he is *unrighteous* (**"There is none righteous"** [*ouk esti dikaios*]). This deficiency is explicitly universal since there is **"not even one"** (*oude heis*) who could be described as *righteous*. [Paul is here paraphrasing Eccl 7:20 in language similar to that found in Psalms 14 and 53.] As a natural consequence, men are deficient in spiritual perception (**"There is none who understands"** [*ouk estin ho suniōn*]), and, as a further result, man

---

thus a series of Biblical quotations all dealing with the same subject given one after another. –RNW

[3] When Hodges speaks of Paul probably quoting from memory, he is speaking of dictation. Paul did not put quill to parchment himself. Instead he dictated the letter to a scribe named Tertius (cf. Rom 16:22) who in turn wrote down all that Paul said. –RNW

is deficient in spiritual devotion (*"There is none who seeks God"* [*ouk estin ho ekzētōn ton Theon*]).[4] Whatever man's religious inclinations may be, these do not manifest themselves in a diligent pursuit of a genuine knowledge of his Creator. (Given the tendency of prepositional prefixes to lose their force in Hellenistic Greek, the verb *ekzētōn* [from *ekzēteō*] can be taken as the equivalent of the simple *zēteō*. But in this context a more intensive connotation would be appropriate, as in our word "search." Paul would no doubt have acknowledged that people may seek God in sporadic, or superficial, ways.)

In place of a search for God, human beings *"have all turned aside"* (*Pantes exeklinan*) to empty, futile pursuits, with the result that *"Together they have become useless"* (*Hama ēchreiōthēsan*). That is, they accomplish nothing worthwhile even when considered as a totality (*together* [*Hama*]). Man's self-directed efforts apart from God[5] are profitless when summed up and weighed in the divine scales.

---

[4] Overthinking Rom 3:11 is common. Many appeal to this verse to prove man's total inability and then label as semi-Pelagian anyone who speaks of man having an active role in receiving everlasting life. The difference between *seeking* and *responding* is huge. Paul categorically states that unbelievers do not seek God. They are not *the initiators* of reconciliation toward God. *God seeks and God initiates.* The fact that man does not initiate seeking toward God does not negate the idea of unbelievers *responding* to God's seeking of them. Cornelius in Acts 10 may look like one seeking God, but ultimately it was a response to a God whose grace was beginning to dawn upon him.

Some may counter-assert that *dead* people cannot respond. But this misinterprets Ephesians 2:5 and 8. Verse 5's parenthetic "you have been saved" equals God (*sunezōopoiēse*) "made [dead people] alive." Verse 8 says that the salvation [being made alive] of v 5 happens *through* faith (*dia tēs pisteōs*). *Through* introduces one action that precedes another. In "The car starts *through* turning a key," turning a key precedes the car starting. Likewise, in "You were saved [made alive] *through faith*," faith precedes being saved [made alive]. Belief precedes being made alive. Timothy R. Nichols, "Dead Man's Faith: Spiritual Death, Faith, and Regeneration in Ephesians 2:1-10" (Th.M. thesis: Chafer Theological Seminary, 2004), explores the impact of *through* upon sequence and the definition of *dead*. *Dead* is alienation from God here, not inability to believe. Ephesians 2:12 defines *dead* as "without Christ," "having no hope," and "without God in the world." Two chapters later, 4:18 explains unbelievers being "without God" as "being alienated from the life of God." Being *dead* focuses on alienation from God and from the life Christ offers, not upon inability. –JHN

[5] In *A Free Grace Primer: The Gospel Under Siege*, 233f, Hodges gives more details about his view of the ability of people to come to faith in Christ: "It is often claimed by theologians that man has no capacity to believe and that faith, like salvation, must be given to him as a gift. But this view is contradicted by 2 Cor 4:3-4 where Paul wrote: 'But even if our gospel is veiled, it is veiled to those who are perishing, whose minds the god of this age (i.e., Satan) has blinded, who do not believe, lest the light of the gospel of the glory of Christ, who is the image of God, should shine on them.'" Hodges then concludes, "From Paul's words it appears that Satan himself does not regard men as *constitutionally incapable* of faith. Instead, from his point of

Not only is mankind collectively *useless*, but there is not a single individual who does **"good...not even so much as one."** The Greek word translated *good* here is *chrēstotēta*, which translates the Hebrew *t£oñbù* in Ps 14:3 [LXX = 13:3]. However, the Greek of Ps 53:4 [LXX = 52:4] employs *agathon* for the same Hebrew word. While *chrēstotēs* in Greek might at times carry a nuance different from *agathos*, it probably does not do so here since, as Psalms 14 and 53 show, either word could render the basic Hebrew word for "good." Thus the main point of v 12 for Paul would be that, whether considered together or individually, mankind is hopelessly unprofitable and produces nothing truly worthwhile. In other words, everything is tainted by sin.[6]

But man is not only guilty of sins of *omission*; he is also guilty of sins of *commission*. Paul now comes to man's *depravities* (vv 13-17). To be noted here is the stress on various parts of man's body—his throat (v 13a), tongue (13b), lips (13c), mouth (v 14) and feet (v 15). By inference, we gather that the members of man's body are the vehicles through which his sinfulness comes to reality, and this subtly prepares the ground for Paul's later discussion about the sinful orientation of our own physical bodies (cf. esp. 7:21-25; 8:10). In all probability, this is not the first time Paul has gathered up the Scriptures of this catena in this careful fashion, but it was probably new to his Roman hearers/readers.

To begin with then, man's throat is like the entranceway into a vast burial cave from which the sealing stone has been rolled away. **"Their throat is an opened tomb,"** Paul charges. The implication is that men's corrupt words, which come out of their *throats*, are like the stench of an open sepulcher, the unmistakable evidence of death within. Moreover, the words that are formed by **"their tongues"** express **"deceit"** (*edoliousan*) all

---

view, men are *in danger of believing* unless he actively blinds them. He must therefore prevent the truth from dawning on their hearts."–JHN

[6] Hodges saw Paul's reference to the doing of good in Rom 3:12 as a reference to an unbeliever's *perseverance* in doing good. We know from Scripture that the unregenerate do good (cf. Isa 64:6; Acts 10:1-4, 35). But the good which men accomplish has no merit before God (Isa 64:6). And certainly men do not *persevere in doing good*. See Hodges' comments on Rom 2:7 above, where unbelievers' works will be found inadequate to grant them life. In *A Free Grace Primer: The Gospel Under Siege*, 271, he cites Rom 3:12 to prove that "One can no more earn eternal life by 'patient continuance' [that is, *perseverance*] in doing good works than one can be justified by keeping the law." See also *A Free Grace Primer: Grace in Eclipse*, 417, where Hodges links Rom 3:12 with Jesus telling the rich young ruler that no one is good but God. – JHN

too readily, while "under their lips" lies concealed venom (*"the poison of asps"* [*Ios aspidōn*]), painful and poisonous to those who hear them.

Finally, the opening of *"their mouth"* (to emit words) discloses mouths that are *"full of a curse"* (*aras* [singular]) *"and bitterness."* (A hendiadys is possible here: *"full of a bitter curse."*) Thus from *throat* to *tongue* to *lips* to opened *mouth*, the words of men exhibit their deep sinfulness. (We have already noted the role of spoken words at the final judgment: see 2:15.) It is little surprise then, as vv 15-17 demonstrate, that man's corrupt *words* are accompanied by equally corrupt *actions*.

Paul's catena now focuses on those actions. The *spiritual* "death" disclosed by *"a throat* [that] *is an opened tomb"* leads in action to the physical death of others, since *"their feet are swift to shed blood."* And on that pathway (*"in their paths"*), men leave not only the blood of their victims but also *"ruin and misery"* for others (one thinks readily of the effects of warfare). Moreover, these effects are continuous inasmuch as *"the path of peace they have not known."* Whether in private matters or in international affairs, men may pursue peace but the path to that experience eludes their grasp. Their sinfulness invites unremitting conflict at every level of experience.

What is the bottom line? It is this: *"There is no fear of God before their eyes."* When all is said and done, mankind refuses to determine its course with reference to the wishes of its Creator. Human beings single-mindedly pursue their own agendas rather than God's. Their paths are not God's paths. Thus it happens that both their words and their actions display a manifest absence of the *"fear of God."* In a sense, therefore, v 18 is both a summary of vv 10b-17 and also an explanation for those verses. Man's words and actions both display, and are rooted in, a tragic loss of the holy fear which is indispensable to the blessing of every human creature. Here we almost return full circle to the "slide" into depravity that was initiated by the solemn fact that "when they knew God, they did not glorify Him as God, nor were they thankful" (1:21). From that deadly root has grown the poisonous plant of humanity's desperate wickedness.

Paul is now ready to state the conclusion toward which he has been moving since 1:18. The catena of Scriptural quotations just given serves him much as a closing argument serves a prosecuting attorney.[7]

---

[7] This catena of OT passages demonstrates that all humanity is estranged from God. All unbelievers and (to some degree) all believers are suppressors of truth, so all suppressors (believers and unbelievers alike) are subject to God's revelation of wrath in the present time (cf.

We must think here, then, of the entire case Paul has constructed since 1:18. Starting with the fact that God's wrath has been "revealed from heaven against all ungodliness and unrighteousness of men" (1:18), Paul proceeds to describe that wrath in terms of the degradation of mankind (1:19-32) and he insists that even the moralizers among men are not exempt from that wrath (2:1-5). But the God who thus displays His wrath is also man's impartial Judge, whose present dealings with His creatures are completely equitable (2:6-11) and whose future judgment of them will be equally equitable (2:12-16). The Jew will have no advantage in the Day of Judgment since his high pretensions are falsified by his actual conduct (2:12-24). The Jew's circumcision amounts to uncircumcision since the Jew himself does not keep the law (2:25-29). That does not mean that it is worthless to be a Jew because the Jews are the recipients of God's Scriptural revelation (3:1-8). But even this superlative privilege will be of no advantage in the Day of Judgment since the very Scriptures the Jews possess condemn them along with all mankind (3:9-18).

What then is the bottom line? Paul now states it in 3:19-20.

**3:19-20. Now we know that whatever the law says, it says to those who are under the law, so that every mouth may be shut and all the world might become accountable to God. Therefore by the works of the law no flesh will be justified before Him, because through the law *comes* the knowledge of sin.**

Paul has just quoted **the law** in the recognized Jewish sense in which it referred to the totality of God's will as made known in the Scriptures. The Scriptures, then, address **those who are under the law** (i.e., the Jews), but in the process of addressing them, *the law* condemns *them* along with *all* humanity. Paul's catena constitutes a sweeping assertion that God does not find *even one person* who can properly be called "righteous" or be described as "one doing good." There is "not even so much as one" such person.

The net result of this Scriptural testimony is that **every mouth**, whether Jewish or Gentile, is **shut** and left without any capacity to counter this condemnation. By that same testimony, as well, **all the world** has **become accountable to God**. The word rendered here by *accountable* (*hupodikos*) carries the idea of being subject to justice or punishment. As we have

---

notes on Rom 1:18 and 8:1). –JHN

seen, God's just punishment of man's sinfulness is already in operation through His present wrath and will culminate when man is condemned at the final judgment. Thus mankind is *being* held *accountable* and *will be* held *accountable* to his utterly impartial Judge.

It is clear from this sweeping condemnation of mankind (drawn from *the law* itself), that *the law* offers man no hope of ever being justified before God. Since the law's condemnation is universal, it follows that **by the works of the law no flesh will be justified before Him**. Not for a moment does this truth clash in any way with Paul's earlier assertion that "it is the doers of the law who will be justified" (2:13) because it remains true that this principle applies to any who can be so described. But in that passage Paul was discussing the *principle* by which God will judge mankind. What Paul states now is the *reality*. All men are sinners who have broken the law. And if so, they can never find justification *by the works of the law*.

Thus what is sometimes called the "Lutheran" Paul is the real Paul, not the quasi-Jewish Paul envisaged by many modern scholars (e.g., Sanders, Dunn, etc.).[8] No doubt the typical Jewish perspective did *not* consider a Jewish man's case to be hopeless if he did not keep the law completely. But Paul left that kind of Jewish thinking on the Damascus road. No such Paul appears in his NT epistles. Instead, the Christian Paul repudiated *works of the law* as completely ineffectual for justification before God. No one ever has attained justification by that means, and no one ever will.

What the law really does, in fact, is to expose humanity's wickedness, **because through the law *comes* the knowledge of sin**. As Paul explains more fully in Gal 3:19-24, the law had an educational function designed to bring people to the Messiah for justification (Gal 3:22). The conviction of sin is precisely the effect God designed for the law, because if man's hopelessness under the law is truly understood, then he is prepared for God's provision. In that case, what he will *not* do is to seek acceptance *by the works of the law*.

In the light of the whole discussion of 1:18–3:20, therefore, it may be said that God's wrath that is presently visible in the world is an unmistakable indicator of humanity's unrighteous state. Indeed that wrath is expressed against precisely this very "unrighteousness and

---

[8] See, for example, E. P. Sanders, *Paul and Palestinian Judaism* (Philadelphia, PA: Fortress Press, 1977) and James D. G. Dunn, *The New Perspectives on Paul* (Grand Rapids: Eerdmans, 2008). –RNW

ungodliness" (1:18). Eternal judgment is the natural outcome to which that "unrighteousness" is leading mankind. But the outcome of this judgment is a foregone conclusion, since in the judgment only the doers of the law will be justified, not its mere hearers. Since there are no such persons, mankind's situation looks hopeless indeed. It is even implicit that man must somehow find a way to *escape the final judgment*, impossible as that seems.[9]

Is there any solution to this distressing situation? Paul now turns to God's solution for man's apparently hopeless condition.

## B. The Unrighteous Can Obtain Righteousness Through Jesus Christ (3:21–5:11)

God does indeed have a solution to man's dismal, distressing, and doomed situation under His righteous wrath. But if that wrath is expressed toward man because of his *un*righteousness, and if righteousness cannot be attained by the law, where can man find righteousness that could be the means of his deliverance from God's wrath? The Apostle Paul now addresses that very question.

### 1. God's Righteousness Has Been Revealed to Men (3:21-31)

#### a. God's Righteousness Is Available by Faith (3:21-22a)

**3:21-22a. But now God's righteousness apart from the law has been manifested, borne witness to by the law and the prophets, that is, God's righteousness through faith in Jesus Christ, *which is* for all and *is* upon all who believe.**

The initial word in the Greek of this new unit (*Nuni* = *now*) is emphatic. (The English word *But* translates the *second* word: *de*.) The emphasis serves to call attention to the new consideration that, despite human *un*righteousness, God has another kind of **righteousness** that is available to mankind. This righteousness is testified to (**borne witness to**)

---

[9] This sentence alludes to John 5:24b and the promise that believers "shall not come into judgment" concerning their eternal destinies. As is evident here, Hodges uses the expression *the final judgment* to refer to the Great White Throne Judgment where *unbelievers* will be judged (Rev 20:11-15). In Hodges' view believers will indeed "escape the final judgment," that is, they will not appear at the Great White Throne Judgment. See his comments under Rom 4:3 for further details. –RNW

**by the law and the prophets**, the very same Scriptural witnesses that Paul has just cited as utterly condemning man for his sinfulness (3:10-20).

In the major section starting at 1:18, Paul began by declaring the wrath of God to be revealed (*Apokaluptetai*) from heaven. The material up to 3:20, in effect, has justified that wrath. Now, however, something else is declared to be "revealed" (*pephanerōtai*), but *this* manifestation is not one of *wrath*, but rather of *righteousness*. Furthermore, this revelation is not to be discerned from human experience, as was the case with wrath (cf. 1:19-32). Instead it is a matter that God has communicated in His inspired word, namely *the law and the prophets*. Unlike the revelation of wrath that can be deduced from visible phenomena, mankind *must be told* about this new kind of *righteousness*.

As a result, God's righteousness about which Paul is now speaking is a matter of faith. Hence, after mentioning this *righteousness*, Paul goes on immediately to define it more precisely: **that is** [= *de*], **God's righteousness through faith in Jesus Christ**.[10] No human mind would or could have imagined such a righteousness had it not been disclosed in Scripture.

Thus justification by faith is not at all a human idea, but a divine idea. The history of the interpretation of Romans, right up to our modern

---

[10] The phrase *pisteōs Iēsou Christou* literally reads "faith of Jesus Christ," which is how the KJV renders it. Over time, most expositors have understood "of Jesus Christ" as an objective genitive (faith in Jesus Christ), as does this commentary. Recently, some have proposed taking the genitive as subjective and *pistis* as *faithfulness* or *faith* (faithfulness of Jesus Christ). Thomas R. Schreiner, *Romans*, BECNT, ed. Moisés Silva (Grand Rapids, MI: Baker Academic, 1998), 185-86, after initially toying with that idea, rejected it when he considered each use of *pistis* in Rom 3:21–4:12:

> In 3:21-31 such a reading [subjective genitive] made good sense. But when I came to Rom. 4 the proposal began to encounter heavy resistance. Paul clearly refers to the faith of Abraham, for he uses the verb *pisteuein* (vv. 3, 5) [with Abraham as subject]. Thus "the faith" (*hē pistis*) reckoned to Abraham as righteousness (v. 9) could only refer to Abraham's personal faith. So too the righteousness of faith mentioned in verse 11 (so also v. 12) must refer to Abraham's personal faith, and the repetition of the verb *pisteuein* in this verse confirms such a judgment. That *pistis* refers to the faith of believers is also apparent in the subsequent verses, for the text alternates between the noun *pistis* and the verb *pisteuein* (cf. 4:13 [n], 14 [n], 16 [n 2×], 17 [v], 18 [v], 19 [n], 20 [n], 24 [v]). My point is this: it seems hard to believe that *pistis* in 3:21-31 is Christ's faithfulness but that in Rom. 4 it denotes the faith of believers. The Romans would have had a terrible time reading Paul if he switched the meaning of *pistis* so violently from chapter to chapter. It is more likely, therefore, that the term in both 3:21-31 and 4:1-25 refers to the faith of believers.

–JHN

day, shows all too clearly how foreign this concept is to the heart and mind of man. Were it not in Scripture, it would have to be dismissed as a mere fantasy. Indeed many commentators have dismissed it that way, not in so many words, but by redefining Paul's concept so as to make it congenial to human thought. Those writers, for example, who take 2:13 as if it somehow represented a factual reality, exemplify this very tendency. It is striking, therefore, that God chose for the exposition of this truth a convert whose unsaved mentality was its direct opposite, the relentless Pharisee named Saul of Tarsus.

But not only is this righteousness one that comes *through faith in Jesus Christ*, it is also one whose potential scope is universal so that it is **for all**. The Greek of this phrase is *eis pantas*, which of course in this context means *for all*, whether they are Jews or Gentiles. It has the same reference as the phrase "all the world" in 3:19. This is, in fact, a righteousness offered by the same God with whom "there is no partiality" (cf. 2:11). The *all* in *for all* is likewise identical with the "all" who "have sinned and come short of the glory of God" (3:23).

Regrettably, the standard modern critical editions of the Greek NT drop the immediately following words, *kai epi pantas* (**and…upon all**), due to their omission by the old Egyptian manuscripts. But this is a mere error of *homoioteleuton* in which the scribe's eye has slipped from the first *pantas* to the second *pantas*, omitting the words in between. It is one of the most common of all scribal blunders. The words *and…upon all* are attested by the vast majority of Greek manuscripts and are printed in *The Greek New Testament According to the Majority Text*.[11]

But although *God's righteousness* is intended *for all* (without distinction), it is actually bestowed **upon all who believe**. The phrase *who believe* is an articular participle construction in Greek (*tous pisteuontas*) that is read most naturally with this last *pantas* only (the one immediately preceding it). Thus Paul is saying that this *righteousness*, which is intended *for all*, is actually bestowed on *believers*, i.e., on those *who believe*.

The last words of v 22, **For there is no difference**, relate primarily to the following verse and will be discussed there.

[11] Zane C. Hodges and Arthur L. Farstad, editors, *The Greek New Testament According to the Majority Text: Second Edition* (Nashville, TN: Thomas Nelson Publishers, 1985). –RNW

### b. Christ Is the Mercy Seat for All Men (3:22b-26)

**3:22b-23. For there is no difference. For all have sinned and fall short of the glory of God,**

Paul has just stated (v 22a) the universal scope of this righteousness of God by declaring it available to any, and to all, "who believe." This universality is founded on an equally universal fact. Indeed, **there is no difference** between Jew and Gentile inasmuch as **all** (whether Jew or Gentile) **have sinned**. It should be noted that Paul in no way qualifies this reality by any phrase like "a great deal" or "too much." From Paul's point of view, the mere fact of sin is sufficient to condemn all mankind.[12]

Paul had already made this clear when he described the final judgment. He had stated that on that occasion "as many as have *sinned* without the law shall also perish without the law" and that "as many as have *sinned* under the law shall be judged by means of the law" (2:12, italics added). It is *sinners* who must fear this eschatological event. But, in fact, that is what everyone is, *for all have sinned.*

It follows inevitably from this simple fact that all *also* **fall short**[13] **of the glory of God**. The sense of the phrase *the glory of God* must not be separated from Paul's thought in the immediate context. Obviously part of God's glory is the absolute perfection of His righteousness. To sin is to flagrantly miss the lofty moral standard of that glorious righteousness. But by implication, if one is granted *God's* righteousness, one is raised thereby to a level consistent with His glory. Man's plight is hopeless unless or until he can receive a righteousness compatible with *the glory of God.*

**3:24. *so that men are* being justified freely by His grace through the redemption that is in Christ Jesus—**

---

[12] Hodges did not believe in original sin as it is commonly taught. That can be seen in a careful reading of his words here. He does not understand *all…have sinned* as a reference to Adam's sin imputed to every man. He sees it as a reference to the fact that all living human beings, both Jews and Gentiles, have sinned in their personal experience. In Hodges' view Adam's sin was not imputed to all. Rather, in his view Adam's sin was passed from father to child as the inclination to sin. See Hodges's discussion of Rom 5:12-21 for further details. – RNW

[13] The verb *fall short* (*husterountai*) is a present tense, unlike the earlier verb *have sinned* (*hēmarton*), which is a past tense (aorist). All have sinned in the past, and all presently continue to *fall short of the glory of God.* –RNW

Paul's statement in v 23 is followed immediately by a participial construction in Greek that is grammatically subordinate to the verbs of that verse. The circumstantial participle *dikaioumenoi* (**being justified**) connects grammatically to *hēmarton kai husterountai* ("have sinned and fall short") in v 23. This poses a challenge for the translator. The participle is most naturally construed as one of manner, stating *the way in which* justification comes to all. But this of course is not the same as saying that such justification does come to each and every sinner. As Paul has already stated, it comes to those "who believe." But the flexible character of the participle in Greek would not have suggested to the Greek hearer/reader that justification comes to every sinner. A translator must, to some extent, paraphrase here.

Thus the words *so that men are* have been added in the translation for the sake of clarity. The meaning simply is that, in view of universal sin, justification comes only in this way. Since "all have sinned," all must find justification in the fashion now described. In particular, sinful men must be **justified freely by His grace**. "God's righteousness," therefore, that comes "through faith in Jesus Christ" (v 22), does not involve any form of synergism with "the works of the law" (cf. v 20), as though these could be "elevated" by the exercise of faith. On the contrary, "God's righteousness" comes *freely* and it comes only *by His grace*. Paul therefore begins his discussion of the doctrine of justification by sharply defining its means in contrast to the ineffectual nature of "the works of the law," by means of which there can be *no* justification (v 20).

This is actually possible, in fact, **through the redemption that is in Christ Jesus**. Here then for the first time in Romans, Paul refers directly[14] to the death of our Lord. [He *has*, of course, alluded to it in 1:4 by his reference to the resurrection.] In this initial reference to Christ's death Paul employs the term *redemption*, a word especially connected in Greco-Roman society with the ransoming of prisoners of war or the manumission of slaves. The implication here is that *Christ Jesus* has

---

[14] By *directly* Hodges means something like *transparently* or *obviously*. The knowledgeable reader, which the believers in Rome were, knew that *redemption* referred to the work of Jesus when He died on the cross for our sins, though neither the cross nor the death of Jesus is mentioned specifically in v 24 or even in the verses which follow. Paul does refer to the blood of Christ in v 25, another reference that the discerning reader grasps as relating to substitutionary atonement. –RNW

bought us out of some form of servitude. Paul will make this concept clearer as he proceeds.

It should also be noted that *the redemption* Paul speaks of is *in Christ Jesus*. As Paul will now go on to show, this *redemption* is not simply procured *by Christ Jesus*, but is actually found *in* Him.

> **3:25. whom God has set forth as a Mercy Seat, through faith, by means of His blood, to serve as proof of His righteousness in passing over, in the forbearance of God, the sins previously committed;**

It is, in fact, the very Person of Jesus Christ that **God has set forth as a Mercy Seat**. The "mercy seat" under the Old Covenant was the golden covering over the ark of the covenant, a sacred box-type object that stood in the Holy of Holies in the Jewish tabernacle and in the later Solomonic temple. (It was lost when Jerusalem fell to the Babylonians.) The sacrificial blood of the Day of Atonement was sprinkled on the mercy seat (Lev 16:1-17); and it was there, above this covering and between the cherubim that were on either end of the ark, that God could meet with Moses or with the Jewish high priest (cf. Exod 25:21-22; Lev 16:2). Here Christ Jesus is identified as the divinely appointed *Mercy Seat* where God and man can meet.

The exact meaning of the Greek word *hilastērion*, translated here (and by the NET Bible) by *Mercy Seat*, has been much discussed. Some meaning like "propitiation" (NKJV, NASB, HCSB) or "sacrifice of atonement" (NIV) are usual. But the primary use of the word in the Greek OT (LXX) as the name for the mercy seat renders it quite likely that this word had that sense for Paul here.[15]

But Jesus Christ is a *Mercy Seat*, of course, only in a metaphorical sense. (In the language of typology we might say that the OT "mercy seat" was a type for which Christ is the Antitype.) Thus He is *a Mercy Seat...* only through faith. The Greek words for *through faith* (*dia...pisteōs*) stand immediately after the word for *Mercy Seat* (*hilastērion*) and are quite naturally taken with it as an expression of "the means through which" (*dia*) Jesus Christ functions as *a Mercy Seat*. His role is to be a "meeting place" between God and man *whenever* man exercises faith in God's Son.

---

[15] For a good discussion of *hilastērion*, see Moo, *Romans*, 231-36. –ZCH

Thus the truth of John 14:6 finds expression here: "No one comes to the Father except through Me."

The NT, of course, knows nothing of any other way to God except through the Person named Jesus Christ (cf. Acts 4:12). The so-called doctrine of "implicit faith" is nowhere taught in the Bible and is a product of the finite human mind. A person cannot believe in Jesus Christ without knowing His name, and thus one cannot encounter the true and living God except in Him. But God has publicly set Him forth as His appointed *Mercy Seat*. Precisely for this reason, His name needs to be proclaimed to every kindred, tribe, and tongue, just as Paul had undertaken to do so far as God enabled him to do it. The human idea that salvation is possible, at least in some cases, without this proclamation is an enormous theological error.

The next words, **by means of His blood**, render the Greek phrase *en tō autou haimati*. The grammar would permit them to be connected with the words for *through faith*, so that we might read the two phrases together as *through faith in His blood* (so KJV, NIV, HCSB). But this reading is very improbable (and is not followed by most modern translations including the NKJV, NASB, ESV, NET). Paul nowhere else speaks of "faith *in* His blood" and there is no good reason to think he does so here (as most commentators point out). Rather, since the OT mercy seat was sprinkled with blood on the Day of Atonement, it is extremely likely that here Paul has chosen this expression as part of his metaphor about Jesus as God's *Mercy Seat*. Our Lord has become a *Mercy Seat*, where God and man can meet, precisely *by means of* the shedding of *His blood* for the world's sins.

No doubt Paul had thought deeply about the way the temple ritual manifested God's saving work in Christ (whether or not he wrote Hebrews). Indeed even the words *set forth* (*proetheto*) suggest that in all likelihood Paul was thinking of the hidden nature of the Old Covenant mercy seat (cf. Heb 9:7-9), in contrast to the public character of the new *Mercy Seat*. God had publicly displayed Jesus Christ as the way to Him, a fact symbolized by the rending of the veil of the temple when Christ died (Luke 23:45). A theologian of Paul's depth was likely to have had all these things in mind here.

The concept of Christ Jesus as *a Mercy Seat...by means of His blood* is now elaborated in terms of its evidential value. The words **to serve as a proof** (lit., "for a proof": *eis endeixin*) are most easily understood when taken with the whole phrase that began with *whom God set forth*. In other words, God has openly displayed Christ as *a Mercy Seat…by means of His blood* as a demonstration (*proof*) of two great facts in particular. The first of these is now stated. (The second is stated in v 26.)

The sacrificial work of Christ on the cross is, first of all, *a proof of* God's **righteousness in passing over, in the forbearance of God, the sins previously committed**. The idea contained in the words translated *the sins previously committed* (*tōn progegonotōn hamartēmatōn*) can hardly have reference to anything other than to *the sins* that men did *before Christ was crucified*.[16] In His dealings with mankind prior to the cross, God had been passing over human sin and dealing with mankind in the light of the future work of Christ. Unless God had anticipated the cross of Christ, mankind could have expected Him to exercise definitive justice rather than the grace and forgiveness that He so often extended. But His righteousness in exercising this kind of *forbearance* (or *clemency*: *anochē*) was not as yet manifested. The public death of His Son was a vindication of God's merciful dealings with sinners in all the preceding ages. Thus it was a *proof of His righteousness* in so conducting Himself with mankind.

> **3:26. *and* for a proof of His righteousness at the present time, so that He may be righteous and justify the person who has faith in Jesus.**

There is no connecting word in Greek between vv 25 and 26. The *and* appears in my translation for the sake of smoothness. The Greek, however, does not require the conjunction and Paul slightly changes the construction here. Whereas the words *serve as proof* (v 25) translate the phrase *eis endeixin*, here the words **for a proof** render the phrase *pros endeixin*. Although the expressions are functionally equivalent, the Greek hearer/reader might have caught a subtle shading in which, lacking the conjunction, the latter phrase could be felt as an outcome of the former, much as we might say, "He did it for (*eis*) this reason with a view to (*pros*)…"

This is to say that God, in the death of Christ, not only offers "proof" of His righteousness in ages past, but that He does so with the specific

---

[16] Some have read their own theology into Paul's words here, suggesting that he means that at the moment of faith the blood of Jesus takes care of one's sins up to that point in his life. Sins committed after that point need to be dealt with by a man-made system of confessing sins to priests, doing works of penance, last rites, communion, etc. As Hodges points out, it is impossible that Paul meant that. He was referring to sins committed prior to Calvary. –RNW

intent (*pros*) of vindicating **His righteousness at the present time**. In other words the first vindication serves also the goal of the second. If God's "forbearance" in the past is shown to be righteous, *ipso facto* He is shown to be righteous in what He presently does. The cross of Christ is not *two* forms of vindication but rather a seamless garment that demonstrates God's righteousness in all of human history. All of mankind's sin, whether past or future at the time of the cross, is dealt with by the death of Christ. He is "the Lamb of God who takes away the sin of the world" (John 1:29).

The result is that God can **be righteous and justify the person who has faith in Jesus**. The English necessarily obscures an obvious Greek word play, since the Greek words for *righteous* (*dikaion*) and *justify* (*dikaiounta*) are cognates joined in Paul's sentence by the simple *and* (*kai*). God, says Paul, is both *righteous and righteous-fier*.[17] This simple assertion is actually the fundamental core of Pauline theology.

Throughout the centuries of Christian history, thinkers of every persuasion have wrestled with Paul's basic ideas. (An excellent, up-to-date treatment of this long-running discussion is available now in Stephen Westerholm's *Perspectives Old and New on Paul* [Eerdmans, 2004].) But at bottom, Paul believed two very basic things. These were: (1) God, apart from man's works, justifies the one who believes in Jesus; and (2) the cross is the basis for this justification and shows it to be a fully righteous act.

Here it is important to say that for Paul these are absolute realities totally independent of anything man does before or after faith. There is no basis whatsoever in Paul's letters to connect human works with justification by faith no matter when these works are performed. Whether done before or after conversion, they remain *works* (i.e., *erga*, *deeds* or *actions*). The distinction drawn by some writers between "works done to attain favor with God" and "works done out of faith or gratitude" is non-existent in the Pauline material. This alleged distinction is a theological fiction.

For Paul, "good works," whether done under or apart from the Mosaic Law, cannot contribute to our justification. To say that somehow they do contribute would really amount to a denial of the simple fact that God *justifies the person who has faith in Jesus*. In that case God would be justifying only the person who has faith plus works, not a person

---

[17] Possibly another way to bring this across in English would be something like *so that He may be righteous and may declare righteous the person who has faith in Jesus*. –RNW

who just has faith. No matter how this idea is articulated, it contradicts Paul's fundamental idea that justification is *"apart from works"* (v 28; see 4:6). Furthermore, to say that "our (post-conversion) works" somehow vindicate God's justification is a denial of the adequacy of the cross for that purpose. The famous statement that "we are saved by faith alone, but not by a faith that is alone" is a Reformation idea, not a Pauline one. *This idea can be found nowhere in Paul's writings.*

To be greatly lamented is the sad fact that, although Reformation soteriology denied good works entrance through the front door, good works were often reintroduced through *the back door.* The resultant theology is hard to distinguish, except semantically, from Roman Catholic theology. The synergism of faith and works in salvation is differently expressed in Protestant and Catholic theology, but its fundamental character is essentially the same: namely, no true justification without good works. Paul knows nothing of this.

Of course, theologians have spilled a tremendous amount of ink trying to show that works have some fundamental role in Pauline soteriology. But in Paul works do not have, and cannot be shown to have, any connection whatsoever with the truth of justification. For Paul, grace and works are opposites. He will later say in this very epistle: "But if it is by grace, it is no longer by works, otherwise grace is no longer grace. But if it is by works, it is no longer grace, otherwise work is no longer work" (Rom 11:6). This is perfectly plain, and theologians have wasted their time trying to qualify, revise, or reinterpret Paul's lucid concept. According to Paul, when you mix faith and works you change the basic nature of both.

Paul concludes the long Greek sentence that began in v 23 with the words *the person who has faith in Jesus* (*ton ek pisteōs Iēsou*; lit. = "the one of [by] faith in Jesus"). Here for the first time since 1:17 we meet Paul's frequent phrase *ek pisteōs* (cf. Rom 3:30; 4:16 [2×]; 5:1; 9:30; 10:6; 14:23 [2×]). All the other instances in Romans (with the exception of 14:23) use the phrase in reference to righteousness or justification coming *by means of* faith. This suggests a second look at its usage in this verse.

In our translation we paraphrase the Greek article (*ton*) with the words *the person who* and the Greek *ek* by *has.* But the Greek is perhaps more likely to mean something like *the by-faith-in-Jesus person.*[18] In that

---

[18] What Hodges means here is that the Greek literally has a sense of *the one of faith in Jesus,* or, less woodenly, *the person who has faith in Jesus,* which is the way he translates this phrase. –RNW

case the Greek article is a functional ellipsis of the idea "the person who receives this justifying action" (cf. *dikaiounta*). Paul's brevity at this point is due to his intention of explicating this idea very shortly.

It is noteworthy that in this direct reference to *faith in Jesus* (*Iēsou* is an objective genitive) Paul uses only the human name (in v 21 he uses "Jesus Christ"). But for Paul, of course, both the words *Lord* and *Christ* were still titles, the latter one indicating Messiahship. The distinctive feature of NT evangelization was that it called on both Jews and Gentiles to exercise faith in the person named Jesus. (Note precisely this idea in John 20:30-31.) After the coming of Christ, it was no longer adequate to believe simply in a Messiah whose identity was unknown. On the contrary, the Christian proclamation was that the Messiah (= Christ) *had now appeared* and that His name was Jesus (hence "Jesus *Christ*" [v 21] = "Jesus the *Messiah*"). Henceforth justifying faith found its true focus not in an unnamed promised Messiah, but in Jesus of Nazareth. It is in fact "the name of *Jesus*" that is above every name and to which every knee will someday bow (Phil 2:9-11). Therefore, too, "there is no other name under heaven given among men by which we must be saved" (Acts 4:12).

The *righteousness of God*, therefore, that is now "manifested" (v 21) in the promised Christ, comes by *faith in* a man named *Jesus*.

### c. Faith-Righteousness Vindicates the Law (3:27-31)

**3:27. So where is boasting? It is excluded. Through what sort of law? Of works? No indeed, but through the law of faith.**

The truth stated in vv 21-26 leads to a triumphant declaration by Paul that boasting has been excluded. This trait (**boasting**) has already been ascribed to the Jews in 2:17-20 and they especially are probably in mind here. (No doubt now that he knows the grace of God, Paul himself is chagrined by his own proud spirit in his unregenerate days.) But if justification is granted only to "the person who has faith in Jesus," then such a person can find no ground for *boasting*.

In fact, boasting is actually excluded ("shut out": *Exekleisthē*) by the very principle **of faith**. (Here Paul obviously uses the term **law** in the sense of a "controlling principle" or an "operating rule.") The sort of law that excludes human pride is definitely not the principle **of works** which, in fact, invites *boasting* (see Eph 2:8-9). On the contrary, the only "rule" that excludes human pride is *the law of faith*, that is, the "rule" that men are justified only by "faith in Jesus" in contrast to justification by "the works of the law" (3:20).

An error often found in contemporary discussions is that "works of gratitude to God" are somehow 'immune' to the temptation to boast. But this is contrary to both experience and Scripture. In fact, in the only passage in the Gospels where our Lord explicitly refers to justification (Luke 18:9-14), a Pharisee is represented as *thanking* God for what he conceives to be his numerous religious virtues (Luke 18:11-12). All experience confirms that even when our theology ascribes our works to God's grace, boasting is *not* excluded. Man is perfectly capable of bragging that his works demonstrate that he is one of God's "elect."[19] In essence, the Jews of Paul's day did that, for Paul charges, "You bear the name of 'Jew,' and you rest in the law and *boast in God*" (Rom 2:17). Justification by faith, and by faith alone, can block this all too human failing.

No system of theology that *includes* works in its soteriology can also *exclude boasting.*

> **3:28-29. So we hold that a man is justified by faith apart from the works of the law. Is He the God of the Jews only? Is He not in fact also of the Gentiles? Yes, also of the Gentiles!**

Functionally v 27 was somewhat parenthetical. In effect it was a triumphant exclamation by Paul that the truth presented in vv 21-26 had successfully locked out boasting. The **so** (*oun*) that opens v 28[20] most probably reaches back to the truth of vv 21-26, as its summarizing nature clearly suggests. The bottom line, Paul states, is that **we hold** (*Logizometha*) **that a man** (*anthrōpon*, generic = man or woman) **is justified by faith apart from the works of the law.**

In making this concluding statement, Paul here slightly expands the phrase "apart from the law" used in v 21. What that phrase meant there is even clearer when expressed, as it is here, as *apart from the works of the law*, since this refers to any and all acts of obedience to the law's commands. It is not just the law as a system that Paul excludes from Christian

---

[19] Hodges often wrote disapprovingly about the tendency of Calvinists to point to their own works as evidence of their regeneration. He sees that essentially as boasting, even with all the caveats normally associated with Calvinism. –RNW

[20] *Oun* is the second word in the Greek sentence (after *Logizometha*); but it opens the sentence logically. –RNW

soteriology, but also *the deeds*, i.e., *the works of the law* that are excluded. As he will shortly say, "to the person who *works* the compensation is not made on the basis of grace, but on the basis of what is owed" (4:4, italics added). Paul will not allow human deeds (*erga*) any role at all in man's justification.

This principle is in fact a universal one. Since *the works of the law* are irrelevant when *a man is justified by faith*, such justification is available to all mankind, whether they possess the law or not. God is not **the God of the Jews only**, but **also of the Gentiles**. The question format which Paul uses here to affirm this truth heightens the rhetorical effect of his declaration. Most emphatically, He is the God of all mankind.

> **3:30-31. Consequently, there is one God who will justify the circumcision by faith and the uncircumcision through faith. So do we annul the law through faith? Far from it! In fact we establish the law.**

Alluding to the familiar Jewish declaration (the Shema, Deut 6:4) about the oneness of God, Paul declares that **there is one God** for all humanity who **will justify** any human being by means of faith. The slight change of construction from **by faith** (*ek pisteōs*) to **through faith** (*dia tēs pisteōs*) should not be overplayed, since the first phrase is the usual one that Paul employs for this doctrine, regardless of racial distinction. But the addition of the article (*tēs*) in the second phrase is perhaps the key to the nuance involved since articles tended to occur with abstract nouns (like *faith*) when the abstract quality was itself under discussion.

It seems probable that a subtle difference is conveyed (perhaps unconsciously since Paul seems quite fluent in Greek). I suggest something like this: (1) the *ek* phrase with its anarthrous noun (*pisteōs*) retains its usual force expressing an operating principle (the "by-faith way"), while (2) the *dia* phrase with the articular noun (*tēs pisteōs*) looks at the abstract term itself ("through this thing called faith"). If something like this is accurate, then the first phrase, referring to Jews (**the circumcision**), retains its implicit contrast with *ex ergōn nomou* (cf. v 20) as the principle on which justification occurs for them. In reference to the Gentiles (**the uncircumcision**), the thought is more that they are justified *through* the very thing just referred to, i.e., *faith*. (Hence the article, *tēs*, is almost an article of previous reference.)

But does this principle of "faith-type justification" for both Jew and Gentile alike mean that the standards of the law are meaningless? This, at least, seems to be the idea involved in Paul's question (**So do we annul the law by faith?**). The most obvious objection to Paul's doctrine from a Jewish viewpoint would be that God's standards are thus ignored and rendered invalid. The verb Paul uses, *katargoumen*, rendered *annul*, suits such an idea well. Paul's reply (*Mē genoito* = **Far from it!**) emphatically disclaims such a result.

On the contrary, Paul claims, **In fact we establish the law**. Paul does not here, or elsewhere in Romans, elaborate this observation. But its meaning for him is fairly obvious. If it is true, as he has affirmed, that "through the law comes the knowledge of sin" (3:20), then the law's revelatory role in regard to sin is fully respected by the corollary truth that "by the works of the law no flesh will be justified before Him" (3:19). To claim that man can find justification under the law, despite his multiple infractions of the law, would seriously diminish the dignity in which all of the commandments of God ought to be held. By contrast, to insist that the law cannot be a means of justification if it is violated at all is the only way that its full integrity and seriousness can be maintained. Therefore, to uphold it in this way is to *establish the law*.

Finally, it must be said that to take 2:13 as a statement that justification by doing the law is somehow possible (as many have) is to denigrate the importance of a full and unflawed obedience. Under this perspective, human beings often imagine that God will not be "too strict" in assessing their lives and will give them "a passing grade" for a deeply flawed performance. But this diminishes the seriousness of the law and is a concept totally foreign to Paul. Only the abandonment of the law as a means for, or an aid to, justification properly validates the full integrity of God's righteous standards.

# Romans 4

## 2. God's Righteousness Is Attested in the OT (4:1-25)

### 4:1. So what shall we say that Abraham our father has obtained with reference to the flesh?

Paul had introduced the subject of "God's righteousness apart from the law" with the claim that it was "borne witness to by the law and the prophets" (3:21). Now that he has made clear that this righteousness comes "through faith in Jesus Christ" (cf. 3:21 and the material following), he returns to the idea of OT authentication. For Paul this was crucial. If he did not have the support of "the law and the prophets," then his message could not claim divine validity. Paul therefore insisted that "the gospel of God" was "promised beforehand through His prophets in the Holy Scriptures" (see 1:1-2). He will now proceed to *demonstrate* that this is in fact the case.

But Paul's segue into this theme is made easier by raising a question that suggests itself naturally from his observations about faith and the law in Rom 3:27-31. In view of Paul's conclusions about justification by faith as over against "the works of the law" (3:27-31), how does all this relate to Abraham who bore in his own physical body (i.e., in the flesh) the sign of circumcision, and in fact bore it long before the Mosaic statutes were enacted? Was circumcision, then, an irrelevant feature of Abraham's relationship to the Lord his God? Such an issue would very readily arise for a thoughtful circumcised Jew, and it probably *had* arisen often in Paul's synagogue debates during his missionary journeys.

The words **what...Abraham our father has obtained** state the issue broadly. What advantage or effect did the *physical* side of Abraham's relationship to God actually have? The phrase **with reference to the**

**flesh** alludes to circumcision, which the typical Jew would take as the necessary mark of God's acceptance of Abraham. If it was not grounds for this acceptance, what did it matter in Abraham's life? Paul is quite ready to respond to this issue since a major OT proof text for justification can now come to the fore.

Some problem of the kind I have described seems implied by Paul's enquiry here about *what…Abraham our father has obtained with reference to the flesh.* The question—**what shall we say?**—probably represents a literary plural equivalent to "What shall *I* say?" or "What should I say about *this*?"

### 4:2. For if Abraham was justified by works, he has something to boast about, but not with regard to God.

"Let's begin," Paul is saying here, "by raising the issue of Abraham's justification." From Paul's perspective **if Abraham was justified by works**, then in that case **he has something to boast about**. But as Paul has just insisted, justification is by faith alone and *excludes* boasting (3:27-28). It follows therefore that if it *can* be said that Abraham *was* in some sense justified by works, it *cannot* be said that this experience grants him boasting that is *Godward* (*pros ton Theon*). Therefore, any such justification cannot be the kind of full judicial acceptance before God that is involved in the justification Paul has been discussing.

An important point must be noted, however. The statement of this verse can be taken to imply that there may be *some* sense in which *Abraham was justified by works.* Paul employs here a so-called first class conditional sentence in which the statement of the "if" clause is assumed (for argument's sake at least) to be true. His statement thus does not deny that Abraham *could* have been *justified by works* in *some other* sense than the kind of justification Paul has in mind.

If (as seems likely) the epistle of James had already been written before Paul wrote this book,[1] the idea was already in circulation that a person's reputation as a "righteous" individual could be established by "deeds" (*works*) that were a superlative expression of his or her righteous

---

[1] In his commentary on the epistle of James (*The Epistle of James: Proven Character Through Testing* [Denton, TX: Grace Evangelical Society, 2009]), Hodges argued that James was the first NT book written. He believed it was written in AD 34-35, within one to two years of the Lord's resurrection and ascension (pp. 10-12). If that is true, James was written decades before Romans. –RNW

character. Paul was no doubt aware of this idea, whether or not he had read James. Thus Abraham could be said to be openly justified as "the friend of God" by his supreme act of obedience (consisting of a series of deeds, or *works*, on his part) "when he offered Isaac his son on the altar" to God (Jas 2:21-23). In the same way, Rahab was also justified before men (and received into Israel) when she not only protected the spies in her house but also sent them safely away (Jas 2:25). James insists that this kind of justification occurs, yet about the idea that our works are indispensable to justification *before God*, James says absolutely nothing at all.

Accordingly, if he *had* already read James, Paul had found nothing to conflict with the gospel he preached. What James had said could be easily granted. Only if someone talked about works producing justification *in reference to God*, would Paul have strongly objected. *Before God* none can boast, though for Paul there were also perfectly legitimate ways in which one *could* boast. (Note that the Greek word for *something to boast about* [*kauchēma*] is found with a positive sense in 1 Cor 9:15, 16; 2 Cor 1:14; 5:12; 9:3; Gal 6:4; Phil 1:26; 2:16; Heb 3:6.) A lesser justification[2] (which occurred before men) *could be* a source of appropriate boasting on Abraham's part. Paul does not wish to deny this to the great patriarch whom all his physical kinsmen revered. But **with regard to God** this great man was on the same level as all other men, as Paul will now go on to show.

### 4:3. For what does the Scripture say? *"Then Abraham believed God, and it was imputed to him as righteousness."*

So far from being in conflict with what Paul has said about justification by faith, Abraham's experience furnishes an explicit example of such justification. Indeed, this is precisely declared in **the Scripture** Paul now quotes from Gen 15:6.

In Pauline theology, the initial call of Abraham in Gen 12:1-3 contained a salvific promise in the words, "And in you all the families of

---

[2] Justification before God is forensic. That is, God the Father legally *declares righteous* all who believe in His Son. Justification before men, however, is interpersonal. This latter sort of justification occurs when someone *is vindicated* before men by his actions. Abraham's act of offering up Isaac was regarded by Jews, and later by Christians, as the greatest example of piety in the history of mankind (with the exception of the death of Jesus on the cross for the sins of the world, to which Abraham's offering up of Isaac pointed as a type). Any time a person is vindicated before men by his works, he has something to boast about *before men*, but not *before God*. –RNW

the earth shall be blessed." This is made clear in Gal 3:8 where this promise is treated as a prediction "that God would justify the Gentiles by faith," so that in fact God had "preached the gospel to Abraham beforehand." Thus Abraham had been informed at his call that Messianic salvation would come through his family line. (It would be naïve to think that the quoted words of Gen 12:1-3 are the total sum of what God said to Abraham on this occasion, not to mention other occasions of divine communication with him as well.) Apparently Abraham had not actually believed this specific guarantee, even though he had acted on God's call. Instead, his unbelief about the Messianic promise of Gen 12:3 is indicated by his words in Gen 15:2 complaining, "Lord God, what will You give me, seeing I go childless, and the heir of my house is this Eliezer of Damascus?"

This time, however, when God reaffirms His promise in terms of a guarantee of physical seed, *"Abraham believed God."* In the light of Gal 3:6-9 we can discern the fact that Messianic salvation was part and parcel of what Abraham believed on this occasion. But that is not Paul's point here in Romans 4.[3] Rather Paul is concerned with validating justification by faith in terms of Abraham's experience as revealed in Scripture. Thus, as his quoted text declares, when *Abraham believed* on the occasion in question, it was then that *"it"* [Abraham's belief in Messianic salvation] *"was imputed to him as righteousness."*

It must be carefully noted that in this statement the word *it* refers back to Abraham's exercise of faith. No other antecedent is really possible, and indeed this understanding is made explicit by Paul in v 9. Thus, as 4:9 declares, "faith was imputed to Abraham as righteousness." This simple fact has not been properly assimilated into Christian theology.

Frequently we are told that "Christ's righteousness" or even "Christ's personal righteousness in fulfilling the law" are imputed to the believer.

---

[3] At first reading, this sentence by Hodges seems self-contradictory. However, it is not if we read him carefully. Hodges' point is that there is a difference between Messianic salvation (i.e., regeneration) and justification. While Hodges does not discuss that here, I know from personal conversations with him that he distinguished regeneration from justification. He said that though both occurred at the same time and both were by faith alone, regeneration is a work of God the Holy Spirit whereas justification is a work of God the Father. In addition, regeneration means being *made alive* (cf. Eph 2:1-5), whereas justification means being *declared righteous.* While both are necessary in order to be fit for Jesus' kingdom, they are not the same thing. These separate acts of two different members of the Trinity both occur at the moment of faith. Hodges' point is that Abraham believed God concerning the promise of regeneration through the Messiah, and when he did, then God (the Holy Spirit) not only regenerated him, but also God (the Father) justified him. –RNW

But such ideas are not found in Paul. God does not, according to Paul, credit us with an obedience to "the works of the law" which we have in fact signally failed to perform. Paul has already stated that "God's righteousness" is "apart from the law" (3:21). This righteousness in no sense represents a non-existent "fulfillment" of the law's works. To say so is to degrade it.

The simple fact of the matter is that God accepts "faith in Jesus" as a fully adequate substitute for any and all works of whatever kind they may be. The perfect righteousness that God gives is nothing less than His accepting faith as a wholly adequate righteousness in and of itself. Abraham's *"faith was imputed to him as righteousness."* The word rendered *as* is the Greek preposition *eis* and we could equally well render the statement: *it was accounted to him for righteousness.* Abraham's *faith* became a substitute for the righteousness he otherwise lacked. For Paul, when *"Abraham believed God,"* the transaction called justification occurred in the absence of works of any kind. For this event, only *faith* mattered.

Thus the atonement of our Lord Jesus Christ (see 3:24-26) has completely removed the demands of God's law from consideration, as well as removing all other forms of working as well. The righteousness Paul can proclaim in the light of the cross is totally separate from works of all kinds precisely because it is a "faith-righteousness." It is this and nothing else, and God is "just" (3:26) in granting this form of righteousness precisely because Christ has fully satisfied God about mankind's sinful works. In short, Christ has paid for our "works-failure" and God gives a "faith-righteousness" (*not* an "imputed works-righteousness") to the believer.

It is important to note in passing that there are no charges to be laid before God's judgment seat in regard to His elect, since "God is the One who justifies" (Rom 8:33). It follows that there can be no "trial" where there are no charges. Since the final judgment is for the *unrighteous* and can only justify "the doers of the law" (Rom 2:12-13), there is no role for this judgment in regard to those who have a *"faith-righteousness"* with which the law has nothing to do. As Jesus Himself said, "Most assuredly, I say to you, he who hears My word and believes in Him who sent Me, has everlasting life, *and does not come into judgment*, but has passed from death into life" (John 5:24, italics added; cf. also 3:18). With this, of course, Paul would have fully agreed.

The persistent idea that there is one final judgment at which all must appear is a myth. The first resurrection occurs a thousand years before the second (Rev 20:5). The final judgment is for the unjustified only. Of course, as we shall see in Rom 14:10-11, Paul *does* believe that Christians will give an accounting for their earthly lives, but by no stretch of the imagination is this a soteriological judgment. The eternal destiny of those who stand there is already evident by their participation in the first resurrection, one thousand years before the Great White Throne Judgment (Rev 20:4-6).

Thus, by being the first individual in the OT record to have his faith *imputed to him as righteousness*, Abraham becomes the prototype for this experience in all succeeding generations.[4] It was faith, not circumcision or any other form of obedience, which rendered Abraham righteous before God. In the prestigious father of his race, Paul sees precisely the same kind of faith-righteousness about which he has been speaking. It goes without saying that he must have used this fact effectively in the synagogues where he proclaimed Christ. It was a superb Biblical proof.

**4:4-5. Now to the person who works the compensation is not made on the basis of grace, but on the basis of what is owed. But to the person who does not work, but believes in the One who justifies the ungodly, his faith is imputed as righteousness.**

Paul now explicitly draws out the conclusion demanded by his pivotal text about Abraham. From Abraham's personal experience of justification by faith one must conclude that the bestowal of righteousness was an act of divine grace. If works had been involved, then this *righteousness* would have been a form of compensation (*ho misthos*: pay, wages) and not **on the basis of grace** at all. Rather it would have been **on the basis of what is owed** (*kata opheilēma*). The reference to *grace* here picks up the idea already expressed in 3:23 where Paul speaks of being "justified freely by His grace." Clearly it was *on the basis of grace* that Abraham was justified, since it was **his faith**, not his works, which was **imputed** to him **as righteousness**.

---

[4] Hodges does not mean that no one before Abraham had been justified (and regenerated) by faith. Clearly many had (e.g., Adam and Eve, Abel, Enoch, Noah, etc.). His point is that Abraham "is the first individual in the OT record" to have this said of him. Indeed, he is the *only* person in the OT record to have said of him that his faith was accounted for righteousness. –RNW

The rendering **is not made** (v 4) represents the underlying Greek phrase *ou logizetai* (from *logizomai*). *Logizomai* is Paul's standard word in Romans for "imputing" righteousness (as in 4:3, 5, etc.). Its use here of both an earned payment (*compensation*), in v 4, and an unearned *righteousness*, in v 5, is comprehensible in the light of this word's commercial sense. We might see the connection in English better by translating this way: "*compensation is not put to his account on the basis of grace*" (v 4), and, "*his faith is put to his account as righteousness*" (v 5).

One might paraphrase Paul's concept as follows: "In God's books, a works-righteousness belongs in the 'earned pay' column, while a faith-righteousness belongs in the 'unearned gift' column."

Thus **the person who works** gets whatever he earns. This is the principle that governs the works-relationship to God. On the other hand, **the person who does not work** and instead believes obtains a graciously bestowed righteousness that is attributed to *his faith*. It would be difficult to make the distinction any sharper than this. There is no such thing in Pauline theology as a man who is justified because *as he works* he believes. Instead this righteousness comes to one *who does not work*. All work is excluded from this faith-righteousness and is thus completely irrelevant to it.[5]

### 4:6. Just as David too speaks of the blessedness of the man to whom God imputes righteousness apart from works:

This verse is best understood as beginning a new sentence. The English versions differ in this regard, with a comma being placed at the end of v 5 by the NKJV and NASB. But a period follows v 5 in the KJV, NIV, NACE, and JB. The initial word, rendered **Just as** (*Kathaper*), here introduces an independent clause and could therefore be translated by something like *In a similar fashion*. The point Paul is making is that David's words testify to the same truth stated by Gen 15:6 in reference to Abraham. Thus the

---

[5] A correct understanding of Rom 4:5 dismantles all attempts to regard works as an integral part of faith (believing). Faith is fundamentally simple, lacking various components that people wish to add. Paul speaks of one "who does not work, but believes." Yet, people speak of "a working faith," as though works were a component of faith. The contrast between working to earn a wage (v 4) and God's gracious accounting of righteousness to the non-working believer could not be sharper. Unfortunately, interpreters love to lessen the contrast by nuancing the meaning of v 5. Paul would denounce in strong terms the infamous mantra, "Faith alone saves, but the faith that saves is never alone." Properly understood, Rom 4:5 stands against any such amalgamation of faith and works in soteriology. –JHN

Biblical testimony is twofold here in accord with the OT law of witness (see Deut 17:6; 19:15; John 8:17).

David, we are told, describes **the blessedness of the** [justified] **man**. The term *blessedness* is chosen here in the light of the following quotation from Psalm 32, which commences with the word *blessed*. Thus the quotation to follow highlights the state of well-being enjoyed by the justified person.

> **4:7-8. "*Blessed are those whose wicked deeds are forgiven, and whose sins are covered. Blessed is the man to whom the Lord does not impute sin.*"**

A twofold "blessedness" is actually described by David in the words quoted from Ps 32:1-2. These are marked by the double use of **blessed** (v 7 and v 8). In v 7, the first "blessedness" is the blessing of forgiveness by which sin is put out of sight. The persons thus *blessed* are said to be **"those whose wicked deeds are forgiven, and whose sins are covered."** This is not the same as the "blessedness" of v 8. In fact, the concept of "forgiveness" is absent from the theology of Romans and this quotation is the only reference to it in the entire book. Its occurrence here is due to the fact that it is preparatory to v 8.

In point of fact, as wonderful as forgiveness is, it is actually less than the blessing of justification. As the Psalm indicates, forgiveness signals that *sins are covered*, that is to say, they are hidden from view and no longer interfere in the forgiven person's relationship to God. But though *covered*, the sins are there. They were properly imputed to the person who did them as *wicked deeds*, but then they are put out of sight. This is not what justification means, however.

What justification means is much more. This is the *second* blessedness described in the Psalm and is quoted in v 8. The justified person is **"the man to whom the Lord does not impute sin."** In terms of justification God charges the justified man with nothing at all (see 8:33). That man's faith, as Paul has already shown, is "imputed as righteousness." Since this is a righteousness totally "apart from works" (v 6), no works of any kind—good or evil—can be factored into it. It stands totally complete and sufficient on the basis of faith alone. From this perspective, the presence or absence of forgiveness is irrelevant.

David's Psalm, at this point, has an ascensive character. A great blessing (forgiveness) precedes an even greater blessing (justification). In the Psalm itself, the words *"the man to whom the Lord does not impute sin"* are followed immediately by "and in whose spirit there is no guile" (Ps 32:2b). Paul does not quote these words, of course, but it is not hard to see how he would have understood them. Given Paul's concept of human depravity (Romans 1–3), even in believers who must struggle with sin (Romans 6–8), no doubt Paul would have taken the unquoted words as a reference to the ultimate transformation (i.e., glorification) which is guaranteed by justification.

That is to say, using the terminology of Rom 8:30, all those "whom He *justifies*, these He also *glorifies*" (emphases added). In an absolute sense, at no time in this present life can a man claim that his spirit is totally free of guile. But that blessing will indeed be experienced by the *glorified*, whose destiny is assured by their having been *justified*. Yet since a reference to that here would be premature in Paul's argument, his quotation stops with the declaration about justification.

> **4:9. Therefore does this blessedness *come* upon the circumcised, or also upon the uncircumcised? For we are saying that faith was imputed to Abraham as righteousness.**

Paul now wraps together his double testimony from Scripture about justification.

**This blessedness** (alluding to David's words) is what has already been mentioned in regard to Abraham. The question now is no longer whether such righteousness can be bestowed since that is proved by Paul's two proof texts. The question rather is whether such a blessing can **come** only **upon the circumcised or** whether it can come **also upon the uncircumcised**.

From Paul's perspective the answer is already obvious from what he has been talking about. **For** what **we are saying**, states Paul, is **that faith was imputed to Abraham as righteousness**. This carries with it the manifest implication that circumcision, like every other kind of work, is not involved and that hence *this blessedness* can indeed come *also upon the uncircumcised*. He will now proceed to nail this point down.

> **4:10. So how was it imputed? While he was circumcised or uncircumcised? Not while he was circumcised, but while he was uncircumcised.**

Paul now delivers the *coup de grâce* to any idea that one must be **circumcised** in order to receive justification. The father of the Jewish race was himself **uncircumcised** when his faith was credited to him as righteousness. Thus circumcision can be no factor at all in the reception of "this blessedness."

> **4:11-12. And so he received the sign of circumcision, a seal of the righteousness by faith which *he received* while he was uncircumcised, so that he might be the father of all those who believe while uncircumcised (in order that righteousness might be imputed to them also), and *might be* the father of circumcision not only to those of the circumcision, but also to those who follow in the footsteps of the faith of our father Abraham which *he had* while he was uncircumcised.**

The conclusion obviously reached in v 10 leads logically to another question. What then was the role of circumcision if it made no contribution to the righteousness that Abraham received by faith? Paul's answer to this implicit question is that circumcision was a sign, that is, it was a **seal of the righteousness by faith which** Abraham had *received* **while he was uncircumcised**.

Paul is referring to Gen 17:1-14 where God enters into a covenantal relationship with Abraham. The distinguishing mark of this covenantal relationship was the circumcision that Abraham and every male in his household were to undergo. The fact that God chose this point in time (*after* Gen 15:6) is important for Paul here. God's willingness to execute a covenant with this justified man was a clear indication that God fully accepted him on the basis of his previous justification. If Abraham were still unrighteous in God's sight, such a covenant would have been unthinkable. Thus the sign of the covenant was also a sign and *seal of the righteousness by faith* that Abraham now had. Like a document formalized by the *seal* affixed to it by its author or sender, so God's *seal* on Abraham was the circumcision that marked him out as standing in special relationship to his Creator.

The words *which he received while he was uncircumcised* are followed by a clause that explains the reason why he received this *righteousness by faith…while he was uncircumcised*. The reason is that thereby he becomes **the father of all those who believe while uncircumcised**. If somehow circumcision had preceded his justification, Abraham could hardly have been perceived as in any sense a true spiritual *father* to uncircumcised believers. But now, as the first Biblical figure to be declared righteous *by faith*,[6] all believing Gentiles can look back to him as their spiritual progenitor.

Even more than that, as is indicated by the words **in order that righteousness might be imputed to them also**, the case of Abraham was actually designed to encourage Gentile belief and justification. By the addition of these words that are parenthetical in my translation, Paul conveys that Abraham was intended as more than a mere prototypical figure exemplifying justification. His case is actually presented in Scripture to encourage Gentiles to believe *in order that* they too might receive *righteousness* in the same way. It does not take much imagination to picture Paul before a Gentile audience telling them that they could receive God's *righteousness* by the same gracious means as the distinguished father of the Jewish race had received it.

But in addition to becoming the spiritual father of uncircumcised believers, Abraham's subsequent *circumcision* made him **the father of circumcision** both to his physical descendants (**those of the circumcision**) and also **to those who follow** his believing footsteps. The words *follow in the footsteps* **of the faith of our father Abraham** are most naturally taken to refer to believing Jews who, like Abraham, receive *righteousness* by means of *faith*. They stand so to speak in the *footprints* of Abraham when, like him, they believe and are justified.

The point of v 12 is that Abraham is not simply *the father of circumcision* to all his circumcised descendants. He is likewise a *father of circumcision* to his circumcised descendants who *also* believe as he did. Thus, in a sense, Abraham has a double fatherhood here: (1) as the physical prototype of all those who are literally circumcised, and (2) as the spiritual prototype of all the circumcised who are justified by faith. This double category is indicated in the Greek text by articles in front of each category (*tois ouk ek peritomēs monon* and *tois stoichousi…Abraam*).[7] Needless to say, Paul must often have appealed to the case of Abraham when urging his

---

[6] See previous note. –JHN

[7] The phrase *tois ouk ek peritomēs monon* has occasioned some difficulty, and it has even been thought that the second article (in front of *stoichousi*) is a textual error. But the problem dissolves if we recognize the phrase as a compressed equivalent of *ouk monon tois ek peritomēs monēs* ("not only to those of circumcision alone"). The phrase *ouk…monon* is predictably followed by the natural correlative words *alla kai* (**but also**), so that the meaning is: "not only to these but also to these." –ZCH

circumcised hearers to be justified by faith in Jesus Christ. Thus they would become Abraham's children in this second, superior sense.

**4:13. For the promise that he would be heir of the world was not made to Abraham or to his seed through the law, but through the righteousness of faith.**

Paul's argument from Scripture here takes a step back historically speaking, and he now refers to **the promise that** Abraham **would be heir of the world**. This can hardly refer to anything other than the original promise made to him at the time of his call and recorded in Gen 12:1-4. In particular it refers to the universal promise made at the conclusion of the call that "in you all the families of the earth shall be blessed" (Gen 12:3).

As we know from Gal 3:8-9, Paul understood Gen 12:3 as a prophecy about the gospel and justification by faith. His words there are these: "And the Scripture, foreseeing that God would justify the Gentiles by faith, preached the gospel to Abraham beforehand, saying, 'In you all the nations shall be blessed.' So then those who are of faith are blessed with believing Abraham." The universality of this part of the promise to Abraham is obvious. In addition, since the world to come will be composed exclusively of those who receive the Abrahamic blessing of justification, Abraham thereby becomes the *heir of the world*. Just as he will "inherit" the physical land of Israel through his *physical* descendants, so also he will inherit the world to come through his *spiritual* descendants.

Obviously *the promise* Paul is referring to came long before the giving of the law and thus **was not made to Abraham or to his seed through the law**. Instead, since *the promise* pertained to the blessing of justification, it can be said to have been made to him **through the righteousness of faith**. (Paul includes here a reference to Abraham's seed since *the promise* of Gen 12:3 is repeated in Gen 26:4 in reference to *his seed*, and in 28:14 in reference to both him *and his seed*. See below under v 16.) The eternal world to come will therefore be populated and possessed by Abraham's *spiritual* descendants, both Jewish and Gentile, all of whom will be recipients of the Abrahamic blessing of *the righteousness of faith*.

**4:14-15. For if those who are of the law are heirs, faith is made void and the promise is annulled. For the law causes wrath, since where there is no law there is no transgression.**

Paul affirms that it is not possible that **those who are of the law** could be heirs of this Abrahamic promise of blessing (i.e., justification). In that case, faith could not be the means by which the blessing is received but would be **made void** (*kekenōtai*, "has become ineffectual"). Equally, **the promise** could not be realized and thus would be annulled (*katērgētai*, "has been nullified"). As Paul has already established, "by the works of the law no flesh will be justified" (3:20), thus **the law** would render *the promise* unattainable.

So far from making the Abrahamic blessing attainable, *the law* actually produces the opposite of blessing, namely, wrath. (Paul has already explained how man's sin calls forth divine **wrath**: see 1:18ff.) Since Paul has previously showed that "through the law is the knowledge of sin" (3:20), it follows that **where there is no law there is no transgression**, so that to introduce law is to disclose *transgression* and thereby to make *wrath* inevitable. Of course, Paul does not say that in the absence of law there is no *sin*. Sin is a violation of God's righteous standards whether this is realized by the sinner or not. But the presence of law confronts the sinner with the fact that his behavior is a *transgression* (*parabasis*) of God's known will and therefore subject to His retributive *wrath* (anger).

> **4:16-17a. For this reason it is by faith, so that it might be by grace, in order that the promise might be confirmed to the entire seed, not only to the *seed* which is of the law, but also to the *seed* which is of the faith of Abraham, who is the father of us all (just as it is written, "*I have made you a father of many nations*").**

Therefore, since the law would have made the promise unattainable to both Jews and Gentiles, God ordained that the promise would be bestowed **by faith, so that it might be by grace**. Man's utter inability to measure up to the law necessitated that God should bestow the promise purely *by grace*, and therefore faith, not works, became the means through which it was received. Faith is the medium for God to act in grace.

The result is that the Abrahamic promise of blessing is **confirmed** (*bebaian*), that is, *made sure and certain*, to believing Jews and Gentiles alike. Thus **the entire seed** (*panti tō spermati*) of believers, both those who are **of the law** and also those who are simply **of the faith of Abraham**, are recipients of the promised blessing. From this standpoint, Abraham can be seen as **the father of us all**, that is, of all believers whether under the law or not.

This kind of fatherhood, in fact, fulfills the Scripture where **it is written, "I have made you a father of many nations"** (Gen 17:5-6). Since *the entire seed* is made up of many believers from the nations (*ethnōn*, from *ethnos*: "Gentile" or "nation"), Abraham's fatherhood is thereby extended to "*many nations.*"

> **4:17b. He believed God, before whom *he stood*, the One who brings the dead to life and speaks about things that do not exist as though they did.**

Paul now segues into a discussion of the kind of faith[8] Abraham had when he was justified, and he will show that, like our own faith, it is a faith in the God who raises the dead.

The opening construction for this new subunit requires attention. The words that begin 17b are *katenanti hou episteuse Theou* (lit., "before whom he believed, *namely*, God"). The prepositional phrase, *katenanti hou*, is evidently designed to link the new discussion conceptually with the subject of the immediately preceding words *tetheika se* ("I have made you," v 17a). Though technically grammatically subordinate to these preceding words, what follows is clearly a new consideration and we have treated it as an independent sentence in our translation. (The words *he stood* are added for clarity.)

The God whom Abraham believed on the occasion of his justification, Paul now says, is **the One who brings the dead to life and speaks about things that do not exist as though they did.**[9] Death and non-existence are not hindrances to Abraham's God since He possesses both resurrection power and the power to bring things into being.

The words rendered *speaks about things that do not exist as though they did* represent the Greek words *kalountos ta mē onta hōs onta*. The exact meaning of *kalountos* (from *kaleō*) here has been debated. The meaning

---

[8] Hodges did not accept the idea that there are different kinds of faith, one saving (the one that includes or results in commitment, obedience, and perseverance) and others which are not saving (e.g., temporary, sign, demonic, intellectual, spurious). Instead, he refers to *the object* of his faith, as the discussion which follows suggests. –RNW

[9] The words *the One* in our translation are not to be taken as implying that there might be other "gods" who do not do this. They simply render the articular participle construction in the Greek that serves to characterize the God Abraham believed. –ZCH

offered for this expression by BDAG is *"the one who calls into being what does not exist"* (p. 503).[10] That suggestion is no doubt wrong since it does not adequately account for Paul's *hōs.*

The more fundamental sense of *kaleō,* "to call, designate, name, address," will fit naturally here, though my phrase *speaks about* is more idiomatic English.

The reference is back to the preceding statement, made by God, that "I *have* made you [not "I *will* make you"] a father of many nations" (v 17a). The Greek verb for *make* is a perfect tense, *tetheika,* most naturally taken of a past event with present effects. This declaration represents a *fait accompli.* Yet it was made long before the fulfillment that Paul has specified in terms of the many believing Gentiles who have now become Abraham's spiritual children (cf. "father of us all," v 16). But the non-existence of these children at the time God spoke was no impediment to God. Since He would fulfill His word, He could speak of Abraham's future children, who *did not yet exist, as though they did.*[11]

But of the two statements about God (that is, that He *brings the dead to life* and that He *speaks about things that do not exist as though they did*), it is the first one which will now be elaborated in the verses that follow. Paul will connect Abraham's justifying faith with our own. Like him, we too believe in a God of resurrection inasmuch as God has "raised Jesus our Lord from the dead" (v 24).

**4:18.** *He is the one* **who beyond hope believed in hope, that he might be** *"a father of many nations,"* **according to what was spoken:** *"So will your seed be."*

---

[10] Frederick W. Danker. *A Greek-English Lexicon of the New Testament and Other Early Christian Literature.* 3d ed. (Chicago, IL: University of Chicago Press, 2000). –ZCH

[11] Verse 17b says, Abraham "believed God, before whom he stood, the One who brings the dead to life and speaks about things that do not exist as though they did" (ZCH). Some see this verse affirming that Abraham believed that God created the universe (cf. Cranfield, *Romans,* p. 1:244; Dunn, *Romans 1–8,* p. 218). Though it is reasonable to conceive of Abraham regarding God as Creator, that hardly seems to be Paul's contextual point. Other commentaries (besides Hodges) seeing the promise *that Abraham would be the father of many nations* (Rom 4:17a) as the referent include Sanday and Headlam, Lenski, Murray, and Schreiner (cf. William Sanday and Arthur C. Headlam, *A Critical and Exegetical Commentary on the Epistle to the Romans,* 3rd ed., ICC, ed. Samuel Rolles Driver, Alfred Plummer, and Charles Augustus Briggs [Edinburgh: Clark, 1898], 113; R. C. H. Lenski, *The Interpretation of St. Paul's Epistle to the Romans* [1936; reprint, N.p.: Hendrickson, 1998], 320f; John Murray, *The Epistle to the Romans* [Grand Rapids, MI: Eerdmans, 1959-65; paperback reprint ed. in one vol., Grand Rapids, MI: Eerdmans, 1997], 147; Schreiner, *Romans,* 237). –JHN

As at 2:6 (see comments there), the relative pronoun *hōs* functions as a virtual independent pronoun and introduces a new sentence. The reference back to Abraham is secured by the normal relative connection with the preceding subject word, in this case, the subject of *episteuse* in v 17. (A simple pronoun could have been misconstrued, at first, as a reference to God.) My phrase **He is the one** who seeks to retain something of the relative pronoun's nuance. (NKJV places a semicolon at the end of v 17, but a period is found in KJV, NASB, NIV, NACE and JB.)

Abraham, Paul states, was a man who **beyond hope believed in hope.** My English rendering attempts to keep the phrases *beyond hope* and *in hope* as close to each other as is feasible, but in Greek they are given one after another (*par' elpida ep' elpidi episteusen*) for rhetorical effect. The sense is that Abraham was well past (*par'*, *beyond*) the point at which he could, humanly speaking, have *hope* for a physical child, yet his faith was based on (*ep'*, *in*) the *hope* that God's promise brought to him. The reference is to Gen 15:6, as is clear from the phrase **"so will your seed be,"** taken from Gen 15:5.

In the Genesis context, Abraham had despaired of having a physical son and saw his possessions as devolving to his servant Eliezer (15:3-4). But God offers him an heir "who will come from [his] own body," whereupon He takes Abraham outside and shows him the stars of heaven and gives him the promise, "So will your seed be" (Gen 15:5). Although there were great physical obstacles to this promise (which Paul will mention in v 19), Abraham's faith rose above those obstacles so that what was out of reach as a physical hope was achieved. He thereby became **"a father of many nations."**

The words **that he might be** translate the Greek *eis to genesthai*. The Greek phrase can be understood as expressing either purpose or result, but is probably somewhere in between (and thus "semi-final") in the sense of "to the end that he became." Necessarily the reference is to *God's* intention, since in the actual situation of Genesis 15 this promise was not yet explicit for Abraham. But God had this outcome in mind when Abraham believed. When later the promise is made explicit (Gen 17:5), it therefore pointed to the outcome of Abraham's justifying faith by which he would become the spiritual father of believing Gentiles.

**4:19-21. And since he was not weak in faith, he did not take into account his own body which was already dead (since he**

**was about one hundred years old) nor the deadness of Sarah's womb. And he did not doubt the promise of God in unbelief, but became strong in faith, giving glory to God and being fully convinced that what He had promised He was also able to do.**

This impressive description of Abraham's justifying faith is highly instructive. In order to believe the promise God made to him (Gen 15:5), it was necessary for Abraham to ignore **his own body** which had lost all potential for *communicating life* by physical means. Thus his body, in this sense, was **dead** due to the fact that **he was about one hundred years old**. But there was also the problem of the corresponding **deadness of Sarah's womb**, since she had always been unable to *conceive life*. This too Abraham had to ignore.[12]

Thus Abraham demonstrated that **he was not weak in faith**. Implicitly he believed in God's resurrection power since his faith was not hindered by "death" either in himself or in Sarah. In fact, **he did not doubt the promise of God in unbelief**. That is to say, his heart did not call God's promise into question because of an inability to believe it (*in unbelief*). On the contrary, he **became strong in faith**.

The words *became strong* translate the Greek word *enedunamōthē*. The standard NT lexicon (BDAG) places the use of the word in this verse under the broad category of meaning "to become able to function or do something" (p. 333). The point Paul is making here is that God's promise did not lie beyond Abraham's capacity to believe it, but instead he found the spiritual strength to do so. (Paul, however, is not dealing with *how* Abraham managed to believe in these circumstances, but rather with the impressive fact that he *did*. It was, so to speak, a mighty exercise of faith.)

In exercising this faith Abraham was **giving glory to God**. This does not mean that he expressed praise on this occasion. Rather the sense is that by taking God at His word he was, in so doing, giving God glory. (The aorist form *dous* [giving] looks at the action as a whole.) In what way precisely he rendered this *glory to God* is now clarified by the words that follow, stating that he was **fully convinced that what He had promised**

---

[12] The word *ignore*, used several times by Hodges here, means "to refuse to take notice of" (Merriam-Webster.com). Abraham had to *overcome* or *get beyond* facts about Sarah and himself by focusing on the One who works miracles. This was what the majority of Israelites failed to do at Kadesh Barnea. They saw giants in the land and considered their own bodies unable to overcome them. But they failed to account for God's promise. Of course, Joshua and Caleb, like Abraham, looked beyond their bodies to the One who made the promise. –RNW

**He was able also to do.** In other words, Abraham glorified God by his strong conviction that God could perform *what He had promised*, however difficult it might seem. He ascribed to God the power to fulfill His word.

The Greek word here translated by *being fully convinced* is *plērophoreō*. It is relatively rare in the NT and is found only elsewhere in Luke 1:1; Rom 14:5; and 2 Tim 4:5, 17. The cognate noun occurs in the NT only at Col 2:2; 1 Thess 1:5; and Heb 6:11 and 10:22. In BDAG, the instance in this verse falls under the semantic domain "convince fully" [p. 827]. The word serves to underline Paul's point that Abraham *did not doubt the promise of God in unbelief.* However much his physical condition, and Sarah's, might have seemed an obstacle to the fulfillment, Abraham was totally persuaded that what God *had promised He was able also to do.*

### 4:22. Therefore also *"it was imputed to him for righteousness."*

Abraham's belief in God's promise to him resulted in his justification. The pronoun **it**, the subject of the verb *"was imputed,"* is not a separate word in Greek but is implicit in the verb (*elogisthē*). The reference can only be to his belief, that is, his faith. This already is perfectly clear from the more general statement of 4:5 where Paul writes, "his faith is counted for righteousness" (*logizetai hē pistis autou eis dikaiosunēn*).

As earlier noted, for Paul justification is by no means a matter of imputing some form of obedience to the law to believers. Justification by faith is exactly what its name says. The believer is justified by his faith because that faith—totally apart from works—is what is accounted *"to him for righteousness."*

> **4:23-24.** Now it was not only written for his sake that it was imputed to him, but also for our sake to whom it would be imputed, *that is*, to those who would believe in the One who raised Jesus our Lord from the dead.

Paul did not treat Scripture as a mere historical record, but as the timelessly relevant Word of God (see Rom 15:4; 1 Cor 9:9-10; 10:6; 2 Tim 3:14-17). Abraham himself was not the sole concern of the declaration of Gen 15:6, although the record of his faith surely commends him. But instead God had definitely in mind the period from Paul's day to the present. The declaration about Abraham was made also for the benefit of **those who would believe in the One who raised Jesus our Lord from**

**the dead**. That is, the record about Abraham's faith was intended to offer Scriptural support to the proclamation about Jesus.

Here again the subject word *it* (used twice in this verse) is most naturally taken in the same way as the *it* of v 22 must be taken. (The words *as righteousness* in v 22 make the reference of *it* to *faith* unmistakable.) Just as *faith* **was imputed to** Abraham "as righteousness," so *faith* **would be imputed** "as righteousness" *to those who would believe in the* same God in whom Abraham believed.

As Paul has just shown in vv 19-22, the faith by which Abraham was justified was *implicitly* a confidence in God's resurrecting power. The God in whom he believed could overcome his own "dead" body as well as the "deadness of Sarah's womb." Paul of course preached the resurrection of Christ (1 Cor 15:3-8) and he could say that "if Christ is not risen, your faith is futile, you are still in your sins" (1 Cor 15:17). So it is in every way probable that, since the cross, justifying faith has never occurred in any heart that thinks Jesus is still dead. Indeed His very offer of eternal life is inseparable from the promise of future resurrection (John 11:25-26).

However, on the other hand, all of the first disciples believed in Jesus for eternal life without realizing that He must die and rise again. This is quite plain from John 20:8-9 (see also John 2:22) and from the fact that the announcement of His resurrection by the women was received in unbelief by the disciples (Mark 16:9-13; Luke 24:11). But despite this lack of understanding on the part of the first disciples, when they believed Jesus' word as the word of the One who sent Him (see John 5:24), they were in fact believing in *the One who would raise Jesus our Lord from the dead*. In short, faith in the God who set Jesus forth as a Mercy Seat (3:25) is faith in a God of resurrection, whether consciously realized or not.

### 4:25. who was delivered for our offenses and raised for our justification.

The God who "raised Jesus our Lord from the dead" (v 24) did so on the third day after the Savior's death for our sins. The word translated **was delivered** is from the Greek verb *paradidōmi*, which has a technical sense related to the police and the courts, meaning to "hand over into [the] custody of" (BDAG, p. 762). This sense no doubt lies in the background here for Paul (as it does also in 1 Cor 11:23b). The verb is used repeatedly in the four Gospels in reference to our Lord's betrayal and arrest.

Nevertheless, Paul is referring ultimately to God. Human beings did in fact deliver Jesus to the authorities seeking His execution, but God was behind all of that (cf. Acts 2:23). It is God, therefore, who delivered Him **for our offenses** just as it was also God who raised Him **for our justification**. Both the death and resurrection of our Lord are the work of God the Father, as is already implicit in 3:25.

The word *for* (used twice in this verse) reflects the Greek preposition *dia*. Here it has its causal sense and might be reasonably (if not perfectly) rendered "for the sake of" in both places in the verse. Our Lord was delivered to execution *for the sake of our offenses*. That is to say, He died as a substitute for us so that those offenses might not remain as an impediment to God's justifying grace to us. His death was necessitated by these offenses if He was to become a *Mercy Seat* (see discussion under 3:25) where man and God could meet in peace.

*Offenses* translates the Greek word *paraptōmata*, used here for the first time in Romans, but occurring a half dozen times in chap. 5. Thus its use here prepares the way for the following discussion. In this verse, however, it can scarcely be distinguished from *hamartēma* (sin), which Paul had used in 3:25. The reference to human sins (*offenses*) in this verse carries us back to the initial paragraph (3:21-26) of the present unit. Indeed the reference in 4:25 to the atoning work of Christ discussed in 3:21-26 serves as an informal *inclusio* marking the end of the whole unit (3:21–4:25).

It is also significant that the words *raised for our justification* are the first direct reference to the resurrection of Jesus since 1:4. The risen life of Christ is a major concern of the material that follows in chaps. 5–8. Here, too, the language of Paul suggests strongly that 4:25 is a "hinge" verse, concluding the unit begun at 3:21, but anticipating what will follow.

Once again, as suggested above, the word *for* can be understood in the sense of *for the sake of*. Just as our sins necessitated the death of Christ, so also *our justification* required His resurrection.[13] This was not because

---

[13] Commentators often struggle to explain what "raised for our justification" means. As Hodges points out, Paul clearly does not mean that there was something "incomplete or inadequate about the atoning death of our Lord." Rather, he sees in Jesus' resurrection a proof that God indeed justifies all who believe in His Son. "Our justification required His resurrection" in the sense of validation, as Hodges says here, and in the sense which he said in his discussion of the previous verse, Rom 4:24, that Jesus' promise of regeneration is inextricably tied with His promise of resurrection in John 11:25-27. The word which Hodges translates as *justification* is not the normal word *dikaiosunē*. Instead it is a word (*dikaiōsis*) used only twice in the NT, here and in Rom 5:18. See note 14 under Rom 5:18 where I suggest that

there was anything incomplete or inadequate about the atoning death of our Lord. Instead, as a demonstration of God's satisfaction with His Son's atoning death, the resurrection provides a valid proof that God is righteous in deciding to "justify the person who has faith in Jesus" (3:26). A dead Savior would provide no such validation of God's act when He grants justification to sinners who believe in Jesus.

Thus Paul succinctly concludes his crucial discussion of *God's righteousness apart from the law* (3:21), the vindicating principle of which is the death and resurrection of Jesus Christ. He is now ready to move on to the implications that this truth has for Christian experience.

---

an alternate translation for Rom 4:25 might be *raised for our righteous living* (i.e., raised that we might live righteously in our experience). –RNW

# Romans 5

## 3. God's Righteousness Makes Spiritual Victory Possible (5:1-11)

Paul is now ready to spell out the splendid spiritual benefits that can follow the experience of justification by faith. This is what he does in 5:1-11. The description of these benefits stands in marked and dramatic contrast with the degradation and spiritual bondage in which humanity stands as a result of God's wrath against human sinfulness (as described in 1:18–2:5).

### a. The Description of This Victory (5:1-5)

**5:1. Therefore since we have been justified by faith, we have[1] peace with God through our Lord Jesus Christ,**

---

[1] There is a textual problem here. The external evidence slightly favors the reading *echomen*, which is an indicative. Hodges, with his translation *we have peace…*, clearly takes that reading. Nearly as many manuscripts (the Majority Text is divided fairly evenly here) reads *echōmen*, which is a hortatory subjunctive and would be translated: "let us have peace." Those who see this as the correct reading believe that the experience of peace with God, rather than the positional reality, is in view. However, the internal evidence strongly supports the indicative here, as the exposition by Hodges shows.

Verlyn D. Verbrugge, "The Grammatical Internal Evidence for ECHOMEN in Romans 5:1," *JETS* 54 (September 2011): 559-72, contends that the wording of Rom 5:3 presupposes the indicative in v 1. Verse 3 starts with *ou monon de* (and not only). The first and third words of the phrase are crucial. *De* links the *echōmen/echomen* (v 1) with *kauchōmetha* (v 3), but *ou* defines what *de* connects. Specifically, *ou* goes with indicatives, while *mē* goes with non-indicatives. Thus, it is *echōmen eirēnē…ou monon de…kauchōmetha* (Not only do we have peace, but we glory). If Paul wanted to say, "Let us not only have peace, but let us glory," he would have written *echōmen eirēnē…mē monon de…kauchōmetha* (underlining added). Although many scribes substituted *echōmen* for *echomen*, manuscript evidence solidly supports *ou*, rather than *mē*. Thus, both external and internal evidence in v 3 support the indicative in v 1. –JHN

In vv 1-5 Paul describes the victory of by-faith justification. Then in vv 6-11 he explains the basis for that victory. Paul now wishes to draw out the implications of the truth he has just expounded. What in fact are the results of the by-faith justification that he has explained so carefully?

The first of these results is the blessing of **peace with God**. This is precisely the benefit we would expect Paul to mention in view of his elaborate description of God's wrath that has been revealed from heaven (see 1:18–2:5). Obviously if mankind stands under the manifestation of divine anger, it does not enjoy anything that can be described as genuine *peace with God*. But when God justifies a sinner who believes in Jesus, a fundamental *peace* is established between the sinner and God.

The nature of this *peace* is of course *judicial*, since justification is the act of God as our Judge. As a result, no charge can be brought against the justified person before God's bar of justice (see Rom 8:33-34). The modern reader should avoid reading into this text the idea of inner tranquility which, even in English, is by no means a regular feature of the word. The *peace* involved here is like that which results when two warring nations are no longer in a hostile relationship to each other.

To use the Pauline image, when a person believes in Jesus he has encountered God at His appointed "Mercy Seat" (Rom 3:25). There the shed blood of God's Son renders this believing encounter a *peaceful*, rather than a hostile, encounter. The sinner is fully accepted as righteous in God's eyes. Thus this *peace* is realized **through our Lord Jesus Christ** who in His own Person is our "Mercy Seat."

> **5:2. through whom we also possess access by faith into this grace in which we stand, and we exult in the expectation of the glory of God.**

However, not only do justified persons "have peace with God," they **also possess access...into this grace**. Here Paul carries us a step beyond the basic experience of justification. That he is not simply repeating himself in this verse is indicated by the word *also* (*kai*). *Access* is therefore an *additional* benefit of justification by faith.

The key to Paul's concept is the word *access* which translates the Greek word *prosagōgēn*. The word occurs in the NT only three times, all in Paul (Eph 2:18; 3:12; and here). Ephesians 2:18 speaks of "access by one Spirit to the Father" and Eph 3:12 may easily be taken in the same sense of access into the presence of God. In secular Greek the word can be found, for example, in the *Cyropaedia* of Xenophon (fifth century BC) in reference to "access to Cyrus for an audience" (see BDAG, p. 876). *Access* to God is the natural sense here in Romans.

As mentioned above, Paul has earlier referred to our Lord as a "Mercy Seat" (3:25), drawing upon the imagery of the tabernacle and temple in the OT. Since the physical mercy seat was located in the Holy of Holies, it was thought of as standing in the presence of God. Only the Jewish high priest had *access* to this part of the sanctuary, and he had it only once a year on the Day of Atonement (see Heb 9:7).

The believer, however, has already met God at the true Mercy Seat. He has already been into the presence of God, so to speak, where he has received a righteousness that is his entirely by grace. Here, in the present verse, Paul appears to be thinking of the presence of God as a place of grace into which we now have a right to enter at any time. His concept is quite similar to the one in Hebrews where believers are encouraged to "come boldly to the throne of *grace*" (Heb 4:16, italics added).

Moreover, Paul's statement that *we also possess access…into this grace* **in which we stand** is strikingly worded. By this assertion Paul affirms that we both *stand* in *this grace* and also that we *possess access into* it. In other words, our possession of God's *grace* in justification is permanent (*we stand* in it) and precisely because it is, we can come at any time into the *gracious* presence of the God who justified us. What is implied is that the resources of divine grace can be drawn upon as we approach God to ask for them. Prayer is the obvious way in which we utilize the *access* we now have as justified persons.

But a third benefit that flows from justification by faith is also mentioned here by Paul. It is nothing less than **the expectation of the glory of God**. (The word *expectation* is chosen for the translation here, rather than the familiar "hope," because the underlying Greek word [*elpis*] does not necessarily carry the nuance of uncertainty that the English word "hope" usually does.[2] See BDAG, pp. 319-20.) So exciting is this *expectation*, in fact, that the justified person can actually **exult** in it.

---

[2] This small translation choice by Hodges wonderfully opens up the meaning of these verses. The traditional word *hope* mistakenly conveys in English, as Hodges points out, a sense of uncertainty. Yet the Greek refers to something which is certain, yet still future. It is something we must wait to obtain. Hence *expectation* is a wonderful choice. It really makes vv 2-5 much clearer to the English reader. –RNW

Justification therefore assures the believer of his ultimate destiny and glorification. As Paul will later say, "whom He justifies, these He also glorifies" (Rom 8:30); that is, God will conform the justified person to the "likeness of His Son" (8:29). But as presented here by Paul, the result of such an *expectation* is more than what we normally mean by *assurance of eternal salvation*. It is that, of course, but beyond that it is a source of *exultation*.

The Greek verb rendered here by *exult* (*kauchōmetha*) occurs in the NT in both a positive and a negative sense. There is a kind of "exultation" which is equivalent to our English concept of "boasting." But there is also a kind of exultation that is essentially selfless. The verb is used twice in the famous Pauline statement, "He who *exults*, let him *exult* in the Lord" (2 Cor 10:17, italics added). In the context here in Romans, in connection with justification by faith, the exultation must inevitably be "in the Lord." It is sourced in the magnificent grace of God made available to us through our Lord Jesus Christ (v 1).

In speaking like this immediately following his reference to *access*, it is quite likely that Paul is thinking especially (though not exclusively) of corporate Christian worship in which assembled Christians come boldly before God to offer exultant praise to their Lord and Savior (see especially Heb 10:19-25).

Paul's initial statement in this unit proclaims a "trinity" of benefits that flow from the experience of justification. These are (1) peace, (2) access, and (3) joy (i.e., exultation), but beyond these lies yet another benefit that is equally remarkable.

**5:3-4. And not only that, but also we exult in afflictions, knowing that affliction produces endurance, and endurance, approvedness, and approvedness, expectation.**

The exultant assurance of future glorification carries with it a further capacity to **exult**. The justified believer can now see his **afflictions** in a new light and can regard them as a process that produces **endurance**. This, in turn, creates an **approvedness** that results in yet further **expectation**.

The words **and not only that** suggest that Paul is now referring to a significant addition to the previously mentioned results of justification by faith. In contrast to unrighteous men who should see their troubles and turmoil as an expression of divine *wrath* (1:18ff.), the person who is righteous by faith can learn to view *afflictions* from a new vantage point.

How this can be true Paul will elaborate later (8:18-38), but for now he simply summarizes the important truth that our *afflictions* can have positive results.

It should be noted here that in the suggested translation the word *approvedness* stands in place of a variety of words used in the English versions ("experience," KJV; "character," NKJV, NIV; "proven character," NASB; "tried virtue," NACE; "perseverance," JB). The underlying Greek word (*dokimē*) is used twice in this verse but nowhere else in Romans. It is derived from the same root as the verb *dokimazō*, used in Rom 1:28; 2:18; 12:2; and 14:22. Especially relevant is the use in 12:2 where Paul speaks of "approving" God's will (see discussion there).

As indicated in the "extended definition" offered by BDAG (p. 256), *dokimē* is defined as "the experience of going through a test with special reference to the result." The "formal equivalents" offered are "standing a test" and "character." Neither of these definitions seems quite right here, however. Though "character" has often been used in the translation of this verse, that English word is now quite general and broad. Used alone it most often means a set of traits that distinguish one individual or group from others. If a positive assessment is wanted, we frequently add an adjective like "good." I therefore suggest here the word *approvedness* which, though rare in contemporary English, refers to the state or quality of being approved.[3]

Paul is saying that our *afflictions* can produce the ability to bear up under difficulties (*endurance*), and this capacity in turn results in our becoming people upon whom God's divine approbation can rest. Just as gold that has passed through the fire of testing comes out purged of disfiguring dross and is "approved" for appropriate use, so the Christian who has endured his *afflictions* can emerge from them as a person of whom God Himself approves (cf. 1 Pet 1:6-9).

---

[3] Approval by Christ is a fairly major theme in Paul. AWANA children's ministries is based on 2 Tim 2:15 and Paul's exhortation to Timothy to "Be diligent to present yourself *approved* to God, a worker who does not need to be ashamed, rightly dividing the word of truth." In Paul's famous statement in 1 Cor 9:27, he said, "I discipline my body and bring it in to subjection, lest, when I have preached to others, I myself should become disqualified (*adokimos*)." The word translated *disqualified* actually should be translated *disapproved* since the same word used in Rom 5:4 and 2 Tim 2:15, *dokimos*, appears here, except that the alpha-primitive is added to reverse the meaning (like *atheist*, *atypical*, or *asymmetrical*). See also Rom 14:18; 16:10; 1 Cor 11:19; 2 Cor 13:7. –RNW

This represents a remarkable progression in human experience. Since God's wrath (see 1:18ff.) expresses His *disapproval* of unrighteous men and their conduct, the justified person can now achieve a state of *approvedness* as a result of his personal conduct under trial. This *approvedness* bestows on him a further endowment of *expectation*, though the exact nature of this *expectation* is not spelled out here. Paul will deal with it more explicitly later (see 8:17-25).

Taking into consideration the whole of vv 1-4, it might be said that both *grace* and the *exultation* that flows from it have a double aspect for Paul. Through justification by faith we both *stand in God's grace* and have *access to it* through prayer. Our standing brings with it *exultation* that is based on our "expectation of the glory of God," while our trials (about which we *pray* [8:26]) bring additional *exultation*. The bottom line for this kind of experience is stated in the following verse.

**5:5. Now expectation does not result in shame, because the love of God is poured out in our hearts through the Holy Spirit who has been given to us.**

The **expectation** that is produced in us through enduring our trials and becoming approved in God's sight, promotes a boldness about our Christian profession. What Paul means is that we can *unashamedly* (i.e., boldly) *confess* such a believing *expectation*. Paul will address the theme of confessing Christ in 10:5-13, a passage in which he affirms that "everyone who believes in Him shall not be ashamed."

The fundamental reason why this freedom from shame can be realized is now traced to a rich inner experience of **the love of God**. So far from our "afflictions" creating a sense of distance and estrangement from God, they can actually usher in a deeper appreciation of His love. As these afflictions are properly endured, producing qualities in us of which God approves, it is as though *the love of God* **is poured forth in our hearts**. That is to say that our hearts are suffused with His love as **the Holy Spirit** makes that love a joyous realization within us.

With these words, Paul has reached the climax of his "staircase" treatment of the benefits of justification. Justification by faith results in *peace with*, and *access to*, the God from whom we were formerly estranged, and is accompanied by an *expectation of future glory*. This *expectation*, in turn, is enhanced by experiencing the afflictions which God uses to mold us into persons who have His approval. And that process itself leads to a grand realization of how much we are *loved* by Him.

Paul's description in 5:1-5 of the rich quality of the Christian's post-justification experience serves as part of a bridge section (5:1-11) leading to a detailed exposition of precisely this experience (Rom 5:12–8:39). But Paul's words already imply how abundantly meaningful is the last phrase of his thematic statement in 1:17: "The one who is righteous by faith *shall live.*"

### b. The Basis for This Victory (5:6-11)

**5:6. You see, while we were still weak, Christ died at the proper time for the ungodly.**

A new subunit begins here. Paul has just described the fullness of the post-justification experience that God designs for the one "who is righteous by faith" (5:1-5). He now wishes to examine in summary form the basis for such an experience. Here, in vv 6-11, Paul answers the natural question about *how* justification leads to an experience as rich as the one he has so eloquently delineated.

The opening words of v 6 in Greek are *Eti gar Christos*. I have chosen to render the conjunction *gar* by the English phrase, **You see.** (This rendering is suggested by BDAG, p. 189, under the category of "marker of clarification.") Paul now wishes to go behind the statements of vv 1-5 to present their rationale.

The position of *Eti* (**still**) at the front of the sentence draws attention. Though *gar* is postpositive and never stands first, *Eti* is not the expected initial word and so is emphatic. In a sense it goes with the words *ontōn hēmōn asthenōn* (**while we were...weak**). The positioning of *Eti*, however, allows Paul to stress the fact that the basis of the experience he has just described in vv 1-5 arises in no way from our own inherent strength. When the whole process began, *we were still weak.*

But God had a solution for this profound weakness on our part, and thus when **the proper time** came, **Christ died...for the ungodly.** By the words proper time (*kata kairon*), Paul no doubt means something similar to his statement in Gal 4:4, "But when the fullness of time had come, God sent forth His Son." The death of Christ, which was *for the ungodly,* came at precisely the point in human history that God had foreordained for it. It thereby became the fundamental starting point by which *weak* and *ungodly* people like ourselves (*hēmēn*) could be brought into the experience of spiritual *strength*. Clearly, a remarkable inner *strength* is implied by the exultation in our afflictions that Paul has just described (5:3-5).

The English necessarily conceals a euphonic combination in this verse. Subsequent to the subject word *Christos* (Christ), the proximity of the two following word groups, *ontōn hēmōn asthenōn* (*while we were...weak*) and *kata kairon huper asebōn* (*at the proper time for the ungodly*), has a quasi-poetic effect. This combination is rhetorically useful in postponing the verb *apethane* (**died**), which has been expected since *Christos*, so that *apethane* becomes effectively climactic. The result is a well-crafted Greek sentence.

> **5:7-8. For only rarely will anyone die for a righteous man, though perhaps for a good man someone might even dare to die. But God demonstrates His own love for us because, while we were still sinners, Christ died for us.**

In order to elaborate the experiential implications of the death of Christ, Paul returns to the theme of divine love that had climaxed in vv 1-5. If we think in human terms, he suggests, we realize that a willingness to **die for a righteous man** is found **only rarely**. (This meaning for the Greek adverb *Molis* is one that is offered by BDAG, p. 657.) On the other hand, the willingness to die **for a good man** can conceivably (**perhaps**) be thought of as more natural. It is something **someone might even dare to do**. The words *even dare* (*kai tolma*, i.e., *even be bold enough*) imply not simply an example of this kind of self-sacrifice, but a case of boldness in doing so.

Clearly Paul means here that mere moral rectitude (i.e., *a righteous man*) *rarely* inspires the laying down of life, while *goodness* (particularly to others) could *perhaps* more readily do so. But in contrast to both examples is the way that **God demonstrates His own love for us**. For although we were neither *righteous* nor *good* (see 3:10-12), but instead **were still sinners**, nevertheless **Christ died for us**. The starting point for all human realization of the Creator's love for His creatures is always the cross of Christ.

The words **while we were still sinners** (*eti hamartōlōn ontōn hēmōn*) clearly evoke the earlier words in v 6, "while we were still weak" (*eti...*

*ontōn hēmōn asthenōn*). The rich experience of God's love for us (v 5) is rooted in neither our own inherent capacity nor in our own inherent goodness, since we possessed neither of these things. Instead the initiating force was divine love demonstrated when *Christ died for us.*

It should be noted that the word rendered here by *demonstrates* is the Greek verb form *Sunistēsi*. This verb is employed by Paul in his writings a total of ten out of its twelve NT uses. In a majority of the cases outside of Romans, the sense seems to be that of "commending" or "recommending" (2 Cor 4:2; 6:4; 7:11; 10:18 [twice]; 12:11), while once it refers to a demonstration or presentation (Gal 2:18). (The remaining instance is intransitive [Col 1:17]). In Romans, the two other Pauline instances split between "demonstrate" (3:5) and "recommend" (16:1). In the present verse either meaning is possible, but in this context one may suspect that, for Paul, the word carries overtones of both ideas. God not only *demonstrates* His love through the cross of Christ, but *recommends* it to us, as Christians, as a source of encouragement and as a basis for trust. This latter concept underlies Paul's splendid paean[4] to that love in 8:37-38.

**5:9. All the more therefore, since we have now been justified by His blood, we shall be delivered from wrath through Him.**

Few verses in this epistle are more crucial to the correct understanding of Paul's letter than the present verse. It may even be said that in this verse and the next we have the most significant hinge verses in the entire epistle. A failure to understand the force and relevance of these verses entails an irreparable loss in comprehending Paul's argument.

The words **All the more therefore** reflect the Greek construction *Pollō oun mallon*. The combination *Pollō...mallon* is employed by Paul in Romans three more times, once in the following verse (5:10), and twice in the following context (5:15, 17). The expression was apparently commonplace in Greek when arguing from something known or assumed to a conclusion that naturally follows from it. As a result, in both Biblical and secular Greek, *pollō mallon* (or, *posō mallon*) often follows a conditional clause (as in fact it does in 5:10, 15, 17). (See BDAG, p. 614.)

Here the Greek participle *dikaiōthentes* (**since we have...been justified**) is the functional equivalent of a conditional clause that is

---

[4] A paean is a song of praise or triumph. In the Greek classical period a paean was typically sung by choirs. –RNW

assumed to be true. Its truth has been established by Paul's argumentation in Rom 3:21–4:25.5 The conclusion to be drawn is naturally expressed in the future tense since it refers to something that is logically expected to follow from it. Thus it should be carefully observed that the verb *sōthēsometha* (**we shall be delivered**) is a *gnomic* future, not a *predictive* one.

The grammars tell us that the *gnomic* future is employed "in order to express that which is expected under certain circumstances (as in classical [Greek])" (see BDF, p. 178). In the type of construction we are looking at here, the term *logical* future might be clearer. This type of future *idea* is nicely illustrated in Matt 6:30 where a future tense verb is not expressed, but clearly implied in the Greek and expressed in the English: "Now if God so clothes [*amphiennusin*] the grass of the field...*will He not* much more [*pollō mallon*] *clothe* you, O you of little faith?" [The Greek presupposes the future of *amphiennumi* in the concluding clause.] But our Lord's statement is a call to *trust* God to do that, not a simple prediction. In view of His care for "the grass of the field," it is *logical* to assume He can be counted on to care for us. But this does not imply (as a predictive future might) that His provision is independent of our trust.

The extended discussion which Paul will begin at 5:12 develops the truth that is expressed in this verse. Paul does not assume that the "deliverance" he is speaking of is independent of our willingness to avail ourselves of God's provision for it. To read some idea of "inevitability" out of the future tense of *sōthēsometha* (*we shall be delivered*), as though it were necessitated by the grammatical form, would be an error that is excusable only in an elementary Greek class.

In addition, it needs to be stated that Paul's assertion must necessarily be understood in the light of the argument of the epistle thus far. When Paul writes that *we shall be delivered* **from wrath through Him**, it is illegitimate to refer the word *wrath* (*tēs orgēs*) to eternal damnation.[6]

---

[5] Neither *save* (*sōzō*) nor *salvation* (*sōtēria*) appear at all in Rom 3:21–4:25, the section on justification by faith, with Rom 5:9 being the first use since 1:16. The words *save* and *salvation* in Romans focus on temporal deliverance from temporal wrath, not on justification/regeneration. On this issue the commentary tradition stands nearly united in opposition to Paul's meaning. The reader may profitably consult this commentary's treatment of Rom 1:16-17. –JHN

[6] This passage recalls Rom 1:16-17, the theme statement for the epistle. Paul gives evidence both here and in 1:16ff. that eternally secure believers need deliverance from wrath. Contrary to popular (and scholarly) opinion, Romans does not use *save* (*sōzō*), *salvation*

No such use of *orgē* occurs in Romans and to so interpret is to commit eisegesis (reading something into the text that is not there).

On the contrary, *orgē* is a high profile word in Romans and occurs in the first few words following Paul's thematic statement in 1:16-17. There (1:18a) Paul declares, "For the wrath of God is revealed from heaven" (*Apokaluptetai gar orgē Theou ap' ouranou*). In the following context, as we have already seen, this "wrath" is clearly identified as God's *present* displeasure with "all the ungodliness and unrighteousness of men" (1:18b; cf. 1:19-32). The only subsequent explicit references to "wrath," prior to our present verse, occur in the *inclusio* (2:5) that ties up the unit (1:18–2:5), and in brief references to it in 2:8; 3:5; and 4:15. The sense of the word is not to be arbitrarily altered in any of these instances.

With the present verse Paul returns to the leading theme of the "body" of this famous epistle—namely, the theme of mankind sunk into the depths of moral depravity because of God's extreme displeasure with its wickedness. But now that Paul has established that God imputes *righteousness* to (i.e., He justifies) the believer in Jesus, the question becomes profoundly relevant: *What is the relationship of the justified believer to this universal display of heaven-sent wrath?*

Paul's answer is that it is reasonable and fully to be expected that the person who has **now been justified by His blood** *shall be delivered from wrath through* this very Jesus.[7] Thus, justification by faith is seen as the "open sesame" to deliverance from the divine penalty imposed on human sin here and now. Needless to say, this implies the necessity of a change in lifestyle and that is precisely the subject Paul will now proceed to discuss (5:12–8:39).

It is important to observe here (and also in v 10) that the word translated *delivered* renders the familiar Greek verb *sōzō* ("to save"). This word has a very wide range of meanings in normal Greek usage. As is indicated in the standard Greek lexicon (BDAG), and as is well known in academia, the word is far from confined in Biblical usage to its standard theological sense today, a sense in which it usually is understood to mean "to save

---

(*sōtēria*), for saving unbelievers from a destiny in the lake of fire. Neither does it use *wrath* (*orgē*) for the lake of fire. –JHN

[7] Paul is arguing from the greater to the lesser in Rom 5:9-10 (see esp. *much more* [*pollō mallon*] in both verses). Since God has guaranteed believers' eternal destiny in justifying and reconciling them (the greater), He will also seek to deliver them from temporal wrath (the lesser). –JHN

from eternal damnation." Correctly BDAG gives as the first extended meaning for *sōzō* the following: "to preserve or rescue from natural dangers and afflictions" (p. 982). Thus we encounter such meanings as "save, keep from harm, preserve, rescue," or "save from death," or "save/ free from disease," etc. (see BDAG, p. 982). The word *delivered* is used in my translation to avoid the almost automatic reflex most readers have that assumes the reference is to salvation from hell. That assumption in vv 9-10 would be false to the progression of Paul's thought.

It should also be noted in passing that the reference to wrath here is expressed in the Greek by an articular use of *orgē* (*apo tēs orgēs* = *from* [the] wrath). Although abstract nouns in Greek, like *orgē*, often employ the definite article where in English we would not use one, it remains true that after a preposition (here, *apo*) an anarthrous noun (i.e., a noun with no article) is to be expected (cf. *en hēmera orgēs* at 2:5). This suggests that here in the phrase *apo tēs orgēs*, the article is an article of previous reference and is intended to refer the hearer/reader back to the previous references to *wrath*.

So important is the transitional statement of this verse that Paul at once repeats it, in carefully altered form, in the next verse.

**5:10. Indeed, if while we were enemies we were reconciled to God through the death of His Son, all the more, since we have been reconciled, we shall be delivered by His life.**

This extremely significant verse rearticulates v 9, but at the same time heightens the logic of Paul's assertion.

In our former condition, as unrighteous people, we were in a state of enmity with God, that is, **we were** His **enemies.** But now through **the death of His Son** our relationship to God has been changed. On the basis of Christ's *death*, by means of which we have been justified (cf. v 9), **we have been reconciled to God.** The fundamental state of enmity has been removed, and God accepts us as *righteous* people on the basis of our faith in His Son.

The verb translated *reconciled* here is the Greek verb *katallassō*. As stated in the extended definition in BDAG (p. 521) it signifies "the exchange of hostility for a friendly relationship." Since "the wrath of God" was "revealed from heaven" precisely because of "the ungodliness and unrighteousness of men" (1:18), in this new relationship God no longer accounts us as fundamentally unrighteous, but rather as "righteous by faith." The new ground on which we stand permits us to have "access" to Him "by faith" and to enjoy a bold "expectation of the glory of God" (5:2).

As a result of standing in this new friendly relationship to God, we can expect to be **delivered by His** [Christ's] **life**. The sense here of course is precisely what we observed in the previous verse. Our "deliverance" is from the *wrath* which formed the starting point of Paul's argumentation at 1:18 and is explicitly referred to in v 9. It is logical in the highest degree that those who have received this "reconciliation" should no longer be objects of divine anger. For the believer to remain under God's wrath would be utterly contradictory to his present acceptance before God.

Contradictory? Yes. But impossible? Definitely not, as Paul will proceed to show.

Before leaving v 10, it should be noted that the contrast set up in this verse is between *the death of* Christ and *His life*. In v 9, however, the contrast was between being justified and being delivered. These contrasts are mutually complementary. The justified person can expect to be delivered from wrath. The former experience was based on Christ's death and is the basis on which we were reconciled to God. The latter experience is a deliverance *by His life*.

Though the phrase *by His life* is used in my translation, it does not quite do justice to the underlying Greek (*en tē zōē autou*). To be sure, the Greek preposition *en* can certainly mean *by* in reference to the means or instrument "by which" something is done. But in the light of the subsequent discussion about the Christian life (chaps. 6–8), it is likely that its extremely common meaning of *in* comes to the fore here. In that case the sense can be paraphrased as follows: **we shall be** delivered *in the experience of His life*. Paul will develop this concept in the following chapters.

> **5:11. And not only that, but also we will be exulting in God through our Lord Jesus Christ, through whom we have now received this reconciliation.**

In this verse Paul brings to a climax his anticipation that a justified person will be delivered from the divine anger under which mankind in general lives. To say that "we shall be delivered from wrath" (v 9) is to say something truly impressive. But that is not all that can be said.

The words **not only that** signal that we can expect something *more* than simple deliverance from wrath. We *should* expect to be delivered,

**but also** we should anticipate that this experience will be accompanied by **exulting in God**. (The Greek participle that is rendered *exulting* [*kauchōmenoi*] is contemporaneous with the time of the verb translated "shall be delivered" in v 10.) Deliverance and joy are therefore the keynotes of the experience Paul will describe in chaps. 6–8.

With his statement about *exulting in God*, Paul alludes to the similar declaration he had made in 5:3. There he had spoken in terms of exulting (*kauchōmetha*) "in afflictions." But, as the extended discussion to follow will show (chaps. 6–8), that kind of exultation is the direct product of a life lived in union with the risen Christ. Thus the kind of exulting that Paul has in mind here is essentially the same as that mentioned in v 3. Exultant living—victorious Christian experience in all our circumstances— constitutes the core of Paul's concept.

But this kind of experience can only come to us **through our Lord Jesus Christ** since He is the One **through whom we have now received this reconciliation**. The reconciliation in view here, of course, is effected by Christ's death (v 10), but must also be received by men. It *is* received when we are justified by faith, for it is then that, so to speak, we meet God at His new Mercy Seat (see 3:25).

This double aspect of reconciliation is also presented by Paul in 2 Cor 5:18-21. There God is seen as "reconciling the world to Himself" at the cross and subsequently sending forth messengers "pleading" with men to "be reconciled to God." True reconciliation with God required God's initiative in the death of Christ, and it requires our response to Him by faith.

With this verse, Paul reaches the conclusion of an extensive section that began in 3:21. His theme has been *the righteousness of God* that sinful man can obtain through faith in Jesus. He has climaxed the unit with a brief consideration of the marvelous results that can follow justification in the life of the believer. But the material contained in 5:1-11 is succinctly given in summary form. Paul wants his readers to know what effects they can look for in their life-experience as an outcome of their Christian faith. And now that he has summarized these effects, and their basis in the work of reconciliation, he is prepared to launch into an extended discussion of the Christian life. In fact, the discussion that follows in 5:12–8:39 is the longest such discussion to be found anywhere in Paul's epistles.

In what follows we meet the fundamental teaching of this great apostle about the nature of, and the means for, a truly Christian life-experience.

### C. Those Who Are Righteous by Faith Can Live Victoriously (5:12–8:39)

### 1. The Sin Problem and Its Solution (5:12-21)

In commencing his consideration of Christian experience, Paul traces our problem with sin to its source in the fall of Adam. This starting point permits him to present the solution to this problem in terms of our union with the Second Adam, Jesus Christ.

> **5:12. Therefore just as sin entered the world through one man, and death entered through sin, and so death came to all men because all have sinned—**

The structure of Paul's opening sentence creates a potential problem to correct interpretation. The words **just as** (*hōsper*) lead to the expectation of a corresponding phrase *so also* (which would be *houtō kai* in Greek: see vv 15, 18, 19, 21). But this phrase is not actually found here in this or in the following verse. The later words of this verse, **and so** (*kai houtōs*), are not meant to be their equivalent. That is to say, *and so* (*kai houtōs*) is not equivalent to *so also* (*houtō kai*).

The fact is that Paul's sentence is never actually finished. Technically this abrupt change in a sentence to a second construction that is inconsistent with the first is called an anacoluthon—from the Greek word meaning "inconsistent." The incompleteness here is generally indicated in the English translations by an em dash after the last word of this verse. As the exposition will show, the idea left unexpressed here is not picked up again by Paul until vv 18-19.

The incomplete sentence does help us to understand the force of **therefore** (*Dia touto* = "on account of this," "in view of this"). The reference of this expression is naturally taken back to the content of vv 9-11, in which Paul has expressed the truth that deliverance from wrath is available through the *life* of the Lord Jesus Christ. He now wishes to say that, in view of (*Dia touto*) the truth just mentioned in vv 9-11, *life has become available* through one Man (Jesus Christ), *just as* **sin**, as well as **death**, have **entered the world through one man** (Adam).

Indeed the entrance of sin and death into mankind's experience has become universal. *And so* (*kai houtōs*) the result of its entrance through one man is that **death came to all men because all have sinned**. This statement is plain and direct. Yet in one of the strangest turns in the exegesis of Romans, this straightforward statement has been made to teach that all mankind sinned in Adam as its seminal head. But no such idea is found here or anywhere else in the Bible. Paul's meaning is quite uncomplicated. Death became a universal experience precisely *because all* human beings *have sinned.* In other words, "the wages of sin is death" (see 6:23).

Paul is not concerned here with the "mechanics" of the transmission of a sinful nature from generation to generation. It is enough to know that what Adam and Eve did in the garden has produced descendants who, *without exception*, have committed sin. Were this fact not so, death would not be a universal experience either. But since everyone is sinful in word and deed, everyone also *dies*.[8] This is the straightforward reality described by Paul here.

**5:13. For until the law sin was in the world, but sin is not itemized when there is no law.**

In a sense, vv 13-17 can be treated as a parenthesis, as is done in KJV and NKJV (but not in NACE, NASB, NIV or JB). Yet at the same time, so long a series of verses is not likely to be strictly parenthetical, but should be seen as directly contributory to Paul's developing argument. JB conceals the disjunction between vv 12 and 13 by translating the initial *Dia touto* as "well then" and terminating the verse with a period. My translation avoids a parenthesis while retaining the em dash found also in NACE, NASB and NIV. But against the last three named translations, I begin this verse with a capitalized **For.**

In this way, my text attempts to show the grammatical disconnection between vv 12 and 13 (using the em dash), while making the material of v 13ff. an independent unit of thought.

Since Paul has just stated that "all have sinned" (v 12), the question might be raised as to how human beings could sin in the absence of God's law. Adam at least had the law forbidding him to eat of the tree of the knowledge of good and evil. But what law did subsequent generations violate in the absence of divine commands? How could they be said to have sinned? Since the word *For* does not really refer specifically to

---

[8] Neither Paul nor Hodges comments on the two exceptions, Enoch and Elijah. In God's grace two sinners never died. They were translated into the presence of God (cf. Gen 5:24; 2 Kings 2:11). Of course, the only reason this could happen was because of the coming death of Christ (cf. Rom 3:25 and Hodges' discussion of it). –RNW

anything in v 12, it can be naturally taken as an indirect allusion to some such problem as, "What about the period before the law? Was sin really **in the world** then?" Paul's reply is: For, despite any suggestion to the contrary, sin *was* in the world even then. (The Greek word for *For* [*gar*] could also be rendered here "in fact.")

Paul flatly asserts that **until the law sin was** *in the world.* There is no real need for him to demonstrate this fact, since even a cursory examination of the book of Genesis would prove it, beginning with the murder of Abel. But Paul had perhaps heard the issue raised and so he wishes to affirm sin's presence *in the world* from the time of Adam's fall and onward.

The only distinction between the pre- and post-law eras is expressed by the words **but sin is not itemized when there is no law**. The key word in this phrase is the one rendered *itemized* (*ellogeitai*).[9] The verb *ellogeō* occurs only twice in the NT (here and in Phlm 18) and is apparently a commercial term meaning to "charge to the account of someone" (BDAG, p. 319). It is found in both inscriptions and in papyri in this general sense.

The available examples of *ellogeō* seem naturally to suggest a record of specific charges which are to be paid at some future date. Thus to Philemon Paul writes that anything Onesimus might have owed Philemon should be placed, not on the slave's account, but on Paul's own so that he can repay it (Phlm 19a). Politely he thereby suggests that he might indeed owe other debts to Philemon which are already listed (though Philemon owes *him* something as well [19b]). Moulton and Milligan cites Papyrus Ryland II (second century AD) in which two women write their steward to "put down to our account everything you expend on the cultivation of the holding."[10] It is more than likely that these ladies expected an itemization of the expenditures.

In the light of such data we have chosen the term *itemized* for the translation here precisely because of its usage in commercial affairs in a

---

[9] Some major translations have *imputed* for *ellogeō* here (e.g., NKJV, KJV, NASB). Yet in every other place in Romans where the translation *imputed* is given, the underlying Greek verb is *logizomai*. And as Hodges goes on to point out, *ellogeō* is only used one other time in the NT and there it clearly refers to a list of charges. For this reason a number of influential translations essentially agree with Hodges' rendering *itemized* ("accounting for," NET; "charged to a person's account," HCSB; "counted," ESV; "taken into account," NIV). –RNW

[10] James Hope Moulton and George Milligan, *The Vocabulary of the Greek Testament: Illustrated from the Papyri and Other Non-Literary Sources* (New York: Hodder and Stoughton, 1919), 204. –ZCH

sense similar to the Greek word. Paul's idea seems to be that in the period before the law a specific list of sins could not be drawn up which had universal application to all men. As he has already told us (in 2:14-16), Gentiles without the law will be judged in terms of their conscience as this is manifested by their discussions about right and wrong among themselves. Though badly defaced, the law is nevertheless written on each conscience in a way that permits God to judge individuals as individuals (see discussion under those verses). But the absence of law means that man's failures cannot be codified into a specific list of infractions.

### 5:14. Nevertheless death reigned from Adam to Moses even over those who had not sinned in a way that resembled the transgression of Adam, who is a type of the Coming One.

Paul begins this verse with a strongly contrastive word (*alla, nevertheless*). Despite the fact that there could be no itemization of sins in the pre-law period, **nevertheless death reigned from Adam to Moses**. This fact was in itself evidence that sin was in the world during that period. But Paul's thought here seems to be primarily that death had an unbroken "reign" over mankind during the pre-Mosaic era. He is moving toward the truth that this "reign" can actually be broken in the lives of believers through their union with Jesus Christ (see v 21).

In view of this direction of thought, the statement that *death reigned* should not be taken as merely a colorful way to indicate that men died, though naturally that is included. Instead Paul is implying that death exercised a tyranny over humanity by which man was somehow enslaved. Indeed the grim reality of death in human experience has motivated all kinds of evil conduct on the part of those who wish to evade it as long as possible. (The writer of Hebrews also takes this kind of view: see Heb 2:14-15.) This makes death part of the spiritual bondage under which humanity lives.

Paul does not at this point do more than to suggest this idea by the use of the word *reigned*, but ultimately he will climax this entire section (5:12–8:39) with a song of triumph over death itself (see 8:35-38). Indeed, the reference to death in the opening verses of this unit—and the explicit reference to it in 8:38—gives 8:38 the character of an *inclusio* that brackets 5:12–8:39 and marks this extended section off as complete.

Moreover, this "reign" of death ensued from the fall of Adam even though the exact form of his sin could not be replicated. It was a "reign"

**even over those who had not sinned in a way that resembled the transgression of Adam**. Hence from a specific and unique instance of sin, death was able to extend its "domain" over all mankind despite the differences between humanity's many transgressions and the single *transgression of Adam*. This fact will play an important role in the comparison/contrast between Adam and Christ in the verses to follow.

In fact, it is at this point that Paul specifically introduces this comparison by describing Adam as **a type of the Coming One**, that is, of Jesus Christ. The discussion that follows reveals what Paul means by this statement. The term type here (*tupos*) can be understood in the sense of "an archetype serving as a model" and therefore with specific meanings like "type, pattern, model" (see BDAG, p. 1020). At the same time, the resemblances between Adam and Christ are of a general nature and entail specific contrasts. Adam is hardly a "model" for Jesus Christ.

Therefore Paul is not really thinking that Adam portrays personal characteristics that delineate characteristics found also in Jesus Christ. On the contrary, the following verses stress the contrast between them. Yet, seen as the *sources* from which flow certain experiences to others, Adam and Christ are indeed of the same type and this idea is conveyed in traditional theology as the two Headships. Adam is the "head" of the fallen race of men since their fallenness is derived from his sin. By contrast, Christ is the "Head" of the redeemed race since He is the source of their redemption.

But it should be noted that Paul does not make the idea of "two races" explicit. We are entitled therefore to wonder whether theology has not introduced a needless rigidity into the comparison/contrast Paul is now going to pursue.

> **5:15. However, the free gift in fact stands in contrast to the offense. For if many died through the offense of that one *man*, much more the grace of God and the gift *given* through the grace of one Man, Jesus Christ, has abounded to many.**

The opening assertion, **however the free gift in fact stands in contrast to the offense**, reflects a more succinct statement in Paul's Greek: *All' ouch hōs to paraptōma, houtō kai to charisma* (literally, "but not as the offense, so also the free gift"). The word *kai* (translated as *in fact*) seems redundant from the perspective of English. The original is perfectly clear but is best handled in an idiomatic way, as my translation attempts to do.

The initial word of the verse, *however* (Gk. *All'*), is once again a strong word of contrast. Though Adam is indeed "a type of the Coming One" (v 14), he is only such in terms of the effect he has had on many although he was only **one man**. Analogously, **one Man, Jesus Christ** has also had, and continues to have, an effect on many. Nevertheless the effects involved stand starkly in contrast. The effect of Adam's offense was that **many died**. The effect of Jesus Christ is the reception of a gift that is bestowed through His grace.

It is notable how Paul's statement here positions the word *offense* as a contrast with **the grace of God** and **the grace of…Jesus Christ**. God is certainly not the Source of Adam's disastrous **offense**, but He is most emphatically the Source of **the gift *given* through** *the grace of…Jesus Christ*. Here Paul gives clear witness to the prevailing testimony of the NT that "God has sent His only begotten Son into the world, that we might live through Him" (1 John 4:9). The grace that men encounter in *one Man, Jesus Christ*, is nothing less than *the grace of God*. The death they encounter in human experience is the result of a single *man's* offense.

Furthermore, the *gift given through the grace of one Man* has not simply entered the human arena to be received by men, but it has in fact **abounded to many**. By the term *abounded* Paul suggests the plentitude, the abundance, which is inherent in this gift. As he has already indicated, those who have been justified by faith can live so triumphantly that they can even exult in God in the face of all their tribulations (cf. 5:3-4, 9-13). This thought will be fully spelled out in the climax of the whole discussion in 8:31-38.

> **5:16. And the free gift is not like *what happened* through one man who sinned. For the judgment *came* for one *offense* to produce servitude *to sin*. But the free gift *brings release* from many offenses to produce righteous action.**

In this verse once again, Paul's Greek is succinct. My translation expands his statements slightly for the sake of clarity, and italics are used where English words are supplied that are not present in (though implied by) the Greek.

The initial statement of the verse translates the following words from the Greek: *Kai ouch hōs di' henos hamartēsantos, to dōrēma* (literally, "and not as through one having sinned, [is] the gift"). My rendering of this statement expands the simple *hōs* to **like *what happened*** to clarify the nature of the contrast. The *effect* of the free gift **is not** *like what happened* when a quite different *effect* was produced **through one *man* who sinned**. The latter resulted in **servitude *to sin***, while **the free gift** results in **righteous action** (or, conduct).

Paul's word for *gift* here (*dōrēma*) is a functional synonym for the word *gift* (*dōrea*) that is used in v 15. I distinguish *dōrēma* in this verse and elsewhere by the rendering *free gift*, though admittedly *free* entails a redundancy.

In the case of the *one man who sinned* the result was that **the judgment came for one offense**. By contrast *the free gift* **brings release from many offenses**. Paul's reference here to *the judgment* (*to krima*) is undoubtedly a reference to the divine decree that brought death to Adam, and to the sinful race which has descended from him, as a result of his single sin. On the other hand (Paul uses the contrastive particles *men...de* in this statement), *the free gift brings release from many offenses. Brings release* is a not entirely satisfactory paraphrase of the implication of the simple Greek phrase *ek pollōn paraptōmatōn*. The reader, however, understands perfectly well that Paul is referring to justification by faith. The *many offenses* of the justified person are not imputed to him (cf. 4:6-8).

Moreover, *the judgment* of death on Adam produced for him and his race *servitude to sin*. This phrase translates simply the Greek *eis katakrima*. The word *katakrima* is used here for the first time in Romans. It occurs also in v 18 and is then picked up again in the important statement of 8:1. Its treatment in the commentaries has been largely inadequate.

BDAG (p. 518) makes the important observation that "in this [word]...the use of the term 'condemnation' does not denote merely a pronouncement of guilt...but the adjudication of punishment." Moulton and Milligan (pp. 327-28) long ago referred to Deissmann's opinion that "the word must be understood technically to denote 'a burden ensuing from a judicial pronouncement—a servitude.'"[11] They give supporting evidence from the papyri and then proceed to say this (p. 328):

It follows that this word does not mean *condemnation*, but the punishment following [a judicial] sentence, so that the "earlier lexicographers" mentioned by Deissmann were right. This not only suits

---

[11] Adolf Deissmann, *Bible Studies: Contributions Chiefly from Papyri and Inscriptions to the History of the Language, the Literature, and the Religion of Hellenistic Judaism and Primitive Christianity* (Edinburgh: T & T Clark, 1903), 264-65. –ZCH

Rom 8:1 admirably, as Deissmann points out, but it materially helps the exegesis of Rom 5:16, 18.

There is no adequate antithesis between *krima* and *katakrima*, for the former never suggests a trial ending in acquittal. If *katakrima* means the result of the *krima*, the "penal servitude" from which *hoi en Christō Iēsou* are delivered (8:1), *dikaiōma* represents the "restoration" of the criminal, the fresh chance given to him.

This is an excellent treatment of this word. Without this distinction, Paul's statement would mean that *the judgment (to krima) is to judgment (eis katakrima)*. That certainly seems like a useless comment. With the distinction defended by Moulton and Milligan, the statement is at once meaningful. *The judgment* passed on Adam led to (*eis*) a *penalty*, i.e., *servitude to sin.*[12] Adam was now spiritually dead, and physically dying, and in this condition he fell under *bondage to sin* (*to sin* is added for clarity and is supported by Paul's following discussion [vv 17-21]).

By contrast with this, however, *the free gift* of justification *from many offenses* leads to (*eis*, translated **to produce**) *righteous action (dikaiōma)*. As indicated in the discussion from Moulton and Milligan, *dikaiōma* is the reversal of *katakrima*, slavery to sin. The suggestion "restoration" is not a bad one but such a rendering loses the obvious connection between *dikaiōma* and *dikaiosunē* (righteousness). The person who has received *the free gift* (imputed *righteousness*) can now be "restored" to an experience consistent with this imputation, so that he can produce *righteous action*.

The Greek word *dikaiōma* occurs ten times in the NT, five times in Paul, all in Romans (here and 1:32; 2:26; 5:18; 8:4) and five times elsewhere (Luke 1:6; Heb 9:1, 10; Rev 15:4; 19:8.) The two extended meanings offered by BDAG (p. 249) are (1) "a regulation relating to just or right action" and (2) "an action that meets expectations as to what is right or just." Under (1) BDAG lists Heb 9:1, 10 and Rom 1:32; 2:6; and 8:4. Under (2) it includes Rev 15:4 and 19:8 plus Rom 5:18. A separate treatment is

---

[12] Other than paraphrases, most English translations of Rom 5:16 render *krima* as *judgment* and *katakrima* as *condemnation*. They render *eis...katakrima* variously as "resulting/resulted in condemnation" (NASB, HCSB, NKJV), "brought condemnation" (NIV, ESV, JB, RSV), "led to condemnation" (NET), "to condemnation" (KJV, Darby), or something similar. However, as Hodges mentions, papyrus discoveries show that the second term, *katakrima*, means *penal servitude*. We have this same idea today, as when we say a prisoner must *serve his time*. Hence, *slavery to sin* better fits the context of Romans. *Krima" eis katakrima* refers to two different court scenes. The first (*krima*) was when God pronounced a guilty verdict; the second (*katakrima*) was the sentencing. The result is that man was sentenced to *servitude to sin*. –JHN

given to Rom 5:16 and the suggestion made that *dikaiōma* was probably "chosen because of the other words [ending] in -*ma*, and [because it] is equivalent in meaning to *dikaiōsis*" (ibid.). But for this suggestion there is no real evidence. Instead, it is quite natural to take the word in the same sense in this verse *and* in v 18 which follows it.

It is certainly reasonable to place Rom 1:32 under category one above, but the treatment of the other Romans passages in BDAG is open to question. Inasmuch as the relevant phrase in 2:26 seems functionally identical to 8:4 (with only a change from plural [2:26] to singular [8:4]), there is no reason not to place them (as BDAG does) under the same category. However, it seems likely that both of them should be placed in category two (not one) along with 8:4. In fact, 8:4 is most naturally taken (as this commentary will seek to show) as a reference back to 5:16, 18.

Thus, on the view of Paul's usage that I have just stated, the translation *righteous action* is appropriate for all three occurrences in the large unit extending from 5:12 through 8:39. Paul means by this word exactly what BDAG's second extended meaning states, namely, "an action that meets expectations as to what is right or just" and, therefore, "righteous deed" (ibid.). The contrasted terms are *katakrima* (*servitude*) and *dikaiōma* (*righteous action*). Adam's sin led to the former (slavery to sin), while *the free gift* leads to the latter (*righteous action*).

**5:17. For if by means of the offense of one *man* death has reigned through that one *man*, much more those who receive the abundance of grace and the gift of righteousness shall reign in life through one *Man*, Jesus Christ!**

It can now be seen more clearly what Paul means by the "reign" of death. Once **the offense of one *man*,** Adam, had occurred, his descendants became "subjects" of death in the sense that their "servitude" to sin (v 16) became inescapable. Adam bequeathed to his descendants an existence in which human sin became inevitable so that death also became inevitable. Man was in the thrall of sin and therefore he inescapably reaped sin's wages, i.e., death (cf. 6:23). Death, therefore, was in control.

Thus it was **through that one *man*,** Adam, that this state of affairs came to be. However, in contrast to this, another **one *Man*, Jesus Christ,** makes possible a different kind of experience. This new experience is described as one in which the participants in it **shall reign in life.** (The future tense in this verse is precisely analogous to the future in 5:9. See the discussion there.)

It should be carefully noted that there is an asymmetry to Paul's contrast here. On the one hand, death itself reigns. But on the other, certain people *shall reign in life*. It is not life per se that reigns, but certain people who *reign in* it. And, as Paul has already said, the life in question is nothing less than the very life of God's Son (5:9-10). Thus the participants in this life are identified as **those who receive the abundance of grace and the gift of righteousness.**

Paul has in mind here those who are "justified freely by [God's] grace through the redemption that is in Christ Jesus" (3:24). But his precise wording is to be carefully noted. The grace that reaches those who are justified is in fact an *abundance of grace* because of its immense potential to produce a spiritually triumphant life (see 5:1-5 and comments under 5:15). It thus enables the recipient to *reign in life* in a world where death reigns over the natural man.

This phrase, *the abundance of grace*, is combined here by Paul with the following (*and the gift of righteousness*), but we are not to think of two distinct things. Instead the words from *the abundance* to *righteousness* are undoubtedly a hendiadys meaning *the abundantly gracious gift of righteousness*. It would be more than generous for God simply to give *the gift of righteousness* and thus to grant us peace with Himself. But for Paul *the abundance of* God's grace is magnified by its enormous potential for transforming human experience.

No wonder that Paul is "not ashamed of the gospel of Christ." The gospel's revelation of "the righteousness of God" discloses also that "the one who is righteous by faith *shall live*" (Rom 1:16-17); that is, he *shall reign in life*. The gospel therefore offers men an *abundantly gracious gift of righteousness*.

> **5:18. Therefore, as through one offense *judgment came* to all men to produce servitude *to sin*, so also through one righteous action *grace came* for all men to produce justification *sourced in* life.**

Paul now recaptures the thought that he had begun, but not completed, in v 12 (see discussion there), and continues it here. This is evident from the fact that the words **as through one offense *judgment came* to all men** pick up the ideas expressed in v 12 by "just as sin entered the world through one man" and by "thus death came to all men." But these ideas are now re-expressed in the terminology of the intervening verses. The *one offense* was that of "one man" (v 12) and the *judgment* that has *come to all men* is the "death" that "came to all men" (v 12). This return to the starting point of v 12 is signaled by a doubled inferential construction in Greek (*Ara oun, therefore*), much as we might return to a previous thought with the words *so then*. At the same time v 18a serves to summarize vv 13-17.

The word *judgment* does not occur explicitly in Paul's text, but it is quite clearly the correct idea here in the light of v 16b (*to men gar krima ex henos eis katakrima*) when that verse is compared to the words in this present verse (*hōs di' henos paraptōmatos...eis katakrima*). In both places (v 16 and here) *katakrima* refers, as I have mentioned, to the *penalty* that was imposed as the result of the *judgment* (= death), namely, the penalty of **servitude** *to sin.*[13] [The words **to produce** paraphrase the sense of the preposition *eis* before *katakrima.*]

It is particularly to be noted that the words "just as" (*hōsper*) in v 12 are resumed here by the word *as* (*hōs*). But in v 12 there was no following "so" to complete the thought and vv 13-17 intervened. Now the thought is completed since the construction introduced by *as* is followed by one introduced by **so also** (*houtō kai*) and fulfills the expectation of a comparison that was left unfulfilled in v 12.

The intervening verses (13-17) have prepared us for the other half of Paul's comparison. As surely as God's *judgment* has brought *servitude to sin, so also* the **righteous action** of "one Man, Jesus Christ" has made available **justification** *sourced in* **life**. [Again, **to produce** paraphrases *eis.*] The Greek phrase translated *justification sourced in life* (*dikaiōsin zōēs*) is unique here in Romans but is a very significant combination of terms. Specifically it combines the two concepts found in Paul's fundamental text, "The one who is *righteous* by faith *shall live*" (1:17; cf. Hab 2:4, italics added).

The noun *dikaiōsis* is found only twice in Romans (or in the NT), that is, here and in 4:25. But its meaning for Paul is clearly fixed by 4:25 as a reference to God's justifying act toward the believer (for which Paul usually uses the verb *dikaioō*).[14] The connection with *zōē* (*life*) is natural

---

[13] The usage of *katakrima* in Rom 5:18 (as well as 5:16 and 8:1) is a strong indicator that the traditional translation (*condemnation*) is unsatisfying. It should be rendered *penal servitude* as Hodges shows. –JHN

[14] In light of Hodges's discussion thus far, it is reasonable to wonder if *dikaiōsis* really means

in view of the transition in thought expressed in 5:9-10 (see discussion there). But the precise connection expressed by the genitive form of *life* (*zōēs*) is not immediately evident.

It is quite conceivable that Paul intended his genitive to retain the ambiguity that is natural to it apart from strong contextual considerations. Thus a translation like *life's justification* may well be as specific as it is possible to get. In that case we will have an idea that might be paraphrased as follows: *a justification that belongs to and is characterized by life* (the so-called genitive of description, = "*a life-kind of* justification"). Or, equally plausible in the light of Pauline theology, would be an idea like: *a justification whose source is life* (the so-called subjective genitive). The fact that the Greek genitive could serve for any of these ideas suggests that Paul chose the construction in order not to exclude any legitimate implication that his whole discussion might convey. But it is this latter option that has been selected for my translation in view of 4:25.

The concept of a *justification sourced in life* is made highly probable in this context by Paul's statement in 4:25, which concludes the previous unit. Not only does that statement contain the only other NT use of *dikaiōsis* (as I noted above), but our justification is linked directly to, and is founded upon, the resurrection of Jesus—i.e., upon His *life*. Paul specifically affirms that our Lord was "raised for our justification," that is, that our *dikaiōsis* springs from, and is founded upon, Christ's own risen life.

In view of the fact that justification is itself a "gift of righteousness" (v 17), Paul's linkage between this concept and life implies that life, in the final analysis, *is also a gift*. In fact, he specifically says so in 6:23. It is not conceivable that Paul was unaware of the NT doctrine that eternal life was God's free gift given to believers in Jesus (see John's Gospel, as well as Eph 2:5, 8; 1 Tim 1:16). It is equally inconceivable that he could have thought

---

*justification* in its only two NT uses (Rom 4:25 and 5:18). Note that Hodges says that Paul usually uses the verb *dikaioō* to refer to justification. Of course, if Paul used a noun to allude to justification, it would likely be *dikaiosunē*, not the rare word *dikaiōsis*. Possibly, like *dikaiōma* and *katakrima*, this word has not been properly understood by most commentators and translators. *Dikaiōsis* might mean *righteous living* (which would be a synonym to *dikaiōma*, righteous action). If we read Hodges' explanation of "raised for our *dikaiōsis*" in Rom 4:25, it sure sounds like he takes it as meaning something other than *justification*. If *dikaiōsis* does not mean *justification*, but instead refers to *righteous living*, then the end of Rom 5:18 would mean, "through one righteous action grace came for all men to produce *righteous living* sourced in [God's] life." And then Rom 4:25 would mean that the Lord Jesus was raised "for our *righteous living*." –RNW

of the possibility that a believer might have one gift (righteousness) but not the other (life). Therefore, *justification sourced in life* is at the very least a new formulation for "the gift given through the grace of one Man, Jesus Christ" (v 15). The link between our life and the risen life of Jesus is fundamental to Paul's whole exposition of Christian experience, starting in chap. 6. We can live the Christian experience because, by a gift of grace, we share that risen life by means of which we have been justified (4:25).

Succinctly put, we have received both justification *and* the life of our Risen Lord as a gift of grace. Of course, this life is *eternal* life (see v 21; cf. 1 John 5:20).

This gift (*justification sourced in life*) in fact is made available **for all men** by means of the cross of Christ, that is to say, **through one** *righteous action*. The phrase *through one righteous action* translates the Greek words *di' henos dikaiōmatos* in which Paul employs the word *dikaiōma*, used in v 16 in the same sense. In contrast to Adam's sinful "action" (his *one offense*) stands the *one righteous action* of Jesus Christ in laying down His life for sinners (cf. vv 6-8). This supremely righteous deed of unselfish love has made God's gift available *for all men*. The words *for all men* render the Greek phrase *eis pantas anthrōpous*, which is identical to the Greek phrase in the first half of the verse that is translated *to all men*. Paul is here playing on the variability of the sense of the Greek preposition *eis*. In the first half of the verse *eis* refers to an actual universal reality, while in the last half it refers to a potential universal reality, since Christ actually died *for all men*.

The italicized words (**grace came**) are easily supplied from the reference to "grace" in v 15. Paul's language here and in the whole of 5:12-21 is particularly succinct, and this is due to the fact that this succinctness effectively highlights the points of comparison and contrast. Although I have supplied the words *judgment* and *grace* in this verse, neither of these two words are a real part of Paul's contrast. The real points of contrast may be said to be: (1) *one offense/one righteous action*; (2) *to all men/for all men* (*to* and *for* both render *eis*), and (3) *to produce* (*eis* each time) *servitude/justification sourced in life*.

In sum, Paul's statement in this verse points to two diametrically opposite experiences traceable to two "men" whose single actions result in widely varying outcomes. On the one hand, Adam's single offense produced universal *servitude to sin*. On the other hand, Christ's *righteous act* on the cross is efficacious *for all men* so that they can now possess, by faith, *righteousness sourced in life*, in consequence of which they will be able to live (1:17).

> **5:19. In fact just as through the disobedience of one man many have been constituted sinners, so also through the obedience of one *Man* many shall be constituted righteous.**

Paul now restates the basic truth of v 18 in a way that tightens the comparison/contrast he is making and links it specifically to two *men* (Adam and Christ). Indeed, although we must understand v 18 in relation to these two, they are not directly referred to there. Instead the point of v 18 is made in terms of the *actions* involved ("one offense"/"one righteous act"), but in this verse the point is the action of **one man** over against the action of another **one *Man***. (We render *gar* here by **in fact** in order to suggest the nuance of recapitulation involved as Paul restates v 18 in the terminology of v 19.)

As a result, v 19 is the climactic back-reference to v 12, completing the back-reference already evident in v 18. The wording of v 12 is here more specifically recalled than in v 18. The phrase *Hōsper di' henos anthrōpou* (v 12) reappears in this verse with only a relatively small addition (i.e., *disobedience*) as follows: *Hōsper...dia tēs parakoēs tou henos anthrōpou.* And, as indicated in v 12 by the words "all have sinned," so here Paul reaffirms this fact in the statement **many have been constituted sinners**.

The word *many* (*hoi polloi*) refers to "all" men, but Paul has chosen it for the purpose of carrying out his comparison/contrast in the last half of this verse, where the same term (*many* = *hoi polloi*) is also used. With the definite article each time, Paul specifies the entire body of those affected by the "two men" of this verse. The initial *hoi polloi* indicates the totality of those who *have been constituted sinners* as a result of **the disobedience of** *one man*. The second *hoi polloi* indicates the totality of those who **shall be constituted righteous** as a result of **the obedience of** *one Man*.

It should also be observed that, in this restatement of v 18, the sinful act of Adam, called an "offense" in v 18, is now labeled as *disobedience*. In contrast, the work of Christ on the cross is called a "righteous act" in v 18, but here it is called *obedience*. Though both terms used of Adam are obvious descriptions of his sin, the term *obedience* has special significance in connection with the death of Christ. It is the clear teaching of the NT, which Paul obviously shares, that Christ died for human sin as a direct response to the will of God the Father, and indeed, to His command (see John 10:17-18; Heb 10:5-10).

Thus the repetition of v 18 in this verse is more than a mere rephrasing. It is also an enrichment that presents the Second Man as the supreme model of obedience to God in a world where *the disobedience of* the first man has wrought the calamitous tragedies of sin and death. Paul is now moving toward a discussion of our own *obedience* to God in the Christian life (chaps. 6–8).

> **5:20-21. Now the law came in so that the offense might become greater. But where sin became greater, grace became superlatively great, in order that just as sin had reigned in *the sphere of* death, so also grace might reign through righteousness unto eternal life through Jesus Christ our Lord.**

Having recapitulated v 12 in vv 18-19 (see above), Paul now picks up the reference he had made to the law in v 13. Since "sin was in the world" even before **the law** (cf. v 13), why then was the law added? The reason, says Paul, is that **the offense might become greater**.

Sin, we must remember, is always a failure in man that brings men short of "the glory of God" (3:23). Yet once the will of God has been made plain to men, an offense against His will becomes greater in the sense that its seriousness is increased and magnified in the light of the divinely revealed standard. Thus the law served the purpose of exposing sin for what it was: an offense against God. A case in point can be discerned in Paul's words in Rom 7:6: "In fact, I would not have recognized sin if not for the law. For I would not even have perceived lust, if the law had not said, 'You shall not lust.'" The recognition of lust as sinful is made possible by the law so that lust is perceived as truly wicked. It takes on greater negative significance than when there was no law that forbade it.

In addition, we can also say that although sin was certainly present in the pre-Mosaic world, it was visibly multiplied by the giving of the law. The total number of known sins also becomes greater. The Greek verb translated *become greater* (*pleonasē*) is sufficiently fluid for Paul's idea here (see BDAG, p. 824) and simply requires us to understand that sin undergoes "enlargement" through the coming of the law. The law is the divine magnifying glass under which man's sinfulness can in no way be minimized.

But in sharp contrast to this grim reality, in which sin has been powerfully magnified by the law, stands God's magnificent grace. The word I have translated **became superlatively great** is the compound Greek verb *huperperisseuō* (cf. 2 Cor 7:4, the only other NT use). The prefixed *huper-* (or *hyper-*) is like a prefixed *super-* and I could even translate here: *grace became super-great* (cf. BDAG's expanded definition "to experience extraordinary abundance" [p. 1034]). However much man's sin was magnified, God's grace can be said to tower over it by virtue of its superlative abundance and plentitude.

This excelling of human sin by divine grace makes possible an astounding result (cf. **in order that**), a result which reverses the reign of sin. Although through Adam "death came to all men" (v 12) and made the world an arena of death in which sin held human beings in bondage, **through Jesus Christ our Lord** a different experience is possible. Thus Paul tells us that **just as sin has reigned in** *the sphere of* **death, so also can grace…reign through righteousness unto eternal life.**

Paul had earlier spoken of the recipients of "the gift of righteousness" as those who can "reign in life through one Man, Jesus Christ" (v 17). Here, however, he speaks of grace itself as reigning. But these are simply verbal variations of the same concept. God's grace reigns when the believer reigns "in life" *through Jesus Christ*. That is to say, when the believer gains victory over sin, **grace** is reigning in his life experience. The means by which this victory is attained is the subject of the following chapters (Romans 6–8). The present passage (5:12-21) is intended as an introduction, stating the fundamental problem and anticipating the solution about to be expounded.

God's grace can reign precisely because it is the source of righteousness and *eternal life*. What was implicit in the earlier phrase *justification sourced in life* (v 18) is now stated more fully. Grace, Paul states, reigns *through* (*dia*, "by means of") *righteousness unto* (*eis*) *eternal life*. The combination of Greek prepositions here is best understood if both of them (*dia, eis*) are taken as connected with the verb for *reign* (*basileusē*). The reign of grace, therefore, is made possible by means of the righteousness that is granted to faith and is a reign realized through the experience of *eternal life*.

Paul's use of *eis* (*unto* [i.e., "to," "into"]) here is best understood under BDAG's fourth category, "marker of goals involving affective/abstract/suitability aspects" (p. 290). We might paraphrase, "grace reigns *as far as/ right into* the experience of eternal life." The phrase *eternal life* thereby expresses the manner in which the reign of grace triumphantly manifests itself.

Implicit here is the inner connection in Paul's thought about righteousness and *eternal life*. If grace is to reign in the experience of people who were formerly under God's wrath (cf. 1:18ff.), it must do so *through righteousness*, since wrath was explicitly manifested because of human *unrighteousness* (1:18). The deliverance from wrath that Paul has in mind (5:9) cannot be affected apart from the bestowal of the righteousness that comes by faith in Jesus Christ.

Yet at the same time, this righteousness does not automatically confer deliverance from wrath since such deliverance must come from the *life* of Jesus Christ (5:10). But it is precisely *His risen life* that is the basis of our imputed righteousness (4:25) and which is part of the gift of grace that is given when we believe (cf. 6:23). Thus God's grace also involves our coming into union with that life (that is, with *eternal life*) and, in fact, it is *into* this kind of life that we enter when we are justified. This truth is made crystal clear in chaps. 6–8 (cf., e.g., 6:10-11).

The unit Paul had commenced in 5:12 closes here with the words *through Jesus Christ our Lord*. The words recall the similar phrase that "bookends" the previous unit in 5:1 and 5:11, though here the designation *our Lord* is climactic. Although the phrase *through Jesus Christ our Lord* could also be construed with *reign*, as the two previous prepositional phrases were (see above), it seems more natural to connect this final phrase directly to *eternal life*. That is to say, when *eternal life* is experienced, as grace reigns in the Christian's life, this experience comes *through Jesus Christ our Lord*. As Paul will show, this is true because we have been united with our Lord in His death, burial *and* in His resurrection *life* (see 6:1-11).

The following unit (6:1-23) expounds the truth stated in the present verse. Exactly the same phrase that ends the material in 5:12-21 (i.e., *Jesus Christ our Lord*) is found at the end of the next unit as well (in 6:23). There it forms an *inclusio* that terminates that unit and marks it as complete. Both in 5:21 and 6:23 the expression *our Lord* is climactic (contrast 5:1 and 11), since we are now about to consider truth which relates directly to the *lordship* of *Jesus Christ* in the life of the believer.

# Romans 6

## 2. Our Freedom from Sin Through Union with Christ (6:1-23)

Paul now embarks on an extended discussion about the means by which *grace can reign* in the life of the one who is *righteous by faith*. In developing this subject, Paul now focuses on the second part of the truth found in Hab 2:4, namely, that "the one who is righteous by faith *shall live*" (cf. Rom 1:16-17). The key concept in this unit, as well as in the units that follow it to the end of chap. 8, is the concept of *life*.

The starting point for the larger discussion, which ends at 8:39, is the present unit (6:1-23). It is essential for the justified believer in Jesus to understand the nature of the union that he now enjoys with Jesus Christ his Lord, and the freedom which that union brings. The entirety of chap. 6 is devoted to the clarification of this union that is basic to all Christian living.

### a. Our Union with Christ in His Death and Resurrection (6:1-11)

**6:1-2. So what shall we say? Do we continue in sin so that grace may become greater? Far from it! How shall we who have died to sin still live in it?**

As Paul has already mentioned, there were people who seriously distorted his doctrine that God is vindicated by human evil (see 3:5-8). He therefore begins this discussion by dismissing a false conclusion that he no doubt had heard articulated by opponents of his theology of grace. Paul might have been the first preacher of grace to be charged with promoting libertinism, but he was by no means the last.

Paul therefore poses a question that needs a direct answer. What conclusion is to be drawn from what Paul has just been saying (in 5:12-21)? Should **we continue in sin so that grace may become greater?** Is the *reign of grace* (5:21) merely God's grace continuously surmounting our ongoing sinful lives? Should we then *continue in sin* to give grace an ever increasing opportunity to be enlarged and thus *become greater?*[1]

The proposition in the question is at once dismissed by Paul with the words, **Far from it!** Such a conclusion is unthinkable. And it is unthinkable precisely because Christians **have died to sin.** Significantly, the concept of dying to sin is here introduced for the first time in Romans. It will be elaborated in the material that immediately follows.

It is evident from Paul's following discussion that our death to sin does not make it impossible for us to *commit* sin. Paul uses the metaphor for death, not to indicate that all sin has been eliminated from our lives, but (as we shall see) that we are no longer in bondage to it. On a formal level, the question **how shall we...still live in it?** expresses an inconceivable choice, not an impossible one. Compare the English, "How could we ever do such a thing?"

On the other hand, Paul will go on to teach that if we *do continue in sin*, it will not be an experience of *life* but rather of *death* (see 8:13 and the discussion there). Thus there is a sense in which **we who** *have died to sin* actually can no longer *live in it* for the simple reason that to do so is not genuine *living* at all. In accordance with 1:17, "the one who is righteous by faith" can "live" only as he experientially appropriates his union with the life of Christ.

But at this point in Paul's discussion the inconceivability of the option to *continue in sin* is undoubtedly to the fore. But the inconceivability of such a choice is later reinforced by Paul with his teaching that it is also functionally impossible. That is to say, what looks like "living in sin" is not true "living." Thus Paul's switch in this verse from the verb *continue* to the verb *live* is fraught with implications. The former signals a possibility, the latter an inconceivable choice that is finally impossible.

---

[1] The manuscripts of the Majority Text are divided on the form of the Greek word for *continue.* The alternatives are: 1. *epimenomen,* 2. *epimenōmen,* or 3. *epimenoumen*; but the variations do not have a discernible effect on the meaning. The alternative translations would be: 1. "do we continue...?" (my translation above), 2. "should we continue...?" or 3. "shall we continue...?" The sense of my translation is: "Is this the choice we are going to make?" Compare our English expressions like, "do we keep on?" or "do we stop here?" –ZCH

Interpreters of the Bible often overlook the issue of the function of an utterance, technically called its *illocutionary force*. Illocution deals with whether an act of speech (oral or written) involves such things as ordering, warning, undertaking, etc. The same set of words may be used for different speech acts. For example, a statement like "you're a capable man" may have a variety of functions. It may be a straightforward statement of praise; it may express an encouragement to accomplish something ("you can do this"); an expression of sarcasm ("a fine capability you have!"); or something else. Needless to say, the context of the utterance determines its illocutionary force.

Thus the illocutionary force of Paul's rhetorical question here, as demanded by the context of his thought in chaps. 6–8, is that of criticism and complaint. The words, *How shall we who have died to sin still live in it?* convey the thought of something that is totally inappropriate for a Christian person. It is much as we might say, "How can loyal Americans cheat on their taxes?" (I mean: "That's unthinkable," even though some might regard it as thinkable.)

Paul therefore wishes to commence the present discussion by announcing that it is utterly unsuitable that believers in Jesus Christ our Lord should go on living their lives *in sin*. That would be in utter contradiction to our relationship to sin, since we have actually *died to* it. By formulating the issue in this way, he manages to introduce the death/life motif which will dominate his discussion in the immediately following verses.

### 6:3. Or don't you know that as many of us as have been baptized into Christ Jesus have been baptized into His death?

But how, in fact, have we died to sin? Paul states the basis for this truth in the form of a question that is once again virtually rhetorical. He does not expect the Romans to be ignorant on this point.

Paul's tone in raising the question, however, suggests that he is still thinking of people who might argue that grace is magnified by our continuance in a life of sin (see discussion of v 1). The words **or don't you know** contain an implicit rebuke of such an idea. If someone advocates that course, they must be ignorant of the fundamental truth Paul has in mind.

What exactly is that truth? Many interpreters have taken Paul's words here as a reference to the rite or sacrament of water baptism. The meaning of Paul's statement is then understood against the background of the interpreter's theology of baptism. If water baptism is regarded as largely symbolic, then Paul might be understood as appealing to a commitment to abandon sin made at the time of our baptism in water. If the interpreter holds to baptismal regeneration, then Paul might be understood as appealing to what happens to us when we are born again in the baptismal waters. That is, as we are **baptized into His death**, we become dead to sin either by renouncing it or by being reborn.

In view of the discussion to follow, however, it is hardly likely that Paul has in mind a mere commitment on our part to abandon sinful ways. Furthermore, the Scriptures really do not support the idea that water baptism is the true point of regeneration (which occurs when we believe). Still less does some mysterious transformation occur in us when we undergo this rite. There is no good reason for taking Paul's statement as a reference to baptism in water.

On the other hand we know that baptism by the Holy Spirit was a doctrine profoundly significant to Paul. In fact this baptism is what forms the body of Christ according to 1 Cor 12:13. Thus our spiritual union with Jesus Christ is affected by the Holy Spirit's baptism, and it is precisely to our union with Him that the following verses in Romans appeal.

Moreover, in no NT passage is water baptism unambiguously referred to as *baptism into Christ Jesus*. Where water baptism is linked explicitly to Jesus Christ, all the clear passages refer to it as being *in His name* (Acts 2:38; 8:16; 10:48; 19:5; 1 Cor 1:13, 15 [by inference]). On the other hand, the terminology used here about being **baptized into Christ Jesus** can easily be taken as synonymous with being baptized into His *Body*.

This conclusion is also supported by Gal 3:27 which is a parallel to our text here in Romans. There Paul writes, "For as many of you as were *baptized into Christ* have put on Christ." But the content of Gal 3:28 is clearly parallel to 1 Cor 12:13 where the reference is explicitly to baptism by the Spirit. When the three texts (Rom 6:3; Gal 3:27-28, and 1 Cor 12:13) are taken together, the reference in all three to baptism by the Holy Spirit becomes the only viable conclusion.

What Paul has in mind in this verse is nothing less than the work of the Holy Spirit that affects our spiritual union with Jesus Christ. It is about this union that Paul elsewhere writes that "we are members of His body, of His flesh and of His bones" (Eph 5:30), and that "he who is joined to the Lord is one spirit" (1 Cor 6:17). As the following elaboration by Paul will show, this dynamic union is the very essence of Christian experience and victory. The baptism of the Holy Spirit, therefore, means that believers **have been baptized into His death**. This union with Christ in **His death** is in fact the key to a new life experience.

> **6:4. Therefore we have been buried with Him through baptism into death, so that just as Christ was raised from the dead through the glory of the Father, so also we might walk in newness of life.**

The spiritual union Paul now describes involves "immersion" into Christ's death. As is well known, the words *baptize* and *baptism* are only transliterations of the Greek verb and noun respectively, and do not actually translate these words. Here the terminology of being **buried** suggests complete removal from view and therefore that the baptism is thought of as an *immersion* into the death-experience of Jesus Christ. The Greek verb and noun can indeed indicate an immersion (though other nuances are possible: see BDAG, pp. 164-65).

In fact, immersion in water was widely practiced in first century Judaism as a purifying rite. This is indicated by the large number of *mikvah*s (pools used for ritual purification) discovered by archeologists in Israel (including numerous ones on the wealthy estate excavated at Qumran). The cultural implication of "purification," associated with such immersions, is no doubt an appropriate part of Paul's imagery here. Baptism into the death of Christ effectively "purifies" the inner man from sin, rendering him dead to it (see vv 5-11; also Titus 3:4-7).

The Christian, Paul is saying, has been united with Christ in His death so that he may also share in the resurrected life of His Savior. Since **Christ was raised from the dead through the glory of the Father**, it is therefore implied that the Christian may **walk in newness of life** by means of that same glory. (Note the words **just as** and **so also**.) Thus *the glory of* God *the Father* is introduced as the dynamic power behind the Christian's new lifestyle in this world.

As Paul will go on to point out, especially in 8:1-13, this glorious resurrection power is precisely what will enable the believer to surmount the impediment of his sinful body. Left to his own strength, the regenerate inner man is unable to overcome the resistance of his body to a walk in holiness. God alone, by means of His Spirit, is able to affect a supernatural victory over the body by means of a resurrection miracle (see 8:11). This truth, which is spelled out in Romans 7–8, is anticipated here by the reference to *the glory of the Father* that raised our Lord Himself *from the dead.*

To be noted here also is the fact that Paul does *not* write: *just as Christ was raised from the dead…so also* **we might** *be raised from the dead.* That is not his point. The Christian in fact is already "alive from the dead" (see vv 11 and 13). But the issue before Paul's mind, both here and up to 8:13, is how those who *are* alive from the dead can live like it. In other words, how can such people *walk in newness of life?*[2] It is *that* issue that governs Paul's discussion from 6:1–8:13.

> **6:5-6. For if we are united with *Him* in the likeness of His death, we shall surely also be *united in the likeness* of *His* resurrection, since we know this: that our old man has been crucified with *Him*, in order that the body of sin might be nullified, so that we might no longer serve sin.**

When the statements of these two verses are taken as a whole, and properly connected with the truth of v 4, it is evident that Paul is not discussing our future resurrection from the dead. On the contrary, he is discussing the walk "in newness of life" that he has referred to in the previous verse.

Inasmuch as **we are united with** Christ **in the likeness of His death** by means of the baptizing work of the Holy Spirit, it follows that we can also expect a similar union with Christ *in the likeness* **of His resurrection**. That is to say, we can expect to "walk in newness of life" just as Christ Himself lives such a life.[3]

---

[2] Paul links believers in Christ with His death by crucifixion and with His subsequent resurrection life. Paul uses the word "walk" (*peripateō*) thirty times in his NT epistles in the Majority Text (Rom 6:4; 8:1, 4; 13:13; 14:15; 1 Cor 7:17; 2 Cor 4:2; 5:7; 10:2f; 12:18; Gal 5:16; Eph 2:2, 10; 4:1, 17; 5:2, 8, 15; Phil 3:17f; Col 1:10; 2:6; 3:7; 4:5; 1 Thess 2:12; 4:1, 12; 2 Thess 3:6, 11). Each use looks at conduct, whether good or bad, whether by believers or unbelievers.

The phrase *newness of life* presupposes that believers possess life. Cf. John 10:10b, where Jesus states His purpose in coming to earth. He came with two purposes: (1) to give everlasting life to people when they believe in Him and (2) to enable believers to have that life more abundantly. Romans 6:1–8:13 develops the truth of 6:4, that Christ's resurrection is the basis for believers living the Christian life. –JHN

[3] The illocutionary force (see discussion on 6:2) of the words **we shall surely also be** *united* is that of strong expectation, not simple prediction. For *alla: surely, certainly,* see BDAG, p. 45 [under 4]. –ZCH

The phrase *united with Him* translates the Greek word *sumphutoi*, used only here in the NT.[4] The Greek adjective *sumphutos* (*sum-* + *phutos*) is derived from the root of the word *phuō* ("to grow up," "come up"). The implicit agricultural image serves nicely in this context where Paul no doubt thinks of our "burial" by baptism into Christ's death as a kind of spiritual "planting." The *Him* of my translation is implied by the prefixed *sum-* ("with").

Paul's use of the word *likeness* should be noted. The broad sense here refers to "a state of having common experiences" (BDAG, p. 707). Paul's argument is that our shared experience of Christ's death can be expected to lead to a shared experience of His resurrection life. (The words *in the likeness*, which I supply before the words *of His resurrection*, are clearly implied in the Greek sentence.) The expectation of this kind of life-experience is based on something instructed Christians know about their union with the death of Christ. Paul now proceeds to state the content of this knowledge.

What is it that we know? We know, Paul affirms, **that our old man has been crucified with *Him***. Since it is obvious that our physical bodies cannot be said to have undergone co-crucifixion with Christ, the reference to *our old man* can only be a reference to the inner self, or persona, which "lived" inside our physical bodies prior to our union with Jesus Christ. This "old self" has died.

This truth implies that a "new man" (that is, a "new inner self") has replaced this *old man*. Paul will speak of this new self later in this section where he calls it "my inward man" with which he delights in God's law (7:22). The "old man/new man" terminology also occurs in Eph 4:20-24, where the idea is that Christians should not "wear" their old self, but their new self.

Underlying this kind of terminology is the well-known Jewish/Christian belief that man is more than the sum of his physical parts. When the body dies, there is a self which enters the spiritual world and lives there consciously. Our Lord's own story about the rich man and Lazarus (Luke 16:19-31) gives emphatic testimony to this belief as do many other Scriptures.

---

[4] BDAG, p. 960, cites a helpful instance of the cognate verb in Dio Chrysostom (ca. 40 – ca. 120 AD) which it renders "growing up together with it" (*sumpephukotes ekeinō*), where *ekeinō* refers to "the divine" (*tou Theiou*). –ZCH

This truth helps us to understand that the events that occur at the moment of saving faith in Christ are not mere illustrative images. When we speak of regeneration and of the baptism of the Holy Spirit we are talking about spiritual events that radically alter the inward reality of our being. When we believe in Christ for eternal life, the inward man is reborn with that life. And when we are baptized at that same moment by the Holy Spirit, we are united with the spiritual body of Christ and thus are also united with Him in His death, burial, and resurrection.

As Paul makes clear in the following discussion, we are to consider ourselves to be *already* "alive to God in Christ Jesus our Lord" (v 11). It follows, then, that the reference in v 5 to the expectation that *we shall…be united in the likeness of His resurrection* does not refer to this co-resurrection *per se*, but rather to the *experiential likeness* to *His resurrection* that results from it. In other words, it refers to our walking "in newness of life" (v 4). However, at this point in the discussion, the focus is on what has been accomplished by our union with Christ's death.

Knowing the truth *that our old man has been crucified with Him* involves also the realization that this has occurred **in order that the body of sin might be nullified**. By the term *body of sin* Paul evidently means the aggregate total of all the sins committed through our physical bodies. Analogous terminology occurs in Col 2:11-15 where Paul speaks of a spiritual circumcision by which we have put off "the body of the sins of the flesh" (Col 2:11, as read by the large majority of Greek manuscripts). Later he will refer to individual sins as "your members" (Col 3:5, where the word for "members" [*mele*] refers to members of a body). Since Paul saw the physical body as the seat of sin in the Christian, this metaphor is quite natural. Thus *the body of sin* is the sum total of its individual "members," that is, the sum of our individual sins.

Paul's point here is this. Our union with Christ in *His death* has as its purpose that this *body of sin might be nullified* **so that we might no longer serve sin**. *The body of sin* (and by extension, the physical body itself) has lost its unbreakable dominion over us. Its power to rule us has been nullified by the fact that in Christ we have died to it (see vv 7-11). In our former (unregenerate) condition we were *slaves* to it, as the Greek word for *serve* (*douleuō*) indicates, and so we did its bidding. But now this slavery **no longer** exists.

**6:7. For he who has died is justified from sin.**

This remarkable statement catches my eye at once. Paul here uses the verb for *justify* (*dedikaiōtai*) to describe our relationship to sin.[5] He has already used this verb ten times in the forensic sense of the divine act of ascribing righteousness to men (2:13; 3:20, 24, 26, 28, 30; 4:2, 5; 5:1, 9) and once of the vindication of God (3:4). Here the required sense is that assigned to it by BDAG, p. 249: "to cause someone to be released from personal or institutional claims that are no longer to be considered pertinent or valid." For Rom 6:7, BDAG offers the translation, "the one who died is freed from sin."

Paul's point is that sin has no claim of any kind on the person who has been united with Christ in His death. Death has freed us from the dominion of sin. As Paul will go on to show, however, this freedom applies to the "inner man" who is still "trapped" in his physical body and the realization of this freedom in personal experience requires the power of the Holy Spirit.

Nevertheless, although this is Paul's meaning here, the use of the verb for *justify* constitutes a word play in which there is an allusion to the truth of justification by faith. After all, it is the believer in Jesus who has been justified by faith who is also united with Christ in His death, with the result that he is justified (that is, *freed*) from sin.

> **6:8-9. Now if we have died with Christ, we believe that we shall also live with Him, knowing that since Christ was raised from the dead, He no longer dies; death no longer has authority over Him.**

The point Paul now wishes to make in reference to our walk in "newness of life" (v 4) involves a fundamental assumption of the Christian faith. If, as Paul has affirmed, **we have died with Christ**, we conclude (**we believe**) as well **that we shall also live with Him**. Here it seems that Paul invokes the Christian conviction about our destiny as those who will live in the presence of our Savior forever, that is, *we shall live with Him* (cf.

---

[5] Hodges' statement here is initially puzzling. What does he mean when he speaks of "our relationship to sin"? Do we have a *relationship* to or with sin? The answer, as Hodges goes on to point out, is a resounding "Yes." Before we died with Christ (Rom 6:1-6), we were slaves of sin. After we died with Him, we were "justified" from sin. As he goes on to say, this means that we are "freed" from sin's dominion. We are no longer slaves of sin. Hodges retains the translation *justified*, however, because he believes Paul wishes the reader to remember that this liberation occurred due to our justification by faith in Christ. –RNW

1 Thess 5:10). But the wording of this statement is such that it can also apply to *the present experience* of the believer.

The words *we shall also live with Him* translate the Greek phrase, *kai suzēsomen autō*. Since Paul is basically discussing our union with Christ by the baptism of the Holy Spirit, the compound verb *suzēsomen* (*sun-* + *zaō* = "live together with") neatly serves his aims here. For Paul, we who will *live together with Him* in the future can *live together with Him* in the present by the resurrecting power of the Holy Spirit (see 8:11).

Thus the truth Paul is beginning to expound about our victory over sin is part of the same basic truth, namely that death *with* Him leads to life *with* Him. The *not yet* of our future experience can become the *already* of our present one.[6] Thus, too, we see the ramifications of the basic statement of 1:17 that "the one who is righteous by faith *shall live.*" *Living with Him* is the true portion and destiny of the justified person, both here and hereafter.

This conviction (*that we shall also live with Him*) is accompanied by the knowledge (**knowing**) **that since Christ was raised from the dead, He no longer dies.** For Jesus Christ the triumph of His resurrection terminated forever any experience of death. He will in no way return to the grave from which He arose. Therefore the life we experience when *we...live with Him* is nothing less than *eternal life.* Precisely this is what we obtained when we received "the abundance of grace and the gift of righteousness" so that we might "reign *in life*" (5:17), for in fact eternal life is God's gift to us "in Christ Jesus our Lord" (6:23). It is this life that we *experience* through our union with Him.

Since, then, Christ will *no longer* die, it follows that **death no longer has authority over Him**. Death has no power, no claim whatsoever, over Jesus Christ our Lord. Thus the life we also share with Him is not under the *authority* of death either. As Paul has just said (v 7), we are "justified (freed) from sin"; that is, sin and death have no claim on us since we have died with Him.

---

[6] Hodges is borrowing the well-known expression *already, not yet*, made famous in eschatology. He does not mean to imply that he agreed with that view of eschatology (though he did believe that there was some sort of mystery form of the kingdom during the Church Age). He certainly did not agree with the way scholars now apply *already, not yet* to soteriology (i.e., we are already justified by faith, but we are not yet finally justified by works, and if we fail to be finally justified by works, then we are off to the lake of fire). –RNW

This reference to death's authority is a significant point for Paul. As he has already pointed out in 5:12-21, as a result of Adam's sin "death reigned [*ebasileusen*] from Adam through Moses" (5:14). However, God's grace was manifested "in order that just as sin had reigned [*ebasileusen*] in the sphere of death, so also grace might reign [*basileusē*] through righteousness unto eternal life through Jesus Christ our Lord" (5:21). The use of the verb *basileuō* shows that Paul conceptualizes death (along with sin) as a tyrant ruling over those who were subject to it. But Christ has voluntarily entered this tyrant's domain and has risen triumphantly from the dead. Thus the tyrant, death, has lost its temporary power over Jesus. *Death no longer has authority (kurieuei) over Him.* The "rulership" conferred on death by the sin of the first Adam, has been broken by the Second.

> **6:10-11. For with regard to the fact that He died, He died to sin once for all; and with regard to the fact that He lives, He lives to God. So also you should consider yourselves to be dead to sin, but alive to God in Christ Jesus our Lord.**

The death **that He died** was a **once for all** (*ephapax*) encounter with sin in which sin was fully atoned for. **He died to sin** permanently. Now that this sacrificial work has been accomplished and He has risen from the dead, **He lives to God**. Sin is no longer something that attaches to Him personally, as it did when He bore it on the cross. From now on, in His resurrection life, the life **that He lives** is fully oriented *to God*. (The words **with regard to the fact that**, in both cases, translate the sense of a Greek relative pronoun [*ho*] that cannot here be precisely reproduced in English.)

The relationship of Christ, both *to sin* and *to God*, is precisely the way believers should relate *to sin* and *to God*. They should, in fact, **consider themselves to be dead to sin, but alive to God in Christ Jesus our Lord**. Here then is the bottom line of the identification truth that Paul introduced at 6:3.[7] Believers have been spiritually united with Christ in

---

[7] The expression *identification truth* comes from the writings of John Nelson Darby (1800-1882) and the early Plymouth Brethren, as well as from the Keswick Convention (started 1875), which gave rise to Keswick theology. Today *identification truth* means different things to different people. Hodges did not agree with all aspects of Keswick theology and exchanged-life teachings. What he lays out here is an excellent overview of his position. For more details see his book *Six Secrets of the Christian Life* (Dallas, TX: Redención Viva, 2004), esp. 29-39. –RNW

His death and resurrection. The first step to walking "in newness of life" is to consider this to be so.

The word rendered *consider* is the Greek verb *logizomai*. This happens also to be the verb that Paul has used repeatedly in chap. 4 of God "imputing" righteousness to the believer (4:3, 5, 6, 8, 9, 10, 11, 22, 23, 24). It is hard to believe that Paul, in choosing this verb here, was not perfectly conscious of his previous use of it in regard to God *considering* believers to be righteous by faith. Thus the man or woman whom God "considers" righteous by faith should consider himself or herself to be now *alive to God*. Thus, at a fundamental level, "the one who is righteous by faith" already *lives* (cf. 1:17), and he should consider that to be his fundamental status.

### b. Acting on Our Union with Christ (6:12-23)

**6:12-14. Therefore do not let sin reign in your mortal body so that you obey it with its lusts, neither turn over your body's members to sin as instruments for unrighteousness, but turn yourselves over to God as people who are alive from the dead, and *turn over* your body's members to God as instruments for righteousness. For sin shall not have authority over you, because you are not under the law but under grace.**

In view of the spiritual reality expressed in the previous verse (v 11), believers should not only consider themselves to be "alive to God," they should actively reorient their behavior in the light of that truth. Whereas formerly, in their unregenerate days, they had allowed **sin** to **reign in** their **mortal body** so that they obeyed **it with its lusts,** they are to do so no longer.

This previous obedience to sin's lusts had been put into effect by their turning over their **body's members as instruments for** doing **unrighteousness.** The *body's members*—its eyes, arms, legs, etc.—had been used in the pursuit and enjoyment of sinful aims and activities. This kind of behavior should now cease.

The new lifestyle is to be marked by conscious commitment to God and to His will. Now they are to **turn** themselves **over to God as people who are alive from the dead.** They are not to think of themselves any longer as subjects reigned over by sin and death. Instead they should see themselves *as people who* have been raised from the dead to walk in newness of life (see 6:4). Their attitude of heart should be, "Here I am, Lord, *alive from the dead* and prepared to live for you."

The Greek verb rendered twice in v 13 by **turn over** (*paristanete* and *parastēsate*), signifies that something is made available for some purpose, that is, it is *"put at someone's disposal"* (see BDAG, p. 778, 1.a.). Paul's point is that, although they previously put the members of their bodies at sin's disposal, they should stop doing so. Now they should put themselves *and* their bodies at God's disposal.

The attitude expressed when they turn themselves *over to God* should be followed by appropriate actions. They are to *turn over* the members of their body to Him **as instruments for righteousness**. That means that they are to employ their eyes, arms, legs, hands, and all their other *members* for the will of God. They are to use them *as instruments for* (that is, they are actually to *do*) *righteousness*. When both the attitude and the actions cohere, Christian living is experienced.

In addition, both the new attitude and the new behavior are appropriate and possible precisely because sin has lost its capacity to **have authority over** them. The future tense in the phrase **shall not** *have authority* (*ou kurieusei*) should be understood as an imperatival future (like: you shall not murder). Paul is saying, "You must not allow sin to rule you."[8]

Why not? Because, Paul insists, **you are not under the law but under grace**. With these words Paul introduces the dominant theme of the discussion to follow (6:15–8:13). Although grace was referred to in 6:1, it has not been directly mentioned since then, and *the law* has not been referred to in this chapter at all. The ineffectual nature of *the law* figures prominently in the discussion that follows.

Contrary to the opinion held even by many Christians in Paul's day (see Acts 15:5), the Mosaic Law was no more an effective instrument

---

[8] Fitzmyer, *Romans*, 447. Exodus 20:13, "You shall not murder," uses the future tense to command (in Hebrew, Greek, and English). Such usage of the future tense is not uncommon in the Bible. The relationship between vv 13-14 shows that the future is imperatival. Verse 14 starts with an explanatory *gar* (for), so it explains v 13. The following paraphrase shows the logic: *do not present…, but present…, for you must not let sin have dominion.* Many commentators treat the future tense in v 14 as predictive, something like, "Do not worry, sin will not dominate you" (cf. Murray, *Romans*, p. 228). If that view were right, why does Paul warn the Romans in v 13, "Do not present your members as instruments of unrighteousness to sin"? Also, v 14 has a *gar*, so how would it explain v 13? The relationship between vv 13 and 14 shows that sin has the potential to dominate a believer. As such, Paul admonishes believers not to allow this to happen. –JHN

for Christian living than it was an instrument for justification (see 3:19-20). Those who lived under it could not truly escape the authority of sin in their lives. In contrast to this, freedom from sin's authority can be experienced by Christian people precisely because they *are not under the law but under grace.*

Paul now wishes to make this truth completely clear.

> **6:15-16. What then? Shall we sin because we are not under the law but under grace? Far from it! Don't you know that to whom you turn yourselves over as slaves in obedience, you are slaves of the one you obey, whether of sin producing death, or of obedience producing righteousness?**

The first question to be raised is whether the fact that **we are not under the law but under grace** gives us a license to sin. The words **far from it** emphatically deny that it does. The underlying Greek (*Mē genoito*) is idiomatic and the phrase is to be translated as best suits each context. Here the words "that's unthinkable" might equally well be used to express Paul's idea.

Indeed, why should such an option even be considered? Paul goes on to suggest the question (**Shall we sin?**) was functionally equivalent to asking whether we should be the slaves of sin. Thus, after dismissing the suggestion categorically (*far from it*), he asks rhetorically, **Don't you know...you are slaves of the one you obey**? "Don't you realize," he says, "that sinning entails slavery to your sinful practices?"

Paul, of course, is not implying that anyone in the Roman congregation didn't really know this. The question is treated as hypothetical and this barbed response is rhetorical, highlighting the absurdity of any suggestion that we *should* sin. The fact was that to whomever they might turn themselves **over as slaves in obedience**, they were *slaves of the one* they obeyed. They could therefore either become slaves to sin or to its opposite, righteousness (cf. v 18).

We should note that in Paul's discussion here, the meaning expressed by the Greek verb *paristēmi* (to *turn over*, see v 13) clearly denotes the idea of actually doing something. The one who turns himself over to sin is on the path that produces death (**whether of sin producing death**). But the one who turns himself over to obedience is on the path that produces righteousness (**obedience producing righteousness**). Stated this way, the only reasonable choice was the obedience that produced righteousness, since who would wish to produce death?

> **6:17-18. But praise *is due* to God that *though* you were the slaves of sin, but you have obeyed from the heart that form of teaching in which you were instructed. And having been liberated from sin, you became enslaved to righteousness.**

Paul is grateful **to God** for the Christian experience of the Roman believers. In their unconverted days they had been **slaves of sin**, but after their conversion they had **obeyed from the heart** (i.e., sincerely) **the form of teaching in which** they had been instructed. That is to say, they had responded obediently to the Christian teaching they had received.

The Greek underlying the phrase *in which* **you were instructed** (*eis hon paredothēte*) is at first surprising. The verb *paradidōmi* can mean "to pass on to another what one knows of oral or written tradition" (BDAG, pp. 762-63), but it is also often used as a technical term for turning someone over to the custody of the police or courts (BDAG, p. 762). Here Paul employs it as a kind of word play, though the literal sense is something like "to which you were handed over." On the one hand, Christian teaching has been "passed on" to the Roman Christians. On the other, however, in accordance with the metaphor about slavery, they have been "turned over" to the authority of that teaching for their lives.

For the sake of clarity, my translation is a paraphrase, since the word play in question cannot really be communicated by a simple rendering. The NKJV translation ("to which you were delivered") is not very meaningful in English. My rendering is also reflected in the Jerusalem Bible, which reads: "you submitted without reservation to the creed you were taught."

The phrase *that form of teaching* suggests that the content of what they were taught followed a particular pattern. The Greek word rendered *form* is *tupos*, which is properly assigned here by BDAG (p. 1020) to the meaning category: "a kind, class, or thing that suggests a model or pattern." Paul is no doubt thinking of the general format in which Christian instruction was generally given to converts to Christianity. This Christian instruction and exhortation is sometimes referred to in technical literature by the term *parenesis*.

The Roman Christians were not total strangers to Paul (see 16:1-20) and he even states that their "obedience" (*hupakoē*) has become widely known (16:19). Since they had obeyed the Christian *teaching in which* they *were instructed*, their personal *experience* had been one of being **liberated from sin** and of being **enslaved to righteousness**. In other words, they had turned away from sin to do what was right in God's sight. Their servitude was now to Him and not to sin.

> **6:19. (I speak in human terms because of the weakness of your flesh.) For just as you have turned over your body's members as slaves to uncleanness, and to wickedness producing wickedness, so now turn over your body's members as slaves to righteousness producing holiness.**

Paul is not altogether comfortable with describing their Christian obedience as being "enslaved to righteousness" (v 18). He has only adopted such **human** terminology due to **the weakness of** their **flesh**.

His concern is for their comprehension of the truth. A more abstract description—even if accurate—would have failed due to their limitations as human beings. The following words in the verse show he is working with an analogy, moving from the familiar (slavery to sin) to the unfamiliar (slavery to righteousness).

In the past they had **turned over** their **body's members as slaves to uncleanness and to wickedness** (*anomia*). The result of this servitude to sinful practices was, of course, simply wickedness. (The phrase **producing wickedness** translates the Greek words *eis tōn anomian*.) Your former slavery, Paul states, was irremediably negative in its effects. It was unclean and wicked and productive of nothing other than an experience of evil.

I have rendered the Greek word *anomia* by the more general word *wickedness*. An examination of its uses in the Greek translation of the OT (the Septuagint) shows that it had become a very general word for what is evil. The modern tendency to interpret it in terms of its derivation ("lawlessness") is most likely an example of the so-called "root fallacy." A word's actual meaning at any given time is determined by usage, not by the meaning of its root.

This past experience in wickedness is the backdrop for understanding Paul's reference to being enslaved to righteousness. As believers, the Roman Christians are **now** to **turn over** their **body's members as slaves to righteousness**. What was once done in submission to sin should now be done in submission to righteousness. The result of this new form of active obedience will be the production of holiness. Thus the evil result of the former servitude can be replaced by the good result of a new servitude.

The phrase **producing holiness** translates *eis hagiasmon*. BDAG (p. 10) reminds us that outside of Biblical literature the word *hagiasmos* frequently signals "personal dedication to the interests of the deity." In the NT it has come to mean especially "the state of being made holy." In this context, however, an element of the basic meaning seems implicit in the context of being *slaves to righteousness*. The Greco-Roman world was familiar with the concept of someone who was permanently attached to a pagan temple as a servant of the god who was worshipped there.

> **6:20-21. For when you were slaves of sin, you were free from righteousness. So what fruit did you have then in the things of which you are now ashamed? For the result of those things is death.**

Paul continues to expand his analogy between the old servitude and the new one. As **slaves of sin** they had been **free from righteousness**. That is to say, righteousness was "powerless" in their lives. It had no control over what they did. It was not their "master."

There could be no positive outcome or result from such a life. It could bear no constructive fruit, and in retrospect, it was a life that **now** made them feel **ashamed**. The rhetorical question, **So what fruit did you have then…?** assumes that there was none at all. How could there be, since **the result** [*telos*, end] **of those things** could only be **death**?

In speaking of death here, Paul no doubt had physical death in mind, but his concept of death is much broader than that. This becomes plain in his subsequent discussion, especially in 7:8-13 and in 8:6-13 (see the comments in both places). For Paul, death is not the mere cessation of physical existence but is also an experience that is qualitatively distinct from true life.

As Paul puts it in Eph 4:18, the unregenerate are "alienated from the life of God, because of the ignorance that is in them." But as he will show clearly in the following two chapters, such "alienation" from God's life is experienced also by the Christian when he submits to the desires of his spiritually dead physical body.

> **6:22-23. But now, since you have been freed from sin and enslaved to God, you have your fruit producing holiness, and the result is eternal life. For the wages of sin is death, but the gift of God is eternal life in Christ Jesus our Lord.**

Despite their unproductive past, the Roman Christians are now in a position to bear real fruit that actually produces (or, consists of) holiness. This is due to the transforming fact of their union with Christ that Paul had emphasized earlier in the chapter (see especially 6:1-11). This union has resulted in their being **freed from sin and enslaved to God**. As Paul expresses it in 6:7, "the one who has died [with Christ] is justified [= freed] from sin." Thus the believer is now to regard himself as "dead to sin, but alive to God *in* Christ Jesus our Lord" (6:11, emphasis added).

A new lifestyle is therefore made possible in which the believer can "walk in newness of life" (6:4). This "newness of life," of course, is nothing less than **eternal life**. The believer's "walk" in this new life is the outcome of possessing that life *in* Christ. Thus the end **result** [*telos*] of **producing holiness** is nothing less than an experience of *eternal life* itself. This idea is already implicit in the Biblical quotation that Paul cites as part of his thematic statement for the entire book: "Now the one who is righteous by faith *shall live*" (Rom 1:17, emphasis added).

Paul can now wrap up the fundamental truths on which the entire unit (6:1-23) is based. On the one hand, death in all its aspects is the *pay-off* (**wages**) **of sin**. The word rendered *wages* (*opsōnia*) is not essentially different than its counterpart in English and refers in ordinary use to *pay* or *compensation*. Obviously a statement like this is deliberately broad enough to embrace all the various aspects in which death is the *compensation* for sin. In other words, it states a principle, and should not be narrowed to an exclusive reference to the *second death*, or the lake of fire (Rev 20:14).[9] Paul will later say to these believers that "if you live in relation to the flesh, you will die" (Rom 8:13) and that concept is one specific aspect of the principle he states here.

With sin, therefore, one receives what one has earned (wages). But **eternal life** is an *unearned* experience because at its core *eternal life* is **the**

---

[9] Hodges has written elsewhere about the atonement (e.g., *The Atonement* [Mesquite, TX: Kerugma, 2006]), arguing that no one is sent to the lake of fire due to his sins, but only because he is not found in the book of life due to his unbelief (pp. 4-5; see Rev 20:15). In addition, Hodges' discussion about death in chap. 6 has stressed that death refers to *physical death* as well as to the *debilitating consequences* of sin in our lives here and now. My best guess is that Hodges is alluding here to the one of two ways a person could gain entrance to the new earth and the Lord Jesus' eternal kingdom: via sinlessness. Hodges taught that the only way a person lacking everlasting life could enter Jesus' kingdom would be because he never sinned. Of course, there are no such people (Rom 3:23; 5:12-21). Thus being a sinner condemns the person lacking everlasting life to the second death, even though the Lord Jesus removed the sin barrier by His substitutionary death on the cross. –RNW

**gift of God** that is given **in Christ Jesus our Lord**. That is to say, by virtue of our being *in Christ* (see 6:3-4) we possess this gift. When we produce holiness we are living out *the gift* that God gave us when we were justified by faith.

The word used here for *gift* (*charisma*) is picked up from 5:15-16 where its occurrences are the first ones in the body of Paul's argument. (It is used in another connection in 1:11.) As is clear from 5:12-21, for Paul righteousness and life are part of one and the same *charisma*. As a result, "those who receive the abundance of the grace and of the gift (*dōreas*) of righteousness shall reign *in life* through one Man, Jesus Christ" (5:17). The whole gracious bestowal can be described as a "justification sourced in life" (5:18, see discussion there). (For the Pauline link between regeneration and justification, see also Titus 3:5-7.)

The closing words of v 23, *in Christ Jesus our Lord*, are identical in Greek to the words that close v 11 (*en Christō Iēsou tō Kuriō hēmōn* [Majority Text]). Thus they form an *inclusio* with v 11 and mark the present sub-unit (vv 12-23) as complete. The repeated words also serve to emphasize the truth that the *eternal life* which is given to us as a gift (by virtue of which we are "alive" [v 11]) is our possession *in union with* the Savior in whom we died and in whom we have been raised to walk in God's paths.

# Romans 7

## 3. Our Means of Victory Over Sin (7:1–8:39)

Paul is now prepared to discuss the basic "nuts and bolts" of Christian experience. In 5:12-21 he has set two experiences sharply in contrast, that is, the experience of sin and death brought to mankind through Adam, and the experience made possible through Jesus Christ. This latter experience is one of "reigning in life" through Him (5:17). In 6:1-23, Paul makes clear that such an experience is rooted in our union with Christ Jesus our Lord in whom we have received the gift of eternal life.

But victorious Christian living is far from automatic. Indeed it can be fraught with struggle and defeat when the means for spiritual victory are not properly appropriated. Paul now wishes to address this problem in some detail. The result is the longest single section of the body of Romans, one that extends from 7:1–8:39. At 8:39 we meet again the phrase that concludes 6:23: *in Christ Jesus our Lord*. Once again it serves as an *inclusio* in 8:39, indicating the completion of the long unit begun at 7:1.

### a. The Inadequacy of the Law for Spiritual Victory (7:1-25)

Although Jewish believers did not constitute the majority in the churches on the Gentile mission fields, their influence in the various bodies of believers must have been enormous. Their knowledge of the OT Scriptures placed them, in many respects, light years ahead of Gentile converts with no such background. As we learn from Acts 15:5, they were quite likely to think that the Law of Moses was an essential element in Christian living. But this was a serious mistake and Paul now wishes to confront it directly.

To have an effective experience of Christian living, the believer must know first of all that any relationship he may have had to the Mosaic Law has ended.

### i. Our relationship to the law has ended (7:1-6)

**7:1. Or are you unaware, brothers (for I am talking to those who know the law), that the law has authority over a man for as long a time as he lives?**

Paul is now addressing those in his audience **who know the law**, in particular, Jewish believers and any Gentiles who may have been connected with the synagogues before coming to faith in Christ. (For examples of such Gentiles, see Acts 2:10; 6:5; 8:27-28; 13:43; 17:4, 17; 18:7.) It was important that such people in the Roman church be fully aware of what Paul intends to say about the law. Of course, the remainder of the congregation will also learn from this.

The basic principle that Paul wishes to state is **that the law** is applicable to people who are alive. It **has authority over** a person only **for as long** as that person **lives**. After all, God's law was promulgated in an earthly setting (Mount Sinai) and applies to the sphere in which it was given. This does not mean that it does not express any timeless principles of righteousness. But as a body of legislation it was intended to regulate life *on earth*. Many of its stipulations are only relevant to our own world (e.g., Deut 25:4, quoted in 1 Cor 9:9). One of these, which Paul will now use as an example, is the law's regulation of marriage.

**7:2-3. In fact, a married woman is bound by the law to a husband who is alive. But if the husband dies, she is released from the law of her husband. So then, while the husband lives, she shall be called an adulteress if she marries another man; but if the husband dies, she is free from the law, so that she is not an adulteress if she marries another man.**

The example chosen by Paul is one intended to teach by analogy the freedom the Christian has from the Mosaic Law. Under the Mosaic legislation (leaving the issue of divorce aside), **a married woman** was not allowed to contract a new marriage while her husband was alive. Only upon his death was another marriage permissible, since otherwise such a second marriage would have been an act of adultery.

> **7:4. Therefore, my brothers, you too were put to death to the law through the body of Christ, so that you might marry Another—the One who was raised from the dead—so that you might bear fruit for God.**

In applying the example just mentioned, Paul draws on the truth of our union with Jesus Christ in His death, burial, and resurrection. This truth, clearly enunciated in 6:3-4, has been at the core of his entire discussion in chap. 6. Now he wishes to explore its implications in terms of our relationship to the law.

The fundamental consideration here is that **through the body of Christ** believers have been **put to death to the law**. This fact is predicated on our being baptized by the Holy Spirit into Christ and therefore into His death (see 6:3-4 and the discussion there). Thus our union with Him has linked us to the experience of His own body in which He bore the penalty that the law required for sin. (In Gal 3:13 we are told that Jesus redeemed us from the law's curse by becoming a curse for us.) The result is that *in Him* we too have died and are free from the law. We can therefore be properly married to **Another** Husband, namely to **the One who was raised from the dead**.

It is clear that the analogy with the married woman whose husband has died is not a perfect fit. Naturally, Paul expects his readership to realize that the comparison he uses is deliberately loose. He therefore plays upon the theme of our *death to the law*. We have indeed died *to the law* just as Jesus Himself did. But strictly speaking it is not the law itself (like a former husband) that has died. Instead, it is Jesus Christ who died, and *in whom* we also have died, so that the effect is the same. Our connection to the law has been broken by death.

The aim of the new marriage is that we **might bear fruit for God**. In the imagery employed by Paul, the children of a marriage are its fruit. But of course, in terms of the application, Paul is thinking of the "fruit producing holiness" to which he has just referred (see 6:22).

Our new marriage to our risen Lord—that is, our spiritual union with Him—is the true source of holiness. When we "walk in newness of life" (6:4) we are realizing our union with him and "giving birth" to deeds of holiness.

**7:5. For when we were in the flesh, the yearnings for sin that the law produced, were at work in our body's members to bear fruit for death.**

In describing this pre-conversion experience, Paul switches from the plural "you" employed in v 4, to the plural "we" in vv 5-6. In this way he signals to that portion of his readership who "know the law" (see v 1) that what he will now set forth had been his experience as well as theirs.

In those days, they all had been **in the flesh** (but they are not so any longer; see 8:9) and such fruit as they "gave birth" to at that time was only **for death** and not "for God" (see previous verse). The end result of their sinful works was always, and only, death.

Thus it can be said of Paul and the others "who know the law" that the law played a role in their experience in their unregenerate days. This role was manifested in **the yearnings for sin that the law produced**. In my translation, the phrase *the yearnings for sin* represents *ta pathēmata tōn hamartiōn* in Greek, usually handled in the English versions by "the [or, our] sinful passions" (NASB; NIV; NACE; JB). However, this popular rendering does not seem quite accurate.

In the NT the word *pathēma* usually refers to *sufferings* (as it does in Rom 8:18; 2 Cor 1:5, 6, 7; Phil 3:10; Col 1:24; 2 Tim 3:11; Heb 2:9, 10; 10:32; 1 Pet 1:11; 4:13; 5:1, 9). Only here and in Gal 5:24 do we have texts that are not easily understood as a reference to *suffering*. For these two texts, BDAG (p. 748) cites extra-biblical support for a meaning of this type: "an inward experience of an affective nature, *feeling, interest.*" But the word used this way is not inherently negative. As Moulton and Milligan note, it has a "properly colorless character" as in terms like *disposition, propensity*. This "vanilla" aspect of the word is illustrated in Plato's *Phaedo* 79d in reference to a search by the soul that is basically intellectual. "Passions" is not a good reflection of this meaning.

In the light of Paul's subsequent statement about the law arousing lust (v 7), it is likely that he has in mind the way negative commands so easily awaken *yearnings for* forbidden sin (taking *tōn hamartiōn* as a collective). These yearnings were ones *that the law* actually produced, as in fact it did in the case of the command not to covet (v 7). Since *pathēma* was frequently used by Paul for actual *suffering*, it is plausible that he is partly trading on that meaning as well. Yearnings for sin can be a form of inward suffering since they frequently create a sense of dissatisfaction and frustration.

In their unregenerate experience, Paul states, these yearnings **were at work in our body's members**. The words, *were at work*, render the Greek verb *enērgeito* in its frequent sense of "to put one's capabilities into operation," with specific meanings such as "*work, be at work, be active, operate, be effective*" (BDAG, p. 335). Paul is thus suggesting that the yearnings to which the law gave rise operated with effect in the physical members of their bodies so that the result was fruit consummated by death.

Such, then, was their law-based experience while they *were in the flesh*. But this need not be their experience any longer.

> **7:6. But now we have been released from the law by dying *to that* by which we were held back, so that we might serve in the newness of the Spirit, and not in the oldness of a written code.**

The contrast with the old experience is emphatically introduced by a strong *now* (*Nuni*). The idea of "release" is expressed with the verb *katērgēthēmen*, which might even be rendered here as "discharged" (see BDAG, p. 526). It is their death in union with Christ that has resulted in this "discharge" from **the law**. Paul has already stated this fact (v 4) and he now refers to it again with the words **by dying *to that* by which we were held back**.

It is notable that here Paul describes their former relationship to *the law* as one *by which we were held back*. The language could perhaps imply a kind of bondage expressed in the word *kateichometha*. BDAG (p. 533) places this instance of *katechō* under the category, "to keep within limits in a confining manner, *confine*" and renders the whole clause by "having died to that by which we were bound." This is certainly possible. But it would be the only instance of this meaning in the NT. (In John 5:4 [Majority Text] it probably ought to be rendered "afflicted" = "hindered." See next paragraph.)

But it is equally plausible that the word here belongs to BDAG's first meaning category, "to prevent the doing of something, or to cause to be ineffective, *prevent, hinder, restrain*" (p. 532). In its only other use in Romans (in 1:18), this is the meaning. (Elsewhere in Paul the same meaning is found in 2 Thess 2:6, 7.) With this meaning, the significance will be that *the law*, so far from being an aid to producing holiness, actually *hindered* them from doing it. As Paul will make clear a little later, this is not a reflection on *the law* itself. On the contrary, it is the result of *the law*'s counterproductive influence on the flesh—an influence he has just referred to in v 5.[1]

This second meaning is more likely in this context and is reflected in my translation by the words *held back*.

Thus *the law* need no longer *hinder* those believers who have been under it, since they have now died to it. Instead, they are now free to **serve in the newness of the Spirit, and not in the oldness of a written code**. With these words Paul picks up important ideas from the discussion that he began at chap. 6:1.

Most notably, Paul uses the word *newness* (*kainotēs*) for the first time since 6:4. (In fact, 6:4 and 7:6 are its only two occurrences in the NT.) The "newness of life" in which it is now possible to walk by virtue of our union with Christ in His death, burial, and resurrection (6:4) is nothing less than a service rendered to God in *the newness of the Spirit*.

In translating the underlying Greek here, I have used the English article twice, but the articles are not found in the Greek phrase (*en kainotēti Pneumatos*). So I could also translate: "in newness of spirit [or, of Spirit]." But in the kind of phrase Paul is using, the absence of the article is fairly normal and hardly indicates anything indefinite. The capital letter *P* is an editorial decision. The original Greek may refer either to the human spirit or to the Holy Spirit. The latter seems more probable here since Paul's word *newness* refers us back to the baptism of the Holy Spirit (see discussion at 6:3-4) by which we have union with Christ.

This *newness of the Spirit*—that is, the new life lived by means of the Spirit—is contrasted with *the oldness of a written code*. These latter words translate *palaiotēti grammatos* (literally, "oldness of letter") and are an obvious reference to the law. Because we have now died to the law, the Mosaic code belongs to the former experience of those who used to

---

[1] Hodges does not discuss the issue of the proper use of the Law of Moses during the previous dispensation, when it was in effect. However, he and I discussed this. His view is that men like King David did not view the law as the means to sanctification. David and other godly believers kept their focus on the coming Messiah as the Source of victory in their daily living. David was a man after God's own heart (1 Sam 13:14). Thus it seems unlikely that he had been enslaved by the law's hindrances. Paul was describing the view of the law held by the Pharisees of his day. Their legalistic devotion to the law, rather than to the One who gave the law, was a terrible error. When Jews came to faith in Christ for everlasting life and gave up trying to be *justified* by means of the law, often they would continue to look to the law as the means of *sanctification* (cf. Acts 15:5, cited by Hodges in the introduction to Rom 7:1-25). –RNW

be under it. For that reason it is "old" in contrast to the "new" spiritual experience that God has made possible for believers.[2]

However, Paul no doubt has more than that in mind. After all, the new life is lived under the *New* Covenant, of which Paul considered himself a minister (2 Cor 3:6-18), and this covenant stands in contrast with the *Old* Covenant of the law (see 2 Cor 3:14). The classic text contrasting the two covenants as new and old is Heb 8:7-13. Thus Paul would have regarded service to God *in the newness of the Spirit* as the experience of New Covenant life in distinction from life lived *in the oldness of the written code.*

Paul's word for *serve* here is the word for slave service (*douleuein*) and picks up from 6:22 his concept of being "enslaved (*doulōthentes*) to God." The service we render to God *in the newness of the Spirit* is an expression of our inner man's complete adherence to God's will. This truth will shortly play a major role in Paul's teaching in this chapter (see especially 7:22-24).

### ii. Our efforts to live under the law fail (7:7-25)

**7:7. So what shall we say? Is the law sin? Far from it! In fact I would not have recognized sin if not for the law. For I would not even have perceived lust, if the law had not said, *"You shall not lust."***

Paul's negative assessment of the law's impact on our experience of sin (v 5) leads to a natural question. **Is the law** itself **sin**—that is, *is the law* an instrument of sin and therefore fundamentally sinful? Such a suggestion must be immediately dismissed. **Far from it** is Paul's familiar response (*Mē genoito*) to unthinkable, or absurd, propositions.

**In fact** (*Alla*), Paul says, the law actually exposes sin so that it can be properly recognized as sin. There could be no better example of this function of the law than the case of **lust**. How could a person **have perceived** certain desires as sin if God had not pronounced them sin with the command, **"You shall not lust"**? But once the law had pointed out lust, human beings could recognize it for what it was—the expression of an evil urge.

---

[2] Since OT saints did not have the permanent indwelling of the Holy Spirit (cf. John 14:17), their spiritual experience was a different one than Church Age believers have. Hodges goes on to discuss the new spiritual experience somewhat in the last two paragraphs of his comments on Rom 7:6. –RNW

**7:8. But sin took advantage *of me* through the commandment and produced in me every kind of lust. For without the law sin is dead.**

This role of **the law** in exposing sin, however, does not make the law itself sinful. On the contrary, sin takes advantage of the sinner **through the commandment** to produce what the law actually forbids. In the specific case Paul is using as an illustration, **sin took advantage** of him to create in him **every kind of lust**—that is, a plethora of lustful desires arose in his heart.

How sin did this has already been suggested (in v 5) in Paul's mention of "the yearnings for sin" that the law awakens. But the responsibility for that lies with sin itself. All that the law actually did was to make Paul aware of the evil dispositions his own heart was capable of harboring. In this way, *sin took advantage* (*of me* is added for clarity) by stimulating and drawing forth from Paul the sinful desires inherent in his sinful nature.

Therefore, insofar as sin lies unrecognized apart from the prohibition that **the law** announces, sin can be said to be dead. In other words, sin as such is not an issue until it takes on the character of sin. It **is dead** because no moral question is at stake in the human heart or mind. But *the law* raises a moral issue so that sin comes to life in an otherwise common, ordinary human attitude.

**7:9. Now I myself was once alive without the law, but when the commandment came, sin came back to life and I died.**

This verse marks an important turn in Paul's discussion of the law. This turn is signaled to the reader by the emphatic **I** (*Egō*) with which the sentence begins (it is actually first in the Greek sentence). Surprisingly, this is the first time in Romans that this personal pronoun appears and this fact helps it to stand out. Furthermore, this instance is one of eight occurrences from 7:9 through 7:25. *Egō* is thus the pivotal word of this section.[3]

---

[3] This passage has 333 Greek words, fifty two of them (pronouns and verbs) are first person singular. That is one in six. Furthermore, the nominative singular "I" (*egō*) appears eight times, as Hodges notes. One of every forty-one words is the nominative first person pronoun (*egō*). In the NT as a whole, *ego* (I) and *kagō* (and I) combined tally one in 322 words. Unquestionably, Paul emphasizes the first person singular here to an extreme level. Paul's emphasis of "I" logically requires understanding this passage as autobiographical. –JHN

The material in 7:1-25 is therefore personal material that Paul draws from his own experience with the law. Moreover, as the content of this experience clearly shows, this must necessarily have been *his Christian experience with the law, not the experience of his unregenerate days.*[4] The view that the *I* of Rom 7:1-25 is somehow impersonal and a generalization of human experience is forced and unnatural in the light of Paul's use here of the emphatic first person pronoun. It is also an example of the reluctance in some quarters to take at face value the NT testimony about the struggles and failures of real-life Christian experience.

Paul continues to trade on the death/life analogy here. Having just spoken about the deadness of sin apart from the law, he now changes the figure to suggest *his own* deadness when he interacts with the law. He himself, he states, **was once alive without the law**, but that condition ended when the law aroused sin, and at that point, Paul affirms, **I died** (*egō de apethanon*). Here again, as at the beginning of the verse, Paul employs the emphatic first person pronoun (*egō*) underlining the personal nature of this experience.

There is no coherent way that an experience like this can be sensibly assigned to the days when Paul was a self-righteous Pharisee.[5] It is one thing to say that the law makes men conscious of sin, but quite another to describe them as *alive without the law*. In fact, as Paul has been at pains to say in 5:12-21, "*death* reigned from Adam to Moses even over those who had not sinned in a way that resembled the transgression of Adam"

---

[4] Nygren, *Romans*, 288, observes a fatal flaw of the view that Rom 7:9 refers to Paul as an unbeliever, "Brunner has stated the message of chaps. 5–8 entirely correctly [i.e., the Christian life, cf. Nygren, 287]. That he [Brunner] cannot fit chap. 7 into this context, but must speak of 'the great interruption of chapter 7,' is due to the fact that he finds in it only a description of man's pre-Christian life under the law. With such a view it is quite impossible to see a single line of thought. Chapter 7 inevitably becomes a 'foreign element.' This must be judged a very weighty objection to such an interpretation." See Emil Brunner, *The Letter to the Romans: A Commentary*, trans. H. A. Kennedy (London: Lutterworth, 1959; reprint, Philadelphia, PA: Westminster, n.d.). –JHN

[5] Commentaries recognizing that Romans 7 describes Paul as a believer include C. K. Barrett, *A Commentary on the Epistle to the Romans*, 2nd ed., BNCT, Henry Chadwick, gen. ed. (London: Black, 1991), 136; Cranfield, *Romans*, p. 1:356; Leon Morris, *The Epistle to the Romans* (Grand Rapids, MI: Eerdmans, 1988), 284-90; Robert H. Mounce, *Romans*, New American Commentary, vol. 27, E. Ray Clendenen, gen. ed (N.p.: Broadman & Holman, 1995), 166f; Murray, *Romans*, p. 256-58; Fung, "The Impotence of the law: Toward a Fresh Understanding of Romans 7:14-25," in *Scripture, Tradition, and Interpretation: Essays Presented to Everett F. Harrison by His Students and Colleagues in Honor of His Seventy-Fifth Birthday*, ed. W. Ward Gasque and William Sanford LaSor (Grand Rapids, MI: Eerdmans, 1978), 42. –JHN

(5:14, emphasis added). "Life," for Paul, when spiritually considered, is sourced in Christ, so that as "*death* has reigned through that one man [Adam], much more those who receive the abundance of grace and of the gift of righteousness shall reign *in life* through one Man, Jesus Christ" (5:17, emphasis added).

Accordingly, the Greek word translated *once* (*pote*) refers to an unspecified time in Paul's *Christian* experience. The wording in this verse about living and dying is intended to anticipate the later, climactic statement that "if you live in relation to the flesh, you will *die*. But if by the Spirit you put to death the deeds of the body, you will *live*" (8:13, emphasis added). Only the Christian can experience both "life" and "death" in the Pauline sense of these terms.

Paul is therefore referring to a time in his Christian experience when he was *living* in harmony with God, that is, he was walking by the Spirit (cf. 8:13). But then the law confronted him with one of its commands (**when the commandment came**) and aroused sin in him, resulting in the end of his experience of life (*I died*).

The statement that **sin came back to life** again translates the Greek words *hē hamartia anezēsen*. The use of the verb *anazaō* is to be especially noted. This verb basically means "to come to life out of a condition of death," but for the statement of this verse BDAG appropriately suggests the idea is "to function after being dormant" and it translates it, "sin became alive" (p. 62).

The point Paul is making is that while he "lived" in harmony with God, sin lay dormant until it was awakened to life by the law's commandment. This "coming to life" of sin terminated the experience of spiritual life[6] that Paul had been having. The sequence here is vital to Paul's idea: *the commandment came—sin came back to life—I died.* Such was the ultimate, deadly effect of the commandment, even though sin itself caused the death Paul experienced.

Paul's experience here has been replicated countless times in the experience of Christians, particularly those young in the faith. After their conversion they were living joyously as Christians. But suddenly they were confronted with a command of the law that they either did not know

---

[6] Hodges does not mean that Paul thought everlasting life can be lost. Instead, he is saying that Paul said that *the experience of everlasting life* can be terminated. That is, one's fellowship with God can be broken by obsessive focus on the law. –RNW

or had forgotten.[7] Their joy was suddenly replaced by a struggle with temptation, their struggle ended in defeat and sin, and their experience of walking with God was terminated. From being alive they had passed over into an experience of death. They had died exactly as Paul later warns (8:13).

> **7:10-11. And the very commandment *intended* to produce life was found to produce death. For sin took advantage of me through the commandment, and deceived me, and through it killed *me*.**

Of course, God *intended* that the commands of the law should have a positive, not a negative, effect. The words translated **the very commandment *intended* to produce life** represent the Greek phrase *hē entolē hē eis zōēn* (literally, "the command, the one for life"). Contrary to its actual purpose to keep man from the deeds that lead to death, through sin's allurement the commandment instead produced for Paul an experience of death. It did this by taking **advantage** of his sinful proclivities, **deceived** him about the value of the sinful act and, once he had committed it, sin had **killed** him. A vibrant experience with God was terminated.

> **7:12-13. Therefore, the law is holy, and the commandment is holy and righteous and good. So did what was good become death for me? Far from it! Instead sin, that it might appear *as* sin, produced death for me through what was good, so that through the commandment sin might become supremely sinful.**

The experience of "dying" that Paul has just described in no way diminishes the sanctity of **the law**. Since sin simply *used* the law as a means of arousing desire and producing sinful behavior (v 11), the law in no sense is culpable for that. Sin is to blame. As a result, the character of the law is untouched. It remains **holy and righteous and good**. These adjectives are probably not intended by Paul to represent distinct characteristics of

---

[7] It is unclear if by "the law" here Hodges means the Law of Moses or merely God's commands. He held the view that Christians are not under the Law of Moses, but that we are under the commands of the NT. Those commands are called *the law of Christ* or *the law of liberty*. Hodges seems to be suggesting here that even the commands of the NT can result in this same deadly experience if believers become fixated on them. –RNW

the law, but rather are a rhetorical instrument for underlining the law's complete moral perfection.

But having said this, must one also say that **what was good** had **become death for** Paul? In other words, holy though it was, was the law a deadly instrument? Was it, so to speak, a sword that slew men instead of helping them? That too would be a very negative assessment of God's law.

Paul's response is that such a perspective is unthinkable. (**Far from it** renders Paul's familiar *Mē genoito*.) On the contrary, the law served its basic purpose of making sin known. As Paul had earlier stated, "by the works of the law no flesh will be justified before Him, because through the law comes *the knowledge of sin*" (3:20, emphasis added). Even in the spiritual "fall" Paul has described (vv 9-11), the law still served its true end which was to expose the character of sin as being just that—sin.

Indeed, sin's successful utilization of the law enhanced the condemnation under which the law had placed it. This happened because sin—to the end **that** (*hina*) **it might appear** *as* **sin**—produced death for Paul **through what was good**. In other words, a desire is proved to be sinful whenever it is confronted by God's **commandment** and refuses to die. The fact that this impulse had led to sin and death in the very face of the commandment forbidding it was further evidence that it was truly sin. In other words, sin used a good thing (the law) to produce death, and it was allowed to do this in order that (*hina*) more than ever *it might appear* as the sinful thing it was.[8]

In this way, the sinfulness of sin was enhanced. Obviously it was sin if the law said so, but the fact that sin acted in defiance of the divine command, producing death, made it **supremely sinful**. These last two words (*supremely sinful*) translate the Greek phrase *kath' huperbolēn hamartōlos* (for which BDAG, p. 1032, proposes "sinful in the extreme"). It is one thing for sin to express itself in the absence of divine law—that is bad enough. But sin becomes sinful "in the extreme" when it does its work in direct contravention of God's known will.

**7:14. Certainly, we know that the law is spiritual, but I myself am fleshly, sold under *the dominion of* sin.**

---

[8] For further information from Hodges about Rom 7:13-25, see *A Free Grace Primer*, p. 221*f*, and *Absolutely Free! A Biblical Reply to Lordship Salvation* (Dallas, TX: Redención Viva; Grand Rapids, MI: Academie, 1989), 71. –JHN

Furthermore, **the law** is not only good, it **is spiritual**. That is to say, it is not mundane or fleshly but partakes of the spiritual nature of the God who gave it. (The word *certainly* translates the Greek conjunction *gar*, taking it in its emphatic sense: BDAG, p. 190, "a marker of inference, *certainly, by all means…*" etc.) Therefore the evil results of sin's manipulation of the law (vv 9-13) are not the result of the law's lack of spirituality. They find their true source in what Paul is himself in his own human nature.

**I myself** (*egō*), says Paul, **am fleshly**. The word rendered fleshly is *sarkikos* and relates (according to BDAG, p. 914) "to being human at a disappointing level of behavior or characteristics, *merely human*" (the same meaning applies also to *sarkinos*, read by the Critical Text [BDAG, p. 914]). At this point in the discussion, Paul categorizes himself as a mere human who lacks a spiritual nature that is congruent with the law, so that he finds himself **under** *the dominion of* **sin** (the words *the dominion of* are added for clarity). Sin rules him precisely because of his basic human nature.

As a *fleshly* person by nature, Paul describes himself as **sold under…** **sin**. Here Paul uses again the concept of man's enslavement to sin (6:16-21) and he uses the terminology of the slave market (*sold*) to make his point. It is doubtful that Paul has in mind any specific occasion on which this selling occurred. The word *sold* seems obviously rhetorical and portrays the complete helplessness of his servitude to sin.

> **7:15. For I don't know what I am accomplishing. For what I wish is not what I do, but what I hate is what I do.**

The initial **For** (again, *gar*) is here truly inferential. Paul's immediately preceding statement implies his frustration with the fact that, although the law itself is spiritual, he is not. In fact he is in bondage to ("sold under") sin. He is now about to explain how this moral gulf has led to a struggle that seems to accomplish nothing. (The statement, **I don't know what I am accomplishing**, is functionally equal to the expression, "I'm not getting anything done.") Indeed, this ineffectual struggle supports his recognition of his bondage: it is plain that he is "sold…under sin" for the very reason (*gar*) that his struggles have no positive result.

Specifically, he does the very opposite of what he wants to do: **what I wish is not what I do, but what I hate is what I do**. Thus, from the very start of this memorable discussion (which goes down to v 25), the problem is focused on the issue of Paul's will. What he *wills* cannot be carried out.

The key word in Paul's statement is the Greek verb *thelō*, translated here by the word *wish*. Previously in Romans, this verb has only been found in 1:13 where Paul *wants* the Romans to know that he has tried to come visit them but has been unable to do so. But in the present section (7:15-25) it occurs seven times. Paul is beginning to show here how Christian living is far more than a determined exercise of the will.[9] Indeed, for true Christian living the Christian's own personal wishes can never accomplish his goals. This is a truth that will emerge clearly by the end of chapter 7.

> **7:16-17. But if I do what I do not wish *to do*, I am agreeing with the law that it is good. So in this situation, it is no longer I myself who accomplishes it, but instead the sin that dwells in me.**

The futility of Paul's struggle with sin, however, leads to a discerning self-analysis. If he is in fact doing what he does **not wish *to do***, it follows from this that at the level of his innermost desires he is **agreeing with the law that it is good**. By this statement Paul no doubt means that when he violates the law in some particular way, his inward desire to do otherwise shows that he fully agrees that what the law commands on this point is good. He is thus aware that what he *actually* does is evil.

But this leads to a further observation. The words **so in this situation** render the Greek words *Nuni de*. The word *Nuni* is emphatic in form and indicates the present circumstances. Given what Paul has just said about his inward—but ineffectual—desire to do what the law prescribes, his disobedience to the law must be ultimately assigned to **the sin that dwells in** him. It is *not* to be assigned to his inner self (**I myself**).

In making the statement that **it is no longer I myself who accomplishes it**, Paul picks up the same word (*katergazomai*) that he had used in v 15: "I don't know what I am accomplishing." His frustration that he cannot *accomplish* what he truly desires (i.e., obedience to God) is now resolved into the realization that his disobedience is in fact the *accomplishment* of sin. Thus at the level of his "inward man" (see v 22) he remains "enslaved" to God's law (v 25). In the words we are looking at,

---

[9] Hodges stressed this point often in both personal conversations and public teaching. Clearly this is what he sees as the essential problem Paul is addressing in Romans 7. –RNW

Paul gives expression to the truth that the Christian's inner self *remains sinless* (see the discussion under v 25).[10]

> **7:18-19. For I know that in me—that is, in my flesh—no good thing dwells. For to wish *to do* lies ready at hand for me, but I do not discover how to accomplish what is good. For the good thing that I wish *to do* I do not do, but the evil thing I do not wish *to do* is what I do.**

The sharp differentiation between sin and himself that Paul has just made (v 17) facilitates the recognition that he is fundamentally incapacitated and lacks the ability to do any good thing. There is **no good thing** that **dwells** in him, that is to say, nothing good can come out of what he is in the flesh. To be sure, his inward man has the capacity to **wish to do** that which is good. The capacity to *desire* this **lies ready at hand for** him. That is not the problem. But the ability **to accomplish what is good** is absent because of his flesh.

With the statements of these verses Paul is beginning to show that "the body [his flesh] is dead because of sin" (8:10). That is to say, his complete inability to *accomplish* [*katergazesthai*] *what is good* is due to the fact that he dwells in a spiritually dead body. Try as he may, he is unable to **discover how** to surmount the impediment of his body in order to obey God's law.

The expression **I do not discover** is of interest. The experience Paul is describing is not simply one in which he futilely tries and fails. It is more than that. It is also an experience of seeking to find out [discover: *Heuriskō*] how to do what God desires him to do. Indeed, his desperation at not making this discovery is aptly expressed in v 24 by the words, "What a wretched man I am! Who will deliver me from the body of this *kind of* death?"

---

[10] Compare Hodges' commentary on 1 John and especially his comments on 1 John 3:9. Hodges believed that everlasting life is more than simply eternal security. It is *life* that lasts forever. In his view that life is and always will be without sin. He would often say that we never sin *as an expression of our born-of-God self*. Sin, he would say, is always an expression of the flesh, of what Paul calls in Romans *our mortal bodies*. Thus even though believers sin until they die (cf. Rom 3:23; 1 John 1:8, 10), their inner selves are not doing the sinning. That is what he means when he says, "the Christian's inner self *remains sinless*." –RNW

Paul's words therefore hint that the believer often does not find the secret of victorious Christian living until he is urgently seeking to discover it.

**7:20. And if I do what I myself do not wish *to do*, it is no longer I myself who accomplishes it, but instead the sin that dwells in me.**

Paul now repeats the conclusion already expressed in v 17. The repetition shows that this point is an important one for Paul. At the level of his innermost self (his "inward man"), he is in complete harmony with God's will (see v 22). Thus Paul can affirm about himself that when **I myself** act contrary to my deepest desire, **I myself** do not in fact really do the evil thing. Instead **the sin that dwells in me** does it.

Both in v 17 and here, the English phrase *I myself* represents an underlying emphatic *egō*. Although it might be theoretically permissible to connect the initial *egō* of this verse with the verb *poieō* (**I do**), the position of the *egō* (the Critical Text brackets this initial *egō*) makes it more likely that it is to be taken instead with *ou thelō* (**I do not wish**). Taken this way, the Greek pronoun in this passage is used consistently as a reference to Paul's deepest, truest self that *wants* to do good.

**7:21. Therefore I discover this law for myself that, when I wish to do what is good, evil lies ready at hand for me.**

Although in the struggle Paul is describing he has not been able to "*discover* how to accomplish what is good" (v 18), he *has* made a discovery. His experience has allowed him to **discover** (*heuriskō*) the fact **that when he wishes to do what is good, evil lies ready at hand for** him. As hard as it is *to do what is good*, by contrast it is extremely easy to do what is evil. Thus, since *evil lies ready at hand* (Greek: *emoi...parakeitai*, "lies alongside me"), he needs, so to speak, only to reach out and pick it up.

This discovery takes for Paul the form of a law (**this law**, *ton nomon*). In this case it is an unbreakable principle that is invariably operative in his human experience. The Greek construction, *Heuriskō...ton nomon tō thelonti emoi poiein to kalon*, is best construed in the sense of "I discover a law applying to myself who wishes to do good..." That is, *this law* pertains to him and impacts his personal experience as he struggles against sin.

Paul does not share the illusion that some modern Christians have that if we have been regenerated then obedience to God's law is both simple and natural. Such Christians are forgetting a fact of which Paul was painfully conscious—that although the Spirit within us is life, the physical body remains completely dead to God's will (see 8:10). In other words, they are forgetting the law Paul is referring to here.

> **7:22-23. For I delight in the law of God with my inward man, but I see another law in my *body's* members waging war with the law of my understanding, and taking me captive by means of the law of sin which is in my *body's* members.**

Paul now elaborates the concept of "law" that emerged in his preceding statement (v 21). We may note several "laws" here: (1) **the law of God**; (2) **another law in my *body's* members**; (3) **the law of my understanding**; and (4) **the law of sin which is in my *body's* members**. It is possible that Paul intends the same thing by numbers two and four, but this is doubtful since "law" number two brings him into captivity **by means of** "law" number four. If we are to track Paul's thought, all four "laws" must be considered carefully. (The translation supplies the word *body's* each time for the sake of clarity: see v 24.)

Of course, by the term *law of God* Paul has in mind chiefly the Mosaic moral code. In that law his **inward man** can and does delight. But *another law* in his *body's members* opposes the willingness of his *inward man* to conform to God's law. That law is actually **waging war with** (*antistrateuomenon*) the desire of his *inward man*. In the light of v 25 (see discussion there) Paul most likely means by this particular law the inveterate inclination of his sinful flesh which always desires the opposite of what the Spirit desires (see also Gal 5:16-17).

The desire of his inward man to obey God's law is expressed by the term *the law of my understanding*. Paul means by this that his *inward man understands* that the law is "holy" and "spiritual" (vv 12 and 14) and that its command is "holy and righteous and good" (v 12). Therefore it is highly desirable. But the *law in* his *body's members* (law number two above) overcomes the desire of the *law of* his *understanding* (law number three). It does so by utilizing *the law of sin which is in* his *body's members* (law number four) so that **by means of** this *law* (number four) he is taken captive.

This final law (*the law of sin*) can be understood as the "reign" of sin in his physical flesh (see 6:12) resulting in the complete subservience of his physical body to its dictates. Thus the impulses of his physical body, by means of their enslavement to *the law of sin*, are invariably aligned against his desire for obedience to God. These impulses thus become a *law in* his *body's members* (#three) that is driven by *the law of sin* (#four). The result is Paul's captivity to "the evil thing" that he does "not wish to do" (v 19).

> **7:24-25. What a wretched man I am! Who will deliver me from the body of this *kind of* death? I thank God through Jesus Christ our Lord! So then, I myself serve the law of God with my understanding, but with the flesh *I serve* the law of sin.**

Paul found the situation he described intolerable. The total disconnect between his inward, holy desires and the impulses/actions of his physical body left him **wretched**. He cried out in perplexity for a deliverer. Since he could not **deliver** himself, he wondered who might be able to deliver him **from the body of this *kind of* death**. Of course, at the time of writing, this cry was simply a rhetorical way of expressing the deep frustration into which this experience of defeat had led him.[11] Its solution became plain to him (v 25).

As the italics indicate, the words *kind of* are supplied in translation to help the English reader. The Greek phrase is actually *ek tou sōmatos tou thanatou toutou*, that is, literally, "from the body of this death." This is functionally equivalent to "this dead body." Paul means exactly what his words suggest here. The Christian person—who has Christ in Him—lives in a spiritually *dead* body, as is plainly stated in 8:10. The body is therefore like a dead albatross hanging around the spiritual "neck" of the regenerate inward man. It continually drags him down to defeat.

Can anyone rescue him from this miserable experience? He states the answer at once. He is thankful that God can, and does so **through Jesus Christ our Lord**. The words *through Jesus Christ our Lord* are probably to be taken as completing an implicit "[God] who does so" or "[God] who delivers." If they are taken as a mere adjunct to **I thank God** (i.e., the thanks is given *through Jesus Christ*), they do not fit the thought here (or

---

[11] Paul was no longer undergoing this struggle. This was a problem he experienced early in his Christian life. Thus while he needed to continue to walk victoriously in this way he had discovered, he was not walking in defeat at the time he was writing. He merely presents it that way for rhetorical effect. –RNW

in chap. 8) as naturally. This triumphant assertion prepares the way for Paul's exposition of victorious Christian living that follows in the next chapter.

But before launching that discussion, he pauses to summarize the conclusions to be drawn from the experience described in 7:7-24. This summation is introduced by the words **so then**, which reflect a combination of the Greek inferential conjunctions *Ara oun*. This doubling of conjunctions is not only emphatic, but serves also to highlight the final statement of this unit of material (7:7-25).

Out of his frustrating experience of spiritual defeat, two basic truths emerge clearly. The first is that **I myself serve the law of God with my understanding**. By this statement Paul obviously means that his "inward man" (see v 22) is completely and intelligently subject to the commands that God's law contains. The term *understanding* translates the Greek word *noi* (from *nous*), a word already used in v 23 of the perceptive faculty that discerns the law's true worth (cf. again, vv 12, 14).

Earlier Paul had spoken of the fact that believers were "enslaved (*edoulōthēe*) to righteousness" (6:18) and here he uses the cognate word *douleuō* (*I serve*, i.e., "serve as a slave"). Inwardly, he is fully submissive to God's will—he is a slave to it—but he is unable to carry it out. His understanding of its value cannot be translated into concrete action. The reason for this failure is due to the second basic truth of the passage, namely, **but with the flesh *I serve* the law of sin.**

The italicized words *I serve* are an obvious phrase to supply from the first part of Paul's statement. His inner servitude to God's law is counterbalanced by his servitude to the law of sin. The former servitude cannot find expression because of the latter servitude. The fruitless struggle described in the preceding verses (vv 15-23) has made this fact plain.

In Paul's Greek the two phrases, *with my understanding* (*tō men noi*) and *with the flesh* (*tē de sarki*), are formally parallel. But the bare dative forms are fluid in the language and Paul no doubt understands each phrase in a slightly different way. Although the dative in both cases could be rendered "as regards the understanding/flesh," Paul's *understanding* is the *sphere* in which the law is served, while *the flesh* is the *instrument* with which he carries out sin's desires.

Finally we must notice that in the first clause of this last statement, Paul employs the Greek phrase *autos egō* (*I myself*). This precise construction occurs only here in Romans and contrasts sharply with the merely implicit first person idea in the second clause. The phrase *autos egō* probably carries with it the overtones of an expression like "the real I" or "the true I." Such an inference is natural in the light of vv 17 and 20 where Paul uses the emphatic *egō* to disassociate himself from the sin he does not want to do. The "real I" does not sin.

Moreover in this kind of treatment of the problem of sin we meet a concept not unlike that found in 1 John 3:9 and 5:18. There the regenerate person is said not to sin nor to be able to sin. (The explanations of these verses based on the use of the present tense are forced and are widely abandoned today.) Due to the fact that God's "seed remains in" the regenerate person, "he cannot sin because he has been born of God" (1 John 3:9). It is easy to see that this "impossibility" that John describes can be conveyed by Paul's metaphor about being "enslaved" to *the law of God*. Paul's "inward man" does not, and cannot, "do" the sin he hates (Rom 7:20-23).

# Romans 8

## b. The Adequacy of the Spirit for Spiritual Victory (8:1-39)

Paul's previous discussion (7:1-25) has focused on the inadequacy of the Mosaic Law as an instrument for effective Christian living. The Christian is in fact dead to it (7:1-6), and his efforts to live under it only issue in defeat (7:7-25). He must necessarily turn elsewhere for the spiritual deliverance that eludes him due to the body's enslavement to the law of sin.

As has already been affirmed by 7:25, such deliverance comes from God through Jesus Christ our Lord. But how exactly is this victory realized? The present unit of material (8:1-38) addresses that question directly and also describes the triumphant form of living that is possible as a result.

In the cry, "Who will deliver me from the body of this *kind of* death?" (7:24), Paul had employed the Greek verb *rhuomai* to express the idea of *deliverance*. But *rhuomai* is a functional equivalent for the idea in the Greek word-group *sōzō/sōteria*, "to save," "salvation."[1] In addition, the *deliverance* for which Paul cries out in 7:24 is obviously a *deliverance* that entails *life*, since Paul is "trapped" in "the body of this *kind of* death."

In the motifs of death/life/deliverance we encounter again the truth of the epistle's thematic statement (Rom 1:16-17). This statement affirms that "the gospel of Christ...is the power of God for *deliverance* (*sōterian*) for everyone who believes" and that "the one who is righteous by faith *shall live.*" Defeated though he was in the experience of 7:15-25, Paul

---

[1] Hodges takes *rhuomai* in Rom 7:24 as a synonym for *sōzō*. The word *rhuomai* occurs eighteen times in the NT, twelve times in Paul (Rom 7:24; 11:26; 15:31; 2 Cor 1:10 [3ˣ]; Col 1:13; 1 Thess 1:10; 2 Thess 3:2; 2 Tim 3:11; 4:17-18). –RNW

could, by "the power of God," experience *salvation* from "the body of this kind of death" so that he might *live*.

Romans 8, especially vv 1-14, shows how this can become a reality.

### i. The spiritual resurrection of our mortal body (8:1-13)

Paul begins his exposition of the means of Christian victory with a basic summary statement.

> **8:1. Therefore there is now no servitude *to sin* for those who are in Christ Jesus, who do not walk in relation to the flesh but in relation to the Spirit.**

The statement of this verse succinctly expresses the core of Christian victory. The manner in which this victory is achieved is the subject discussed in vv 2-13.

In referring to the issue of **servitude *to sin*** (*katakrima*) Paul has reference to the problem discussed in the previous chapter. But in fact the problem Paul had wrestled with in his personal life was simply a manifestation of the larger problem he had discussed in 5:12-21. Paul's own struggles were only a manifestation of sin's reign in the sphere of death (5:21), a reign over *all* men that was initiated by the disobedience of the *first* man, Adam.

As Paul's exposition in 5:12-21 has shown, "through one offense [that is, Adam's sin] judgment" has come "to all men to produce *servitude to sin*" (5:18; cf. 5:16). In both 5:16 and 18 Paul has used the Greek word *katakrima*, which is used again and for the last time here in 8:1. The rendering, *servitude*, has been discussed and justified under the exposition of 5:16.

Contrary to the widely held opinion that in 8:1 Paul is discussing the truth of justification as the removal of all *condemnation*, Paul's statement has a quite different meaning.[2] Paul is referring to the reign of sin and death that was initiated by the fall of Adam. Since Paul lives in a "body of...death," sin reigns in his physical body. "With his flesh" Paul "serves

---

[2] Before becoming aware of Hodges' explanation and defense of this understanding, and before accepting the Majority Text view (during the doctoral program at DTS), I had thought this was a verse about the believer's freedom *from condemnation*. Yet once I came to see what the text really was, and what the word *katakrima* meant, the verse came alive to me. Hodges is certainly understating the case to say that the result is "a quite different meaning." This meaning is the exact opposite of the traditional understanding. –RNW

[as a slave to] the law of sin" (see the discussion under 7:25). His problem has been "deliverance" from this *servitude to sin* (the translation adds *to sin* for clarity).

This *servitude to sin*, Paul declares, does not exist for those of whom two things are true. These two things are: (1) they **are in Christ Jesus**, and (2) they **do not walk in relation to the flesh but in relation to the Spirit**. Regrettably the words *who do not walk in relation to the flesh but in relation to the Spirit* (found in KJV, NKJV) are omitted by most modern translations (e.g., NIV, NASB, JB).[3] This omission by modern translators is due to their reliance on a few older Greek manuscripts that differ from the Majority Text.[4]

The first part of Paul's statement specifies that one must be *in Christ Jesus* to experience this freedom from sin's bondage: **there is now no servitude to sin for those who are in Christ Jesus**. The truth that we *are in Christ Jesus* does not come into play in Romans until we reach 6:1-11 where it leaps to prominence in Paul's exposition. Chapter 6, in fact, begins Paul's response to the problem of the reign of sin and death that has occupied him in 5:12-21.

In 6:1-11 it is made clear that our union with Christ (by the baptism of the Holy Spirit) is the foundation for our "walk in newness of life" (6:3, 4). By virtue of this union we have been united with Christ in His death and resurrection so that now we are "dead to sin, but alive to God *in Christ Jesus* our Lord" (6:11, emphasis added). The words "in Christ Jesus" in 6:11 (*en Christō Iēsou*) are precisely the words used here: [*those who are*] *in Christ Jesus* (*en Christō Iēsou*).

---

[3] Some may imagine that omitting the phrase "who do not walk in relation to the flesh but in relation to the Spirit" (as in NA[27]) would negate Hodges' exposition of v 1. It does not. NA[27] has *katakrima* (penal servitude) here, as well as in Rom 5:16, 18, speaking of a futile servitude of sin in the present age. Pretend that the critical text's omission of walking by the Spirit were right. Would the verse then suggest that all believers would automatically escape penal servitude? No, both prior and following context teach that the escape is not automatic. It requires walking by the Spirit. Romans 7:13-25 described Paul as a believer making a futile effort to escape penal servitude by the flesh. Romans 8:1ff sets forth walking by the Spirit as the only way for believers to escape penal servitude. The majority family of manuscripts strongly favors including the whole statement, but even those following the critical text should catch the meaning of Rom 8:1. –JHN

[4] The vast majority of Greek manuscripts (undivided Majority Text and even codex Alexandrinus, a key Critical Text manuscript) support the longer reading. So does the context. In v 4 the idea of walking not according to the flesh but according to the Spirit is repeated. Yet the UBS editors call the reading that omits this phrase "virtually certain" (by giving it an A rating). Hodges would say that *the longer reading* is certain. –RNW

Being *in Christ Jesus* is absolutely essential to victory over sin but, as Paul's previous discussion has shown, by itself it is not enough. The second step to victory therefore is how the Christian person *walks*. He must *not walk in relation to the flesh but in relation to the Spirit*. Here we pick up the word *walk* that Paul has used in 6:4.

The verb *to walk* (from *peripateō*, from which we get words like *peripatetic*, walking about) is a familiar one in the Pauline literature and describes the process of living, or the manner in which one behaves. BDAG (p. 803) gives as meaning category number two: "to conduct one's life, *comport oneself, behave, live* as habit of conduct." Whether the conduct or behavior is thought of as positive or negative depends on context (see, e.g., 1 Cor 3:3; 7:17; 2 Cor 5:7; Eph 2:2; 4:1, 17; 5:15; Phil 3:17-18; Col 1:10; 4:5, and many other texts). Here there is obviously an option in which a positive mode of behavior is to be chosen if one is to be free from *servitude to sin*.

But the statement of this option (repeated in v 4 and also in v 13) introduces a component that was not present in Paul's struggles as described in 7:15-25. The new element is expressed by the phrase *in relation to the Spirit*, since *the Spirit* was not a factor at all in those struggles. His introduction into the process of Christian living is, for Paul, the key to spiritual victory. The role of *the Spirit* will be immediately expounded in the following section (vv 2-13).

The words *in relation to* translate the wide-ranging Greek preposition *kata*. Both here and in v 4 the most common rendering of *kata* is "according to" (NKJV, NASB, NIV) and this is certainly a permissible translation. JB, however, translates (in v 4): "who behave not as our unspiritual nature but as the spirit dictates." But this is not quite the same idea.

In fact, it is doubtful that either of these ideas would have clearly suggested themselves to the Greek reader in this kind of context. Instead, it is likely that a more general nuance would have been felt, such as my translation conveys. (For the meaning *in relation to* see BDAG, p. 513, definition 6.) A paraphrase might be: "those who walk flesh-wise," and "those who walk Spirit-wise," that is, with a fleshly or with a spiritual orientation.

What this actually means experientially will become clearer as Paul's exposition proceeds.

**8:2. For the law of the Spirit of life in Christ Jesus has freed me from the law of sin and death.**

The word *for* is significant here. The reason that servitude to sin does not exist for those described in v 1 is that **the Spirit of life** liberates them from **the law of sin and death**. *The Spirit of life* is in fact *the Spirit* who has baptized believers into **Christ Jesus** (see 6:3-4) so that *the Spirit* now dwells in them (see 8:9).

But the liberation being described is experiential and cannot be automatically predicated of all believers. As the discussion of chapter 7:15-25 makes clear, it could not be predicated even of Paul at one time in his Christian experience. But now it *can* and therefore he personalizes the statement—**has freed *me* from the law of sin and death**. The fact that he does not say "us" is not an accident. Each believer must claim this victory in his own experience. Paul could not know that everyone in the Roman congregations had done so.

What exactly **the law of the Spirit of life** is in Christian experience awaits the exposition in the following verses. Nevertheless, very clearly, this new law overrides the opposing *law of sin and death* which had prevented Paul from fulfilling his holy desires (7:15-25). Though chap. 7 has made the role of *the law of sin and death* quite clear, it is the present chapter that will elaborate *the law of the Spirit of life* for Paul's readers.

**8:3. For in regard to the incapacity of the law, in that it was weak because of the flesh, by sending His own Son in the likeness of sinful flesh and as a sacrifice for sin, God pronounced sentence on sin in the flesh,**

Paul's statement here in the original Greek is somewhat difficult, although its general meaning is quite clear. My translation treats the opening Greek construction (*to…adunaton tou nomou* = **the incapacity of the law**) as an accusative of general reference.[5] This construction in turn is qualified by the words **in that it was weak because of the flesh** (a relative clause in Greek). *The incapacity of the law* was due to the impediment that *the flesh* posed to Paul's fulfillment of its holy demands. *The law*, therefore, *was weak because of the flesh* and could not aid Paul in the resolution of this problem.

---

[5] For the grammatical possibilities, see Robertson, *Grammar*, 491. –ZCH

But precisely **in regard to** this very problem (the weakness of *the law*), God, by means of **sending His own Son**, has imposed a **sentence on sin in the flesh**. The word translated *pronounced sentence on* is *katekrine* and my rendering accords with that word's basic sense. The extended meaning for *katakrinō* offered by BDAG (p. 519) is "pronounce a sentence after determination of guilt," i.e., "*pronounce a sentence on.*"

Paul's thought in this verse flows out of v 2 and is intimately tied up with it as the conjunction *for* (*gar*) indicates. The reason Paul has been freed from "the law of sin and death" (v 2) is due to God's action as described in Paul's statement here. Sin in Paul's flesh no longer has unfettered freedom to rule Paul. On the contrary, it stands under divine sentence and its power over him has been annulled.

How has God brought about this new state of affairs? He has done so **by sending His own Son in the likeness of sinful flesh and as a sacrifice for sin**. Paul refers here both to the incarnation of God's Son (*in the likeness of sinful flesh*) and to His work on the cross (*as a sacrifice for sin*). Indeed, He is a sinless *sacrifice for sin* because He did *not* come *in sinful flesh*, but only *in the likeness of sinful flesh* (literally, "in [the] likeness of [the] flesh of sin," *en homoiōmati sarkos hamartias*).

The phrase *as a sacrifice for sin* reflects the underlying Greek words *peri hamartias*. The Greek expression was a common way of referring to the atoning purpose, or effect, of a sacrifice in the Jewish religious system (BDAG, p. 798, meaning 1g; see especially Heb 10:6, 8, quoting Ps 40:6-7, which use exactly this Greek phrase, by itself, in the sense given in my translation).

Apart from the coming of God's Son as a man to offer Himself *as a sacrifice for sin*, the dominion of sin in the experience of all sinful human flesh would be a fully legitimate expression of divine wrath against human sinfulness. Paul insists on the legitimacy of God's wrath in human experience in 1:18-32. That wrath, as Paul plainly stated, comes "against all the ungodliness and unrighteousness of men" (1:18). Human beings have no reason to expect the lifting of this wrath so long as they remain unrighteous in God's sight. But the cross of Christ changed all that.

As Paul has been at pains to show (see 3:21-26; 4:23-25), by His death Christ has made it possible for God to "be righteous and [to] justify the person who has faith in Jesus" (3:26). Such a person now becomes righteous *in Christ* (see 3:22, 24; 5:1; see also 8:1 where Paul indicates the one in Christ has the potential to become righteous *in his experience* if he walks in relation to the Spirit and not in relation to the flesh). Thus the death of Christ is also a sentence of doom upon *sin in the flesh*, destroying its present power and presaging its final removal from the experience of the one who is "righteous by faith" (1:17).

Or in other words, "since we have now been justified by His blood, we shall be *delivered from wrath* through Him" (5:9, emphasis added). This means that "the one who is righteous by faith *shall live*" (1:17, emphasis added). Therefore, "the law of sin and death" (v 2) has no right any longer to rule the experience of the justified man or woman. That man or woman has died in Christ and sin has no legal claim on them, "for he who has died is justified from sin" (6:7). He or she can now *live* to God (6:11).

Paul now goes on to say exactly that in the following verse.

> **8:4. so that the righteous action of the law might be fulfilled in us who do not walk in relation to the flesh but in relation to the Spirit.**

The very thing Paul found himself unable to do as he strove to obey the law (7:15-25) has now become possible for him by means of the Spirit. Since he has been united with Christ in His death (6:5), the sentence pronounced on "sin in the flesh" at the cross (see previous verse) applies directly to sin in *Paul's* flesh because he is "in Christ Jesus" (see 8:1). **The righteous action of the law** can **be fulfilled** by him as he walks **in relation to the Spirit.**

The phrase *the righteous action of the law* deserves careful attention. Paul uses here the Greek word *dikaiōma* (*righteous action*) which he has used previously in Romans only at 1:32; 2:26; 5:16, 18. Particularly relevant to the present verse are the occurrences in 5:16, 18, which are a part of the larger unit 5:12–8:39. In fact, 5:16 specifically contrasts *katakrima* and *dikaiōma*, the very words used in 8:1 (*katakrima*) and here (*dikaiōma*).

In actuality, 5:16 anticipates the truth being elaborated here by Paul. In 5:16 Paul has stated that whereas "the judgment" (*krima*) that Adam's sin brought on man led to "servitude (to sin)" (*katakrima*), the free gift (*charisma*) leads to "righteous action" (*dikaiōma*). In Romans 5, however, Paul was not yet ready to explain exactly *how* this is realized. But in Romans 8 he is.

However, Paul's statement in 8:4 has been seriously misconstrued in the NIV (1984). Incredibly, the NIV translation offered for the Greek words *hina to dikaiōma tou nomou plērōthē en hēmin* this rendering:

"in order that the righteous requirements [plural] of the law might be fully met in us." If this translation is intended to convey that a Christian can fully keep the law in his Christian walk, it expresses an incredible delusion and would stand in stark contradiction, for example, to 1 John 1:8. Neither Paul nor any other NT writer shared such a delusion.

For the requirements of the law to be "fully met" they must be *fully* met. As James has said so plainly: "For whoever shall keep the whole law, and yet stumble in one point, he is guilty of all" (Jas 2:10). Paul made the same point in Gal 3:10. Thus the rendering of this verse by the NIV necessarily implies the possibility of sinless perfection.

To be sure, something quite similar to the NIV's rendering is found in the JB: "that the law's just demands [plural] might be satisfied in us." That rendering partakes of the misperception expressed in the NIV, but the NIV accentuates the flawed rendering with the words *fully met.* Perhaps the JB could be argued to imply by the word *satisfied* something less than "fully met."

Much to be preferred is the translation given by the NKJV ("that the righteous requirement [singular] of the law might be fulfilled in us"), the NET ("so that the righteous requirement [singular] of the law may be fulfilled in us"), and the NASB ("in order that the requirement [singular] of the law might be fulfilled in us"). In these translations the *singular* of *dikaiōma* has been retained, as over and against the NIV and the JB which treat the singular form in a collective sense.

However, it has been argued at 5:16 that the Greek word *dikaiōma* should be rendered there, not as "justification" (NKJV, NASB [JB = "verdict of acquittal"]), but in conformity to 5:18 as "righteous act" (NKJV), "act of righteousness" (NASB), or "good act" (JB). In both places in chap. 5, therefore, as well as here, I choose the translation *righteous action.* (See the discussion in 5:16.)

In contrast to the NKJV and NASB, I place the use of *dikaiōma* in Rom 8:1 under the second meaning category in BDAG, p. 249, ("an action that meets expectations as to what is right or just") rather than the first ("a regulation relating to just or right action"). The difference is semantically small, but theologically significant to Pauline thought.

As Paul has already asserted, the Christian is "not under the law but under grace" (6:14). Thus Paul does not mean here that a Christian can operate *under* the law and carry out its "requirements," but rather that *the righteous action* which the law stipulated, but failed to produce (see

7:15-25), can be achieved *under grace*. Understood this way, the singular of *dikaiōma* is important.

The singular occurs because Paul's statement is a statement of principle. What Paul is affirming is that *the thing that couldn't be done by living under the law can in fact be achieved by walking in relation to the Spirit.* The law addresses our sinful flesh and cannot deliver us from walking **in relation to the flesh** (see v 2). Now, however, we have died to the law (7:6) in order that we might walk in a newness of life that comes to us because we are *in* Christ Jesus (see 6:4). *The righteous action (i.e., any righteous action)* that *the law* tried but failed to produce in men is within the reach of those who walk in the liberty that the Spirit can give. That is to say that any such *righteous action* can be realized (*fulfilled, plērōthē*) through the power of the Spirit.

But, as already indicated in 8:1, freedom from "servitude to sin" (*katakrima*; see discussion there and in 5:16) depends not only on being "in Christ Jesus" but also, as repeated here, on not walking *in relation to the flesh but in relation to the Spirit*. Paul will now proceed to discuss this Spirit-led walk (8:5-13).

> **8:5. For those who are in relation to the flesh have their minds set on the things of the flesh, but those who are in relation to the Spirit *have them set* on the things of the Spirit.**

Paul's exposition of the Spirit-led *walk* must begin with a clarification. As indicated in my explanation under 8:1, the Greek phrases *kata sarka* and *kata Pneuma* are essentially general and therefore vague, and of course Paul was aware of that. Paul now wishes to make the concept expressed by these phrases more specific.

In the present verse Paul clarifies the basis on which he can affirm the "righteous action of the law" is carried out only by those who "walk…in relation to the Spirit." This is true because (**for**, *gar*) the phrases he uses to describe a person's *walk* suggest an individual's *orientation*. That is to say, **those who are in relation to the flesh** (*Hoi…kata sarka*) describes people who are oriented to **the things of the flesh** (*ta tēs sarkos*). But in contrast, **those who are in relation to the Spirit** (*hoi…kata Pneuma*) are people oriented to **the things of the Spirit** (*ta tou Pneumatos*). It is this latter orientation that is crucial to spiritual victory.[6]

---

[6] Hodges unwittingly (or possibly intentionally) chose a word, *orientation*, that is now very

The key word in this concept is the Greek verb *phroneō*, translated here by **have their minds set on**. This verb occurs for the first time in Romans in this verse (and elsewhere in Romans only at 12:3, 16; 14:6; and 15:5, in different settings). Here, however, the cognate noun *phronēma*, as well, occurs in 8:6, 7, 27 and nowhere else in the NT. The concept involved in these two words is crucial to Paul's thought in this section (8:1-13).

The use of *phroneō* in Rom 8:5 belongs under the second category of meaning given by BDAG, p. 1065, as "to give careful consideration to something, *set one's mind on, be intent on.*" The meaning of *phronēma* corresponds to *phroneō* in the sense of "the faculty of fixing one's mind on something, *way of thinking, mind-set*" (BDAG, p. 1066).

The orientation of the individual Christian—that is, their focus, or mind-set—is seen by Paul as a pivotal element in the Christian "walk." But this should not be understood simplistically as though the fleshly "mind-set" meant only something like, "to be fond of sin." On the contrary, Paul is describing the root of the very problem he so vividly records in 7:15-25.

While striving for holiness under the law, Paul had found himself focused *on the sins* that the law forbade. Indeed, he declares, "I would not even have perceived lust, if the law had not said, 'You shall not lust.' But sin took advantage of me through the commandment and produced in me every kind of lust. For without the law sin is dead" (7:7b-8). In short, the law had focused him on "lust" so that his mind-set was *fleshly*: "I must steer clear of all lust." This fleshly orientation doomed him to commit the very sin he sought to avoid.

Simply put, if one lives with a fleshly orientation—even if it is the result of a vigorous effort to keep the law—they are going to fail because it is the *wrong* mind-set.[7]

**8:6. For the mind-set of the flesh *is* death, but the mind-set of the Spirit *is* life and peace.**

---

widely used to refer to heterosexuals, homosexuals, and transgenders: *sexual orientation*. Paul here speaks of one's *spiritual orientation*. Is one spiritually oriented to the things of the Spirit, or to the things of the flesh? –RNW

[7] The same thing can be seen in Paul's letter to the Galatians. In the epistle to the Galatians, to walk in the flesh is to follow the legalistic teachings and practices of the Judaizers. To walk in the Spirit is to have one's mind focused on Christ and on the power of the Holy Spirit to give life to these mortal bodies. –RNW

Paul now describes the basic difference between the two opposing types of mind-sets. Although in the English the copula *is* must be supplied, here this does not help very much. Paul is not so much *defining* these mind-sets as he is giving their fundamental distinction.

We get closer to the true force of Paul's statement with a more literal rendering: *the flesh's mind-set—death. But the Spirit's mind-set—life and peace.* These two mind-sets, Paul affirms, are poles apart. One belongs to the sphere of, and results in, death. The other belongs to a contrasting sphere with contrasting results, **life and peace**.

Although the translation of Rom 8:6 by the JB is not above criticism, it is not too wide of the mark: "It is death to limit oneself to what is unspiritual; life and peace can only come with concern for the spiritual." Although handled differently by the JB in each clause, the underlying *phronēma* (*mind-set*) is treated with a fluid sense of the basic thought: i.e., "limit oneself to" and "concern for." But it is difficult to give a fully adequate rendering of Paul's pregnant concepts here.

Paul is saying that there is a reason why (note again **for**, *gar*) "the righteous action of the law" is beyond the reach of those who walk "in relation to the flesh" and attainable for those who walk "in relation to the Spirit." The reason is found in the differing spheres to which each mind-set fundamentally belongs. **The mind-set of the flesh** operates in the sphere of death, while **the mind-set of the Spirit** operates in the sphere of life. In this latter sphere alone one finds peace.

One might illustrate this idea (however inadequately) by the example of a man walking through a funeral home grieving over the death of all around him but unable to change anything. But if he is walking out in the field in the bright light of nature, he is energized by the signs of life that are everywhere and he himself experiences what it means to be truly alive.

The trap into which a Christian falls when he is principally concerned with the law itself is that he cannot escape a preoccupation with the spiritual deadness within and around him.[8] The mind-set of the Spirit, however, lifts his preoccupations to the level of supernatural *life and peace*. Paul's discussion (to the end of chap. 8) proceeds to explore this concept.

---

[8] Note that Hodges understands Paul to be denouncing a legalistic mind-set, not willful rebellion against God. While the latter is surely wrong and is a problem for believers (e.g., Luke 15:11-32; Gal 6:1-2; Jas 5:19-20), that is not what Paul is discussing here. The fleshly mindset that concerns him in Romans 8 is that of the legalistic Christian who thinks that by focusing on the commands (rather than the loving Commander) he can achieve life and peace. –RNW

**8:7. For this reason the mind-set of the flesh *is* hostile toward God, because it does not submit to the law of God, nor indeed is it able to.**

As Paul has learned by painful experience (see 7:7-11), the law commanded what the flesh really did not want to do and it forbade what the flesh wanted to do. Instead of suppressing lust, for example, the law had the effect of multiplying lust in Paul (7:7-8). In his personal striving to obey the law, Paul was hopelessly enmeshed in a quagmire of fleshly preoccupations (i.e., a mind-set) that were inherently resistant (hostile) to God and to His revealed will in the law. There was no way those fleshly inclinations could become submissive to the divine will.

The word translated **for this reason** (*Dioti*) is a strong one and draws a conclusion that is important to Paul's discussion. Since **the mind-set of the flesh** is inescapably preoccupied with the sphere of sin and death (v 6), it cannot be rescued from this preoccupation and from all the evil inclinations that manifest themselves in that sphere. Thus Paul's experience of spiritual defeat—an experience of death itself—could not be changed as long as this mind-set remained unchanged.

The flesh's mind-set not only **does not submit to the law of God**, it is completely incapable of doing so. In the expression **nor indeed is it able to**, the word *indeed* renders *gar* (taken as emphatic) although a causal sense is possible ("it is not subject *because* it cannot be"). For a Christian to be trapped in the wrong mind-set is to be trapped in a life of continuous defeat, precisely as Paul has described in 7:7-25.

**8:8-9. So those who are in the flesh are unable to please God. But you are not in the flesh but in the Spirit, if indeed the Spirit of God dwells in you. Now if anyone does not have the Spirit of Christ, he does not belong to Him.**

If the readers had not been Christians they could not have hoped to escape the bondage Paul has described. Unregenerate persons (that is, the unjustified) are people **who are in the flesh**. Since the mind-set of *the flesh* is the only one possible for them, they are completely **unable to please God**. The true Christian life can be lived only by Christians.

It is important to keep in mind that walking in relation to the flesh (see vv 1, 4) is not, in Paul's thought, the exclusive experience of those who are *in the flesh*. The Christian still has the sinful flesh in his physical body (e.g., 7:22-25; cf. 8:13) and can therefore walk in relation to the flesh, but he also has another option. At the level of his innermost man (see 7:22, 25) he is **not in the flesh but in the Spirit**. This means that he can also walk in relation to the Spirit.

This is the first time in Romans that Paul has used the terminology *in the flesh* and *in the Spirit*,[9] but it is clear that they are the functional equivalents for him of the "unjustified" and the "justified." The distinguishing feature in the contrast here is whether or not the person has **the Spirit of Christ**. If someone **does not have** *the Spirit of Christ*, that person **does not belong to Him** at all.

Paul has already spoken about the baptism of the Spirit without directly referring to the Spirit (6:3-4). There is also a clear allusion to the Spirit in 7:6 (see discussion there). Otherwise the only overt reference to the Holy Spirit prior to this chapter has been at 5:5 in a unit that anticipates the discussion of 5:12-8:39. It is evident that the reticence to directly mention the Spirit up until the present chapter is a part of Paul's literary technique. It is in chap. 8 that the Holy Spirit becomes the center of the truth Paul is expounding. Until now, the Spirit has been kept mainly in the background of Paul's presentation.

> **8:10. But if Christ** *is* **in you, the body** *is* **dead because of sin, but the Spirit is life because of righteousness.**

In the light of the presence of **the Spirit** within his believing audience—that is to say, the presence of Christ within them—they must recognize a dual reality. On the one hand their physical bodies remain spiritually **dead**. On the other hand, the inner presence of the Spirit gives them **life** within those very same dead bodies.

Paul does not mean here that the Christian's physical **body** is dead *physically*. Instead his statement must be understood in the light of the discussion in the previous unit (7:13-25) which had climaxed with a cry

---

[9] What Hodges means here is evident. When Paul speaks of being *in the flesh*, he is speaking of being in that state in one's position. He is not speaking of walking in that state in one's experience. Hodges is suggesting that Paul uses the precise words "in the flesh" (here and Rom 7:5, though 2:28 is a different sort of use as Hodges' discussion there shows) or "in the Spirit" when referring to one's *position*. Hodges believes that when Paul uses the similar but different expression *in relation to* (or "according to," NKJV) *the flesh* and *in relation to* (or "according to," NKJV) *the Spirit* in Rom 8:1, 4, 13 he is referring to one's *experience*. Believers are *in the Spirit*, but may walk *according to the Spirit* or *according to the flesh*. Unbelievers are *in the flesh* and only walk *according to the flesh*. –RNW

for deliverance from *the body of this kind of death* (7:24). The body is spiritually unresponsive (i.e., dead) to God's will precisely because it is the seat of "the law of sin which is in my *body's* members" (7:23).

By means of this description of the Christian's physical body as dead Paul makes clear that the Christian's body it is incapable of producing the life of God on its own. This is precisely what Paul had discovered in the fruitless struggles recorded in 7:15-25. Apart from some kind of intervention by the Spirit, the resulting spiritual defeat cannot be reversed. Paul will now state explicitly what the nature of this intervention by the Spirit must be.

> **8:11. And if the Spirit of the One who raised Jesus from the dead dwells in you, the One who raised Christ from the dead will also bring to life your mortal bodies on account of His Spirit who dwells in you.**

Although Christians live in physically mortal bodies that are already spiritually dead because of sin (v 10), **the Spirit** can impart to these **mortal bodies** an experience of life. In its context here, this statement must not be taken as referring to our future resurrection. Instead, it refers to the life and peace produced by the mind-set of the Spirit (v 6b). Thus the Spirit can overcome the death that characterizes the fallen state of our present mortal bodies (v 10) and can make them vehicles for expressing the divine life within us.

The Spirit through whom this amazing action is accomplished is none other than the Spirit **of the One** (that is, God the Father) **who raised Jesus from the dead**. With this statement we come full circle back to Rom 6:4. There Paul had stated that our union with Christ had an important goal: that "just as Christ was raised from the dead by the glory of the Father, so we also might walk in newness of life."

Accordingly, the resurrecting power of God the Father (**the One who raised Christ from the dead**), exercised through **His Spirit**, can bring us into experiential union with the risen life of Christ so that we actually walk in that "newness of life" that He Himself possesses.

It should be noted that this verse does not precisely say that all this is done *through* **His Spirit who dwells in you**, but rather **on account of** *His Spirit who dwells in you*. Of course, Paul's whole discussion makes it clear that God does act through His Spirit to produce this new experience of life. But the words *on account of* (*dia*) suggest also the nuance that the indwelling Spirit is *the reason for,* and *the ground of,* this whole experience. It occurs *because of* His presence, not merely *by means of* His presence. It occurs, fundamentally, *for His sake,* not ours.

As Paul will shortly say (8:26-27), "the Spirit Himself makes intercession on our behalf" (8:26) and He does so "in harmony with God" (*kata Theon,* 8:27). It is obvious that a victorious Christian life is in a real sense an answer to the Spirit's intercessory prayers and thus is realized *on account of* Him. Indeed, to the extent that our own prayers are in accord with His, this agreement as well is evidence of His work within us. In every respect the "resurrection" of the believer's mortal body that Paul describes here is accomplished *on account of His Spirit who* indwells us.

> **8:12-13. So then, brothers, we are not obligated to the flesh to live in relation to the flesh. For if you live in relation to the flesh, you will die. But if by the Spirit you put to death the deeds of the body, you will live.**

Paul now brings this unit of his discussion (8:1-13) to a close. He does so by setting forth clearly the two options his Christian readers have before them. To begin with, they are no longer inwardly in bondage to sin. They are, in fact, "dead to sin" (6:11) and, since "he who has died is justified from sin" (6:7), sin has no claim on them. Though sin still remains in their mortal flesh, they need not allow "sin to reign in their mortal body so that [they] obey its lusts" (6:12). In short, we Christians are in no way **obligated to the flesh to live in relation to the flesh.**

But Paul is far from denying the possibility of this. In fact, he bluntly warns his Christian readers that **if you live in relation to the flesh you will die.** Since those who "are in relation to the flesh have their minds set on the things of the flesh" (8:5), and since the "mind-set of the flesh is death" (8:6), death will be the experience of any who *live in relation to the flesh.*

In fact Paul had already tasted a "death experience" in the days when he struggled unsuccessfully against his sinful impulses. He wrote earlier: "Now I myself was once alive without the law, but when the commandment came, sin came back to life and *I died*" (7:9, emphasis added; see discussion there). And he adds (7:11), "But sin took advantage of me through the commandment, and deceived me, and through it *killed me"* (emphasis added). Thus a kind of "spiritual death" had occurred, cutting him off from the experience of God's life.[10]

Every born again Christian understands this experience. After walking with the Lord in a spirit of harmony with Him, suddenly sin erupts and creates a sense of distance from God. The vitality of Christian experience dies then, and the new inner self (see 7:22-25) is now cut off from the vibrant experience of divine life. Such is the reality created by the dominance of the flesh, whether momentary or continuous.

By contrast, **if by** the ministry of **the Spirit** we **put to death the deeds of the body**—that is, if we cease to obey the body's desires—then we can enjoy the eternal life that God has given to us as a free gift (cf. 6:22-23). That is to say, spiritually speaking, we **will live**.[11]

The word translated **you will live** is *zēsesthe* and it recalls the word *zēsetai* in 1:17 ("Now the one who is righteous by faith *shall live*"). Precisely in the manner outlined in Rom 8:1-13, the justified person can realize, by the power of the Spirit, the life that is an integral part of the status of justification. "Justification rooted in life" (5:18) issues, therefore, from life lived by the Spirit of God.

## ii. Our spiritual triumph over suffering (8:14-39)

Paul has already indicated that Christian experience leads to a remarkable result, namely, that we exult in sufferings (5:4). This expectation stands in stark contrast with the modern church's tendency to think that Christianity results regularly in a happy and more comfortable life. But Paul knew better, as even a casual reading of 2 Cor 4:7-18 clearly shows.

Thus in the following section, Paul sets before us a splendid reality. The Christian person who is led by the Spirit can experience suffering as a grand prelude to eternal glory. As he experiences every manner of hardship, he can view himself as a "conqueror" through the Lord Jesus Christ who loved him. This is done in the certainty that nothing can separate him from this wonderful divine love.

---

[10] Cranfield, *Romans*, 1:394, has completely lost sight of context: *"mellete apothnēskein.* The periphrastic future is used to emphasize that the consequence is necessary and certain, since it is God's judgment. *Apothnēskein* is pregnant: the meaning is not merely that they will die (those who live according to the Spirit have also to die—compare v. 10), but that they will die without hope of life with God." Rather, Paul urges believers to live life. –JHN

[11] See Nygren, *Romans*, 326-27. –RNW

Paul has just concluded a section on victorious Christian living. His final statement was, "But if by the Spirit you put to death the deeds of the body, you will live" (8:13). Such an experience can obviously be described as one in which the justified person is "led by the Spirit of God." Thus the statement of 8:14 connects with that of 8:13, but it also marks a new theme: triumphant suffering.

### 8:14. In fact, as many as are led by the Spirit of God, these are God's sons.

In the preceding section, 8:1-13, Paul has expounded what it means to "walk in relation to the Spirit" as over against walking "in relation to the flesh." Clearly the life experienced in the Spirit's pathway is appropriately described as being **led by the Spirit of God**.

In the context of Romans 8, this has nothing to do with what is often described as "the leading of the Lord." That concept is essentially an appeal to some "inner direction" that is more mystical than Biblical. Here the larger context suggests a life in conformity to the revealed will of God as found in His Word. In such a life, "the righteous requirement of the law" can be "fulfilled" in the believer who walks "in relation to the Spirit" (see 8:4 and discussion there).

Strikingly, this is Paul's first use in Romans of the Greek word for *son* (*huios*) other than in reference to Jesus Christ (as in 1:3, 4, 9; 5:10; 8:3). This statement does not simply mean that those *led by the Spirit* are Christians. Neither is Paul's point to be related to some supposed proof of one's eternal salvation.

In Paul's much earlier epistle to the Galatians, he clearly distinguished between a *minor child* (*nēpios*) and a *son* (*huios*). The former is a child "not yet of legal age" (see BDAG) who is under the governance of a tutor (the law), while the latter is the "adult son" who is no longer under this tutor (see Gal 4:1-7). If the Galatians passage is compared carefully with Rom 8:14-17, their similarities will be quite obvious.

Both passages contain the words for *son* (Gal 4: 4, 6; Rom 8:14 [also vv 19, 29, 32]) and *heir* (Gal 4:1, 7; Rom 8:14, 17). Both refer to the Spirit's cry, "Abba, Father" (Gal 4:6; Rom 8:15), and both use the word *adoption* (*huiothesia*: Gal 4:5; Rom 8:15) in the technical sense of "adoption of children" (see BDAG).

In the light of Paul's teaching in Gal 4:1-7, it is natural here to take the expression *the sons of God* (*huioi Theou*) as a reference to the life-experience of the adult son who is not under the law. In contrast to the earlier struggle (described in Rom 7:7-25) in which the regenerate inner man strived vainly to fulfill God's law, now the one *led by the Spirit* lives the life of an adult son who is no longer under the law (note especially 6:14).

**8:15. For you have not received again a spirit of bondage producing fear, but you have received a spirit of adoption as sons, by means of which we cry out, "Abba, Father!"**

The underlying principle of v 14 is stated here quite clearly. The reference to *bondage* (*douleias*) is naturally taken as a reference to the law since Paul describes those under it as being in bondage (cf. Gal 4:26-27; 5:1; for the connection of this passage with Galatians, see the discussion under v 14; cf. also Acts 15:10). Thus to be under the law is to experience **a spirit of bondage**, that is, to live under coercion and not in spiritual liberty. This spirit says, "I *must* do this," rather than, "I *want* to do this."

Such bondage had the effect of **producing fear**, since disobedience to the law stood under the threat of retribution. Man's inability to keep the law resulted in him living continuously under this retributive threat. As Paul puts it in Gal 3:10, "For as many as are of the works of the law are under the curse; for it is written, 'Cursed is everyone who does not continue in all things which are written in the book of the law, to do them.'"

But those who believe in Christ have not received this *spirit of bondage*. Instead the believer has received **a spirit of adoption as sons**. The transparent implication is that such *a spirit* is not *a spirit of bondage* but *a spirit* of freedom. Or, as Paul has already put it, the believer is "not under the law but under grace" (Rom 6:14).

As is frequently true in Paul, it is difficult to decide whether I should print *a spirit of adoption* or *a Spirit of adoption*. The contrast with the phrase *the spirit of bondage* suggests the former, but the capitalized form would be equally good. Unquestionably, as this context plainly suggests (v 16), Paul has the Holy Spirit in mind as he also does in the similar passage in Gal 4:1-7.

The word *again* in the phrase **you have not received again** is of special interest here. The new life experience which the believer in Christ has begun is not just a reiteration of life under the law. Believers are not once again under that principle of living. Instead, as Paul made clear in

Rom 6:4-14, the believer has entered into "newness of life" by virtue of his union with Christ in His death, burial, and resurrection. This union, in fact, was effected by the work of the Spirit (see discussion under 6:4). The Spirit did not again place us under the law.

All of this is what is intended by the expression **a spirit of adoption**. The term rendered *adoption* (*huiothesias*) refers here (as it does also in Gal 4:5) to the status of the adult son who is no longer under the tutorial control of the law. He lives, so to speak, a "grown-up" life which, for Paul, means a life "led by the Spirit of God" (v 14). This grown up son, moved **by means of** the Spirit, is able to **cry out, "Abba, Father!"**

### 8:16. The Spirit Himself bears testimony along with our spirit that we are the children of God.

But not only does our own spirit cry out "Abba, Father!" thus testifying to our awareness **that we are the children of God** (v 15), the Holy Spirit does likewise. As Paul will shortly say, the Spirit is involved in our prayer life and personally makes intercession for us (vv 26, 27). He does this precisely because we are God's children and thus He adds His testimony to ours that God is our Father.

This verse is often misunderstood as a reference to some kind of inner (mystical) witness *to* (as opposed to *with*) our human spirit that gives us a subjective assurance that we are born again.[12] Paul knows nothing of this kind of "inner witness." This false conclusion is usually based on the English translation which sounds like it could mean that.[13] But as BDAG

---

[12] The popular view is that the Holy Spirit witnesses *to* our human spirit, rather than *along with* our spirit. Morris, *Romans*, PNTC, 316, admits that his (the common) view has grammatical difficulties: "There is a problem as to whether we should understand him to say that the Spirit bears witness 'to' our spirit or that he bears witness 'with' our spirit. The form of the verb [*summarturei*, "bear witness along with another"] might be held to favor the latter, but this is not conclusive." In a footnote Morris says why he dismisses the form of the verb as inconclusive: "*Summarturei* means strictly 'bear witness along with another,' though in usage this is weakened to 'agree' (cf. 2:15)." Morris is wrong. Compare the present commentary's note on Rom 2:16. The context of Rom 2:14-16 is a divine courtroom. In that legal setting, God will call on each defendant's conscience to testify concerning that person. The courtroom setting of 2:15 is fatal to Morris' assertion that *summartureō* weakens to *agree*. Morris himself acknowledges that the form of the word, if taken seriously, argues for seeing both the Holy Spirit and our human spirit jointly giving testimony that we are regenerate, because both know that we believed Christ's promise of everlasting life. –JHN

[13] Some commentators suggest that the *sun-* (*with*) prefix in *summartureō* does not refer in Rom 8:16 to *witness with*, but that it instead merely intensifies the meaning of the verb, thus referring to a very powerful testimony to our spirit. However, as Hodges shows, that does not

rightly points out, the meaning of the verb used here (*summartureō*) is "to provide supporting evidence by testifying, [to] confirm, support by testimony" (p. 957). Thus the Holy Spirit *supports* the testimony of our human spirit when we claim God as our heavenly Father as we cry, "Abba, Father." It is as though the Spirit said to the Father as we prayed, "This is Your child."[14]

The result of this "twofold witness" (our inner spirit and the Holy Spirit) is that in the heavenly audience room our status before God as children of His has the firmest possible claim on His divine attention. Our conviction that God will indeed listen to our prayers is thereby strengthened, even when we are unsure exactly what we should pray for (vv 26, 27).

This assurance is foundational to what Paul is now about to say. Paul is prepared now to launch into the subject of Christian suffering. In the midst of such suffering we must not doubt that God fully receives us before His throne. Christian sufferings are not an indication we have lost favor with God, or have been somehow separated from His love (see v 38). Instead they are a means by which we can "more than conquer through Him who loved us" (v 37).

**8:17. And if *we are* children, *we are* also heirs—heirs, on the one hand, of God, and on the other hand, co-heirs with Christ**

---

fit the context. In addition, Paul uses this same verb only two other times in Romans and in both cases it clearly refers to consciences which also *bear witness with* the person(s) involved (Rom 2:15; 9:1). Paul uses a number of *sun-* prefix verbs in Romans. The others refer to a mutual verbal action (cf. Rom 1:12, "encouraged together with you"; 7:16, "I agree with the law"; 8:17, "suffer together with Him"; and "glorified together with Him"). Taking Rom 8:16 as a verse about assurance of everlasting life not only misunderstands the passage entirely, but actually strips believers of assurance since they cease looking to Christ's promise only (e.g., John 5:24). Instead, they now look introspectively for some sort of mysterious feeling. Such a practice is self-defeating since our feelings cannot be objectified or trusted. –RNW

[14] Romans 9:1 may be the clincher. It is in the same book as 8:16 and the two verses have parallel grammar. Brackets enclose a minor addition to Hodges' translation: "I am telling the truth in Christ, I am not lying (my conscience bears witness along with me [bearing witness to you] in the Holy Spirit), that there is great grief for me and unceasing pain in my heart." The word *me* (*moi*) is dative, serving as the object of the prefixed preposition (underlined) on *summartaurousēs*, just as the dative, *tō pneumati*, is the object of the prefixed preposition (underlined) on *summartaurei* in 8:16. Romans 9:1 does not say that Paul's conscience testified truthfully *to himself*, but that both Paul himself and his conscience testified truthfully *to the Romans*. –JHN

**if we suffer together *with Him* so that we may also be glorified together *with Him*.**

Precisely because of our status before God as His children, we have also the status of heirs. To begin with, we are **heirs...of God**. This fact indicates that we have an inheritance by virtue of our fundamental relationship to God the Father as children. What this heirship entails is indicated in v 18ff. where Paul discusses the future manifestation of God's sons and refers to "the glorious liberty of *the children* [*tōn teknōn*] of God" (v 21, see discussion there).

The children of God are therefore destined for a "glorious liberty," which certainly includes freedom from sin, suffering, corruption, and death. The NT Scriptures testify to this ultimate freedom in many places (cf. especially, 1 Cor 15:42-58).

But in the text before us, Paul has *two forms of heirship* in mind. This double heirship is clearly signaled by the *men...de* construction that we have rendered **on the one hand...on the other hand**. Not only are God's children *heirs of God*, but they may also become **co-heirs with Christ** on the condition that they "co-suffer" with Him.[15]

According to OT inheritance law, the firstborn son in a family normally received twice as much as the other sons (Deut 21:17). It should not be assumed that Paul is working outside of this OT conception of heirship. In fact, a few verses further on he actually describes the Lord Jesus Christ as "the Firstborn among many brethren" (v 29).[16] To be

---

[15] Commentators who agree that co-heirship with Christ is conditioned on suffering with Christ and/or who punctuate the text the way Hodges does include James Denney, "St. Paul's Epistle to the Romans," in *Expositor's Greek Testament*, ed. W. Robertson Nicoll (1897–1910; reprint, Grand Rapids: Eerdmans, N.D.), 2:648; Ernst Käsemann, *Commentary on Romans*, trans. Geoffrey W. Bromiley (Grand Rapids, MI: Eerdmans, 1980), 229; William R. Newell, *Romans: Verse by Verse* (Chicago, IL: Moody, 1938), 317-18; Eric Sauer, *In the Arena of Faith* (Grand Rapids, MI: Eerdmans, 1966), 163; Sanday and Headlam, *Romans*, p. 204; Wilbur Smith, *The Biblical Doctrine of Heaven* (Chicago, IL: Moody, 1968), 193; James D. G. Dunn, *Romans*, 2 vols., WBC (Dallas, TX: Word, 1988), 1:456; Joseph A. Fitzmyer, *Romans: A New Translation with Introduction and Commentary*, Anchor Bible (New York, NY: Doubleday, 1993), 502; and possibly Henry Barclay Sweet, *The Holy Spirit in the New Testament* (N.P.: Macmillan, 1910; reprint, Grand Rapids, MI: Baker, 1964), 219. –JHN

[16] Verse 29 portrays Jesus Christ as the firstborn among many brethren. The firstborn's inheritance is twice that of the other sons. This is a huge clue that co-heirship with Christ is something special—involving special inheritance rights not shared by all believers. All children of God enjoy the basic inheritance as heirs of God, but those sons who suffer with Christ enjoy a co-heirship with God's firstborn Son (Jesus Christ). The relevant literature fails to link vv 17

*co-heirs with Christ* is to be *co-heirs with* the Firstborn. A special kind of heirship is implicit here against the backdrop of OT familial inheritance. In the Christian family there are both children (*heirs of God*) and also a Firstborn Son. The former are all heirs of God, but the inheritance of the Firstborn can be shared as well (*co-heirs with Christ*).[17]

This second heirship—co-heirship with Christ—is predicated on "co-suffering" that leads to "co-glorification." Paul's Greek text emphasizes the "co-" element by a repeated use of words with the *sun*-prefix.[18] Thus Paul speaks of our being co-heirs (*sugklēronomoi*) who "co-suffer" (*sumpaschomen*) and who then can expect to be "co-glorified" (*sundoxasthōmen*).[19] The word *if* (*eiper*) indicates the conditional nature of this statement. It is false grammar to say that the "if" clause treats this as a definite fact. The construction means no more than the expression "on the assumption that" and leaves fully open the opposite possibility.

It is this last aspect of our heirship that leads Paul directly into the theme of suffering which will occupy him until the end of the chapter (8:39). At this point Paul begins to elaborate on the statement made at the conclusion of the unit 3:21–5:11 affirming that even beyond our justified standing before God (5:1-2), we can "also exult in afflictions, knowing that affliction produces endurance; and endurance, character; and character, a *sure hope* (*elpida*)" (5:3-4).

Here in this verse, then, *co-heirship* is the "sure hope" that suffering in fellowship *with Christ* can bring.[20]

---

and 29. –JHN

[17] See G. H. Lang, *Firstborn Sons: Their Rights & Risks* (London: Roberts, 1936; reprint, Miami Springs, FL: Conley & Schoettle, 1984), 123; George N. H. Peters, *The Theocratic Kingdom*, 3 vols. (New York, NY: Funk & Wagnalls, 1884; reprint, Grand Rapids, MI: Kregel, 1952), 1:570. –JHN

[18] See notes 12 and 13. –RNW

[19] *Sun* is a Greek preposition typically translated *with*. When it serves as a prefix, the *n* will often change in relation to the letter that starts the word. For example, *sun + martureō* becomes *summartureō*, not *sunmartureō*; *sun + kleronomoi* becomes *sunklēronomoi*; *sun- + paschomen* becomes *sumpaschomen*. –RNW

[20] Hodges in essence lays out v 17 as a chiasm:

    A  if children,
        B  then heirs of God
            C  on the one hand,
            C′  and on the other hand
        B′  co-heirs with Christ,
    A′  if we suffer with Christ.

When set forth in this way, the two heirships leap off the page. Unfortunately, much of the

The mention of the suffering/glory motif in v 17 turns Paul's discussion toward the intrinsic relationship between these two things in the experience of God's children/sons. It also leads him to the natural now/then correlation which those two themes suggest. Suffering is a *present* experience, while glory is a *future* one.

**8:18. Now I consider that the sufferings of the present time *are* not worthy to be compared with the glory that is going to be revealed for us.**

In Paul's Greek text the word *gar* (**now**, in second position in the Greek sentence) connects Paul's thought with the preceding statement (v 17). But the usual translation "for" would be misleading since the connection is not causal. Instead, the particle's use here fits under BDAG's extended definition: "marker of clarification: *for, you see*," under which there is the comment, "in many instances *gar* appears to be used adverbially like our 'now'…'well, then,' 'you see'" (p. 189).

Having raised the suffering/glory theme in v 17, Paul now wishes to underline the huge disparity between the two kinds of experiences. Although our **sufferings** in **the present time** so often seem dreadful and nearly unbearable, they are dwarfed by the superlative greatness of the glory to which they lead. So much is this the case that our sufferings cannot stand any real comparison with **the glory that is going to be revealed for us**.

The Greek words rendered here by *for us* (*eis hēmas*) have been understood in different ways. The familiar KJV translation, "in us," is followed by NKJV, NIV, and NACE. The NASB translates them "to us." In my judgment, however, JB captures the sense best with its quasi-paraphrase, "…can never be compared to the glory, as yet unrevealed, *which is waiting for us*" (italics added).

Since Paul has spoken of co-glorification in v 17, he is not likely to mean here that the glory is simply revealed *to* us. And while "in us" makes acceptable sense, this idea would more likely have been conveyed in Greek by *en hēmin*. The Greek phrase here (*eis hēmas*) is more naturally taken in the sense of **for us**. (BDAG observes that, "As in Modern Greek, it is used for the dative, especially, the dative of advantage, but also = *for* in general" [p. 290].)

---

literature seems oblivious to what Paul is saying here. –JHN

Paul's point is that the glory God has prepared *for us* far exceeds in worth and value the temporary deprivations that sufferings entail. The principle is the same one he states in 2 Cor 4:17: "For our light affliction, which is but for a moment, is working for us a far more exceeding and eternal weight of glory." This glory will be revealed when Christ Himself is revealed (see Col 3:4).

But as the following context (vv 19-32) discloses, Paul is not simply thinking of the glorification of the individual person, but rather of his participation in the glorious transformation *of the entire creation.* This glorious transformation, Paul will say, is something that will occur for our benefit (v 32).

**8:19-21. For what is eagerly desired by the creation waits for the revelation of the sons of God (since the creation has been made subject to futility, not willingly, but because of Him who subjected *it to this* in hope), because the creation itself also will be released from bondage to corruption into the liberty of the glory of the children of God.**

It is a measure of the greatness of "the glory that is going to be revealed *for us*" (v 18) that it entails nothing less than the liberation of the whole creation. To make this significant point, Paul employs a personification of nature that presents nature as yearning for its ultimate release from corruption.

The words **what is eagerly desired** translate the Greek noun *apokaradokia* (eager expectation). It is as though the creation, because of the very presence of corruption and death, expresses an intense longing by nature to attain release from these things. Anyone who has ever been deeply moved by the beauty of God's creation has surely felt that such beauty did not exist simply to perish. Nature cries out inarticulately, so to speak, for a better destiny.

But such a release can only come when there is a **revelation of the sons of God**. That is to say, the creation cannot find its freedom until God's sons have been manifested. In the words *the sons of God* Paul picks up the terminology of 8:14, 15 where this phrase is linked with the expression "adoption as sons" (*huiothesias*, see discussion under v 15). The adult status possessed by all believers, and experienced as they are "led by the Spirit" (see discussion under v 14), will be on full and glorious display at the coming of Christ, and that display will result in the liberation of **creation itself** from its **bondage to corruption**.

Verse 20 is best treated as a parenthetical comment, and v 21, with its initial *because (hoti)*, picks up the link with v 19. Verse 19 asserts that the creation desires something that awaits *the revelation of the sons of God*, while v 20 explains exactly what the creation stands in need of.

The creation, in fact, has been subjected **to futility**. This latter word renders the Greek noun *mataiotēs*. BDAG (p. 621) defines it as "state of being without use or value, *emptiness, futility, purposelessness, transitoriness*," and translates Rom 8:20 by "*the creation was subjected to frustration*." BDAG thus nicely signals the broad implications of Paul's word. The hollowness and vacuity of so splendid a creation suffering unremitting deterioration is the idea Paul has in mind.

Moreover the futility to which the creation has been subjected was not due to any act of the will on its part (continuing Paul's figure of speech). Rather the creation was subjected to this *unwillingly* (**not willingly**) as a result of man's fall in Eden (see Gen 3:17-19). This subjection to futility was an act of God (**because of Him**) Who did this with special reference to man's hope for the future (**in hope**).

By the words *in hope (ep' elpidi)* Paul probably has in mind the fact that the fallen state of nature was designed to stimulate in mankind a desire for the better world of the future. (BDAG places the *ep[i]* of Rom 8:20 under the meaning category of "marker of basis for a state of being, action, or result" [p. 364].) Man was to live in this fallen world grounded *in hope*.

Indeed, just as God offered hope to mankind in general (Gen 3:15), so also that hope, by implication, was extended to the creation that Satan's triumph had damaged. The Serpent's head was to be "crushed" (Gen 3:15, NIV, JB), with all that this prophecy implied. The later prophets also spoke of this hope (Isa 11:6-9; 65:25; Hos 2:18) as part of Israel's expectation when her kingdom was established by Messiah.

Having specifically articulated the dire condition of nature (in v 20), Paul returns to the point stated in v 19, namely, **the creation waits for** God's sons to be manifested. The reason it does so is indicated by the clause introduced by **because** *(hoti)*. It waits precisely because when *the revelation of the sons of God* takes place, then **the creation itself will be released from bondage to corruption**. That is to say, corruption and death will be completely removed from the natural world. Nature will no longer be in bondage to these things.

This deliverance will allow creation to share **the liberty of the glory of the children of God**. As a result of their being "heirs of God" (8:17), these children will at that time have fully entered into the privilege of their "adoption as sons" (8:15). They will be totally free from all the effects of sin, corruption and death.[21] This, of course, is exactly what it means to be resurrected (or, "transformed" at the Rapture). The new body will be a body of glory (cf. 1 Cor 15:43), fully at liberty from all sin-related bondage. Such is the glorious heirship of every "child" of God whether or not he attains to co-heirship with Jesus Christ (8:17). Into that kind of liberty, *the creation* also will come.

> **8:22-23. Now we know that the whole creation groans together and suffers labor pains together right up until now. And not only *the creation*, but also we who have the first fruits of the Spirit—even we ourselves groan within ourselves as we wait for *our* adoption as sons, *namely*, the redemption of our body.**

In his vivid personification of nature, Paul now describes **the whole creation** as racked with severe pain. Only in this verse the image suggests a woman's anguish as she is in the process of giving birth. The creation not only **groans together** (*sustenazei* from *sun-* and *stenazō*) but also **suffers labor pains together** (*sunōdinei*). Both Greek verbs are compounds in which the *sun-* prefix is used and both verbs therefore suggest the idea of "in unison." In unison, the entire created natural order (*pasa hē ktisis*) is undergoing agonies that look toward a new age (that is to say, the realization of the "hope" Paul has already referred to [v 19]).

In the expression **right up until now** (*achri tou nun*) Paul has in mind the long history of creation's travail that has lasted since the fall of man *right up until* the present time (*tou nun*). Yet in its long-extended, sorrowful "bondage to corruption," creation itself is now joined by those in whose lives the Holy Spirit has been at work.

---

[21] Hodges' point here is that though believers have everlasting life, we still experience many grievous effects from the fall, including the deterioration of our own bodies culminating in our own deaths (unless the Rapture occurs first), the physical deaths of our friends and loved ones, the corruption of our world and universe, and the wickedness that exists in our world. We are not yet free from such things. But we shall soon be. –RNW

Thus Paul proceeds to affirm that it is **not only *the creation*** that groans, but that **also we who have the first fruits of the Spirit** do the same. In the words *the first fruits of the Spirit* we meet an expression that has been variously interpreted. It has been understood in the sense of *the first fruits which are the Spirit.* That is grammatically possible, but not likely in this context.

The previous discussion found in 8:1-13, immediately preceding the unit to which v 23 belongs (that is, 8:14-38), gives us exactly the work of God's Spirit that suggests the image of *first fruits* used here. The Greek word *aparchē (first fruits)* is used only eight times in the NT, six times by Paul, three of them in Romans. It has no apparent fixed meaning in Paul's usage.

In 1 Cor 15:20, 23 it is used of Christ as the *first fruits* of the resurrection. In 1 Cor 16:15 and Rom 16:5 *aparchē* is used of some of the first converts in Achaia. In Rom 11:16 it is used in a statement of principle (see discussion there). Thus the usage here is unique for Paul and the present context must guide us.

Paul has already spoken of a spiritual resurrection of our bodies that is accomplished by the power of *the Spirit* (8:11) and which empowers us to live in newness of life (8:12-13; see 6:4). Yet such resurrection life is never perfectly realized in our "mortal bodies" (8:11) and awaits a total fulfillment. That will come when we are resurrected/transformed into our future bodies to enjoy "the liberty of the glory of the children of God" (8:21). That is to say, it awaits what Paul in this verse calls **the redemption of our body**.

The result of experiencing this kind of *first fruits of the Spirit* is to produce an intense desire for its full realization in the future. Consequently, *we who have the first fruits of the Spirit,* and therefore walk in newness of life, do indeed **groan within ourselves** (*en heautois stenazomen*)[22] precisely because we long for the complete realization of ***our* adoption as sons** (see 8:15)—namely, *the redemption of* this present mortal body.

---

[22] The verb *stenazō* (*I groan*) only occurs six times in the NT. Three of the six uses are in Paul: Rom 8:23 (v 22 has the related verb *sustenazō*); 2 Cor 5:2, 4. The two usages in 2 Corinthians 5 are identical in sense to the usage in Romans 8. Our deteriorating bodies should cause us to groan for the glorified bodies and the righteous kingdom which is to come. The other three NT uses (Mark 7:34; Heb 13:17; Jas 5:9) have different senses (sighing, grief, and grumbling, respectively). –RNW

In other words, we long for complete victory over all sin. Our spiritual resurrection is therefore *the first fruits* of our physical one.

In the language of the harvest, we have tasted *the first fruits* (and they are wonderful) and we eagerly wait for the entire harvest—the full realization of our status as sons.

**8:24-25. For we have been delivered in hope, but hope which is seen is not hope, since why does anyone also hope for what he sees? But if we hope for what we do not see, we wait *for it* with endurance.**

Paul now returns to a fundamental theme of Romans with the words, **we have been delivered in hope**. Once again he uses the word *sōzō* ("to save, deliver") which is a pivotal term for him in this epistle. As we have seen, the cognate words *sōzō/sotēria* have been employed in the thematic statement of 1:17 (*sotēria*) and again in 5:9, 10 (*sōzō*), but nowhere in the material from 1:18 to 5:8. That includes the whole discussion of justification by faith in 3:21–4:25, from which the idea of "deliverance" is absent.

In Pauline thought, "justification" is not to be directly identified with the "saving" (= "delivering") experience and never serves as a substitute for the word "saved." This is true throughout his epistles. Instead, spiritual "salvation" for Paul meant to have, receive, or experience eternal life (see, e.g., 1 Tim 1:15-16; 2 Tim 1:9-10). In Romans, "justification" is presented as distinguishable from "life," although intimately connected with it. Thus the thematic statement of 1:17 preserves this fundamental Pauline distinction: "Now the one who is righteous by faith shall live." In other words, it is the *justified* person who *lives*.

Accordingly, in 5:9-10, justification is presented as a fact that is *related to* the experience of being delivered, but clearly not *identical with* it (see discussion there). Furthermore, in those verses, to be "delivered from wrath through Him [Christ]" (5:9) means to be "delivered by His [Christ's] *life*" (5:10). Or, as Paul puts it shortly afterward, it means to "walk in newness of life" by virtue of our union with Him in His death, burial, and resurrection (6:4).

Now it is precisely this experience of walking in newness of life that Paul has expounded in Rom 8:1-13. Those who so walk, "walk in relation to the Spirit" (8:1, 4), experience the Spirit's quickening of their "mortal bodies" (8:10-11) and thus "by the Spirit" they "put to death the deeds of the body" (8:13). Paul says, if you do that, "*you will live*" (8:13). It is precisely in this way, therefore, that "the one who is righteous by faith *shall live*" (1:17).

This then is the "deliverance" Paul has in mind in the context of our verse. The present "spiritual resurrection" of our bodies by the power of the indwelling Spirit is, by its very nature, a "first fruits" of our final resurrection and of our entrance into the unhindered experience of eternal life forever and ever. It is quite natural that "we who have the first fruits of the Spirit" should long for its full, eternal realization. And that is what Paul meant when he wrote that "we ourselves groan within ourselves as we wait for *our* adoption as sons, *namely*, the redemption of our body" (v 23).[23]

Thus *we have been delivered in hope*, since the very experience of the Spirit's power in our mortal bodies accentuates and deepens our longing and expectation (hope) for the *full* experience (that is, "the redemption of our body"). In fact, the statements in these verses apply basically to "*we* who have the first fruits of the Spirit" (v 23) and not necessarily to all believers without distinction. If a believer has not experienced the "deliverance" Paul is talking about, the statements are not directed at him. Paul, of course, is among the "we" who have experienced it. And those who share this experience with him, share also the arousing of this hope.

But this is hope and not reality as yet. However wonderful our present experience of the Spirit's "delivering" power may be, it does not fulfill our ultimate longing which is for a *perfect deliverance*. This "deliverance" **we do not see** yet, for if we did see it, it would no longer be hope. On the contrary, **hope which is seen** (that is, realized) **is** no longer a hope, but a reality. So why, if the hope is realized, should **anyone also hope for** it still?

Thus we find ourselves in the same condition as the creation around us, longing for the realization of our hope for complete deliverance (v 23). This is an important point in Paul's discussion. Both we and the creation share the experience of suffering in "the present time" (v 18), and we and the creation share the hope to which this suffering points, that is, full liberty from corruption and death (v 21).

Since this hope is not yet a reality, either for the creation or for ourselves, the groanings of both it and ourselves express our mutual longing and expectation. And when *our* hope is realized, so will also be

---

[23] See previous note. –RNW

realized the hope of creation itself (v 19). Paul thus carefully intertwines our experience with that of the natural world around us. He will draw upon this intimate connection in v 28.

In the meantime, as **we hope for what we do not see**, we should do so **with endurance**. With the mention of the word *endurance* (*hupomonēs*), Paul will now turn to the intensely practical issue of how we bear up under our sufferings as **we wait** for the ultimate glorious reality which inspires our hope.

By resurfacing the concept of *endurance* here, Paul is returning to the themes he had mentioned in the final paragraph (5:1-11) of the larger unit on justification by faith (3:21–5:11). In that paragraph, he had anticipated his later discussion of suffering (see 5:3-5). By way of anticipation, he had presented "afflictions" as a grounds for joy since "affliction produces endurance [*hupomonēn*]" (5:3), which in turn produces "hope" that "does not result in shame" (5:4-5).

Paul is now ready to elaborate further on the seminal ideas found in 5:3-5.

How then can we endure sufferings? Paul addresses this in 8:26-32. His answer is twofold. We can do so (1) by means of Spirit-assisted prayer (8:26-27), and (2) by keeping our focus on the outworking of God's purpose which can bring us to co-heirship with Christ (8:28-32).

> **8:26-27. But likewise also the Spirit gives us help in our weaknesses. For we do not know what to pray for as it is necessary *to do*, but with *our* inarticulate groanings the Spirit Himself makes intercession on our behalf. And the One who searches the hearts knows what the aspiration of the Spirit is, because He makes intercession on behalf of the saints in harmony with God.**

Paul now very deftly transitions to the theme of how to bear up under suffering. The initial Greek words of v 26 are *Hōsautōs de kai* (**But likewise also**). Although it is true that our sufferings cannot be compared with the coming glory (8:18), still we are weak and groan even in the midst of Christian victory (v 23). Thus we urgently need divine **help in our weaknesses**. And this is precisely what we receive through the indwelling Spirit, who *likewise also* (in addition to producing His first fruits within us [v 23]) gives us this help.

In fact, *our weaknesses* are manifest precisely in our times of prayer when, under the pressures of suffering, we try to make intelligent requests from God. But we have no real ability to assess any stressful situation we are in and to know precisely what it is really necessary for us **to pray for** at such times. Into this gap, Paul assures us, comes the intercessory work of **the Spirit** who dwells within us.

Consequently, in the midst of our own **inarticulate groanings, the Spirit Himself makes intercession** for us. Although some commentators have thought that the *groanings* (*stenagmois*) referred to here are those of *the Spirit*, this seems quite improbable.[24] The preceding context speaks clearly of our own groanings (*stenazomen*, v 23) and the reference is surely to that. When our own inability to know how to pray in the necessary way results in inarticulate (*alalētois*) expressions of anguish and concern, the Spirit intervenes. He prays the requests we ourselves do not know to pray.

Naturally, we do not know what the Spirit is praying for since, if we did, we ourselves could also pray for that. But, says Paul, we don't need to know, because God knows. **The One who** alone searches all human hearts, searches ours at such times and knows therefore what His Spirit within us desires (His aspiration). The Greek expression that is rendered here by **the aspiration of the Spirit** is *to phronēma tou Pneumatos* and is not a new one. This is precisely the phrase that Paul also employs in 8:6 in the statement "but the mind-set of the Spirit is life and peace" (*to de phronēma tou Pneumatos zōē kai eirēnē*). The Greek noun *phronēma*, though translated differently in 8:6, nevertheless has much the same sense in that verse and here. The realization of the Spirit's "mind-set" is after all a realization of His aspiration for us. In Christian living (8:6) He desires us to experience "life and peace." There is no reason to doubt that the aims of His intercessory work for us are exactly those things. In fact, when suffering is borne "with endurance" (8:25), it enhances our experience of "life and peace."

---

[24] The major translations suggest that it is the Holy Spirit who is groaning, not believers (e.g., KJV, NKJV, NASB, ESV, NIV, NET). As pointed out above in note 22, all of the Pauline uses of the verb *stenazō* deal with believers. None of them refer to the Spirit groaning. Indeed, the three non-Pauline uses all refer to people, not the Spirit, as well (see note 22). Certainly the addition of the word *inarticulate* shows this must be people, since it would be impossible for the Spirit to be unable to find the right words to express what He was thinking or feeling. –RNW

Thus suffering is also a way in which "the one who is righteous by faith" can "live" (cf. 1:17) as a result of the Spirit's ministry within our hearts.

That the intercession of the Spirit is unquestionably effective on our behalf is declared in the words **because He makes intercession on behalf of the saints in harmony with God**. This statement contains the first reference to believers as saints in Romans since 1:7. But it is most suitable here since both the presence of, and the intercession by, *the Spirit* within us clearly mark us out as those who have been set apart to God. God already knows the desires of *the Spirit* for us, Paul is saying, because those desires are basically His own as well (cf. Matt 6:8).

Thus the Spirit's prayers on our behalf are in complete conformity to what is pleasing to God. They are *in harmony with* God's mind for us. (Literally, they are *kata Theon*, "according to God.") Naturally this is what we would expect, assuming we have a clear theology of the Spirit, but Paul is a pastor at heart and any reassurance of this fact is always appropriate for suffering believers. In the Holy Spirit we have the ideal Intercessor in time of testing precisely because He and **the One who searches the hearts** are united in their aspiration for the saints.

> **8:28. Now we know that all things work together with those who love God to *produce* good, *that is*, together with those who are called in harmony with *His* purpose.**

There is also a second basis for our ability to endure sufferings and this is found in the purpose of God. Whatever we might go through, we have the assurance that this is a part of *His* **purpose**.

However, this famous Pauline statement has been misunderstood. The usual reading of the verse partakes heavily of the natural inclination in modern Christianity to think of Christian experience in an overly individualized (self-centered) way. Thus it is usually thought to express the idea that all events in our personal lives (or at least, all negative events) actually produce good results. But this well-known understanding of the verse is in part the result of an inadequate English translation.

It is important to re-examine and reconsider what Paul's claim here actually means. To do this we must look especially at the meaning of **all things** (*panta*) and **work together with** (*sunergei*).

(1) *All things* (*panta*). As just observed, the traditional understanding of Rom 8:28 takes *panta* in some vague general sense like "all events"

or "all sufferings." It is hardly clear which is meant. This very vagueness should raise exegetical doubts.

Moreover, this view ignores the larger context which is discussing *all things* in the sense of the entire creation (vv 19-23). We should especially note the phrase *pasa hē ktisis* ("the whole creation," "all the creation") in v 22. In general Greek usage, the neuter form *panta* (with or without the article) stood often for the totality of existing things.

This use is especially plain in Heb 2:8-10. There the statement of Psalm 2 is quoted, "You [God] have put all things [*panta*] under His [Christ's] feet" (2:8a). This reference to the entire creation is then picked up in vv 8b-10, where the articular form *ta panta* is used in v 8b (twice) and v 10 (twice) in subsequent references to the *panta* in 8a. Likewise, in the present passage, the *panta* in this verse is followed shortly by *ta panta* in v 32. The article in *ta panta* (v 32) is natural as an article of previous reference, that is, it refers to *panta* in this verse.

Moreover, the sense I am suggesting here occurs again in the following unit, 9:1–11:36 (note *epi pantōn*, 9:5, and *ta panta*, 11:36).[25] This well-established usage is easily the most suitable in context and should be accepted here and in v 32. Paul's text is much more than a vague statement that "everything will turn out all right."

From Paul's perspective, as we suffer, our groanings are part of the larger travail of "the whole creation" (*pasa hē ktisis*) which "groans together and suffers labor pains together right up until now" (v 22). But this groaning and this travail of the whole creation are in symphony with our own, since not only does the creation do it, "but also we who have the first fruits of the Spirit" do it too (v 23). The creation is waiting as we are for the "birth" of the new age which will bring freedom from corruption both to us and to the natural world (v 21). This freedom from sin and death, of course, is the ultimate good.

In this experience, *all things* (*panta*) *work together with* our own experience toward the same splendid goal, the age to come. Both creation's groanings and ours are "labor pains" (v 22) that occur together and are full of "hope" (vv 20, 24-25). This shared experience is goal-oriented toward the good of the age to come.

(2) *Work together with* (*sunergei*). The verb *sunergeō* occurs only five times in the NT, three in Paul counting the one here. In all four of the

---

[25] See BDAG, 783 1dβ and p. 784 4dβ for the lexical information. –RNW

other cases the idea is cooperative or coordinated activity that is done with someone or something. Accordingly, BDAG (p. 969) defines the verb: "to engage in cooperative endeavor, *work together with, assist, help.*"[26]

Thus in 1 Cor 16:16, following the phrase *panti tō sunergounti* ("everyone who works with"), an "us" [NKJV] or a "you" is implied [JB = "them"]. In 2 Cor 6:1, after *Sunergountes* ("working together with"), "either *theō*...or *humin*...can be supplied" [BDAG, p. 969], or the third person singular pronoun, "Him" [NKJV]. In the famous faith/works discussion in Jas 2:22, we meet the statement *hē pistis sungergei tois ergois autou* ("faith cooperated with his works"). In Mark 16:20 an implied "them" [NKJV] is entailed by the participial phrase *tou Kuriou sunergountos* ("the Lord working with" [them]).

In my text the dative phrase *tois agapōsi ton Theon* (**those who love God**) is thrown forward for emphasis and expresses the direct object of *sunergei* (this *sun-* compound takes the dative of direct object). The familiar English preposition "for" ("work together...*for* those who love God") is not really suggested by the Greek construction.

The meaning will be that *all things* (i.e., *panta*, "all creation") *work* harmoniously *together with those who love God* **to *produce*** the **good** (*eis agathon*) that lies ahead in the age to come. Another way of putting this idea is that when we suffer as Christians we participate in God's larger goal of preparing for the day when God's children are manifested (vv 19-21). The sufferings and groanings of the creation itself are part of one and the same total experience with our own sufferings. *That is*, they work *together with* ours to "give birth" (note, *sunōdinei*, v 22) to the new world. We and the creation are going through "labor pains" *together*.

Paul has thus succeeded in placing our individual and personal sufferings on a cosmic level. They are no longer to be thought of as merely "my personal troubles" but rather as a part of God's glorious purpose for creation and for His "sons" whose "glory" is about to be revealed (v 18-19). True Christian suffering is therefore an intrinsic part of a cosmic drama that is currently unfolding. In this cosmic drama, sufferings—both ours and creation's—are preparing the way for the advent of the age to come. They *work together* to that end. To understand them that way is to find strength to endure them.

---

[26] The English word *synergy* comes from this word. –RNW

Yet it must be noted that the emphatic position (in Greek) of the words *those who love God* highlights the basic condition for this statement to be a reality. There are many sufferings that Christians bring on themselves as a consequence of their sinfulness, and Paul is not talking about these.[27] He is talking rather about the sufferings of those "who have the first fruits of the Spirit" (v 23) and are thus being led as grown-up sons by the Spirit of God (vv 14-15). With *those* Christians all creation (*panta*) "cooperates" toward the ultimate goal of final deliverance and victory.

In short, *those who love God* share deeply in God's cosmic plan. They do so precisely because they may also be described as **those who are called in harmony with** *His purpose*. Especially to be noted is the phrase *in harmony with His purpose (kata prothesin)*.

Here again we must resist the temptation to individualize Paul's thought. In the immediate context, God's purpose is clearly seen to be the release of *all things (panta)* from bondage to corruption at the same time as this release is manifested in the sons of God. As v 19 affirms, "the creation waits for the revelation of the sons of God" so it can share in "the liberty of the glory" of God's "children" (v 21). God's purpose is that both God's children, and the created order, should experience this splendid freedom. The sufferings that both endure are focused in that direction.

But what exactly does it mean to be *those who are called in harmony with* that splendid *purpose*? The following two verses make this clear.

> **8:29-30. Because those whom He knew in advance He also predetermined to share the likeness of His Son, so that He might be the Firstborn among many brothers. And whom He predetermined, these He also called, and whom He called, these He also justified, and whom He justified, these He also glorified.**

In a beautiful statement about God's eternal goal for believers in Christ, Paul gives us the reason (*because, Hoti*) why the statement of v 28 is true. In the suffering we now endure, "all things" (*panta*) suffer along with us on the trajectory that leads to eternal "good" (v 28a). We who

---

[27] Hodges' view is that the words *those who love God* do not refer to all believers as is commonly taught. They refer to believers who currently love God and hence willingly suffer for Him. *All things*, that is, all of creation, work together with believers who love God to produce the good which is the coming righteous kingdom (along with the redemption of our bodies and of all of creation). –RNW

"love God," yet suffer, are "those who are called in harmony with" God's eternal "purpose" (v 28b). This "calling" is the *reason why* our sufferings lead to what is "good."

That "calling," however, was preceded by God's foreknowledge and His predetermining will. Thus in the chain laid out in these verses, the "calling" stands *precisely in the middle* of the series (third of five). So we have these elements: [God] (1) **knew in advance**, (2) **predetermined**, (3) **called**, (4) **justified**, (5) **glorified**. Each of these five elements requires our attention.

(1) *Knew in advance.* Individual Christians in no way catch God by surprise when they become believers. In fact, God knew such believers far in advance of their exercise of faith. Much ink has been spilled on trying to solve the question of whether the Greek word here (*proegnō*) refers to simple prescience (foresight) or whether it implies more than that.

It is certainly true that the verb can signal simple foresight, as is indicated by its use in 2 Pet 3:17. This fact is acknowledged by BDAG (p. 866) in their first meaning category, "to know beforehand or in advance," for which Peter's text is cited along with extra-biblical references. But their second category is "choose beforehand," where they place Rom 8:29 and 11:2. In 11:2, at least, a reference to mere foresight would almost make the statement pointless (see discussion there). In 11:2, the idea is obviously that God was, so to speak, in a personal relationship with His people (Israel) before they even existed. He "knew" them as if they already existed. If the word "choose" is not precisely expressed (despite BDAG), it is not unfair to say that it is implied in 11:2.

It seems likely in a text where divine purpose and activity are in the forefront, as they are here, that the meaning of *proegnō* is similar to that of 11:2. Of course, this does not solve the question of *how* or *why* God knew us *in advance.* But to eliminate any element of divine choice from the word *proegnō*, as used here, seems contrived and forced. The context certainly does not suggest that this whole grand design by God depended ultimately on what He knew ahead of time that we would do. To say that God is not the Originator of the entire process given here, is to diminish the dignity Paul obviously attaches to the whole sequence of statements.

This conclusion is completely harmonious with Paul's way of thinking as is indicated by 2 Tim 1:9: "[God] saved us and called us with a holy calling, not according to our works, but *according to His own purpose and grace which was given us in Christ Jesus before time began.*" There is clearly nothing here about God's purpose depending on His foreknowledge of our faith. It is God's "purpose and grace" that are determinative.

(2) *Predetermined.* On the basis of His pre-temporal relationship with us (**those whom He** *knew in advance*), God predetermined (*proōrise*) that those so known should **share the likeness of His Son.** This "predestination," however, is not simply for our sakes (as beneficial to us as it is) but is preeminently for the sake of His Son. God did it so that Jesus Christ **might be the Firstborn among many brothers.**

It should be observed, however, that what is expressed by the term *predetermined* is not a "predestination" to eternal salvation per se, but rather to its superlative result—likeness to God's Son. The thought of an eternal relationship to God is clearly present in the preceding statement about *those whom He knew in advance.* But to be eternally saved does not necessarily suggest likeness to the Son of God. Thus the statement here about what God predetermined goes beyond the concept of being eternally saved.

The eternal purpose (*prothesin*) of God (referred to in 8:28) has always had Jesus Christ at its center. This truth need not be made explicit here since Paul could assume that the Christians in Rome knew it quite well. Paul could surely take for granted that his readers possessed a recognition of this divine goal. As he stated in Eph 1:9-10, God has "made known to us the mystery of His will, according to His good pleasure which He purposed (*proethetō*) in Him [in context: 'in Christ'] for the stewardship of the fullness of the times, *that is*, to head up all created things (*ta panta*) in Christ—things in heaven and things on earth—in Him." This deeply significant statement embodies the perspective Paul also has here in Romans as regards God's purpose for "all things."

Thus to refer to Jesus Christ as **the Firstborn** is to declare His heirship of all things [*panta*, v 28] in accordance with the divine purpose [*prothesin*, v 28] being discussed in this passage. We should not take this title as though Paul simply meant it in the sense of **so that He might be** *the eldest of* **many brothers.** That, though true, would be to interpret here independently of the larger context and to sharply diminish the real force of Paul's statement. Jesus Christ is *the Firstborn* in the sense that He is the *Preeminent Heir* among [*en,* "in the midst of"] *many brothers* who are also heirs (see v 17).

Our destiny that God has predetermined for us is to share the likeness of this Firstborn Heir. But as we noted under v 17, in the OT the firstborn son inherited twice as much as the rest of the sons. Since all the children of God are "heirs of God" (see v 17), they have heirship as a facet of this future likeness. But as v 17 also declares, *co-heirship* is also a possibility since if we *co-suffer* with Him we shall also be *co-glorified* with Him (see discussion under v 17).

In Romans 8 *to share the likeness of His Son* is not simply to be morally and spiritually like Him, marvelous beyond words though that is. But in this passage (8:17-30), the preeminent emphasis lies on our sharing His *destiny* as the Heir of all things (*panta*) which are headed toward full deliverance from all corruption (cf. Heb 1:2: "whom He has appointed heir of all things"). The real role of vv 29-30 in Paul's larger discussion is only properly perceived if we understand the centrality of Jesus Christ in God's eternal purpose for creation.

(3) *Called.* It is precisely this middle term in Paul's series of divine actions that connects directly with v 28. According to v 28, those with whom "all things" are cooperating toward eternal "good" are those who have been "*called* in harmony with *His* purpose." It is now clear, by means of v 29, that this "calling" was preceded by God's pre-knowledge of us and by His pre-determination of our destiny to *share the likeness of* Jesus Christ.

In Pauline doctrine, to be "called" is not merely to be "invited" (though *kaleō* can certainly mean "to request the presence of someone at a social gathering" [BDAG, p. 503]). Rather, as BDAG states (p. 503), "from the meanings 'summon' and 'invite' there develops the extended sense *choose for receipt of a special benefit or experience, call.*" It is this sense that predominates in Paul's usage of the cognate words *kaleō*, *klēsis* ("calling"), and *klētos* ("called"). Note for *kaleō*, among other texts, 1 Cor 7:15, 17, 18, 20; Eph 4:1; 1 Thess 2:12; 4:7; 5:24; 2 Tim 1:9. For *klēsis* note Rom 11:29; 1 Cor 1:26; Eph 4:1; 2 Thess 1:11. And for *klētos* see Rom 1:6, 7; 1 Cor 1:2, 24.

Theologians sometimes refer to this kind of "call" as an "effectual call," and that is certainly necessitated by this verse. In Paul's series here *called* cannot refer to the general, universal invitation to eternal salvation for the obvious reason that Paul goes on to state that those **whom He called, these He also justified** and **glorified**.

This *calling* is the starting point of our personal experience of God's eternal design. The truth that He knew us *in advance* and predetermined our likeness to *His Son*, belongs to His eternal counsels. It is with the experience of being called (i.e., eternally saved)[28] that His plan in eternity past touches our personal experience in present time. Therefore the "called," with whom all things suffer together toward the final "good," are those to whom the truth of v 28 refers right here and now.

(4) *Justified.* Those who have obtained this "calling" are also justified. This truth, as we have seen, is the main topic of 3:21–5:11. From Paul's perspective in Romans, it is this judicial event that results in the declaration that the "called" are righteous by means of faith. As justified people we have both "peace with God" and also "access by faith into this grace wherein we stand" (5:1-2). It is precisely this righteous standing, possessed by the "called," that creates the needed sense of harmony with God and access into His presence to obtain the grace He can provide (see discussion under 5:2).

In a context where suffering is the major concern, it is crucial that our fundamental relationship to God involves justification with its accompanying peace and access to the divine throne. Only in the assurance that such a relationship with God exists for us can we find the spiritual strength to endure our sufferings. For with such assurance we can turn aside the voice of a false conscience, or of Satan himself, accusing us of deserving what we are going through.

The concept involved here is more fully explicated in vv 31-34. But it has already been anticipated in the summary verses in 5:1-11, where the privileges of justification (5:1-2) lead directly to triumphant and hope-filled suffering (5:3-4).

---

[28] I'm not sure why Hodges suggests that *called* means *eternally saved* in Rom 8:30 other than it is preceded by "predestined" and followed by "justified." He does not discuss any other passages in which this is true. Nor does he develop why it means that in this context. Possibly he specifically had Rom 1:6-7 in mind (which he does mention as verses to note). Concerning 1:7 he said, "Specifically he is writing to all those *in Rome* who have become the recipients of God's gracious love and now have the status of saints, to which status He had summoned (called) them." In other words, in 1:7 Hodges understands *called* to mean *summoned to be saints.* That is different, however, from how he takes *called* in 8:30. No longer is it being *invited* to be saints, but it is instead *the experience of being eternally saved.* Note that he specifically says concerning *called* in Rom 8:30, "to be called is not merely to be invited." I wish he were still with us so that I could get him to expand on his understanding here. Might the calling in v 30 be the same as the calling in v 29? Might the justification in v 30 refer to *vindication* at the Bema of the believers who respond properly to the call (and not to forensic justification)? Might the glorification be co-heirship with Christ (8:17b) as Hodges himself seems to imply in his comments that follow? Indeed, note this statement at the end of his discussion of v 32: "Instead co-heirship with the Firstborn stands at the end of the long chain of divine actions: 'those whom He knew in advance…He also glorified.'" –RNW

(5) *Glorified.* It is often noted that although glorification is actually future, here it is presented in the same past tense (aorist) as are the statements that precede it in this series. It is probable, however, that the Greek reader would not note this fact with the same perspective as the English reader. Since an aorist is quite capable of what the grammarians call a "gnomic" sense, its use as a statement of a fixed principle or a regular action is natural. All five of the aorists could well be rendered as "gnomic"—i.e., "those whom He knows in advance...predetermines... calls...justifies...glorifies."

Here Paul picks up the theme of "glory" mentioned first in v 17 and then developed in vv 18-21. The climactic statement of v 21 specifies the shared "glory" of the creation and the "children of God," which is perfect freedom from the "bondage to corruption." So it is clear that "all the creation" (v 21) participates in the glory to which all the children of God are heirs. But the mention in v 29 of the Firstborn Heir also recalls the fact that Paul has already suggested that there is a *co-heirship* predicated on suffering (v 17b). But what does this mean in the present context?

The following verses make that clear.

> **8:31-32. What then shall we say about these things? If God *is* for us, who *is really* against us? He who did not even spare His own Son, but delivered Him up on behalf of us all, how shall He not also graciously give us, together with Him, all things?**

What an encouragement the truth of vv 29-30 ought to be for the suffering believer. **What then shall we say about these things?** Paul asks rhetorically. There is really nothing that we (Paul or anyone else) can adequately say in the face of such an overwhelming reality.

Thus we "who are called according to His purpose" (v 28) can take enormous comfort in the reality that God's overarching relationship to us stretches from eternity past to eternity future. What He willed for us when He knew us in eternity past is something He is in the process of accomplishing right now. Having called and justified us, He is preparing us for the final stage of this whole experience, namely, glorification.

No matter what kind of opposition the suffering believer (who has the Spirit's "first fruits," v 23) faces, it really amounts to nothing. Who can *really* oppose us, if God is on our side? In the statement, **If God *is* for us, who *is really* against us?** the italicized words are added for clarity, but they conceal the dramatically elliptical nature of Paul's Greek statement (*Ei ho*

*Theos huper hēmōn, tis kath' hēmōn?*). Again, the question is rhetorical and has no meaningful answer. Who can truly oppose God?

But beyond this stabilizing fact, the believer also can expect, as a result of his sufferings, a tremendous compensation. Paul has already indicated this in v 17b. There He has said that we are "co-heirs with Christ if we suffer together *with Him* so that we may also be glorified together *with Him*" (the italicized words are implied by the Greek). The reward of co-suffering is nothing less than co-glorification with Jesus Christ.

But will the reward be worth it? Paul declares that it will be, since God actually desires to give us **all things**—namely, creation itself. This is the staggering meaning of v 32, where *ta panta* refers in this context to "the whole creation" (v 22; see discussion under v 28). The Firstborn Son is the Heir of *all things* and those who are co-heirs **together with Him** are also heirs *together with Him* of *all things*. When He is glorified as the Ruler of all creation, they will be co-glorified *together with Him* sharing the same rulership.

It should be noted that in Paul's text the words *together with Him* are emphatic. Most frequently they have been taken in the sense that since God gave Him *to* us He will also give *to* us *all things* (in whatever sense construed). This is not likely to be the meaning, however. Paul does not really say that God has given **His own Son** *to* us, but **on behalf of us all** (*huper hēmōn pantōn*). That is, Christ died in place of us and for our eternal salvation. There is no concept here that God gave Him *to* us.

On the contrary, the expression *together with Him* utilizes the word *sun-* (i.e., *sun autō*). In compound words, *sun-* has been prominent in the material from 8:17 to here (note the words *sugklēronomoi, sumpaschomen, sundoxasthōmen* [v 17], *sustenazei, sunōdinei* [v 22], *sunantilambanetai* [v 26], *sunergei* [v 28]). It is most reasonable to conclude that in the statement of this verse the words *together with Him* signify that God is giving *all things* to Him and that He is willing to give them to us as well so that we share them *together with* the Son.

Paul's logic is clear. God **did not even spare** the life of *His own Son* **but delivered Him up** to lay it down *on behalf of us all*. If our eternal interests required God to make so enormous a sacrifice, why would He hesitate to give us the whole creation (*ta panta*) *together with* the Son He refused to spare?

The word Paul uses here for *delivered...up* (*paredōken*) is striking. It is the very one commonly used in the Gospels of the action of Judas in "turning over" Jesus to the authorities (among many texts see, e.g., Matt 26:2, 15, 16, 21, 23, 24, 25, 45, 46, 48). But in Romans Paul has also used it of the exercise of judgment by God who has "turned [men] over" to the consequences of their sin (Rom 1:24, 26, 28). Although the word itself hardly means more than the phrase "hand over," it is not unlikely that Paul was quite conscious of these background connotations. What Judas had done was in reality the action of God, and if man suffers in measure the consequences of his sin here on earth (Rom 1:18-32), Jesus suffered sin's eternal consequences in full measure on the cross. God "handed Him over" to that.

Unquestionably, the holy life sacrificed on our behalf was worth more than all creation put together. God is therefore fully willing to give *all things* to us that we might share them with the Savior-King. The greater benefit (the death of God's Son) makes the lesser one (*all things*) reasonable, even though both benefits are staggering to the human mind.

Here then we meet a theme that is extremely prominent in the NT. It is the theme of co-reigning with Jesus Christ. Paul understood and taught it. In fact it is succinctly expressed in 2 Tim 2:12a: "If we endure [*hupomenomen*], we shall also reign with Him." Second Timothy 2:12a states the same truth as Rom 8:17b. (See also Rev 2:26-28; 3:21.) The future King will rule *all things* and so will we *together with Him* if we endure [cf. *di' hupomonēs*, v 25] suffering for His sake. To co-suffer leads to being co-glorified with Jesus Christ in His exaltation over all creation.

The verb rendered here by **graciously give** (*charisetai*) stands at the end of Paul's sentence in v 32 and thus carries a certain emphasis. As BDAG (p. 1078) points out under the meaning "*to give freely as a favor, give graciously*," it is "a common term in honorific documents lauding officials and civic-minded persons for their beneficence." Although co-rulership is indeed a reward, it is nevertheless an act of divine grace since no amount of endurance could merit this benefit. Instead co-heirship with the Firstborn stands at the end of the long chain of divine actions: "those whom He knew in advance...He also glorified."

All of God's children will indeed be glorified (8:21), but those who share their Lord's suffering will also share in His special glory as the Possessor of all things (8:17b).

In the anticipatory unit in 5:1-11, Paul had spoken of exulting in our afflictions (5:3) because they produce an expectation (hope) that does not result in shame (5:5). Now, in the climax to his discussion of suffering as the divinely ordained route to co-glorification with Jesus Christ, Paul breaks into a paean of triumphant praise that is justly famous. But naturally, Paul hopes and expects that his readers will share this exultation by appropriating the truth he has just set before them in 8:18-32.

> **8:33-34. Who shall bring a charge against God's chosen ones? God *is* the One who justifies. Who *is* the one who condemns? Christ *is* the One who died, and moreover who also rose, who also is at the right hand of God, who also intercedes on our behalf.**

All that Paul has been saying in 8:18-32 has been predicated on the truth that we stand justified before God. That is why after concluding his exposition of justification in 3:21–4:25, Paul had proceeded to anticipate the results of this in triumphant, hope-filled suffering (5:1-5). Paul has now elaborated this suffering/glory theme and he proceeds in vv 33-34 to tie it again to the truth of justification.

In the midst of any experience of suffering there is almost always the temptation to say, "I am guilty and I deserve this." If our conscience does not produce it, the suggestion will almost certainly be made by Satan himself through the agents he uses to inflict that suffering or to add to it. Paul had much experience of that as the book of Acts shows clearly and as he himself acknowledged (1 Cor 4:9-13).

But there is no legitimate condemning voice against the believer who co-suffers with Christ. Who can **bring a charge against God's chosen ones**? God Himself is the Justifier of such persons. Of course, the Greek term rendered here by *chosen ones* is the usual one normally translated as "the elect" (*eklektōn*). As v 29 makes clear these *chosen ones* are those whom God "knew beforehand" in eternity past (see discussion under v 29). In Eph 1:4 Paul states the same truth: "He chose (*exelexatō*) us in Him [Christ] before the foundation of the world."

God does not accept charges against His *chosen ones* who are already in the stream of His plans for them which end in eternal Christlikeness (vv 29-30). After all, He *is* **the One who justifies** them. Nor can this justification be properly challenged by anyone (**Who is the one who condemns?**), since it is based on the fact that **Christ is the One who died** and **who also rose**. Paul has already made quite clear the centrality of Christ's death and resurrection as the basis for God's act in justifying us by faith (cf. 3:21-26; 4:22-25).

But here Paul adds two further elements that he has not previously explicitly mentioned. (His threefold use of *kai* [also] here has the effect of reinforcing his point step by ascending step.) *The One who died*, **and moreover** *who also rose* is a Person **who also is at the right hand of God** and there **also intercedes on our behalf**. Although the last truth expressed here is highlighted by the anonymous author of Hebrews, Paul nowhere else in his epistles refers to the intercessory work of Christ on our behalf in the presence of God. (He has referred to the intercession of the Holy Spirit within us: 8:27.)

Obviously Paul could assume that his Roman readers needed no explanation of this truth. Here he invokes it as a way of saying that in God's presence (*at the right hand of God*) we have a completely qualified Intercessor. Christ's intercessory work is effective precisely because He died and rose again for us. Or, as the Apostle John puts it, "We have an Advocate with the Father, Jesus Christ the righteous. And He Himself is the propitiation for our sins..." (1 John 2:1-2).

In short, our total and unqualified acceptance before God on the basis of our full justification cannot be challenged. In the court of heaven no accuser has any standing at all because of what Christ did (died, rose) and because of what He *is* doing (intercedes). Paul may have in his mind here the story of Satan's accusations against Job (who suffered enormously). That Satan is still engaged in such accusatory efforts is clear from Rev 12:10. But any such attempts (by "angels," "principalities," or "powers") are utterly ineffectual as Paul will triumphantly affirm in 8:38. No accuser can get through our Intercessor.

> **8:35-37. Who will separate us from the love of Christ? *Will* tribulation, or hardship, or persecution, or famine, or nakedness, or danger, or sword? Just as it is written that, "*For your sake we are put to death all day long, we are accounted as sheep for slaughter.*" On the contrary, we are more than conquerors through Him who loved us.**

Here again Paul returns to a concept that he had surfaced in the concluding paragraph (5:1-11) of his discussion about justification (3:21–5:11). This is the rich theme of God's love. Paul had already spoken there of how "the love of God is poured out in our hearts through the Holy Spirit" as the result of the hope engendered by suffering (5:3-5). He has also made the cross of Christ the central demonstration of that love (5:8).

Here, however, Paul explicitly refers for the first time in Romans to **the love of Christ**. Yet this is one and the same thing as "the love of God which is in Christ Jesus our Lord" (v 38). But since Christ is the One who died, rose, ascended, and intercedes for us (v 34), it is appropriate here to refer to His personal love (as Paul also does so explicitly in Gal 2:20). Our Intercessor is more than a disinterested defense attorney—His intercession is motivated by love.

Considering all that Christ has done, and is doing, for us, **who will separate us from** such love as that? The Greek word translated *who* is *Tis* and covers both persons and things (whereas the neuter would have implied only "things," i.e., *what will separate us*). Paul's list (seven items) is intended to refer to all eventualities, whether living beings or any possible experience.

However, the accumulation of words in v 35 is not intended to indicate matters that are fully distinct from one another. Instead, the accumulation of seven negative terms has a rhetorical effect equivalent to "nothing whatever." Nevertheless the choice of words also suggests a wide range of experiences that, though often overlapping, have their own particular emphasis.

The first two, **tribulation** (*Thlipsis*) and **hardship** (*stenōchōria*), are general words and are close to being synonymous. But the following five terms (**persecution, famine, nakedness, danger, sword**) suggest the various forms in which *tribulation* and *hardship* often come.

Such troubles are attested by Scripture as experiences of the godly. Paul now takes up the words of Ps 44:22 and applies them to himself and to other suffering believers. It happens to them **just as it is written**, namely, **that,** *"for Your sake we are put to death all day long."* As the previous verses of the Psalm disclose (and as Paul certainly knew), this was not the result of sin. Rather in the Psalm there is a claim to innocence: "If we had forgotten the name of our God, or stretched out our hands to a foreign god, would God not search this out? For He knows the secrets of the heart" (Ps 44:20-21, NKJV).

As Paul was well aware from personal experience, the godly often endure day-long danger from imminent death. It was like dying many times in one day (*we are put to death all day long*). In this way, the godly are treated (accounted) as if they were sheep singled out *"for slaughter"* on a day of feasting and revelry (cf. 1 Sam 25:1-11). The Psalmist vividly captures the torment of being hunted down for the purpose of execution.

But tragic as the experience he describes may appear, **on the contrary** (i.e., despite appearances) in all these things we **more than** conquer. I retain here the familiar idea, **we are more than conquerors**, for *hupernikōmen* (cf. KJV, NKJV, NIV, NASB; but contrast "we overcome," NACE and "we triumph," JB). It is doubtful how much the force of the prefixed preposition (*huper-*) was felt in Hellenistic Greek, but the choice by Paul here of *hupernikōmen* over the simple *nikōmen* suggests that for him *huper-* had some intensifying effect. The extended meaning in BDAG (p. 1034), "prevail completely," is probably not far from the mark.

This ultimate victory, Paul asserts, is achieved **through Him who loved us**. With the phrases "love of Christ" (v 35) and "the love of God which is in Christ Jesus our Lord" (v 38), Paul employs a triad of references to his Savior's love that tie vv 35-38 together as a unit.

In fact, in this splendid consummation to the whole body of material from 1:18–8:39, the concluding unit (8:33-38) is constructed from two fundamental questions: (1) "Who shall bring a charge against God's chosen ones?" (v 33; answer, v 34) and (2) "Who shall separate us from the love of Christ?" (v 35a; answer, vv 35b-38). The first question pertains to our judicial standing before God (as justified), and the second to our experience of God in suffering (as beloved by Christ Jesus our Lord). The suffering believer's situation is impregnable and moves irresistibly toward complete and unequivocal victory.

> **8:38-39. For I am persuaded that neither death nor life, nor angels, nor principalities, nor powers, nor things present nor things to come, nor height, nor depth, nor any other created thing, will be able to separate us from the love of God which is in Christ Jesus our Lord.**

In a superbly elegant paean of praise to the permanence of God's love in Christ,[29] Paul brings the entire first movement of his *probatio* (1:18–8:39) to a climactic conclusion. This virtual song of triumph is composed of ten elements combined into a strophic arrangement of 2+3/2+3. Paul

---

[29] Hodges told me privately, and it can be seen in his discussion of 8:31-38 if read carefully, that he did not see Rom 8:31-38 as dealing with the doctrine of eternal security. The issue, he said, was our *present experience* of God's love in Christ. The believer who is walking according to the Spirit is one who is experiencing God's love even when he is undergoing persecution for his faith. –RNW

affirms his complete conviction (**I am persuaded**) that none of the entities enumerated can divorce him from the ongoing reality of divine love.

The experiences or forces named are: (1) **neither death nor life** (that is, nothing in our experience of living, nor in the cessation of that experience); (2) **nor angels nor principalities nor powers** (that is, no supernatural being whatever its exalted position); (3) **nor things present nor things to come** (that is, no eventuality already present or that will be present in the future); **nor height nor depth nor any other created thing** (that is, nothing at the highest level of existence or the lowest level or anything in between).

In the final threefold enumeration, Paul is probably thinking of beings (like Satan) with access to heaven (height), of beings whose sphere is in the bowels of hell (depth), and of created beings [*ktisis*] wherever they may be. One might compare with this Eph 1:19-23 and Phil 2:9-11.

The risen and exalted One who is at the right hand of God (v 34), is for Paul the Possessor of absolute power over every experience and every being. He is the ultimate bulwark that shields us from separation from God's love, inasmuch as that love is found in Him who is **Christ Jesus our Lord**!

# Romans 9

## D. Parenthesis: God's Faithfulness Will Bring Deliverance to Israel (9:1–11:36)

As has already been pointed out in my introduction to the main body of Romans, the evidence of the epistle itself suggests the nature of the false opinions that were voiced in Rome about Paul's gospel. The fact that Paul preached that the Jewish Torah (the law) was ineffective for acceptance before God was one salient point of criticism. Paul has defended his view of the Torah's inadequacy in the first major unit of the body (namely, 1:18–8:39). The law can be neither the basis for justification before God nor the effective means for Christian living.

But such a sweeping negative assessment of the Torah was accompanied by the bald fact that Paul's efforts were heavily oriented toward Gentile evangelism. The charge must inevitably have arisen that Paul had a negative attitude toward the Jewish nation and toward that nation's place in the program of God. Such a charge, inevitable enough, was of course a calumny. In fact, Paul cared very much about Israel and had a very high view of its final destiny. This second unit of the body is designed to establish Paul's true appraisal of national Israel.

### 1. Introduction: Paul's Grief for Israel (9:1-5)

**9:1-2. I am telling the truth in Christ, I am not lying (my conscience bears witness along with me in the Holy Spirit), that there is great grief for me and unceasing pain in my heart.**

In the strongest of terms Paul now affirms his deep concern for the spiritual state of Israel (see vv 3-5). That a new unit has begun

245

is signaled here by asyndeton (lack of a connective) in v 1 and by the emphatic position, in Greek, of the word *truth* (*Alētheian*), first in Paul's sentence = "truth is what I'm speaking." Paul wants there to be no mistake about what he feels.

Correctly, Jewett observes (p. 559), "This [verse] completes the most extensive affirmation of Paul's truthfulness in any of his letters, strongly suggesting his conviction that at least some members of the audience are inclined to doubt the sincerity of his devotion to Israel." In fact, this long affirmation has three constituent elements, conforming to the OT law about two or three witnesses (Deut 17:6; 19:7). His assertion about Israel is thus shaped by Israel's law of testimony.

The initial element is a double affirmation about Paul's verbal veracity (positive: **I am telling the truth**; negative: **I am not lying**) in which he claims to speak in submission to Jesus Christ (**in Christ**). This is followed by an appeal to two inward realities (first, **my conscience**; second, **the Holy Spirit**). Though closely connected here, these "witnesses" are obviously not identical.

The words rendered **my conscience bears witness along with me** (*summarturousēs moi tēs suneidēseōs mou*) carry the natural sense of the compound verb *summartureō*: "to bear witness along with" (BDAG, p. 957, "to provide supporting evidence by testifying") as the verb does also in 8:16 (see discussion there). Paul is expressing the thought that in support of his verbal claim (*I am telling the truth*) there is an inner awareness (*my conscience*) that his grief for Israel is real and appropriate.

Paul's word *suneidēsis* was not a precise equivalent of what English speakers usually mean by *conscience* (i.e., the presence or absence of guilty feelings). But Paul's general use of the word is close enough to justify translating it here as *conscience* (see BDAG, pp. 967-68). Paul knows his feelings are true and justifiable. His conscience is definite and clear **in the Holy Spirit**.

The phrase *in the Holy Spirit* should not be taken as a mystical formulation. As the remainder of chaps. 9–11 confirm, Paul's attitude toward Israel is predicated on what the Scriptures reveal about that nation's relationship to God. As is evident from v 4 on, Paul could rightly attribute his deep feelings to the effect that God's declarations about Israel have had on him. Naturally these feelings are mediated to him by God's Spirit. If Paul's inner response to Israel's need were simply a matter of his emotional attachment to his native people, they would not have the same resonance that they do. Paul's feelings are truly his own, yet at the same time they are also the product of the work of the Holy Spirit within him through the Scriptures.

Thus (1) Paul's words, (2) his conscience, and (3) *the Holy Spirit* all attest his profound sadness over his nation.

Paul's emotional reaction to Israel's situation is one of both grief and **pain in** his **heart**. The noun *odunē* (*pain*; also *distress*, etc.) actually appears in the sense of *pain* in Greek medical literature. It is so rendered here in line with the English metaphor "it pains me in my heart." The two attributes of Paul's emotional state, expressed by *great* (modifying *lupē*, *grief*) and *unceasing* (modifying *odunē*), are juxtaposed in Paul's text in order to highlight them (literally, "grief for me is great, and unceasing *is* pain in my heart"). His feelings for Israel are neither shallow nor intermittent.

As has been noted by others, the person hearing Romans read in public might listen to 9:1-2 with some surprise after the triumphant climax of 8:33-38. They might well wonder, "What suddenly causes such sorrow as this?" This element of suspense, however brief, would have been rhetorically effective.

**9:3. For I myself could wish to be accursed from Christ for the sake of my brothers, my fellow-countrymen according to the flesh,**

Paul now makes a statement that has caused much discussion in the literature. It is clear enough from this statement that the grief he has expressed in v 1 relates to his nation, Israel. That they are for the most part unbelieving and hostile to his gospel need not be stated explicitly. Presumably the Roman Christians knew this quite well.

But how, one might ask, could Paul even bear the thought, much less desire, that he could be eternally separated **from Christ** for the good of Israel? This is the wrong question and proceeds on a false assumption about what is meant by the term **accursed** (*anathema*).[1]

---

[1] Interpreters who think that Paul offers to go to the lake of fire inadvertently sabotage his whole argument. How secure would God's promises to Israel be if Paul could overturn God's promises to himself? Paul entertains no theoretical compromises to either God's faithfulness to Israel or to believers' security. Instead, he expresses a willingness to be *anathema*, that is, a believer under divine displeasure. –JHN

Jewett (p. 561) is not correct to say that "in some sense Paul offered his own damnation on behalf of his fellow Jews and that his prayer was rejected." There is nothing in the general usage of this word, either in the NT or the LXX, to suggest that Paul's expression had the theological nuance that Jewett and others[2] have given it.

Of particular linguistic interest is the statement of the conspirators of Acts 23:14 that, "we have put ourselves under a curse" (*Anathemati anethematisamen*, i.e., "cursed ourselves with a curse," "utterly cursed ourselves"). Needless to say, they were not condemning themselves to hell in the event of failure. Indeed the phrase in Acts 23:14 occurs also in the LXX at Deut 13:15[16] and 20:17. In both cases the idea is "to utterly destroy" (13:16, a city and its goods; 20:17, the people in Canaan). The conspirators of Acts are no doubt expressing the idea that if *Paul* does not die, *they* should. Their oath was a pledge not to eat again if their attempt to assassinate him failed (Acts 23:12, 14, 21).

Paul himself used the term *anathema* only here in Romans and only elsewhere in the NT at 1 Cor 12:3; 16:22; and Gal 1:8-9. It would be entirely gratuitous to read "damnation" into any of the Pauline passages. There seems to be no evidence in the Greek Scriptures for the idea that the word *anathema* implies that Paul was willing to go to hell for Israel. Summary destruction (e.g., execution) appears to be the worst implication that can be linguistically supported, but the term *anathema* itself is not specific and might be expected to be realized in diverse ways.

Furthermore, the imperfect verb expressing Paul's thought (*Euchomēn*, **I...could wish**) must not be taken as though it can only be understood as an actual prayer or wish. This ignores the delicate suppleness of this particular tense. When Agrippa says (Acts 25:22a), "I myself also could wish (*Eboulomēn*) to hear this man," he is not making a frontal request that will put his host (Festus) in an awkward position. Instead he indicates that it is not inconceivable that he could find such an opportunity interesting. Festus's reply thus comes over as a favor: "'Tomorrow,' he said, 'you shall hear him'" (Acts 25:22b).

---

[2] Cranfield, *Romans*, p. 2:457-58, unfortunately misconstrues Paul's meaning: "Here in Rom 9.3 *anathema einai* clearly means 'to forfeit final salvation.' Both the suggestion that what is referred to is some such suffering in this present life as that which is reflected in 2 Cor 1.8f; 2.13; 7.7; 12.7 and the suggestion that what is referred to is an act of ecclesiastical discipline must surely be rejected as incompatible with the extreme solemnity of v. 1. Nothing less than final exclusion from that glory which is going to be revealed can be meant." What folly! –JHN

We should not suppose that Paul is saying here that he actually did once desire, or request, *to be accursed from Christ*. Rather, we should take the idea as equivalent to "I was about to wish" or "I almost wish." A. T. Robertson calls this type of imperfect the "potential imperfect" and cites both Acts 25:22 and Rom 9:3, among other texts, as examples (pp. 885-86).

Still we should also ask what it might have meant to Paul to "almost wish" such a thing. In fact, Paul's doctrine of the cross includes the conviction that "Christ has redeemed us from the *curse* of the law, having become a *curse* for us" (Gal 3:13, using the noun *katara* twice). We may therefore suppose that he refers in this verse to some kind of vicarious death like His Savior's own death. Thus, just as Christ was separated from God in that death (Matt 27:46), so Paul could almost contemplate a similar separation from Christ. The definite article here with Christ (*tou Christou*) is most easily understood as one of previous reference, picking up the word *Christ* from v 1 (*en Christō*). Though he now speaks truth *in his union with* Christ (v 1), what he here suggests would involve *separation from* Him.

Such an idea as this was not far from Pauline consciousness. He could speak, for example, of sharing in "the fellowship of His [Christ's] sufferings, being conformed to His death" (Phil 3:10). He also wrote, "Therefore I endure all things for the sake of the elect, that they may obtain the salvation which is in Christ Jesus with eternal glory" (2 Tim 2:10). The vicarious nature of this statement is obvious.

It is likely therefore that this deeply Christ-like man might at times almost have wished that he could undergo death for his **brothers**, his **fellow-countrymen according to the flesh**, just as Jesus had done for him. But, of course, no such possibility was available to him and it is in the highest degree improbable that he could ever have seriously asked God to allow it. But Paul is speaking here out of very deep emotions. He should be understood, therefore, not at a literalistic level, but at the level of heartfelt anguish.

One might recall David's lament, "O my son Absalom—my son, my son Absalom—if only I had died in your place! O Absalom my son, my son!" (2 Sam 18:33).

**9:4-5. who are Israelites, to whom belong the adoption as sons, and the glory, and the covenants, and the legislation, and the**

> sacred service, and the promises, to whom belong the fathers
> and from whom *came* Christ according to the flesh, the One
> who is God over all, blessed forever. Amen.

Paul's grief for Israel is based on far more than his participation in that nationality. Rather it is chiefly founded on, and accentuated by, that nation's profoundly significant relationship to God. In vv 4 and 5 Paul briefly enumerates those matters which make his nation special in the highest degree.

First of all, those whom he calls "brothers" and "fellow-countrymen according to the flesh" (v 3) **are Israelites**. This special designation for his "fellow-countrymen" originated in the renaming of Jacob by God in Gen 32:28. "Israel" thus becomes a national designation redolent with the implication of special divine favor. It is striking that Paul employs the term *Israel/Israelite* no less than twelve times in Romans 9–11 and nowhere else in this epistle. The name by which they were known among Gentiles (*Ioudaioi*, "Jews") is used in all references to them in the other chapters (9:24 also has one reference to "Jews").

The nature of the special privilege of being Israelites is now elaborated in a list of six divine blessings. The structure of Paul's sentence indicates the commencement of this list by means of the introductory word *hōn* (**to whom belong**, literally, "of whom") followed by six divine benefits. A close consideration of the series suggests that Paul has arranged them in roughly chronological order. It is the foundational history of the nation that primarily concerns him here, especially as recorded in Exodus through Deuteronomy.

The first blessing is that of **adoption as sons** (*hē huiothesia*). It was at the very beginning of Israel's history as a nation that this privileged status was conferred on it. Following the end of the patriarchal period recorded in Genesis, Exodus commences the national history. There, in the call of Moses, God announces, "Then you shall say to Pharaoh, 'Thus says the Lord: "Israel is My son, My firstborn. So I say to you, let My son go that he may serve Me. But if you refuse to let him go, indeed I will kill your son, your firstborn"'" (Exod 4:22-23). The national privilege of Israel is thus analogous to the individual privilege of Christian believers (see 8:15: *Pneuma huiothesias*, "a spirit [or, Spirit] of adoption as sons").

The second blessing is **the glory** (*hē doxa*). In the experience of Israel nationally it was subsequent to the Exodus from Egypt that God's glory (that is, the Shekinah glory) was manifested to Israel. This happened soon after the crossing of the Red Sea when Israel murmured because they lacked food (Exod 16:2, 3). Under divine direction, "Moses and Aaron said to all the children of Israel, 'At evening you shall know that the Lord has brought you out of Egypt. And in the morning you shall see the *glory* [Hebrew: *kābôd*; Greek (LXX): *doxa*] of the Lord...' Now it came to pass, as Aaron spoke to the whole congregation of the children of Israel, that they looked toward the wilderness, and behold, the *glory* of the Lord appeared in the cloud" (Exod 16:7, 10, emphasis added).

Similarly, at Mount Sinai, God's glory became visible to the nation, after which Moses went up into the mountain (Exod 24:16-18). God's glory appeared again at the institution of the tabernacle (Exod 40:34, 35). This repeated manifestation of divine splendor was unique to Israel's experience. To no other nation did God manifest His glory in this way.

The third blessing is **the covenants**. The plural term has puzzled commentators who tend to take it in a generalized sense, with special reference to the Abrahamic covenant. But the coupling of that covenant with other unspecified ones is unexpected. The position of this third blessing in Paul's series is also puzzling.

We should remember that Paul is dealing here with Israel as a national entity and the covenant with Abraham is not said to be made with Israel. Indeed, Moses distinguishes between a covenant with the fathers and one with the nation. He says explicitly of the covenant made at Sinai, "The Lord did not make this covenant with our fathers, but with us, those who are here today, all of us who are alive" (Deut 5:3). An additional covenant is also made with the nation in Moab at the border of the Promised Land. Of this covenant it is said, "These are the words of the covenant which the Lord commanded Moses to make with the children of Israel in the land of Moab, *besides the covenant* which He made with them in Horeb" (Deut 29:1, emphasis added).

It is reasonable to assume that the phrase *the covenants* here refers to these two covenantal arrangements that were mediated through Moses before Israel entered the land.

The fourth blessing is **the legislation** (*hē nomothesia*). The word *nomothesia* does not occur in the canonical books of the LXX, but it does occur in 2 Maccabees 6:23; 4 Maccabees 5:35 and 17:16, where in the first two instances the Oxford edition of *The Apocrypha* translates it simply "law." The rendering *legislation*, however, is given for the third instance. It is very doubtful that Paul intended the word here to be a mere equivalent to the word *nomos* (law), which he uses so frequently elsewhere in Romans. The reference will then be to all of the very numerous, specific stipulations that flowed from both of the Mosaic covenants.

The fifth blessing is **the sacred service** (*hē latreia*). The reference here is no doubt to the cultic arrangements connected with the tabernacle and later with the temple. In particular these are elaborated in Leviticus. Only Israel possessed a God-ordained system of worship.

The final blessing is **the promises** (*hai epangeliai*). As the final member of the series, it no doubt summarizes the many subsequent promises made to the nation, including the promise of Messiah and of an eternal kingdom. Again there is no need to refer this to "the promises made to the fathers" (Rom 15:8) or to Abraham personally (Rom 4:13-14, 16, 20-21). But Paul may well have in mind, among other promises, "the gospel of God, which He *promised* beforehand through His prophets in the Holy Scriptures" (Rom 1:1-2, emphasis added).

All of these superlative benefits heighten the sense of Israel's special privilege and at the same time deepen the pathos of Paul's grief for the nation.

A change in structure now signals two further privileges that the nation enjoys. The series in v 4 had begun with *hōn* (**to whom belong**), and in v 5a we again encounter *hōn*, while in 5b we meet *ex hōn* (**from whom**). The sequence *hōn—hōn—ex hōn* (the latter climactic) must have been rhetorically pleasing when the epistle was read aloud at Rome.

By specifically stating **to whom belong the fathers** Paul accentuates this privilege because it is the real key to God's goodness, grace, and mercy to the nation. He will shortly say of his people, "With regard to the gospel, they are enemies for your sake, but with regard to God's choice they are beloved for the fathers' sake [*dia tous pateras*]" (11:28). Historically, Israel has benefited enormously, and in the future *will* benefit enormously, from being descendants of Abraham, Isaac, and Jacob. Their descent from the godly patriarchs is a superlative blessing.

But above all other things—and climactically—it must be said that this is the nation **from whom** *came* **Christ according to the flesh**. Although some have stressed the presence of the article with *Christ* (*ho Christos*) as a specific reference to Him as "the Messiah," this is quite doubtful. The three uses of *Christos* in 9:1-5 (v 1, no article, vv 3, 5, articular) are perfectly idiomatic and not representable in English.

That the nation of Israel produced "the Savior of the world" (see John 4:22, 42) is indeed the very pinnacle of divine privilege. Christians should never forget that from the standpoint of His human nature (*according to the flesh*) our Savior was Himself an Israelite. It is clear that Paul certainly had not forgotten it.

But Christ was much more than a mere Israelite. He was also God incarnate, and Paul rounds off his enumeration of divine blessings to Israel with an affirmation of this truth. After all, Christ personally is **the One who is God over all, blessed forever**. Could there be anything at all more elevating to the Jewish nation than that the Eternal God, who rules *over all* things, became an Israelite? No climax could be as superlative as this one.

Naturally, this understanding of Paul's text has been debated. Scholars who do not think that Paul here refers to Christ as God have argued that a full stop (a period) should come (1) after the words *to kata sarka* (*according to the flesh*) or (2) after *ho ōn epi pantōn* (*who is…over all*). The remaining words in the Greek text (*Theos eulogētos eis tous aiōnas. Amēn*) thus become a doxology by themselves ("God *be* blessed forever. Amen.") or in connection with the four preceding words ("God who is over all *be* blessed forever. Amen").

However neither option is the most natural reading since, for one thing, in an independent doxology it is normal for the word *eulogētos* to stand first. Cranfield regards this point "as so strong as to be in itself almost conclusive" (2:468). There is little reason to doubt that Paul's statement in this verse would have been almost universally read as translated here were it not for the ascription of deity to Christ, which bothers not a few scholars. But the author of Phil 2:6, among other texts, is not likely to have had such inhibitions. (For a full discussion of the issue, see Cranfield, 2:464-70.)

With this doxology, then, Paul concludes his summary of Israel's special relationship to God that underlies his own grief on their behalf. He must now discuss the problem that their unbelief brings clearly to the surface: "Why does Israel reject the fulfillment of its ancient Messianic hope?"

## 2. Argument: God's Promises Are Being Fulfilled (9:6–11:36)

Paul's fundamental answer to the problem of Israel's unbelief is that this unbelief is consistent with Scripture and is part of the outworking of God's purposes related to mankind.

### a. Israel's Unbelief Is Consistent with Scripture (9:6-33)

### (i) God's Grace Is Selectively Channeled (9:6-13)

In dealing with the current experience of Israel, Paul wishes to show that divine selectivity is the key to understanding it. God channels His purposes through those whom He selects for that role. This selectivity, in fact, has been manifest even in God's dealings with the immediate descendants of the patriarchs. That is to say that, before there was a nation called "Israel," this principle was established in the two previous generations.

Paul demonstrates this principle through two examples: (1) the choice of Isaac over Ishmael (9:6-9) and (2) the choice of Jacob over Esau (9:10-13).

> **9:6. Now it is not as though the word of God has failed. For Israel does not consist of all who are part of Israel.**

To begin with, Paul affirms, there has been no failure on the part of God's word. His opening words, **Now it is not as though** (*Ouch hoion de hoti*), are about equivalent to the statement "it is not the case that…" No one should suppose that anything **has failed** which **the word of God** had promised or foretold. As Paul will carefully show, Israel's future is firmly guaranteed by that word and nothing that has happened in the current behavior of Israel alters this ultimate reality.[3]

But to grasp this point clearly, it is important to realize that a formal racial connection with Israel is not what really constitutes Israel. The formal connection with Israel is expressed by the Greek words *pantes hoi ex Israēl* which we render by **all who are part of Israel** ("all who are members of the nation"). But, states Paul, **Israel does not consist of** all those (*ou…houtoi Israēl*) who are related to it in that way.

Paul's phrase *houtoi Israēl* is brief and pointed, leaving the verbal idea (an implied *eisin*, "are") unexpressed. (My rendering is a paraphrase to capture the thought.) "Not all those who belong to Israel are Israel," Paul is saying. This recalls his earlier statement that "a person is not a Jew who is outwardly so…but he is a Jew who is inwardly so" (2:28, 29). For Paul, it is one thing to be an Israelite in the natural sense of that word, and another

---

[3] Clearly Hodges did not believe in replacement theology (i.e., the view that the Church replaces Israel). And neither did the Apostle Paul. –JHN

thing to be an Israelite spiritually. He will now proceed to establish this principle more clearly.

> **9:7-9. Neither because they are Abraham's descendants *are they* all *his* children, but rather, "Through Isaac shall the descendants be called your own." That is, *it is* not the children of the flesh who *are* children of God, but the children of promise are accounted as descendants. For this is the word of promise: *"At this time I will come and Sarah shall have a son."***

Although the opening word of v 7, *Neither* (*oud'*), is a formal continuation of v 6, it serves in fact to support the principle Paul has stated about Israel. This same principle can be seen in the experience of Abraham, the nation's revered father. Just because there is a physical descent from Abraham, that descent is not necessarily spiritual in character. This can be seen in the case of Ishmael and Isaac.

Paul is clearly thinking here of Ishmael, although he does not refer to him by name. But the quotation from Gen 21:12 shows what he has in mind. The words, **"Through Isaac shall the descendants be called your own,"** are part of a response by God to Abraham regarding Sarah's request that Ishmael and his mother, the bondwoman, should be expelled from Abraham's home. God says, "Whatever Sarah has said to you, listen to her voice; for in Isaac your seed shall be called" (Gen 21:12, NKJV).

The quotation by Paul from Gen 21:12 follows exactly the highly literal LXX rendering of the Hebrew text. A more idiomatic translation of the Hebrew would be, "Through Isaac seed will be reckoned to you," but this is the intended sense as well of the LXX version. Thus, by the announcement of God Himself, Isaac is designated the "true" seed of Abraham, leaving Ishmael with a physical link to him but no spiritual standing as the divinely designated line of descent.

Paul is appealing to this fact for the distinction he wishes to affirm here. Simply because people **are Abraham's descendants** does not mean that **they** are **all** **his** **children**. And by this he means, as he goes on to state in v 8, that **it is not the children of the flesh who are children of God**. To be truly children of Abraham, Paul implies, is to be the *children of God*.

Here the phrase *children of God* means—first of all—that Isaac was God's direct gift to Abraham through his miraculous birth, when Abraham was too old to beget seed. But the word *children* is a generalizing plural. By way of analogy, therefore, believing Israelites are *children of God* by faith in Christ, in contrast to unbelieving Israelites who are not. Instead, as mere physical descendants of Abraham, they are actually *children of the flesh*. As Paul states it in Gal 3:7, "Therefore know that those who are of faith are sons of Abraham."

For Paul, then, there is a true spiritual sonship to Abraham by faith in Christ. Such persons are also *children of God*. Isaac is the Biblical prototype for this truth, while Ishmael is the prototype of the unbelieving descendants of Abraham. Like Ishmael, unbelieving Israelites can only speak of a physical connection with Abraham.

Further, these *children of God* are, like Isaac was, **children of the promise**. It is the *children of the promise* who **are accounted as descendants** of Abraham. In other words, Isaac was born to Abraham as a result of God's special promise (v 9) and could be truly called a child of that promise. But the word *children* is again plural. By analogy, those who are right now *the children of God*, and of Abraham, by faith in Jesus Christ, can also be called *children of the promise*.

In the case of believers, however, the promise in question is no doubt *the promise* of the Abrahamic blessing (Gen 12:3). As Paul makes plain in Gal 3:8-9, this promise was essentially a gospel promise: "And the Scripture, foreseeing that God would justify the nations by faith, preached the gospel to Abraham beforehand, saying, 'In you all the nations shall be blessed.' So then those who are of faith are blessed with believing Abraham."

However, it must also be said that the Abrahamic promise of Gen 12:3 and *the promise* about Isaac (Gen 15:2-6; 18:10, 14) are not really separate promises, but part and parcel of the same Messianic hope. If Gen 12:3 "preaches the gospel to Abraham beforehand," it is also true that *the promise* of Isaac confirms that earlier gospel promise and is a genuine part of it. The statement that *through Isaac shall the descendants be called your own* means in fact that the original promise of Gen 12:3 will be fulfilled for Abraham through Isaac's descendants, not Ishmael's.

Thus Paul now quotes **the word of promise** about Isaac as the climax of this initial sub-unit (8:7-9). His point is that Scripture itself distinguishes between *the children of the flesh* and *the children of God/ children of promise*. Isaac is the Biblical pattern for this distinction. His birth resulted directly from the divine promise found in Gen 18:10, 14. Isaac's selection over Ishmael establishes the divine channel for fulfilling God's purposes through Israel. God Himself chose this channel.

Finally, we may note that the quotation Paul gives in v 9 combines both Gen 18:10 and 18:14 as they are translated by the LXX: *"At this time"* (*Kata ton kairon touton,* Gen 18:10, LXX) *"I will come"* (*eleusomai,* Paul's paraphrase) *"and Sarah will have a son"* (*kai estai tē Sarra huios,* Gen 18:14). This combination subtly reminds the knowledgeable hearer/ reader of Romans that God's promise about Isaac's birth was given twice in Genesis 18, thus emphasizing its certainty.

**9:10. And not only *that*, but also Rebecca, when she was pregnant by one man, Isaac our father—**

The case of Isaac is now reinforced by another example of Paul's principle that mere physical descent from Israel (cf. v 6) is not enough. This descent must also have the sanction of divine promise, as Isaac's choice by God in preference to Ishmael has shown. The same principle is now exemplified by the choice of Jacob over Esau in accordance with yet another divine promise.

The opening words, **And not only *that*** (*Ou monon de*), indicate the supplemental nature of the new example. It is *not only* the case that Isaac was chosen on the basis of promise, so also was Jacob.

Paul's statement here is slightly elliptical, but clear enough. The reader or hearer naturally supplies some idea like *there is* (an implicit *estin*) to fill out the idea: "We don't have only the example just given, *there is* **also Rebecca, when she was pregnant by one man**" (*Rhebekka ex henos koitēn echousa*). The pregnancy of Rebecca with the twins Esau and Jacob is the starting point of the new example.

It is significant that Paul stresses here that this pregnancy was *by one man*. Whereas in the example of Isaac and Ishmael two different mothers were involved, here the parentage of Esau and Jacob is identical. In theory an opponent might argue that Isaac was chosen over Ishmael because of the differing status of the two mothers, but no such difference existed for Esau and Jacob. The one mother was pregnant *by one man*. And this *one man* was **Isaac our father**, that is, the father of every Israelite. No Israelite descended from Esau, though Isaac and Rebecca were his parents as well.

Paul will now state that this reality is rooted in God's choice.

**9:11-12. for even though *the children* were not yet born nor had they done anything good or bad, in order that God's purpose in accordance with *His* choice might remain *firm* (not by works**

but by Him who calls), it was said to her that, *"The older* child *shall serve the younger* one."

Once again, the example Paul is dealing with here contrasts significantly with his first one. The promise about Isaac that Paul quotes in v 8, from Gen 21:12, was occasioned by Ishmael mocking Isaac at the feast given for Isaac's weaning (Gen 21:8-9). God's words in Gen 21:12 might be misconstrued as based on this unkindness by Ishmael. But this consideration is totally absent from the second example.

In fact, Esau and Jacob had **not yet** been born when God's word came to Rebecca, so naturally neither of them **had...done anything good or bad**. Thus the case in question has nothing to do with the behavior or character of either of the twins. Instead, the favorable status of the younger son is due entirely to **God's purpose in accordance with *His* choice**.

The particular phrase just mentioned reflects a "compact articular" construction in Greek that places the words *in accordance with His choice* inside the article and noun that are translated here by the word *purpose* (*hē kat' eklogēn prosthesis*). We could literally render it: "The by choice purpose." Paul means by this that the purpose in question was based on a choice made by God Himself and was not based on anything done or not done by the twins. Unlike the case of Isaac and Ishmael, in which one might incorrectly assert that the choice was based on something done (i.e., works) by Ishmael, nothing but the divine purpose was involved here.

We shall be making a mistake, however, if we construe the statement here as if it referred to the eternal destiny of Esau and Jacob. Paul was certainly not discussing whether Esau and Jacob will be in God's eternal kingdom.[4] Indeed, there is no real reason to believe that either of them will *not* be.[5] Instead Paul is simply reemphasizing that God sovereignly chose the vehicle through which His purpose for Israel was to be realized.

---

[4] Romans 9 does not address the issue of individual soteriological election to everlasting life. In regard to Jacob and Esau, the issue is: through whom will Abraham's seed be called (God chose only one to be in the line through which the Messiah would come, based on Gen 12:3; 22:18)? This is the same issue raised between Isaac and Ishmael. Other passages discuss soteriological election, but not Romans 9. –JHN

[5] Nothing in the OT suggests that Ishmael or Esau were unbelievers. Despite being Gentiles, both were beneficiaries of the Abrahamic blessing. Hodges, *A Free Grace Primer*, 465, offers evidence from Heb 12:16 that Esau was a believer. Specifically, the verse warns believers against selling their birthright (as rewardable partakers) as did Esau. –JHN

Natural, physical descent is not the basis for God's sovereign choice. Ishmael and Esau were both the "seed" of Abraham, but neither was the divinely chosen seed from which the nation itself would come.

The words **in order that** *God's purpose...***might remain** *firm* are of special interest (*firm* is added in the translation for clarity). This clause is introduced by the Greek conjunction *hina* (*in order that*) and the purpose it refers to is given in the statement **it was said to her that...** That is, the prophecy was given *in order that* this result (i.e., that God's purpose would remain firm) might be realized.

The word rendered in my translation by *remain* is the fluid verb *menō*. It is likely that Paul meant that the prophecy about Esau and Jacob was given so that it might be evident that this prophecy transcended all of the events that followed the birth of these twins. God's purpose regarding them was not to be perceived as fluctuating with, or influenced by, what Esau and Jacob did or did not do after they were born. It was already announced and, therefore, settled.

In fact, it was so independent of the future actions of the two men that it could be truly said that God's favor toward Jacob was **not by works but by Him who calls**. This means in the first instance that Jacob was in no sense being rewarded for his works by being made the progenitor of the nation instead of his brother. On the contrary he became that progenitor because God sovereignly called him to that role. The privilege came through *Him who calls*.

Naturally Paul here expects the hearers of Romans to pick up the parallel between the special privilege accorded to Jacob and the one to which God had "called" them. In fact, in the previous chapter Paul had spoken of those whom God "knew in advance" and whom He had also "called" and "justified" (8:29-30). Justification, therefore, came *by Him who calls* and it was *not by works* (4:4-5). The analogy is manifest.

But the theology sometimes tortured out of these statements is *not* manifest. Paul leaves completely unaddressed the question of *why* God chose Jacob over Esau. It is illogical to deduce from this silence that there was nothing at all about Jacob that made him a suitable object of divine grace. A purely arbitrary decision on God's part is an illicit conclusion that in no way acknowledges His perfect wisdom. The fact that it is unrevealed leaves men with nothing to say about it.

Of course, this has not stopped them from saying something. But even theologians should take seriously the truth of Deut 29:29, "The secret things belong to the Lord our God, but those things which are revealed belong to us and to our children forever." In so far as God chooses to "know" us "in advance" (8:29), the reasons for this choice are as mysterious as they are in reference to His choice of Jacob.

But in Jacob's and Esau's case, *God's purpose in accordance with His choice* dealt with their *positions* relative to one another in God's plan. The prophecy spoken to Rebecca made the older boy subservient to the younger one (Gen 25:23). The statement that *"the older child shall serve the younger one"* had its initial realization when Jacob received the blessing of the firstborn son instead of Esau, who was the physical firstborn (Gen 27:26-40).

This in fact is explicitly stated by Isaac when Esau complains about losing the blessing (Gen 27:36). Isaac responds, "Indeed I have made him your *master*, and all his brethren [or, *relatives*, NIV, NASB] I have given to him as *servants*; with grain and wine I have sustained him. What shall I do now for you, my son?" (Gen 27:37). Esau thus received a status inferior and subservient to that of his younger brother, Jacob. As Paul will further point out in the next verse, this status was confirmed by events.

**9:13. Just as it is written, *"Jacob have I loved, but Esau have I hated."***

Paul now quotes from Malachi 1 to demonstrate that the status that Jacob obtained through the blessing of Isaac was borne out by subsequent events. Malachi's message opens in 1:2-3 with the words, "'I have loved you,' says the Lord. 'Yet you say, "In what way have You loved us?" Was not Esau Jacob's brother?' says the Lord. *"Yet Jacob have I loved; but Esau have I hated, and laid waste his mountains and his heritage for the jackals of the wilderness."'*

The suitability of this quotation to the point Paul is making from Genesis 23 and 27 is transparent. The "heritage" of Esau (that is, his inheritance/land) was clearly inferior to Jacob's. Whereas the recipients of Malachi's prophecy were now restored to the "heritage" of Jacob (fifth century BC), after the exile in Babylon, no such restoration had occurred for the descendants of Esau. Instead, Esau's inheritance was still desolate.

In the relative and unemotional sense in which "love/hate" could be used in Semitic speech (cf. Luke 14:26), God's treatment of Jacob's heritage vis-à-vis His treatment of Esau's heritage was like the contrast between love and hate. There is nothing here about some kind of divine hostility to Esau as a person. Still less is this a reference to his eternal damnation. Such concepts are foreign to the point Paul is making.

Instead, Paul means that a special and superior destiny was given to the descendants of Jacob as compared with the descendants of Esau. The Israelites of Malachi's day could see this truth in the contrast between God's mercy to Israel and his judgment on Edom. The status of Jacob's heritage was in fact an extended fulfillment of the promise to Rebecca that "the older child shall serve the younger one." But this destiny was awarded to Jacob and his descendants before Jacob was even born and thus was "not by works but by Him who calls" (v 12).

Once more Paul is suggesting an analogy that is central to his point about Israel's present spiritual condition. The Israelites of Paul's day, as well, could be divided between those who were simply descendants of Abraham and Isaac (like Ishmael and Esau were) and those whom God had "called" and "justified" apart from works.

Indeed Paul may even be thinking of the fact that the Israelites of Malachi's day were a mere remnant of the nation. But that remnant had experienced God's gracious restoring mercy. In the same way, the present believing remnant of Israel (as Paul will go on to show) experiences God's mercy in contrast to their unbelieving brethren who are "vessels of wrath" (cf. vv 22-24 and discussion there).

The true force of Rom 9:7-13 is that there is clear Scriptural precedent for God's present dealings with His chosen nation. Israel has never received God's gracious mercy on the basis of mere physical descent from the patriarchs, nor has God's mercy been based on their works. This Scriptural precedent is fundamental to Paul's conviction that God's word has not failed (9:6).

### ii. Scripture Validates God's Mercy and Wrath in Reference to Israel (9:14-29)

God's sovereign choice of both Isaac and Jacob leads to an obvious question. In making such choices, is God acting unrighteously? Is God being unfair and unjust? Paul now wishes to address this question. After all, he has declared in his thematic proposal for Romans, "I am not ashamed of the gospel of Christ" (1:16). Would he not have cause to be "ashamed," however, if his gospel led to the conclusion that God's present dealings with His ancient people were unjust?

In fact, in both of the cases already discussed (Isaac and Jacob), God had deliberately ignored primogeniture (i.e., the rights of the firstborn, Ishmael and Esau). Did not these very examples suggest that there was something unrighteous about God's ways? We may be reasonably confident that Paul had heard these objections before, particularly from Gentiles. Did not the bypassing of the firstborn sons, Ishmael and Esau, imply that Paul's God was arbitrary and unjust? Such an issue could not be ignored by Paul, and it is given full treatment in this section.

> **9:14-16. So what shall we say? There isn't *any* unrighteousness with God, is there? Far from it! In fact He says to Moses: *"I will have mercy on whom I will have mercy, and I will have compassion on whom I will have compassion."* So then *this matter* is not from the one who wishes, nor from the one who runs, but from the God who shows mercy.**

The new section is signaled by the frequent Pauline formulation, **So what shall we say?** (*Ti oun eroumen?* cf. Rom 3:5; 4:1; 6:1; 7:7; 8:31; and also 9:30). Paul brings the unavoidable issue forward for consideration. The question is about whether God acts unrighteously, but Paul will not put it that baldly. Instead he uses the format of a Greek interrogative statement that implies that the appropriate answer is negative: **There isn't *any* unrighteousness with God, is there?**

"Of course not!" Paul replies. His actual words, **Far from it** (*Mē genoito*), are once again quite similar to the expression "perish the thought!" Such a conclusion is not thinkable for Paul. One must not forget that God has prerogatives in regard to such matters.

What are those prerogatives? The words spoken to Moses (in Exod 33:19) express them. It should be noted here that the quotation Paul draws from that text is one in which God promises to allow His glory to pass before Moses as Moses had requested (Exod 33:18). God declares, *"I will make all My goodness pass before you, and I will proclaim the name of the Lord before you."* And then follow the words Paul quotes here: **"I will have mercy on whom I will have mercy, and I will have compassion on whom I will have compassion."** Accordingly, it is part of the very glory of God to bestow mercy and compassion upon whom He will.

Paul's quotation from Exod 33:19b follows the LXX rendering exactly. The Greek words for "have mercy" (twice) are *Eleēsō* (future of *eleeō*) and *eleō* (present active subjunctive of *eleeō*) and translate the Hebrew verb *h£ānan*;

while the words for "have compassion," *oikteirēsō* and *oikteirō*, translate the Hebrew verb *rāḥam*. The Hebrew verbs, like their Greek counterparts here, cannot be sharply distinguished, so that it is likely that Paul's quotation involves "synonymous parallelism." That is, both statements mean essentially the same thing and reinforce each other.

It should be noted that it is the Hebrew verb *ḥānan* that is translated by the Greek verb *eleeō* in Paul's quoted text. This is the Hebrew verb that is used consistently in the LXX for *all* the instances of the Greek verb *charizomai* ("to be gracious," or, "to give graciously"). However, *charizomai* is many times rarer in the LXX than *eleeō*. But the choice of the Exodus text as the keynote for the present unit (9:14-29) serves Paul's purposes well. The underlying Hebrew word can function as an equivalent for the concept of either *eleos* (mercy) or *charis* (grace).

In fact, mercy becomes the pivotal concept in Romans 9–11. The verb for mercy (*eleeō*) occurs seven times in these chapters and only once more in Romans (12:8) The noun (*eleos*) occurs two times and only once more in the epistle (15:9). Altogether Romans 9–11 contain nine out of eleven uses of this root in the epistle. But for Paul this concept is essentially identical with the concept of *charis*. Thus when Paul uses the term *charis* four times in Rom 11:5-6, it is not to be distinguished from *eleos*.

The point Paul is making through the Exodus text is that when it comes to mercy/grace, God asserts His own prerogative to exercise this attribute toward the person, or persons, He Himself selects. But to state this fact is to make the case. No man can lay a legitimate claim on God for His mercy. It is man's need, inadequacy, or failure that calls forth mercy in the first place. To make it a human entitlement is to destroy its gracious character and turn it into a divine obligation. Thus if God acts in mercy/grace toward Isaac or towards Jacob, there is no unrighteousness in doing so. Neither Ishmael nor Esau was deprived of anything he had a right to claim.

The bottom line in **this matter** of mercy is that mercy does not occur simply because someone wishes it (*ou tou thelontos*) or because someone runs, i.e., strives, for it (*oude tou trechontos*). Rather it comes from the God who sovereignly bestows mercy (*tou eleountos Theou*) *on whom* He will. Man's "will" and "desire" (*thelontos*) do not produce mercy, nor do his most strenuous efforts (*trechontos*), like those of a "runner" in a race. God, not man, determines who receives His mercy.

If we ask the question, "Whom does God choose to have mercy on today?" the Pauline answer is transparent. God has chosen to have mercy upon believers, both Jew and Gentile. This is precisely Paul's point in 11:28-32 where he concludes by saying, "For God has enclosed *all men* in unbelief so that He might have mercy upon *all*" (11:32, emphasis added). God's desire to have mercy upon *all* is clearly stated in this text. The same truth is found also in 1 Tim 2:4 where we are told that God "desires *all men* to be saved and to come to the knowledge of the truth."

Neither here nor elsewhere in Romans does Paul suggest that anyone is prevented from believing by means of some kind of negative predestination in eternity past. He would have been very surprised, no doubt, to discover that his words have been put into service to such a harsh concept. At the same time, Paul would not have agreed that faith occurs without divine intervention (cf. 2 Cor 4:6). But Paul never makes an attempt to "harmonize" these realities.[6]

> **9:17-18. You see, the Scripture says to Pharaoh:** *"For this very thing I raised you up, that by means of you I might demonstrate My power, and that My name might be declared in all the earth."* **So then He has mercy on whom He wishes, and whom He wishes He hardens.**

There is a corollary, however, to God's sovereign prerogative to "have mercy on whom [He] will have mercy" (v 14). This corollary is introduced by the word *gar*, which my translation places under BDAG's extended meaning 2 ["*marker of clarification*," p. 189]. I render it, **You see.** From Paul's vantage point, the right to show mercy involves also the right *not* to show mercy. But in the withholding of mercy, God is free to harden **whom He wishes.**

The Pharaoh of the Exodus is Paul's illustration of this principle. And once again, the issue is not that of being predestined to eternal damnation. Paul here does not address at all the question of Pharaoh's eternal destiny, even though there is no known reason to expect Pharaoh to appear in God's kingdom. The issue is far narrower than that. If God so chooses, He has a right to harden anyone **He wishes.**

---

[6] Neither did Hodges try to harmonize the fact that all are free to believe in Christ and yet none will unless God opens the heart (cf. Acts 16:14). He did believe that God elected certain people to everlasting life and others He did not. Yet he also believed that anyone could come to faith and be born again and that God wanted any and all to be eternally saved. –RNW

From the perspective of Israel, the Pharaoh in question was the very epitome of resistance to Israel's God. God's demand was, "Let My people go, that they may hold a feast to Me in the wilderness" (Exod 5:1; cf. 4:23; 7:16; 8:1, 20; 9:1, 13; 10:3). It is precisely this point on which God hardened Pharaoh's heart. This is explicitly stated before Moses even goes in to see Pharaoh. God tells Moses, "When you go back to Egypt, see that you do all those wonders before Pharaoh which I have put in your hand. But I will harden his heart, so that he will not let the people go" (Exod 4:21).

The hearer/reader of Romans, however, would be likely enough to think, "Well, Pharaoh deserved it," as indeed he did. But Paul leaves Pharaoh's merits, or lack of them, out of the discussion here. Instead he quotes God's own declaration to Pharaoh, preceding the seventh plague, in which the reason for the hardening is presented from the divine perspective. The fundamental reason for hardening Pharaoh's heart lies in God's words, *"For this very thing I raised you up, that by means of you I might demonstrate My power, and that My name may be declared in all the earth."* In short, Pharaoh was hardened that God might be glorified.

It should be pointed out that Paul's quotation of Exod 9:16 is obviously not the form of the verse found in the standard edition of the LXX today (i.e., Rahlfs's edition). The verbal differences are too numerous for that. It is not conceivable that these differences can be traced to Paul (*contra* Jewett, p. 584). Instead we must postulate that Paul quotes from a version of the Greek translation that we no longer possess. The later labors of Origen and others on the textual criticism of the LXX bear tribute to the variety that existed in the manuscripts in Origen's time, and subsequently in the time of Eusebius and Pamphylus, who used his famous Hexapla.

There is no reason to think that Paul could not check his quotation against the original text, and the version he quotes here is actually closer to the Hebrew text than the one printed in Rahlfs. The only significant difference is that the Masoretic Hebrew text underlying Exod 9:16 reads, "that I might make *you* [sing.] see My power." This varies only slightly from Paul's text, as quoted here, which reads *hopōs endeixōmai en soi tēn dunamin mou* (*that by means of you I might demonstrate My power*). In fact, the rendering Paul quotes was probably considered by the translator(s) as a paraphrase of the Hebrew text consistent with the following words, *and that My name might be declared in all the earth.*

It is probable that Paul understood the Greek text in the same sense. God would indeed demonstrate His power *to* Pharaoh, but Pharaoh was simply the means by which this demonstration became world-wide. God's fame was, in fact, spread by the Exodus events. This is clearly shown in Josh 2:9-10; 9:9; and 1 Sam 6:6. In the latter text, the hardening of Pharaoh's heart is referred to in the words of the Philistines, "Why then do you harden your hearts as the Egyptians and Pharaoh hardened their hearts? When He did mighty things among them, did they not let the people go, that they might depart?"

Paul does not quote this divine statement carelessly. On the contrary, it follows shortly after the first direct statement that God *did* actually harden Pharaoh's heart. Although, in 4:21 and 7:3, the Lord had declared His intention to do exactly that, it is not until Exod 9:12 that we are specifically told, "But the Lord hardened the heart of Pharaoh; and he did not heed them, just as the Lord had spoken to Moses" (Exod 9:12). Between 7:3 and 9:12, however, the hardening process is attributed to Pharaoh himself (Exod 8:15, 32).

We may be sure Paul knew all this. God's stated intention was to "harden Pharaoh's heart, and multiply My signs and wonders in the land of Egypt" (Exod 7:3). Had Pharaoh repented after only a few of the ten plagues, God's **power** would not have been fully demonstrated. The Lord would not allow that to happen until His mighty demonstration was complete. But it is unmistakable that all that God really does is to confirm and extend a process of hardening that Pharaoh himself had initiated.

No doubt Paul expects perceptive hearers/readers of Romans to put these facts together. But his point is not at all to justify what God did, but to insist that God had every right to do it. His conclusion involves an emphatic construction consisting of two inferential conjunctions (*Ara oun*) rendered here as **So then**. The bottom line for Paul is not only that God **has mercy on whom He wishes** (as stated in v 16), but also that **whom He wishes He hardens**.

Both points matter for Paul's argument. God in fact is presently having mercy on both Jews and Gentiles who believe (see 9:23-24; 11:30-32). But He has also hardened unbelieving Israel (11:25). Both are sovereign prerogatives that God exercises as He wishes. But the case of Pharaoh is instructive, since Pharaoh hardened his own heart before God hardened it. Paul would no doubt have said the same of Israel. Its hardness to the gospel of Jesus Christ was a process Israel itself began and which God has merely confirmed. This national hardness will continue "until the fullness of the Gentiles has come in" (Rom 11:25).

But Paul's development of this theme also shows that God will still have mercy on any individual Israelite who believes. Paul leaves undiscussed any particular factors that might distinguish believing and unbelieving Israelites, either in his time or in ours. The attempts to penetrate the unrevealed counsels of God on this point are futile.

In the previous unit (9:6-18) Paul has established the divine prerogative of either extending mercy or of hardening the human heart as God so determines. But this issue was no doubt far from new to Paul, who must have encountered it both in the synagogues and also in the market places where he held discussions (cf. Acts 17:17). The objection to his position, to which he now turns, must have been quite familiar.

> **9:19-21. You will say to me therefore, "Why does He still blame *anyone*? For who withstands His will?" On the contrary, O man, who are you to answer back to God? The thing molded won't say to its Molder, will it, "Why have you made me this way?" Or does not the potter have authority over the clay, to make out of the same batch of clay one vessel for honor and another for dishonor?**

The obvious comeback to Paul's statements in 9:7-13 was one he had probably heard many times. The words, **You will say to me therefore**, suggest this familiarity.

"If you're right," an objector might say, "then **why does God still blame *anyone*? For who withstands His will?**" If God hardens the human heart, how could anyone do anything differently, and therefore why would God blame him for what he does? But Paul does not consider this a worthy question. Indeed it is utterly inappropriate since it intrudes the creature into the counsel of his Creator.

The words, **On the contrary, O man, who are you to answer back to God?**, disallow the right of the questioner to raise this issue at all. He is, in fact, trying *to answer back* to his Maker. The articular Greek construction that Paul uses here (*ho antapokrinomenos tō Theō*) might be taken to be a shade scornful, as in the English, "Who are you—this person who answers back to God!" That is, "Who do you think you are to answer God back?"

This kind of reply suggests that Paul does not regard the objection as weighty. What right, he asks, has a creature to tell his Creator what He can blame him for? This is not a way of saying that God has the privilege of being totally arbitrary. Such a view of God is unworthy of God. But it suggests the extreme limitations on knowledge that all human beings possess. How can I, a mere human, possibly know in any case of hardening, the extent to which there is human culpability? As we have seen, the Exodus story indirectly indicates that Pharaoh "had it coming" and that God's own hardening action merely complemented what Pharaoh did to himself.

So the objection Paul is dismissing is a conceptual mismatch. One could not imagine, says Paul, that **the thing molded** could **say to its Molder…"Why have you made me this way?"** The analogy is apt, for the artisan's wisdom and skill cannot for a moment be truly understood— much less questioned—by an inanimate, non-sentient object molded by him. The absurdity of such a thing is apparent. But no less absurd is a human who tries *to answer back to God*.

A potter, in fact, was well within his rights to take a lump from a **batch of clay** and make a beautiful vessel out of it (e.g., a piece of fine dishware). But equally he could draw from **the same** *batch* the clay needed for a vessel used in the labors of a scullery maid or some other household servant. The former was a **vessel for honor** proudly displayed to the guests in a household. The latter was a vessel of another kind. Since it was used for ignominious tasks it could be said to be **for dishonor** and so was kept out of sight in the kitchen area or in a closet.

This down-to-earth illustration from the daily experience of anyone of even modest wealth in Paul's time carries its point. God is the eternal "Molder" and "Potter." In His infinite wisdom and skill He fashions and forms human "clay" as it pleases Him to do. To the vessel that reflects His glory, there is *honor*. To the one that serves as the dark backdrop for that glory, there is *dishonor*. Man has no standing at all to challenge this!

Paul therefore refuses to be put into the position of defending God, even if—as in the case of Pharaoh—he might easily have done so. But any debate on such a matter implies that one might in fact delegitimize God's prerogatives. This is something Paul declines even to consider.

**9:22. But *who can object* if God, because He wishes to demonstrate *His* wrath and make known His power, has borne with great patience the vessels of wrath fitted for ruin,**

The Greek words that open these verses follow smoothly from what Paul has just said. I have supplied the phrase ***who can object*** for clarity, but the actual Greek text has only *Ei de* (lit., "And if"). The effect of this short phrase, which has no strict grammatical completion in this verse, is something like the English term, "So what of it!" "What about it if God does thus and so?" Paul is saying. As he has just affirmed in vv 19-21, God acts as He "wishes" because He is the Divine Potter. Paul will now continue that figure with a discussion of the Potter's differing types of vessels.

The Divine Potter has a right, Paul insists, to **demonstrate His wrath and make known His power**, if that is what He wishes to do. The word for **wishes** (*thelōn*) picks up the same verb that Paul uses in 9:16 (once) and 9:17 (twice). Its force is better felt when the participial form is rendered circumstantially as a causal clause (**because He wishes**). What God has done with regard to **the vessels** Paul now speaks of, was done simply because that is what God wanted to do. The reasons are not within man's knowledge and, even if they were, they are not open to man's challenge.

The reference here to wrath immediately recalls the words of 1:18: "For the *wrath of God* is revealed from heaven against all the ungodliness and unrighteousness of men who suppress the truth by unrighteousness" (emphasis added). Pharaoh was a classic case in point. He wished to deny God's right to take His people out of Egypt. His refusal to obey God's command was an unrighteous effort to *suppress the truth* about the God of Israel.

Pharaoh's contemptuous words reflect human arrogance perfectly: "Who is the Lord, that I should obey His voice to let Israel go? I do not know the Lord, nor will I let Israel go" (Exod 5:2). Accordingly, God chose to deal with Pharaoh, as He has also with mankind as a whole (Rom 1:18), in a way that displayed His righteous wrath and at the same time manifested His divine power. Pharaoh clearly belonged among **the vessels of wrath fitted for ruin**.

But Paul uses the plural *vessels* here. Pharaoh is now simply a case in point. At this stage of the discussion Paul wishes to apply the principles he has enunciated (vv 17-21) to the current situation of Israel. What has happened is that God has chosen *to demonstrate His wrath and make known His power* in reference to unbelieving Israel. Paul has in mind the basic fact that "with regard to the gospel" unbelieving Israelites "are enemies for [the Gentiles'] sake" (11:28). Thus Israel in unbelief has become a focus for God's wrath.

As Paul's discussion of God's wrath in 1:18-32 shows, the term *wrath* does not really suggest what we call *eternal damnation*.[7] In Romans 1 God's wrath is manifestly a temporal divine anger and to make it more than this is a serious error. The idea that God will be eternally angry at the lost who are condemned to hell is a serious distortion of God's character. The psalmist was right to say, "The Lord is merciful and gracious, slow to anger, and abounding in mercy. He will not always strive with us, nor will He keep His anger forever" (Ps 103:8-9). And again, "For His anger is but for a moment" (Ps 30:5).

In the Bible *all* divine anger belongs to time; *none* of it belongs to eternity. The destiny of the lost is an issue of justice, not an expression of anger. We are not therefore on legitimate ground to take Paul's statement here as God's determination that unbelieving Israelites must necessarily remain unbelieving because they are currently objects of God's wrath. As Paul will show in chaps. 10 and 11, any unbelieving Israelite may respond in faith to the gospel even now. Justified Gentiles, too, were once under God's wrath in terms of Rom 1:18-32.

In fact, God has been implicitly merciful to *the vessels of wrath*. This is seen in the fact that He **has borne** them **with great patience**. Paul no doubt has in mind here the fact that God's judgment had not yet fallen in full force upon his nation. Paul was most certainly aware of our Lord's prophecies about the calamities that would overtake them (e.g., Matt 24:1-2; Luke 13:3-5), and which did so in the Jewish war of AD 66–70. But all this lay ahead.

Nevertheless, the Jews' repeated opposition to the proclamation of Jesus as the Christ had deeply affected them. As Paul states in 1 Thess 2:15-16, the Jews had "killed both the Lord Jesus and their own prophets, and have persecuted us, and they do not please God, and are contrary to all men, forbidding us to speak to the Gentiles that they may be saved, so that they always keep their sins filled up. And *wrath* has overtaken them to the uttermost" (author's translation and emphasis). It would be hard to imagine a more vigorous description of divine wrath than this.

---

[7] Moo, *Romans*, 607, presents God as decreeing eternal condemnation in eternity past to vessels of wrath. He says, "…the agent of 'prepared' is indeed God: Paul considers the 'vessels on whom God's wrath rests' as prepared by God himself for eternal condemnation." Such an interpretation errs in two fundamentals: the passage mentions no divine decree and the NT uses *wrath* for temporal, not eternal, judgment. –JHN

Yet despite their appalling full measure of sin, the calamities prophesied for Israel had not yet come to pass. This delay was precisely because God had *borne with great patience* these *vessels of wrath*. But of this, too, Pharaoh was an example. God's repeated grace in withdrawing the plagues when Pharaoh begged Moses for that (Exod 8:8, 28; 9:27-28; 10:16-17) was a manifest divine mercy to this rebellious ruler. At the same time, the resulting multiplication of the plagues continued *to demonstrate* God's wrath and *His power.*

God had therefore also shown mercy to Israel in Paul's day. But disaster lay ahead, because these *vessels of wrath* were obviously *fitted for ruin*. The Greek phrase that is rendered by *fitted for ruin* is *katērtismena eis apōleian* and should not be understood in context to mean "fitted for hell." The word *apōleia* could certainly be used of eternal damnation (e.g., Matt 7:13; John 17:12; Rev 17:8, 11). But it is also used in the NT in reference to the "waste" of ointment (Matt 26:8; Mark 14:4) or in reference to "death" (Acts 25:16 [Majority Text]). Likewise, the cognate Greek verb (*apollumi*) in the NT means primarily "to cause or experience destruction" (BDAG, p. 115). It is used many times in the NT of temporal calamity and, in reference to persons, especially of death (in Matthew alone note 8:25; 12:14; 21:41; 22:7; 26:52; 27:20; see BDAG 1 a, pp. 115-16).

In general Greek usage, therefore, the word group to which *apōleia* belongs was general rather than specific. TDNT (1:463) points out that in classical Greek "the ideas conveyed by this group of words usually involve injury (of a violent nature), destruction or the final end of earthly existence." The exact nature, or form, of these experiences must always be determined in the NT by context. NT commentators should resist the "knee-jerk" reaction of equating the term *apōleia* with hell.

Each NT passage requires close consideration (including the six uses in 2 Peter), while the numerous instances of the word (over one hundred) in the LXX overwhelmingly refer to some form of temporal calamity. In fact, *apōleia* in the LXX actually reflects as many as twenty-one Hebrew words or phrases. It has no technical sense in Biblical Greek at all, much less a technical sense referring to eternal damnation.

On the analogy with Pharaoh, Paul's prototype for the vessels of wrath, we ought to think in this context of the national disaster that lay ahead of Israel in Paul's time. The judgment of AD 70, with its destruction of Jerusalem and of the splendid Jewish temple, along with the death of 1.1 million people (mainly Jews [Josephus, *War* VI, ix. 3]), was fully worthy of the term *apōleia* or *ruin*. One is reminded of the way the servants of Pharaoh admonished him, "How long shall this man be a snare to us? Let the men go, that they may serve the Lord their God. Do you not yet know that Egypt is destroyed?" (Exod 10:8; LXX: "destroyed," *apolōlen*, from *apollumi*).

As has often been noticed, Paul does not directly assign the process of fitting for ruin to God. Although he clearly believes that Israel is under God's judgment (see 11:25-27), it is also apparent that they themselves have contributed heavily to the spiritual condition which makes them ripe for disaster. The verb form translated by *fitted* (*katērtismena*) means approximately what I mean by the word *prepared* and more should not be read into it than that. There is nothing here to suggest that Paul is thinking of a mysterious divine decree before time began. The behavior of his nation in Paul's own day sufficiently explained Israel's ripeness for ruin (cf. again 1 Thess 2:15-16), just as Pharaoh's behavior explained his.

> **9:23-24. and *also wishes* to make known the wealth of His glory upon the vessels of mercy, which He has prepared beforehand for glory—*that is*, upon us whom in fact He has called, not only from among the Jews, but also from among the Gentiles?**

These verses continue the sentence begun in v 22. Paul has just said that "God…wishes to demonstrate His wrath and make known His power" and so He bears "with great patience the vessels of wrath." Verse 23 then begins with a purpose clause (introduced by *hina*) which is connected with this idea. In all probability we should take the *hina* here as grammatically dependent upon *thelōn* ("because He wishes," v 22).

The *hina* clause is therefore semantically parallel with the Greek infinitives *endeixasthai* and *gnōrisai* ("to demonstrate," "to make known," v 22). In fact, the *hina* in v 23 is followed by *gnōrisē* which picks up the earlier *gnōrisai* of v 22. The words *also wishes*, supplied in my translation, are intended to clarify this structure for the English reader.

Paul is affirming that God "wishes" to do two things: (1) manifest "His wrath" and "His power" (v 22); and (2) manifest **the wealth of His glory** (v 23). The former He does with reference to "the vessels of wrath," while the latter is done **upon the vessels of mercy**. These *vessels of mercy* are identified in v 24 as both Jews and Gentiles.

In connection with the "vessels of wrath," God's patience with them has lengthened the time for the demonstration of His "wrath" and "power," just as did His patience with Pharaoh. But it has also afforded an opportunity for God to display Himself as well in terms of *the wealth of His glory* (*ton plouton tēs doxēs autou*). This glory is nothing less than the richness (*plouton*) of His mercy since that mercy has now been extended to Jew and Gentile alike (v 24), who are equally *the vessels of mercy*.

In short, the recalcitrance of Israel which has called forth divine wrath has also been the catalyst for demonstrating how rich God is in mercy. Paul means by this that God's mercy has overleaped the boundaries of Israel itself and has gone out to the Gentile world. God is not so "poverty-stricken" that He must confine His mercy to Israel.[8] The growing number of Gentile believers proves *the wealth of His glory* in terms of God's measureless mercy. As Paul will soon say, the "transgression" of Israel "is the enriching (*ploutos*) of the world and their failure is the enriching (*ploutos*) of the Gentiles" (11:12).

Moreover *the vessels of mercy* themselves are vessels which the Divine Potter **has prepared beforehand for glory**. This last phrase has reference to the truth Paul expressed in 8:30, in which the divine work in believers is traced from His pre-knowledge of them onward, that is, through the steps identified by the terms *called*, *justified* and *glorified*. God's pre-knowledge, call, and justification of believers is precisely what *has prepared* them *beforehand* for participation in God's eternal glory.

*The vessels of mercy* that have been prepared in this way are identified in v 24 as **us whom in fact He has called**. The words *whom in fact* translate the Greek phrase *hous kai*, and a rendering like "whom He also" would be misleading here (notwithstanding NIV, NASB). The *kai* is left untranslated by KJV, NKJV, NACE and JB. (JB paraphrases, "Well, we are those people.") In Zerwick's discussion of *kai*, he correctly points out that "A very frequent usage…is that where *kai* immediately follows the relative

---

[8] Cranfield, *Romans*, 2.497f, rightly notes the close connection between v 23 and v 24. He also notes that relative clauses rarely serve as independent (rather than embedded) sentences. This leads to translating *kai* as *also*, rather than as *and*. In other words, "us, whom He called, not of the Jews only, but also of the Gentiles" (v 24) further defines "vessels of mercy" (v 23).

The phrase "which He prepared beforehand for glory" refers back to Rom 8:28-30. Sanday and Headlam, *Romans*, 263, rightly say, "the best commentary on these words is Rom. viii. 28-30." The yet future glory will be revealed in us when creation is released from its bondage (Rom 8:18*ff.*).

Combining these ideas, God's calling and justification now prepare Jewish and Gentile believers for that future glorification. Calling plus justification guarantees glorification for all believers in Jesus Christ. –JHN

pronoun without there seeming to be any special reason for its insertion"
(p. 156; and see his footnote 1). Here we are no doubt in the presence of
an idiom and my own translation offers the colorless phrase *in fact*.

It is quite improbable that Paul thought that God's call was *in addition
to* His preparation of *the vessels of mercy* ahead of time (beforehand). The
idea in the words *has prepared beforehand* (*proētoimasen*) is that this glory
lies ahead and God has been at work to get us ready for it. In fact, in light
of 8:30, God has both called and justified the believer in anticipation of
future glory. Paul's point here is that God's preparatory work of calling has,
*in fact*, already been in operation on *the vessels of mercy*. Those vessels are
variegated in character (like the work of any talented potter) and consist
**not only** of people **from among the Jews, but also** of people **from among
the Gentiles**.

> **9:25-26. As indeed He says by Hosea, "*I will call them who
> were not My people, My people, and her who was not beloved,
> beloved.*" "*And it shall be that in the place where it was said to
> them, 'You are not My people,' there they shall be called sons of
> the living God.*"**

Paul now begins to enforce his point with a catena, or chain, of OT
proof texts. Ever since the introduction to the major unit covering chaps.
9–11 (that is, since 9:1-5), Paul has rounded off each sub-unit with an OT
citation. Thus, the sub-unit 9:6-9 ended with a quotation from Genesis
18; the sub-unit 9:11-13 with one from Malachi 1; but the much lengthier
sub-unit (9:14-29) concludes with a series of such quotations. This fact
speaks to the importance of this longer unit in conveying Paul's thought.

In this lengthy unit, Paul has argued that God is dealing with
unbelieving Israel through a wrath that is tempered by long patience with
them, and that He has taken the opportunity thus provided to extend
His mercy beyond the boundaries of Israel to Gentiles, who were not
previously God's people at all.[9] Is this mode of operating true to God's
revealed character? The answer is "yes," as two quotations from Hosea
demonstrate. The introductory phrase, **as indeed He says by Hosea**, is
not equivalent to saying that the prophet's words are *fulfilled* by Paul's

---

[9] Individual Gentiles were, of course, born again during the time before the Church Age. But
there was no corporate entity made up of Gentile believers before the birth of the Church. The
only group of believers then was Israel. –RNW

application of them. The word *as* suggests simple conformity with the situation Paul is discussing.

Both quotations refer in the context of Hosea to the northern kingdom of Israel, which God had rejected because of its spiritual harlotry expressed in idolatry. But for Paul's purposes the words of Hosea sufficiently establish the principle that those at one time rejected as the people of God can be received by Him as His people. Since the vessels of mercy are composed of both Jews and Gentiles (vv 23-24), God's loving action in having mercy on them makes the principle exhibited in Hosea applicable to both.

The two quotations Paul uses are presented in reverse order to their sequence in Hosea. Verse 25 quotes Hos 2:23 (LXX: 2:25), while v 26 quotes 1:10 (LXX: 2:1b). The sequence in Paul is probably dictated by the fact that Hosea 2:23 is directly connected with the theme of mercy highlighted by Paul in Rom 8:23-24. Hosea 1:10 further elaborates that mercy.

It should be pointed out in passing, however, that although the quotation of Hos 1:10 agrees verbatim with the LXX (2:1b), Hos 2:23 does not precisely reflect the Septuagint as we know it today. It is probably an exercise in futility to try to explain the variations in terms of Pauline rephrasing. The likelihood is that Tertius (16:22), or Paul himself, checked their Greek version of Hosea, especially for a formal treatise like Romans. As already noted, Paul appears to use a form of the LXX that differs at various points from the form we now know.

In fact, the quotation of Hos 2:23 actually reverses the Hebrew and LXX order of the two quoted statements (identified here as #one and #two). It is altogether plausible to conclude that *Kalesō ton ou laon mou 'laon mou'* renders Hebrew clause #two (MT = 2:25b), which can be handled literally in English as, "I will say to not-My-people, My people—you." The following words in Paul's quotation, *Kai tēn ouk ēgapēmēnen 'ēgapēmēnen,'* are also easily seen as an equivalent of Hebrew clause #one (MT: 2:25a), literally, "I will love [Heb: *piel of rāḥam*] her-not-loved" [Heb: *pual of rāḥam*]. In the sequence Paul gives here, then, the two clauses of the Hebrew text (#one, #two) have been reversed, so that #two precedes #one.

The total LXX quotation involved would then be: "*I will call not-My-people, My people, and her-not-beloved, beloved.*" Though this reverses the order of the underlying Hebrew clauses, it does not really affect the sense. The flexible Hebrew verb *'āmar* (to say) is rendered by *Kalesō*, which is allowed to govern both clauses (when reversed). The result is a smooth translation that captures the basic thought. It is in the highest degree probable that this is what Paul (and/or Tertius) found in their Greek translation and, like the quotation in v 26, they repeated it verbatim.

Paul's Greek text, therefore, rendered Hos 2:23 (MT and LXX, 2:25) using a form of *agapaō*, but Paul would no doubt have been aware that the Hebrew word underlying both instances (*ēgapēmenēn* twice) was *rāham*. This Hebrew verb was a suitable equivalent for the Greek verb *eleeō* ("to be merciful"). *Eleeō* occurs in the standard edition of the LXX more than twenty times as a translation for *rāham* (nine of them in Hosea). Paul's OT text is chosen precisely because it dealt with the theme of God's mercy, which, after all, is not really distinct from His love.

Together the two quotations from Hosea present God's loving acceptance of those upon whom He shows mercy, since He acknowledges them as His people and as **"sons of the living God."** This acceptance is experienced by "the vessels of mercy," namely, "those whom He in fact has called, not only from among the Jews, but also from among the Gentiles" (Rom 9:23-24). In the very broadest sense, then, the divine action referred to by Hosea applies to all who experience new birth and who thereby become God's sons and are members of His eternal family. What Hosea applied to Israel refers to nothing less than the wealth of mercy that God bestows on all who are part of His true people, whether they are Jews or Gentiles.

> **9:27-28. And Isaiah cries out concerning Israel: *"Though the number of the sons of Israel should be as the sand of the sea, the remnant shall be delivered, for He is doing a reckoning, completing it and cutting it short in righteousness, because the Lord will carry out a reckoning that is cut short on the earth."***

In his second quotation, taken from Isa 10:22-23, Paul wishes to establish the additional point that God's mercy to Israel takes the form of mercy to a greatly reduced segment of the whole nation. In other words, Paul is expressing what we might call "remnant theology" as it relates to Israel's present and future.

Once again Paul's quotation essentially follows the LXX but contains variants that suggest a slightly different version of it than mine. We may begin by dismissing the Critical Text variants here (that is, *hupoleimma* for *kataleimma* and the omission of *en dikaiosunē*; the former is a stylistic change, the latter likely a scribal accident). The Majority Text is identical at these points with the current form of the LXX.

On the other hand, Paul's quotation contains the Greek words *Ean hē ho arithmos tōn huiōn Israēl* (**"though the number of the sons of Israel should be"**) which differ slightly from the underlying Hebrew: "for if Your people Israel shall be" (LXX: *kai ean genētai ho laos Israēl*). But Paul's form is simply a paraphrase of the underlying Hebrew. In addition, Paul's quotation has *epi tēs gēs* (on the earth) instead of the LXX's *en tē oikoumenē holē* (on the entire inhabited earth) for the Hebrew of "in the midst of all the earth." Once again, the version cited by Paul seems to slightly paraphrase the original Hebrew text.

It is crucial to understanding the point of Paul's citation that the Greek term *Logon* (used twice) be correctly understood. In my translation I have rendered it by the word *reckoning*, which reflects a well-known semantic category for *logos* (BDAG, pp. 600-601). In the NT we meet this usage again in Rom 14:12, as well as in Matt 12:36; 18:23; 25:19; Luke 16:2; Acts 19:40; Heb 13:17; 1 Pet 4:5. The Greek translators, therefore, selected this sense of *logos* for the Hebrew word *killāyôn* in Isa 10:22 and repeated it for clarity in 10:23.

The Isaiah passage (Isa 10:20-27) is fundamentally eschatological and points towards the end time calamities which are to fall on the entire world (namely, the Great Tribulation). From these calamities only a remnant of Israel will **"be delivered"** and survive to enter the kingdom. Jesus was speaking of these very calamities in His Olivet Discourse when He said, "And unless those days were shortened, no flesh would be saved; but for the elect's sake [i.e., for Israel's sake] those days will be shortened" (Matt 24:22). Israel will survive though in greatly reduced numbers, precisely because of God's mercy and fidelity to them. Only a remnant of them will enter God's kingdom.

It is important to note that Paul has selected here a prophetic utterance about Israel's future deliverance (or, salvation) from temporal divine wrath. The statement that **"the remnant shall be delivered"** (Greek: *sōthēsetai*) picks up Paul's important word group *sōzō/sōtēria*. This ties the Isaiah text back to Rom 8:24; 5:9-10; and, finally, to the theme in 1:16. Isaiah, we are being told, foresaw the wrath that Israel would undergo and knew that her survival would be realized only by a small remnant of the whole nation. As Paul will shortly say, "also at the present time there is a remnant [*leimma*] according to His choice by grace" (11:5).

In the eschatological perspective of Isaiah, the reckoning that God would make with mankind **"on the earth"** would be brief. Isaiah sees the Lord **"completing it and cutting it short in righteousness."** God's righteous work of judgment will be swiftly completed and brought to an end. This fact is emphasized by its repetition in the final words of Paul's citation: **"the Lord will carry out a reckoning that is cut short on the earth."** It is highly probable Paul was thinking here of His Lord's words that were spoken to the same effect (see again Matt 24:21-22). God's mercy would finally bring His wrath to its swift consummation.

> **9:29. And just as Isaiah had previously said, "If the Lord of Hosts had not left us descendants, we would have become like Sodom, and we should have been comparable to Gomorrah."**

The unit (9:14-29) is now rounded off by a final quotation, this one also drawn from Isaiah (i.e., Isa 1:9). By **previously said** Paul intends to indicate that he is about to quote an Isaianic statement made earlier than the one he has just used. Obviously Isa 1:9 precedes 10:22-23, but the present quote is so near the beginning of Isaiah's prophecy that Paul may have thought of it as virtually thematic in character.

The quotation agrees verbatim with our present version of the LXX and accurately reflects the Hebrew of the MT. Still, it should be noted that the word for *descendants* that Paul picks up from his LXX version is the Greek *sperma*. This renders the underlying Hebrew *śārîḏ* (survivor). Thus the thought of the Hebrew text coheres closely with the "remnant theology" Paul has discussed in this unit of material. The *sperma* in this context is in fact the remnant, the survivors of the eschatological day of wrath.

Once again Paul selects a passage which transparently reproduces his fundamental concept of God's wrath as a temporal manifestation (as in 1:18ff). The destruction of the wicked cities of Sodom and Gomorrah is not an example of eternal damnation, but of devastating temporal judgment. The OT prophet is declaring that, but for God's mercy, Israel might be as completely wiped out as were these two notorious cities.

Thus, Paul has now laid the Biblical groundwork for what he is about to say about the contemporary situation. The chain of quotations has established the fact the God who sovereignly bestows mercy on whom He wishes (9:14-18) is acting now in a way consistent with Biblical revelation. As the Divine Potter, answerable to no one, He both postpones His ultimate judgment on the vessels of wrath while dealing mercifully with the vessels of mercy, both Jewish and Gentile (9:19-24). The dramatic reduction in the number of Jews who actually receive that mercy produces a mere remnant of the whole nation. But none of this is surprising as the words cited from Hosea and Isaiah (in 9:25-29) make clear.

### iii. Conclusion: Israel Has Stumbled over Christ (9:30-33)

Paul is now prepared to state the bottom line in his argument so far. Israel is the object of God's wrath, and the Gentiles of His mercy, because of Israel's rejection of Christ. This is a conclusion he will elaborate in the following discussions (chaps. 10 and 11). But it was important for Paul to show that what he postulates about God's actions in wrath and mercy can be validated from the Word of God. These actions are consistent with God's actions in the past and in the prophesied future. He now summarizes the present situation.

**9:30-31. So what shall we say? That the Gentiles who were not pursuing righteousness, have obtained righteousness, but *it is* a righteousness that is by faith. But Israel, while pursuing the law of righteousness, has not attained to the law of righteousness.**

Paul opens the concluding sub-unit of the section 9:30-33 with the same words that opened the preceding sub-unit (9:14-29). The question **So what shall we say?** invites attention to the conclusion to be drawn from his presentation thus far.

As he has already stated, Gentiles are among those who are now vessels of mercy (9:24). This leads to the startling result that the notoriously unrighteous Gentiles have actually **obtained righteousness**. Indeed, God's mercy is such that this is true even though these Gentiles previously **were not pursuing righteousness** at all. God's great mercy has overtaken them through the gospel.

This righteousness is not based on their conduct, since they were not even pursuing such a goal. On the contrary, according to Paul's gospel expounded earlier in Romans (that is, in 3:21–5:11), this righteousness is bestowed on them on the basis of faith. The word translated *pursuing* (*diōkonta*) is a strong one that suggests diligent pursuit. Paul is not denying that **the Gentiles** might at times fitfully or half-heartedly pursue righteousness. Moreover he is speaking generally in terms of overall

Gentile culture. No Jew was likely to question this kind of summary of Gentile life.

The explanatory words, **but *it is* a righteousness that is by faith**, are intended to highlight the contrast with Israel that follows immediately. The righteousness that has been obtained by Gentiles is quite different in character from the kind pursued by Israel.

That nation actually *is* pursuing a form of righteousness, Paul says. But it is not a faith-righteousness that they pursue, but rather **the law of righteousness**. That is to say, they are seeking righteousness before God by means of Torah, *the law* that prescribes righteous conduct. But this pursuit, as Paul has already shown in Romans (see 3:19-20) has failed, with the result that **Israel has not attained to the law of righteousness**. The Greek verb for **attained** (*ephthase*) carries a connotation like our word *reach*. Though Israel pursued legal righteousness with zeal (see 10:2), such righteousness is in fact *out of their reach*. They have not reached their goal.

> **9:32-33.** Why? Because *they did* not *seek it* by faith, but as *if it came* by the works of the law. For they have collided with the Stone of collision, just as it is written, *"Behold, I place in Zion a Stone of collision and a Rock of entrapment, and everyone who believes in Him shall not be ashamed."*

The reason for Israel's failure to attain righteousness is now specified precisely. They were seeking righteousness in the wrong way, that is, by means of **the works of the law** rather than by means of faith. This misdirection of effort on Israel's part resulted in a serious collision with the true Source of divine righteousness, the Lord Jesus Christ.

In my translation the phrase *"Stone of collision"* replaces the traditional English expression "stumbling stone" (KJV, NKJV, NASB, NIV, NACE, JB). The idea of "stumbling" is too weak here. In Paul's statement (based on Isa 28:16 quoted in the next verse) a cognate noun and verb are used (*Prosekopsan, proskommatos*: collided, collision). The verb *proskoptō* is fundamentally stronger than "to stumble" and has the extended meanings "to cause to strike against something" and "to make contact with something in a bruising or violent way" (BDAG, p. 882).

Obviously Israel had collided violently with her promised Messiah, Jesus Christ, with the result that He died a violent death at her hands.

But this collision was foretold by Isaiah the prophet. Once again, as in all of the sub-units of 9:6-33, this final sub-unit is concluded with an OT citation. Paul's quotation itself is sometimes thought to be a combination of Isa 8:14 and 28:16.[10] But a comparison of these two verses as they are found in the MT and in the LXX makes such a combination improbable. For one thing the LXX varies significantly from the MT of both verses. Indeed, the LXX of Isa 28:16 can hardly have been translated from the MT as we now have it. By contrast, Paul's quotation is quite close to the MT.

In fact, Paul's quotation can be read from the MT of Isa 28:16 with only one significant textual difference. The words *"a Stone of collision and a Rock of entrapment"* correspond with the Hebrew text except that in the MT there is no word for *collision*. The Hebrew text in English would be, "Behold I lay in Zion a stone, a stone that puts to the test."

The Hebrew word for "put to the test" is *bōḥan* and is treated in HALAT as a unique instance of the word (p. 37).[11] More likely, it is a participle form of the Hebrew verb *bachan* ("to test"). It is not unlikely that at one time a participle also followed the first instance of the Hebrew word "stone." This could have been, for example, a form of the Hebrew verb *nāgap̱*, which actually is rendered by *proskoptō* four times in the LXX. Thus a participle form of this verb could well have been represented by *proskommatos*.

The data suggest the following probable conclusions: (1) the words *lithon proskommatos kai petran skandalou* accurately reflected the Hebrew text from which they were translated; (2) this Hebrew form of the text existed in Paul's day and was known to Paul; (3) the participle following the first *'ā̱ben* ("stone") in the Hebrew text had been lost (or was not found) in the sources that reached the Masoretes (sixth–tenth century AD). (4) Paul's text is likely to have been the original form of the Hebrew.

It should also be noted that the words *a Rock of entrapment* were the Greek translators' interpretation of the Hebrew *e̱ben bōḥan* ("a stone putting to the test"). The Greek rendering, *petran skandalou* construed the Hebrew *bōḥan* as a reference to some form of ensnaring trial. This cohered well with the earlier words *lithon proskommatos*. Both phrases refer to the devastating and destructive mistake that Israel made in rejecting her Messiah.

---

[10] See Gleason Archer and Gregory Chirichigno, *Old Testament Quotations in the New Testament: A Complete Survey* (Chicago, IL: Moody, 1983), 97. –ZCH

[11] Walter Baumgartner, Ludwig Koehler, and Johan Jacob Stamm, eds., *Hebräisches und aramäisches Lexicon zum Alten Testament* (5 vols.; Leiden: Brill, 1967-1997). –ZCH

Finally, it is important to note that Paul extends his quotation from Isa 28:16 to include the words about the believer not being ashamed. To reach these words, however, he skips over a portion of the MT that does not serve his immediate purpose. (The skipped words in the MT are difficult but may possibly be rendered by "a valuable corner(stone) for a foundation *that is* founded"). But the words immediately following the omitted phrase are those with which Paul concludes his quotation here.

This concluding statement from Isa 28:16, *"And everyone who believes in Him shall not be ashamed,"* is important to the following discussion found in Romans 10 and it is cited again in 10:11. Its use there suggests that Paul understood these words as a command (e.g., "you shall not kill") rather than as a statement (e.g., "you will not kill"). Its force, then, is that despite the rejection of Christ by Israel, for whom He is *a Stone of collision*, the believer in Jesus should never *be ashamed* of Him and of his identification with Him. The ramifications of this truth will emerge in the next unit of material (10:1-21).

# Romans 10

### b. Israel's Deliverance Requires Faith
### and Confession (10:1-21)

Paul has now set forth the present spiritual situation of Israel and has shown it to be anticipated by Scripture (9:6-33). The Word of God has not failed (9:6a), even though Israel has. What then is the solution to this dilemma? Paul will now proceed to discuss that issue.

### i. Israel's Need for Righteousness (10:1-4)

**10:1. Brothers, the desire of my heart, and my prayer to God on behalf of Israel, is for *their* deliverance.**

The new unit is opened with the word **Brothers**. This is the only time in Romans that the word *brothers* opens a sentence. Its effect (especially on an audience hearing Romans being read aloud) would be arresting: "Brothers, listen!"

The obvious major thrust of the preceding unit is that Israel as a whole is an object of divine wrath (9:22), like Pharaoh was at the time of the Exodus (9:17-18), or like Sodom and Gomorrah (9:29). The nation has had a devastating "collision" with their own Messiah (9:32-33). What they urgently need is deliverance from their present status, that is, deliverance from divine wrath. The term for *deliverance* (*sōtērian*) is to be taken here consistently with the use throughout the epistle of the word group *sōzō/sōtēria* (see discussions at 1:16; 5:9,10; 8:24; 9:27). Its reference is to rescue from the temporal display of God's anger.

But though it is true that Israel is under God's wrath, Paul strongly affirms that his desires for Israel are positive. **The desire of** his **heart**, as well as his **prayer to God**, is that their spiritual situation might be radically altered by the experience of deliverance. This assertion carries us back to Paul's statements in 9:1-3 where he also insists strongly on his love for Israel. As indicated in the discussion there, it seems likely that Paul was at times accused of a negative attitude toward his own nation.

The question might well be raised whether the Pauline ministry to the Gentiles did not, in fact, show a basic hostility toward God's ancient people. But Paul would have been *ashamed* to preach a gospel that was overtly, or implicitly, hostile to national Israel. The gospel of Jesus Christ implied no such attitude on his part and he was unashamed to preach it (1:16). In fact, as he will now say specifically, his gospel was precisely what Israel needed.

> **10:2-3. For I bear witness about them that they have a zeal for God, but not according to knowledge. For since they are ignorant of God's righteousness and are seeking to establish their own righteousness, they have not submitted to the righteousness of God.**

Despite the frequent persecutions that his fellow Jews had unleashed against Paul (cf. Acts), he still is able to find something in his nation to praise. They do after all **have a** real **zeal for God** (which a lesser person than Paul might have written off as spurious). Paul can **bear witness** to that fact, especially since that zeal had often been misdirected in hostility toward him (cf. Acts 22:3).

But this zeal is not properly guided by **knowledge**. Instead it is founded on ignorance about **God's righteousness**. By *God's righteousness* (*tēn tou Theou dikaiosunēn*) Paul means exactly the same thing as he meant by "God's righteousness" (*dikaiosunē Theou*) in 3:21. It refers to the righteousness that comes "through faith in Jesus Christ, which is *for* all and is *upon* all who believe" (3:22, emphasis added). For Paul, no other righteousness is adequate in the sight of God.

Israel, therefore, is both ignorant of God's righteousness and is also trying (**seeking**) **to establish** their own righteousness. The result is that they have not submitted to the righteousness of God. Despite the offer of righteousness by faith alone, Israel rejects that offer rather than accepting it. When the offer is preached to them, they refuse to *submit* to it as the Word of God. Instead, they resist it, revile it, and persecute those who preach it. They then continue their efforts to achieve their own righteousness by the works of the law.

In short, Israel refuses *God's righteousness* in an ignorant preference for **their own righteousness**. In the words, *seeking to establish*, Paul has reference to the futility of this effort since "by the works of the law no flesh will be justified before" God (3:20).

### 10:4. For Christ is the goal of the law as regards righteousness for everyone who believes.

Although Israel pursues an endless and unreachable goal in search of "their own righteousness," what they need is near at hand. **Christ** Himself, whom they have rejected, provides what Israel wrongly thinks is attainable by the law. In Christ alone is found the realization of the otherwise impossible **goal of the law**, namely, perfect **righteousness**.

The underlying Greek phrase rendered here by *the goal of the law* (*Telos… nomou*) could also be translated as "the end [termination] of the law." If so rendered it would refer to some kind of cessation for *the Law* of Moses. But this can hardly be what Paul means here. Paul never taught that the law was done away with (not even in Romans 6), but rather that because we are alive in Christ we are no longer under it (6:10-14). But that is different than a statement that the law has somehow ended. Even Jesus declared that He did not come to destroy *the law* but to fulfill it (Matt 5:17-18).

Righteousness was indeed the true *goal of the law*. But as Paul understood, *the law* can do nothing for those who are dead in their sins. Thus he tells the Galatians, "For if there had been a law given which could have given life, truly righteousness would have been by the law" (Gal 3:21). Though no divine law could accomplish that, Christ could do it **for everyone who believes**. For Paul, it is only "the one who is righteous by faith" who "shall live" (1:17). In Christ the unattainable *goal of the law* is achieved.

In the words *for everyone who believes*, Paul has in mind the universal offer of righteousness that applies with equal validity to the believing Jew or Gentile alike. But in this context Paul no doubt had particularly in mind the fact that, despite Israel's national unbelief, the offer had validity for any individual Jew who believed it.

## ii. Israel's Need for Paul's Gospel (10:5-15)

**10:5. For Moses writes about the righteousness which is by the law that, *"The man who has done these things shall live by means of them."***

Paul now begins to spell out in specific detail how the gospel that he proclaims about Jesus Christ is exactly what his nation needs. They have failed to submit to God's righteousness (v 3) despite the fact that **Moses** himself is a witness to their need. According to Moses, **the righteousness which is by the law** could only be obtained "at the end of the road" after a person had done the things *the law* required. Paul does not need to say again how conspicuously Israel has failed in this regard (see 2:17-29; 3:9-20).

Paul here quotes from Lev 18:5. His citation varies slightly from the LXX and once again it is likely Paul is quoting verbatim the Greek version of Leviticus that he had (although an adaptation of the LXX to this context is possible). The Greek words *ho poiēsas auta anthrōpos zēsetai en autois* (***"the man who has done these things shall live by means of them"***) probably reflect the translators' attempt to make an independent clause out of the *'asher* construction in Hebrew. Paul has exactly the same words in the same sequence when he quotes the same text in Gal 3:12.

It is noteworthy that Paul's citation does not use the term *righteousness* and instead refers to *life* (*zēsetai, shall live*). For Paul, the failure of *the law* was not simply a failure to make righteousness possible, but specifically an inability to impart life. As he states in Gal 3:21, it was the law's inability to bestow life (*zōopoiēsai*) that made it impossible to obtain righteousness by means of *the law*. In fact, as Paul's citation here shows, life was available under *the law* only to the person who *has done these things*. In Pauline theology that excluded all flesh whether Jewish or Gentile (3:19-20).

This principle is exemplified by the words the Lord Jesus Christ spoke to the enquiring expert in *the law*. After the lawyer had quoted the law's two great commandments on love, Jesus said, "Do this and you will *live*" (Luke 10:25-28, emphasis added). That should have convicted the lawyer of sin (and in a sense it did: Luke 10:29) and should have destroyed any hope that he might gain *eternal life* that way (Luke 10:25). This incident, recorded only by Paul's traveling companion Luke, perfectly reflected Paul's own theology about gaining life through *the law*.

As Paul will proceed to show in this section (10:5-13), Israel needed the experience of *life* in order to be free from divine wrath. They needed to live, which they could not do *by means of* Moses' Law. Only Paul's gospel made such a life possible.

> **10:6-7. But the righteousness which is by faith speaks this way, *"Do not say in your heart, 'Who will go up into heaven?'"* (that is, to bring Christ down), or, *"'Who will go down into the Abyss?'"* (that is, to bring Christ up from the dead).**

Paul now draws a sharp contrast between "the righteousness which is by the law," as spoken through Moses (v 5), and **the righteousness which is by faith** that speaks (as it were) in the gospel Paul proclaimed. To do this he adapts wording drawn from Deut 9:4; 30:12-14; and Ps 107:26 to his purpose. The result is a collage of Scriptural phraseology. But Paul's words are not to be understood as a quotation from Scripture, and are not introduced as such. Rather they are an evocative utilization of familiar terminology employed to clothe his presentation.

*The righteousness which is by faith* (i.e., Paul's gospel) says clearly to anyone who hears it, *"Do not say in your heart"* the question Paul then asks. (The Greek phrase is drawn verbatim from the LXX of Deut 9:4: *Mē eipēs en tē kardia sou.*) It is important for Paul to draw attention right away to what goes on in the heart since the attitude of the heart is the key to Israel's deliverance from wrath (see v 10).

The heart attitude, therefore, must not reflect the mind-set that Messiah (the Christ) had yet to come and needed to be brought down from heaven by someone. Naturally, in rejecting Jesus as God's Christ, Israel had adopted the attitude that Messiah was yet to appear. But in Paul's day, the view of many was that the coming of the Messiah could be *hastened* by Jewish obedience to *the law*.

Jewett appropriately observes:

> The reference to ascending to heaven to 'bring Christ down' is neither a 'fanciful' allusion to 'looking high and low for Christ,' nor a warning against spiritual journeys to master heaven's secrets or to gain access to the inaccessible Wisdom revealed in Christ. It is instead a historically apt depiction of the goals of some of the Jewish parties in Paul's time. They sought to hasten

the coming of the divinely appointed *Christos* (= 'anointed one, king) by religious programs associated with the law).[1]

Such a "program," Paul insists, is foreign to the perspective of *the righteousness which is by faith*. The Christ has *already* come down from heaven in the person of Jesus the Messiah.

But in addition, neither should one say in his heart that the Christ was still in Sheol (i.e., Hades). Paul's reference here to **"the Abyss"** is naturally construed as a reference to the abode of the departed, at least as understood by Pharisaic Judaism. (The Sadducees did not believe in resurrection: Luke 20:27.) In his exchanges with unbelieving Jews, Paul often must have heard the retort, "Well, if your Jesus is the Christ, He's a dead One!"

Thus the two interrogatives presented here represent the two extremes of Jewish unbelief about Jesus. On the one hand, "Christ has not yet come; who can go and get Him?" and on the other, "Your Christ is dead; who can raise Him up?" But such attitudes, insists Paul, are not the message of the gospel that proclaims *the righteousness which is by faith*. In fact, they are the opposite of the truth that Paul preached.

> **10:8. But what does it say? *"The word is near you, in your mouth and in your heart"*—that is the word of faith which we preach,**

What then does Paul's gospel ("the righteousness which is by faith") actually say? Unlike the statements of unbelief he has just rejected (vv 6-7), **the word of faith** Paul preached presented something quite **near** at hand and readily available. Jewish unbelief spoke of the necessity of waiting for the Christ to come down from heaven, or waiting for Him to arise from the dead, but Paul's message spoke of the realization of both things. What was now needed was an immediate response with the mouth and with the heart.

To express this concept Paul utilizes terminology found in Deut 30:14. Perhaps again he draws verbatim upon his Greek translation of the Torah, except that he drops the Greek word *sphodra* ("exceedingly"; [Heb, *mᵉʿōḏ*]). However, the reference in Deuteronomy is to the fact that Israel already had the law. Therefore, the individual Israelite could recite it (LXX: *en tō stomati sou*, in your mouth), remember it (LXX: *en tē kardia*

---

[1] Jewett, *Romans*, 626-27

*sou*, in your heart), and obey it (LXX: *kai en tais chersin sou auto poiein*, and in your hands to do it [or, that you may do it). These last words are not used by Paul and did not fit the broad analogy he is creating here.

Paul's gospel declared the fulfillment of Israel's hope for the coming of Messiah, the Messiah's triumph over death by means of resurrection, and the immediate availability of "the goal of the law" (cf. v 4) in terms of a "righteousness which is by faith" (v 6). As a result, the *deliverance* that Paul earnestly desired and prayed that Israel might receive (v 1), was available to them if only they would respond correctly with their mouth and with their heart.

It was not as though Israel had not heard the truth (cf. v 18). On the contrary, just as the law had been near the Israelites of Moses' day (Deut 30:11-14), so now Paul could say that, ***"The word** [**that is**, *the word of faith* **which we preach**] *is presently **near you, in your mouth and in your heart."*** As in the OT text on which Paul's words are modeled, so here the words for *you/your* are all singular. The response that the *individual* Israelite should make is now to be stated explicitly.

> **10:9. that, If you confess with your mouth "Lord Jesus," and believe in your heart that God has raised Him from the dead, you will be delivered.**

The response of the mouth should be a confession framed in terms of directly addressing Jesus with the designation Lord attached to it. As will be seen shortly, this confession is explicitly connected by Paul to a supplication made to Jesus in prayer (vv 12-13). It is not simply an acknowledgement of His lordship, but in fact an appeal to His lordship for the needed deliverance from divine wrath.

The Greek phrase that Paul uses here deserves attention. The words *ean homologēsēs en tō stomati sou Kurion Iēsoun* are variously rendered. Following "if you confess with your mouth" we find "the Lord Jesus" (KJV, NKJV), "Jesus as Lord" (NASB), "Jesus is Lord" (NIV, JB), and "Jesus is the Lord" (NACE). However, the renderings that make *Kurion* predicate ("Jesus is/as Lord") are not a likely reading of the Greek, for which we would have expected the sequence *Iēsoun Kurion* if that were the sense. But the rendering "*the* Lord Jesus" is not much more likely, for in that case we would expect the definite article (as in Acts 16:31: "Believe on <u>the</u> Lord Jesus Christ," where we have *Pisteuson epi <u>ton</u> Kurion Iēsoun Christon*; cf.

the article also at Acts 9:29; 11:17, 20; 15:11, 26; 19:13, 17; 20:21; 21:13; 28:31).

The prevailing practice in Acts is reflected almost everywhere in Romans for the sequence "Lord Jesus" (note the article at 5:1, 11; 13:14; 15:6, 30; 16:18, 20). The exceptions are in prepositional phrases, specifically at 1:7, and also in 14:14 where many witnesses read *Christō* for *Kuriō*. Robert Jewett (p. 621) is no doubt correct to give us the rendering "Lord Jesus!" which fits the Greek construction comfortably.

But as is obvious, this direct appeal to Jesus,[2] with the accompanying title "Lord," necessitates that the one who makes the appeal should believe that Jesus is *alive* to hear it. Thus the attitude of the heart is crucial. When one calls on **Jesus** with his mouth in order to be delivered, he therefore must have faith in his heart **that God has raised Him from the dead.** When these two conditions obtain, the person who calls on Him **will be delivered** (see v 13 below).[3]

The wrath of God under which Israel now stands, according to Paul, cannot be averted for any individual Jew by faith alone, as necessary as that faith is. A converted Jew might feel strongly inclined to keep his faith in Jesus secret in view of the overt hostility of his fellow Jews. But if he *did* keep it secret, he would *not be delivered*.[4] Paul now proceeds to clarify this point.

**10:10. For with the heart He is believed for righteousness, but with the mouth He is confessed for deliverance.**

Needless to say, the message Paul proclaimed to a Jewish audience did not differ fundamentally from what he preached to a Gentile one. Yet at the same time this splendid communicator knew how to adapt his message to its hearers. The present passage in Romans is concerned

---

[2] Note well that Hodges sees the words "If you confess…'Lord Jesus…'" to be "a direct appeal to Jesus." That is, this is not someone telling another person, "Jesus is Lord." It is instead a direct appeal to the Lord Jesus for deliverance from the current wrath. –RNW

[3] Confessing, "Lord Jesus" (vv 9-10) equals calling upon His name (vv 13-14). Hodges implies that here and says that directly in discussing Rom 10:13. –JHN

[4] Two authors catalog views and their proponents concerning the salvation in Rom 10:9-13: John F. Hart, "Why Confess Christ? The Use and Abuse of Romans 10:9-10," *JOTGES* 12 (Autumn 1999): 3-35; René A. Lopez, *Romans Unlocked: Power to Deliver* (Springfield, MO: 21st Century, 2005), 210-12. The existence of six different evangelical approaches to these verses testifies to their perceived difficulty. Five of six equate salvation with justification or receiving everlasting life. This commentary has argued throughout its pages against such an equation (cf. comments on Romans 1:16-17 and 5:9-10). Once again, context differentiates salvation in Romans from justification. Recognition of this is the key to the book. –JHN

especially with God's truth as the Jews needed to hear it. We should keep this in mind as we consider these well-known verses. The Jewish backdrop is often neglected.

The natural timidity which a Jewish convert to faith in Christ might feel is something Paul is very sensitive to right here (cf. John 12:42-43). This verse and the two that follow are aimed directly at discouraging such timidity. Jewish believers must not be ashamed of their faith in Jesus. Why? What happens in the heart, though vital, is not enough **for deliverance**.

Of course, **the heart** is where it all begins. But the benefit derived from faith in Christ in our hearts is *righteousness*. By this Paul means justification by faith. For Paul, righteousness for human beings is always conditioned on faith and only on faith (see 3:21–4:25). That principle is affirmed right here: *with the heart* **He is believed for righteousness**. One gets righteousness by the believing response of *the heart*.

Paul's mode of expression is interesting. He employs a passive form of the verb for "believe" (i.e., *pisteuetai*) that obviously has the object of faith (i.e., Christ) as its subject. There is no adequate reason to understand an "it" as the subject (e.g., "that God has raised Him from the dead" [so BDAG, p. 817]). The parallelism of the two clauses (with *believed/confessed*) indicates that the subject of both clauses is the same.[5] It is the Lord Jesus who is confessed and is the conceptual subject of v 9. It is awkward (and needless) to make the subsidiary idea of 9b the functional subject of both verbs in v 10.

Although this usage of *pisteuō* is a natural use of its passive voice, the passive of *pisteuō* with a subject of the person believed is not found elsewhere in the NT. It occurs, however, in the Septuagint rendering of 1 Sam 27:12 (LXX: 1 Kings 27:12; *kai episteuthē David en tō Anchous*, "and David was believed by Achish"). It also occurs in secular Greek. BDAG (p. 817, 1.*d*.f) recognizes this semantic category ("I am believed, I enjoy confidence") and references Xenophon, Diodorus Siculus, Josephus, and a papyrus text. They would have done well to place Rom 10:10 in that category.

---

[5] Hodges' translation and discussion here is both simple and profound. Instead of the vague "For with the heart <u>one believes unto righteousness</u>" and "with the mouth <u>confession is made unto salvation</u>" (NKJV; the NIV, NASB, NET, and ESV all have essentially the same translation), Hodges' rendering is much clearer and more grammatically accurate (preserving the passives): "For with the heart <u>He is believed</u> for righteousness, but with the mouth <u>He is confessed</u> for deliverance." –RNW

Thus in the matter of obtaining righteousness, Jesus is the object of faith. But in the same way, He is also the object of our confession: **but with the mouth He is confessed for deliverance.**[6] In my translation the word *but* renders the Greek word *de*, normally described as a "mild" adversative, that is, a "weak" *but*. It is frequently translated simply by "and," which tends to conceal for the English reader any sense of contrast. Not surprisingly, the English versions have perpetuated the traditional "and" here (so KJV, NKJV, NIV, NASB, NACE).

The Jerusalem Bible, however, captures the actual sense almost perfectly. JB drops any connective word and manages by so doing to convey the implicit contrast: "By believing from the heart you are made righteous; by confessing with your lips you are saved." It is precisely this contrast that is the point here. Although the Jewish believer may be assured that God has granted him righteousness on the basis of faith in his heart, God will *not* grant him deliverance on the basis of that faith alone. For *deliverance* from God's wrath the Jewish convert must not suppress the truth he believes. He must confess with his mouth.[7]

Let us recall here a fundamental statement about God's wrath that Paul makes at the very beginning of the main body of the epistle. In Rom 1:18 Paul affirms that, "the wrath of God is revealed from heaven against all the ungodliness of men who *suppress the truth* by unrighteousness." The words "suppress the truth" (*tēn alētheian…katechontōn*) are directly related to Paul's point here. Paul went on immediately in Rom 1:19-22 to describe how men failed to glorify the God revealed in creation and exchanged that glory for idolatrous images. Thus the truth about God was "suppressed" by man's wickedness and idolatry.

No person, Jew or Gentile, who continues to *suppress the truth* about God can expect to be delivered from His wrath. To be justified by faith in

---

[6] Romans 10:10a says that believing *alone* results in righteousness (justification). Since confession occurs after one is justified, the deliverance must necessarily be something potentially obtained after one's eternal destiny is settled. Once again, salvation/deliverance (*sōtēria*) in Romans is not salvation from the lake of fire. –JHN

[7] Not only does confession happen after believing, but it produces a different result. The chiastic structure of Rom 10:9-10 makes clear that believing results in righteousness (justification), while confession results in salvation:

   A    that if you confess with your mouth the Lord Jesus (9a), and

      B    believe in your heart that God raised Him…you will be saved (9b).

      B'    For with the heart one believes unto righteousness (10a),

   A'    and with the mouth confession is made unto salvation (10b).

–JHN

the heart but to refuse to confess "Lord Jesus!" with the mouth will leave the believer tragically still exposed to God's temporal anger. To the Jewish portion of his audience Paul is saying, "Don't be ashamed of what you believe." He will now go on to elaborate this point.

**10:11. For the Scripture says,** *"Everyone who believes in Him shall not be ashamed."*

At this point Paul returns to the last statement of the quotation with which he concluded the preceding unit of material (Rom 9:14-33). Using the prophecy of Isaiah to drive home the point that Jesus had been a "Stone of collision" for Israel, Paul's final quoted words there (Rom 9:33) are identical with those he quotes in the present verse (dropping only the initial "and"). The quotation's relevance here is apparent.

Despite the fact that Israel has "collided with the Stone of collision," no Jewish believer in Him should be put off by that fact. The believer should not hesitate to confess the Lord Jesus Christ. If the Jewish person had put faith in this "Stone of collision," he should also fulfill the admonition of the prophet that he should "not be ashamed."

The underlying Hebrew word rendered here by *kataischunthēsetai* (ashamed; the LXX has *kataischunthē*) is apparently the hiphil of the verb *hûš* (*to hurry*) which is rare in the Hebrew OT. The translators seem to have understood the text as a poetic metaphor for being embarrassed and "hurrying" on (to get away from the embarrassing collision with the Stone?). There is no reason not to accept this understanding, which Paul obviously did.

Once again it appears that Paul is quoting from a version which is not identical with the LXX we now possess. Paul's version read: *pas ho pisteuōn ep' autō ou kataischunthēsetai,* while the LXX has: *kai ho pisteuōn ou mē kataischunthē.* The differences are not consequential and the *pas* in Paul's version may be simply an interpretive rendering of the Hebrew, which may be taken to imply it.

Obviously as a follow-up from v 10 Paul construes the necessity to *"not be ashamed"* as the functional equivalent of a command to confess Jesus Christ.[8] Contrary to much contemporary theology, neither Paul nor the

---

[8] The quotation of Isa 28:16 in Rom 9:33 and 10:11 forms an inclusio. Translations of these verses render the future indicative with an indicative sense (e.g., NKJV, "whoever believes on Him *will not be put to shame*"). This commentary understands the future indicative here as an imperatival indicative. This suggestion meets the conditions set forth by Wallace, *Grammar,*

rest of the NT requires confession as a condition for receiving everlasting life (cf. Acts 16:31; Eph 2:8-9; 1 Tim 1:16). One should note especially John 12:42-43 where Johannine doctrine requires us to understand the non-confessing rulers as possessors of eternal life who lacked the courage of their convictions.

What Paul exactly has in mind here is made clear in the following verses.

**10:12-13. For there is no difference between either Jew or Greek, since the same Lord of all deals richly with all who appeal to Him. For *"whoever shall appeal to the name of the Lord will be delivered."***

Although the text of these verses (especially v 13) has been used innumerable times as though it referred to a cry for salvation from hell, in context the verses are no such thing. The "deliverance," as I previously noted, is a deliverance from wrath. God's anger rests heavily upon unbelieving Israel and their first step must be to believe in their Messiah for righteousness (v 10a). But though necessary, this alone will not bring deliverance from God's temporal anger. In fact, deliverance comes by confessing "Lord Jesus!" with the mouth (v 10b).

How exactly does this come about? The answer is found in the truth affirmed by yet another quotation from the Jewish Scriptures, this time from Joel 2:32. But in leading up to this quotation, Paul emphatically declares the measureless capacity of the Lord Jesus to respond lavishly to **all who appeal to Him**. Since, in fact, Jesus is **Lord of all**, His ability to respond applies to all, **either Jew or Greek**. All human beings, without distinction (**there is no difference**), now stand under His lordship.

---

569, "The future indicative is sometimes used for a command, almost always in OT quotations (due to a literal translation of the Hebrew)."

Although not common outside of Matthew, Daniel B. Wallace, *Greek Grammar Beyond the Basics: An Exegetical Syntax of the New Testament* (Grand Rapids, MI: Zondervan Publishing House, 1996), 570, lists Rom 7:7 and 13:9 as examples in Romans. The commentary translates the future indicative as "shall not be ashamed," understanding the word *shall* as an exhortational indicative, as in 1 Pet 1:16, "You shall be holy, because I am holy." Perhaps a slight paraphrase of the translation by Zane Hodges of Rom 9:11 and 10:10 ("let him not be ashamed") will help: "...everyone who believes in Him—Let him not be ashamed." Believers who become ashamed of Christ will not confess Him and will not receive that deliverance. Paul introduced the concept of shame and the believer early in the book, in Rom 1:16: "For I am not ashamed of the gospel of Christ, since it is the power of God for deliverance for everyone who believes, both for the Jew first and for the Greek" (ZCH translation). –JHN

Accordingly, His abundance can be directed toward anyone who will appeal to Him as the Lord that He truly is.

The words *all who appeal to Him* (*pantas tous epikaloumenous auton*) are heavily freighted. According to Luke (Paul's travelling companion), in Paul's unconverted days he had persecuted "all who call on [the Lord's] name" (Acts 9:14; cf. 9:21). That is to say, Paul persecuted those who were Christians "out-in-the open" (he could hardly persecute secret Christians). But prior to the Gentile mission this surely meant he persecuted Jewish believers (note Acts 9:1-2) who assembled together for worship and prayer. Furthermore, after Paul's own conversion, Ananias instructed him to get baptized, "calling on the name of the Lord" (Acts 22:16). This fact is reported by Luke in a speech Paul gave to a *Jewish* audience with whom he seeks to identify himself (Acts 22:1-3).

Quite naturally, then, the terminology becomes a Pauline way to identify all Christians (*either Jew or Greek*) who assembled together and invoked **"the name of the Lord"** (1 Cor 1:2; 2 Tim 2:22). Also relevant is the fact that the verb in question (*epikaleō*) is the technical term in Acts for Paul's legal appeal to Caesar, the empire's highest authority (Acts 25:11, 12, 21, 25; 26:32; 28:19). Thus believers who gather in Christian assemblies acknowledge the Lord Jesus with their mouths and publically appeal to His name for all that they need.

It is evident that, as a description of Christians, to *appeal to the name of the Lord* does not describe a one-time event. It becomes a basic description of them (see again, 1 Cor 1:2; 2 Tim 2:22) precisely because it was done *habitually*, especially in gatherings for Christian worship and prayer. In the process of doing so, they were *habitually* confessing Jesus as the universal Lord, higher by far than Caesar himself. (Caesar was also referred to as *kurios*: Acts 25:26; see BDAG, p. 577 [2 b B].)

The concept of a one-time event of confession, used by many evangelists, is the product of an ill-conceived evangelistic use of Rom 10:9-13. The idea of a two-step "conversion," that is (1) faith in the heart, and (2) public acknowledgement of this (i.e., "I just accepted Christ," etc.), is quite far from Paul's thought here. Confessing "Lord Jesus" is what Christians do regularly and it is what marks them as believers in Jesus Christ.

But here Paul is concerned with one of the chief benefits of this Christian practice. Though many benefits are available to those who appeal to this exalted name, those who openly appeal to the lordship of Jesus receive what Paul is actually discussing—deliverance from divine wrath. Since Jesus is now *Lord of all*, the extension of such a benefit to those who appeal to Him is an expression of His superlative generosity.

That is to say, as Lord He **deals richly with** them. The word rendered *deals richly* (*ploutōn*) recalls the earlier statement that God desires "to make known the wealth (*ton plouton*) of His glory upon the vessels of mercy" (9:23). For Paul, God's glory is made known by the "richness" of His dealings with these "vessels of mercy." Not only are they *justified* with a perfect righteousness through what they believe in their heart, but they are also *delivered* from God's wrath by appealing, with their mouth, to the power of the exalted Lord.

This privilege, Paul affirms, is stated in the Scripture that says, **"whoever shall appeal to the name of the Lord will be delivered."** The quotation is drawn from Joel 2:32 and follows the LXX exactly. Paul introduces it with a *gar* (*For*) that indicates its connection with his statement of v 12. The context in Joel from which Paul draws it is precisely in harmony with Paul's subject matter here in Romans. Joel's words refer to the manifestation of God's wrath in Israel during the end times (i.e., the Tribulation).

A simple reading of Joel 2:30-32, in its larger context, suffices to show that the prophet is concerned with temporal wrath and with the end times. In particular the words of Joel 2:30-31 are the OT background for our Lord's famous prophetic declaration in Matt 24:29-30. Through Joel God announces: "And I will show wonders in the heavens and in the earth: blood and fire and pillars of smoke. The sun shall be turned into darkness, and the moon into blood, before the coming of the great and terrible day of the Lord" (Joel 2:30-31, NKJV).

This statement is immediately followed in Joel 2:32 by the words, "And it shall come to pass that whoever calls on [*shall appeal to*] the name of the Lord shall be saved [delivered]. For in Mount Zion and in Jerusalem there shall be deliverance, as the Lord has said, among the remnant whom the Lord calls" (NKJV). In its context, Joel's words are not concerned with "salvation from hell." To read them as though they were is to insert an illegitimate theological gloss into the Biblical text, not only into Joel's text but into Paul's as well. As Paul has already made clear (and will do so again in vv 14-15), this *appeal to the name of the Lord* is not the same thing as receiving righteousness by faith in one's heart (v 10).

It is significant that the relevance of Joel's quotation to Israel's spiritual condition after the crucifixion of Christ was recognized at the founding of the Church on the Day of Pentecost. In fact it is the first Biblical quotation in Peter's famous Pentecostal sermon and is explicitly applied by him to "the last days" (see Acts 2:14-17). The Petrine words, "and it shall be in the last days, God says" (Acts 2:17), are apparently an interpretive (midrashic) formulation of Joel's statement in Joel 2:28a: "and it shall be afterwards" (Heb: *ăharê-kēn,* "after thus"). Though Peter quotes Joel 2:28-31, pointing to the fulfillment of the promise of the Spirit (Joel 2:28-29), the subsequent material (vv 30-31) is noteworthy precisely because it was *not* fulfilled (but might have been) at that time.

Peter's words thus set the tone of the NT as a whole in which Christians are seen to be living in "the last days." The author of Hebrews dramatically affirms this with his assertion that "God…has in *these last days* spoken to us by His Son" (Heb 1:1-2, emphasis added; see also 1 Pet 1:20; 1 John 2:18). Paul himself could say in 1 Cor 10:11, "Now all these things happened [in OT times, vv 1-10] to them as examples, and they were written for our admonition, on whom *the ends of the ages* [*ta telē tōn aiōnōn*] have come" (emphasis added). For Paul, Joel's prophecy was relevant at the very time in which Paul and other believers currently lived.

Therefore, the wrath of God that had been revealed from heaven, according to Paul (1:18), was on a continuum with the woes that Joel had announced for the last days. The last days were *already* upon the world, whatever might be the judgmental intensification that would be manifest just before Christ appeared. It followed that Joel's text was applicable at the present time to both Jew and Greek, that is, to whomever it was who appealed to the name of the Lord Jesus for deliverance.

Thus too, on the basis of Joel's text, it could be said that "the one who is righteous by faith" could "live" (cf. 1:17). What else was Joel promising but the continuation of a believer's *life* into the kingdom itself despite a period of wrath that threatened to extinguish *all* natural life (cf. Matt 25:22)? The words of Joel 2:32a are thus a superlatively suitable text for Paul, and especially so since their Jewish orientation in Joel's context is so manifest. The Jewish believers during the Great Tribulation will have this motivating promise to sustain them until the dawning of the age to come. But so do believers today.

Thus the Jewish believer (and the Gentile one as well) should not stop with faith in the heart, vital as that was. But he should join the fellowship of others who made it a habit to appeal to the name of the Lord with the mouth. As he joined in this confessional process, and as he appealed to his Lord for the necessary enablement, the believer could indeed *live* in freedom from divine wrath. Or, as Paul has already put it, "if by the Spirit you put to death the deeds of the body, you will *live*" (Rom 8:13, emphasis added). No person who was ashamed of the Stone of collision could *live* like that. He needed to openly and regularly confess, "Lord Jesus." He needed to rely steadily on the name of the Lord who deals richly with all who appeal to Him.

Romans 10:13 has been read for so long in its traditional sense that its actual meaning is hard for many to grasp. The fundamental terminology had a different connotation for a Greek reader than it does for a contemporary English reader. As the NT usage of the terminology *epikalesētai to onoma Kuriou* shows, a one-time confession is not in view. Instead it has to do with an activity that was regularly practiced in Christian gatherings. In NT times, a person who did not participate in such gatherings could hardly be said to be "confessing" the Lord. But those who regularly appealed to His name with their mouths confessed Him repeatedly by making precisely that appeal. And those who did so could expect this Lord to hear their appeal and grant deliverance from the debilitating and ruinous impact of God's wrath that was so manifest in the world at large (1:18-32).

> **10:14. How then shall they appeal *to Him* in whom they have not believed? And how shall they believe *in Him* of whom they have not heard? And how shall they hear without a preacher?**

Paul is not ashamed of his gospel (1:16). Paul's gospel in no way implies a belittling of Israel. The very fact that Israel stands under divine wrath and needs deliverance from it (10:1) necessitates the preaching of Paul's gospel. In the present verse he draws out the logical necessity for this preaching.

If Israel needs to appeal to the Lord Jesus in order to be delivered (and they do), then how could they possibly do so without first believing in Him? **How then shall they appeal *to Him* in whom they have not believed?** But it follows also that if they must first believe in Him before they can *appeal to Him*, how can they do this without first hearing about Him? **How shall they believe *in Him* of whom they have not heard?** The human preacher is therefore a necessity, even for the Israelites, for **how shall they hear without a preacher?**

Despite the false charges that Paul apparently had heard, he is not only deeply concerned for Israel but actually preaches his gospel to them. As Acts records, Paul customarily began his evangelism in a new city by going first to the synagogue and preaching his gospel to the Jewish audience there. So far from this message implying a minimizing of Israel's importance, his was a message for them first of all. The gospel of Christ that Paul preached was "for the Jew *first* and for the Greek" (Rom 1:16, emphasis added). As regards his nation, Paul's gospel is something he is not ashamed of precisely because it acknowledged the priority of the Jewish recipient.

In the process of drawing out this logical sequence, Paul speaks in a way that clearly shows the distinction between "believing in" and "appealing to" the Lord Jesus. They are obviously *not* synonymous terms, but are in fact sequential. Believing in Him *must precede* appealing to Him. This reaffirms the exegesis I have given above to Rom 10:9-13.[9]

**10:15. And how shall they preach unless they are sent? Just as it is written, *"How beautiful are the feet of those who proclaim good news about peace, Who proclaim good news about good things!"***

But to be a legitimate bearer of the gospel message, one must be sent by God to preach it. That Paul claimed to have been sent for this purpose is plain as early as the first verse of this epistle. There Paul asserts that he was "called to be an apostle who is set apart for the gospel of God" (Rom 1:1).

This commission to preach, which he and others were fulfilling, was a preliminary realization of an OT passage that pertained directly to Israel. The words **just as it written** introduce the passage Paul has in mind which comes from Isa 52:7. Paul's text of Isa 52:7 differs in various ways from the LXX. In addition, many NT manuscripts do not have the words *tōn euangelizomenōn eirēnēn* (***"of those who proclaim good news about peace"***). But this appears

---

[9] If one starts at the end of v 14 and works backwards, the sequence is undeniable. What comes first, the preacher preaching or hearing the preacher? Obviously the preaching comes first. What comes first, hearing the words of the preacher or believing the words of the preacher? Obviously the hearing must precede the believing. And then to the first question of v 14, what comes first believing in the Lord or appealing to Him? Obviously the believing precedes the appealing. If one then goes back to v 13, it is clear that the ones being "saved" there are believers, not unbelievers. –RNW

to be a simple scribal error (technically called *homoioteleuton*) in which the scribe's eye skips from a similar syllable or word to another of the same letters, thus omitting the intervening words. The text rendered here can confidently be taken as original.

As noted in *OTQNT* (p. 119), "in Romans 10:15 Paul is much closer to the MT than the LXX is." The context of Isa 52:7 relates to the same eschatological era, the end times, as did Joel 2:32 quoted in v 13. Israel's ultimate deliverance is in view. Those who proclaim this deliverance are extolled as persons with **"beautiful...feet,"** since their feet carry them to Israel with this good news. Indeed, the immediately following portion of Isa 52:7, which is not quoted by Paul, is very significant for the context of Paul's thought.

Directly following the quoted material from Isa 52:7a are these words: "...who proclaim salvation, who says to Zion, 'Your God reigns'" (Isa 52:7b). Thus the Isaiah context speaks of salvation (deliverance) precisely as does the passage in Joel 2:32. The underlying Hebrew word for salvation in the Isaiah text is *yeshuah* (in the LXX it is rendered by *tēn sōtērian*). In fact, Isa 52:8-10 speaks of the joy of Jerusalem because it has been rescued by God before the eyes of all mankind. Verse 10 concludes with the words: "And all the ends of the earth shall see the salvation of God," where again salvation is *yeshuah/tēn sōtērian* (MT/LXX).

Clearly Paul is choosing OT proof texts that deal directly with the issue of Israel's deliverance from divine wrath. These texts refer in fact to the end of the age when the nations have assembled against Jerusalem and when that city is dramatically delivered from their attack by the direct intervention of the Lord Jesus Christ. The good news with which Israel will be evangelized in that day is the **"good news about peace"** and about the **"good things"** that come with God's deliverance. Paul will refer again to the events foreseen by Isaiah when he writes Rom 11:26-27.

Paul is proud to preach this gospel, both to Jew and Gentile. His own feet which trudged over many a weary, dangerous road, were beautiful in the sight of His Lord and of all who believed in Him.

### iii. Israel's Need for Faith (10:16-21)

The solution to Israel's dire situation was right at hand. God's Word in the form of the gospel Paul preached was near them, in their mouth and in their heart (10:8). What then was lacking? The answer obviously was:

faith in the preached Word (cf. v 15). Paul will now highlight the sad state of Jewish unbelief as it was clearly foreseen in the OT.

**10:16-17. But they have not all obeyed the gospel. For Isaiah says, "Lord, who has believed our report?" So then faith *comes* from the report, and the report by means of the word of God.**

It is striking that Paul now has recourse to the great "Servant" prophecy found in Isa 52:13–53:12. In that passage is found the richest discussion in OT Scripture of the rejection of Messiah and His vicarious suffering on behalf of His nation. In addition, the passage on God's Servant that begins at Isa 52:13 follows the last quoted material (Isa 52:7a) by only a few verses.

In v 16, Paul of course is quoting Isa 53:1, where the prophet laments the general rejection by Israel of the report about Messiah's sufferings, death, and resurrection (Isa 53:2-12). The quotation by Paul agrees with the MT and LXX, but follows the LXX in introducing the word *Lord*. As OTQNT (p. 121) observes, the vocative word *Kurie* (*Lord*) "was probably inserted to clarify to the reader that the prophet begins his query to God."

The question, ***"Lord, who has believed our report?"*** suggests the meagerness of the believing response by Messiah's own people. This text, as employed by Paul, is very telling as a proof that **they** [that is, Israel] **have not all obeyed the gospel.** Israel as a whole has not *obeyed the gospel* precisely because it has neither believed the message of Christ in the heart nor confessed the Lord Jesus with the mouth (cf. vv 8b-10).

But here Paul is also concerned with the fact that Isaiah's words show that faith should have been the response to his report. Yet the prophet's declaration has not been believed. Israel has spurned the *means* God has used to proclaim deliverance to them.

For Paul, it follows (**So then**) from Isaiah's words that a report was needed to produce faith. That is to say, **faith *comes* from the report** (*hē pistis ex akoēs*). *The report* was God's instrumentality to awaken faith. But this report is nothing less than the gospel Paul himself preached. So far from being ashamed of that gospel (1:16), as though his gospel diminished Israel, Paul knew the absolute necessity for Israel to hear it if they were to believe and be delivered from God's wrath.

The traditional rendering for the word *akoē* in v 17 (*hearing*: KJV, NKJV, NASB, NACE) is misleading. It is the same word used in the question in v 16 and rendered there by *report* (KJV; NKJV; NASB;

NACE). The choice of a different English word in each verse conceals the obvious connection Paul has in mind. Much better is the NIV's "message" used all three times for *akoē* in these verses, although "message" (in its usual sense) sounds a bit too informal. The JB has the following felicitous rendering for the three instances of *akoē*: "As Isaiah said, *Lord, how many believed what we proclaimed?* So faith comes from what is preached, and what is preached comes from the word of Christ." This is right on target.

The last part of v 17, **and the report by means of the word of God**, makes clear the process Paul has in mind. (The term *God* is found in most of the manuscripts of Romans, while "Christ" is read by only a few, mainly the ancient Egyptian copies; it is no doubt secondary: see the Introduction.) Just as faith is derived from believing the preached report, just so the preached report is in turn derived from the very mouth of God, that is, *the report* [comes] *by means of the word of God* (*hē de akoē dia rhēmatos Theou*). The use of *rhēma* here (rather than *logos*) implies the *spoken word of God*. Paul's gospel is not merely what *he* says; fundamentally it is what *God* says.

> **10:18. But I say, it's not that they haven't heard, is it? On the contrary, "Their voice has gone out into all the earth, And their words to the ends of the world."**

Israel's problem does not lie in the fact that the gospel has not been preached to them. Obviously if they had not heard the report (that is, the gospel) they would not be able to believe it. The preacher of the gospel must first proclaim it to them (see v 14). But this is exactly what has been done.

Paul is thinking here not only of the preaching that had occurred in Israel itself since the founding of the Church (see Acts 1–7), but also of the spread of the same message to the Jews in the Diaspora all over the Roman world. Paul himself was a major bearer of this report, but he was by no means the only one.

This proclamation was indeed universal in character in accordance with the words of Ps 19:4 (MT = 19:5). It is important to observe that here the Biblical words cited by Paul lack a "citation formula" such as "Scripture says" (v 11), "as it is written" (v 15), "Moses says" (v 19) or "Isaiah is so bold as to say" (v 20). What Paul is doing is simply formulating his observation by using Biblical terminology. Undoubtedly he is aware that Ps 19:4 does not refer to the preaching of the gospel but to the testimony of nature. Yet just as that testimony is for all, so is his gospel.

The words of Ps 19:4 follow exactly the form found in the LXX which must also have been the form found in Paul's version of the Greek OT. No doubt this translation was of special usefulness to Paul. The Greek translators had chosen to render the Hebrew expression for **"to the ends of the world"** by a phrase that suited Paul's needs at this point: *eis ta perata tēs oikoumenēs.* The word *oikoumenē* translates the Hebrew *tēbēl* (= "world"), but in Paul's time it was often used as a functional equivalent of the Roman Empire (BDAG, p. 699 [2]). Paul is probably not commenting on the precise extent to which his gospel had spread all over the globe, but instead is affirming that it had spread throughout the empire. If this is the case, the expression **"into all the earth"** signifies the outward thrust of the gospel that has brought it *to the ends of the* [Roman] *world.* The point would be that through the voice of its many messengers (i.e., **"their voice"**) the gospel **"has gone out"** (*exēlthen*) as a universal proclamation destined to reach everywhere.

Yet by the date of Romans (c. AD 56 or 57) the gospel must have been carried far beyond the confines of the empire. (Tradition reports that the Apostle Thomas preached in India.) Paul might well have known of this wider spread of the message, especially since he is writing under inspiration. In any case, he probably regarded his words as a prophetic declaration of the gospel's ultimate extension to all mankind. Even so, in this context, the rhetorical question Paul asks (**it's not that they haven't heard, is it?**) must mainly have signified that most Jewish communities that were situated in the Roman Empire (*oikoumenē*) had received the message about Jesus Christ.

In fact, even though Paul was planning a missionary trip to the unreached regions of Spain (see 15:20, 21, 24, 28), it does not follow that no word about Jesus Christ had yet reached any of the synagogues in that land. On the contrary, missionaries like Apollos (who preceded Paul in Ephesus: Acts 18:24-25) had probably already borne the message of Christ to the synagogues in Spain.

**10:19. But rather I say, it's not that Israel hasn't known, is it? First Moses says, "I will stir you to jealousy by those who are not a nation, And I will make you angry with a foolish nation."**

The opening words of this verse (*Alla legō*) repeat the same Greek words as those that open v 18. But here they probably have an ascensive force (cf. 2 Cor 7:11 [BDAG, 4 b, p. 45]) so that I render them, **But rather I say**. Not only is it true that Israel has *heard* (v 18), they have also known (**It's not that Israel hasn't known, is it?**). The rhetorical form of the questions in vv 18 and 19 is the same, so that the change of verb (*ēkousan*, "heard"; *egnō*, "known") is thereby highlighted.

This progression of thought is significant for Paul's argument. The gospel has indeed been preached to the Jews (they *have* heard). But their inclination is to resist and reject it because so many Gentiles have believed (cf. Acts 13:45-51). But this angry rejection has already been revealed in Scripture and has thus been made known to them.

Paul will now show from a pair of Scriptures that this spirit of jealousy and anger should not be a surprise to Israel itself. First, it was revealed through Moses and then also through Isaiah (v 20). Israel *knows* what its Scriptures say even if the nation will not acknowledge their truth in the present situation.

The quotation in this verse is from Deut 32:21 and is very close to the LXX, which in turn follows the MT. The differences in Paul's text are: (1) *egō* for *kagō* (*I* for *and I*) and (2) *humas* for *autous* (*you* for *them*). Although the second change has been ascribed to Paul himself by commentators, there is no necessity for doing this. Both could well have stood in his Greek copy of Deuteronomy, and in that case, the second change is an interpretive aid introduced by the translators or a reflection of the Hebrew text from which they worked. Whatever its origin, the intent of the text is not changed at all by *humas*.

The words of Moses specifically predict that God would arouse the jealousy and anger of Israel through His dealings with Gentile people. The references to *"those* who *are not a nation"* and to *"a foolish nation"* clearly indicate Gentiles. Paul probably understood this text as signaling God's intent to call particular Gentiles from various nations. Thus they did not constitute a whole nation (*ep' ouk ethnei*) like Israel did. Yet by gathering them from many nations, these Gentiles themselves became a nation (1 Pet 2:9, "you are...a holy nation"), but one which initially lacked the understanding of God that Israel possessed (*epi ethnei asunetō*). The OT words are rhetorically designed to convey this truth through formally, but not actually, contradictory statements. Israel is to be humbled by a "not-nation" and an "ignorant nation."

As Paul will shortly say, God's intent was to "stir them [Israel] to jealousy" for the purpose of bringing them to divine deliverance (cf. 11:11-14). As often happens in life's many circumstances, an initial angry reaction can be followed by a deeper comprehension of a given situation. God's provocation of Israel had exactly this goal.

**10:20-21. Then Isaiah is so bold as to say, *"I have been found by those who did not seek Me, I have been revealed to those who did not ask for Me."* But to Israel he says, *"All day long I have stretched out My hands to a people who disobey and contradict Me!"***

Two final OT citations conclude this unit on Israel's need for faith (10:16-21). Whereas the citation in v 19 was from the Torah (i.e., Deut 32:21), these are from the section of Israel's canon known as the Prophets, specifically from Isa 65:1 and 2.

The opening words, **Then Isaiah is so bold as to say** (*Ēsaias de apotolma kai legei*), should be read as a follow-through from the word *First* (*Prōtos*) in v 19. *Moses first* said, *then Isaiah* said thus and so. The situation of Israel as described by Paul was prophesied as far back as Moses, whose testimony is confirmed much later by the great prophet Isaiah.

Here again we are faced with the Greek version employed by Paul/Tertius, which was not identical with our standard modern edition of the LXX. It appears that in Isa 65:1 the LXX has transposed the two verb forms (1) *herethēn* (**"I have been found"**) and (2) *emphanēs egenomēn* (**"I have been revealed"**), so that the LXX reads the sequence the opposite way that Paul does: "I have been revealed to those who did not ask for Me; I have been found by those who did not seek me." But the NT order is closer to the MT since *herethē* then stands loosely for the Hebrew *niḏraštî* ("I let Myself be sought," "I was found") and *emphanēs egenomēn* represents the Hebrew *nimṣē'tî* ("I was found"). In the LXX order, *emphanēs egenomēn* is a less probable rendering for *niḏraštî*. No doubt *eurethēn* seemed like an "improved" equivalent for *nimṣē'tî* but, when the verbs were transposed, *emphanēs egenomēn* for *niḏraštî* became problematic.

The second quotation (from Isa 65:2) is essentially the same in the MT, LXX, and Paul's version. However a transposition of *"all day long"* from its primary position in Paul's citation to a position after *"My hands"* in the LXX could well be another effort at "improvement" since it conforms to the position of the corresponding Hebrew phrase. Again, no significant difference is involved.

These two final OT citations (Isa 65:1 and 2) form a conceptual *inclusio* with Rom 9:30-33 and thus mark the end of the larger unit of 10:1-21. In 9:30-31, Paul had stated that "the Gentiles, who were not pursuing righteousness, have obtained righteousness" (9:30), whereas Israel has missed this righteousness and instead has "collided with the Stone of collision" (9:31-33). Isaiah's prophecy confirms both points, the former from Isa 65:1 and the latter from 65:2.

God's declaration (Isa 65:1) that He has *been found* and has *been revealed* to those who neither sought Him nor asked for Him, is fulfilled by the Gentiles in obtaining a righteousness by faith that they were not seeking (Rom 9:30). And God's further declaration (Isa 65:2) that *all day long* He has **"stretched out** [His] **hands to a people who disobey and contradict** [Him]**"** is fulfilled by Israel's continued stubborn rejection of this same righteousness (9:31-33).

With these two prophetic statements from Isaiah, Paul finalizes his explanation of Israel's present unbelieving situation. That situation is in fact a realization of Israel's own God-given Scriptures. The question that must now be addressed is whether or not this rebellious condition is permanent for national Israel. That important issue is the subject of 11:1-36.

# Romans 11

## c. Israel's National Destiny Will Be Realized (11:1-32)

In this final major subunit of the larger unit 9:6–11:32, Paul brings his discussion of national Israel to a superb culmination. Although Israel is temporarily set aside to the benefit of Gentile humanity, God's purposes for His nation will ultimately be realized. Israel will one day cease to be the object of God's wrath and will experience His deliverance through the coming of the Deliverer.

The new unit (11:1-27) is clearly structured. Two explanatory units are introduced by the same Greek words, *Legō oun* (*So I say*), in 11:1 and 11:11. Both units are concluded by OT citations as has been Paul's practice since the beginning of the larger section about Israel (chaps. 9–11). The first subunit here (11:1-10) concludes with the citations found in 11:8-10. The second subunit (11:11-27) concludes with the citation found in 11:26-27. There follows in 11:28-36 a conclusion to the entire section on Israel (chaps. 9–11) that is climaxed by a doxology.

### i. National Israel has been blinded (11:1-10)

**11:1. So I say, God hasn't cast away His people, has He? Far from it! In fact I myself am an Israelite, of the descendants of Abraham, of the tribe of Benjamin.**

The description of Israel's rebellious and unbelieving state, as presented in 10:16-21, leads naturally to the question Paul raises here. Introducing this new turn in the discussion by **So I say** (see above), he asks whether God is through with Israel. The Greek form of his question implies a negative response: **God hasn't cast away His people, has He?** And Paul quickly states that response: **Far from it!** (*Mē genoito*).

The Greek word rendered cast away (*apōsato* from *apōtheō*) carries meanings like "push aside," "reject," and "repudiate" (BDAG, p. 126). Is God's response to Israel's hostility to the gospel to be understood as a repudiation of *His people*? The words *His people* are telling here since it is plain from the Scriptures that God acknowledged Israel as His people over and over again (cf. Isa 1:2-4 and many, many other texts). Has this ancient, Biblical link between God and the nation been irrevocably broken? Does God now repudiate this relationship?

This question is relevant even today. Over the centuries of Christian history right up to the present day many have claimed in one way or another that Israel's special relationship to God is over. This is often softened into the concept of a new Israel which the largely Gentile Church supposedly fulfills. But Paul knows nothing of this. His concern here is not about a so called spiritual Israel, but about the real, physical nation that goes by that name. No suggestion of anything like a spiritual counterpart to Israel can be discovered anywhere in chaps. 9–11.

For Paul, an Israelite was an Israelite. **In fact** (*Kai gar*), he asserts, he himself was still one of them. He remained, even after his new birth, one of the physical **descendants of Abraham** and a member **of the tribe of Benjamin**. He is therefore living proof that God has not rejected His ancient people. He will state this truth directly in the next verse.

**11:2. God has not cast away His people whom He foreknew. Or don't you know what the Scripture says in regard to Elijah? How he intercedes to God against Israel, saying,**

The rhetorical question of v 1a is emphatically answered by the words, **God has not cast away His people whom He foreknew.** Paul himself is proof of this (1b). But now the explicit declaration of our verse is followed at once by proof that is drawn from OT **Scripture.** The OT situation referred to by Paul is a famous incident involving **Elijah** the prophet, recorded in 1 Kgs 19:9-18.

It should be noted that Paul's statement here identifies Israel as a nation *whom He foreknew.* Modern Christian readers are strongly inclined to read these words as a reference to God's eternal foreknowledge of all things. The question is then asked how this foreknowledge relates to the doctrine of predestination. But these issues are not at all likely to be what Paul had in mind.

We must not forget that, throughout his whole discussion of Israel in chaps. 9–11, Paul's thinking is fully informed by Scripture itself. A reference here to a hidden doctrine of foreknowledge/predestination has nothing in the larger context to commend it. (And certainly not, as we have seen, in Rom 9:6-24.) Instead, we should ask on what Biblical grounds Paul based this statement. If we ask that question, the answer is obvious. He based it on God's promises to Israel's father, Abraham.

In fact he has already referred to God's statement that, "through Isaac shall the descendants be called your own" (9:6, quoting Gen 21:12). Since Isaac was not even born yet, God *foreknows* his birth and that of the race of which he became the ancestor. Moreover, in Paul's highly favored text about Abraham's justification, Abraham believed what God *foreknew*, namely a seed as numerous as the stars of heaven (Gen 15:5-6). Paul has already made much of this faith as it related to Abraham's offspring (cf. Rom 4:19-22).

We ought to take the statement that God foreknew the nation of Israel as a reference to God's ancient promise about the birth of the nation long before the nation actually existed. It was therefore unthinkable that a nation God so impressively anticipated and promised would now be *cast away*. Paul rejects such an idea categorically.

This rejection is supported by the experience of Elijah. Elijah, who lived during the ninth century BC and first appears during the reign of Ahab, lived in a day of deep apostasy in Israel. The words of Elijah quoted in the following verses by Paul are from 1 Kgs 19:10 (repeated in 19:14) and express Elijah's profound displeasure with Israel. Indeed Paul perceives them as intercession **to God *against*** [*kata*] **Israel**. Elijah is exasperated with Israel and his statements imply that they deserve nothing further from divine benevolence.

> **11:3-4. "Lord, they have killed Your prophets, and torn down Your altars, and I myself am left alone and they seek my life." But what does the divine response say to him? "I have kept for Myself seven thousand men who have not bent a knee to Baal."**

The words cited here by Paul were actually spoken twice by Elijah (1 Kgs 19:10 and then in 19:14). After the first statement God responds with a series of signs (1 Kgs 19:11-12) and then He repeats the question of 19:9, "What are you doing here, Elijah?" (19:13). When Elijah repeats his complaint, God responds verbally. It is to this second response by God that Paul refers in the statement, **What does the divine response say to him?** So it is really the *repetition* of the complaint (in 1 Kgs 19:14) that Paul is discussing here. Only a word from God puts an end to Elijah's intercession against Israel.

Elijah's complaint against Israel is serious indeed. It involves nothing less than the rejection of God's messengers (*"they have killed Your prophets"*), the rejection of the worship of Jehovah (**"they have…torn down Your altars"**), and the relentless pursuit of the Lord's one remaining messenger (*"I myself am left alone and they seek my life"*). No doubt Paul thought that all three features of Israel's sin in Elijah's day were analogous to the contemporary situation, but he leaves the readers to perceive that for themselves.

The exact wording of the quotation in vv 3-4 does not follow exactly either the MT or the LXX, but the differences are basically insignificant and do not really affect the meaning of the OT text. It is doubtful that Paul intended a verbatim quotation at this point, just as we do not when we say, "He said to me etc., etc.," and we give the basic sense. We do this all the time and in the absence of any misrepresentation of the speaker there is no problem in repeating his words in that way. The same observations apply to God's words reported in vv 3-4 of our text.

The fact is that Rom 11:3-4 are the only citation of the book of 1 Kings (LXX: *Basileiōn G'* [3 Kingdoms]) in the Pauline epistles. As we have seen, in Romans 9-10 there are frequent citations of Isaiah (for example), which give the impression Paul is quoting directly from a Greek text. It is plausible to suggest that in the household of Gaius, Paul's host (cf. Rom 16:23), a codex or scroll of the Greek Isaiah was available for use by Paul and his amanuensis, Tertius (Rom 16:22), but that no such codex/scroll was available for 1 Kings.

The word translated *divine response* is *chrēmatismos*. It was widely used in Greek to refer to an utterance by a divinity, whether directly or speaking through an oracle. (The corresponding verb [*chrēmatizō*] is found nine times in the NT, mainly of a communication by God [but not in Rom 7:3; see the comments there].) In our verse it refers to a direct statement by God to Elijah. Paul's use of it here is no doubt intended to highlight the stark contrast between the all-too-human sentiments of Elijah and the sovereign divine purpose of Israel's God.

From Elijah's point of view, the rebellion of Israel was complete, leaving only the prophet himself as a true servant of God. But Elijah is wrong, since God's response informs him, *"I have kept for myself seven thousand men who have not bent a knee to Baal."* In Elijah's perception the entire nation had given way to Baal worship as promoted by Ahab and his notorious wife, Jezebel. In fact, the grace of God had preserved *seven thousand men* (that is, *males [andras]*) as true worshippers of Himself. These men had never *bent a knee* to this abomination. But if they were males, it followed in ancient culture that their households had largely followed their example and they too had not bowed before Baal. Thus the actual number would have been much larger than *seven thousand*, once women and children were counted as well.[1]

Paul will now apply this OT narrative to the contemporary situation of Israel.

**11:5. In the same way then, there is also at the present time a remnant according to *His* choice in grace.**

Precisely as it had been in Elijah's day (**In the same way then,** *Houtōs oun*), so also it was in Paul's day (**at the present time**). God had graciously chosen to preserve for Himself **a remnant** of Israel.

God had not "cast away His people whom He foreknew" (vv 1, 2). Not only does Paul himself illustrate that fact (v 1b), but so does the reality of the many Jews in Paul's day who were believers in Jesus Christ.[2] In all probability, the number of Jewish believers in the Roman church was not insignificant. Paul relies heavily in the present section (chaps. 9–11)

---

[1] This is a common phenomenon in Scripture. For example, John 6 reports that Jesus fed five thousand men (John 6:10, again using *anēr* [*andres* is the form in the text]) with a few loaves and fish. But many of their wives and children were surely also present. Hence commentators speculated there were over twenty thousand fed in the so-called *feeding of the five thousand*. –RNW

[2] Hodges' point here is powerful in light of the context of Romans 9–11 (see esp. 11:11-32 and his comments there). Replacement theology explains these verses by saying that though Israel *corporately* has forever forfeited its right to be God's people, God has not abandoned the Jews *individually* in that they can now be part of the new chosen people, the Church. But Hodges rightly sees in Paul the exact opposite point. The Church is not an exclusively Gentile people. That Jews are part of the Church shows that there is a remnant today, and presages a day in which "all Israel will be saved" (Rom 11:26). *All Israel* is clearly corporate. Any reading of Romans 11 that somehow sees in the Church a replacement of Israel is a serious misreading of the text. –RNW

upon Scripture that would be especially meaningful to Israelites. This sufficiently indicates that his audience was far from exclusively Gentile.

The remnant in Paul's day was a product of God's choice exercised **in grace**. The phrase **according to *His* choice** *in grace* represents the corresponding Greek phrase *kat' eklogēn charitos*. We must strongly resist the temptation to translate *eklogēn* using the word *election*. That word is now so heavily weighted with theological implications that it impedes our understanding here.

Unless we invoke the theology of the post-Biblical church, there is no good reason to see here a reference to election before time, although such a doctrine can be found in Paul (cf. Eph 1:4; 1 Thess 1:4).[3] In Romans that concept has been previously suggested, in 8:29-30, by the word *foreknew* (*proegnō*, 8:29) and by the word *predetermined* (*proōrise*, 8:29, 30), both words using the prefix *pro-* signaling the pre-temporal reference. It is easy to forget that the Greek noun *eklogē* basically means *choice* and does not in itself connote the same thing that *election* does in an English theological discourse. If we forget this we will be guilty of reading later theological discussions back into this text.

The simplest and most obvious meaning of the phrase in question [*eklogēn charitos*] is something like "the choice God has made in grace." The genitive word may be designated as a genitive of quality (cf. BDF, p. 91) and indicates an idea like "a grace-choice." In more idiomatic English, we may handle it as *His choice in grace*. Just as in Elijah's day God had "kept for" Himself those who had "not bowed the knee to Baal," so also in Paul's day God had *kept for Himself* those who had responded to His grace in Christ.

Understood in this way, Paul is not addressing the issue of *how* such people were able to believe, which is much more a philosophical issue than a Biblical one. Rather Paul is referring to the fact that those who

---

[3] Although Hodges believed in the doctrine of unconditional individual election, he did not believe that there were many references to it, as this discussion suggests. In private conversations he told me that he considered it *unconditional* only in the sense that no condition was stated. He thought it likely (or certain?) that God chose some rather than others for some reason He has not told us. He thought that reason *might be* the responsiveness people would show to God's revelation. He cited texts like Acts 17:11, 27; Heb 11:6 to show that one's response to revelation is related to whether one believes or not. It could even be argued that there is no text which teaches election *to everlasting life*. Election seems to be primarily to a task. However, Hodges did not completely break from the idea of election to everlasting life. –RNW

*did* believe were God's choice to be *a remnant* belonging to Him within a largely unbelieving nation. Since God sent His message of grace to Israel first (cf. 1:16), it was a certainty that this message would not return to Him void, even in Israel. Paul believed the general Biblical truth that God must enable faith (2 Cor 4:6; John 6:44; Acts 16:14), but the precise interplay between sovereignty and the human will is never addressed by Paul anywhere in his letters.

Here then Paul is concerned with the fact that grace is the basis upon which God has chosen the remnant of Israel *at the present time.*

> **11:6. But if *it is* by grace, *it is* no longer by works, otherwise grace is no longer grace. But if *it is* by works, *it is* no longer grace, otherwise work is no longer work.**

This statement reinforces what we have already seen. Paul's concern is not basically with *how* God affected His choice. Instead Paul's concern is rather with the basis on which Israelites become a part of this choice. They do so by coming to God on the ground of **grace** rather than on the ground of **works**. This was precisely what Israel as a whole did not understand (see 10:1-4). God's remnant in Israel was formed quite apart from meritorious deeds of any kind.

Since God's selection of the Jewish remnant was conditioned on grace, there could be no intermingling of that with the works of the law or with works of any kind at all. In the present verse we hear the echo of the controversies recounted in Galatians as well as in Acts 15. Even in Jerusalem there were believers who thought that the Gentiles should submit to the law as a way of life (see Acts 15:5; cf. 15:10, 11).

The emphatic statements of the present verse once again suggest that in Rome there were those in Paul's audience who were sympathetic to the charge that Paul's sweeping dismissal of Torah was extreme, if not actually wrong. But for Paul there could be no mixing of grace with works without destroying the character of both.

If God's acceptance of a man was grounded on grace, to add works to that as a condition would strip grace of its true nature. It would be unmerited favor **no longer**. But if God's acceptance was predicated on man's works, it was certainly *no longer* by grace. If one spoke of this acceptance as being by grace, the term *works* would be a misnomer inasmuch as we could not be talking about real works. The term would be emptied of meaning: work would **no longer** truly be work.

Needless to say, even in our own day, there are theologies that argue, directly or indirectly, that grace and works can be mixed. The sophisticated articulations of this thought take many forms. For example, one frequently hears an appeal made to the Reformation statement that "we are saved by faith alone, but not by a faith that *is* alone." But this is double talk. We are either eternally saved by faith alone or by faith plus something else. If the latter is true we can only call it *grace* by making grace something it is not. The simple fact remains that if we are eternally saved by grace, it can have nothing to do with works. Otherwise, as Paul insists, **grace is no longer grace**.

As over and against those in the Roman church today who might still have attached value to the works of the law as an avenue of acceptance before God, Paul here categorically excludes any and all such theological mixtures. God's "choice" of a Jewish remnant in the midst of an unbelieving nation was not predicated on the moral superiority of that remnant, nor upon anything done by it. Instead His choice was precisely those Israelites who received His grace in Christ.

> **11:7-8. What then? That which Israel is seeking, it has not obtained. But the chosen *group* has obtained *it*, and the rest have been hardened, just as it is written, "*God has given them a spirit of stupor—eyes so that they cannot see, ears so that they cannot hear, to this very day.*"**

The words, **What then?**, draw out the point of Paul's argument so far. Although the believing remnant of Israel demonstrates that God has not "cast away His people" (11:1), this is after all *only* a remnant (11:5). **The rest**, the majority in Israel, **have been hardened**.

This situation exists because Israel is still seeking the impossible, namely, acceptance before God by the works of the law. Paul had earlier affirmed that "since they are ignorant of God's righteousness and are seeking to establish their own righteousness, they have not submitted to the righteousness of God" (10:3). But here he adds that, in this process of seeking such a righteousness, they not only have not obtained God's righteousness but have actually *been hardened* to it.

By contrast, **the chosen *group* has obtained *it***, that is, they have obtained the righteousness of God by faith. Here Paul reuses the word for *choice* (*eklogē*) found in v 5 (see discussion there), but employs it as a metonymy of the adjunct[4] to refer to those actually participating in this choice. Hence I render it *the chosen group*. Those who have received God's righteousness in Christ constitute a select group that demonstrates that God has not cast away His people. God has *chosen* this remnant for the purpose of demonstrating this fact.

The emphasis of these verses, however, is upon the fact that *the rest have been hardened*. And this reality is now attested from Scripture (**just as it is written**), beginning with a citation from Isa 29:10. Many writers take the words beginning with **"God has given"** and extending as far as **to this very day** as a Pauline conflation of Deut 29:4 and Isa 29:10. But even a cursory examination of the LXX of these two texts shows how implausible this hypothesis actually is. The alleged Pauline conflation produces what amounts to a *new* text not reflected in either Deuteronomy or Isaiah.

Two far more plausible options exist: (1) The Isaiah scroll from which Paul quotes here contained the text he actually quotes. If this is the case, the words from *eyes* to *day* have probably dropped out of the Masoretic tradition. In fact the MT is difficult here and this may well be the case. (2) The words *"God has given them a spirit of stupor"* acceptably render the Hebrew of Isa 29:10a, and what follows is a Pauline commentary on the quoted words that draws primarily on verbiage found in Isa 6:9-10. The punctuation in my translation reflects this second option.

In either option the meaning is the same. God is responsible for the *"spirit of stupor"* that has blinded Israel's eyes and "stopped" their ears so that they do not believe the gospel. That God has hardened Israel in judgment is almost commonplace in NT doctrine. Note Matt 13:14-15 and Acts 28:26-27, both of which are extended quotations of Isa 6:9-10. Although Paul does not refer here to the Exodus narrative, this divine judgment on Israel recalls God's similar dealings with Pharaoh (cf. Rom 9:17-18).

> **11:9-10. And David says, *"Let their table become a snare and a trap and something to trip over and a retribution for them; let their eyes be darkened so that they cannot see, and make their back bend down always."***

---

[4] See E. W. Bullinger, *Figures of Speech Used in the Bible Explained and Illustrated* (Grand Rapids, MI: Baker, 1979), 589. –ZCH

The testimony of Isaiah is now reinforced by the testimony of David. Paul's OT citation in these verses is taken from Ps 69:22-23 and is extremely close to our current version of the LXX. It appears, however, that Paul used a Greek text that read the Hebrew words for "before them" (*enōpion autōn*) as "for a snare" (*eis pagida*) and the immediately following Hebrew words as "for a trap" (*eis thēran*). Paul's text added also a clarifying phrase (*"for them,"* *autois*) at the end of the verse (Ps 69:22). This is the simplest explanation of the differences between Paul's Greek text and our LXX. The overall sense, however, is identical.

The poetic language of the Psalm refers to *"their table,"* i.e., Israel's provisions and blessings (taking table as another metonymy of the adjunct; cf. v 7). Their very blessings have *"become a snare and a trap...for them."* What was intended for their benefit has instead become *"something to trip over"* (*eis skandalon*) and a form of *"retribution"* (*eis antapodoma*) to them.

In Paul's mind *their table* would most likely be a reference to the special provisions and blessings God had granted to the nation (enumerated in 9:4-5). Their very sense of privilege and blessing (an undoubted source of Jewish pride) had lured them into a feeling of "worthiness" that motivated them to vainly seek righteousness by means of the law (11:7; 10:3). But this vain search for law-based righteousness was *a snare* as well as *a trap* into which they had fallen; their search should have convicted them of their sinfulness and led them to the righteousness of God (Rom 3:19-22).

The remainder of the quotation (Rom 11:10, quoting Ps 69:23) is identical in form to our standard LXX. The words, *"Let their eyes be darkened so that they cannot see,"* reinforce the citation from Isa 29:10a (in v 9) which states that *God has given them a spirit of stupor.* It also confirms a portion of Paul's following comments (v 9: "eyes so that they cannot see"). Israel as a whole has fallen into a blinding spiritual stupor.

The last line of the cited text presents Israel as bearing a heavy burden (*"and make their back bend down always"*). The LXX rendering differs from the English of NKJV which reads, "make their loins shake continually." This is no doubt largely due to the translators' interpretation of the rare Hebrew verb *mā'ad* which occurs only six times in the OT. If taken in the sense suggested by the Greek word *sunkampson* ("to cause to bend") the image will be of a man bending over at the waist, so that the word *nōton* (back) is a rough paraphrase of the Hebrew noun *māṯnayim* ("loins").

In Pauline thought, as previously expressed in this passage, Israel is the object of the wrath of God that has fallen upon them in their unbelief (cf. 9:22, 29, 32-33). Poetically conceived, the nation labors under this burden like a slave who is continually bent over by the weight of the load he must carry.

### ii. National Israel will be restored (11:11-32)

Thus far Paul has simply demonstrated that God has not completely washed His hands of His ancient nation. The "chosen group," proves this. But unanswered as yet is the obvious question whether the present situation is permanent. Is the spiritual collapse of Israel as a national entity final? Are they no longer to be a special nation through which God's purposes will be fulfilled? Are the unique benefits enumerated in 9:4-5 mere matters of past history? What is the nation's real future?

This is obviously an important issue. It is likely that in the Roman church there were those who thought that Israel no longer had a special national destiny. Or at least, there were those who believed that Paul himself thought that way (see the introduction to chaps. 9–11). No doubt some Gentile believers might naturally feel sympathetic to this point of view, while Jewish believers would be appalled at the idea.

In the present unit Paul reaffirms his belief in the national future of Israel while at the same time warning Gentiles not to get proud about their present privileges. This extremely effective section skillfully wraps up Paul's treatment of the problem of national Israel. It therefore stands as a timeless rebuttal to all who think that the nation God dealt with so particularly in OT times is now simply to be subsumed under a predominantly Gentile entity, the Church.

Such a view is not only unbiblical. It is also an expression of Gentile vanity.

Paul introduces this new movement in his thought by addressing the obvious question of why God has allowed Israel to commit the offense of rejecting the message of Christ. Is this offense a sign that Israel is finished as a national instrument in God's program?

**11:11. So I say, they haven't stumbled just to fall, have they? Far from it! Instead, by their offense *there is* deliverance for the Gentiles, in order to stir them to jealousy.**

The words **So I say** (*Legō oun*) introduce the new point Paul now wishes to address. This point is expressed by a question, the Greek of which implies a negative answer: **they haven't stumbled just to fall, have they?** (*mē eptaisan hina pesōsi?*). The conjunction *hina* (which I have rendered *just to*) raises the point, "Is this what it's all about?" Is the fact that they have stumbled (*eptaisan*) merely the indicator of a final collapse (*pesōsi*)?

Paul at once denies any such idea with his familiar expression *Mē genoito*: **Far from it! Instead** (*Alla*) God intends that **their offense** in rejecting the gospel should become the occasion **for the Gentiles** to receive **deliverance**. Even this mercy to the Gentiles is not for the Gentiles' sake alone, but rather is intended **to stir** [Israel] **to jealousy** so that they too can obtain mercy.

We must notice that Paul here returns to the theme enunciated in 10:1 where he expresses his strong desire that *deliverance* (*sōtērian*) should come to his nation. This in turn picks up the theme stated in 1:16 that the gospel conveys "the power of God for deliverance," that is to say, deliverance from *wrath* (5:9-10; cf. 1:18ff.). Thus here (as in 10:1) the term *deliverance* (*hē sōtēria*) means more than simply salvation from eternal judgment. It goes without saying that Paul does not want his nation to be eternally damned. In fact, he wants much more than that. He wants them to cease to be "vessels of wrath" (9:22) who constantly fight the truth of the gospel. He wants them in fact to experience the wonderful "rescue" from divine wrath which so many Gentiles are now experiencing.

If *there is deliverance for the Gentiles*, Paul perceives in this fact God's continuing concern for Israel. God's intention is *to stir them to jealousy* (*eis to parazēlōsai autous*) through His mercy to the Gentile world. In fact, in Rom 10:19, Paul has already cited Scripture for this perception using the words of Deut 32:21, "I will stir you to jealousy by those who are not a nation." These words are currently finding their reality in the grace that has gone out to so many Gentile believers in Christ. God desires that Israel should want what the Gentiles are receiving and, as a result, turn to the Lord Jesus Christ in faith.

**11:12. Now if their transgression *is* the enriching of the world and their loss *is* the enriching of the Gentiles, how much more *will* their fullness *be so*.**

To put the situation he has just described into perspective, Paul immediately points out that **the world** has actually benefited from the **transgression** and **loss** of Israel. But if that is so, **how much more** would it benefit the world if Israel were to be restored to a harmonious relationship with God? In the background are the many OT texts that predict the blessing of the Gentile nations when Israel itself is blessed (cf., Isa 60:1-3; 62:1-3; Mic 4:1-4; Zech 8:11-13, 20-23).

Thus the transgression and loss that are at present so apparent in Israel have given God occasion for **the enriching of the world** (*ploutos kosmou*), that is to say, **the enriching of the Gentiles** (*ploutos ethnōn*). By this Paul means the *enrichment* brought to Gentile mankind by the gracious deliverance available through the gospel (cf. v 11). The results of this enrichment are even more apparent after nearly two thousand years of human history, and the Christian gospel has had positive ramifications not only at a strictly religious level, but also in countless ways at a societal level (e.g., in the administration of justice; in the freeing of slaves; in the countless Christian-inspired charities; and so on).

The word here translated *loss* is *hēttēma*. This noun and its cognate verb (*hēttaomai*) are rare in the NT, and outside of Romans they occur a total of only four times (1 Cor 6:7; 2 Cor 12:13; 2 Pet 2:19-20). In the LXX the noun occurs only at Isa 31:8 (9). The verb, however, occurs numerous times in the LXX and appears to be well known in extra-Biblical literature (see BDAG, p. 441). It seems to be primarily used in the general sense of being "defeated" (as in 2 Pet 2:19, 20). It is probably not wrong to take *hēttēma* in this verse in the sense of a "defeat" or a "severe setback" (cf. Moulton and Milligan, p. 282).

Israel's transgression has led to a huge loss of opportunity and blessing, and the sequence of these words in this verse suggests that Paul has this connection in mind. But viewed from either angle, whether as sin or as a severe setback, Israel's experience has nonetheless issued in Gentile blessing. It follows that the reversal of these effects will have an even greater (*how much more*) impact for good upon the Gentiles themselves, the full realization of Israel's destiny (**their fullness**) is therefore much to be desired.

**11:13-14. For I am talking to you Gentiles. Inasmuch as I am an Apostle to the Gentiles, I glorify my service, if somehow I**

might stir to jealousy *those who are* my flesh and deliver some
of them.

The Gentiles in Paul's audience are particularly in mind (**For I am
talking to you Gentiles**). As I have also noted earlier, there was in all
probability some sentiment among the Gentile members of the Roman
church that inclined to the view that Israel's special destiny had been
forfeited by its "offense" in rejecting the gospel of Christ. In all likelihood
Paul was sometimes invoked as a proof of that perspective. After all, did
he not primarily work among Gentiles?

Yes, says Paul, since he was indeed **an Apostle to the Gentiles**, he
attempts to maximize this ministry (**I glorify my service**) precisely for
the reason that he desires the deliverance of his fellow Jews (**if somehow
I might...deliver some of them**). The Gentiles should not be under the
illusion that he has focused on his Gentile **service** (*diakonian*) simply
because he has washed his hands of the rebellious Jewish nation. On the
contrary, his very ministry to Gentiles has the same intent as that of God
Himself.

Paul has already insisted on God's deliberate intention to **stir** [Israel]
**to jealousy** by granting "deliverance for the Gentiles" (v 11). Paul's Gentile
labors are accordingly directed to exactly the same end. The expression
*I glorify* (*doxazō*) refers no doubt to the fact that Paul puts this service
on highly visible display. His success in Gentile evangelism, wherever he
went, was intended to arouse a holy jealousy among his fellow Jews so
that at least he might *deliver some of them*. His goal is that the Jews should
say, "We want that too."

As everywhere in Romans, so here in 11:14, the sense of the word
group *sōzō/sōtēria* remains consistent with the initial uses found in 1:16
and 5:9-10. The reference is to a "deliverance" from God's wrath that is
made possible by the gift of righteousness (justification). The first person
subjunctive form *sōsō* (*I might...deliver*) is to be taken as a metonymy of
the effect.[5] The "deliverance" actually wrought by God is in fact the effect
which Paul produces through preaching the gospel.

Paul clearly intends the statements of these verses to reinforce his
repeated claims to be deeply concerned for Israel (see 9:1-3; 10:1). Instead
of saying that he wishes to *stir* Israel *to jealousy*, he says he wishes to do this
to *those who are* **my flesh** (literally, simply *my flesh, mou tēn sarka* [*mou*

---

[5] Bullinger, *Figures of Speech*, 560-67.

is emphatic]). No one should suppose, therefore, that he begrudgingly carries out the divine intent of stirring God's ancient people *to jealousy*. On the contrary, these people are as important to him as his very flesh itself.

**11:15-16. For if the throwing aside of them *is* the reconciling of the world, what *shall be* their reception but life from the dead? For if the first fruits *are* holy, so *is* the batch of dough; and if the root *is* holy, so *are* the *branches*.**

The divine purpose for Israel which Paul serves (vv 11-14), namely the effort to stir them to a jealousy that will lead to faith, is a purpose eminently worthwhile. For if, as he has already pointed out, the Gentile world has benefited profoundly from Israel's fall, how much more would it benefit from Israel's full restoration? To express this truth, however, Paul chooses his words with care.

What he has previously called Israel's "transgression" and "loss" (v 12), he now calls **the throwing aside of them** (*hē apobolē autōn*). After all, despite the existence of a believing remnant in Israel, this remnant can by no means hide the fact that nationally, and as a whole, Israel has been set aside. The noun *apobolē* draws its meanings from *apoballō* ("to throw away," "to shed," "to take off," even "to depose," etc.; cf. BDAG, pp. 107-108). *Apobolē* is no doubt to be understood here in the general sense of "casting aside" in contrast to the stronger idea in 11:2 expressed by *apōsato* ("cast away," "reject," "repudiate"). God has *not* definitively repudiated Israel, but He *has* cast them to one side.

This *throwing aside* in fact has already led to **the reconciling of the world** (*katallagē kosmou*). In referring to the concept of "reconciliation" Paul no doubt has in mind the same truth he has already referred to in 5:10-11. There the believer is represented as having "received the reconciliation," i.e., he has entered into "peace with God" (5:1) through our Lord's reconciling work on the cross (see discussion at 5:11). But for Paul that reconciling work was accomplished for all mankind, thus making possible the reconciliation of each believer when he turns to Jesus Christ in faith (cf. 2 Cor 5:19-20). Reconciliation is inherently a two-party process, but the first step was taken at the cross where God reconciled *the world* to Himself by imputing their sins to Christ (2 Cor 5:19). Therefore *the world* is no longer estranged from God by an unbridgeable gulf of sin.

As a result, the believer can experience personal reconciliation to God by faith (2 Cor 5:20).

Thus the whole world has been reconciled as a result of Israel's fall. In the process of rejecting Messiah and crucifying Him, Israel precipitated her own *throwing aside*. But the result of this tragic loss of opportunity and privilege was *the reconciling of the* entire *world*. In the cross, Israel's supreme sin becomes God's supreme act of reconciling love (5:8) to all mankind.

But if such a superlative benefit accrues to *the world* through throwing Israel aside, how could one describe the potential benefit of Israel being received back into God's gracious favor? Such a reception (*proslēpsis*) of Israel would mean nothing less than a resurrection of the world itself. The restoration of Israel would be like **life from the dead** (*zōē ek nekrōn*).

Paul has already alluded to such a "world-resurrection" in the discussion found in 8:18-21. He has declared that the entire natural order will be liberated from the "bondage to corruption" (8:21) which currently holds it in thrall. This will take place when the sons of God are manifested in their glory (8:19). But this latter event also obviously involves resurrection—specifically the resurrection of the saints.

Indeed, the Lord Jesus Himself described the new age to come as "the regeneration" (that is, *tē Palingenesia* = "the rebirth," Matt 19:28). Jesus states that prophesied era will be the time "when the Son of Man sits on the throne of His glory" and the apostles themselves "sit on twelve thrones judging *the twelve tribes of Israel*" (Matt 19:28). This same new age is also the period described in Rev 20:4-6 and characterized there as "the first resurrection" (20:5-6).

Paul therefore has in mind here the eschatological consummation and he will later, at the climax of the unit 9:1–11:36, refer to it with a decisive Scriptural citation (11:26-27). It is then that Israel will be received back into its favored position. When this occurs, the entire world will experience such a transformation for the better that this transformation can be appropriately described as *life from the dead*.

No one should conclude that Israel has become simply an unholy thing now permanently separated from its holy connections and origins. On the contrary, the believing remnant should be construed as a kind of **first fruits** which prefigure the future transformation of the entire **batch of dough**, that is, of the entire nation. For ultimately "*all* Israel will be delivered" (11:26, emphasis added). The holy status that now pertains to the *first fruits* will someday pertain to the complete *batch of dough.*

But from another perspective, Israel's **root is holy** with the result that **the branches** that have sprung from it are likewise holy. By the term *root* it is natural to understand a reference to Abraham who is physically the source of the entire nation. Paul has already made clear that it was Abraham's faith in a resurrecting God that produced his countless natural offspring despite the deadness of his body and of Sarah's womb (4:17-22). Thus the very existence of *the branches* was sourced in Abraham's faith by which Abraham himself became holy; so despite the catastrophic fall of the nation, the *branches* sprung from the Abrahamic root remain holy to God.

With these two vivid metaphors Paul manages to look both forward and backward. The metaphor of *the first fruits* points to a future reality, while the metaphor of *the root* points to the past, that is, to the nation's origin. However viewed, whether in terms of its future destiny or in terms of its beginning, Israel is holy. Has Israel "stumbled just to fall?" Paul's answer is "Far from it!" The nation remains holy in the plans and purposes of God.

The imagery of "the root" and "the branches" that Paul has just employed raises an important question. Has not God obviously rejected most of the branches in "throwing" Israel "aside"? How can one say that the branches are "holy," if they have been separated from God's ongoing purpose? Paul wishes now to address this issue and, for his purpose, continues the root-branch metaphor in a different and more elaborate form.

One must keep in mind here that Paul shared the NT expectation that the Lord Jesus Christ could return in his lifetime. For example, when he spoke of the Second Coming in detail (e.g., 1 Thess 4:13-18) he is completely comfortable in saying, "Then *we* [not 'they'] who are alive and remain shall be caught up together with them in the clouds to meet the Lord in the air" (1 Thess 4:16). In this present passage, it would be a mistake to suppose that Paul conceived of a very long time period between the writing of Romans and the eschatological consummation. As far as Paul was concerned, he might live to witness the Second Advent, and its consequences, himself.

It follows that the figure of the olive tree and its branches does not presuppose that a great length of time intervenes before the restoration of the natural branches. On the contrary, the branches cut off and those grafted back in must not be construed as two separate groups, one alive in Paul's day and the other living in an undetermined future day. The imagery could well have had its full realization in Paul's own time.

> **11:17-18. Now if some of the branches were broken off, and you who were a wild olive tree were grafted in among them and have become a sharer in the root and richness of the olive tree, do not exult over the branches. But if you do exult, *it is* not you *who* bear the root, but the root *bears* you.**

The Greek connective rendered by **Now** (*de*) is to be understood as belonging to BDAG's second extended meaning: "a marker linking narrative segments, *now, then, and, so, that is*" (p. 213). No contrast is implied by *de*, but instead a new direction to the discussion. Paul now focuses on the Gentile response to the setting aside of Israel.

The warning to Gentiles contained in these two verses and in the unit as a whole is not likely to be a concern drawn out of thin air. On the contrary, it is natural to suppose that Paul's fervent claim to a deep concern for Israel (9:1-3; 10:1) counters a negative opinion about Israel on the part of some Gentiles who falsely took Paul's Gentile ministry as a piece of supporting evidence. Implicit in the whole discussion is the claim, probably not infrequently made even in Paul's day, that God's rejection of Israel for its unbelief was a permanent state of affairs.

To reply to this point of view Paul employs the diatribal format. Verses 17-24 are tied together by the rhetorical device of a single interlocutor, to whom Paul presents himself as responding. This fact is not evident to the English reader since our second person word "you" may be either singular or plural. But starting with v 17 the Gentiles are treated as personified by a single person and all the second person Greek forms (whether pronouns or verbs) that occur up through v 24 are singulars. Note in particular the phrase in v 17, *su de agrielaios ōn* (**you who were a wild olive tree**), where the *su* introduces this collective personification as a tree (*agrielaios*), not as a branch.

The view that Israel's present status was permanent could easily lead to what amounted to prideful Gentile exultation that in this new situation the Gentiles themselves were God's favored people. Paul's warning is that they should by no means **exult over the branches**. After all, the Gentiles did not have any legitimate roots in God's *olive tree*. They were merely branches taken from *a wild olive tree* and **grafted in among** the original branches after many of those **branches were broken off**.

In the figure Paul is using, the contrast is obviously between a carefully cultivated *olive tree* and an uncultivated, and hence *wild, olive tree*. Historically the cultivation of Israel as a channel for the divine purposes in the world began with the patriarch Abraham. It is thus natural to think of Paul's reference here to *the root* as a reference to Abraham from whom the entire nation had sprung. The uncultivated *olive tree* is accordingly the Gentile world which had never received the special efforts God made through Jewish history to spiritually cultivate the chosen people.

If the Gentiles had been *grafted in* it was not at all the case that they brought inherent value to **the olive tree** to which they were now spiritually connected. On the contrary, it was they who benefited from **the root and richness** of the cultivated *olive tree*. They had simply **become a sharer** (*sunkoinōnos*) in the spiritual advantages that flowed from *the root* into the tree. In no sense could they be said to **bear the root**. Instead it was **the root** that bore them. Humility was thus in order for Gentile believers rather than an attitude of triumphalism in regard to unbelieving Israel.

In speaking of *the root and richness of the olive tree*, Paul has clearly in mind that the Gentiles have profited enormously from being grafted into the cultivated tree. The figure Paul is using is indeed an apt one. The engrafting of which he speaks has nothing to do with the concept that Gentiles have become what some call the new Israel. To the contrary, their position in *the olive tree* is not permanent (cf. vv 19-22). Backing off from the spurious new Israel motif, it is not hard to see what Paul means.

By virtue of the evangelization of the Gentile world, Gentiles have been placed into *intimate connection* with God's ongoing purposes with His chosen nation. Most obviously, the Jewish Messiah, Jesus Christ our Lord, has become the Savior of countless Gentiles. But in addition to this, the preaching of Christ brings Gentiles into vital contact with the Jewish Scriptures with all the immense spiritual profit that this entails. At this distance from Paul's words we can also see the further enrichment brought by the production of the NT Scriptures, all of which as far as I can tell was written by Jewish men. (Not even Luke is likely to be an exception to this, despite the widespread opinion that he was a Gentile.) Beyond this, the Judeo-Christian tradition has been the channel of enormous benefits to Gentile society.

But everything springs from the Abrahamic root and it is in fact the blessing of Abraham (that is, justification by faith) that the Gentiles who believe have received (cf. Gal 3:6-14). Yet the richness Paul mentions goes well beyond this fundamental blessing. It suggests all the ensuing benefits that come from being placed in close connection to God's ongoing purposes with His ancient people. After all, Paul has just stated that the Gentiles are being blessed precisely because God wishes to use them as a means of provoking His unbelieving people to jealousy (cf. vv 11-15).

> **11:19-21. So you will say, "Branches were broken off so that I could be grafted in." Very well. In unbelief they were broken off, but you stand by faith. Don't be haughty, but be afraid. For if God did not spare the natural branches, *be afraid* lest He not spare you either.**

One possible response from high-minded Gentiles to Paul's previous statements (vv 17-18) could be, "Well after all, they were broken off so that we could replace them, weren't they?" As I have already noted, in Paul's presentation of this proud response he is continuing the format of a diatribe. The speaker is presented as a single person (*Ereis*, **you** [singular] **will say**), the typical interlocutor of the diatribe. He speaks as the personified representative of Gentile pride (**"so that I could be grafted in"**). I, he proudly affirms, am the one for whom the branches were removed.

Paul admits that fact (**Very well**). But it is not a legitimate ground for pride since the issue is not "merit" (i.e., works) but rather an issue of unbelief and faith. What **the natural branches** lost in their unbelief, the Gentiles gained **by faith**. But it was not simply that they *gained* it *by faith* but instead that they now **stand** *by faith*. The verb for *stand* is *hestēkas* and signals here that the Gentiles (i.e., *you* [*su*]) can only retain their position on the olive tree if they maintain their faith.

This, of course, has nothing to do with the issue of individual perseverance in the faith, or with anyone's individual eternal destiny.[6] Paul's *su* is a collective personification of the Gentiles that intends to describe their present privileges as the product of their believing response

---

[6] Newell, *Romans*, 422f, likewise sees this as corporate and not individual; and deliverance from temporal judgment (that results in worldwide temporal blessings), not individual salvation from eternal condemnation. –JHN

to the gospel. The implication is that should this believing response cease, the situation can change. In fact this is precisely what Paul is warning about in vv 20b-21.

Accordingly he cautions his interlocutor, **Don't be haughty, but be afraid**. The implicit arrogance of the interlocutor is inappropriate. Instead he should *be afraid* that the Gentiles might fail to continue standing *by faith*, since God could do to the new branches exactly what He did to the old ones. **If God did not spare** *the natural branches*, the personified Gentile representative should *be afraid* (these words are supplied for clarity) that He might **not spare you** (still the singular, *sou*) **either**.

Very simply put, should the Gentile world cease to be a responsive instrument for the gospel, God could return His focus to Israel. This would mean the cessation of the present period of Gentile privilege and a return to the original privilege of Israel as the chief vehicle for the divine message.[7] This, of course, is exactly what will happen as a close reading of the Olivet Discourse and the book of Revelation show. The 144,000 who evidently proclaim the gospel during the Great Tribulation will be *believing Jews* who are the first fruits of a new worldwide evangelistic outreach (cf. Matt 24:9-14; Rev 7:2-9; 12:17; 14:1-7).

A case can be made that this change in Gentile responsiveness is already far advanced. Today the Gentile world largely rejects the gospel in the form in which it was preached by Paul and by the Lord Jesus Christ Himself. That is not the same as saying that Christendom has disappeared. It has not, but its message is no longer really the message that Paul proudly preached (Rom 1:16-17).

Much that passes as Christianity today in the Gentile world is not Biblical Christianity at all. Just as the Judaism of Jesus' day rejected the true Christian gospel, so also does much of Gentile Christianity in our own day and time. The issue for Paul was not whether Judaism continued in his own time (it did), but whether the Gentiles might actually fall into the same pattern of unbelief as Judaism had. If they did, they would lose their present privileged place in the good olive tree.

---

[7] Hodges' comments here mirror those of classic Dispensationalism. The Church has a very limited run, from Pentecost when the Church was born until the Rapture when the roles of the Church are closed. After the Rapture, no one else will be added to the Church. Prior to Pentecost, no one was in the Church. After the Rapture all Jews who believe in the Lord Jesus for everlasting life will be members of Israel, and all Gentiles will be members of the nations. That is, of course, the same situation that existed from the birth of Israel until the Church began at Pentecost. –RNW

As a matter of fact, Jesus prophesied this degeneration in the parables of Matt 13:31-33. Christendom, having grown from its tiny beginnings into a huge worldwide tree (religion), now finds its branches weighed down by every satanic evil bird (Matt 13:31-32; cf. 13:4 and 19). In addition, the truth of God, like three measures of wheat flour, is now fully mixed with the leaven of false doctrine (Matt 13:33; cf. Matt 16:12). Gentile failure is thus more and more evident as time passes.

> **11:22-23. Look therefore at the kindness and severity of God— toward those who fell, severity; but toward you, kindness, if you remain in that kindness. Otherwise you too will be cut off. And they too, if they do not remain in unbelief, shall be grafted in, since God is able to graft them in again.**

Once again Paul utters a warning to his interlocutor, that is, to this personification of Gentile pride. The singulars of the diatribe format continue here: *Ide* (**Look**), *epi de se* (**toward you**), *kai su* (**you too**). The Gentiles ought to think seriously about both **the kindness** (*chrēstotēta*) and the **severity** (*apotomian*) **of God**. God's kindness was the source of their present privilege, while those whom God originally favored with His kindness (i.e., the Jews) had now tasted His severity. The loss of the former resulting in the latter could easily be repeated for the Gentiles.

The choice of the word *chrēstotēs* (*kindness*) here is felicitous. The word was generally used of a human virtue that suggested things like "goodness," "kindness," or "generosity" (cf. BDAG, p. 1090). In Paul's collage of quotations from the Psalms (Rom 3:10-18), it is presented as a quality that no human possesses (3:12: *Ouk estin poiōn chrēstotēta*; see discussion there). The Gentiles, therefore, are not in their present position due to *their own chrēstotēs* but due to God's.

This unmerited *kindness* from God must be valued in the light of God's severity with His chosen nation (**toward those who fell**). It should not be taken for granted. The Greek word *apotomia* (*severity*, or sharpness) is derivationally related to the cognate verb *apotemnō* (I cut off). Its suitability here in the metaphor about the olive tree is obvious. God has "pruned" His olive tree with the sharp instrument of His judgment. That same "instrument" could be turned in all its sharpness on the Gentiles as well. [Cf. the cognate *apotomos* in a Roman inscription where it has been taken as a reference to "regular sharp weapons dealt out to gladiators": Moulton and Milligan, p. 71.]

Thus the kindness that the Gentiles currently enjoy (*toward you, kindness*) is conditional: **if you remain in that kindness**. If the Gentiles do not *remain in* God's *kindness*, that is, if they do not continue to be responsive to the truth of the gospel (see discussion under vv 19-21), they can be removed from the olive tree: **Otherwise you too will be cut off**. This means that the Gentiles collectively will forfeit their privileged place in the ongoing purposes of God and will cease to be the primary instrument for the spread of the gospel (see discussion above).

But if the Gentiles are *cut off*, the restoration of Jewish privilege can also take place, provided that **they** (the Jews themselves) **do not remain in unbelief**. The Gentiles should not regard this eventuality as unlikely or remote, for the simple reason that **God is able to graft them in again**. The growing belief over the centuries among Gentiles that Israel will never again be at the center of God's purposes is therefore an arrogant misconception on their part. It misperceives what God truly desires and is fully able to do.

The issue hinges on whether the Jews continue their massive rejection of the gospel message. However, *if they do not*, the Jewish nation **shall be grafted in**, precisely because God is fully able to put them back where they were in the first place. That is, He will *graft them in again* (*palin*, emphatically positioned in Paul's text). That Paul knew with certitude that this would indeed be the final outcome is made unmistakably clear in 11:25-27 (see the discussion there).

We must not miss both the solemnity and grandeur of Paul's expectations for his nation. His words in Rom 11:17-24 are in effect a prophecy about the future even though they are couched in the form of a warning to Gentile humanity. But Paul obviously knew that this warning would be ignored (as it already has been) and that the ancient promises to his nation would truly come to pass. Today it is only a matter of time before this prophecy catches up with Gentile self-satisfaction and pride.

The picture drawn by our Lord in Matthew 24–25 and by the Apostle John in Revelation 7 and 14 (as we saw above) makes clear that a brand-new forward thrust of the gospel will occur immediately prior to the glorious appearing[8] of our Lord and Savior Jesus Christ. This highly fruitful evangelism will reap a great abundance of souls (Rev 7:9-17). And

---

[8] Hodges is not referring here to the Rapture. He is referring to the Second Coming. –RNW

it will be Jewish missionaries, primarily, who are our Lord's instruments in this final worldwide harvest.

> **11:24. For if you were cut off of an olive tree that is wild by nature, and contrary to nature were grafted into a good olive tree, how much more shall they who are natural *branches* be grafted into their own olive tree?**

There should be no doubt about God being "able to graft them in again" (v 23) since, says Paul, that process would be more natural than the one that the Gentiles had undergone. Thus he warns his Gentile interlocutor to remember where he came from: **you** (*su*) **were cut off of an olive tree that is wild by nature** (*ek tēs kata phusin exekopēs agrielaiou*). The source from which the Gentiles were taken was the uncultivated *olive tree* of Gentile humanity which was utterly undisciplined (i.e., *wild by nature*). The Gentiles lacked the spiritual cultivation that God had administered to Israel over the centuries so that Gentile religion was marked by ignorance (cf. Acts 17:22-30) and Gentile conduct was marked by every form of sin.

Yet God had grafted the Gentiles **into a good olive tree** and that was an act **contrary to nature**, that is to say, it defied natural wisdom. No orchard keeper would want to do something like that since it might adversely affect the soundness of the *olive tree* into which the wild branches **were grafted**. The implication that lies just below the surface here is that such a horticultural move in everyday life carried with it a risk to the *olive tree* itself, i.e., the danger of a disease-bearing branch. Such an engrafting might easily prove a failure.

And so it would in the case of the Gentiles. This Paul clearly implies with the words **how much more shall they who are natural *branches* be grafted into their own olive tree**. The engrafting that the Gentiles had experienced was even more likely to happen to the *natural branches*, since that would be *according to nature*. In light of his earlier words ("Otherwise you too will be cut off," v 22), the removal of the Gentiles is therefore strongly suggested.

In the following verse, Paul makes explicit the fact that the present Gentile situation is not destined to last (v 25). In the imagery Paul has drawn here from nature itself, there is no room on the one *olive tree* for both types of branches, just as there would be none on a literal olive tree. If one set of branches is engrafted it is because another set has been removed. This premise is basic to Paul's discussion in this crucial passage.

What has already been clearly implied during Paul's dialogue with his Gentile interlocutor (11:17-24) is now made explicit. The setting aside of Israel is temporary and her final deliverance from divine wrath is certain. Thus the position of the Gentiles on the olive tree of the divine purpose and program is temporary. It will last only as long as God's present purposes are in process of realization.

> **11:25. For I do not want you to be uninformed about this mystery, brothers, so that you may not be wise in your own estimation—*that is*, that partial hardening has happened to Israel until the fullness of the Gentiles has come in.**

The reason (**For**, i.e., *gar*) Paul has engaged in his dialogue with the imaginary Gentile interlocutor (11:17-24) is for the instruction of his Christian audience (that is, his **brothers**). He does not want them **to be uninformed** (i.e., to be ignorant: *agnoein*) about God's intentions. This assertion no doubt implies that some among his audience probably *were* uninformed on this significant point related to Israel. From the very beginning of the unit covering chaps. 9–11, Paul has clearly hinted at his concern that his own view of **Israel** has been misrepresented. That view allows no room for the idea that the Gentiles are a permanent replacement for the Jewish "branches."

In fact, the truth Paul has been discussing can be called a mystery. The mystery involved here is no doubt the same one that is referred to in the doxology of Rom 14:24-26 (though this is traditionally and wrongly placed at Rom 16:25-27). In the doxology, **this mystery** is said to have been "kept silent through past eternal times, but now has been manifested, and has been made known to all the *Gentiles*" (14:24-25, emphasis added). It also recalls the Pauline statements of Eph 3:4-6: "...the mystery of Christ, which in other ages was not made known to the sons of men, as it has now been revealed by the Spirit to His holy apostles and prophets, that the *Gentiles* should be fellow heirs, of the same body, and partakers of His promise in Christ through the gospel" (NKJV, emphasis added).

Very simply put, the incorporation of converted Gentiles into the olive tree itself, elevating them to the same privileged status as the remaining natural branches, was a situation not explicitly revealed in the OT. This includes (but is not identical with) the truth that the Church is a unique body in which the Jew/Gentile distinction, found in OT history and prophecy, is set aside. But this new state of affairs has a *terminus ad quem*, that is, **until the fullness of the Gentiles has come in**. Thereafter the former natural branches will replace the wild ones and God's world program as it centers on Israel will resume.

Ignorance about *this mystery*, Paul cautions, is spiritually dangerous. It can cause his brothers to become **wise in your own estimation** (*par' heautois phronimoi*; cf. BDAG, p. 1066). Gentile believers whose attitude reflected that of the interlocutor of 11:19 might well feel that they possessed a discernment in these matters not perceived by their Jewish fellow believers. Thus they might ill-advisedly "exult over the branches" (11:18).

But *this mystery* (to which such Gentiles ought to attend) disclosed that only a **partial hardening** had **happened to Israel** and that when *the fullness of the Gentiles* had *come in*, this hardening would be lifted (v 25). God had never totally cast away His people in the first place (11:1ff.). The existence of a believing remnant showed His ongoing concern for them, and Paul himself was a case in point (11:1b). Thus the Gentiles might well expect that there was a limit on the duration of God's action in setting Israel aside. And so there was.

This limit is clearly specified by the word *until* (*achris hou*). The *terminus ad quem* was the realization of *the fullness of the Gentiles* (*to plērōma tōn ethnōn*). In Rom 16:5 Paul uses the term *first fruits* (*aparchē*) to describe the initial evangelistic results in Achaia (see also 1 Cor 16:15), and it is likely here also that harvest imagery is in his mind. (For this he had precedent in our Lord's own use of such harvest imagery: Matt 9:37-38; Luke 10:2; John 4:35-38.) The word *fullness* will in that case refer to the entire harvest of Gentile converts and the words *come in* (*eiselthē*) will signify the "bringing in" of the harvest crop (cf. John 4:36).

Therefore, the evangelistic thrust into the Gentile world in Paul's day had a specific goal. This goal could be stated in terms of a *complete harvest* which must be brought in. In the afterlight of the more than 1,950 years that have intervened since the writing of Romans, it is evident that this harvest is not yet quite complete. Its precise numerical extent is a figure known only to God, but whenever that figure is reached God will turn once again to His purposes with Israel.

But although this is so, there is plenty of evidence in the events taking place on the world stage today that the harvest is nearly reaped. In fact, the recapture of Jerusalem by Israel in 1967 terminated the "times of the Gentiles" according to Luke 21:24. Luke's phrase for "times of the Gentiles" is *kairoi ethnōn* and is probably best understood as the period of Gentile privilege and opportunity that Paul has discussed in Rom 11:17-24. If this is in fact the case, then in the light of Rom 11:25 we might infer that the harvest proper is over and that what remains is the "gleaning," that is, the final sweep of the harvest field to "bring in" whatever was left from the major harvesting operation.

**11:26-27. And thus all Israel shall be delivered, just as it is written, "The Deliverer shall come from Zion, and shall turn away ungodliness from Jacob; and this is My covenant with them, when I shall take away their sins."**

As has been the case throughout the section covering Romans 9–11, the conclusion of a unit is signaled by a Scriptural quotation (cf. 9:13, 29, 33; 10:15, 20-21; 11:10). Here too Paul's discussion of Israel's future (11:11-27) is climaxed by the Scriptural citation in these verses. The citation is drawn mainly from Isa 59:20-21 culminating with a final phrase derived from Isa 27:9.

Paul introduces these citations with the declaration, **And thus all Israel shall be delivered** (*sōthēsetai*). Throughout this commentary I have consistently rendered the Greek verb *sōzō/sōtēria* by the English term *deliver* in order to avoid the common reflex of a supposed reference to "salvation" from hell (see Introduction). With this in mind, we should understand Paul to be talking about "deliverance from wrath" in all these passages, a connection that is set up by the proximity of *sōzō* and *orgē* (wrath) in 1:16 and 18, and made explicit in 5:9.

In the present verse the link between "deliverance" and "wrath" is signaled by the word ungodliness (*asebeias*: Isa 59:20, LXX). The same word has been used in Rom 1:18 to express a fundamental cause for the divine wrath. Paul had written there: "For the wrath of God is revealed from heaven against all the ungodliness (*pasan asebeian*) and unrighteousness of men." Since Paul has described unbelieving Israel as "vessels of wrath" (9:22; see discussion there), Israel's full deliverance from wrath requires that *"the Deliverer"* (Jesus Christ) should *"turn away ungodliness from Jacob."* That is to say, after believing in their hearts for justification (Rom 10:10a), Israel must also "appeal to Him", "confessing" Him as Lord with their mouths (Rom 10:10b-13; see discussion there). When the nation as a whole does this, it will be delivered: "For whoever shall appeal to the name of the Lord will be delivered" (10:13).[9]

But this triumphant spiritual revival will take place only when *the Deliverer* comes *"from Zion"* at His Second Advent. This very repentance and spiritual renewal is graphically portrayed in Zech 12:10: "And I will pour on the house of David and on the inhabitants of Jerusalem the Spirit of grace and *supplication*; then they will look on Me whom they have pierced; they will mourn for Him as one mourns for his only son, and grieve for Him as one grieves for a firstborn" (emphasis added). After this magnificent event, Israel will be a holy nation no longer living under God's wrath but instead walking in the experience of His measureless mercies. Thus the whole nation (*all Israel*) *shall be delivered* and become vessels of mercy (cf. 11:23).

The quotation from Isa 59:20-21 follows the Masoretic Text and the LXX closely with one exception. For the Hebrew *lᵉṣîyôn* (= *lᵉ* + *Ṣîyôn*) in the Masoretic Text, the LXX has *heneken Siōn* ("for Zion's sake") while Paul's text has *ek Siōn* (*from Zion*). It is now known from comparative Semitics that the preposition *lᵉ* (in *lᵉ* + *Ṣîyôn*) could mean *from*, so Paul's reading is no doubt an older rendering of this word in contrast to our standard LXX edition. The reference will be to Zion as the starting point of this national deliverance, since our Lord will descend to the Mount of Olives when He returns.

The brief quotation drawn from Isa 27:9a is more difficult. The MT is not easy to interpret, but it appears that Paul's version of the LXX understood the Hebrew words *kol-pᵉrî* as equivalent to "as a result of" (and thus: *Hotan,* *"when"*) rather than "all the fruit of" (NKJV; cf. NACE, NIV) or "the full price of" (NASB). Such an interpretation is a reasonable semantic option for the term "fruit" (note Isa 3:10), and this is true even in our own language where fruit can be a metaphor for "result." Otherwise Paul's text differs here from the MT and LXX only in taking the collective "his sin" (*autou tēn hamartian*) as a plural (*tas hamartias autōn*: *"their sins"*) since Israel is in view. None of the divergences from the LXX in either citation (Isaiah 59 or 27) needs to be attributed to Paul.

The words Paul has quoted from Isa 27:9a are followed in the LXX by a statement predicting the destruction of Israel's false objects of worship

---

[9] For another work that understands Rom 11:25-27 as a future deliverance of ethnic Israel, see Arnold Fruchtenbaum, *Israelology,* [3ʳᵈ ed.] (Tustin, CA: Ariel Ministries, 1994), 796. –JHN

(Isa 27:9b-10 [NIV]: "when he makes all the altar stones to be like chalk stones crushed to pieces, no Asherah poles or incense altars will be left standing"). No doubt Paul understood the words of Isa 27:9b-10 to describe the same eschatological period as the words of 59:20-21. Thus he has employed Isa 27:9a as a commentary on the words that follow the phrase, *"And this is My covenant with them,"* in Isa 59:21.

This handling of the two texts is significant. In Isa 59:21, the words *"and this is My covenant with them"* are followed by *"My Spirit who is upon you, and My words which I have put in your mouth, shall not depart from your mouth, nor from the mouth of your descendants, nor from the mouth of your descendants' descendants,' says the Lord, 'from this time and forevermore"* (NKJV). The "you" in this statement is Israel and the prophecy relates to Israel's future fidelity to the words, or will, of God. Paul obviously wanted to cite the reference to the New Covenant (*My covenant*), found in Isa 59:21a, but instead of the elaboration of its effects found in the rest of Isa 59:21, he was satisfied with the words drawn from Isa 27:9a. Paul's point about the turning away of Israel's sins in the quoted portion of Isa 59:20 is thus reiterated by the phrase drawn from 27:9a.

In the quoted material the statements that (1) *"the Deliverer...shall turn away ungodliness from Jacob,"* and (2) *"when I take away their sins"* are parallel statements. The deliverance in view is not simply justification by faith, though that of course is essential (10:9-10), but instead it is freedom from sin's dominion over Israel's conduct. As in the Christian experience that Paul has described in Rom 8:1-13, so also it will be for Israel: "the one who is righteous by faith shall live" (1:17).

Thus in the quotations found in the verses under discussion, Paul brings to an effective climax the unit begun at 11:11. Israel has not stumbled simply to fall permanently (cf. 11:11). On the contrary, once "the fullness of the Gentiles has come in" (11:25), the triumphant return of the Lord Jesus Christ, Israel's Deliverer, will bring final deliverance from wrath to God's chosen people. The Messiah will *"turn away ungodliness"* permanently from this presently rebellious people. Thereafter they will walk harmoniously with God by the enablement of His Spirit (cf. Isa. 59:21b). God will *"take away [Israel's] sins"* from the life of that nation so that they may walk forever in harmony with Him.[10]

---

[10] Hodges is not suggesting that from the time of the Second Coming onward no Israelite would ever sin again. Clearly during the Millennium there will be sin on the part of the multitudes that will be in natural bodies, as evidenced by the final rebellion at the end of

Paul has now elaborated God's purposes with Israel and the Gentiles (9:6–11:27). These purposes constitute a divine mystery that has now been disclosed for the instruction of believers in Christ (cf. 11:25). What final conclusions should Paul's readership draw from these things?

There are basically two fundamental conclusions to be drawn and both are expressed in this final subsection of the large unit covering chaps. 9–11. The first conclusion (11:28-32) is that the Gentiles are currently the recipients of *God's mercy* precisely because of the unbelief of Israel, which is only temporary. Israel remains the object of God's electing love and the future object of His mercy.

The second conclusion (11:33-36) is that God's dealings with Israel and the Gentiles display in splendid relief *His astounding wisdom* for which He must receive glory. Therefore, the two key words in the overall conclusion (11:28-36) are *mercy* and *wisdom*.

> **11:28-29. With regard to the gospel, *they are* enemies for your sake, but with regard to *God's* choice *they are* beloved for the fathers' sake. For the gracious gifts and the calling of God *are* irrevocable.**

The Greek of Rom 11:28 is much more abrupt than my English translation suggests. Neither clause contains a verb, nor is the sentence introduced with any connective word. The omission of a connective (asyndeton) is an effective stylistic means of beginning a new unit or a new subunit. In this staccato fashion Paul calls attention to the summarizing nature of his statement, literally: "As to the gospel, enemies on your account; as to election, beloved on the fathers' account."

The bottom line for Paul, as we have seen, is that God is not through with His ancient people. Even though they are currently at enmity with God (i.e., they are His enemies) on account of their rejection of **the gospel**, they remain His chosen people. Thus they are still beloved because of God's commitment to the patriarchs Abraham, Isaac, and Jacob. **God's choice** of this nation lay in His promises to these men and thus Israel remains in special divine regard **for the fathers'** [i.e., Abraham, Isaac, and

---

the Millennium (cf. Isa 65:20-26; Rev 20:7-9). What Hodges seems to mean is that glorified Israelites will never sin again and that ultimately, after the Millennium, no Israelite will ever sin again. –RNW

Jacob's] **sake**. His choice of them remains unchanged precisely because **the gracious gifts and the calling of God are irrevocable**.

The word *eklogēn* (*choice*) here concerns God's definitive decision to accomplish His purposes in the world through the descendants of the patriarchs. It has no reference at this point to the issue of eternal salvation from hell.

The expression *ta charismata* is translated here by *the gracious gifts* to distinguish it from the more simple word for gift, *dōrea* (Rom 5:15, 17). *Charismata*, with its obvious derivation from the root of *charis* (*grace*), is used by Paul more often than *dōrea* in this epistle (c.f., 1:11; 5:15, 16; 6:23; 12:6). Its coupling with *the calling* (*hē klēsis*) forms a phrase that can be regarded as a hendiadys. Thus *ta charismata kai hē klēsis tou Theou* can be understood in the sense of "the gracious gifts *bestowed by* God's calling."

God's "call" of Israel into a special relationship with Himself will not be forfeited, any more than any of the "gifts" bestowed by that calling. These gifts have already been enumerated in 9:4-5. Both calling and gifts are completely irrevocable (*Ametameleta*: not to be regretted [BDAG, p. 53]). God has not, and will not, revoke them. The failure of Israel in Paul's day, and in ours, in no way diminishes their basic standing and privileges in God's sight.

> **11:30-31. For just as you too at one time disobeyed God, but now have received mercy by means of their disobedience, so also they have now disobeyed, so that by means of your mercy they too might receive mercy.**

How then should the Gentiles regard their present privileges? The answer for Paul was simple: they **have received mercy**. But Paul expresses this idea in a long sentence that covers vv 30-31. Its structure consists of two clauses shaped by the correlative conjunctions *Hōsper* (**just as**) and *houtō* (**so**). The Gentile experience of God's mercy ought to be understood in the light of, and compared with, His mercy to Israel.

In Jewish thought both Gentile religion and Gentile conduct were grossly disobedient to God, so Paul now reminds the believing Gentiles that **you too at one time disobeyed God**. The pagan background of his Gentile readers is obviously in mind. But *just as* this had been true of them, **so also** it was now true of Israel since **they** (emphatic *autoi*) **have now disobeyed**.

But there was another side to this comparison as well. The formerly disobedient Gentiles *now have received mercy* **by means of** Israel's **disobedience**. As Paul has emphatically stated, God's mercy to the Gentiles was occasioned by His desire "to stir" Israel "to jealousy" (11:11). It was **by means of their disobedience** (*tē toutōn apeitheia* that His mercy had been released in a special way to Gentile mankind. But just as this was the case, so also the reverse would prove true.

The Jews who had *now disobeyed* could and would benefit from God's mercy to the Gentiles. Their present disobedience would be ended if they responded properly to what God was doing. That is to say, **that by means of your** [the Gentiles'] **mercy, they** [Israel] **too might receive mercy**. What is especially significant about Paul's words here is that they follow the Scriptural declaration he has just given in 11:26-27. Paul did not entertain the idea that God's efforts to "stir" Israel "to jealousy" might fail. On the contrary, they would succeed as Scripture itself made clear.

It is important to note that the statement *they have now disobeyed* (*houtoi nun ēpeithēsan*) is followed by a purpose clause *so that [hina] by means of your mercy they too might receive mercy*. The structure of this *hina* clause is unusual although not unique, since a portion of the clause precedes *hina: tō humeterō eleei hina kai autoi eleēthōsi*. Examples of this kind of construction with *hina* may be found in 2 Cor 2:4; Gal 2:10; Col 4:16; and Acts 19:4. The sense derived from this is very natural and the phrase about mercy that is thrown forward is therefore emphatic.

Nevertheless, a significant number of interpreters have taken the phrase *tō humeterō eleei* to be connected with the preceding verb *ēpeithēsan*. This yields a sense like "they too have not now believed by reason of the mercy shown to you" (NACE) or "so those who are disobedient now—and only because of the mercy shown to you—will also enjoy mercy eventually" (JB). Similarly, Jewett (p. 694) has, "so also have they now been disobedient because of the mercy you received." A variant rendering, produced by the same grammatical analysis, is exemplified by Moo (p. 711) who translates "so also they have disobeyed [accidentally dropping "now"?] for the sake of mercy for you" (cf. also Dunn, p. 676).

These solutions are not acceptable. For one thing, Paul's argument in chaps. 9–11 shows that Israel's disobedience was sourced in its "collision" with her Messiah (cf. 10:20-21) and not in God's mercy to the Gentiles, which only came later. The variant idea that Israel's disobedience had occurred "for the sake of" God's mercy to the Gentiles is not supported by Paul's preceding discussion. It also requires the improbable expedient of giving a nuance to the phrase *tō humeterō eleei* that is different from that of the earlier phrase *tē toutōn apeitheia* (v 30), to which it is clearly parallel. As pointed out above, the structure of the *hina* clause in no way compels such conclusions.

Therefore this commentary concurs with the interpretation supported by Cranfield, KJV, NKJV, NASB, and NIV.

More than 1,950 years have elapsed since Paul wrote Rom 11:28-32. If we are inclined to posit the "failure" of God's effort to "stir" Israel "to jealousy," we are being premature. God has measureless patience. His work among the Gentiles for some 2,000 years will yet achieve its goal in arousing a "holy jealousy" in Israel which will be followed by a revival under the two witnesses of Revelation 11 and by national repentance at the Second Advent.

### 11:32. For God has enclosed all men in disobedience so that He might have mercy on all.

The bottom line in regard to God's dealings with Jew and Gentile alike is that all have become potential objects of mercy as a result of their disobedience. The Gentiles are currently the special object of His mercy despite their past history of disobedience to God (v 30). But the Jews who are currently disobedient will one day be the renewed objects of that same mercy (v 31). Mercy will overtake Israel just as surely as it has overtaken the Gentiles.

The verb here rendered **enclosed** (*Sunekleise*) signals the truth that God has now put everyone on the same level, namely, a status of disobedience before Him. The nuance of the verb must be handled with care and we should probably not interpret it in terms of ideas like "imprison" or "confine." There is nothing in the overall Pauline discussion to suggest that the disobedience in question is some kind of special "prison" for men (as implied, e.g., by JB), beyond the fact that sin is always an enslaving experience (cf. Rom 8:6-8; John 8:34).

An analogy with the use of this very verb in Luke 5:6 (its only NT occurrence outside Paul) is suggestive. There it is employed to describe a net enclosing a great number of fish. What God has done is to "catch" all mankind (**all men:** *pantas*) in His "net," so to speak, so that their only way out is by means of the divine mercy found in Jesus Christ. The Jewish people, in particular, needed to learn that their standing before God was fundamentally the same as that of the Gentile world. Despite centuries of feeling "superior" to other nations, Israel must now face divine actions designed to puncture all such feelings. God had designed to confront the chosen nation with its desperate need for His delivering mercy.

The term used here for **disobedience** (*apeitheian*) is the same one used in v 30 (*apeitheia, disobedience*). It is of course cognate with the verbs employed in vv 30-31 (i.e., *ēpeithēsate, you...disobeyed; ēpeithēsan, they have...disobeyed*). The basic sense of "disobedience" seems demanded by the general nature of Paul's remarks. And that concurs with the fundamental meaning of both the verb and noun in Greek usage.

However, a number of interpreters prefer to render the verb and/or the noun by words like "disbelieve" or "unbelief" (as in KJV; NACE; NRSV; REB). Such a rendering may occasionally be plausible for the noun. But in the case of the verb, those who abandon the standard meaning "with less probability render *a.*[=*peitheō*] 'disbelieve' or an 'equivalent'" (BDAG, p. 99). Of course, Paul certainly has in mind Gentile/Jewish unbelief, but his statements cannot reasonably be confined to this. Undoubtedly, my rendering is preferable and is also found in NKJV, NASB, NIV, and JB.

God's purpose has mercy as its ultimate objective. Mankind has been "caught" in its **disobedience so that** God **might have mercy on all**. Paul's gospel, which he proclaims without embarrassment, is, "for the Jew first and for the Greek" (1:16).

### d. God's Wisdom Is Unknowably Profound (11:33-36)

As a climax to the entire discussion begun in 9:1, Paul draws the inescapable conclusion that is expressed in this last subunit and here presented in the form of a paean of worship. The seeming tragedy of Israel's disobedience to the gospel is in reality a triumph of divine wisdom. The tragedy is real, but God designs mercy as its ultimate goal.

> **11:33: O the depth of the wealth and wisdom and knowledge of God! How unsearchable *are* His judgments and *how* untraceable *are* His paths.**

God, Paul declares, has measureless depths of wisdom. The Greek phrase rendered by **the wealth and wisdom and knowledge of God** is a kind of tripartite hendiadys. The three coordinated words (*wealth, wisdom, knowledge*) are all grammatically dependent upon the term

**depth** (*bathos*) and are qualified by the genitive *Theou* (*of God*). The entire construction might be rendered: "*O the depth of the wealth in God's wise knowledge.*" But the hendiadys carries a rhetorical impact that a more commonplace formulation would not have carried.

Paul is moved by the profundity of a divine wisdom that can rise so far above the tragedy and evil of human disobedience and unbelief. And precisely because the divine plan was drawn from the wealth of God's *wisdom and knowledge*, it was previously a "mystery" (cf. v 25 and the discussion there). It was therefore utterly unknowable apart from being revealed to men. Thus God's judgments are declared by Paul to be **unsearchable** (*anexereunta* [Majority Text; the Critical Text has *anexeraunēta*]) and **His paths** are extolled as **untraceable** (*anexichniastoi*, i.e., "not to be tracked out"; cf. BDAG, p. 77).

The word **judgments** is appropriately chosen, since the present state of Israel is the result of God's judgment, by which "partial hardening has happened to Israel until the fullness of the Gentiles has come in" (11:25). But this very judgment is unsearchable since its surprising outcome will ultimately be the restoration of the nation God has judged (11:26-27).

Thus the ways of God—*His paths* (*hai hodoi autou*)—are untraceable because no one could have foreseen where God "was going" with His judgment. The divine effort to stir jealousy in His chosen nation by means of His mercy to the Gentiles was a track no human being could have perceived or followed.

Paul therefore praises God for the matchless wisdom that has devised such a plan as this.

> **11:34-35: "Who indeed has known the mind of the Lord? Or who has been His counselor?" "Or who has given first to Him, so that it shall be paid back to him?"**

It has been Paul's custom throughout the unit covering chaps. 9–11 that subunits are concluded by a Scriptural citation. The conclusion of the entire larger section starting at 9:1 (that is, 11:33-36) now employs the same pattern. Following his worshipful paean to God in v 33, Paul at once adds a final, climactic reference to the OT.

The first part of the Scriptural citation (questions one and two, from **"Who"** to **"counselor?"**) is drawn from Isa 40:13. Paul's quotation follows the LXX almost exactly (though LXX has *Kai*, "And," for *Ē*, **Or**), and the Greek is basically equivalent to the MT. The second part of the citation (question three, from the second *"Or"* to *"him?"*) is taken from Job 41:11 and is found in the words God speaks in rebuke to Job. Here, however, the LXX diverges sharply from Paul's Greek citation.

Inasmuch as Paul's citation of Job 41:11 much more closely follows the MT than LXX does, there is no reason to think that Paul is not citing the rendering found in his own Greek version of Job. It has been noted that while the MT reflects the fact that God is the speaker, the Pauline quotation does not. (Cf. the English: *"Who has preceded Me, that I should pay him?"* [NKJV].) It is not impossible that in this case Paul himself adopted the third person reference to God (i.e., Him). But there is not adequate reason in Romans for the oft-repeated claim that Paul often did not cite his Scripture text exactly, but molded it to his own use. Thus another explanation seems more probable.

It is quite conceivable that the translators of Paul's version read the Hebrew text as Paul cites it. This would have required only that the Hebrew verb and its suffix, *hiqdîmanî*, be read simply as *hiqdîmanô*, a very slight difference in Hebrew script. If this form was read in that way, the translators then avoided a "clash" in the personal references by translating the first person singular of the following Hebrew verb by a passive in Greek (*antapodothēsetai*). In such a rendering of Job 41:11 the point of the citation for Paul remained the same.

The two quotations combined summarize Paul's thought quite well. God's dealings with Israel partake of the divine inscrutability. The "mystery" of Israel's hardening (v 25) was God's secret (***"Who indeed has known the mind of the Lord?"***) and was in no way a result of human "counsel" or "advice" (***"Or who has been His counselor?"***). At the same time, God's plans for Israel do not flow from any merit on Israel's part, as though they had given Him something He needed to repay (***"Or who has given first to Him, so that it shall be paid back to him?"***). God's actions toward His ancient people, as well as toward the Gentiles, are pure and simple products of His mercy.

**11:36: Because all things *are* from Him and through Him and for Him. To Him *be* the glory forever. Amen.**

Although every preceding section of the material contained in Romans 9–11 is concluded by a Scriptural citation and nothing more, here Paul makes an exception. Following the quotations from Isa 40:13 and Job 41:11, Paul concludes the entire unit (Romans 9–11) with a doxology.

Rhetorically considered, the doxology marks the definitive climax, not of a subunit, but of the entire discussion begun at 9:1.

The doxology continues to express Paul's awe at the unfathomable "depth" of God's wisdom (v 33). But it also adds a new thought. In fact, the doxological thrust of Paul's words is that God is the divine Source of everything (**all things are from Him**) as He is also the medium through which everything is realized (*all things are...***through Him**) and that finally everything is done with a view to His own interests (*all things are...* **for Him**).

As we have already seen, the Greek phrase translated here by *all things* is *ta panta* and in the Greek of Paul's day was often a reference to the universe (see discussion at 8:32). Paul's thought then is likely to be that the entire universe, and all of the things and events that the universe contains, begin and end with God, who orders them according to His own matchless wisdom. This most definitely includes, but is not limited to, His amazing "paths" (v 33) with Israel and the nations.

God therefore fully deserves a glory which is far more than temporal. The glory He is owed is forever.

A solemn **Amen** is added, which the hearers of Romans might well have echoed orally when the letter was read aloud to them in the various Roman congregations (cf. Rom 16:3-15).

# Romans 12

## E. God's Will Worked Out in the Lives of the Delivered (12:1–15:13)

We have now come to the third major unit of the main body of the Epistle to the Romans. In the first unit of the main body (1:18–8:39), Paul has dealt with a highly inflammatory issue: the role of the law (Torah) in his gospel. He has insisted that the law cannot be, nor was ever intended to be, a means of justification before God or a tool for effective Christian living.

In the second unit of the main body (9:1–11:36), Paul has insisted that Israel has not been permanently set aside. On the contrary, Paul argues, Israel is beloved for the sake of the Patriarchs. God's gifts to, and His call of, His chosen nation are irrevocable. Indeed, Paul's gospel is precisely what Israel now needs.

But the discussion up to this point leads to an obvious problem that would easily suggest itself to those nurtured on the Law of Moses. If the law is no more effective for Christian living than for justification, does this not lead to lawlessness? Already, as Paul has indicated, there were those who claimed that Paul taught men to do evil that good might result (cf. Rom 3:8). In the final analysis, was Paul an antinomian?

This unit answers that question. And it does so, not by an overt defense of Paul's moral standards, but rather by an appeal to his readers to live lives worthy of God's mercy on them. Had the Gentiles become objects of God's mercy? Yes, they had. Let them therefore live lives that reflected that mercy. This is the message of the final unit of the main body, namely, Rom 12:1–15:13.

The goal of this final unit is to round off Paul's defense of his gospel, a gospel that he preaches without embarrassment (1:16). There are three

344

reasons he is not ashamed, corresponding to the three divisions of the main body: (1) His view of the role of the law accords with OT Scripture (cf. 3:19-20); (2) His view of Israel accords with OT prophecy (cf. 11:26-27); and (3) His view of Christian morality as a life of love is a fulfillment of God's moral law (cf. 13:8-10).

## 1. Introduction: The Call to Be a Living Sacrifice (12:1-2)

**12:1. I exhort you therefore, brothers, by the mercies of God, that you present your bodies *as* a sacrifice *that is* living, holy, pleasing to God—*which is* your rational service.**

The new discussion that begins here commences in striking fashion. For the first time in Romans, Paul opens a major unit with a direct exhortation (contrast 1:18; 9:1). Until this point, Paul has been discussing what in modern terminology is called "theology." He has been concerned mainly with expounding on a pair of fundamental truths that undergird his gospel. As we have seen, these truths relate to the role of Torah (the law) in Paul's gospel (1:18–8:39) and to the place of Israel in God's unfolding purposes (9:1–11:36). He has now reached the point where the practical implications of his theology can be spelled out as they relate to actual personal behavior.

This rhetorical shift to a hortatory mode is effective for Paul's goals. If he had continued in the less personal doctrinal style he has employed up to now, it might have suggested a measure of detachment on his part. Instead he begins the entire unit with a word of appeal. The words **I exhort** translate the Greek verb *Parakalō* (so NACE; "urge," NASB, NIV; "beg," JB; "beseech," KJV, NKJV). The charge Paul referred to in Rom 3:8, that he encouraged doing evil in order to produce good, is thereby challenged by the very first word of this section.

Paul's appeal to his Christian brothers is founded on a theme he has just expounded in chaps. 9–11, namely, **the mercies of God**. The Greek word rendered *mercies* here is *oiktirmōn* and occurs only in this place in the epistle (though the verb occurs twice in 9:15). It is a synonym for the noun *eleos*. That noun and the cognate verb *eleeō* occur a total of eleven times in Romans, all but two of them in Romans 9–11. The choice of the alternative word (*oiktirmos*) in this verse is probably for rhetorical effect.

The new word arrests attention while evoking the same theme Paul has just discussed (see especially 11:30-31).

The phrase *by the mercies of God* employs the Greek preposition *dia* (by), which is probably not to be reduced to a mere formulaic sense expressing urgency (as apparently BDAG, p. 225 3f). Instead the sense seems to approach a causal meaning (such as BDAG [p. 225 #5] suggests for Rom 8:3; 2 Cor 9:13). Paul is basing his appeal on the very mercies that he has expounded in the preceding unit. But since "because of" would probably overplay the causal nuance a bit, *by* remains my choice here with KJV, NKJV, NASB, NACE (NIV: "in view of"; JB has: "think of God's mercy"). The *therefore* (*oun*) is harmonious with the causal idea I am discussing since it underlines the connection with what has gone before.

What follows this appeal based on God's mercies is a call to a conscious religious orientation to life. Indeed one might say the appeal evokes the image of a believer-priest through Paul's use of the term **service** (*latreian*). The word *latreia* was previously employed by Paul in 9:4 in reference to the ceremonial system of the Law of Moses (which is precisely its sense in Heb 9:1, 6 and John 16:2, the only three other NT uses of the noun outside of the two in Romans). The three uses of *latreia* in the LXX of the Pentateuch all refer to the Passover ritual (Exod 12:25, 26; 13:5). The cognate verb, *latreuō*, occurs frequently in the Pentateuch in reference to the ceremonial services related to Israel's God, or by contrast to false gods (cf. Deut 7:4-5).

The English word *worship* is likely to be misunderstood here (cf. NASB, NIV, JB) since it so often represents an attitude rather than a prescribed religious ritual. Indeed, in the Exodus account, the word *latreuō* is closely linked with the offering of sacrifice (note Exod 10:7, 8, 11, 24, 26 [2×]), which was presumed to be a feature of the activity of "serving" God. Thus the connection in this verse between *service* and *sacrifice* is intrinsic to the image that Paul has in mind. But since in Judaism only priests officiated at sacrifices, the implication arises that Paul is talking here about his readers' role as believer-priests. This truth is well attested in the NT (cf. 2 Pet 2:5, 9; Heb 13:15, 16), but it is striking that Paul himself never uses the Greek word for priest (*hiereus*) at all.

Thus to call upon his brothers to **present** their **bodies as a sacrifice**, which in turn was a *service* to God, was to urge them to live in the atmosphere of priestly activity. That this *sacrifice* was not a literal, physical act is indicated by the term **rational** (*logikēn*). The adjective *logikēn* clearly evokes the recollection of Paul's use of the verb *logizomai* in 6:11 in his discussion of Christian living.

The variations in the translation of *logikēn* in the English versions testify to the difficulty of choosing the best term. So we meet "reasonable" (KJV, NKJV), "spiritual" (NASB; NIV; NACE), and "worthy of thinking beings" (JB). The problem with all of these options is that they lose the connection with 6:11. They therefore ignore the fact that 12:1-2 recapitulates Paul's doctrine of the Christian life as expounded in Romans 6–8. I discuss this recapitulation below. Even the word *rational* is not a perfect choice, but it does retain the implication of well-reasoned mental activity that underlies *logizomai* in 6:11. It is hard to do better.

With evident rhetorical skill, Paul deftly indicates the actual nature of the sacrifice he urges his readers to make. Not only does *logikēn* (*rational*) indicate that the sacrifice is related to the mind and to our reasonable (mental) processes, but the descriptive term *zōsan* (*living*) likewise sets this service sharply apart from its OT analogue. Here, too, with the word **living** we are back with the truth expressed in Romans 6, in particular Rom 6:11. The believer, Paul has said there, should mentally "consider" (*logizesthe*) himself to be "dead to sin, but alive (*zōntas*) to God in Christ Jesus our Lord."

Moreover, at the climax of his argument (in 8:9-13), Paul has insisted that our physical bodies (*sōma*), though dead to God (8:10), can be made alive (*zōopoiēsei*) as a vehicle for our new lives (cf. 8:10-11). By the Spirit's power we can "walk in newness of *life*" (*zōēs*, 6:4, emphasis added). If this in fact occurs, then (as Paul states in 8:13) believers in Christ will actually put to death "the deeds of the body" (*tas praxeis tou sōmatos*) with the result that they "will *live*" (*zēsesthe*, emphasis added).

Thus against the background of this teaching it is clear that when believers present their *bodies as a sacrifice*, it is in fact the *deeds* of the body that are put to death, but the body itself is *living* because it is alive with the very life of God. From that perspective, this is truly the sacrifice of a living body—not merely "alive" in the physical sense—but above all "alive" in a spiritual sense. The entire life of Christian obedience to God, as empowered by the indwelling Spirit, is therefore a superlative act of sacrifice by the justified believer in Christ.

The three attributes of the sacrifice specified here are found in the terms **living** (just discussed), **holy**, and **pleasing to God**. The two additional terms likewise pick up concepts from chaps. 6–8. The fruit of Christian experience is in fact "holiness" (6:22), and this in turn is *pleasing to God* (the adjective *euareston, pleasing,* shares the root of the verb *areskō,* "to please" [Rom 8:8]). If Christians live in the quickening power of the Spirit of Christ, their behavior in so living will have these very attributes.

Such then is the sacrifice Paul enjoins his Christian brothers to present. Not surprisingly, the Greek word for *present* is *parastēsai,* from the verb *paristēmi/paristanō* (see BDAG, p. 778), and it is an important one. The verb occurs a total of five times in Romans 6 (vv 13 [2×], 16, 19 [2×]) and serves as a key term in that chapter. It does not occur again until the present verse (and only twice more in the epistle: 14:10; 16:2). The sense in Romans 6 of to "put at someone's disposal" (BDAG, p. 778) blends easily with the sacrificial context found here.

In this initial verse of the final major section of the main body Paul manages to link the section with the two preceding ones (that is, with 1:18–8:39 and 9:1–11:36). With his reference to *the mercies of God,* he connects with the latter section, while the terminology of the appeal itself connects with the former. In this way, the interrelated nature of the entire main body is clearly signaled.

> **12:2. And do not be conformed to this age, but be transformed by the renovation of your understanding, so that you may put to the proof what *is* the good and pleasing and perfect will of God.**

If Christian living can be described as the presentation of a "living sacrifice," the process involved in such living can be characterized as a process of *transformation.* Neither in Romans, nor elsewhere in his epistles, did Paul regard Christian experience as a simple, automatic transition from defeat to victory. Instead he regarded Christian living as a *process* of spiritual change accomplished by the work of the Holy Spirit.[1] This truth is succinctly stated in 2 Cor 3:18. Its principles are more fully elaborated in Rom 8:1-13.

Romans 12:2 may then be regarded as summarizing the fundamental methodology by means of which the sacrifice urged in v 1 can be carried

---

[1] As the previous sentence shows, Hodges does not mean that this process automatically results in transformation in the lives of every born-again person. Rather, he means that the Holy Spirit is committed to this process. As long as a believer keeps listening to and submitting to the clear teaching of God's Word, he will progress. –RNW

out. The first point is a negative one. If his brothers are to make a living sacrifice of their bodies, they must not allow themselves to **be conformed to this age**.[2] The second point is positive: they are to **be transformed** in order to experience the **will of God**.

Fresh wording is used to express the negative part of the charge. The command **do not be conformed** is expressed by the Greek phrase *mē suschēmatizesthe* (the verb is used only here by Paul). Likewise the phrase *to this age* (*tō aiōni toutō*) occurs only here in Romans, although it is not uncommon elsewhere in Paul's writings.

This new wording once again recapitulates the truth found in Romans 8, in particular vv 5-7. As Paul stated there, "those who are in relation to the flesh" manifest a mind-set focused on "the things of the flesh" (8:5), whose final fruit can only be "death" (8:6). As a result, this mind-set is both hostile to God and incurably insubordinate to God's law (8:7). Clearly such features as these are precisely the characteristics of the present age. The Christian's life ought not any longer to manifest conformity to such a spirit and to the resulting forms of conduct.

On the contrary, Paul wants his brothers to undergo the spiritual change that comes through inward renovation. The words **the renovation of your understanding** translate *tē anakainōsei tou noos humōn*. In the NT, *anakainōsis* ("renewal": BDAG, pp. 64-65) is found only here and in Titus 3:5. The cognate verb (*anakainoō*) is used only by Paul in the NT, and only in 2 Cor 4:16 and Col 3:10. It seems clear that in this verse *the renovation of your understanding* is the inward counterpart to being transformed in outward behavior, i.e., in obedience to the *will of God*.

As Paul taught in Rom 8:1-6, "the righteous requirement of the law" can be "fulfilled" in those "who do not walk in relation to the flesh but in relation to the Spirit" (8:4). This righteous experience requires "the mind-set of the Spirit" (*to...phronēma tou Pneumatos*, 8:6), which results in "life and peace" (8:6). The noun for *understanding* in this verse is *nous*, a term Paul previously used twice in Romans 7 (vv 23, 25) to describe the inner self that delights in the law of God but is unable to carry it out (7:22-23). Paul's reference to *the*

---

[2] Romans 12:1-2 does not indicate that the successful Christian life is automatic or guaranteed. Yet Peter Stuhlmacher ("The Theme of Romans," in *The Romans Debate*, rev. ed., Karl P. Donfried, ed. [Peabody, MA: Hendrickson, 1991], 341) blatantly expresses perseverance theology, seeing Romans 12–15 dividing those who really believe from those who do not. See also John MacArthur, Jr., *Romans 9–16*, *The MacArthur New Testament* (Chicago, IL: Moody, 1994), 140. –JHN

*renovation of your understanding* (or, "mind") is thus most naturally taken as the production of the new mental outlook, "the mind-set of the Spirit," wrought by the Spirit Himself through His work on our understanding. This renovation of our mind produces practical holiness (see discussion in chapter 8).[3]

The result of the transformation in conduct that is effected through this *renovation of* the believer's understanding is the realization of God's will in his life experience. The purpose construction introduced by the Greek preposition *eis* is probably best linked with the main idea of the clause, conveyed by the command *be transformed*. The realization of the divine will is the intended result of this transformation.

This raises the question of how exactly to render the verb *dokimazein*, which I translate as **put to the proof** (see *Oxford English Dictionary*, "proof," *sv.* 4a). The versions offer various options: "prove," KJV, NKJV, NASB; "discern," NACE; "discover," JB; "test and approve," NIV. It may be admitted that no rendering here is totally satisfactory, primarily because English does not have a verb whose semantic connotations are identical with *dokimazō*.

It is not likely that the idea of "discover" or "discern" is appropriate here since the earlier discussion (in Rom 6:1–8:13) does not deal with *finding out* God's will, but with *doing* it. Equally, the word *prove* is easily misunderstood since it can suggest that God's will is either dubious until it is performed, or that it is a matter of discovery through experimentation. "Test and approve" (NIV) heightens the unnecessary notion of experimentation.

By my rendering I suggest that doing God's will results in an experiential demonstration of its excellence. This is akin to our colloquial phrase, "Try it, you'll like it!" In line with its semantic overtones of successfully undergoing examination, *dokimazō* neatly captures this idea. Paul is saying that when we actually perform the *will of God* in our lives, we will discover for ourselves that His will is **good and pleasing and perfect**.

In this view, these three qualities do not suggest an ascending series of levels in discerning, or experiencing, God's will. Rather they specify three fundamental attributes of God's will that are manifest when it is performed. A single article (*to*) unites all three of them. Thus the divine will has an intrinsic excellence (*good, agathon*). It has a favorable effect on

---

[3] See also 1 Cor 2:14-16 where Paul discusses the spiritual man. He is one who has "the mind of Christ," meaning that he thinks as Christ thinks. –RNW

God (*pleasing, euareston*; cf. v 1). And it possesses an inherent superiority and completeness (*perfect, teleion*; cf. BDAG, p. 995 #1, "pertaining to meeting the highest standard"). All these characteristics belong to the will of God at one and the same time.

In the opening two verses of this final unit of the main body (12:1–15:13), Paul has skillfully re-articulated the fundamental Christian truth about life, which is more fully expounded in 6:1-13.[4] His re-expression of this teaching is verbally arresting and at the same time opens new windows of comprehension of the truth involved. It is an extremely effective rhetorical technique that prepares the ground for the practical admonitions to follow.

## 2. Presenting Our Bodies to God in Holy Living (12:3–14:26)

Paul will now spell out in some detail the moral and spiritual standards that ought to be manifested in Christian living. In presenting our bodies to God in holy living (12:1-2), there are several areas of experience which Paul feels should be stressed for the benefit of his Roman readers. These areas constitute the subdivisions of the large body of material found in 12:3–15:6. The subdivisions are the following: (1) personal standards (12:3-21); (2) societal standards (13:1-14); and (3) ecclesiastical standards (14:1–15:6). Just as 12:1-2 provides an introduction to this large unit, so 15:7-13 furnishes a conclusion.

### a. In Personal Conduct (12:3–13:14)

Personal character was an important consideration in the Greco-Roman world in which Christianity was born. Greek and Latin biographers show this by their careful attention to it in describing the lives of their subjects. Greco-Roman moralists also had much to say about the qualities that made men either admirable or disreputable. The ancient Israelite traditions about personal holiness thus flowed freely and naturally into Christian thought. Readers of Romans would take for granted that moral standards mattered in general.

---

[4] This commentary's distinction between justification and deliverance (*sōtēria*) harmonizes well in Rom 12:1-2. If those justified (by faith alone in Christ alone) call upon Him for post-justification deliverance, they will not be put to shame. –JHN

### i. Maintaining perspective on one's
### role in the church (12:3-8)

**12:3. I say then through the grace that has been given to me, to everyone who is among you, not to aspire beyond that to which one ought to aspire, but to aspire to what is sensible— each person as God has distributed to him faith's portion.**

The opening words in Paul's detailed elaboration of Christian living, **I say then** (*Legō gar*), signal the new unit. In the light of his statements in vv 1-2, he now wishes to stress certain particulars and begins logically with matters related primarily to the individual himself. Naturally such matters relate also to behavior towards others, but they must first of all be the personal concern of each individual Christian.

This approach is evident here in Paul's call to modesty, or proper perspective, in regard to one's own role in the Christian body (12:3-8). Paul's admonition, he states, comes via (**through**) his own experience of **the grace that has been given to** him. Though he speaks as an apostle (cf. 1:1), this is a role attained only *through the grace* of God. He therefore models the modesty he enjoins on the Romans.

As an experienced church planter, Paul knew only too well that God's grace to Christians could easily morph into a source of prestige, especially with regard to newfound spiritual gifts, but to treat one's spiritual capacities as a badge of honor was to become "conformed to this age" (v 2). Paul therefore urges **everyone who is among you** (none are immune) **not to aspire beyond that to which one ought to aspire, but to aspire to what is sensible**. These words in Greek involve an obvious wordplay which ought to be looked at carefully.

With rhetorical calculation Paul uses three words here that are etymologically related. These are: *huperphronein* (*to aspire beyond*); *phronein* (*to aspire*, 2×); and *sōphronein* (*is sensible*). As Goetzmann points out in his discussion of the word group,[5] "unlike *phronēma* and *phronēsis*, the verb tends to retain its ordinary meaning; it is, so to speak, more neutral and requires a context to indicate its true sense" (p. 617).

The context is especially crucial to the nuance of *phroneō*. Goetzmann thinks this passage shows how the verb "used absolutely, acquires its

---

[5] See "Mind: *phronēsis*," *The New International Dictionary of New Testament Theology*, Colin Brown, ed., (Grand Rapids, MI: Zondervan, 1975), 2:616-20. –ZCH

proper meaning only from its immediate grammatical context, e.g., from its use with the prefix *hyper-*, think more highly (Rom 12:3), or with some characteristic word like *sōs* (as in *sōphronein* also in Rom 12:13 [*sic* for 12:3], 'to think with sober judgment')" [NIDNTT, 2:617]. In the light of the ensuing discussion of gifts, I suggest the meaning *aspire* for *phroneō* here.

The translation *aspire* falls under BDAG's second meaning category, "to give careful consideration to something, *set one's mind on, be intent on*" [p. 1065]. BDAG itself renders Rom 12:3a under its first category as "*not to think more of oneself than one ought to think*" [*ibid.*]. But this is too general and does not cohere as well with the following discussion of gifts. On the other hand, our rendering coheres nicely with the later use of this verb in v 16 (see that discussion). See also the same verb in parallelism with *zēteite* ("seek") in Col 3:1-2.

As a man with extensive pastoral experience, Paul had already encountered the self-centered aspirations that could exist when gifts were taken as badges of status within the Christian community. (1 Cor 12:12-26 should be read carefully with this in mind.) A man with a lesser gift might easily *aspire* to one that was more prestigious. Even James warned, "My brethren, let not many of you be teachers, knowing that we shall receive a stricter judgment" (Jas 3:1). The opportunity to "teach" could easily become an occasion for self-display.

Instead of aspiring beyond their actual capacity, believers should *aspire to what is sensible* (*phronein eis to sōphronein*). That is, they should aim for service in the church that conformed to their actual ability and gift. This sensible approach meant that **each person** should take account of the manner in which **God** had **distributed to him faith's portion** (literally, "to each as God has measured the measure of faith").

Commentators have frequently been misled by wrongly understanding the term *metron* here. The reference can hardly be to the "degree" or "extent" of one's faith, which is not really relevant in context. Instead, *metron* should be taken to indicate what has been "measured" out to them as a result of their Christian faith, namely, their spiritual gift. The phrase *metron pisteōs* (*faith's portion*) is to be understood as the functional equivalent of the phrase in v 6, "gifts differing according to the grace that has been given to us." Underlying this concept is Paul's teaching that God does not give every gift to every person, but instead the Spirit sovereignly determines the role each person will have in the Body of Christ (cf. 1 Cor 12:13-31).

The versions here struggle to construe the correct sense: e.g., "the measure of faith" (KJV, NACE); "a measure of faith" (NKJV, NASB); "the measure of faith God has given you" (NIV); "by the standard of the faith God has given him" (JB). This confusion is due to the failure to recognize that, contextually, *emerise metron* (lit, "He [God] has measured a measure") entails a metonymy of the cause in which *metron* stands for the gift imparted by God's action of measuring it out.

Paul's readers are being urged to sensibly assess their giftedness and not to *aspire beyond* the spiritual status that God has assigned to them in the Christian Church.

> **12:4-5. For just as in one body we have many members, but all the members do not have the same function, so we *who are* many are one body in Christ, but members individually of one another.**

The connection of these verses to what Paul has just said is clearly indicated by the words **For just as** [*Kathaper gar*]. (The words of vv 4-5 also remind us of 1 Cor 12:12 and the discussion that follows there [12:13-31].) To "aspire to what is sensible" (Rom 12:3) involves the realization that the Christian Church is analogous (*Kathaper*) to a physical body which has **many members**. The words **we have** are generalizing: "what exists for all of us in our **one body** are its *many members*." The result is that there is a variety in the functions performed by these members.

This analogy should be applied, Paul says, to the Church. The **so** (*houtōs*) of v 5 picks up the *just as* of v 4. We should recognize the basic fact that **we *who are* many** in number are all a part of a single whole (**one body in Christ**) and therefore we are individually (*ho...kath' heis*: each individual) members who actually are part **of one another**.

If a believer "aspires" to some gift that God has in fact bestowed on another believer rather than on himself, such an attitude fails to recognize the diversity in function (*praxin*; cf. BDAG, p. 859 #1) which is inherent in the *one body*. It also fails to remember that we do not live separate, isolated lives any longer, but rather we are **members individually *of one another*.** Rather than to "aspire beyond" one's actual gift, believers should recognize that they are part of a team. They should function in collaboration with each other and not as discrete individuals. Thus, each member should perform the function that he or she was intended to perform in the *one body.*

> **12:6-8. Now since we have gifts differing according to the grace that has been given to us, if *we have* prophecy, *let us do this* in agreement with the faith; if *we have the gift of* service, *let us be engaged* in service. If *we are* a teacher, *let us be engaged* in teaching; if *we are* an exhorter, *let us be engaged* in exhortation. The giver *should give* with generosity; the leader *should lead* with diligence; the one who shows mercy *should do so* with graciousness.**

A glance at the original text of vv 6-8 shows that Paul's Greek is very elliptical in these verses, even though the meaning is clear enough. The italicized words in my translation attempt to bring out what is simply understood when Paul's text is read. In a general way, Paul enjoins the exercise of each gift whatever it may be.[6] If a believer "aspires to what is sensible" (v 3), this is precisely what he will do.

The premise on which the exhortation rests is stated clearly in the words **since we have gifts differing according to the grace that has been given to us.** Inasmuch as the functions of the members of the body are not identical (as Paul has stated in vv 4-5), it follows that each person should apply himself to the exercise of his own particular gift. In that way, *the grace that* had *been given to* each one can be used for the profit of the whole body. Implicit is the fact that the Body of Christ benefits when every gift is actually exercised (cf. Eph 4:11-16).

It is noteworthy that Paul does not here include the term *apostle* among the gifts mentioned. There were no apostles in the Roman church[7], since this preeminent gift (1 Cor 12:28) was apparently a closed group among which only fourteen individuals can be identified with confidence (see Acts 1:13, 21:16, 14:14). But the second ranked gift, according to 1 Cor 12:28, was that of prophecy, and this gift was obviously present at Rome. Paul thus addresses the use of this gift first.

The one who possesses the gift of prophecy should exercise this gift **in agreement with the faith** (*kata tēn analogian tēs pisteōs*).[8] The meaning

---

[6] Romans 12:6b-8 is not an exhaustive list of spiritual gifts, but offers parameters for using one's gift, whatever it is. –JHN

[7] The apostles did take note of some in the church of Rome as 16:7 shows. –RNW

[8] The common theological expression *the analogy of faith* comes from Rom 12:6. The word

of this phrase in Greek has raised questions in the minds of interpreters, but the translation given here seems by far the most natural (cf. BDAG, p. 67, where "*in right relationship to, in agreement with, or in proportion to*" are suggestions for *katā analogia*). The articular expression *the faith* (*tēs pisteōs*) can be most naturally taken in the sense given in BDAG, p. 820 #3: "that which is believed, *body of faith/belief/teaching.*"

For the Greek words *tēs pisteōs*, the meaning, "the share of commitment one has" (see BDAG, p. 67), is improbable here. Paul does not use *pistis* as an equivalent to *fidelity* in any place in Romans, and more specifically its normal sense (*faith*) is preferable also in v 3. The paraphrase in BDAG actually masks the vagueness of the idea that must be (with difficulty) extrapolated from the single word *pisteōs*. The extrapolation in turn depends on an equally improbable idea supposedly found in *pisteōs* in v 3 (i.e., "commitment or fidelity adequate for implementing the gift" [BDAG, *in loc.*]). It is more than dubious that any hearer of the epistle in the Roman congregations would have detected this kind of meaning in either verse.

By contrast the meaning my translation conveys is clear. Paul recognized the latent danger in allowing prophecy to take place in the churches if it was untested against the established truths of *the faith*.[9] At Corinth (1 Cor 14:29) he commanded, "Let two or three prophets speak, and let the others judge" (*diakrinetōsan*: pass judgment on). The possibility was all too real that individuals claiming prophetic inspiration might express ideas that ran counter to true Christian doctrine. The true prophet does what Paul enjoins here: he prophesies *in agreement with the faith*.[10]

But the next gift mentioned, service, is quite a different sort of gift. Whereas prophecy is a speaking gift, service is an activity. Indeed, Peter summarizes all the gifts by mentioning these two categories (1 Pet 4:10-11). The "open" nature of early Christian meetings (they were not preaching services) created a danger that people who had no speaking

---

*analogy* is from the Greek word *analogia* in the expression "*in agreement with* [or in proportion to, or in keeping with] the faith." –JHN

[9] The nature of the restriction on prophecy is debated: some think it is to be *in proportion to* the prophet's faith. But actually it is to be according to the analogy of the faith (i.e., according to revealed truth). Prophecy that is not *in accordance with* (*kata*) the analogy of the faith, is an inappropriate use of the gift, just as self-service violates the serving gift, etc. –JHN

[10] Among those arguing for this view are: Cranfield, *Romans*, 621; Fitzmyer, *Romans*, 647; Moo, *Romans*, 765f, agrees (his comments on v 3, 760f, clarify his view of v 6). –JHN

gift would engage in unprofitable speech (cf. Jas 3:1-2). The juxtaposing here of these two types of gifts reinforces Paul's admonition. Each believer should *aspire* to use his own gift well, and thus serve according to the grace that had been given to him.

Various kinds of service existed in the Church of Paul's day. One could think of service to widows exemplified by the *deacons* in Acts 6:1-6 and again mentioned in 1 Tim 5:3-16. Orphans might need service of one kind or another (Jas 1:27) as also might the sick (1 Thess 5:14).

With the mention of the next gift, Paul alters his grammatical structure slightly and in my translation this is signaled by a period following **in service**. I render the next words (*eite ho didaskōn*) by **if *we are* a teacher**. The definite article (*ho*) is the generic article that signals the category being discussed (cf. BDF, pp. 131-32). (It does not suggest that there was only one teacher in the Roman churches.) *A teacher*, then, should be occupied **in teaching**. It is noteworthy that although *a teacher* stood third in the hierarchy of gifts (1 Cor 12:28), it is here placed after the more humble gift of service (see Luke 22:26-27).

The same principle is true of **an exhorter**: he should utilize this gift in the activity of exhortation. (In the Greek, definite articles precede both teaching [v 7] and exhortation [v 8a] and mark the specific function under discussion.) The gift in question here was no doubt a hortatory one, although the Greek word *parakaleō* often implies "comfort" or "consolation" (cf. BDAG, pp. 764-65). We should not think of these aspects (exhortation and comfort) as mutually exclusive.

The exhorter was skilled at stirring the proper response to truth, whereas the teacher (v 7) would be particularly gifted in expounding and explaining truth. This does not mean that the teacher did not exhort or that the exhorter could not explain Biblical truth. What is observable in churches where the use of all the gifts is encouraged is the simple fact that these gifts are clearly distinguishable when they are actually used. The skill of exposition excels in one, while that of motivating excels in the other.

In the middle of v 8, Paul's construction again changes slightly. The series commences in v 6b with *eite* and continued by this word three more times (twice in v 7 and finally in 8a) ends after the term *exhortation*. If this is not merely a rhetorical effort at variation, it may in fact signal a subtle transition. In this latter case, we would no longer be listing gifts (*charismata*, v 6a), and this explanation is probably correct since the activities now mentioned are more general. Furthermore, the three items in v 8b provide a smooth transition into the material of vv 9ff that clearly leaves the subject of gifts behind.

The fact that **the giver** (*ho metadidous*) **should give with generosity** is therefore best understood as applicable to *all* who give. Giving is a general Christian responsibility (Eph 4:28; cf. Luke 3:11) and is never elsewhere called a gift. Paul's word here for *generosity* (*haplotēti*) is employed three times in Paul's chapters on giving in 2 Corinthians (8:2; 9:11, 13). The model of Jesus Christ Himself is the inspiration for true Christian generosity (cf. 2 Cor 8:9).

The following activity, however, is not a general one like giving. Instead the type of person indicated by the term *ho proïstamenos* (**the leader**) would include especially anyone who held the office of elder. (Note *proïstēmi* in 1 Thess 5:12; 1 Tim 3:4, 5, 12.) The office of elder was strictly a local church office and those who held it might, or might not, have the gift of teaching (cf. 1 Tim 5:17). But irrespective of their individual gifts, the various leaders should vigorously apply themselves to their ruling responsibilities. These responsibilities should be carried out **with diligence** (*en spoudē*). In all probability Paul had met a few leaders whose efforts in the church were too casual, lethargic, or unfocused.

The third item in this brief transitional list of three is the activity of showing mercy. Like the other two activities in the series (giving, leading), mercy is a general responsibility for Christians when the occasion for it occurs (cf. Matt 5:7; Jas 2:13). *The giver* meets the material needs that happen to confront him, *the leader* deals with the concerns that his situation entails, while **the one who shows mercy** extends it to those whose circumstances are difficult or distressing. In the latter case, the mercy should not be given grudgingly or under duress, but **with graciousness** (*hilarotēti*). For the noun *hilarotēs*, I have chosen the more contemporary term *graciousness* instead of the familiar "cheerfulness" (KJV; NKJV; NACE; NASB; "cheerfully": NIV, JB), which despite the versions is slightly antiquated in this context.

### ii. Maintaining godly character (12:9-13)

The verses in this new unit are very general in nature and are a natural follow-through for the general commands of v 8b. In broad strokes Paul gives admonitions that pertain to good Christian character, beginning with the supreme Christian virtue of love.

**12:9. Love *should be* without hypocrisy. *We should* hate what is evil, cleave to what is good.**

The leading admonition in the new section might almost be a summary for the entire section. The superlative Christian virtue is **love** (cf. 1 Corinthians 13) and, as Paul will shortly say, "love is the fulfillment of the law" (Rom 13:10). No doubt the exhortations that follow are in a sense a commentary on what it means to have love.

The essential attribute of love is sincerity. It *should* be **without hypocrisy**. In the Christian community, where love was the supreme mark of Christian character, it was all too easy to feign love in order to conform to the ethos of the church. That, in fact, has been true from Paul's day to our own. It will always be a temptation to hypocritically profess love while disguising hostility or selfishness in the heart.

Although Paul does not explicitly draw the connection between *love* and the immediately following words, that connection is obvious. It is in the nature of love not only to be sincere, but also to be pure. Love, Paul tells us elsewhere, "does not rejoice in iniquity, but rejoices in the truth" (1 Cor 13:6). Thus it will be accompanied by true disgust with **what is evil**.

The word translated by **hate** (*Apostugountes*, abhor) is a participle in form and has here an imperatival sense (cf. BDF §468.2). But the participle's continuative force can also be felt: "let love be real *while* you abhor what is evil." True Christian love does not involve a softening of one's attitude toward evil.

Neither does it involve less than full loyalty **to what is good**. Instead, a Christian ought to **cleave** *to what is good*. Here the sense of the Greek term *kollōmenoi* (cleave) is probably that suggested by BDAG, p. 556, "*be attached* or *devoted to what is good*." Sincere love entails a commitment to what is truly good in general, and in particular for those who are loved.

**12:10. In regard to brotherly love, *have* strong affection for one another; in regard to honor, lead one another's way *to it*;**

At this point Paul commences a series of admonitions which all begin with a quality expressed in the Greek dative case. This construction extends through v 13a. I have rendered each of the qualities in question with the English phrase **in regard to**. Whereas v 9 was quite general,

Paul now deals with specific matters that are relevant to good Christian character.

How then is **brotherly love** to be manifested? Paul's answer employs the Greek adjective *philostorgos* which no doubt bears the sense here of **strong affection** (BDAG, p. 1059). Genuine brotherly love should not be reduced to a mere superficial cordiality but involves a real feeling for the worth and welfare of our brothers and sisters in Christ.

What about honor? It is natural to seek it for ourselves (even inside the church) but that would be self-centered and unloving. Instead, Paul urges here that **in regard to honor**, the believer should be in the forefront of bestowing it on others. He should be leading his fellow believers' **way to it.**

The Greek phrase *allēlous proēgoumenoi* (**leading one another's** *way*) has been given various senses resulting in differing translations: e.g., "in honor giving preference to one another," NKJV (similarly, KJV, NASB); "honor one another above yourselves," NIV; "anticipating one another with honor," NACE; "have a profound respect for each other," JB. It seems most likely that the basic meaning of the verb *proēgeomai*, "to go first," "to lead the way," is the fundamental meaning here. Note the first lexical entry in BDAG, p. 869: "to go first and lead the way, *go before and show the way*."

When it comes to giving honor, the believer should lead the way; that is, he should be a model of bestowing honor on others in the church rather than grasping for honor himself. The words *to it* in my translation are added for clarity. It is just possible that Paul's choice of words was intended to evoke the image of an awards ceremony (e.g., in a public assembly) in which the "presenter" of honor might be expected to lead the honoree forward to stand before the assembled group (whatever the group might have been). So also in the Christian assembly, the believer is encouraged to be a "presenter" of honor, rather than a recipient of the same.

> **12:11. in regard to diligence, *we should* not *be* lazy; in regard to *our* spirit, *we should be* zealous; in regard to the Lord, *we should* do slave-service;**

Paul's list of qualities continues with a comment on diligence, i.e., "earnest commitment in discharge of an obligation or [in] experience of a relationship" (BDAG, p. 939). BDAG (*ibid.*) observes that in Greco-Roman literature and inscriptions the word refers to "extraordinary commitment to civic and religious responsibilities." Thus the Christian should be a person who takes his responsibilities very seriously, especially in the church, and who discharges them with commendable energy and effort.

This injunction leads easily to a consideration of what **our spirit**, i.e., our attitude, **should be**. The Greek expression *tō pneumati*, like the previous items in the series (brotherly love, honor and diligence) and those that follow (Lord, hope, affliction, needs) are all articular. This is a perfectly normal Greek idiom when considering particular qualities and traits. We should avoid the error of thinking of the expressions as containing some extra nuance simply on the grounds that in English such a list would *not* use the article. The languages differ in this respect.

Paul would undoubtedly acknowledge that the Holy Spirit is the ultimate Source of Christian zeal, but his text does not directly refer to this divine Person. The participle here (*zeontes*) is defined by BDAG, p. 426, as "to be stirred up emotionally, *be enthusiastic/excited/on fire*." The choice of the best English term for this is not easy in our cultural context. Most translations tend toward the traditional *fervent* (KJV, NKJV, NASB, NACE), *[keep your spiritual] fervor* (NIV); but JB has *great earnestness*. Other options are possible.

I have chosen the word **zealous** because of its easy association with religious commitments in our contemporary culture, though it is not confined to that. The definition of *zeal* in the *American Heritage Dictionary* is almost exactly what is needed here: "enthusiastic and diligent devotion in pursuit of a cause, idea, or goal" (p. 1405). In terms of his inner spirit, the Christian should possess an obviously strong dedication to all his genuine responsibilities.

This conception of Paul's words leads naturally to the next command, which he specifically relates **to the Lord**. The fact that the participle here is *douleuontes* and naturally takes the dative has caused translators to ignore the obvious fact that the construction is exactly the same as those preceding and following it in vv 10-13a. It is not to be translated as a simple participial phrase ("serving the Lord": KJV, NKJV, NASB, NACE, NIV). Instead, in conjunction with the series of which it is a part, it should be read as **in regard to the Lord, *we should* do slave-service.**

The previous command to be a zealous person in spirit was evidently general in nature. It was not intended just to define the believer's attitude toward his religion, but to specify a character trait. He should be an enthusiastic person in every worthwhile pursuit. If he had responsibilities in any area of his life, he was to manifest diligence (v 11a) and *be zealous* about them (v 11b). Since there would be many slaves in the Roman congregations, such admonitions were very much to the point (cf. Col 3:22-24).[11]

But specifically *in regard to the Lord*, this diligence and zeal should translate into genuine *slave-service* (*douleuontes*). Paul always taught the Christian slave not to do his service as if his human owner were his true master. Rather he was to serve as a slave *to the Lord* (1 Cor 7:22-23; Col 3:22-23). This truth resonates in Paul's statements here, without at the same time singling out the Christian slaves in Rome. Indeed all Christians, not simply those with the social status of a slave, should regard themselves as doing *slave-service* for *the Lord*. But the hearers in Rome who were actually slaves would get the implication that their diligence and zealous efforts should be manifestations of their relation to their exalted Master, Jesus Christ.

**12:12. in regard to hope, *we should* rejoice; in regard to affliction, *we should* endure; in regard to prayer, *we should* persevere;**

To do slave-service to the Lord was to labor in **hope** (expectation, anticipation). Paul taught exactly that in Col 3:22-25. There the submissive slave is invited to anticipate the reward that his work for his earthly master could merit. He could expect to be recompensed by none other than the Lord Christ (Col 3:24). Thus the basic attitude of believers in all their endeavors should be characterized by the joyous expectation of future glory and reward. No one has more to look forward to than Christians do. They should always be able to rejoice (cf. Phil 4:4).

However, rejoicing may often seem impossible in the face of earthly affliction. But the proper attitude toward any such experience is not despair or depression. Instead, the Christian is called to **endure** (*hupomenontes*, a form of *hupomenō*, the regular NT word for bearing up under hardship and suffering). This cannot be done without prayer, and the habit of persisting in prayer is valuable at all times, and especially in

---

[11] Estimates vary, but it is widely held that over one-third (and possibly over half) of the population of the Roman Empire of the first century was made up of slaves. –RNW

times of stress. The Christian should habitually persevere in prayer as a fundamental practice of his spiritual life (cf. 1 Thess 5:17).

**12:13. with regard to the needs of the saints, *we should* share *with them*. Pursue hospitality.**

The final member of the series (that began with "in regard to brotherly love," v 10) focuses on the obligation to be charitable to fellow Christians (**the saints**) who have material **needs**. The verb **share** (*koinōnountes*) is used several times in the NT (in its noun and adjective forms as well) of the process of alleviating the material needs of other Christians (e.g., Rom 15:26, 27; 2 Cor 9:13; Phil 1:5; 4:15; Heb 13:16).

The initial command, "love should be without hypocrisy," has no expressed verb (a form of *eimi* is to be understood). The following two commands simply employ the imperatival participle. But then follows the series we have just looked at where an initial quality expressed in the dative case is followed by the imperatival participle. In the latter part of the present verse, Paul drops the dative construction for *tēn philoxenian diōkontes*, i.e., **pursue hospitality**. This looks very much like a stylistic *inclusio*. Verses 9b to 13b begin and end with the same construction in reverse order (12:9b has participle + accusative substantive, while 13b has accusative substantive + participle). When we examine the structure of Paul's material in the present sub-unit (12:9-13), we can see that it is far from haphazard.

Thus the sub-unit, vv 9-13, is structured with an initial broad command to love (9a) which is then elaborated in 9b-13b, concluding with the virtue of hospitality as a final manifestation of Christian love. Here, as elsewhere in Paul's letters, hospitality is regarded as an appropriate Christian virtue (cf. 1 Tim 3:2; Titus 1:8; cf. also Heb 13:2; 1 Pet 4:9). In particular, Christians who traveled benefited from the hospitality of their fellow Christians since accommodations for travelers in the empire were poor and often disreputable.

### iii. Maintaining good relationships (12:14-21)

It is a very natural transition for Paul to move now beyond the general admonitions for manifesting Christian love, to specific issues that pertain to interpersonal relationships. Believers live in contact with each other and with the world outside the church, but certain types of actions (or non-actions) have a pronounced effect on our relations with other people. To these kinds of matters, Paul now turns.

### 12:14. Bless those who persecute you; bless and do not curse.

The new sub-unit is signaled by the employment of three imperatives (*bless* [2×]: *Eulogeite*; *curse*: *katarasthe*). These are the first finite verbs Paul has used since v 5. The intervening commands are expressed (if a verb is used at all) exclusively by participles. To a Greek-speaking listener the change of construction would at least register sub-consciously. In English this is missed when the Greek construction from vv 6-13 is not strictly followed (as it is not in my own translation).

The conceptual contrast with the last previous command ("pursue hospitality," v 13) is equally striking. Thus a new direction is indicated for these and the commands to follow (through v 21). How do we deal with our relationships, particularly when they present problems to our behavior?

We should not assume that the command to **bless those who persecute you** is exclusively applicable to our non-Christian relationships. Obviously it is usually the case that *those who persecute* us are the unregenerate, but this is far from being the only source of persecution. As is abundantly illustrated in the history of Christian churches, even within the Christian fellowship vendettas easily arise. These may be motivated by personal or doctrinal matters, or by both.

Whenever we feel anyone is against us and seeking to harm us in some way (not necessarily physically), it is then we are tempted to use harsh and disparaging language either about them or to their face. It is this type of verbal assault that Paul is forbidding. Instead, we should wish such people well or express the hope that God's goodness will be theirs. In that way we bless rather than curse, and in doing so we manifest the love of Christ (cf. 1 Pet 4:21-25).

### 12:15. Rejoice with those who rejoice, and weep with those who weep.

In the commands that follow the three imperative forms in v 14, Paul varies his hortatory word, using infinitives (this verse), and participles in the initial three commands of v 16. Rhetorically he is no doubt aiming for variety, since the use of only one type of imperative form would diminish the oral effectiveness of his words.

The command to wish people well ("bless") instead of wishing them ill ("curse") that was given in v 14 is obviously reinforced by the commands of this verse. We could, in fact, express "blessing" with our lips and have little real concern for the person addressed (it often happens). But here the command is to *feel* the feelings of others, that is, to possess true sympathy.

We are reminded of the compassion of our Lord Jesus Christ who wept for the bereaved even as He was about to raise Lazarus from the dead (John 11:35). The appeal by Paul challenges Christians to desire that their emotions should be appropriate to the circumstances of others.

**12:16. Have the same aspirations for each other. Do not aspire to high things, but associate with humble *people*. Do not become wise in your own sight.**

In this series of injunctions Paul picks up a Greek verb (*phroneō*) that he had employed in v 3. As in that verse, the best meaning is "to aspire" (cf. discussion under v 3). Thus the Greek phrase used here, *To auto eis allēlous phronountes*, refers, as does v 15, to one's inner attitudes towards others. (The participle is again imperatival in force.) To **have the same aspirations for each other** instructs us to desire that others should experience what we ourselves would like to experience. This contrasts sharply with what often actually happens in a church, where one's own ambition is to "get ahead" of others.

The command just stated is achievable if we **do not aspire to high things** (*Mē ta hupsēla phronountes*). Overweening ambition is a trap into which self-centered persons easily fall. They then have no real concern for the aspirations of others since they are consumed by their own unrealistic goals. As Paul has already admonished in v 3, a sober perspective on what we are, and on what we are able to accomplish under God, is the true Christian attitude.

Instead of unrealistically aiming for *high things* (status, reputation, etc.), we should instead **associate with humble *people***. The Greek phrase *tois tapeinois sunapagomenoi* (*associate with humble people*) might also be understood in the sense *accommodate yourself to humble ways* [BDAG, p. 965 (2)]. The Greek original permits either view, and the word *ways* presumes a contrast with *ta hupsēla* in the preceding phrase (and thus takes *tois tapeinois* as neuter). But the reference to *people* assumes *tois tapeinois* is masculine. On the whole, Paul's stress in this context on inter-personal relations seems to favor the reference to *people*.

As the data offered by BDAG (p. 965) suggests, the most probable meaning for *sunapagō* is "to join the company of others, *associate with*." This is the sense which is found "generally" in "the ancient versions and Chrysostom" [ibid.] for this verse. It is also this meaning that is represented by NKJV ("associate with the humble"), NASB ("associate with the lowly"), NIV ("be willing to associate with people of low position") and, creatively, by JB ("make real friends with the poor").

Among other concerns, as a godly spiritual shepherd Paul must surely have been aware that in a church cliques could easily form around persons of wealth and stature in society. Poorer believers could be tempted to cultivate relationships with such persons and to ignore people whose societal status was not significant. The present verse provides a decided warning against such behavior. Believers should be only too happy to associate with fellow Christians who were of humble status.

Finally, Christians should **not become wise in** their **own sight**. This seems to be the meaning of the phrase *Mē ginesthe phronimoi par' heautois*, which is paralleled by Prov 3:7 (*mē isthi phronimos para seautō*: LXX), where the underlying Hebrew reads "do not be wise in your (own) eyes."

As the previous statements of this verse show, Paul is here especially concerned with the "social climbers" who might be in the various Roman congregations. The effort of aiming after *high things* could lead easily to a self-presentation that stressed one's own knowledge, skill, and insight. In other words, it was easy to pose as, and actually believe that one was, a person possessing special wisdom that should impress other people. This, says Paul, is not correct Christian behavior.

### 12:17. Repay no one with evil in return for evil. Make provision for things that are good in the sight of all men.

As important as it is to maintain positive attitudes, it is also equally vital to avoid negative attitudes. Verses 14-16 have stressed the need to "bless" others, share their joys and sorrows, and treat humble people with dignity instead of pursuing personal social status. But even a basically positive person can have his spirit poisoned by focusing on the injustice of other people. Paul now turns to deal with this issue, one of the most commonly occurring problems in Christian churches.

Paul begins by admonishing that believers are to **repay no one with evil in return for evil**. Paul's text emphasizes the word for *no one*

(*Mēdeni*) which appears first in the clause. There should be no exception to the principle he is stating (such as, "but *he* really deserves it!"). The impulse to get even is intrinsic to our sinful nature, and rationalizations for retributive actions are easy to come by. Paul knows this, of course, so he emphasizes that such actions are not justified toward *anyone at all*.

In fact, a line of behavior is to be pursued which is the direct opposite of the one Paul has just forbidden. Instead of seeking retribution, Christians should **make provision for things that are good in the sight of all men**. The verb here for make provision (*Pronooumenoi* from *pronoeō*) implies forethought and perhaps even *careful* forethought (as BDAG, p. 872, suggests).

There is an implicit connection between the two commands of this verse, which Paul does not make explicit but which is obvious. One of the chief sources of conflict, both inside and outside the church, is the opinion by one party that another party has behaved improperly. This leads the first party to actions that offend the second party, who in turn may try to "get back at" party number one. Such conflicts can be dramatically reduced if everyone is careful to give a little forethought to how their actions will be perceived.

Paul's word for *good things* (*kala*), with no specifying article, shows the breadth of his admonition. Whatever actions one takes, in or out of the church, they should stand up under scrutiny. We should aim for our actions to look truly good to whoever observes them, that is, *in the sight of all men*. The ramifications of this command as regards our personal, family, business, social, or church experience, are as extensive as they are important.

### 12:18. If possible, on your part be at peace with all men.

The admonition of this verse is a logical extension of the previous verse. If we are not to return evil for evil received, and if we are to be careful how our actions are perceived by others, it follows that our real aim is, or should be, **peace with all men** to the extent to which we are able to achieve this. The qualifying phrase **on your part** (*to ex humōn*) is an obvious recognition that this may not always be **possible**. But if it is not possible in any given case (Paul himself often faced this impossibility), at least we should seek that the cause for the conflict does not lie within ourselves. The Christian attitude should be: "I, for my part, have no hostility against him/her."

**12:19. Do not take revenge for yourselves, beloved, but leave room for wrath, since it is written, *"Vengeance is mine, I will repay,"* says the Lord.**

Despite his best efforts, the believer will in all probability face injustice and undeserved mistreatment in one form or another (cf. 2 Tim 3:12). When this occurs, however, he must be careful not to pursue **revenge**.

It might be thought that this command is essentially the same as the one given in v 17 and in one sense it is. But at another level, there is a distinction. It is always easy to give tit for tat (evil for evil) in our dealings with others, so that, for example, we say: "he's nasty with me so I'll be nasty with him." Revenge, however, goes further and aims for a balancing of accounts. With such a mentality we are seeking to settle the score. In the process, we easily consume time and energy on how exactly the score ought to be settled. Paul forbids that kind of behavior.

Remarkably, when we decline to avenge ourselves we **leave room for** the expression of God's **wrath** toward the offending party. As BDAG (p. 1012) understands it, the Greek statement, *dote topon tē orgē*, suggests that we should *"give the wrath (of God) an opportunity* to work out its purpose." The idea is that we should not preempt God's action through our own vengeful behavior. Paul made it clear as early as chapter 1:18ff. that God deals with mankind by bringing His wrath to bear in an appropriate way. Our own ill-considered or inappropriate revenge can short-circuit what God would otherwise do Himself.

After all, as Scripture itself declares (**it is written**), *"Vengeance is mine, I will repay,"* **says the Lord**. Here Paul is quoting from Deut 32:35 and the Greek text he apparently employed is closer to the MT than to our standard LXX. (It is likely that the translators took the Hebrew consonants *wšlm* [MT = *wᵉšīllēm*] as representing a piel infinitive absolute that could be rendered here by *I will repay*.) Paul has added the expression familiar from the OT, *says the Lord*, to mark out the preceding words as spoken by the Lord Himself.

Vengeance, therefore, is a divine prerogative. Human beings should not take it into their own hands.

**12:20-21. So *"If your enemy is hungry, feed him; If he is thirsty, give him a drink; For by doing this you will heap coals of fire on his head."* Do not be overcome by evil, but overcome evil with good.**

How then should a Christian respond to a person who is hostile to him? Paul gives the answer in words drawn from Prov 25:21-22. He should show him kindness by meeting his needs when the occasion presents itself.

It is interesting that Paul does not introduce the quoted words with a citation formula of any kind (such as "it is written"). But he is certainly not paraphrasing, since the cited words are almost identical to the LXX as we know it. [Paul's text had *psōmize* for *"feed"* rather than the LXX's *trephe*.] In all probability the immediately preceding statement in v 19, "says the Lord," here fills the role of such a formula. Though the phrase "says the Lord" refers to the statement quoted from Deut 32:35, Paul's text deftly adds something else that *the Lord says*. The word **So** (oun) is added by Paul as a connecting word (it is not in the LXX).

By running the second quotation directly into the first one without a break, Paul deftly links together the truth of Deuteronomy and of Proverbs. Both are from the mouth of God.

It is clear that from the perspective of divine wisdom, acts of kindness to one's enemy place that enemy in a more precarious position than would a refusal to assist him. In the light of v 19, and especially of the command to "leave room for wrath," to perform such kindness to one's foe is to *"heap coals of fire on his head"* and thus to augment divine wrath against him.

Some people may feel that it is totally inappropriate for Christians even to think of God's vengeance as a substitute for their own. But Scripture gives no support to this humanistic idea. The God of the Bible is a God of justice and His providence ordains that "whatever a man sows, that will he also reap" (Gal 6:7). Paul's point in Rom 12:19-20 is not that we should pretend that nothing wrong has been done. His point instead is that vengeance is not our business but God's. We should not be involved in it and, to the contrary, our wisest course is always kindness to those who oppose us.

In fact, behaving in this way is in reality a victory over **evil**. To behave in a vengeful and ungracious way toward an enemy is to be conquered (*overcome, nikaō*) by the very evil that animates and controls that enemy. But to rise above such evil and to behave in a truly Christian way is to conquer (overcome) that evil by means of the good we do. In short, kindness to our enemies is a significant spiritual triumph.

# Romans 13

### iv. Obeying those in authority (13:1-7)

In the deeply practical section covered by Rom 12:3–13:14, Paul's progression from unit to unit is carefully conceived. Romans 12:3-8 discuss the believer's specific (gifted) role in the church, which then broadens out to a consideration of his general personal character in 12:9-13. This section in turn is followed by a consideration of his behavior towards others in 12:14-21.

The new section is the broadest yet and deals with the believer's relationship toward the secular power under which he lives his life. This was obviously a subject very close to home for readers who lived in Rome itself.

> **13:1. Let every person submit to the governing authorities. For there is no authority if _it is_ not _bestowed_ by God, and the present authorities are established by God.**

In all societies the temptation exists for Christians to regard the secular state as unworthy of their allegiance and obedience. This can lead to the claim that a Christian is subject to _God's_ authority, not to _man's_. Paul does not countenance any such idea as that. Indeed his words here suggest that he may wish to directly contradict it. It is not unlikely that in the Roman congregations were more than a few converts who seethed with resentment against the Roman power. Many of them may have been slaves, but the well-to-do also often develop a prejudice against government based on some real or imagined wrong done to them.

Paul begins by making clear that he conceives of no exceptions to what he is now saying.[1] The words **every person** (*Pasa psychē*) make this point unmistakable. The phrase **governing authorities** translates the Greek expression *exousiais huperechousais* (BDAG, p. 1033). The command is succinct and to the point. Paul will now state the reason for it.

The subjection enjoined here is based on the simple fact that **there is no authority if *it is* not *bestowed*** by God. The words *if it is not bestowed by God* try to capture the basic sense of the Greek phrase *ei mē hupo Theou*. The words do not exactly say "except from God," which would have been written *ei mē apo Theou*. [A few manuscripts do read *apo*.] It may be suggested that *hupo* emphasizes a bit more pointedly than *apo* would have that God is the actual *Agent* in establishing *the governing authorities*. God does not merely *allow* certain men to rule, He *arranges* it.

This point is now explicitly applied (*gar*) to the present situation. No one should attempt to divert the application to other times or circumstances. It is **the present authorities** that **are established by God**. The Greek phrase for *the present authorities, hai (de) ousai exousiai*, carries an obvious stress on their current (*ousai*) position. One might compare the expression cited by BDAG, p. 283, from *Papiri greci e latini*, 229.11: *tou ontos mēnos*, "the current month."

In affirming that *the present authorities are* in fact *established by God*, Paul uses a Greek verb phrase (*tetagmenai eisin*) that is quite close to our English expression "put in place." The verb *tassō* has a wide semantic range, but seems to have had a significant military use. This is indicated by the evidence from Polybius and Diodorus Siculus cited by BDAG (p. 991), where it was used of being put under someone's command. On a political level, the verb might mean "to appoint" (active) or "to be appointed" (passive). Moulton and Milligan (p. 626) cite a papyrus which refers to "those who had been appointed [*tōn...tetagmenōn*] to the administration in Serapeum," and another that refers to the "governor of the prison of Zeus" (*tō tetagmenō pros tē tou Dios phulakē*).

Therefore, the word *tetagmenai* suggests that *the present authorities* in Paul's day were actually "put in place," that is, they were "appointed" *by God* to the governmental role they currently possessed. They were

---

[1] Hodges is not saying that there is no basis at all for disobeying any government about anything on conscientious grounds. He means that *every person* is to be subject to the governing authorities. There is no exception *in that sense*. See Hodges' comments under v 2 for times when one is free to disobey the commands of government. –RNW

not in the final analysis imperial or senatorial appointees, but God's own appointees. By implication, they served at His pleasure. Their authority derived directly from Him. By extension we must say also that, in America, our elected officials are in reality "appointed" by God. Regardless of our party affiliation, or our political views, Christians need to take this fact seriously. God still "rules in the kingdom of men, and gives it to whomever He chooses" (Dan 4:25; cf. 4:17, 32).

> **13:2 Therefore the person who resists the authority resists the ordinance of God, and those who resist *it* will receive judgment for themselves.**

Verse 2 follows inescapably from Paul's statements in v 1. Resistance to earthly authority is resistance to God Himself. The simple term **the authority** (*tē exousia*) is here a metonymy of the attribute for the person who exercises it (as was also the plural used in v 1). That is to say that to resist *the authority* of the emperor is to resist the emperor, or to resist *the authority* of the governor is to resist the governor, and so on. But behind the emperor or the governor is **the ordinance of God** Himself who "appointed" these human authorities.

By *the ordinance of God* (*tē tou Theou diatagē*) Paul refers to the God-ordained authority wielded by earthly officials. Since these could have no authority at all apart from God granting it to them (v 1), resistance to their authority is resistance to God. It is His ordinance, not man's, that is being flouted.

This raises many questions for modern minds. But it will help if we remember that Paul is stating the basic principle. His statement in no way authorizes an earthly official to command direct disobedience to God. If that happens, Peter and the other apostles demonstrated the Biblical approach. When confronted with the Sanhedrin's command not to preach in the name of Jesus Christ, they replied, "We ought to obey God rather than men" (Acts 5:29). What is implicit in such a statement is that the human command went counter to a divine command. It was the divine command that had to take precedence.

But in modern "democracies" there is a temptation to categorize laws as good or bad, where the latter category furnishes justification for disobedience. But unless the law runs counter to a *direct divine command*, there is no Biblical authorization to disobey it. On the contrary, this passage commands obedience. Moreover, Paul warns that the failure to submit to this authority entails consequences.[2]

The words **those who resist** *it* **will receive judgment for themselves** are forceful. The believers in the Roman churches should not suppose that, by virtue of being Christians, they could elude the consequences of resisting the empire's authority (in whatever form they did so). On the contrary, such conduct would bring them judgment (*krima*). Although the word *krima* could refer to a legal verdict (usually negative) it could also refer to the consequence of the verdict, that is, to the *punishment* that was received (cf. BDAG, p. 567 #4 b). The latter meaning is most natural here.

In making this statement, Paul does not make specific whether the judgment will come from *the authority* itself or from God who is behind *the authority*. No doubt he thought that even cases that escaped the attention of the earthly power could still entail judgment from God, who could administer it either directly or indirectly. Nevertheless, the thought of retribution from *the authority* itself is uppermost, as the following verse makes clear.

**13:3. For rulers do not cause fear about good works, but about evil** *works*. **Now do you wish not to be afraid of the authority? Do what is good and you will have praise from it.**

A Christian need not have fear about "judgment" (v 2) from the earthly authority so long as his conduct is good. Paul's statement in Greek here is more concise than my English rendering. The Greek expression is a metaphor in which the action itself is put for the one(s) doing the action: *phobos tōn agathōn ergōn* (lit., "a fear of [for] good works") followed by *alla tōn kakōn* (lit., "but of [for] evil *ones*)." My translation (**rulers do not cause fear about good works, but about evil** *works*) is a paraphrase.

The Roman believers can avoid such fear if they **do what is good**. In fact they can expect to receive praise from the earthly authority for such

---

[2] Robert Jewett observes that a multitude of interpretations have been imposed on Romans 13 through the years: "The interpretation of this pericope has swung from abject subservience to political authorities viewed as virtually divine to critical submission on the basis of their advancement of justice. The endless stream of studies has been marked by advocacy of various appraisals of the role of government shaped [often contorted] by denominational traditions and by modern ethical considerations" (*Romans*, pp. 382-83). Hodges takes a position between both extremes mentioned by Jewett. However, he is clear that one must never disobey the clear commands of God over and against the clear commands of government. –JHN

behavior. Paul was well aware of potential exceptions to these words,[3] but he is giving the basic principle. All things being equal, good citizens have nothing to fear from government (which usually has its hands full with the other type of citizens). Law-abiding citizens may even expect to be commended if they are exemplary (**you will have praise from it**).

A slightly ironic tone may be present in Paul's question, **Now do you wish not to be afraid of the authority?** Even if Paul did not have detailed knowledge of the Roman congregations, his knowledge of individuals was extensive (Rom 16:3-15) and he must have known others who had visited the congregations there. It is probable enough that he knew there were people in the Roman assemblies who professed to fear, or actually did fear, the imperial government. This attitude could not only promote sedition, but could be a motive for eluding official attention, e.g., in the matter of not fully paying one's taxes. (Paul will address that issue shortly in vv 6-7.) *Do you wish* might be a piece of irony equal to, "Is this what you really want?"

The real way *not to be afraid of the authority* was to be a good citizen in every respect. A government is not normally in the habit of dealing out "judgment" (v 2) to those who are good citizens. Instead such people are normally praised. Further, the Roman readers lived under Nero, whose early reign, at least, contained much that could rightly be called *good* (see Suetonius, *The Lives of the Caesars* VI. x-xix). Most probably Romans was written well before the church had problems with Nero. But even so, these problems were an aberration in Roman government and not at all the norm. The book of Acts, as well, takes a largely positive view of the Roman authorities. Paul is addressing normal life under the empire.

> **13:4. In fact he is God's servant to you to *produce* what is good. But if you do what is evil, be afraid, because he does not bear the sword in vain. For he is God's servant, an avenger to *bring* wrath on the person who does evil.**

With some elaboration, Paul reiterates the truth he has just stated. His restatement here suggests the likelihood that he had reason to be concerned about these issues. I have already noted that he had plenty

---

[3] Paul wrote the book during a three-month stay in southern Greece (Acts 20:3). Earlier, Paul complained formally that Roman officials beat him, an uncondemned Roman (Acts 16:37*ff*). Shortly after writing Romans, Paul appealed to Caesar (Acts 25:11). Paul's willingness to claim his rights as a Roman citizen is well known. –JHN

of conduits for information about the Roman congregations. No doubt many of their members were slaves, or others of a lower social order, who might feel victimized in some way by imperial authority. Paul wants to make his call to submission as emphatic as possible.

Rather than view "the authority" (that is, in the final analysis, the emperor) as an isolated source of arbitrary human power, they should keep in mind that "the authorities that exist are established by God" (v 1). That meant that this authority (the emperor) worked for God. (The subject, which I render here by *he*, is contained within the verb *esti* [*is*] and could refer back to "the authority" in v 2, or more specifically to the emperor.) The emperor was **God's servant to** them.

This might represent a new perspective for some of the Christians in Rome. They should regard the emperor not as an oppressor, but as an *agent* of God. The Greek word translated *servant* here is *diakonos*, a very general word that indicated neither a slave nor an official. Words like *agent, intermediary,* or *assistant* are illustrative of its connotations (cf. BDAG, p. 230). Moreover, God's "agent" was intended **to *produce* what** was good for the people, not evil. No doubt Paul has in mind the good order and societal tranquility which was a major function of government.

**But if** in fact the Christians did what was evil, they should indeed **be afraid**, since the government had the power of **the sword**. The words, **he does not bear the sword in vain**, remind the Christian readers that this power of *the sword* was no empty threat but a reality in the government's dealings with evildoers. Christians too could feel its effect if they refused obedience to the proper authorities.

This leads to the point that the Emperor was **God's servant** (again, *diakonos*) not simply *to produce what* was good, but also to punish evildoers. Thus the Emperor was **an avenger to *bring* wrath on the person who** did wrong. The word *wrath* here is significant in the larger context of Romans. The Greek word (*orgē*) occurs twenty-one times in the Pauline epistles, of which twelve are in Romans. The pivotal nature of this word in Romans is signaled by its extensive treatment early in the main body of the Epistle (1:18–2:5).

In Rom 1:18–2:5 Paul had discussed in some detail God's providential governance of the world and how He dispensed justice to ungodly men. The statement here is obviously a part of that general providential activity. The imperial government was not the only instrument of this exercise of judgment, but it was *an* instrument. Paul had already expounded for his Roman readers how the justified person can be "delivered from wrath" (cf. Rom 5:9-10; and 5:12–8:13). Here his words are a salutary warning that resistance to constituted authority would once again bring a believer within the range of God's wrath, this time as conveyed through governmental authorities.

> **13:5. Consequently it is necessary to submit, not only because of the wrath, but also because of conscience.**

For Paul, the conclusion was obvious (**Consequently**: *Dio*). Obedience to the imperial government was necessary (*ananke*) and was constrained not merely by a fear about **the wrath** Paul has just mentioned, but by **conscience** itself.

The Greek phrase rendered **not only because of the wrath but also because of conscience**, employs parallel expressions using the definite article with both nouns (*dia tēn orgēn* and *dia tēn suneidēsin*). Greek often employs the article with abstract nouns where English does not, so the parallel constructions here suggest that both articles are present for that reason (i.e., because the nouns are abstract). Still, the article with *orgē* carries some of the force of an article of previous reference and I have translated it (i.e., put the word *the* before *wrath*) for that reason. *The wrath* is the same wrath referred to in v 4.

That the conscience of believers should also motivate them to obey constituted authority is likewise obvious. If "the authorities that exist are established by God" (v 1) and "the person who resists" those authorities "resists the ordinance of God" (v 2), then a good conscience toward both God and men will naturally urge submission (cf. Acts 24:16).

> **13:6. For this reason also, pay taxes, since they are God's ministers who are devoted to this very thing.**

Paul's previous comments about submission were general. No doubt he mainly had in mind obedience to Roman laws as a whole. But now he turns specifically to the issue of taxes. This was doubtless a controversial subject in the minds of some of his readers. Probably many of them regarded the taxation rate to be exorbitant. Indeed, throughout the Empire the tax gatherers ("publicans" in the Gospels) were notorious for overcharging and thereby enriching themselves with the additional funds extracted from taxpayers.

But the same reason for general submission applied to taxes. It is possible to take the word **also** (*kai* in Greek) either with **For this reason** or with **pay taxes**, but to read *for this reason also* leaves obscure what the other reason might be. On the other hand, it is clear that the call to general submission required *also* the payment of taxes.

Once again the authorities are referred to here, but the switch from singular to plural should be noted. In v 4 we twice have the words, "For he is God's servant" (*Theou gar diakonos esti/estin*, both times), whereas in the present verse we meet *leitourgoi gar Theou eisin*: **they are God's ministers**. In the former verse we think chiefly of the Emperor. But in this verse the reference seems obviously to the tax collectors themselves. Moreover their "sanctity" is enhanced by calling them *leitourgoi*, a term which had "sacred connotations" in Biblical literature (BDAG, p. 591).

It was certainly contrary to the general conception of tax collectors to regard them as ministers of divine things. Yet Paul's words are clearly chosen to reinforce the divine right of the Empire's tax gathering mechanism. To refuse to give these ministers their taxes, whether done overtly or covertly, was to refuse to give them what belonged to God. The question of the Herodians, "Is it lawful to pay taxes to Caesar, or not?" (Matt 22:17) is here answered in the spirit of our Lord's own reply to that question (Matt 22:21). The payment of taxes to Caesar is analogous to rendering to God what is due to God.

The final words, **who are devoted to this very thing**, are no doubt intended to continue the metaphor suggested by *leitourgoi*. The phrase *are devoted to* renders the Greek verb form *proskarterountes*. The verb *proskartereō* occurs a total of ten times in the NT and involves "sacred" activity not only here and in Rom 12:12, but also in Acts 1:14; 2:42, 46; and 6:4. From this perspective, Paul is suggesting, tax collectors are engaged in a sacred duty.

> **13:7. Therefore render to all what they are owed: a tax to whom** *one owes* **the tax; a customs duty to whom** *one owes* **the customs duty; respect to whom** *one owes* **respect; and honor to whom** *one owes* **honor.**

Paul's command in v 6 has further implications that need to be spelled out. No one must think that their duty is fulfilled if they pay just one kind of tax. What Paul seeks is a broad, general compliance that results in the

Christian rendering **to all what they are owed**. Whatever the form of tax might be, **a customs duty** for example, the Christian should pay it.

Nor is this submission to taxation to be accompanied by a rude and abrasive manner. If the agents of tax gathering are indeed "God's ministers," they deserve **respect**, as indeed do all duly constituted officials of the government. The Greek term rendered here by **respect** is *phobos*, usually translated *fear*, but it should not be handled that way here because its English connotations are wrong for this context. Paul obviously means *respect*. Closely related to *respect* is **honor**. A middle level official is at least owed the former, while one at a higher level may be entitled to the latter.

However, Paul's goal is clearly to inculcate in his believing audience, located as it was at the seat of imperial power, a genuine spirit of compliance with that government. It seems probable that the two pairs of contrasting terms, tax/customs duty (*phoron/telos*) and respect/honor (*phobon/timēn*), ought not to be too sharply distinguished. It is dubious, for example, that *telos* means strictly a *customs duty*[4] or that *honor* is actually a higher term than respect. More likely Paul employs each pair rhetorically to indicate the full range involved in his admonition. No required tax is to be neglected; no official given less than the deference he deserves.

### v. Living in the light of the Lord's return (13:8-14)

Paul has now reached the conclusion of the unit begun at 12:3 and extending to 13:14, which I have called "Living in Personal Holiness." The subjects covered were these: "maintaining perspective on our role in the church" (12:3-8); "maintaining godly character" (12:9-13); "maintaining good relationships" (12:14-21); and "obeying those in authority" (13:1-7). It is now time to summarize the essence of this unit, and this takes the form of a conclusion with principles which are quite broad.

> **13:8. Owe no one anything except to love one another. For the one who loves another has fulfilled the law.**

---

[4] The expression *customs duty* is relatively rare in English. By this Hodges meant something like "revenue obligation, indirect tax, [or] toll-tax" (BDAG, p. 999a). The word *telos* more normally means *end, termination, conclusion,* or *goal.* The only other place in the NT where it carries this meaning is Matt 17:25. –RNW

From the responsibility not to owe unpaid taxes, Paul now proceeds to urge the payment of all debts, except the one debt that can never be fully paid: **to love one another**. The Greek text lays stress on the words **no one** (*Mēdeni*) and **anything** (*mēden*, literally *nothing*),[5] which precede the verb for **owe** in Paul's sentence. Whatever one owes to anyone should be paid. But after that is done, one still owes love.

Paul is obviously thinking here of love for other Christians as the words *love one another* show. While Paul believed in showing love beyond the range of the Christian family (see Gal 6:10), he is especially concerned here with mutual Christian love (cf. for example, 1 Cor 16:14; 2 Cor 2:8, 8:24; Gal 5:13; Eph 1:15, 4:2, 15, 16; Phil 2:2; 1 Thess 4:9). But loving relations within the church are likely to have an overflow beyond it.

It is significant that Paul here explicitly affirms that **the one who loves another has fulfilled the law**. As we have seen, the Epistle to the Romans is especially concerned with Jewish issues as they pertain to Paul's gospel. Paul has spent a great deal of time examining the Jewish law, both in reference to justification (Romans 3–4) and in reference to Christian living (Romans 5–8). He has found this law inadequate for both. But this did not mean, as his opponents had evidently alleged (Rom 3:8), that a Christian should live without regard to the moral standards of that law. On the contrary, obedience to the law was implicit in a life lived in love.

The words *has fulfilled the law* do not contradict Paul's earlier assertion that no one does this in reference to the law as a whole (cf. Rom 3:19-20). Instead, Paul's words here are very precise. Paul is talking about someone *who loves another* (*ho gar agapōn ton heteron*) and is pointing out that when one treats another person with love he is doing what the law requires. In so far as he treats a person that way, he *has fulfilled the law* as regards *that* person. But a broad fulfillment in all areas of conduct is impossible for a sinful human being and is not at all in view here.

**13:9-10. For this *matter of "You shall not commit adultery,"* *"You shall not murder," "You shall not steal," "You shall not covet"*—and if *there is* any other commandment, it is summed up in this statement, namely, *"You shall love your neighbor as***

---

[5] The emphasis is both because of their placement at the front of the sentence and the fact that they are identical except for the addition of one letter (*iōta, i*) at the end of the first word (which changes its meaning and catches the attention of the listener/reader). –RNW

*yourself.*" Love does not produce what is bad for a neighbor, so love is the fulfillment of the law.

Paul now supports his claim that a person fulfills the law when he loves. The proof is extremely simple. The familiar commands not to *"commit adultery,"* not to *"murder,"* to *"steal,"* or to *"covet"* are all designed to prevent wrong treatment of another (*"your neighbor"*). They can therefore be summed up by the second of the two great commandments of the law, *"You shall love your neighbor as yourself"* (cf. Matt 22:34-40). When we act in love, we do not treat our neighbor wrongly. Thus we fulfill these commands of the law by the way we treat our neighbor.

One should note here that *love* (*agapē*) is not defined by feelings, but by actions. Love's basic principle is that it does **not produce what is bad for a neighbor**. In our culture which glorifies feelings, Christians sometimes feel guilty if they do not have *emotions* towards another Christian that they can identify as love. But the Greek words *agapē*/*agapaō* were not strongly emotional in general Greek usage. Both the noun and the verb have become the standard words for God's love, and Christian love, in the NT Scriptures. (Cf. the discussion in NIDNTT, 2:542-43.)

For Paul the demands of God's law were more than a mere issue of morality, but went deeper than that. At its core, the law sought the expression of true love toward one's neighbor. One does not have to be *under* the law to love,[6] and in fact love is the supreme Christian virtue (1 Cor 13:13). Christian love should grow spontaneously out of true Christian experience that is empowered by the Holy Spirit. That is what Paul had in mind when he wrote that "the righteous requirement of the law [could be] fulfilled in us who do not walk in relation to the flesh but in relation to the Spirit" (Rom 8:4).

One might very well ask what motivates the justified believer to love in a world largely characterized by the pursuit of self-interest. Why

---

[6] This comment helps explain Hodges' point under his discussion of Rom 13:8, where he says, "He has found this law inadequate for both [justification and sanctification]. But this did not mean, as his opponents had evidently alleged (Rom 3:8), that a Christian should live without regard to the moral standards of that law. On the contrary, obedience to the law was implicit in a life lived in love." Hodges' point is that while believers are no longer *under* the Law of Moses (Rom 7:6; Gal 4:5-7, 10-11, 21-31), they ultimately fulfill it since the commands of the NT likewise center on love for one's neighbor. A by-product of Christians heeding the Law of Christ (Gal 6:2) is meeting the moral standards of the law of Moses, even without knowing the law of Moses. –RNW

should we wish to give love to others whether or not they give it to us? The answer lies in the nature of true Christian *expectation*. Or to use a word that Paul elsewhere associates with love (1 Cor 13:7, 13), it lies in our *hope*. Paul therefore brings the unit begun in 12:3 to a climax with a focus on the Christian's hope and its impact on our lives.

**13:11. In fact *you should do* this, since you know the time, that the hour for us to awake out of sleep *is* already *here*. For now is our deliverance nearer than when we believed.**

The opening words of this verse in Paul's Greek text are a simple *Kai touto*. But their sense here requires careful attention. The KJV's rendering "and that" is obscure, while JB's "besides" looks like a guess. Much to be preferred are the renderings which make *touto* the object of an implied verb "do" ("and do this," NKJV, NIV; "and this do," NASB, NACE). This understanding makes the neuter *touto* refer naturally to the previous discussion on love.

Love, then, is to be motivated by the realization that our final destiny is not far away. Paul assumes that a Christian church in Rome would share the same eschatological hope he himself had. This meant that his readers already **know the time**. The word rendered *time* here is *kairos* and it is a term often found in eschatological contexts (cf. 1 Cor 4:5; 1 Thess 5:1; 2 Thess 2:6; 1 Tim 4:1; 2 Tim 3:1; 4:1; Rev 1:3; 11:18; 22:10). Clearly that is true here as Paul's following statements show.

In the phrase **the hour for us to awake out of sleep**, Paul draws upon a familiar eschatological image, namely, that of the sleeper who is abruptly awakened by the unexpected arrival of prophesied events (Matt 24:43-44; Luke 21:36; Mark 13:35-36; 1 Thess 5:4-7). His readers know that this was no *time* to be sleeping and that they should be wide awake and watching. They should not "put off" the determination to be alert, for the time *to awake* has *already* (*ēdē*) arrived. That is to say, **our deliverance** is **nearer** than ever.

With the words **now is our deliverance nearer than when we believed**, Paul refers again (as he did in 8:23-25) to the hope of a full and permanent deliverance from sin and from sin's impeding impact on our Christian life.[7] Such deliverance involves a full escape from the experience of God's

---

[7] The literature recognizes that Paul speaks of eschatological deliverance to something, but tends not to ask: "From what will the Church be delivered?" It will be a final and complete

wrath (cf. 1:18-32; 5:9-10) through the acquisition of resurrection life. Paul has called this "the redemption of our body" (8:23). Obviously our present taste of this deliverance is a mere "first fruits" (8:23) of its full, eternal realization.[8]

In other words, from Paul's standpoint, once a person has believed and obtained justification, he can immediately begin to experience deliverance (5:9). But this process only *begins* with our present life in the Spirit (8:13, 23). The consummation of this deliverance is accomplished at the coming of the Lord. And since His coming is *nearer than* it was when we entered this process (i.e., *when we believed*), the passage of time means that this consummation is closer than ever.[9]

**13:12. The night has moved on, and the day has drawn near. So let us take off the works of the darkness and clothe ourselves with the equipment of the light.**

Paul's earlier exposition of God's work of deliverance from sin and wrath (Rom 6:1–8:13, referred to in the previous verse) is still in his mind here. This is made plain by his use of the word *hopla* (**equipment**), only found elsewhere in the epistle at 6:13 (twice). In Romans 6 the word may be taken in its simple sense of "instruments" or "tools." Here, however,

---

deliverance *from wrath and from a futile penal-servitude of sin.* Compare the commentary's discussion of Rom 1:18-32; 5:9-10. Paul, as a believer, cried out: "Who will deliver me from the body of *this kind* of death?" (Rom 7:24, ZCH translation). The commentary's exposition of Rom 8:23 speaks of walking by the Spirit as "first fruits" of deliverance from sin, wrath, and futility; while Rom 13:11 speaks of the "full, eternal realization" of deliverance. The literature is oblivious to Paul's message in Romans: regenerated believers need to receive salvation/deliverance from sin, wrath, and penal servitude. –JHN

[8] Many commentators believe that Paul is speaking about what they call *final salvation* or *eschatological salvation*. By that they think Paul is referring to avoiding eternal condemnation by being justified by works before God at *the final judgment* (which they see is the Great White Throne Judgment, which they think is the same as the Judgment Seat of Christ). Hodges has deftly avoided such false connotations by his discussion here. He understands Paul to be speaking of deliverance from sin and its impact on our lives when we are glorified. The issue it is not eternal destiny. The issue is deliverance from our fallen, sinful bodies and from the wrath which comes upon us as a result. –RNW

[9] Some commentators (e.g., Paul J. Achtemeier, *Romans*, Interpretation, ed. James Luther Mays [Louisville, KY: Knox, 1985], 211) suggest that Paul was wrong here, and elsewhere (e.g., 1 Thess 5:1-11), when he suggested that the return of Christ was imminent since two thousand years have now passed. Achtemeier wrongly attributes error to Scripture. The Rapture was actually imminent then and it has remained imminent since then. –JHN

the imagery draws upon the Greek word's more specific use in reference to military *equipment* (cf. BDAG, p. 716).

The Christian should be aware that his "deliverance is closer than when" he "believed" (v 11). This means that the era of spiritual darkness (**the night**) is far along (**has moved on**) toward its consummation in a brand new day when righteousness shall reign on earth. The phrase *has moved on* renders *proekopsen* which is to be understood here in a temporal sense. The result is that **the day**, the new era of God's kingdom, **has drawn** that much nearer.

Christians should therefore "get dressed" for the arrival of *the day*. The image of dressing is conveyed by the Greek words for **let us take off** and **clothe ourselves** (*Apothōmetha, endusōmetha*). (Cf. BDAG, p. 123 #1a and p. 333 #1.) The Christian should not be caught wearing "night clothes," that is, **the works of the darkness**. Instead he should dress himself in "day clothes," or in an outfit that is suited for the arrival of *the day*. The image Paul has in mind here is suggested by his use of the word *hopla* that I noted above. Paul is probably visualizing a fully armored Christian soldier such as the one he describes in Eph 6:11-17 (which begins also with the verb *Endusasthe, put on*).

At the coming of the Lord to bring us our final deliverance, the Christian ought to be fully identifiable as a "soldier" **of the light**. He should have laid aside the kind of conduct (*the works*) that characterizes people who belong to this era of moral *darkness*. In short, he should be ready for the arrival of the conquering King (Rev 19:11-16).

> **13:13. Let us walk circumspectly as in the day, not in carousing and drunkenness, not in sexual misbehavior and licentiousness, not in strife and jealousy.**

As an experienced shepherd to God's people, Paul will not leave what he means in the previous verse (v 12) vague or general. The type of misconduct (i.e., "works of darkness") that he has in mind is now specifically indicated and the proper mode of behavior is elaborated briefly in the following verse (v 14).

In the Greek text, the words **as in the day** (*Hōs en hēmera*) stand first and are emphatic. What he enjoins is what is truly suitable to the arriving day. In fact, his turn of phrase suggests that Paul is urging the readers to behave *as* if *the day* was already here and he and they were living in it.

Christians should therefore **walk circumspectly**, that is, in a morally decent and decorous way. The Greek adverb *euschēmonōs* (*circumspectly*) is quite broad and signifies such ideas as being "correct," "decorous," "appropriate," "decent," "becoming," etc. To walk in this way, believers should avoid "ugly" and "shameful" forms of misbehavior.

This meant that they should avoid **carousing and drunkenness** (*kōmois kai methais*). Paul uses these two words also in Gal 5:21 (in reverse order), and *kōmos* is found in 1 Pet 4:3 while *methē* occurs in Luke 21:34. In all four passages the words are part of vice lists and they were probably common terms in such lists. (See references in BDAG, pp. 580 and 625.) Together they probably suggested the image of undisciplined revelry accompanied by excessive drinking (cf. BDAG, p. 625).

The initial pair of words is followed by two other pairs, that is, **sexual misbehavior and licentiousness** (*koitais kai aselgeiais*) and **strife and jealousy** (*eridi kai zēlō*, also in Gal 5:20 in this same order). The sequence of the three pairs does not seem accidental. *Carousing and drunkenness* easily lead to *sexual misbehavior* and crass immorality (*licentiousness*), or equally the first pair often produced envy and contentious brawls (*strife*). Paul had had ample opportunity to observe all the types of behavior he names here. Whether causally related or not (the sequence implies they could be), Christians ought to studiously avoid all the evil conduct Paul mentions.

**13:14. Instead, clothe yourselves in the Lord Jesus Christ, and take no forethought to *accommodate* the desires of the flesh.**

To conclude the section, Paul returns to the verb *enduō* that so often means to "put on a garment." He had used it in v 12 (*endusōmetha*) of putting on "the equipment of the light." Here in a further figure of speech he urges his readers to **clothe** themselves (*endusasthe*) **in the Lord Jesus Christ**. Since for Paul "to live [was] Christ" (Phil 1:21), he obviously thinks that if *Jesus Christ* is manifest in a believer's conduct that this is the essence of true Christian experience (see also Gal 2:20). Christians should "wear" Jesus Christ their Lord.

But this positive undertaking ("wearing" their Lord) was to be accompanied by a negative undertaking. They should **take no forethought** for **the flesh**. The Greek word rendered here by *forethought* (*pronoian*) could refer either to actual thought or consideration ahead of time or to the result of that, i.e., the provision to which forethought led.

Acts 24:2 exemplifies this latter use and is, along with this text, the only other place where this noun is found in the NT. The corresponding verb itself, *pronoeō,* occurs only three times in the NT (i.e., Rom 12:17; 2 Cor 8:21; and 1 Tim 5:18). But both noun and verb were common enough in general Greek and many instances occur (cf. BDAG, pp. 872-73).

Not surprisingly the English versions are split here between the two options for the Greek phrase *pronoian mē poieisthe.* KJV, NKJV and NASB have "make no [KJV, not] provision"; but NACE reads "take no thought for." The NIV has "do not think about how [to gratify the desires of]," while JB quite freely renders "forget about satisfying [your bodies]."

It would appear, however, that the choice between these two alternatives ought to be made on the basis of Paul's exposition of Christian experience in Rom 8:1-13. As we have seen he has recapitulated that teaching as recently as Rom 12:1-2. In both passages a special emphasis is placed on the "mind" (cf. 8:5-8; 12:2), which for Paul is the arena in which the transforming work of the Holy Spirit is accomplished. Here then it would be wise to see a similar reference. The Christian is not to "set his mind" on the things of the flesh and thus pre-condition himself to fulfill its desires. He should *take no forethought* for that and instead cultivate a spiritual perspective by "putting on" *the Lord Jesus Christ.*

The words *of the flesh* (*tēs sarkos*) stand first in the second half of v 14 in Paul's text (...*and of the flesh do not make forethought for its desires*), although they most naturally connect with the last word, *desires* (*epithumias*). This extreme displacement makes them emphatic and their positioning closely juxtaposes them with the words *the Lord Jesus Christ.* It is possible to capture the sense with a paraphrase like this: "clothe yourselves in the Lord Jesus Christ and, as for the flesh, take no forethought."

The final Greek phrase of the verse (*eis epithumias*) is rendered **to accommodate the desires**, adding the word *accommodate* to signal more clearly the nuance of intention that *eis* seems to contain. The Christian should not spend time thinking about how he could or would facilitate the sinful desires of his flesh. His mental and moral focus should be on Jesus Christ.

With these memorable words, then, Paul brings to a climax a section begun in 12:3 that deals with the theme of living in personal holiness. His words here effectively summarize what Paul's doctrine calls upon believers to pursue in terms of practical, everyday living. In particular, the present verse can be said to be Christian living in a nutshell. Such living does not center on our worthless fleshly desires but on the Son of God Himself.

# Romans 14

## b. In loving others (14:1-26)

**14:1. Accept the one who is weak in the faith, *but* not to engage in disputes about opinions.**

Paul was evidently well aware that disputes on certain matters existed in the Roman congregations.[1] His fundamental principle was mutual acceptance (15:7) and this acceptance must include **the one who is weak in the faith**. As the following discussion shows, *the one who is weak in the faith* signifies a person who does not fully grasp his personal freedom in Christ in regard to mere earthly things. Paul is not talking about basic morality.

The Greek word translated *Accept* (*proslambanesthe*) can signify *"to receive in(to) one's home or circle of acquaintances"* (BDAG, p. 883). Jewett (p. 835) is probably correct to observe that the word "in this context carries the technical sense of reception into the fellowship of the congregation, that is, to the common meal." What Jewett means is that the weak are to be welcomed *to the Lord's Supper* regardless of their personal scruples about certain foods.

---

[1] As noted in the Introduction, Hodges reappraised his earlier estimates of the size of Paul's Roman audience. In his book *Absolutely Free* (p. 231, n. 2), he estimated there were only fifty or so believers in the Roman church(es). In working on this commentary on Romans, he found Robert Jewett's case for multiple tenement congregations helpful. Hodges was working on Rom 14:15 when he died. Hodges cites Jewett twice directly in vv 1-2 and he makes five apparent allusions to him in his discussion of Romans 14. The Introduction also discusses how the various Roman congregations stratified along ethnic and linguistic lines: Latin-surnamed, Greek-surnamed, and Jewish. Paul, writing from Corinth, sought to prevent Roman Christians from becoming as hopelessly divided as the Corinthians. –JHN

Evidently, sometimes in the Roman churches a certain pseudo-acceptance was extended to the weak. But its real intent was to convert them to the opinions of those stronger *in the faith*. Paul makes clear here that this is not the kind of acceptance he has in mind. Disputes over such matters revealed that true Christian acceptance had not occurred. We should keep in mind that the open character of the gatherings at the Lord's Supper permitted all but the women to participate verbally (cf. 1 Cor 14:26-40). This freedom could easily lead to **disputes about opinions** of the type Paul has in mind. Paul is warning against such debates, especially at the Lord's Table.

The phrase translated as *about opinions* renders the Greek noun *dialogismōn*. Although generally in the NT this noun may be translated simply as "thought(s)" or "reasoning(s)" (e.g., Matt. 15:19; Mark 7:21; Luke 2:35; 5:22; 6:8; 9:46, 47; 1 Cor 3:20), here the meaning *opinions* suits the context perfectly (cf. BDAG, p. 232). Paul here refers to conclusions drawn from a person's own thought processes, rather than those drawn directly from God's Word.

> **14:2-3. One person believes he can eat everything, but another who is weak eats vegetables. The person who eats should not scorn the person who doesn't eat, and the person who doesn't eat should not condemn the person who eats, for God has accepted him.**

The problem of differing opinions about foods is the first question that Paul brings forward here. Commentators often conclude that this problem was essentially a Jew/Gentile problem and mainly involved the OT regulations about clean and unclean foods. There is no reason to doubt that these issues were likely to arise in the mixed congregations at Rome. But this need hardly be the full extent of the problem.

According to 1 Cor 8:1-8, a question existed at Corinth about the suitability of eating meat from animals offered in sacrifice to idols. Even Gentile converts might have scruples about eating such meat. Paul's language here is general enough to include this issue as well. Further, in a complex, multi-racial society such as was found at Rome, an even larger range of food issues is not hard to imagine. Some of these were probably mainly cultural or could stem from pre-Christian pagan scruples.

Jewett (p. 835) notes that "in view of Greco-Roman ascetic ideals present at Rome, it is altogether possible that the **weak** also included ascetics from pagan backgrounds." His subsequent discussion (p. 837) is illuminating on this point. Paul's words are no doubt deliberately broad so as to include whatever food issues might exist in the Roman congregations.

In the present context, Paul's words imply that some of the believers at Rome were vegetarians by conviction. The idea that this refers mainly to Jews who could not obtain kosher meat in the Roman markets is not very persuasive. The people Paul has in mind ate vegetables, in contrast to those who felt free to **eat everything**. If the issue had been simply a matter of kosher meat, such meat must have been easily available from merchants who catered to Jewish customers.

Instead we have here an apparent scruple similar to the one referred to in 1 Tim 4:3a where the influence of demons is mentioned in connection with "abstaining from foods" (NKJV). The subsequent statements (1 Tim 4:3b-5) strongly imply that "meat" from animals is mainly in view. Here in Romans, however, there is no suggestion that such scruples are of demonic origin. Rather the person who has them *is weak* in the faith.

It is important for those who are *not* weak in the faith not to scorn the people who are. If **the person who eats** looks down on **the person who doesn't eat**, he has not accepted him in a truly Christian manner. But conversely, **the person who doesn't eat** should not adopt a judgmental attitude toward **the person who eats**. The word for **condemn** (*krinetō*) is the basic word for *judge*, but obviously here the judgment referred to would be negative. The scrupulous Christian must not censure (whether verbally or in his heart) the brother who does not share his scruples.

Experience shows that both the lack of scruples and the possession of scruples often result in spiritual pride. Out of pride over one's superior grasp of the faith, those who are "strong" (cf. 15:1) easily fall into the habit of scorning those who are weak and overly scrupulous. But pride in one's superior scrupulousness is equally a danger and is an expression of self-righteousness. Thus the condemnation of those lacking one's own scruples is equally common among the scrupulous.

To the scrupulous, in particular, Paul now adds an additional warning. They must not refuse to accept someone whom **God has accepted**. The fact is that every believer is justified by faith in Christ. Even if he does not hold to one's own personal opinions about what can or cannot be eaten, it is clear that *God has accepted him*. To refuse acceptance to someone whom *God has accepted* amounts to putting oneself above God.

Paul adds here a subtle counterpoint to the admonition given in v 1. The strong, who no doubt dominate the various Roman churches, were told to accept (*proslambanesthe*) the one *who is weak* (v 1). Now Paul admonishes the weak not to judge the strong because God Himself *has accepted* (*proselabeto*) the person he judges. Implicit is an irony that often happens; a (weak) believer finds acceptance in a congregation but inwardly does not accept those who accepted him. Such a believer must rise above his scruples and recognize the acceptability before God of his less scrupulous brothers.

Through the centuries, an uncountable number of Christians have held proud personal opinions that encouraged them to look down on those who welcomed them into the Christian fellowship. Paul obviously understood this fact and is warning against it here.[2]

> **14:4. Who are you to judge another person's house servant? He stands or falls to his own lord. But he shall be enabled to stand, because God has power to enable him to stand.**

In Paul's Greek text, v 4 begins with the personal pronoun **you** (*Su*) which is emphatic here (as we might say, "who are *you of all people* to…"). The point is that no one has the right to pass judgment on someone else's **house servant** because only his master has that right. It is arrogant overreaching if a believer imagines he can pass judgment on a fellow Christian who, in fact, is God's *house servant*.

The word for *house servant* here is *oiketēn*. Paul liked to think of the Christian Church in terms of a household. For this particular image he could employ the term *oikos* or related words (cf. 1 Tim 3:5, 15 [*oikos*]; Gal 6:10; Eph 2:19 [*oikeios*]; 2 Tim 2:20 [*oikia*]). Thus, **to judge** a fellow Christian was to usurp the prerogative of the divine Lord of the Christian household.

In my translation, the word **lord** (*kuriō*) might well have been capitalized, depending on whether we are thinking of the general truth or the specifically Christian one. The *lord* of the typical *house servant*

---

[2] The issue of strong versus weak could potentially create warring factions *within* individual congregations, but also *between* the fifteen (or more) assemblies. The Introduction shows that stratification of assemblies. Groups showed little mixture between those with Greek versus Latin surnames; Gentiles seemed separate from Jews. Rome could easily become a second Corinth. The Corinthian epistles correct divisions, while Romans aims to prevent schism. – JHN

represents the Lord of the *Christian house servant* in the Church. In the Greek, the words **to his own lord** stand first (as *you* did in the previous sentence) and are emphatic (*"He stands or falls to his own lord"*).

The statement that **he stands or falls** most naturally refers to the issue of whether the lord of the house servant ultimately approves or disapproves of his conduct. The typical scrupulous Christian, however, would be tempted to think that his less scrupulous brother would surely *fall*. That is to say, God would ultimately disapprove of his conduct. But Paul here denies this censorious conclusion. On the contrary, Paul insists that **he shall be enabled to stand.**

This statement by Paul invites thought. If the issue he is addressing is simply a way of saying "God will ultimately approve" of the strong Christian's freedom, his words are puzzling. In fact, in the following statement Paul adds, **because God has power to enable him to stand** (the Greek is *dunatos gar estin ho Theos stēsai auton*). This does not sound like a mere question of approval or disapproval. Rather it sounds like an exercise of divine strength.

In all probability, the issue Paul has in mind is one that often arises when so-called doubtful things are in question. The scrupulous Christian frequently believes that even if a particular matter is not in itself wrong, it can easily lead to doing what *is* actually wrong. That is to say, the matter in question facilitates sin. Thus the scrupulous brother might say, "You shouldn't do that because it will lead you into sin—you will fall."

One might well imagine the sensitive vegetarian saying to his strong brother, "If you buy meat in the meat market, you may well buy meat that has come from a pagan animal sacrifice, and thus you will sin." Paul would not have agreed with that of course (1 Cor 10:25-33), but he would hardly have denied that one could indeed slip into sin in connection with eating meat (cf. 1 Cor 8:10-13). Paul was nothing if he was not deeply practical and realistic.

So what about the weak brother's concern that the less scrupulous Christian must surely fall? Paul's answer is simple: God can prevent that. *God has power to enable him to stand.* Paul does not mean by this that regardless of the attitude of the strong Christian, he will inevitably *be enabled to stand.* Instead he means that by relying on God's strength this enabling will be granted so that this brother avoids sin. The scrupulous (weak) brother is underestimating God's power on behalf of his more confident brother.

**14:5. One person regards *one* day above *another* day, and another regards every day *the same*. Let each person be fully assured in his own mind.**

To some extent v 4 was parenthetical (though crucial) to Paul's teaching in this passage. Paul now returns to the major theme, namely that different opinions should be respected (vv 1-3). What has been said about differences of conviction concerning foods, can also be said about differences concerning special days. The structure of Paul's sentence in this verse is quite similar to the structure of v 2 (cf. the correlatives *Hos men…ho de* [v 2] and *Hos men…hos de* [here]).

It is probable that BDAG [p. 567] is basically correct in its treatment of the verb *krinō* that Paul uses here. Under extended definition 1, the lexicon suggests "prefers" in v 5a and "recognize," "approve," or "holds in esteem" for v 5b. However, I have selected the rendering *regards* in order to represent the fact that Paul is using the same verb in both halves of v 5.

The issue of observing certain days as special would surely have involved questions related to the feast days of the Jewish religious calendar. But other religious/cultural scruples might also have been involved in the multi-cultural congregations that must have been found among the Roman house churches (including the tenement churches). Here again, as with the issue about foods, one can scarcely reduce the problem to differences between Jewish and Gentile believers.

The important question for Paul was not whether such scruples about special days were correct or not. The important thing was that each individual should **be fully assured in his own mind**. The verb for fully assured (*plērophoreisthō*) is a strong one whose only other use in Romans is to describe Abraham's complete conviction that God could fulfill His promise (4:21). Paul does not want differences in regard to special days to be superficial or ill-considered ideas.

Differences about the religious importance of certain days were potentially more disruptive than differences about diet. Dietary matters could be more easily overlooked because of their very personal nature, but elaborate regulations often adhered to, for example, Jewish feast days. The ostentatious observance of these rituals could easily breed a sense of division in a congregation. Paul will not forbid the observance itself, but he wants believers to undertake them only out of deep conviction. Implied is the need to respect such deeply held convictions (cf. vv 1-3).

**14:6. The person who esteems the day, esteems *it* with reference to the Lord. And the person who does not esteem the day, with reference to the Lord he does not esteem *it*. So too the person who eats, eats with reference to the Lord, since he gives God thanks. And the person who does not eat, with reference to the Lord he does not eat, and he gives God thanks.**

Assuming that the conviction is deeply held, the observance of certain days, or the non-observance of certain days, will be a matter of conscience before the Lord. Thus both observance and non-observance should be seen as part of the individual's relationship to God. Christian tolerance of the opinions of others is fundamentally inseparable from the realization that their convictions are oriented to the Lord.

The Greek word *Kuriō* occurs four times in this verse and in every case I translate it **with reference to the Lord**. This maintains the same fundamental sense in all four instances. The fourfold use of *Kuriō* within the short span of this verse indicates that Paul hardly saw any difference in meaning between the four instances. He is not trying to specify the precise way the action has **reference to the Lord** in each case, although he is more explicit in the examples about eating.

In the case of special days, Paul points out that whether **the person…esteems the day** (*Ho phronōn tēn hēmeran*) or not (same expression plus the negative *mē* after *ho*), it is with the Lord in view. This no doubt means that the one who observes the day observes it with a desire to please the Lord, while the non-observer feels his relationship to God does not require this observance. In other words, the non-observer (i.e., the strong Christian) is expressing his Christian liberty in not observing the day.

In the case of foods, the Christian who feels free to eat certain foods (rejected by his weaker brother) shows that he is doing this in **reference to the Lord** by the fact that **he gives God thanks** for that food. But conversely, the brother **who does not eat** those foods is also acting in **reference to the Lord**. This is demonstrated by the fact that he too **gives God thanks** for what he does eat. He could hardly do so if he felt that he was eating what he should not have been eating. Thus the thankfulness of both parties attests to their God-consciousness in what they choose to eat or not to eat.

This new reference to foods (cf. vv 1-3) serves as a sort of *inclusio* that marks 14:1-6 as a unit.

**14:7-8. After all no one of us lives with reference to himself** *alone* **and no one dies with reference to himself** *alone.* **For if we live, we live with reference to the Lord; and if we die, we die with reference to the Lord. So whether we live or die, we are the Lord's.**

Paul now addresses yet another reason why believers should be careful not to pass judgment on each other in matters of personal opinion. He reminds the Romans that **After all** (*gar*) no Christian lives in isolation as if his experience concerned only himself. On the contrary, the Christian's experience is inextricably related to the Lord to whom the Christian belongs. This means that each Christian will "render an accounting of himself to God" (v 12; cf. vv 9-12).

The truth that is involved here has already been elaborated earlier in Romans. The believer is already joined with Jesus Christ through union with Him in His death, burial, and resurrection (Rom 6:4). In fact, he has died to the law that he might be married to "the One who was raised from the dead" and so "might bear fruit for God" (7:4). Moreover, beyond the range of death, the believer is destined to be "glorified" (8:30). He can never be separated from God's love in Christ by anything whatsoever, including "life" or "death" (8:38). If all of this is taken seriously, it is manifest that **whether we live or die, we are the Lord's.**

It is inevitable that in living we do so in **reference to the Lord** and in dying we also do that in **reference to the Lord.** Verse 8 gives the reason (**For,** *gar*) why v 7 is true.

Paul is not speaking here of a choice we make, but instead he is speaking of the inescapable reality that *we are the Lord's* and that we cannot avoid our connection with Him in whatever we do or in whatever happens to us. This leads quite naturally to a discussion of the *Bema,* or, the Judgment Seat of Christ.

**14:9. In fact, to this end Christ both died as well as rose and lived, so that He might exercise lordship over both** *the* **dead and** *the* **living.**

The logical connection of this verse with the previous one is better expressed by rendering *gar* **in fact.** As believers we are indeed "the Lord's" (v 8), but the broader fact is that **Christ both died as well as rose and lived** to be *everybody's* Lord, whether they are dead or living. The words **to**

**this end** translate the Greek phrase *Eis touto* and express an intended goal of the Savior's death and resurrection. By undergoing death He obtains **lordship over...*the* dead**, and by rising and living, He obtains lordship over *the* **living**.

The statement of Paul here should be understood in the light of our Lord's own statement that the Father "has committed all judgment to the Son" (John 5:22). This authority to judge is based on His being "the Son of Man" (John 5:27). Beyond the Messianic implications of the title "Son of Man," there is also the simple fact that Jesus Christ was a human being who *died as well as rose and lived*. Thus His God-given Lordship relates to those in the sphere of death and relates *as well* to those in the sphere of life. Mankind's Judge will Himself be a man who tasted both death and resurrection, as all men[3] are destined to do. He is qualified, therefore, to exercise the ultimate Lordship, i.e., to exercise judgment.

The Greek phrase *kai apethane kai anestē kai ezēsen* (*both died as well as rose and lived*) caused trouble for some of the scribes in the NT manuscript tradition and has led to textual error. The main error was probably a simple accident in which the scribe wrote the second *kai* and then his eye skipped to the third *kai* and he proceeded to write *ezēsen*, omitting *anestē kai* (a frequent scribal fault known as *homoioteleuton*). The initial *kai* before *apethane* may also have seemed problematic to a scribe/editor (due to the threefold repetition here) or may have been dropped by accident as well. In any case the full text used here has the support of the majority of the surviving Greek manuscripts.

The threefold construction with *kai* is perfectly good Greek (cf. BDAG, p. 495 #1f). But it cannot be translated into English simply by the words "both...and...and." It is clear, however, from the following phrase, *kai nekrōn kai zōntōn* (*both the dead and the living*), that Paul has essentially two categories in mind. Thus I render the threefold construction to indicate this: *both died as well as rose and lived*.

At first glance, the phrase *rose and lived* is unexpected. But this may be due mainly to our perspective after 1900 years of Christian theology. In the Greco-Roman world a belief in immortality beyond the grave was unexceptional, but a belief in physical resurrection certainly was

---

[3] Of course Hodges is speaking generally here. There have been two exceptions, Enoch and Elijah, who did not die. And there will be many more exceptions in the future. Those believers alive at the time of the Rapture will not die, but will be changed (1 Thess 4:15-17; 1 Cor 15:51-52). –RNW

exceptional. Paul encountered a disbelief in physical resurrection on Mars Hill (Acts 17:32) and later in the church at Corinth (1 Cor 15:12). Here the addition of the words *and lived* makes clear that a return to physical life is involved. The word *rose* cannot in that case be referred to some "spiritual" emergence from the experience of death. In Rome, especially, with its multiple house and tenement churches, Paul might have anticipated the possibility of a problem similar to the one at Corinth.

> **14:10. But as for you, why do you judge your brother? Or you too, why do you scorn your brother? For we must all appear before the Judgment Seat of Christ.**

Paul now draws the obvious conclusion from what he has just said. Since Jesus is Lord both of the dead and the living, what business do believers have judging a Christian **brother**, or alternatively, scorning a Christian **brother**? The "weak" brother was tempted to do the former, while the "strong" brother was tempted to do the latter.

Paul makes his point by employing the emphatic personal pronoun *su* in both of the questions in this verse. In the first question, *Su* stands first and I translate it **as for you**. In the second question, the emphasis is plain in translation, so I render *Ē kai su* by **Or you too**. The weak and the strong in the Roman churches are pointedly addressed.

Paul is reiterating the point he made earlier in v 4. The lord of a servant is the only person qualified to **judge** that servant. Since Jesus is Lord by virtue of both His death and resurrection, He alone has that prerogative in regard to our Christian brothers and sisters. It follows that we have no right to either *judge* or **scorn** our fellow servant. This is all the more true since we too **must...appear before** our Lord to be judged. All believers, in fact, must do this, a point Paul stresses in Greek by placing the word **all** (*pantes*) first. No Christian should think himself exempt.

The phrase **the Judgment Seat of Christ**[4] occurs in this form only here and in 2 Cor 5:10.[5] The word for *Judgment Seat* in the Greek text

---

[4] A minority of manuscripts reads the *Judgment Seat of God* [*tou Theou*]. The majority of manuscripts read the *Judgment Seat of Christ* [*tou Christou*]. There is every reason to accept the majority reading here, especially in light of the parallels with 2 Cor 5:10 (see next note) and the fact that the Lord Jesus said, "For the Father judges no one, but has committed all judgment to the Son" (John 5:22). –RNW

[5] The wording is similar in both verses. Both say that all believers (*pantes*) must stand or appear before the Judgment Seat of Christ (*bēmati/bēmatos tou Christou*). –RNW

(*bēmati* from *bēma*), though it had other meanings, evidently had wide currency in the sense of *judicial bench* (cf. BDAG, p. 175). Despite the occurrence of the precise phrase in only two NT passages, there are other clear references, including Paul's famous text in 1 Cor 3:12-15 (cf. also 1 Cor 4:1-5; 2 Tim 2:12, 15; 4:6-8; 1 John 2:28; 4:17-19).[6]

The concept, however, is not originally Pauline, but instead goes back to the teaching of our Lord about the judgment of His servants. Two pivotal passages on this theme are to be found in Luke 19:11-27 and Matt 25:14-30. In both narratives it is the servants of the king who are in question, since they have received responsibilities from their lord (i.e., minas or talents). In Luke 19:27 the servants of the king are explicitly distinguished from his "enemies." It is clear that here in Romans the theme of "servant/ Lord" (found in the teaching of Jesus) is formative for Paul's thinking (cf. v 14). *The Judgment Seat of Christ* is for the servants of Christ.[7]

**14:11. For it is written: *"As I live, says the Lord, every knee shall bow to Me, and every tongue shall confess to God."***

Paul now gives Scriptural proof for his statement that all believers must give an accounting to God. For this purpose he draws upon a divine declaration found in Isa 45:23. This inspired pronouncement asserts that all humanity must someday **bow** the knee and **confess to God**.

The Isaiah passage as quoted here varies somewhat (though not significantly) from both the MT and the LXX. The MT lacks the word *and* as well as the words *to God*. Both the MT and the LXX do not have the introductory oath formula, **As I live, says the Lord**. It seems likely once again that the text as cited by Paul is the one found in the Greek Isaiah

---

[6] Hodges gives representative NT references here. He has remarked that hardly a page in the NT does not touch on the doctrine of eternal rewards. That is certainly true, as well, of the Judgment Seat of Christ. For when eternal rewards are in view, then the Judgment Seat of Christ is at least in the background. –RNW

[7] This verse speaks of Christians appearing at the Judgment Seat (*Bēma*) of Christ (*MajT*). It says nothing about the judgment of unbelievers, which will separate, at the Great White Throne (Rev 20:11-15). In v 11 Paul cites Isa 49:18 and 45:23 as the basis for asserting that the works of believers will be judged. The universality of the Isaiah passages need not cause consternation. Believers will bow and confess at the *Bēma*; unbelievers will do so at the Great White Throne. Paul's argument through the book aims toward the *Bēma*. God offers deliverance from present wrath, which God offers to those who are righteous by faith (Rom 1:16-17). Believers who avail themselves of this deliverance will receive commendation at the *Bēma*. –JHN

scroll from which he quotes often in Romans. This would include also the insignificant transposition of *pasa glōssa* to before *exomologēsetai*.

The text Paul used looks like an effort to improve on the clarity of MT and may, in fact, represent the original form of the LXX. Alternatively, the oath formula could have been added later by an editor. In any case, Paul's quotation is true to the basic sense of the Hebrew text regardless of these verbal variations.

It must be pointed out that the Isaiah prophecy is broad and general and leaves room for the differing situations we encounter in the NT. The unregenerate dead are judged before the Great White Throne after the initial one thousand years of the kingdom of God (Rev 20:5, 11-15).[8] In this judgment, born-again believers have no part (cf. John 5:24; cf. 3:17-18 [Gk.][9]). Instead, believers will stand before the Judgment Seat of Christ when He returns to inaugurate His kingdom (cf. Luke 19:15; note esp. the clear pre-kingdom sense of Luke 19:17, 19).

It is significant that two features of divine judgment are specified in Isaiah: (1) submission (**bow to Me**) and (2) acknowledgment of responsibility (***confess to God***). This latter action should not be construed as simply a reference to praising God (BDAG, p. 351). On the contrary, the flow of thought in Paul's passage shows clearly that he is talking about *accountability*, not simply *acknowledgement* or *worship* (cf. v 4). This is plain in v 10, and emphatically so in the wording of v 12 (*logon dōsei*: "render an accounting").

The sinful history of mankind would not be adequately completed apart from such a day of reckoning in which both of these acts are performed by every human being. Though the Judgment Seat of Christ does not determine the final destiny of believers, it nevertheless is part of the completion that God has ordained for every earthly life. Its certainty is guaranteed (even in the Hebrew of Isa 45:23) by a divine oath.

---

[8] Hodges refers to the Millennium as "the initial one thousand years of the kingdom of God." He did not believe, as most Dispensationalists do, that the Millennium will be a separate kingdom from Jesus' eternal kingdom that will be on the new earth. In his mind the Millennium was the start of the eternal kingdom (cf. 2 Pet 1:10-11). –RNW

[9] Hodges's point about the Greek of John 3:17-18 can be seen by a more literal translation of it: "For God did not send His Son into the world in order that He might *judge* [*krinē*] the world, but in order that the world might be saved through Him. The one who believes in Him *is not judged* [*ou krinetai*]; but the one who does not believe *has already been judged* [*ēdē kekritai*] because he has not believed in the name of the only begotten Son of God." –RNW

**14:12. So then each of us shall render an accounting of himself to God.**

With this statement, Paul concludes the short section begun at v 7. The words **So then** represent a doubled inferential conjunction in Greek (*Ara oun*), and they signal that the statement is the final one in this subunit (vv 7-12). Individual believers should get out of the business of either judging or scorning their fellow servants (v 10), since those we judge or scorn, as well as ourselves, are subject to a final accounting to be rendered **to God**. Any serious consideration of this fact should cause us to focus on our own day of accounting, rather than the presumed failures of other Christians.

**14:13. Therefore, let us no longer judge one another, but decide this instead: that *we* not create an impediment or a snare for *our* brother.**

The new subunit draws an inference (**Therefore**: *oun*) from what Paul has just declared about our future accounting before God. Rather than passing judgment on one another, we should be seriously concerned that we ourselves not incur judgment at the Judgment Seat of Christ. That such judgment of others was actually going on is implied by the word for **no longer** (*Mēketi*). What we should do instead (*alla*: **but…instead**) is, in fact, to pass judgment on our own behavior.

This point is implicit in a word play Paul employs here which our English cannot exactly represent. The Greek word translated **judge** (*krinōmen*) is the same verb translated **decide** (*krinate*) in the following clause. Believers, Paul says, should focus their judgmental capacity on their own conduct and determine whether or not it is harmful to their Christian brother.

That means that their conduct should not **create an impediment** for their fellow Christians. The Greek phrase for *create an impediment* is *tithenai proskomma* and seems clearly to express a metaphor similar to our "place a stumbling block" (in someone's path). Both the verb and the noun of this phrase occur together in Rom 9:33 (quoted from Isa 28:16) in an analogous expression: *tithēmi…lithon proskommatos* ("I lay…a stone of collision" [or, "stumbling"]). Our own conduct must not constitute an impediment over which a brother might well trip or fall.

Neither should our conduct produce **a snare** (*skandalon*) **for our brother**, i.e., a trap in which he might be caught. This second word, taken together with *proskomma*, appears to have a slightly heightened sense for Paul. We are neither to "trip up" *our brother* (*proskomma*), nor cause him to be "ensnared" (*skandalon*).

Seriousness in the light of our future accounting before God should lead to careful consideration of how our behavior affects others.

> **14:14. I know and am persuaded in the Lord Jesus that *there is* nothing unclean of itself, except that to a person who considers something to be unclean, to that person *it is* unclean.**

Paul wants to make clear that what is involved here is not concurrence in some fashion with the unjustified scruples of the weak. The concern for the sensitivities of others that he urges does not involve submission to their principles. To make this point he starts with himself.

On his own part he has complete assurance that nothing is **unclean of itself**. This assurance is at once both knowledge (**I know:** *Oida*) and conviction (**am persuaded:** *pepeismai*). That is to say, it is both based on what he knows to be true and it is also a matter of firm certitude. In saying this, Paul fortifies the strong by assuring them that he holds their view of things. This assurance, he affirms, is **in the Lord Jesus**; that is, it comes from *the Lord* Himself and carries the Lord's approval.

The statement that *there is* **nothing** *unclean of itself* refers to what may be called the mundane, or ordinary, things of human life. Violations of God's moral law are not in view. Instead, Paul is thinking of the matters previously referred to, i.e., negative restrictions pertaining to foods and the observance of special days (vv 2, 5). None of the actions forbidden in these activities can be considered inherently defiling.

The idea of inherent uncleanness is conveyed by the phrase *unclean of itself* (*koinon di' autou* [*heautou*]). The word *koinon*, however, is especially used of what is "profane" ("non-sacred") as BDAG makes clear under usage 2 (p. 552). But a scrupulous person would probably not usually draw a distinction between this term and the corresponding word for moral impurity (*akathartos*). This can be seen in the conjoining of the two words in Acts 10:14 (*koinon ē akatharton*). To the sensitive heart of the weak believer, either term might apply to the same action.

At whatever level the weak perceive something as **unclean**, this impurity is not intrinsic to the nature of the thing in question. On the contrary, whatever uncleanness there may be lies in the perception of the individual. Thus, **to a person who considers something to be** *unclean*, it is actually **unclean** for **that person**. In other words, if such a person does not share Paul's knowledge and conviction (see above), his freedom *in the Lord Jesus* is inhibited.

**14:15. Now if because of your food your brother is grieved, you are no longer walking in love. By your food, do not ruin that person for whom Christ died.**

But where such inhibitions exist, the strong Christian must be fully sensitive to them. He cannot simply run roughshod over the feelings of his weaker brother. Indeed, if he does nothing more than grieve his brother, he has done too much. To do that is to stop **walking in love** and to live selfishly. A person who says, "I don't care how my brother feels about this; no one can take my liberty away," is a person who reveals his lack of Christian love.

Paul no doubt has in mind here the basic Christian meeting, with its regular observance of the Lord's Supper, that is, the eating of a communal meal.[10] On such occasions a strong Christian might be tempted to flaunt his freedom to eat non-kosher meat (for example) and thus his weaker brother would be grieved. But the cost of such conduct could be that he would **ruin that person**, who is in fact an individual **for whom Christ died**. Love demands that this consequence be avoided, particularly in the light of the love of Christ for that very individual (cf. 5:6-8).

In the command, **do not ruin** (*Mē apollue*),[11] Paul is using a Greek verb (*apollumi*) which is rarely associated with eternal condemnation in the NT (six times in John's Gospel, none elsewhere).[12] However, here it has its normal meaning of temporal loss or destruction. In this case,

---

[10] Hodges (a Plymouth Brethren from his college days onward) believed that Christians should not only take the elements (bread and juice) *each week*, but that the remembrance should be part of *a meal, an actual supper*. The meal would begin with the taking of the memorial bread and then after supper the cup would be taken (1 Cor 11:25, "He also took the cup after supper"). He viewed the teaching of God's Word to be a vital part of this meeting and often cited Acts 20:7-12 (cf., v 9, *dialegomai*, speaking or *dialoguing*). –RNW

[11] This is where the text of Hodges' commentary ended (near the end of his comments on Rom 14:15) when he went to be with the Lord on November 22, 2008. The text from here to the end is mine, except for the translation and outline, which Hodges completed entirely.–RNW

[12] By my count *apollumi* refers to eternal condemnation only six times in the NT (John 3:15, 16; 6:39; 10:28; 17:12; 18:9). That is only six percent of the time (six of ninety-two). For a detailed discussion see Robert N. Wilkin, *The Ten Most Misunderstood Words in the Bible* (Corinth, TX: Grace Evangelical Society, 2012), chap. 4. –RNW

the *destruction* (NKJV) or *ruin* (Hodges' translation) is that of a fellow believer.

*Ruin* is the opposite of edification (cf. 14:19-20). If a believer is led to violate his own conscience, he has actually sinned against God as Paul makes clear at the end of this discussion (14:23).

**14:16. So do not let your good *activity* be defamed.**

Paul clearly wants no one to blaspheme or speak evil of that which is good. But what exactly does he mean by **your good *activity*** (*humōn to agathon*), which could also be translated "your good" (NKJV)?

If Paul has the stronger brother alone in view here (and not both the stronger and weaker brothers), which seems likely, then *your good activity* refers to the eating of foods that the weaker brother considers inappropriate to eat.

He is referring to the foods which the stronger brother enjoys, but which the weaker brother conscientiously avoids. If the stronger brother bulls ahead when in the presence of the weaker brother and eats foods which he considers good, but which the weaker brother considers bad, then he will injure his brother and that brother will likely be moved to speak against what he has done. He will decry the food his brother ate and the eating of it in his presence.

**14:17. For the kingdom of God is not food and drink, but righteousness and peace and joy in the Holy Spirit.**

Of course, the Lord Jesus did say that He would partake of wine once again when He returned to establish His kingdom (Luke 22:18). Thus there will be eating and drinking in Jesus' kingdom. That is not Paul's point here.

Is Paul speaking, as many commentators suggest (e.g., Cranfield, Murray), of *the present experience* of God's kingdom?

The kingdom is not yet. Christ is not ruling and His kingdom is not currently in effect (John 18:36; Acts 1:7; Heb 12:2; Rev 3:21). His kingdom will come when He returns to earth after the Tribulation.

However, it is possible that Paul is speaking of current experiences that are foretastes of the kingdom. The Lord said to His disciples, "There are some standing here who shall not taste death till they see the Son of Man coming in His kingdom" (Matt 16:28). The Lord was referring to the fact that six days later (Matt 17:1, the very next verse) Peter, James, and John saw the Lord Jesus transfigured before them. They caught a glimpse of the glory of God which is to come (cf. 2 Pet 1:16-19). They were not literally in the kingdom. But they experienced it when the saw the King in His coming glory.

Compare 1 Cor 4:20, where the same construction is used by Paul: "For the kingdom of God is not in word but in power."

Paul's point is that **the kingdom of God is not food and drink** in the sense that our freedom to eat or drink is not what will be the defining characteristics of the coming kingdom. Rather, that which defines the kingdom to come is **righteousness and peace and joy in the Holy Spirit.** Many other texts of Scripture link the coming kingdom with *righteousness and peace and joy* (cf. Matt 25:21, 23; Luke 2:14; 19:42; Rom 8:18-30; 11:26-27; 2 Cor 5:1-8; Heb 1:8; 12:2; 1 John 3:2). Whenever we as believers today experience *righteousness, peace, and joy,* we are getting a foretaste of what will be our experience forever, except to a much greater degree.

Thus, it makes no sense to live in a manner that is inconsistent with a focus on the life to come.

### 14:18. Indeed, the person who serves Christ in these things is pleasing to God and approved by men.

The believer **who serves Christ**, rather than his belly and his own private desires, **in these things**, that is, in "righteousness, peace, and joy," **is** [well] **pleasing** [*euarestos*] **to God.** In light of 14:10-12 and 2 Cor 5:9 (where the same word is used in a context dealing with the Judgment Seat of Christ), the reader should realize that there is eternal significance to this matter of treating our fellow believers well. Of course, the issue is not *eternal destiny,* but one's eternal rewards are directly related to what he does in this life.

In addition to pleasing God, *the one who serves Christ in these things* is also **approved** (*dokimos*) **by men.** Here we find a term, *dokimos,* Paul loves to use in relation to *Christ's approval.* Six of its seven NT uses are in Paul, and five of those six directly refer to the importance of having God's approval (e.g., Rom 16:10; 1 Cor 11:19; 2 Cor 10:18; 13:7; 2 Tim 2:15; cf. 1 Cor 9:27 and 2 Cor 13:5-7 where the antonym, *adokimos, disapproved,* appears). The word *men* here looks at fellow believers from within one's own assembly. They approve of such service of Christ. The world does not.

**14:19-20. Therefore let us pursue the things *that produce* peace and the things *that produce* edification for each other. Do not tear down the work of God for the sake of food. All *foods* indeed are pure, but *it is* evil for the man who causes an impediment *for someone* by eating *it*.**

Peace between believers is essential for edification to occur. Mature believers **pursue the things *that produce* peace and the things *that produce* edification for each other**. That means a giving up of one's liberties if the exercise thereof would harm one's fellow believers.

The stronger brother knows that there are no longer any unclean foods. Thus he might well reason that he will not give up *foods* that God has given him to enjoy simply because of the sensitivities of an ignorant fellow believer. After all, he might think, *my eating might well help him snap out of his weakness.*

Yet this is not a proper way to treat the weaker brother. The stronger brother is the one who should freely give up his rights so as not to hurt his fellow brother.

Of course, Paul is not discussing the issue here that came up in Antioch (cf. Gal 2:11-21). The issue here is not the person who says that one must keep the OT dietary laws to be born again.

Probably this is not even a sanctification issue for the weaker brother, or else Paul would have surely raised an objection (cf. Gal 2:19-20; 5:13-26). The issue is the brother who simply believes that for him to eat such foods would be wrong.

**14:21. It is good not to eat meat nor to drink wine nor *to do anything* by which your brother runs into an impediment or is ensnared or made weak.**

The first word in the Greek text here is **good** (*Kalon*). It is clearly in contrast to the word *evil* (*kakon*) in the previous verse. In fact, there is a minor sound play involved (*Kalon* vs. *kakon*). The *good* is **not to eat meat nor to drink wine. Anything** which causes one's **brother** to run **into an impediment or** to be **ensnared** or to be **made weak** is that which is evil and **not good**.

Paul conveyed the same idea in 1 Cor 8:13: "Therefore, if food makes my brother stumble, I will never again eat meat, lest I make my brother stumble." Of course, the apostle was adamant that the OT food restrictions were no longer in place and that believers may eat whatever they wish (cf. Gal 2:12; Col 2:21; see also Rom 6:14-15). Even meats that had been offered to idols, the subject under discussion in 1 Cor 8:13, were not off limits *as long as one was not harming the conscience of another* (1 Cor 8:4-13; 10:23-31).

Edification of our fellow believers (vv 19-20) is the goal in all we do, including eating and drinking. To tear down our spiritual brothers and sisters for any reason, especially for the sake of petty preferences in food or drink, reveals a carnal rather than spiritual mindset (1 Cor 2:14–3:4).

Paul is concerned here with what we eat and drink *when in the presence of other believers.* He is not saying that in the privacy of one's own home he should avoid meat or wine since there may be some believer in his church who is a vegetarian or teetotaler. Of course, what one eats or drinks in private is to remain private if discussing it would hurt a weaker brother.

> **14:22-23. Do you have faith? Have it by yourself before God. Blessed is the person who does not condemn himself *for the thing* which he treats as acceptable. But the person who is doubtful is condemned if he eats, because *he does* not *do so* by faith. And whatever *is* not by faith is sin.**

Commentators are divided as to whether Paul is exclusively addressing weaker brothers in vv 22-23 or the stronger brothers in v 22ab and weaker brothers in v 22c-23.

If v 22ab addresses weaker brothers, then both verses exhort them not to violate their own consciences by eating meat (14:6, 21). If v 22ab addresses stronger brothers, then Paul is exhorting them to enjoy meat privately (before God), not before weaker brothers, which would be tempting them to violate their consciences. Paul's words indicate no change of audience, so the addresses of both v 22ab and vv 22c-23 are weaker brothers.

The question for the weaker brother is to the point: **Do you have faith?** The intended answer is yes. The question concerns not saving faith, but faith regarding the eating or non-eating of meat.

Paul's command is to **have** this faith **by yourself** [i.e., personally and privately] **before God.**

The blessing here is to **the one who does not condemn** [or, *who does not judge, ho mē krinōn*] **himself *for the thing* which he treats as acceptable** [or, *in what he approves, en hō dokimazei* (from *dokimazō,* the verb form of *dokimos*, found in v 18)]. It is better, Paul says, not to eat certain foods or certain drinks if the result of that eating or drinking is that one has violated his own conscience.

Paul concludes his discussion of food and drink with a general statement that overarches the issue of dietary choices and weaker brothers: **And whatever *is* not by faith is sin.** In other words, the way in which we live the Christian life is by living out what God has impressed upon us from His Word (Rom 12:2; 2 Cor 3:18). If our actions are not *by faith*, that is, if our actions contradict what we believe the Scriptures teach, then they are sinful actions, not godly ones.

> **14:24-26. Now to the One who is able to establish you in accordance with my gospel and the message of Jesus Christ, in accordance with the revelation of the mystery *which was* kept silent through *past* eternal times, but now has been manifested, and has been made known to all the Gentiles through prophetic Scriptures in accordance with the command of the eternal God, to produce the obedience of faith—to God *who* alone *is* wise *be* glory forever through Jesus Christ. Amen.**

At this point the vast majority of Greek manuscripts of Romans contain three verses which the Critical Text reserves till the last three verses of the entire book. Not only is that reading not supported by the external evidence, but it is unlikely contextually that Paul would add a benediction after he gave his famous closing words, "The grace of our Lord Jesus Christ be with you all. Amen." In none of his other epistles where this saying occurs with an *Amen* are any other words given (i.e., Gal 6:18; Phil 4:23; 1 Thess 5:28; 2 Thess 3:18; Phlm 25). Only once, in 1 Cor 16:23-24, does Paul even add anything after this saying. But there no *Amen* appears with it. And what follows is short and is not a benediction: "my love be with you all in Christ Jesus. Amen."

The Hodges-Farstad *Greek New Testament According to the Majority Text* lists these three verses as Rom 14:24-26. In English translations, including the NKJV, which is somewhat based on the Majority Text, these verses appear as Rom 16:25-27.

This is a fitting conclusion to chap. 14 and Paul's admonition to show love to the weak. Treating other believers in a loving manner requires an ongoing focus on God, **the One who is able to establish** us (*stērixai* from *stērizō*). BDAG says of *stērizō* in this verse, "to cause to be inwardly firm or committed, *confirm, establish, strengthen*" (p. 945 #2).

Here Paul hearkens back to something he said in the opening verses of the letter. In Rom 1:11 he said, "I long to see you so that I may impart some spiritual benefit to you in order that you may be strengthened [*stērichthēnai* (from *stērizō*) *humas*]."

Believers are not guaranteed that they will please God. But they are guaranteed that God *is able* to cause them to please Him. If believers fail to please Him, the problem lies with them, not with a failure on God's part. Such strengthening/establishing comes from the teaching of the Word of God applied by the inner work of the Spirit of God to the lives of believers who are open to instruction (cf. Rom 12:1-2 and the discussion there).

Paul's readers knew this to be true based on Paul's gospel, **the message** [or preaching] **of Jesus Christ**, and based on **the mystery** [*mustērion*]. When Paul uses the expression *the mystery* he is referring to something not previously known. Specifically he is talking about the Church, the Body of Christ, made up of Jews and Gentiles united in one body, *which was* **kept silent through** *past* **eternal times.**[13]

The Church Age is a fulfillment of the **prophetic Scriptures.** Though without the further revelation of the NT one would not understand the OT texts which prophecy about the Church, such texts reveal that Gentiles would one day have a prominent God-honoring role in God's household. The Church is designed to be a God-honoring body, and to do so there must be unity and love.

Paul here repeats a phrase, **to produce the obedience of faith** (*eis hupakoēn pisteōs*), which he first presented in Rom 1:5 ("to bring about obedience by faith," Hodges' translation). See the discussion of that phrase there. The obedience which God desires to flow from faith in Christ includes, indeed is epitomized by, stronger brothers showing loving deference to weaker brothers.

After the prayer of vv 24-25, Paul ends this powerful chapter with a doxology. It is not uncommon for Paul to insert doxologies well before

---

[13] Hodges affirmed that the church was an unrevealed mystery in the OT (cf. Eph 3:5-6). That is, he believed that one reading the OT with a legitimate hermeneutic before the apostolic era would never conclude that God planned to create a new entity in which Gentiles and Jews would be equals with equal access to God. Even so, he sensed that a few OT passages (e.g., Psalm 45), when read through the lens of NT revelation, contained divinely intended references to the Church, but that these references were veiled in OT times. –RNW

the end of his letters (cf. Gal 1:5; Eph 3:20-21; 1 Tim 1:17). To **the eternal God...*who* alone is wise *be* glory forever through Jesus Christ**. Paul here sees ahead to the new earth. *Forever* we will bring *glory* to God *through Jesus Christ*. **Amen**.

The third and final part of Paul's discussion of God's will worked out in the lives of the delivered (15:1-13) is at hand. Delivered believers are to seek the glory of God in three ways, by accepting others as Christ has accepted us (15:1-7), by worshipping God (15:8-11), and by abounding in hope (15:12-13).

# Romans 15

3. Conclusion: Seeking the Glory of God (15:1-13)

    a. By Accepting Others as Christ Accepted Us (15:1-7)

**15:1. Now we who are strong ought to bear with the weaknesses of the weak and not to please ourselves.**

The apostle contrasts **we** [Paul includes himself] **who are strong** (*dunatoi*) with **the weak** (*adunatōn*). The two groups are strong and weak, direct opposites in terms of their scruples. *Dunatoi* and *adunatōn* could even have been translated as *we who are strong* and *the ones who are not strong.* The only difference in the Greek is the addition of the alpha prefix, which reverses the sense, something we do in English as well (e.g., atypical vs. typical).

Strong believers are enjoined **not to please** [*mē areskein*] themselves. (Of course, this injunction has general application well beyond the issue of eating and drinking. This is a great principle for marriage, sports teams, work, driving, neighborhoods, and all of life.) While there is nothing wrong with believers enjoying the things God has given us to enjoy (cf. 1 Tim 6:17), we must not stubbornly do so while knowingly injuring other believers in our church. The Lord Jesus does not want us using our freedom to hurt fellow believers.

That is what Paul means when he says that we **ought to bear with the weaknesses of the weak.** The way we do that is by freely giving up rights we have in order not to injure weaker brothers.

**15:2. Let each of us please his neighbor in what is good, to produce edification.**

Paul repeats the verb *areskē* from v 1. Rather than pleasing oneself, **each of us** is to **please** [*aresketō*, a third person imperative] **his neighbor in what is good**. Note that Paul does not say *let each of us please the Lord*... While that is certainly what we should do, in this case to please one's *neighbor* is also to please the Lord.

The *good* here might refer to the good of the neighbor (hence the NKJV supplies *his* before *good*) or it could refer to the good of the entire body (implied by Hodges' translation). The latter is most likely in view. The result of such selfless action is **edification** of the church body.

Of course, questions abound about how far we should go in application. For example, if I know there are believers in my church who believe it is wrong to drink wine, must I avoid drinking wine in the privacy of my own home for fear that they might come over and see a wine bottle in the house? If I know a fellow believer in my assembly considers it sinful to mow the lawn on Sunday, must I refrain for fear he might drive by and see me mowing my lawn? While Paul does not seek such detail, it is instructive that what Paul has in mind are situations where the weaker brother is directly present; that is, any time we are breaking bread together. We are not enjoined to live in fear that our *private actions* will hurt the weaker brother. We should simply make sure that we do not flaunt our liberty. So if we know the brother who thinks it is wrong to drink wine comes to our house, we should put the wine out of sight—not to be secretive, but to avoid offending.

In the early 1980s I was a young pastor. We had a New Year's Eve gathering at the home of one of the elders. The elder brought out wine and most people started drinking. I am a teetotaler and I was slightly bothered. Since they knew I did not drink, having come from an alcoholic family, I thought the hosts should have asked me whether I would rather they not drink wine in my presence. I've since been asked that many times at churches where I speak, since it is well known I don't drink. I always tell people that is fine with me if they drink. I am not tempted to drink when others around me do so. I know that the Bible does not forbid drinking. It only forbids drunkenness. But I'm pleased if people who know I'm a teetotaler take the time to ask.

**15:3. For even Christ did not please Himself, but as it has been written, "*The insults of the ones who insulted You fell on Me.*"**

The Lord Jesus Christ is Paul's prime example of one who **did not please Himself**. He lived to please God the Father. The OT quote is from Ps 68:9b (Ps 69:9b in English). The Greek Paul cites is identical to the LXX which we use today.

The first half of that verse is quite famous as well: "Zeal for Your house has eaten me [Me] up" (cf. John 2:17). The same Man who overturned the tables of the money changers in the temple as an expression of His zeal for the temple also willingly went to the cross. There He bore *"the insults"* [or reproaches] of men who were, in reality, angry with God the Father (cf. John 5:23, 43; 8:41-42, 48-49).

The two halves of Ps 69:9 illustrate the fact that our aim in life is to please God, not ourselves, and not even our neighbors per se. Now if pleasing the weaker brother pleases God, then we must please the weaker brother. But if pleasing the legalistic works-salvation advocate on their view of evangelism (by not voicing any objections to their view, or worse, even saying we find no fault in their approach) displeases the Lord, then we must turn over their tables and resist their efforts. There is really no contradiction between the Suffering Servant of Isaiah 53 and the Lion of Judah of Rev 5:5. Jesus overturned tables as the Lion of Judah. He went to the cross as the Suffering Servant.

> **15:4. In fact, whatever was written beforehand, was written beforehand to give us teaching, so that by means of the endurance and the encouragement *derived* from the Scriptures we might have hope.**

The OT Scriptures are in view in the expression **whatever was written beforehand**. Paul is not only thinking of prophetic Scriptures dealing with Christ's sufferings (v 3), though such texts are surely prominent in his thinking. He is thinking of all of the OT Scriptures (cf. 1 Cor 10:11). Of course, his words also apply to the NT writings which had already been written (e.g., James and Galatians) and to NT writings which had yet to be written as well.

The **hope** (or, *expectation*) of which Paul speaks is the certain expectation of the Second Coming of Christ and of the establishment of His kingdom. That *hope* can and should engender in the believer who is focused on it **endurance and encouragement** (cf. 1 Cor 9:24-27; 2 Tim 4:6-8). Of course, the Judgment Seat of Christ is not far from Paul's mind in what he is saying here (cf. Rom 14:10-12).

Though Paul does not elaborate, he might have written much about how the giants of the OT should spur us on to endurance. Hebrews 11, likely written by one of Paul's co-workers (Barnabas?), gives many examples. People like Abel, Enoch, Noah, Abraham, Moses, Rahab, Gideon, Samson, David, and Samuel all were examples of those who lived in expectation of eternal reward in the life to come. For example, of Moses we are told that he "refused to be called the son of Pharaoh's daughter, choosing rather to suffer affliction with the people of God than to enjoy the passing pleasure of sin, esteeming the reproach of Christ greater riches than the treasure in Egypt; for he looked to the reward" (Heb 11:24-26).

> **15:5-6. Now may the God of endurance and encouragement grant that you may have the same aspirations for one another in harmony with Christ Jesus, so that with united purpose you may glorify the God and Father of our Lord Jesus Christ with one voice.**

Paul launches into a prayer. He desires that **the God of endurance and encouragement** (cf. v 4) would grant the believers in Rome a common mindset (**the same aspirations for one another**), one that was **in harmony with Christ Jesus** (*kata Christon Iēsoun*). That in turn would result in a corporate glorification (*hina...doxazēte,* **so that...you may glorify**) of **the God and Father of our Lord Jesus Christ.**

The prepositional phrases **with united purpose** and **with one voice** actually occur together in the Greek text. While Hodges' translation is better English, a more wooden rendering of the Greek is actually: *so that with united purpose [homothumadon] with one voice [en heni stomati,* lit., *with one mouth] you may glorify God.* The major translations handle this in a great variety of ways, including, "so that with one accord you may with one voice..." (NASB), "so that with one heart and mouth you may glorify..." (NIV), "that together you may with one voice glorify..." (ESV, NET), "so that you may glorify the God and Father of our Lord Jesus Christ with a united mind and voice" (HCSB), and "that you may with one mind and one mouth glorify..." (NKJV). Paul's point is that corporate glorification of God occurs when believers are unified inwardly (*homothumadon*) and outwardly (*en heni stomati*). Compare Acts 1:14 and Acts 2:46-47 where *homothumadon* is joined with a speaking expression related to God (*praising God, ainountes ton Theon*).

**15:7. Therefore accept one another just as also Christ has accepted us, to the glory of God.**

The Majority Text is split here, with part reading *Christ has accepted you* [*humas*] and part reading **Christ has accepted us** [*hēmas*, NKJV, Hodges's translation]. The acceptance (or reception) in view is a bit vague. What does Paul mean when he says that *Christ has accepted* [*proslambanō*] *us?*

This is the only place in the NT which specifically refers to *Christ* having accepted (or received) us. In Rom 14:3 Paul says "God has accepted him"; that is, God has accepted the believer who believes it is acceptable to eat meat.) See the discussion there. Apart from those two places in Romans, we do not find any other references in Scripture to Christ or God accepting people. Of course *the concept is found throughout the NT, just not the actual wording* (e.g., John 3:16-18, 36; 5:24; 6:35-40; 11:25-26; Eph 2:8-9; Titus 3:5).

*Christ has accepted us* probably refers to the fact that He has died for us and given us everlasting life in spite of the fact that prior to our new birth we were "not only 'powerless' (5:6, lit., 'weak') but also 'ungodly' (5:6), 'sinners' (5:8), and 'enemies' (5:10)" (John A. Witmer, "Romans," in *The Bible Knowledge Commentary*, NT Edition, p. 495).

It is important to distinguish between Christ's *acceptance* and His *approval*. He *accepts* all believers. But He only *approves* of those believers who are walking in the truth (cf. Rom 16:10; 1 Cor 11:19; 2 Cor 10:18; 13:6-7; 2 Tim 2:15).

The same verb, *proslambanō*, was also used by Paul in Rom 14:1. There Paul called for the strong *to accept* the weak, evidently at the Lord's Supper meeting. See the discussion there.

Here Paul extends the call to all believers to **accept one another.** While this certainly applies contextually to the matter of eating and drinking, it has more general application regarding any non-essential matters (e.g., facial hair or no facial hair, tattoos, jewelry, women wearing slacks).

Paul does not mean that we should accept one another when a fellow believers has departed *on an essential issue*, whether moral (e.g., unrepentant immorality) or doctrinal (e.g., denial of the deity of Christ). We must be united in the essentials. But in non-essentials there is to be liberty.

## b. By Worshipping God (15:8-11)

**15:8-9. Now I say that Christ Jesus has become a minister to the circumcised on behalf of the truth of God so that *He* might confirm the promises made to the fathers, and *so that* the Gentiles might glorify God for His mercy, just as it is written: "For this reason I will acknowledge You among the Gentiles, and sing praise to Your name."**

The glory of God is achieved as Gentiles and Jews together worship God within the Church.

**Christ Jesus has become a minister to the circumcised** in the sense that He taught and helped the house of Israel during His earthly ministry and His apostles continued that ministry. He and His apostles shared **the truth of God** with Israel for two reasons: **so that *He* might confirm the** OT **promises made to the fathers and *so that* the Gentiles might glorify God for His mercy.**

Jesus often pointed out that what He said and did was a fulfillment of OT promises (cf. Matt 12:40; 15:1-20; 21:42; 22:44; 26:31; John 5:39-47; 6:31-51, 58; 19:28).

The reference to *the Gentiles* (or nations) *glorifying God for His mercy* as a result of Jesus' ministry is Paul's recognition that Jesus' ministry had as a secondary purpose to prepare the way for the birth and development of the Church, with Jews and Gentiles together in one body.

The OT quotation is found in two separate texts, 2 Sam 22:50 and Ps 18:49 (17:49 LXX). The citation is identical to our LXX today with one minor exception: our current version of the LXX has *Lord* (*Kurie*) after *"I will acknowledge You"* in both texts.

The references to *You* and *Your* in these OT citations are Messianic. Paul and the other apostles confessed the Messiah among the Gentiles and sang praises to His name wherever they went.

**15:10. And again it says: "Rejoice, O Gentiles, along with His people."**

This quotation is from a portion of Deut 32:43. The form is identical to our LXX today. The remainder of that verse goes on to say that "He will avenge the blood of His sons, and He will render vengeance and recompense justice to His enemies, and will reward them that hate Him;

and the Lord shall cleanse the land of His people" (translation of LXX). Whether Moses expected that fulfillment in his lifetime, or knew it would be future, this has not happened yet. In the Tribulation God will avenge the slain saints of all eras. He will deliver His people Israel (Rom 11:26). He will recompense those who hate Him with terrifying temporal judgments. He will purge the land of His people.

The rejoicing the Gentiles should and will do *"along with His people* [Israel]*"* will be during the eternal reign of Jesus, starting with the Millennium and continuing forever on the new earth (Revelation 21–22).

Paul applies this verse to the present. If Gentiles will one day rejoice with Jews in the kingdom, believing Gentiles should also rejoice with believing Jews today within the Church.

### 15:11. And again: "Praise the Lord, all you Gentiles, and extol Him, all you peoples."

Here Paul quotes verbatim from the LXX translation of the shortest Psalm (Ps 117:1; 116:1 LXX). It too shows that Gentiles and Jews were to **praise the Lord.** While the ultimate fulfillment of Psalm 117 looks ahead to the Millennium and the new earth, it was applicable in the Mosaic economy and it is applicable in the Church Age.

Paul now shifts from speaking about glorifying God by worshipping Him (15:8-11) to glorifying Him by abounding in expectation of the coming kingdom.

### c. By Abounding in Hope (15:12-13)

### 15:12. And again, Isaiah says: "There shall be a root from Jesse, and One who will arise to rule the Gentiles; in Him the Gentiles will put their hope."

Paul ends his concatenation of OT citations with Isa 11:10, a Messianic prophecy. The Greek in lines two and three is identical to the LXX today. The first line omits the words "in that day" (*en tē hēmera ekeinē*) which come after *"There shall be"* and before *"a root from Jesse."* The sense is the same.

Paul cites this text in order to remind his readers that Jesus is "*a* [or the] *root from Jesse"* and that He *"will arise to rule the Gentiles."* The *"hope"* of the Gentiles spoken of here is the *"expectation"* of the establishment by

Messiah of His righteous kingdom when He soon returns. The Gentile believers in Rome had that expectation. By abounding in that hope (v 13) they would glorify God.

> **15:13. Now may the God of hope fill you with all joy and peace as you are believing, so that you may abound with hope by the power of the Holy Spirit.**

**The God of hope** probably refers to God the Father, since Jesus is mentioned in v 12 and the Spirit at the end of this verse, thus bringing in all three members of the Trinity. Paul either means that God the Father is the One who gives us hope, or He is the One who is the object of our hope. The latter is intended. We are to have great expectation for God's promise that Jesus will return soon.

The prayer is that *the God of hope* would fill the readers **with all joy and peace as** they **are believing**. *Joy and peace* are directly linked only one other time in the NT, Rom 14:17, "For the kingdom of God is not food and drink, but righteousness and peace and joy in the Holy Spirit." As we believe, *joy and peace* should be the immediate result.

When believers are filled with *all joy and peace as* they *are believing*, the extended result is that they **may abound with hope by the power of the Holy Spirit.** This repetition of *hope* within the same sentence shows that God is not only the object of our expectation, but that He, that is the Holy Spirit, also enables that same expectation. We can only abound in this hope *by the power of the Holy Spirit*.

The exact expression *by the power of the Holy Spirit* (*en dunamei Pneumatos Hagiou*) occurs only here in the NT. (The Majority Text of Rom 15:19 reads *en dunamei Pneumatos Theou*.) However, we know from other texts that the Holy Spirit enables believers to understand and apply God's Word (cf. Luke 24:32, 45; Acts 6:3; 7:51; 9:31; 11:24). He does this for all who are open and responsive to the truth they have already received. Thus if a believer seeks out a solid Bible-teaching church, he will regularly hear about Jesus' imminent return and the Judgment Seat of Christ. That teaching, if believed, will result in *joy and peace* and in the Holy Spirit producing abundant expectation of Christ's soon return.

The body of the letter ends with a powerful focus on the work of the Spirit in the lives of believers in producing abundant hope, that is, attention upon the soon return of the Lord Jesus.

IV. Conclusion: Final Remarks To The Roman
Christians (15:14–16:20)

A. Paul's Role in the Gentile World (15:14-21)

**15:14. Now my brothers, I am personally persuaded about you that you yourselves are full of goodness, filled with all knowledge, competent also to admonish others.**

Paul begins his discussion of his role in the Gentile world by expressing his confidence (**I am personally persuaded,** *epeismai*, from *peithō*) that his spiritual brothers, the readers, **are full of goodness.** Paul, in his epistles, often after giving commands or even serious correction, follows with a statement about his positive expectations for the readers (cf. 2 Cor 2:3; Gal 5:10; 2 Thess 3:4). What he has written in 12:1–15:13 in no way was meant to discourage the readers or to give the impression that he doubted their intentions or even their spiritual maturity. It is spiritual believers who are **competent also to admonish others.**

*Admonishing* is a counseling word, *noutheteō.* We get the expression *nouthetic counseling* from this word. *Noutheteō* only occurs eight times in the NT, seven of the eight times in Paul's writings (Rom 15:14; 1 Cor 4:14; Col 1:28; 3:16; 1 Thess 5:12, 14; 2 Thess 3:15) and the final one in the recorded words of Paul in Acts 20:31. Selter comments on this term in relation to counseling in the church:

> Admonition as a form of spiritual counseling is (in addition to apostles and church leaders) also the task of the whole church towards one another (Col. 3:16), provided that it is spiritually fit to do so like the church at Rome (Rom. 15:14).[1]

BDAG says that *noutheteō* means, "to counsel about avoidance or cessation of an improper course of *conduct, admonish, warn, instruct* with accusative of person(s)" (p. 679). In most if not all of its uses, the Judgment Seat of Christ is either explicitly or implicitly in view. Believers are warned that their present behavior will directly impact their eternal rewards.

Only spiritual believers are *competent...to admonish others* (cf. 1 Cor 2:14-16; Gal 6:1; Acts 20:31, directed to the Ephesian elders). And they

---

[1] *NIDNTT*, 1:569. –RNW.

are to do so with a spirit of humility, knowing that they too might fail (cf. Eph 6:1).

That they have been **filled with all knowledge** suggests that Paul knows they are well grounded in the Word and in sound doctrine.

> **15:15-16. And I have written very boldly to you, brothers (in part, to refresh your memories), because of the grace that has been given to me by God, that I should be a priestly minister of Jesus Christ for the Gentiles, serving as a priest with the gospel of God, so that the offering up of the Gentiles, sanctified by the Holy Spirit, might be acceptable.**

Paul knows he has **written very boldly**, or daringly, on some points (**in part**), to the **brothers**[2] in Rome, so as **to refresh** their **memories**. Of what? Paul does not say. Probably he has in mind the theme of the letter, deliverance from God's wrath by holding fast their confession of Christ.

Paul does state *why* he gave the reminder: **because of the grace** [or favor] **that has been given to me by God, that I should be a priestly minister of Jesus Christ for the Gentiles.** Paul here refers to his authority. Then he goes on to state, in OT sacrificial terms, the intended aim of his reminder.

In the OT the priests handled the sacrifices and the Levites assisted them by taking care of the temple and its surroundings. Some have suggested that Paul is alluding not to the work of a priest here, but to the work of the Levite who assists the priest. In this view Jesus is the priest and Paul is the one assisting Him.

More likely, Paul is figuratively referring to himself as a priest (obviously under the High Priest, Jesus Christ) who handles not animal

---

[2] Paul's epistles use eighty-three vocative plurals. Seventy-nine designate readers as believers: seventy-one uses of *adelphoi, brothers* (Rom 1:13; 7:1, 4; 8:12; 10:1; 11:25; 12:1; 15:14-15, 30; 16:17; 1 Cor 1:10-11, 26; 2:1; 3:1; 4:6; 7:24, 29; 10:1; 11:2, 33; 12:1; 14:6, 20, 26, 39; 15:1, 50, 58; 16:15; 2 Cor 1:8; 8:1; 13:11; Gal 1:11; 3:15; 4:12, 28, 31; 5:11, 13; 6:1, 18; Eph 6:10; Phil 1:12; 3:1, 13, 17; 4:1, 8; 1 Thess 1:4; 2:1, 9, 14, 17; 3:7; 4:1, 10, 13; 5:1, 4, 12, 14, 25; 2 Thess 1:3; 2:1, 13, 15; 3:1, 6, 13); seven of *agapētoi, beloved* (Rom 12:19; 1 Cor 10:14; 15:58; 2 Cor 7:1; 12:19; Phil 2:12; 4:1), and one of *teknia, little children* (Gal 4:19).

Paul's other vocative plurals are: *Gentiles* (Rom 15:10); *Corinthians* (2 Cor 6:11); *foolish Galatians* (Gal 3:1); and *Philippians* in Phil 4:15.

Seventy-two of his vocatives involve *brethren* or *little children*. Both derive their meaning from regeneration. The fact that God is our Father makes believers brothers. Cf. Jas 1:18 and Heb 2:11. –JHN

sacrifices, but **the gospel of God**. The expression *the gospel of God* is a relatively rare one. Of the seventy-seven NT uses of *euangelion* (most of which are unmodified), this is one of only seven references to *the gospel of God* (cf. Rom 1:1). Almost twice as common is "the gospel of [Jesus] Christ," occurring thirteen times (cf. Rom 1:16; 15:19).

Paul is evidently thinking of the good news that those who faithfully serve God are delivered from His wrath (Rom 1:16-17; 5:9-10; 10:9-10).

The intended result of Paul's *priestly* handling of *the gospel of God* is **so that the offering up of the Gentiles, sanctified by the Holy Spirit, might be acceptable** to God. The believers in Rome were not bringing animal sacrifices. Their *offering* was their very lives (Rom 12:1-2). Paul's reminder is designed to ensure that their *offering* would *be acceptable, sanctified* (or set apart) *by the Holy Spirit.*[3]

This priestly ministry of the gospel is set by Paul within a Trinitarian context. Note his references to God the Father, Jesus Christ, and the Holy Spirit in vv 15-16.

### 15:17. Therefore I have reason for exaltation in Christ Jesus in things related to God.

Paul had reason for exaltation (*kauchēsis* = exaltation, boast; BDAG, 537#1, says, "acts of taking pride in something, *boasting*"). That reason was sourced in Christ Jesus in things related to God.

His ground for boasting was not based on something inherently praiseworthy in him. It was based on *things* pertaining or related *to God*. Paul saw his ministry as God working through him.

The theme of boasting about those to whom he had ministered is one found often in Paul's epistles using *kauchēsis* (2 Cor 1:12; 7:4, 14; 8:24; 9:4; 1 Thess 2:19). While Paul is clear that God gave him this ministry and gave him the power to fulfill it, he also boasted about it since he worked hard (cf. 2 Tim 2:6). Paul joined in Christ's sufferings as he ministered to people as he lays out so clearly when he boasts in 2 Cor 11:22-33 (*kauchēsis* is found in 11:10, 17).

It is an error for believers to speak as though all they have done for Christ is solely their own labor, with no help from the Lord. But it is also

---

[3] The churches in Rome had apparent stratification between Jews and Gentiles. See the introduction. Roman Christianity needed to recognize that Jewish and Gentile believers are brothers with a common Father, God. Such a truth might prevent a recurrence of the problem of divisions in the church of Corinth (cf. 1 Cor 1:10–4:21). –JHN

wrong to act super spiritual and to claim that we had nothing to do with it, that it was simply the Lord using us like marionettes. If we were not to take any credit for our ministries, then Paul could not boast about his ministry.

In the next four verses Paul continues to discuss the ministry that Christ accomplished through him.

> **15:18-19. For I will not dare to speak about any *of the things* that Christ has not accomplished through me to produce obedience by the Gentiles, *whether* by word and deed, *or* by the power of signs and wonders, *or* by the power of the Spirit of God, with the result that I have completed *the spread of* the gospel of Christ from Jerusalem and all around as far as Illyricum.**

The same verb Paul used in v 15 ("Now I have written *daringly* to you") appears again here (*tolmaō*). Paul would write *daringly* about the work of God, but he would **not dare to speak about** anything other than **the things** that **Christ** had worked through him.

Paul includes both his words and his deeds (**by word and deed** [or work]). The phrase **to produce obedience by the Gentiles** is similar to "the obedience of faith" found in 1:5 and 16:26 (14:25 MajT and Hodges' translation). Paul's words and deeds had been used by God *to produce obedience by the Gentiles*, but Paul dared not claim this as something he did independently of Christ.

This obedience was facilitated **by the power of signs and wonders**[4] which Paul did **by the power of the Spirit of God** (cf. 15:13). In Acts Luke tells us about many of the *signs and wonders* God accomplished through Paul (and Peter). For example, in Lystra, Paul healed a man who had been lame from birth (Acts 14:8-10). In Philippi, he cast a spirit of divination out of a slave girl (Acts 16:16-18). In Corinth, Paul healed many who were sick and cast out many who were demon-possessed (Acts 19:11-12). He restored Eutychus to life after he fell from a third story window in Troas (Acts 20:9-12). And on the island of Malta Paul suffered no ill effects from

---

[4] The OT set forth expectations that both God's prophets and His Messiah would do signs. First Corinthians 1:22 says, "Jews request a sign, and Greeks seek after wisdom," often leading people to infer that signs only pertained to Jews. Not so. Even though Gentiles did not seek for signs from God, He used signs to cause both Jews and Gentiles to obey the command to believe in Jesus Christ. –JHN

being bitten by a deadly viper and he healed many people there (Acts 28:3-9). In each case the *signs and wonders* validated his evangelistic preaching.

The contemporary charismatic movement suggests that God still wants to validate our preaching with signs and wonders. However, the NT shows that the sign gifts for the Church Age ended by the end of the ministry of the apostles (cf. Eph 2:20; 2 Tim 4:20). We do not need signs and wonders today since those have already been given during the ministry of Jesus and of His apostles. The same was true in the OT, when there were only a few brief periods of signs and wonders (e.g., Moses and Aaron, Enoch and Elijah). Signs and wonders have never been a normative experience either in Israel or in the Church. (Of course, after the church is raptured, signs and wonders will be part of the ministry of the two witnesses during the first half of the Tribulation.)

The result of the signs and wonders Christ accomplished through Paul is that he **completed** [or *fulfilled, plēroō*] **the spread of the gospel of Christ**. The NKJV translates *plēroō* here as "fully preached," but Paul could have used a word that means *preaching* if he intended that. Instead Paul is thinking, as Hodges' translation suggests, of the fact that he fulfilled *the gospel of Christ*. He might mean that there is a potential in Christ's gospel which he released. Paul, after all, saw the gospel as powerful (cf. Rom 1:16). Or, more likely, Paul means that he *fulfilled the gospel of Christ* in the sense that he spread the message far and wide, as Hodges' translation suggests.

Paul's gospel ministry extended **from Jerusalem**, the heart of Judaism, **and all around as far as Illyricum** (which today consists of parts of Albania, Croatia, and Bosnia & Herzegovina). There is no other NT reference of Paul having gone to this region, unless this refers to the portion of Macedonia where people from Illyricum settled.

> **15:20-21. And *I have done*** so having an ambition to proclaim the gospel where Christ was not named, so that I might not build on another person's foundation, but instead as it is written: "They to whom nothing about Him had been announced shall see, and they who had not heard shall understand."

Paul's **ambition** was **to proclaim the gospel** (or *to evangelize*, since this is the verb *euangelizō*, unlike v 19 which has the noun *euangelion*), but he had a specific aim in terms of the sphere of his evangelistic efforts. He wanted *to proclaim the gospel* in places **where Christ was not named**.

That expression either refers to areas where Jesus Christ was unknown or to areas where no one was confessing Him and calling upon Him in worship. Most commentators adopt the latter position. However, in light of the quote from Isa 52:12 which Paul gives (see discussion below), the former is probably true. In either case, Paul's point is that he wants to plant churches in areas where there are none. In this foundational stage of the Church Age (Eph 2:20), it was vital that the apostles did much of the heavy lifting in ministry.

Paul considered this important **so that** he **might not build on another person's foundation**. He cites Isa 52:15b in support of this *ambition* (again quoting the LXX). Clearly, in order to fulfill this text, those evangelizing had to go where no man had gone before. Paul felt it was his task, as Apostle to the Gentiles, to move from place to place evangelizing and planting churches. He did not look for a place to settle down.

Many modern missionary endeavors have followed this plan. As long as there are still people groups who have not heard the gospel, reaching them is rightly a priority in world evangelization.

Paul is not suggesting he would not and did not visit already existing churches. In Romans 1 he indicates his long-held desire to visit the various assemblies in Rome (cf. Rom 1:8-15). In the section immediately following (i.e., in 15:22-33), he announces his plan to visit the churches in Rome soon. Yet none of the churches in Rome had been planted by Paul. And in his very early ministry he visited and ministered in churches planted by others (e.g., Acts 13:1-2). But Paul's *modus operandi* was to evangelize where the locals had not yet heard about Christ.

B. Paul's Plan to Visit Rome (15:22-33)

**15:22. This is also why I have been hindered many times from coming to you.**

Paul had similarly indicated at the start of the letter, "Now I don't want you to be uninformed, brothers, that many times I have planned to come to you (and have been prevented until now) so that I might have some fruit among you also, just as I have had among the rest of the Gentiles" (Rom 1:13). Here near the end of the letter he takes the time to give more details.

A major reason **why** Paul had **been hindered many times from coming to** Rome was because of his missionary efforts thus far. The phrase **This is also** translates *Dio*, which could also be translated *Therefore*. It is likely that he intends the reader to understand that since there already was a strong gospel presence in Rome, he first went to places where there was no such presence (cf. vv 23-24).

> **15:23-24. But now, since I no longer have *any* room in these regions, and since I have had a desire for many years to come to you, whenever I go to Spain I will come to you. For I hope to see you as I pass through and to be assisted by you on my trip there, provided that first I am at least partially filled up with your company.**

Since his work **in the other regions** (Paul was writing from Corinth in Greece and likely has Greece and Asia Minor in mind) is now on solid footing (**I no longer have any room**), Paul now believes that the Lord will open the way for him to visit them when he journeys **to Spain.**

There is no reason to think that Paul had limited knowledge of the extent of the Roman Empire of his day. Paul was very well educated and well-traveled. He was not saying that there was nowhere in the entire Roman Empire (e.g., Britain, India, Africa) that was yet un-evangelized. He is simply saying that he has fulfilled his calling of planting churches in Greece and Asia Minor.

Paul's **desire** to minister in Rome has lasted **for many years**. He expresses here a desire for their material support (**and to be assisted by you on my trip there**), something he also does in his other epistles (cf. 1 Cor 9:1-18; 2 Cor 8-9; Phil 4:14-17). While Paul often ministered without support from the places in which he worked (cf. 1 Cor 9:1-23; Phil 4:15; 2 Thess 3:7-9), he would ask for support when he was convinced it was appropriate. He expects to enjoy his time with them (i.e., to be **filled up**). Paul found great joy in teaching and having fellowship with other believers.

> **15:25. But right now I am going to Jerusalem to serve the saints *there.***

His expected journey to Spain and Rome will not be immediate, however. Paul informs them that first he is **going to Jerusalem to serve** [or, *minister to*] **the saints *there*.** As the apostle to the Gentiles, Paul had many concerns and priorities. Though his ministry was primarily to Gentiles and to planting churches where Christ had not been named, he certainly wished to maintain good ties with the Jerusalem church as well.

As the next verses show, Paul's ministry to *the saints* in Jerusalem included a financial gift to them from the Gentile churches (cf. Acts 24:17; 1 Cor 16:1-4; 2 Corinthians 8-9). Earlier in his ministry Paul had also taken a financial gift to Jerusalem from the Gentile churches (cf. Acts 11:27-30; 12:25; Gal 2:10b). Of course, he certainly would have edified them as well by telling them of the fruit of his ministry among the Gentiles.

The word *saints* (*hagioi*) refers not to super believers as many employ it today. For Paul *all believers* are saints in their position (cf. Rom 1:7; 8:27; 12:13; 15:26, 31; 16:2, 15). Saints are those who have been *set apart* into God's family, the household of faith (Gal 6:10). When Paul wishes to speak of believers who have distinguished themselves in service, he calls them *approved* (e.g., Rom 16:10), *fellow workers in Christ Jesus* (Rom 16:3), those *who are of note among the apostles* (Rom 16:7), and other such expressions.

> **15:26. For Macedonia and Achaia have been pleased to make a certain contribution to the poor among the saints who are in Jerusalem.**

**For** (*gar*) is explanatory. Verse 26 explains v 25. Paul is going to serve the believers in Jerusalem by bringing a financial gift from the churches in **Macedonia and Achaia.**

The word translated **contribution** is *koinōnia*, often translated as *fellowship*. But it is sometimes used in contexts where the fellowship in question is a financial sharing in the work of ministry. Paul uses *koinōnia* in this same way in Phil 1:5-6. Giving to the ministry or needs of other believers is a sharing in their Christian lives, a sharing that has eternal significance (cf. Matt 6:19-21; Phil 4:17).

The Gentile believers in *Macedonia and Achaia* had **been pleased** [or, thought it good, *eudokeō*] **to make a certain contribution to the poor among the** Jewish believers *in Jerusalem*, which underscores the fact that compassion crossed ethnic lines in the Body of Christ (cf. Gal 2:10).

While Paul certainly promoted this giving to the church in Jerusalem (cf. 1 Cor 16:1-4; 2 Corinthians 8–9), the contribution was nonetheless a free-will offering as suggested by *eudokeō*. Paul did not twist any arms. He merely encouraged the believers who already wished to make such a gift to follow through with their intentions (e.g., 2 Cor 8:10-11).

**15:27. Indeed they have been pleased, and they are debtors to them.** **For if the Gentiles have shared in their spiritual *benefits*, they also are under obligation to render priestly service to them in *their* physical *concerns*.**

The believers in the churches of Macedonia and Achaia were mainly **Gentiles**. The believers in the church of Jerusalem were mainly Jews. Since the Christian message went forth from Jerusalem, all of the Gentile churches in a sense owe their very lives and growth to the Jewish believers in Jerusalem.

**They have been pleased** (*Eudokēsan*) is an exact repetition from v 26. Similarly, Paul uses the verbal cognate to *koinōnia* (*koinōneō*) found in v 26 when he says, **the Gentiles have shared in their spiritual *benefits*.**

**Physical *concerns*** (*sarkikois*) here refers to material possessions. Its use here lacks the negative connotations of that term in 1 Cor 3:1, where it refers to fleshly-minded (or carnal) people.

Paul is here using a variation of his teaching in Gal 6:6 ("Let him who is taught the word share in all good things with him who teaches"). In this case, though the believers in Jerusalem did not directly teach the believers in Macedonia and Achaia, they are worthy of their support since they indirectly sent Paul and his team.

Of course, when Gentile believers aided the Jewish believers in Jerusalem, they strengthened the unity in the Body of Christ. When believers manifest the love of God to one another, they are fulfilling Paul's earlier injunction, "Owe no one anything except to love one another. For the one who loves another has fulfilled the law" (Rom 13:8).

**15:28. So when I have completed this *task* and have sealed to them this fruit, I shall go by way of you to Spain.**

Paul's plan to come to the believers in Rome is so firm that he speaks of it as a certainty, **I shall go by way of you to Spain.** After he goes to Jerusalem with the gift, he plans to head out for Rome, and then to Spain. Most likely he is not speaking prophetically here (cf. vv 22-24). He is merely expressing his firm intention.

Here Paul returns to the point with which he began this section (vv 22-24). After he has finished the task at hand—the giving of the gift—and after he has sealed (*sphragizomai*) this fruit, then he will travel to Rome.

Commentators are puzzled by Paul's choice of *sphragizomai* here. We might expect Paul to speak of *delivering the fruit* or something of that nature. While there is much speculation as to what this means, the point is clear enough for those who believe in the doctrine of eternal rewards as distinguished from the doctrine of justification by faith alone. While the idea of *sealing fruit* occurs only here in the NT, the idea of *sealing* is fairly common (fifteen uses in the Majority Text). The tomb where Jesus was buried was sealed, indicating that it was carefully *secured* by the Roman authorities (Matt 27:66). Believers have been sealed with the Holy Spirit, meaning that their eternal destinies are *secure* (Eph 1:13; 4:30). Sealing conveys *security*. Thus fruit which has been *sealed* means that once Paul completes this gift, then the future eternal reward for the believers in Macedonia and Achaia for what they did in this matter will be guaranteed. There is a clear allusion to the Judgment Seat of Christ here (cf. Phil 1:22; 4:17; see also Matt 6:19-21).

### 15:29. And I know that when I come to you, I will come in the fullness of the blessing of the gospel of Christ.

As in the previous verse, Paul reiterates his conviction: **I know…I will come to you**. On his trip to Jerusalem he was bearing material blessings to the believers there. When he comes to Rome he **will come in the fullness of the blessing of the gospel of Christ**.

*The gospel of Christ* is the good news about Him, including His death and resurrection and His soon return to establish His righteous kingdom (cf. Rom 1:1-6, 16-17; 2:16; 16:25). Paul began this epistle expressing his desire to proclaim to the church in Rome (Rom 1:15), *the gospel*, which is a message of blessing for the obedient believer. Paul emphasizes *the blessing* by speaking of *the fullness of the blessing of the gospel of Christ*.

*The gospel* is a rich spiritual blessing capable of providing *fullness* of blessings to believers. If believers take *the gospel of Christ* to heart and live each day in light of it, then they will be delivered from God's temporal wrath; they will be fulfilling their purpose on earth of glorifying God; and they will be well prepared for the Lord's soon return and the Judgment Seat of Christ.

**15:30-32. Now I urge you, brothers, by our Lord Jesus Christ and by the love of the Spirit, that you contend along with me in *your* prayers for me to God, that I might be delivered from those in Judea who don't believe and that my ministry to Jerusalem might be acceptable to the saints, so that I might come to you with joy by the will of God and *that I might* find rest with you.**

Paul ends his discussion of his proposed trip to visit them with an appeal that they pray for him. The word translated **that you contend along with** is *sunagōnizomai*. It is a term that speaks of mutual work. Prayer, according to Paul, is not a passive activity. It is work. Compare Col 4:12 where the same verb is used without the *sun-* (with) prefix: "*laboring fervently [agōnizomai] for you in prayers*."

Paul's concern is fourfold. First, he is disturbed about **those in Judea who do not believe**. The words translated *those who do not believe* are *tōn apeithountōn*. They can also be translated *the disobedient ones*. In this context, as John 3:36 shows (where the same word is used), the disobedience in view is a failure to believe in Jesus for everlasting life. Compare Rom 11:31. Paul wishes prayers so that he **might be delivered from** unbelieving Jews in Judea. Most likely in view is his health, his freedom from imprisonment, and his life itself.

Second, he desires prayer that his **ministry to Jerusalem might be acceptable** [*euprosdektos*] **to the saints**. *Euprosdektos* is also used in Rom 15:16 concerning the offering of Gentiles being acceptable. Here it is used "with the dative of the one to whom something is acceptable" (BDAG, p. 411 #1). Compare 2 Cor 8:12 where Paul speaks of God *accepting* gifts that are given willingly. Paul wants the believers in Rome to pray that his ministry in Jerusalem will be maximally effective in building up the saints in the church of Jerusalem.

Third, he also wishes them to strive in their **prayers** concerning his proposed trip to Rome. He asks them to pray that he **may come to** them **with joy by the will of God**. He knows that his visit depends on the will of God (cf. Jas 4:13). His life is in God's hands. And he can only come *with joy* if his ministry in Jerusalem is effective.

Fourth, he asks for prayer that he *might* **find rest with** them. In other words, he wants them to pray that his visit to Rome results in mutual refreshment, encouragement, and edification (cf. Rom 1:11-12).

**15:33. Now may the God of peace be with you all. Amen.**

Paul ends with a prayer of his own, a prayer that **the God of peace** might **be with** them **all**. Paul uses the expression *the God of peace* one other time in this letter (Rom 16:20) and three times in his other letters (2 Cor 13:11; Phil 4:9; 1 Thess 5:23). What Paul desires for the church in Rome is the blessing of God upon them.

Cranfield goes too far when he suggests, "Here in the present verse it [the expression *the God of peace*] probably signifies the sum of all true blessings, *including final salvation*" (*Romans*, Vol. 2: 780, italics added). The moment a person believes, he is eternally secure (John 5:24; 6:35; Rom 3:21–4:25; 8:31-39). The believers in Rome needed no prayers from Paul regarding their eternal destiny (which is what Cranfield means by the expression *final salvation*). However, Cranfield is correct that Paul desires for God to shower them with "the sum of all true blessings."

# Romans 16

## C. Paul's Commendation of Phoebe (16:1-2)

**16:1-2. Now I commend to you Phoebe our sister, who is a deaconess of the church which is in Cenchrea, so that you may welcome her in the Lord *in a way* worthy of the saints, and make yourselves available to her in whatever matter she may need you, inasmuch as she herself has been a patroness to many and even to me.**

Evidently Phoebe is the bearer of the letter from Paul to the Romans. The word translated **a deaconess** (*diakonos*) can also be translated *a servant, an agent,* or even *a courier.* At the least Paul means that Phoebe served well in the church in Cenchrea (the eastern port of Corinth). He probably also means that she was the courier of the letter as his following instructions concerning her suggest.

Paul wants the church to **welcome** [or receive] **her in the Lord *in a way* worthy of the saints.** That is, they were to house her, feed her, show her warm hospitality, and send her on her way with provisions. They were to assist her (lit. *stand with her*) **in whatever matter she may need** help from the believers in Rome. She deserves such treatment because **she has proved to be a patroness** [or, *helper*] **to many and even to** Paul.

## D. Paul's Greetings to the Roman Christians (16:3-16)

**16:3-5a. Greet Priscilla and Aquila, my fellow workers in Christ Jesus, who have risked their own necks for my life, to whom not only I am thankful, but also all the churches of the Gentiles; and *greet* the church that is in their house.**

See the introduction for comments on the tenement churches and on the greetings of Romans 16.

Paul in vv 3-16 is evidently listing every single house church or tenement church in the church of Rome in which he knows someone. Fifteen times he uses the verb **greet**. Most likely these are structural indications that there were fifteen small churches in Rome of which Paul was aware of at least some of the members. Most likely there were more churches than that.

The size of most of these churches was probably ten or so people. One family would have church in the tiny room in which they lived, possibly convincing a few friends, family, or neighbors to worship with them.

Possibly a few of these were big enough that we might call them *house churches*. Those churches might have had twenty or more members.

Paul lists twenty-six names and mentions the mother (v 13) and sister (v 15) of two of those named. While we cannot be certain how many total people were in the fifteen assemblies that Paul is greeting here, it surely was a small number by today's megachurch standards. Most likely the church in Rome, counting all of its house and tenement churches, had fewer than one thousand members.[1]

The first people he mentions are **Priscilla[2] and Aquila**, whom he calls **my fellow workers in Christ Jesus.** He mentions the wife first. This puzzles many commentators since the normal style of the day was to mention the husband first. Various suggestions are made as to why Paul does this. Possibly Priscilla came to faith before her husband and may even have led him to faith. Or it is conceivable that her ministry in service for Christ was greater than that of her husband. Jewett suggests that "[t]he precedence of the female name in Rom 16:3 appears to reflect Paul's knowledge of a Roman perception of Prisca's higher [social] status

---

[1] Hodges told me on one occasion that he believed the church in Rome likely had around fifty to seventy-five members based on the people Paul greets in Rom 16:3-16. He felt that idea of mega churches, while not forbidden by Scripture, was not consistent with the NT pattern and was not something to strive after. However, a few years ago Hodges was influenced by Jewett's commentary on Romans and concluded there were fifteen or more house or tenement churches, at a minimum. That would mean at least one hundred fifty people, but possibly one thousand or more if there were lots of house and tenement churches in which Paul knew no one to greet. –RNW

[2] The Greek is literally *Prisca* (*Priska*), not *Priscilla* (*Priskilla*, Acts 18:2), here. However, Hodges chose to translate it as *Priscilla* since this is clearly the wife of Aquila. *Prisca* is merely a more formal version of Priscilla, which is a diminutive (like *Lynnette* or *Jeannette* as compared with *Lynn* or *Jean*). –RNW

[than Aquila], a perception that was not present in Ephesus or Corinth, as reflected in 1 Cor 16:19."[3] Possibly, Paul's mention of her first is merely stylistic. Paul mentions this couple three times in his letters, twice listing her first (here and 2 Tim 4:19) and once listing him first (1 Cor 16:19). In addition Paul's ministry partner Luke mentions him first (Acts 18:26). Paul commends them in that they **risked their own necks for** his **life** [*psychē*, often translated *soul*]. They risked their very lives in an effort to protect his life (cf. Acts 19:23-40 for a possible situation in which they did this). Paul indicates that **not only** is he thankful for them, but so also are **all the churches of the Gentiles.**

*Priscilla and Aquila* were a married couple who, like Paul, were tentmakers by trade. When Paul was in Corinth he stayed and worked with them (cf. Acts 18:1-4). When he left for Syria, they were with him (Acts 18:18). Later when they heard Apollos speak, "they took him aside and explained to him the way of God more accurately" (Acts 18:26).

The close connection between Cenchrea and Corinth and also between 16:1-2 and 16:3-5a might suggest that Phoebe knew Priscilla and Aquila. If so, she might well have hoped to stay in their home while in Rome. See the Introduction under *Date and Place of Writing* for more details (including the suggestion that Phoebe delivered Paul's letter to Priscilla and Aquila).

That Paul tells the readers to *greet* **the church that is in their house** (for essentially the same expression see Col 4:15; Phlm 2) shows that there was more than one house church in Rome. The early church had no church buildings like we do today. All church meetings took place in homes or tenements until the third century or so.

Since *Priscilla and Aquila* are mentioned first, and since he refers to *the church that is in their house*, their church probably was the largest of the churches in Rome.

> **16:5b-9. Greet my beloved Epaenetus, who is the first fruits from Achaia for Christ. Greet Miriam, who has toiled much for us. Greet Andronicus and Junias, my relatives and fellow captives, who are highly regarded among the apostles, who also were in Christ before me. Greet Amplias, my much-loved *one* in the Lord. Greet Urbanus, our fellow worker in Christ, and my much-loved Stachys.**

---

[3] Jewett, *Romans*, 955 n. 29. –RNW.

Between vv 3 and 15 each time Paul says **Greet** (*Aspasasthe*), he is introducing a new house or tenement church.[4] He mentions people whom he knew from within those churches and makes brief comments about them.[5]

The remarks concerning those in vv 5b-13 are much shorter than those about *Priscilla and Aquila*, suggesting Paul's special love and appreciation for them.

**Epaenetus**, mentioned only here in the NT, is identified as **my beloved** and as **the firstfruits from Achaia for Christ**. *Achaia* was the region in Greece next to Macedonia. Paul means that he was either the very first believer in the region, or at the least, one of the first (cf. 1 Cor 16:15).

**Miriam** (or *Mary*), whom Paul says **has toiled much for us** (the Critical Text reads *humas, you*, but there is no reason to go against the Majority Text reading) was likely Jewish, as Hodges' translation (based on the Majority Text reading) suggests.

**Andronicus and Junias** receive special commendation from Paul: they **are highly regarded** [or *notable*] **among the apostles**. Several questions arise here. First, is this *Junia*, a female, or *Junias*, which could refer to either a female or male? Jewett cites studies examining each of 250 extant examples of this name in Latin texts. He found no evidence for taking *Iounian* as a masculine.[6] Second, what does *highly regarded... among* [or *by* or *to*] *the apostles* (*hoitines eisin episēmoi en tois apostolois*) mean? Some commentators think that Paul is saying that Andronicus and Junias were apostles, either in the fullest sense, or in a lesser sense of being traveling missionaries. Others think that they were merely well known *by* or *to* the apostles. The latter is surely the case, regardless of whether we translate *en tois apostolois* as *among the apostles* or *by the apostles*. If someone was well known to the apostles they were also well known among the apostles. (If I said that the former governor of Alaska was well known among the U.S. senators, that would not mean that she was a senator, merely that she was well known by or among the senators.)

---

[4] In v 16 Paul uses *aspasasthe* not to greet named individuals, but instead to urge them to greet one another with a holy kiss. This also let readers know that the churches of Christ greet them as well. See comments on Rom 16:16. –RNW

[5] The Claudian edict targeted key Christians in the synagogues, that is, leaders. Exiled leaders met Paul and later returned to Rome, and Paul greets them as flock leaders in Romans 16. –JHN

[6] Jewett, *Romans*, 961. –RNW

In other words, the apostles had a very favorable opinion of these faithful servants of Christ. Paul uses his famous **in Christ** expression to indicate that they were born again before he was. Paul came to faith one to two years after Jesus' crucifixion and resurrection (i.e., in AD 34 or 35). They came to faith in Christ at an even earlier point, possibly even during Jesus' earthly ministry, though more likely around the time of the birth of the Church on Pentecost (Acts 2).

Paul refers to both **Amplias** and **Stachys** as **my much-loved** (or, *beloved*), a sort of generic expression of his affection for them (cf. v 5b). He refers to **Urbanus** as **our fellow worker in Christ**. That Paul refers to him as <u>our</u> *fellow worker* and not <u>my</u> *fellow worker* (as in v 3) most likely signifies that he did not serve with Paul, but that Paul knew of his service for Christ.

> **16:10-12. Greet Apelles, an approved *one* in Christ. Greet those *who are* in the family of Aristobulus. Greet Herodian, my fellow countryman. Greet those *who are* in the family of Narcissus, who are in the Lord. Greet Tryphena and Tryphosa, who have toiled in the Lord. Greet the much-loved Persis, who toiled a lot in the Lord.**

A passing comment about **Apelles** is quite telling. Paul says *Apelles* is **an approved one** [*dokimos*] **in Christ**. He does not say he is confident that one day *he will be approved* by Christ. Instead, Paul says he is currently *approved in* [or *by*] *Christ*. Christ's approval is not something every believer has. But for this verse, we might think that His approval is merely a potential future reward (cf. 1 Cor 9:27; 2 Tim 2:15). Here, however, we learn that one can be in a current state of approval. If *Apelles* perseveres in his service for Christ, then he will remain approved and will receive Christ's approval at His Judgment Seat.

This seems to suggest that it might be possible, in this life, for a believer to know that he is currently in a state of Christ's approval. Of course, since our works are imperfect (1 John 1:8, 10) and since many of us tend to be overly critical of ourselves (1 John 3:20), it is probably best to say that while we can and should remain certain of our eternal destiny (John 5:24), we at best have reason to believe that we are in a current state of His approval. Paul's point in 1 Cor 4:5 is appropriate: "Therefore judge nothing before the time [i.e., before the Bema], until the Lord comes, who will both bring to light the hidden things of darkness and reveal the counsels of the hearts. Then each one's praise will come from God."

Paul also greets two families or households, those **of Aristobulus** and **of Narcissus.**[7] He does not say of either family what he said of Priscilla and Aquila in v 5: "Likewise *greet* the church that is in their house." This suggests that these churches met not in homes, but in tenements (very small apartments on the upper floors of buildings owned by wealthy persons).

**Tryphena and Tryphosa** are commended by Paul as those **who have toiled in the Lord**. These two women might have been sisters, since they are mentioned together and their names are similar.

Another woman, **Persis**, is said to have **toiled a lot** [or *much*] **in the Lord**. While the addition of the word *a lot* (*polla*) might imply that she did more than *Tryphena and Tryphosa* (see also Mary in v 6 of whom he says the same thing), it seems more likely that Paul is simply varying his style in his brief comments about various people.

> **16:13-14. Greet Rufus, a chosen *one* in the Lord, and *greet* his mother and mine. Greet Asyncritus, Phlegon, Hermas, Patrobas, Hermes, and the brothers *who are* with them.**

Paul says that **Rufus** is a **chosen *one*** [or *the elect, ton eklekton*] **in the Lord**. Likely this is not a reference to election to eternal life, or even election to some ministry, since no additional information is given. BDAG says, "Perhaps Rom 16:13 *ho e[klektos] en kuriō* [means] *the outstanding Christian*" (p. 306 #3). Paul means that *Rufus* is an *outstanding person* in Christ. This probably is the same *Rufus* whom Mark mentions: "Then they compelled a certain man, Simon a Cyrenian, the father of Alexander and Rufus, as he was coming out of the country and passing by, to bear His cross" (Mark 15:21).

That Paul refers to the **mother** of *Rufus* as also his own mother suggests that at some time she had displayed motherly affection and extended hospitality to Paul.

---

[7] Since Paul does not greet these men directly, but instead those of their household, Aristobulus and Narcissus might be 1) attending patriarchs of two families, 2) deceased patriarchs, 3) non-attending patriarchs, or 4) masters/slaveholders. –RNW

As Paul is winding down those whom he is greeting, he has less to say about people. Likely this is because these were people about whom Paul has less knowledge.

In v 14 Paul mentions five men **and the brothers who are with them**. The latter suggests that these five men and the unnamed *brothers* were part of a house church together.

> **16:15-16. Greet Philologus and Julia, Nereus and his sister, and Olympas, and all the saints *who are* with them. Greet one another with a holy kiss. The churches of Christ greet you.**

**Philologus and Julia** are probably husband and wife (or brother and sister). **Nereus and his sister** might be their children. **Olympas** was another person in their house church, and so were **all the saints *who are* with them**.

The call to **greet one another with a holy kiss** is a common one in Paul's letters (cf. 1 Cor 16:20; 2 Cor 13:12; 1 Thess 5:2). Evidently when the early church met to celebrate the Lord's Supper they would *greet one another with a kiss* on the cheek. Greeting someone *with a kiss* was also common among Jesus' disciples when they walked with Him. This is evident in that Judas greeted Jesus with a kiss when he betrayed Him at Gethsemane (Matt 26:29).

Paul ends his greetings to individuals in the churches of Rome with a reminder of the love all churches have for them: **The churches...greet you**. All churches are bound together since they all belong to and serve the Lord Jesus Christ.

### E. Paul's Warning about Divisive People (16:17-20)

> **16:17-18. But I urge you, brothers, to take note of those who cause divisions and snares contrary to the doctrine that you have learned, and avoid them. For such people do not do serve our Lord Jesus Christ, but instead their own belly, and so with smooth talk and flattery they deceive the hearts of the unsuspecting.**

Having completed his greetings (vv 21-23 are greetings given by Tertius, the amanuensis), Paul now turns to a significant closing concern.

Unity is a great thing (cf. v 16), but it is not to be maintained at the cost of truth. If people in a church **cause divisions and snares** (or *offenses*) that are **contrary to the doctrine** (or *teaching*) of the apostles, then the church should **avoid** (or *turn away from*) **them**. The Majority Text has an aorist imperative here (*ekklinate* = avoid) whereas the Critical Text has a present imperative (*ekklinete*). The former is preferred due to its external and internal support. Aorist imperatives typically refer to urgent "right-now" commands. For example, in 2 Cor 8:11, Paul used an aorist imperative when he commanded, "Now also complete [*epitelesate*] the doing," referring to completing the giving of a financial gift to the church in Jerusalem. Present imperatives, by contrast, are used with commands that are timeless, like "*Love* your enemies, *do good*, and *lend*" (Luke 6:35), where three present imperatives are used. Paul means that the church is to break fellowship with troublemakers like this (cf. 1 Cor 5:9-13; 2 Thess 3:6).

Divisive people like this may have **smooth talk and flattery**, but their message is false. These people **do not serve our Lord Jesus Christ, but instead their own belly**. That is, they are saying things that will bring them money so they can eat well. And with their false teaching **they deceive the hearts of the unsuspecting** (or *simple*).

The church must protect its members by not allowing people with contrary teaching to spread their false doctrines. Doctrine matters and must not be overlooked.

> **16:19-20. For *the report of* your obedience has reached to all. So I rejoice over you, but I want you to be wise regarding what is good and innocent regarding what is evil. Now the God of peace shall crush Satan beneath your feet soon. The grace of our Lord Jesus Christ *be* with you.**

The believers in Rome whom Paul is greeting are not like the divisive people about whom he is warning them. ***The report of*** the readers' **obedience has reached to all**. That is, their godly behavior and sound doctrine is well known among all the Gentile churches. Thus Paul rejoices over them.

Yet he still is concerned and wants them **to be wise regarding what is good and innocent regarding what is evil**. This describes what the role of elders in a local church should be. They ensure that sound doctrine is taught in the church; keep defective doctrine from being taught; and warn the flock about false teachers and false doctrines when necessary (cf. Acts 20:28-32; Heb 13:17).

What precisely does Paul mean when he says, **Now the God of peace shall crush Satan beneath your feet soon**? Surely these words allude to the protoevangelium in Gen 3:15. Paul is here referring to the Parousia. When Jesus returns He will *crush Satan* under the feet of all believers. That the return of Jesus is *soon* is in keeping with the fact of imminency which Jesus Himself taught (e.g., Matt 24:42-51; 25:13). All of the NT authors believed and taught that the Lord Jesus would return soon (e.g., Jas 5:9; 2 Pet 3:9-13; 1 John 2:18; Rev 22:20).

For a discussion of the benediction ending v 20, see the comments on v 24 (where it is repeated).

## V. Postscript and Benediction (16:21-24)

**16:21. Timothy, my fellow worker, greets you, and *so do* Lucius and Jason and Sosipater, my fellow countrymen.**

In vv 21-23 Paul sends greetings from various other people. The first person he mentions is naturally his beloved spiritual son and trusted aide, **Timothy**, whom he here calls **my fellow worker** (cf. 1 Cor 4:17; 16:10-11; Phil 1:1; 2:19-23; 1 Tim 1:2; 2 Tim 1:2).

The name **Lucius** is only found one other time in the NT (Acts 13:1), but in the other use he is specially identified as *Lucius the Cyrene* (a place in North Africa). This is not likely to be the same Lucius. Hence we know nothing about him, unless Paul is referring to Luke, the beloved physician and traveling companion of Paul. In Greek, Luke, *Loukas*, is very close to Lucius, *Loukios*. However, as they are not identical, it is uncertain that Paul is referring to Luke (even though he was with Paul during the time when Paul wrote this letter).

**Jason** is a common Jewish name often used as a substitute for *Iēsous*, *Jesus* (Heb. *Yeshua*). This may well be the *Jason* from Thessalonica mentioned in Acts as having been associated with Paul (cf. Acts 17:5-9).

**Sosipater** is likely the same person who accompanied Paul to Asia and who is called "Sopater of Berea" in Acts 20:4. Paul is using the more formal version of the name and Luke in Acts uses the less formal variation. (Likewise, Luke refers to the wife of Aquila as Priscilla, a diminuitive form of her name, whereas Paul in Rom 16:4 calls her by her more formal name, Prisca.)

**16:22. I, Tertius, who wrote this epistle in the Lord, greet you.**

Paul did not write out his epistles himself. Rather, he dictated them to an amanuensis. **Tertius** here identifies himself as the one **who wrote this epistle.**[8] He too sends his greeting.

The words **in the Lord** either modify the verb *I wrote* or the verb *I greet*. If the latter, then he is showing his solidarity with the believers in Rome. If the former, which is preferred, then he is emphasizing the fact that he realizes that this epistle is a very important one. It may even suggest that he realizes he has been used by *the Lord* to record Scripture.

**16:23. Gaius, my host and *the host* of the whole church, greets you. Erastus, the city treasurer, greets you, and *so does* Quartus, a brother.**

**Gaius** was evidently a fairly wealthy man as he was Paul's host in Corinth as he wrote this letter and he was **the host of the whole church**. Most likely the man who is here greeting the Roman believers is the Gaius of 1 Cor 1:14.

**Erastus, the city treasurer**, also greets the church in Rome. This likely is the Erastus of Acts 19:22 and 2 Tim 4:20. In any case, it shows the growing influence of Christianity that an important official in an important Roman town would openly identify himself as a disciple of Jesus Christ and a member of His Church.

The final greeting comes from **Quartus**, whom Paul simply calls **a brother.** He is not mentioned anywhere else in the NT.

**16:24. The grace of our Lord Jesus Christ *be* with you all. Amen.**

Paul often ended his epistles with the benediction: **The grace of our Lord Jesus Christ *be* with you all** (cf. 1 Cor 16:23; 2 Cor 13:14a; Gal 6:18;

---

[8] Tertius identifies himself as the one who penned Romans. Much ink has been spilled over the degree of latitude Paul granted to Tertius. Did he record Paul's dictation in shorthand before transcribing it longhand? Or did Paul give him an outline, which Tertius expanded into a letter? Moo, *Romans*, 935, n. 14, rightly concludes, "Most scholars agree that the directness of the style of Romans, as well as the similarity to the style of Galatians and 1 Corinthians, suggest that the wording of Romans is Paul's own. Tertius probably simply copied out Paul's dictation." –JHN

Phil 4:23; Col 4:18c; 1 Thess 5:28; 2 Thess 3:18; 1 Tim 6:21b; 2 Tim 4:22b; Titus 3:15c; Phlm 25). *The grace,* or favor, *of our Lord Jesus Christ* was not merely some sort of catchy religious phrase for Paul. It was a key to his life and ministry. He knew that the only way anyone could please the Lord was by His favor being continually poured out on them.

Though most translations have three more verses here (Rom 16:25-27), they actually belong at the end of chap. 14, where they are found in the majority of manuscripts. This ending is a perfectly natural one.[9] See comments on Rom 14:24-26 for commentary on those three verses.

With these words Paul's grand letter to the Romans ends. Properly understood, this letter is not an evangelistic tract (e.g., the Romans Road). Instead, it is a primer on deliverance from God's temporal wrath by means of the gospel that Paul preached, the gospel of Christ. The gospel is "the power of God for deliverance for everyone who believes, both for the Jew first and for the Greek" (Rom 1:16). God through His gospel offers the believer abundant life (Rom 1:17), life as He intended us to experience it. Life and peace are experienced by any believer who sets his mind on the Spirit (Rom 8:6).

May you experience the peace and fullness of life that God intends for every believer.

---

[9] The reason why this ending is repeated twice, in vv 20 and 24, is because Paul essentially ends the letter in v 20. But after adding in some final greetings by others, Paul feels the need to repeat the benediction with only minor modification (adding the words *all* and *Amen*). Evidently he did not wish to end the letter with the words "a brother" (v 23). –RNW

# Bibliography

## Works by Zane C. Hodges

Hodges, Zane C. and Arthur L. Farstad, editors, *The Greek New Testament According to the Majority Text: Second Edition*. Nashville: Thomas Nelson Publishers, 1985.

Hodges, Zane C. *Absolutely Free! A Biblical Reply to Lordship Salvation*. Dallas, TX: Redención Viva; Grand Rapids, MI: Academie, 1989.

—. *Six Secrets of the Christian Life*. Dallas, TX: Redención Viva, 2004.

—. "The Moralistic Wrath-Dodger: Romans 2:1-5," *Journal of the Grace Evangelical Society* 18 (Spring 2005): 15-21.

—. *The Atonement*. Mesquite, TX: Kerugma, Inc, 2006.

—. *The Epistle of James: Proven Character Through Testing*. Denton, TX: Grace Evangelical Society, 2009.

—. *A Free Grace Primer: The Gospel Under Siege*. Denton, TX: Grace Evangelical Society, 2011.

## Works Cited

Achtemeier, Paul J. *Romans*, Interpretation, ed. James Luther Mays. Louisville, KY: John Knox, 1985.

Archer, Gleason, and Gregory Chirichigno. *Old Testament Quotations in the New Testament: A Complete Survey*. Chicago, IL: Moody, 1983.

Barrett, C. K. *A Commentary on the Epistle to the Romans*, 2nd ed., BNCT, Henry Chadwick, gen. ed. London: Black, 1991.

Baumgartner, Walter, Ludwig Koehler, and Johan Jacob Stamm, eds., *Hebräisches und aramäisches Lexicon zum Alten Testament*, 5 vols.; Leiden: Brill, 1967–1997.

Brown, Colin ed., *The New International Dictionary of New Testament Theology.* Grand Rapids, MI: Zondervan, 1975.

Brunner, Emil. *The Letter to the Romans: A Commentary*, trans. H. A. Kennedy. London: Lutterworth, 1959; reprint, Philadelphia, PA: Westminster, n.d.

Bullinger, E. W. *Figures of Speech Used in the Bible Explained and Illustrated.* Grand Rapids, MI: Baker, 1979.

Cranfield, C. E. B. *A Critical and Exegetical Commentary on the Epistle to the Romans*, ICC, J. A. Emerton and C. E. B. Cranfield, gen. eds. Edinburgh: Clark, 1975–79.

Danker, Frederick W. *A Greek-English Lexicon of the New Testament and Other Early Christian Literature.* 3rd ed. Chicago, IL: University of Chicago Press, 2000.

Deissmann, Adolf. *Bible Studies: Contributions Chiefly from Papyri and Inscriptions to the History of the Language, the Literature, and the Religion of Hellenistic Judaism and Primitive Christianity.* Edinburgh: T & T Clark, 1903.

Denney, James. "St. Paul's Epistle to the Romans." *Expositor's Greek Testament*, ed. W. Robertson Nicoll. Grand Rapids, MI: Eerdmans, N.D.

Dunn, James D. G. *Romans 1–8*, ed. Ralph P Martin, WBC, vol. 38A, Bruce M. Metzger, David A. Hubbard, and Glenn W. Barker, gen. eds. Nashville: Nelson, 1988.

—. *Romans*, 2 vols., WBC. Dallas, TX: Word, 1988.

—. *The New Perspective on Paul.* Grand Rapids, MI: Eerdmans, 2008.

Elkins, Steve. *The Roman Road Revisited: New Vistas on the Road to Resurrection Living.* Dallas, TX: Allie Grace, 2005.

Fitzmyer, Joseph A. *Romans: A New Translation with Introduction and Commentary*, Anchor Bible. New York, NY: Doubleday, 1993.

Fruchtenbaum, Arnold. *Israelology.* 3rd ed. Tustin, CA: Ariel Ministries, 1994.

Fung, Ronald Y. K., "The Impotence of the Law: Toward a Fresh Understanding of Romans 7:14-25," in *Scripture, Tradition, and Interpretation: Essays Presented to Everett F. Harrison by His Students and Colleagues in Honor of His Seventy-Fifth Birthday*, ed. W. Ward Gasque and William Sanford LaSor. Grand Rapids, MI: Eerdmans, 1978.

Hart, John F. "Why Confess Christ? The Use and Abuse of Romans 10:9-10," *JOTGES* 12, Autumn 1999.

Jewett, Robert. Assissted by Roy D. Kotansky. *Romans: A Commentary*, ed. Eldon Jay Epp, Hermeneia. Minneapolis, MN: Fortress, 2007.

Käsemann, Ernst. *Commentary on Romans*, trans. Geoffrey W. Bromiley. Grand Rapids, MI: Eerdmans, 1980.

Lang, G. H. *Firstborn Sons: Their Rights & Risks*. London: Roberts, 1936; reprint, Miami Springs, FL: Conley & Schoettle, 1984.

Lenski, R. C. H. *The Interpretation of St. Paul's Epistle to the Romans*. Peabody, MA: Hendrickson, 1998.

Lopez, René A. *Romans Unlocked: Power to Deliver*. Springfield, MO: 21st Century, 2005.

MacArthur, John, Jr. *Romans 9-16*, The MacArthur New Testament. Chicago, IL: Moody, 1994.

Moo, Douglas J. *The Epistle to the Romans*, NICNT, Gordon D. Fee, gen. ed. Grand Rapids, MI: Eerdmans, 1996.

Morris, Leon. *The Epistle to the Romans*. Grand Rapids, MI: Eerdmans, 1988.

Moulton, James Hope, and George Milligan. *The Vocabulary of the Greek Testament: Illustrated from the Papyri and Other Non-Literary Sources*. New York, NY: Hodder and Stoughton, 1919.

Mounce, Robert H. *Romans*, New American Commentary, vol. 27, E. Ray Clendenen, gen. ed. Nashville, TN: Broadman & Holman, 1995.

Murray, John. *The Epistle to the Romans*. Grand Rapids: Eerdmans, 1959-65; paperback reprinted in one vol., Grand Rapids, MI: Eerdmans, 1997.

Newell, William R. *Romans: Verse by Verse*. Chicago: Moody, 1938.

*New International Dictionary of New Testament Theology*, Colin Brown, ed. Grand Rapids, MI: Zondervan, 1975.

Nichols, Timothy R. "Dead Man's Faith: Spiritual Death, Faith, and Regeneration in Ephesians 2:1-10," Th.M. thesis: Chafer Theological Seminary, 2004.

Niemelä, John H. "Evidence for a First Century 'Tenement Church,'" *JOTGES* 24. Spring 2011.

Nygren, Anders. *Commentary on Romans*. Philadelphia, PA: Fortress Press, 1988.

Peters, George N. H. *The Theocratic Kingdom*, 3 vols. New York: Funk & Wagnalls, 1884; reprint, Grand Rapids, MI: Kregel, 1952.

Plato, *Phaedo*.

Robertson, A. T. *A Grammar of the Greek New Testament in the Light of Historical Research*, 4th ed. Nashville, TN: Broadman Press, 1934.

Sanders, E. P. *Paul and Palestinian Judaism*. Philadelphia, PA: Fortress Press, 1977.

Sanday, William and Arthur C. Headlam, *A Critical and Exegetical Commentary on the Epistle to the Romans*, 3rd ed., ICC, ed. Samuel Rolles Driver, Alfred Plummer, and Charles Augustus Briggs. Edinburgh: Clark, 1898.

Sauer, Eric. *In the Arena of Faith*. Grand Rapids, MI: Eerdmans, 1966.

Schreiner, Thomas R. *Romans*, BECNT, ed. Moisés Silva. Grand Rapids, MI: Baker Academic, 1998.

Smith, Wilbur. *The Biblical Doctrine of Heaven*. Chicago, IL: Moody, 1968.

Stuhlmacher, Peter. "The Theme of Romans," in *The Romans Debate*, rev. ed., Karl P. Donfried, ed. Peabody, MA: Hendrickson, 1991.

Sweet, Henry Barclay. *The Holy Spirit in the New Testament*. N.P.: Macmillan, 1910; reprint, Grand Rapids, MI: Baker, 1964.

Tacitus. *Annals*.

Verbrugge, Verlyn D. "The Grammatical Internal Evidence for ECHOMEN in Romans 5:1," *JETS* 54 (September 2011): 559-72.

Wallace, Daniel B. *Greek Grammar Beyond the Basics: An Exegetical Syntax of the New Testament*. Grand Rapids, MI: Zondervan, 1996.

Wilkin, Robert N. *The Ten Most Misunderstood Words in the Bible*. Corinth, TX: Grace Evangelical Society, 2012.

# Author's Translation of Romans

### Paul Greets the Roman Christians

1 Paul, a bondservant of Jesus Christ, called to be an apostle who is set apart for the gospel of God ²(which He promised beforehand through His prophets in the Holy Scriptures), ³ which is about His Son, the One who came from David's seed as regards the flesh, ⁴ the One who was designated as the Son of God with power, as regards the Spirit of holiness, by means of the resurrection of the dead, *namely,* Jesus Christ our Lord— ⁵ through Him we have received grace and apostleship to bring about obedience by faith for His name's sake among all the Gentiles, ⁶ among whom you too are called by Jesus Christ—

7. To all who are in Rome, beloved by God, called *to be* saints: Grace to you and peace from God our Father and the Lord Jesus Christ.

### Paul's Desire to Visit Rome

8. First, I thank my God through Jesus Christ for all of you because your faith is proclaimed throughout the whole world. ⁹ In fact, God, whom I serve in my spirit with the gospel of His Son, is my witness that I mention you constantly, ¹⁰ requesting always in my prayers that perhaps now at last I might succeed by the will of God in coming to you. ¹¹ For I long to see you so that I may impart some spiritual benefit to you in order that you may be strengthened— ¹² that is *to say,* that we might be encouraged together among you through the faith that is in each other, both your *faith* and mine. ¹³ Now I don't want you to be uninformed, brothers, that many times I have planned to come to you (and have been

prevented until now) so that I might have some fruit among you also, just *as I have had* among the rest of the Gentiles too. [14] I am a debtor both to Greeks and to barbarians, both to the wise and to the unwise. [15] So there is a readiness on my part to preach the gospel also to you who are in Rome.

## The Theme of Romans

**16.** For I am not ashamed of the gospel of Christ, since it is the power of God for deliverance for everyone who believes, both for the Jew first and for the Greek. [17] For in it is revealed the righteousness of God by faith, granted to faith, just as it is written, *"Now the one who is righteous by faith shall live."*

## God's Wrath Against Man's Unrighteousness

**18.** For the wrath of God is revealed from heaven against all the ungodliness and unrighteousness of men who suppress the truth by unrighteousness. [19] Because what is knowable about God is evident among them, because God has made it evident to them. [20] For His invisible *attributes* are seen clearly by means of the creation of the world since they are discerned from the things that have been made, *namely*, both His eternal power and Deity, so that they are without excuse. [21] Because when they knew God, they did not glorify Him as God, nor were they thankful, but engaged in their empty reasonings and so their senseless heart was darkened. [22] Claiming to be wise, they became fools [23] and exchanged the glory of the immortal God for an image made in the likeness of mortal man, and of birds, and of four-footed creatures, and of reptiles.

**24.** Therefore God also turned them over, in the lusts of their hearts, to uncleanness so that they dishonored their bodies with each other, [25] because they had exchanged the truth of God for a lie and worshipped and served the creature rather than the Creator who is blessed forever. Amen.

**26.** For this reason, God turned them over to dishonorable passions. For on the one hand, their females exchanged their natural practice for an unnatural one; [27] and on the other hand, in a similar way the males also left their natural practice with a female and burned in their desire for one another, males with males doing what is shameful and receiving back in themselves for their error the recompense which was due them.

**28.** And just as they did not see fit to retain God in *their* knowledge, God turned them over to a debased mind so that they did unseemly things, [29] *becoming* people filled with all unrighteousness, immorality, wickedness, greed, malice; full of envy, murder, strife, deceit, malignity. *They are* whisperers, [30] slanderers, God-haters, insolent, arrogant, boastful, inventors of evil things, disobedient to parents, [31] undiscerning, unfaithful, unloving, irreconcilable, unmerciful. [32] Although they know God's righteous standard, that people who do such things are deserving of death, they not only do them, but they even approve of those who do them.

## The Coming Day of Wrath

**2** Therefore you are without excuse, O man (anyone who judges). In fact, because in the matters for which you judge someone else, you condemn yourself, since you who pass judgment do the same things. [2] And we know that God's judgment against people who do such things corresponds to the truth. [3] So do you suppose, O man—you who judge people who do such things and you do them too—that you yourself will escape God's judgment? [4] Or do you despise the wealth of His kindness and tolerance and long-suffering, not realizing that God's kind *behavior* is drawing you to repentance? [5] And by means of your hardness and your unrepentant heart are you storing up wrath against yourself in a day of wrath, and of revelation, and of the righteous judgment of God? [6] He will repay each person according to his works: [7] to those who seek glory and honor and immortality by persisting in good work, eternal life; [8] but to those who are selfish and disobey the truth, but obey unrighteousness *instead*, anger and wrath—[9] tribulation and distress for every human soul who does what is evil, for the Jew first and for the Greek; [10] but glory and honor and peace to everyone who does what is good, both to the Jew first and to the Greek.

## What Good Is It to Be a Jew?

**3** What then is the advantage of the Jew, or what is the benefit of circumcision? [2] Much in every way. For first *is the fact* that they were entrusted with the declarations of God. [3] For what if some did not believe?

Their unbelief can't annul the faithfulness of God, can it? [4] Far from it! Let God, then, be true and every man a liar, just as it is written:

> *"That You might be justified in Your words,*
> *And might conquer when You are condemned!"*

[5] Now if our unrighteousness demonstrates the righteousness of God, what shall we say? God, who brings wrath to bear, isn't unrighteous, is He? (I am talking in a human manner.) [6] Far from it! Otherwise how will God judge the world? [7] For if God's truth excels to His glory by means of my lie, why am I myself still judged as a sinner? [8] And why not (as we are slandered and as some claim that we say): "Let us do wicked things so that good things may happen"? The judgment *passed on* such people is deserved.

## All Are under Sin

**9.** What then? Are we offering a defense? Not at all! For we have previously charged that both Jews and Greeks are all under sin, [10] just as it is written:

> *"There is none righteous, not even one,*
> [11] *There is none who understands,*
> *There is none who seeks God.*
> [12] *They have all turned aside,*
> *Together they have become useless;*
> *There is no one doing good,*
> *There is not even so much as one!"*
> [13] *"Their throat is an opened tomb,*
> *They have spoken deceit with their tongues."*
> *"The poison of asps is under their lips."*
> [14] *"Their mouth is full of a curse and bitterness."*
> [15] *"Their feet are swift to shed blood;*
> [16] *Ruin and misery are in their paths;*
> [17] *And the path of peace they have not known."*
> [18] *"There is no fear of God before their eyes."*

[19] Now we know that whatever the law says, it says to those who are under the law, so that every mouth may be shut and all the world might

become accountable to God. [20] Therefore by the works of the law no flesh will be justified before Him, because through the law *comes* the knowledge of sin.

## God's Righteousness by Faith

**21.** But now God's righteousness apart from the law has been manifested, borne witness to by the law and the prophets, [22] that is, God's righteousness, through faith in Jesus Christ, *which is* for all and is upon all who believe. For there is no difference. [23] For all have sinned and fall short of the glory of God, [24] *so that men are* being justified freely by His grace through the redemption that is in Christ Jesus—[25] the One whom God has set forth as a Mercy Seat, through faith, by means of His blood, to serve as a proof of His righteousness in passing over, in the forbearance of God, the sins previously committed; [26] *and* for a proof of His righteousness at the present time, so that He may be righteous and justify the person who has faith in Jesus.

## Boasting Is Excluded

**27.** So where is boasting? It is excluded. Through what sort of law? Of works? No indeed, but through the law of faith. [28] So we hold that a man is justified by faith apart from the works of the law. [29] Is He the God of the Jews only? Is He not in fact also of the Gentiles? Yes, also of the Gentiles! [30] Consequently, there is one God who will justify the circumcision by faith and the uncircumcision through faith. [31] So do we annul the law through faith? Far from it! In fact we establish the law.

## God's Impartial Judgment

**11.** For there is no partiality with God. [12] In fact as many as have sinned without the law shall also perish without the law; and as many as have sinned under the law shall be judged by means of the law. [13] Because it is not the hearers of the law who are righteous before God, but *it is* the doers of the law who will be justified. [14] However, whenever the Gentiles, who do not have the law, instinctively do the things that are in the law, *then*, though they do not have the law, they constitute a law for themselves. [15] They show the work of the law inscribed on their hearts, because their conscience will be a witness, *as will* also their discussions with each other condemning or even defending *one another,* ¹⁶ in the day when God will judge men's secrets through Jesus Christ according to my gospel.

## The Guilt of the Jews

**17.** Look! You bear the name "Jew," and you rest in the law and boast in God. ¹⁸ And you know His will and you discern the things that really matter, because you are instructed out of the law ¹⁹ and you have confidence that you yourself are a guide for the blind, a light for those in darkness, ²⁰ an instructor of the ignorant, a teacher of babes, since you have the formulation of knowledge and of truth in the law. ²¹ So, you who teach another person, don't you teach yourself? You who preach not to steal, do you steal? ²² You who say not to commit adultery, do you commit adultery? You who despise idols, do you rob temples? ²³ You who boast in the law, do you dishonor God by transgressing the law? ²⁴ For *"the name of God is blasphemed among the Gentiles because of you,"* just as it is written.

**25.** After all, circumcision is profitable if you do the law. But if you are a transgressor of the law, your circumcision becomes uncircumcision. ²⁶ So if an uncircumcised person should keep the righteous standards of the law, will not his uncircumcision be credited as circumcision? ²⁷ And will *not* the physically uncircumcised person who fulfills the law judge you, a transgressor of the law who *has its* written *form* and circumcision? ²⁸ For a person is not a Jew who is outwardly *so*, nor is circumcision something outward in the flesh. ²⁹ But he is a Jew who is inwardly *so*, and circumcision *is* of the heart in the spirit, not in the letter *of the law*, and its praise *comes* not from men, but from God.

## The Justification of Abraham

**4** So what shall we say that Abraham our father has obtained with reference to the flesh? ² For if Abraham was justified by works, he has something to boast about, but not with regard to God. ³ For what does the Scripture say? *"Then Abraham believed God, and it was imputed to him as righteousness."* ⁴ Now to the person who works the compensation is not made on the basis of grace, but on the basis of what is owed. ⁵ But to the person who does not work, but believes in the One who justifies the ungodly, his faith is imputed as righteousness.

### Justification According to David

**6.** Just as David too speaks of the blessedness of the man to whom God imputes righteousness apart from works:

> [7] *"Blessed are those whose wicked deeds are forgiven,*
> *And whose sins are covered.*
> [8] *Blessed is the man to whom the Lord*
> *does not impute sin."*

### Justification and Circumcision

**9.** Therefore does this blessedness *come* upon the circumcised, or also upon the uncircumcised? For we are saying that faith was imputed to Abraham as righteousness. [10] So how was it imputed? While he was circumcised or uncircumcised? Not while he was circumcised, but while he was uncircumcised. [11] And so he received the sign of circumcision, a seal of the righteousness by faith which *he received* while he was uncircumcised, so that he might be the father of all those who believe while uncircumcised (in order that righteousness might be imputed to them also), [12] and *might be* the father of circumcision not only to those of the circumcision, but also to those who follow in the footsteps of the faith of our father Abraham which *he had* while he was uncircumcised.

### The Promise Was Based on Faith

**13.** For the promise that he would be heir of the world was not made to Abraham or to his seed through the law, but through the righteousness of faith. [14] For if those who are of the law are heirs, faith is made void and the promise is annulled. [15] For the law causes wrath, since where there is no law there is no transgression. [16] For this reason it is by faith, so that it might be by grace, in order that the promise might be confirmed to the entire seed, not only to the *seed* which is of the law, but also to the *seed* which is of the faith of Abraham, who is the father of us all [17] (just as it is written, *"I have made you a father of many nations."* He believed God, before whom *he stood*, the One who brings the dead to life and speaks about things that do not exist as though they did. [18] *He is the one* who beyond hope believed in hope, that he might be *"a father of many* *nations,"* according to what was spoken: *"So will your seed be."* [19] And since he was not weak in faith, he did not take into account his own body which was already dead (since he was about one hundred years old) nor the deadness of Sarah's womb. [20] And he did not doubt the promise of God in unbelief, but became strong in faith, giving glory to God [21] and being fully convinced that what He had promised He was also able to do. [22] Therefore also *"it was imputed to him for righteousness."* [23] Now it was not only written for his sake that it was imputed to him, [24] but also for our sake to whom it would be imputed, *that is,* to those who would believe in the One who raised Jesus our Lord from the dead, [25] who was delivered for our offenses and raised for our justification.

## Triumphing in Trouble

5 Therefore since we have been justified by faith, we have peace with God through our Lord Jesus Christ, [2] through whom we also possess access by faith into this grace in which we stand, and we exult in the expectation of the glory of God. [3] And not only that, but also we exult in afflictions, knowing that affliction produces endurance, [4] and endurance, approvedness; and approvedness, expectation. [5] Now expectation does not result in shame, because the love of God is poured out in our hearts through the Holy Spirit who has been given to us.

## The Justified Can Be Delivered from Wrath

**6.** You see, while we were still weak, Christ died at the proper time for the ungodly. [7] For only rarely will anyone die for a righteous man, though perhaps for a good man someone might even dare to die. [8] But God demonstrates His own love for us because, while we were still sinners, Christ died for us. [9] All the more therefore, since we have now been justified by His blood, we shall be delivered from wrath through Him. [10] Indeed, if while we were enemies we were reconciled to God through the death of His Son, all the more, since we have been reconciled, we shall be delivered by His life. [11] And not only that, but also we will be exulting in God through our Lord Jesus Christ, through whom we have now received this reconciliation.

## Sin and Death Enter the World

**12.** Therefore just as sin entered the world through one man, and death entered through sin, and so death came to all men because all have sinned— [13] For until the law sin was in the world, but sin is not itemized when there is no law. [14] Nevertheless death reigned from Adam to Moses even over those who had not sinned in a way that resembled the transgression of Adam, who is a type of the Coming One.

## The Transgression and the Free Gift

**15.** However, the free gift in fact stands in contrast to the offense. For if many died through the offense of that one *man*, much more the grace of God and the gift *given* through the grace of one Man, Jesus Christ, has abounded to many. [16] And the gift is not like *what happened* through one *man* who sinned. For the judgment *came* for one *offense* to produce servitude *to sin*. But the free gift *brings release* from many offenses to produce righteous action. [17] For if by means of the offense of one *man* death has reigned through that one *man*, much more those who receive the abundance of grace and of the gift of righteousness shall reign in life through one *Man*, Jesus Christ!

## Grace Triumphant

**18.** Therefore, as through one offense *judgment came* to all men to produce servitude *to sin*, so also through one righteous action *grace came* for all men to produce justification *sourced in* life. [19] In fact just as through the disobedience of one man many have been constituted sinners, so also through the obedience of one *Man* many shall be constituted righteous. [20] Now the law came in so that the offense might become greater. But where sin became greater, grace became superlatively great, [21] in order that just as sin had reigned in *the sphere of* death, so also grace might reign through righteousness unto eternal life through Jesus Christ our Lord.

## New Life in Christ

**6** So what shall we say? Do we continue in sin so that grace may become greater? [2] Far from it! How shall we who have died to sin still live in it? ³ Or don't you know that as many of us as have been baptized into Christ Jesus have been baptized into His death? ⁴ Therefore we have been buried with Him through baptism into death, so that just as Christ was raised from the dead through the glory of the Father, so also we might walk in newness of life. ⁵ For if we are united with *Him* in the likeness of His death, we shall surely also be *united in the likeness* of *His* resurrection, ⁶ since we know this: that our old man has been crucified with *Him*, in order that the body of sin might be nullified, so that we might no longer serve sin. ⁷ For he who has died is justified from sin. ⁸ Now if we have died with Christ, we believe that we shall also live with Him, ⁹ knowing that since Christ was raised from the dead, He no longer dies; death no longer has authority over Him. ¹⁰ For with regard to the fact that He died, He died to sin once for all; and with regard to the fact that He lives, He lives to God. ¹¹ So also you should consider yourselves to be dead to sin, but alive to God in Christ Jesus our Lord.

### Don't Let Sin Reign

**12.** Therefore do not let sin reign in your mortal body so that you obey it with its lusts, ¹³ neither turn over your body's members to sin as instruments for unrighteousness, but turn yourselves over to God as people who are alive from the dead, and *turn over* your body's members to God as instruments for righteousness. ¹⁴ For sin shall not have authority over you, because you are not under the law but under grace.

### Holy and Unholy Slaves

**15.** What then? Shall we sin because we are not under the law but under grace? Far from it! ¹⁶ Don't you know that to whom you turn yourselves over as slaves in obedience, you are slaves of the one you obey, whether of sin producing death, or of obedience producing righteousness? ¹⁷ But praise *is due* to God that *though* you were the slaves of sin, but you have obeyed from the heart that form of teaching in which you were instructed. ¹⁸ And having been liberated from sin, you became enslaved to righteousness ¹⁹ (I speak in human terms because of the weakness of your flesh.) For just as you have turned over your body's members as slaves to uncleanness, and to wickedness producing wickedness, so now turn over your body's members as slaves to righteousness producing holiness.

### From Fruitlessness to Fruitfulness

**20.** For when you were slaves of sin, you were free from righteousness. [21] So what fruit did you have then in the things of which you are now ashamed? For the result of those things is death. [22] But now, since you have been freed from sin and enslaved to God, you have your fruit producing holiness, and the result is eternal life. [23] For the wages of sin is death, but the gift of God is eternal life in Christ Jesus our Lord.

### Freedom From the Law

7Or are you unaware, brothers (for I am talking to those who know the law), that the law has authority over a man for as long a time as he lives? [2] In fact, a married woman is bound by the law to a husband who is alive. But if the husband dies, she is released from the law of her husband. [3] So then, while the husband lives, she shall be called an adulteress if she marries another man; but if the husband dies, she is free from the law, so that she is not an adulteress if she marries another man. [4] Therefore, my brothers, you too were put to death to the law through the body of Christ, so that you might marry Another—the One who was raised from the dead—so that you might bear fruit for God.

### The Old and the New Experience

**5.** For when we were in the flesh, the yearnings for sin that the law produced, were at work in our body's members to bear fruit for death. [6] But now we have been released from the law by dying *to that* in which we were held back, so that we might serve in the newness of the Spirit, and not in the oldness of a written code.

### Is Something Wrong with the Law?

**7.** So what shall we say? Is the law sin? Far from it! In fact I would not have recognized sin if not for the law. For I would not even have perceived lust, if the law had not said, *"You shall not lust."* [8] But sin took advantage *of me* through the commandment and produced in me every kind of lust. For without the law sin is dead.

## Paul's Experience with the Law

**9.** Now I myself was once alive without the law, but when the commandment came, sin came back to life and I died. ¹⁰ And the very commandment *intended* to produce life was found to produce death. ¹¹ For sin took advantage of me through the commandment, and deceived me, and through it killed *me*.

## The Role of the Law

**12.** Therefore, the law is holy, and the commandment is holy and righteous and good. ¹³ So did what was good become death for me? Far from it! Instead sin, that it might appear *as* sin, produced death for me through what was good, so that through the commandment sin might become supremely sinful. ¹⁴ Certainly, we know that the law is spiritual, but I myself am fleshly, sold under *the dominion of* sin.

## The Vain Struggle with Sin

**15.** For I don't know what I am accomplishing. For what I wish is not what I do, but what I hate is what I do. ¹⁶ But if I do what I do not wish *to do*, I am agreeing with the law that it is good. ¹⁷ So in this situation, it is no longer I myself who accomplishes it, but instead the sin that dwells in me. ¹⁸ For I know that in me—that is, in my flesh—no good thing dwells. For to wish *to do* lies ready at hand for me, but I do not discover how to accomplish what is good. ¹⁹ For the good thing that I wish *to do* I do not do, but the evil thing I do not wish *to do* is what I do. ²⁰ And if I do what I myself do not wish *to do*, it is no longer I myself who accomplishes it, but instead the sin that dwells in me. ²¹ Therefore I discover this law for myself, that when I wish to do what is good, evil lies ready at hand for me. ²² For I delight in the law of God with my inward man, ²³ but I see another law in my *body's* members waging war with the law of my understanding, and taking me captive by means of the law of sin which is in my *body's* members. ²⁴ What a wretched man I am! Who will deliver me from the body of this *kind of* death? ²⁵ I thank God through Jesus Christ our Lord! So then, I myself serve the law of God with my understanding, but with the flesh *I serve* the law of sin.

## Freedom through Walking by the Spirit

**8** Therefore there is now no servitude *to sin* for those who are in Christ Jesus, who do not walk in relation to the flesh but in relation to the Spirit. [2] For the law of the Spirit of life in Christ Jesus has freed me from the law of sin and of death. [3] For in regard to the incapacity of the law, in that it was weak because of the flesh, by sending His own Son in the likeness of sinful flesh and as a sacrifice for sin, God pronounced sentence on sin in the flesh, [4] so that the righteous action of the law might be fulfilled in us who do not walk in relation to the flesh but in relation to the Spirit.

## The Flesh and the Spirit Contrasted

**5.** For those who are in relation to the flesh have their minds set on the things of the flesh, but those who are in relation to the Spirit *have them set* on the things of the Spirit. [6] For the mind-set of the flesh *is* death, but the mind-set of the Spirit *is* life and peace. [7] For this reason the mind-set of the flesh *is* hostile toward God, because it does not submit to the law of God, nor indeed is it able to. [8] So those who are in the flesh are unable to please God. [9] But you are not in the flesh but in the Spirit, if indeed the Spirit of God dwells in you. Now if anyone does not have the Spirit of Christ, he does not belong to Him.

## Resurrected Life by the Spirit

**10.** But if Christ *is* in you, the body *is* dead because of sin, but the Spirit *is* life because of righteousness. [11] And if the Spirit of the One who raised Jesus from the dead dwells in you, the One who raised Christ from the dead will also bring to life your mortal bodies on account of His Spirit who dwells in you. [12] So then, brothers, we are not obligated to the flesh to live in relation to the flesh. [13] For if you live in relation to the flesh, you will die. But if by the Spirit you put to death the deeds of the body, you will live.

## The Experience of Sonship

**14.** In fact, as many as are led by the Spirit of God, these are God's sons. [15] For you have not received again a spirit of bondage producing fear, but you have received a spirit of adoption as sons, by means of which we cry out, "Abba, Father!" [16] The Spirit Himself bears testimony along with our spirit that we are the children of God. [17] And if *we are* children, *we are* also heirs—heirs, on the one hand, of God, and on the other hand, co-heirs with Christ if we suffer together *with Him* so that we may also be glorified together *with Him*.

## From Suffering to Glory

**18.** Now I consider that the sufferings of the present time *are* not worthy to be compared with the glory that is going to be revealed for us. [19] For what is eagerly desired by the creation waits for the revelation of the sons of God [20] (since the creation has been made subject to futility, not willingly, but because of Him who subjected *it to this* in hope), [21] because the creation itself will be released from bondage to corruption into the liberty of the glory of the children of God. [22] Now we know that the whole creation groans together and suffers labor pains together right up until now. [23] And not only *the creation*, but also we who have the first fruits of the Spirit—even we ourselves groan within ourselves as we wait for *our* adoption as sons, *namely*, the redemption of our body. [24] For we have been delivered in hope, but hope which is seen is not hope, since why does anyone also hope for what he sees? [25] But if we hope for what we do not see, we wait *for it* with endurance.

## The Spirit's Help in Sufferings

**26.** But likewise also the Spirit gives us help in our weaknesses. For we do not know what to pray for as it is necessary *to do*, but with *our* inarticulate groanings the Spirit Himself makes intercession on our behalf. [27] And the One who searches the hearts knows what the aspiration of the Spirit is, because He makes intercession on behalf of the saints in harmony with God.

## The Glory of Those Who Love God

**28.** Now we know that all things work together with those who love God to *produce* good, *that is*, together with those who are called in harmony with *His* purpose. [29] Because those whom He knew in advance

He also predetermined to share the likeness of His Son, so that He might be the Firstborn among many brothers. [30] And whom He predetermined, these He also called; and whom He called, these He also justified; and whom He justified, these He also glorified.

## God Is on Our Side

**31.** What then shall we say about these things? If God *is* for us, who *is really* against us? [32] He who did not even spare His own Son, but delivered Him up on behalf us all, how shall He not also graciously give us, together with Him, all things? [33] Who shall bring a charge against God's chosen ones? God *is* the One who justifies. [34] Who *is* the one who condemns? Christ *is* the One who died, and moreover who also rose, who also is at the right hand of God, who also intercedes on our behalf.

## God's Unfailing Love

**35.** Who will separate us from the love of Christ? *Will* tribulation, or hardship, or persecution, or famine, or nakedness, or danger, or sword? [36] Just as it is written that,

> *"For Your sake we are put to death all day long,*
> *We are accounted as sheep for slaughter."*

[37] On the contrary, we are more than conquerors through Him who loved us. [38] For I am persuaded that neither death, nor life, nor angels, nor principalities, nor powers, nor things present, nor things to come, nor height, nor depth, nor any other creature, will be able to separate us from the love of God which is in Christ Jesus our Lord.

## Paul's Burden for Israel

**9** I am telling the truth in Christ, I am not lying (my conscience bears witness along with me in the Holy Spirit), [2] that there is great grief for me and unceasing pain in my heart. [3] For I myself could wish to be accursed from Christ for the sake of my brothers, my fellow-countrymen according to the flesh, [4] who are Israelites, to whom belong the adoption as sons, and the glory, and the covenants, and the legislation, and the sacred service, and the promises, [5] to whom belong the fathers and from whom *came* Christ according to the flesh, the One who is God over all, blessed forever. Amen.

## God's Word Has Not Failed

**6.** Now it is not as though the word of God has failed. For Israel does not consist of all who are part of Israel. [7] Neither because they are Abraham's descendants *are they* all *his* children, but rather, "*Through Isaac shall the descendants be called your own.*" [8] That is, *it is* not the children of the flesh who *are* children of God, but the children of the promise are accounted as descendants. [9] For this is the word of promise: "*At this time I will come and Sarah shall have a son.*" [10] And not only that, but also Rebecca, when she was pregnant by one man, Isaac our father—[11] for even though *the children* were not yet born nor had they done anything good or bad, in order that God's purpose in accordance with *His* choice might remain *firm* (not by works but by Him who calls), [12] it was said to her that, "*The older child shall serve the younger one.*" [13] Just as it is written, "Jacob have I loved, But Esau have I hated."

## God Is Sovereign

**14.** So what shall we say? There isn't *any* unrighteousness with God, is there? Far from it! [15] In fact He says to Moses:

"*I will have mercy on whom I will have mercy,
And I will have compassion on whom
I will have compassion.*"

[16] So then *this matter* is not from the one who wishes, nor from the one who runs, but from the God who shows mercy. [17] You see, the Scripture says to Pharaoh: "For this very thing I raised you up, that by means of you I might demonstrate My power, and that My name might be declared in all the earth." [18] So then He has mercy on whom He wishes, and whom He wishes He hardens.

## The Potter and the Clay

**19.** You will say to me therefore, "Why does He still blame *anyone*? For who withstands His will?" [20] On the contrary, O man, who are you to answer back to God? The thing molded won't say to its Molder, will it, "Why have You made me this way?" [21] Or does not the Potter have authority over the clay, to make out of the same batch of clay one vessel for honor and another for dishonor?

**22.** But *who can object* if God, because He wishes to demonstrate *His* wrath and make known His power, has borne with great patience the vessels of wrath fitted for ruin, [23] and *also wishes* to make known the wealth of His glory upon the vessels of mercy, which He has prepared beforehand for glory—[24] *that is,* upon us whom, in fact, He has called, not only from among the Jews, but also from among the Gentiles? [25] As indeed He says by Hosea,

> "I will call them who were not My people, My people,
> And her who was not beloved, beloved."
> [26] "And it shall be that in the place where it was said to them,
> 'You are not My people,' there they shall be called sons of the
> living God."

[27] And Isaiah cries out concerning Israel:

> "Though the number of the sons of Israel should be as the sand of
> the sea,
> The remnant shall be delivered,
> [28] For He is doing a reckoning, completing it and cutting it short
> His word in righteousness,
> Because the Lord will carry out a word cut short on the earth."

[29] And just as Isaiah had previously said,

> "If the Lord of Hosts had not left us descendants,
> We would have become like Sodom,
> And we should have been comparable to Gomorrah."

### Israel's Present State

**30.** So what shall we say? That the Gentiles, who were not pursuing righteousness, have obtained righteousness, but *it is* a righteousness that is by faith. [31] But Israel, while pursuing the law of righteousness, has not attained to the law of righteousness. [32] Why? Because *they did* not *seek it* by faith, but as *if it came* by the works of the law. For they have collided with the Stone of collision, [33] just as it is written,

> "*Behold, I place in Zion a Stone of collision*
> *And a Rock of entrapment,*
> *And everyone who believes in Him*
> *Shall not be ashamed.*"

## Israel Needs God's Message

**10** Brothers, the desire of my heart, and my prayer to God on behalf of Israel, is for their deliverance. [2] For I bear witness about them that they have a zeal for God, but not according to knowledge. [3] For since they are ignorant of God's righteousness and are seeking to establish their own righteousness, they have not submitted to the righteousness of God. [4] For Christ is the goal of the law as regards righteousness for everyone who believes.

## The Message Paul Preaches

**5.** For Moses writes about the righteousness which is by the law that, "*The man who has done these things shall live by means of them.*" [6] But the righteousness which is by faith speaks this way: "*Do not say in your heart, 'Who will go up into heaven?'*" (that is, to bring Christ down), [7] or, "'*Who will go down into the Abyss?*'" (that is, to bring Christ up from the dead). [8] But what does it say? "*The word is near you, in your mouth and in your heart*"—that is the word of faith which we preach, [9] that, If you confess with your mouth "Lord Jesus," and believe in your heart that God has raised Him from the dead, you will be delivered. [10] For with the heart He is believed for righteousness, but with the mouth He is confessed for deliverance.

## Deliverance through Confession

**11.** For the Scripture says, "Everyone who believes in Him, shall not be ashamed."

[12] For there is no difference between either Jew or Greek, since the same Lord of all deals richly with all who appeal to Him. [13] For "*whoever*

*shall appeal to the name of the Lord will be delivered."* [14] How then shall they appeal *to Him* in whom they have not believed? And how shall they believe *in Him* of whom they have not heard? And how shall they hear without a preacher? [15] And how shall they preach unless they are sent? Just as it is written,

> *"How beautiful are the feet of those*
> *who proclaim good news about peace,*
> *Who proclaim good news about good things!"*

## The Unbelief of Israel

**16.** But they have not all obeyed the gospel. For Isaiah says, *"Lord, who has believed our report?"* [17] So then faith *comes* from the report, and the report by means of the word of God. [18] But I say, it's not that they haven't heard, is it? On the contrary,

> *"Their voice has gone out into all the earth,*
> *And their words to the ends of the world."*

[19] But rather I say, it's not that Israel hasn't known, is it? First Moses says,

> *"I will stir you to jealousy by those*
> *who are not a nation,*
> *And I will make you angry with a foolish nation."*

[20] Then Isaiah is so bold as to say,

> *"I have been found by those who did not seek Me,*
> *I have been revealed to those who did not ask for Me."*

[21] But to Israel He says,

> *"All day long I have stretched out My hands*
> *To a people who disobey and contradict Me!"*

## The Present Jewish Remnant

**11** So I say, God hasn't cast away His people, has He? Far from it! In fact I myself am an Israelite, of the descendants of Abraham, of the tribe of Benjamin. ² God has not cast away His people whom He foreknew. Or don't you know what the Scripture says in regard to Elijah? How he intercedes to God against Israel, saying, ³ "Lord, they have killed Your prophets, and torn down Your altars, and I myself am left alone and they seek my life." ⁴ But what does the divine response say to him? "I have kept for Myself seven thousand men who have not bent a knee to Baal." ⁵ In the same way then, there is also at the present time a remnant according to *His* choice by grace. ⁶ But if *it is* by grace, *it is* no longer by works, otherwise grace is no longer grace. But if *it is* by works, *it is* no longer grace, otherwise work is no longer work.

## Israel's Situation Was Prophesied

**7.** What then? That which Israel is seeking, it has not obtained. But the chosen *group* has obtained *it*, and the rest have been hardened, ⁸ just as it is written,

> *"God has given them a spirit of stupor*
> *—eyes so that they cannot see,*
> *ears so that they cannot hear,*
> *to this very day."*

⁹ And David says,

> *"Let their table become a snare and a trap*
> *And something to trip over and a retribution for them;*
> *¹⁰ Let their eyes be darkened so that they cannot see, And make*
> *their back bend down always."*

## Israel's Rejection Not Final

**11.** So I say, they haven't stumbled just to fall, have they? Far from it! Instead, by their offense *there is* deliverance for the Gentiles, in order to stir them to jealousy. ¹² Now if their transgression *is* the enriching of the world and their loss *is* the enriching of the Gentiles, how much more *will* their fullness *be so*? [13] For I am talking to you Gentiles. Inasmuch as I am an Apostle to the Gentiles, I glorify my service, [14] if somehow I might stir to jealousy *those who are* my flesh and deliver some of them. [15] For if the throwing aside of them *is* the reconciling of the world, what *shall be* their reception but life from the dead? [16] For if the first fruits *are* holy, so *is* the batch of dough; and if the root *is* holy, so *are* the *branches*.

## The Good Olive Tree

**17.** Now if some of the branches were broken off, and you who were a wild olive tree were grafted in among them and have become a sharer in the root and richness of the olive tree, [18] do not exult over the branches. But if you do exult, *it is* not you *who* bear the root, but the root *bears* you. [19] So you will say, "Branches were broken off so that I could be grafted in." [20] Very well. In unbelief they were broken off, but you stand by faith. Don't be haughty, but be afraid. [21] For if God did not spare the natural branches, *be afraid* lest He not spare you either.

**22.** Look therefore at the kindness and severity of God—toward those who fell, severity; but toward you, kindness, if you remain in that kindness. Otherwise you too will be cut off. [23] And they too, if they do not remain in unbelief, shall be grafted in, since God is able to graft them in again. [24] For if you were cut off of an olive tree that is wild by nature, and contrary to nature were grafted into a good olive tree, how much more shall they who are natural *branches* be grafted into their own olive tree?

## The Restoration of Israel

**25.** For I do not want you to be uninformed about this mystery, brothers, so that you may not be wise in your own estimation—*that is*, that partial hardening has happened to Israel until the fullness of the Gentiles has come in. [26] And thus all Israel shall be delivered, just as it is written,

> "*The Deliverer shall come from Zion,*
> *And shall turn away ungodliness from Jacob;*
> [27] *And this is My covenant with them,*
> *When I shall take away their sins.*"

[28] With regard to the gospel, *they are* enemies for your sake, but with regard to *God's* choice *they are* beloved for the fathers' sake. [29] For the gracious gifts and the calling of God *are* irrevocable. [30] For just as you too at one time disobeyed God, but now have received mercy by means of their disobedience, [31] so also they have now disobeyed, so that by means of your mercy they too might receive mercy. [32] For God has enclosed all men in disobedience so that He might have mercy on all.

### Paul's Worship

**33.** O the depth of the wealth and wisdom and knowledge of God! How unsearchable *are* His judgments and *how* untraceable *are* His paths.

> [34] *"Who indeed has known the mind of the Lord?*
> *Or who has been His counselor?"*
> [35] *"Or who has given first to Him,*
> *So that it shall be paid back to him?"*

[36] Because all things *are* from Him and through Him and for Him. To Him *be* the glory forever. Amen.

### The Living Sacrifice

**12** I exhort you therefore, brothers, by the mercies of God, that you present your bodies *as* a sacrifice *that is* living, holy, pleasing to God—*which is* your rational service. [2] And do not be conformed to this age, but be transformed by the renovation of your understanding, so that you may put to the proof what *is* the good and pleasing and perfect will of God.

### God's Will in the Church

**3.** I say then through the grace that has been given to me, to everyone who is among you, not to aspire beyond that to which one ought to aspire, but to aspire to what is sensible—each person as God has distributed to him faith's portion. [4] For just as in one body we have many members, but all the members do not have the same function, [5] so we *who are* many are one body in Christ, but members individually of one another. [6] Now since we have gifts differing according to the grace that has been given to us, if *we have* prophecy, *let us do this* in agreement with the faith; [7] if *we have the gift of* service, *let us be engaged* in service. If *we are* a teacher, *let us be engaged* in teaching; [8] if *we are* an exhorter, *let us be engaged* in exhortation. The giver *should give* with generosity; the leader *should lead* with diligence; the one who shows mercy *should do so* with graciousness.

## God's Will for Our Character

**9.** Love *should be* without hypocrisy. *We should* hate what is evil, cleave to what is good. [10] In regard to brotherly love, *have* strong affection for one another; in regard to honor, lead one another's way *to it* [11] in regard to diligence, *we should* not *be* lazy; in regard to *our* spirit, *we should be* zealous; in regard to the Lord, *we should do* slave-service [12] in regard to hope, *we should* rejoice; in regard to affliction, *we should* endure; in regard to prayer, *we should* persevere, [13] with regard to the needs of the saints, *we should* share *with them.* Pursue hospitality.

## God's Will for Our Relationships

**14.** Bless those who persecute you; bless and do not curse. [15] Rejoice with those who rejoice, and weep with those who weep. [16] Have the same aspirations for each other. Do not aspire to high things, but associate with humble *people.* Do not become wise in your own sight. [17] Repay no one with evil in return for evil. Make provision for things *that are* good in the sight of all men. [18] If possible, on your part be at peace with all men. [19] Do not take revenge for yourselves, beloved, but leave room for wrath, since it is written, "*Vengeance is mine, I will repay,*" says the Lord. [20] So

> "*If your enemy is hungry, feed him;*
> *If he is thirsty, give him a drink;*
> *For by doing this you will heap coals of fire on his head.*"

[21] Do not be overcome by evil, but overcome evil with good.

## Submit to Government

**13** Let every person submit to the governing authorities. For there is no authority if *it is* not *bestowed* by God, and the present authorities are established by God. [2] Therefore the person who resists the authority resists the ordinance of God, and those who resist *it* will receive judgment for themselves. ³ For rulers do not cause fear about good works, but about evil works. Now do you wish not to be afraid of the authority? Do what is good and you will have praise from it. ⁴ In fact he is God's servant to you to *produce* what is good. But if you do what is evil, be afraid, because he does not bear the sword in vain. For he is God's servant, an avenger to *bring* wrath on the person who does evil. ⁵ Consequently it is necessary to submit, not only because of the wrath, but also because of *one's* conscience. ⁶ For this reason also, pay taxes, since they are God's ministers who are devoted to this very thing. ⁷ Therefore render to all what they are owed: a tax to whom *one owes* the tax; a customs duty to whom *one owes* the customs duty; respect to whom *one owes* respect; and honor to whom *one owes* honor.

## Love: The Ongoing Obligation

**8.** Owe no one anything except to love one another. For the one who loves another has fulfilled the law. ⁹ For this *matter of* "You shall not commit adultery," "You shall not murder," "You shall not steal," "You shall not covet"—and if *there is* any other commandment, it is summed up in this statement, namely, "You shall love your neighbor as yourself." ¹⁰ Love does not produce what is bad for a neighbor, so love is the fulfillment of the law.

## Be Ready for the Coming of Christ

**11.** In fact *you should do* this, since you know the time, that the hour for us to awake out of sleep is already here. For now is our deliverance nearer than when we believed. ¹² The night has moved on, and the day has drawn near. So let us take off the works of the darkness and clothe ourselves with the equipment of the light. ¹³ Let us walk circumspectly as in the day, not in carousing and drunkenness, not in sexual misbehavior and licentiousness, not in strife and jealousy. ¹⁴ Instead, clothe yourselves in the Lord Jesus Christ, and take no forethought to *accommodate* the desires of the flesh.

## Concerning Doubtful Things

**14** Accept the one who is weak in the faith, *but* not to engage in disputes about opinions. [2] One person believes he can eat everything, but another who is weak eats vegetables. [3] The person who eats should not scorn the person who doesn't eat, and the person who doesn't eat should not condemn the one who eats, for God has accepted him. [4] Who are you to judge another person's house servant? He stands or falls to his own lord. But he shall be enabled to stand, because God has power to enable him to stand. [5] One person regards *one* day above *another* day, and another regards every day *the same*. Let each person be fully assured in his own mind. [6] The person who esteems the day, esteems *it* with reference to the Lord. And the person who does not esteem the day, with reference to the Lord he does not esteem *it*. So too the person who eats, eats with reference to the Lord, since he gives God thanks. And the person who does not eat, with reference to the Lord he does not eat, and he gives God thanks. [7] After all, no one of us lives with reference to himself *alone* and no one dies with reference to himself *alone*. [8] For if we live, we live with reference to the Lord; and if we die, we die with reference to the Lord. So whether we live or die, we are the Lord's.

## The Judgment Seat of Christ

**9.** In fact, to this end Christ both died as well as rose and lived so that He might exercise lordship over both *the* dead and *the* living. [10] But as for you, why do you judge your brother? Or you too, why do you scorn your brother? For we must all appear before the Judgment Seat of Christ. [11] For it is written:

> "As I live, says the Lord,
> Every knee shall bow to Me,
> And every tongue shall confess to God."

[12] So then each of us shall render an accounting about himself to God. [13] Therefore, let us no longer judge one another, but decide this instead: that *we* not create an impediment or a snare for *our* brother.

## Guided by Love

**14.** I know and am persuaded in the Lord Jesus that *there is* nothing unclean of itself, except that to a person who considers something to be unclean, to that person *it is* unclean. [15] Now if because of your food your brother is grieved, you are no longer walking in love. By your food, do not ruin that person for whom Christ died. [16] So do not let your good *activity* be defamed. [17] For the kingdom of God is not food and drink, but righteousness and peace and joy in the Holy Spirit. [18] Indeed, the person who serves Christ in these things is pleasing to God and approved by men.

**19.** Therefore let us pursue the things *that produce* peace and the things *that produce* edification for each other. [20] Do not tear down the work of God for the sake of food. All *foods* indeed are pure, but *it is* evil for the man who causes an impediment *for someone* by eating *it*. [21] It is good not to eat meat nor to drink wine nor *to do anything* by which your brother runs into an impediment or is ensnared or made weak. [22] Do you have faith? Have it by yourself before God. Blessed is the person who does not condemn himself *for the thing* which he treats as acceptable. [23] But the person who is doubtful is condemned if he eats, because *he does* not *do so* by faith. And whatever *is* not by faith is sin.

## God Can Establish Us

**24.** Now to the One who is able to establish you in accordance with my gospel and the message of Jesus Christ, in accordance with the revelation of the mystery *which was* kept silent through *past* eternal times, [25] but now has been manifested, and has been made known to all the Gentiles through prophetic Scriptures in accordance with the command of the eternal God, to produce the obedience of faith—[26] to God *who* alone *is* wise *be* glory forever through Jesus Christ. Amen.

## Bearing the Burden of the Weak

**15** Now we who are strong ought to bear the weaknesses of the weak and not to please ourselves. [2] Let each of us please his neighbor in what is good, to produce edification. [3] For even Christ did not please Himself, but as it has been written, *"The insults of the ones who insulted*

*You fell on Me."* [4] In fact, whatever was written beforehand, was written beforehand to give us teaching, so that by means of the endurance and the encouragement *derived* from the Scriptures we might have hope. [5] Now may the God of endurance and encouragement grant that you may have the same aspirations for one another in harmony with Christ Jesus, [6] so that with united purpose you may glorify the God and Father of our Lord Jesus Christ with one voice. [7] Therefore accept one another just as also Christ has accepted us, to the glory of God.

## The Worshipping Gentiles

**8.** Now I say that Christ Jesus has become a Servant to the circumcised on behalf of the truth of God, so that *He* might confirm the promises made to the fathers, [9] and *so that* the Gentiles might glorify God for His mercy, just as it is written:

> *"For this reason I will acknowledge You*
> *among the Gentiles,*
> *And sing praise to Your name."*

[10] And again it says:

> *"Rejoice, O Gentiles, along with His people."*

[11] And again:

> *"Praise the Lord, all you Gentiles,*
> *And extol Him, all you peoples."*

[12] And again, Isaiah says:

> *"There shall be a root from Jesse,*
> *And One who will arise to rule the Gentiles;*
> *In Him the Gentiles will put their hope."*

[13] Now may the God of hope fill you with all joy and peace as you are believing, so that you may abound with hope by the power of the Holy Spirit.

## Paul's Priestly Service

**14.** Now my brothers, I am personally persuaded about you that you yourselves are full of goodness, filled with all knowledge, competent also to admonish others. [15] And I have written very boldly to you, brothers (in part, to refresh your memories), because of the grace that has been given to me by God, [16] that I should be a priestly minister of Jesus Christ for the Gentiles, serving as a priest with the gospel of God, so that the offering up of the Gentiles, sanctified by the Holy Spirit, might be acceptable.

## Paul's Gospel Ministry

**17.** Therefore I have reason for exultation in Christ Jesus in things related to God. [18] For I will not dare to speak about any *of the things* that Christ has not accomplished through me to produce obedience by the Gentiles, *whether* by word and deed, [19] *or* by the power of signs and wonders, *or* by the power of the Spirit of God, with the result that I have completed *the spread of* the gospel of Christ from Jerusalem and all around as far as Illyricum. [20] And *I have done* so having an ambition to proclaim the gospel where Christ was not named, so that I might not build on another person's foundation, [21] but instead as it is written:

> *"They to whom nothing about Him had been*
> *announced, shall see,*
> *And they who had not heard shall understand."*

## Paul's Plans to Visit Rome

**22.** This is also why I have been hindered many times from coming to you. [23] But now, since I no longer have *any* room in these regions, and since I have had a desire for many years to come to you, [24] whenever I go to Spain I will come to you. For I hope to see you as I pass through and to be assisted by you on my trip there, provided that first I am at least partially filled up with your company. [25] But right now I am going to Jerusalem to serve the saints there. [26] For Macedonia and Achaia have been pleased to do make a certain contribution to the poor among the saints who are in Jerusalem. [27] Indeed they have been pleased, and they are debtors to them. For if the Gentiles have shared in their spiritual *benefits*, they are also under obligation to render priestly service to them in *their* physical concerns. [28] So when I have completed this *task* and have sealed to them this fruit, I shall go by way of you to Spain. [29] And I know that when I come to you, I will come in the fullness of the blessing of the gospel of Christ.

## Paul Requests Prayer

**30.** Now I urge you, brothers, by our Lord Jesus Christ and by the love of the Spirit, that you contend along with me in *your* prayers for me to God, [31] that I might be delivered from those in Judea who don't believe and that my ministry to Jerusalem might be acceptable to the saints, [32] so that I might come to you with joy by the will of God and that I might find rest with you. [33] Now may the God of peace be with you all. Amen.

## Paul Commends Phoebe

**16** Now I commend to you Phoebe our sister, who is a deaconess of the church which is in Cenchrea, [2] so that you may welcome her in the Lord in a way worthy of the saints, and make yourselves available to her in whatever matter she may need you, inasmuch as she herself has been a patroness to many and even to me.

## Paul Greets the Roman Christians

**3.** Greet Priscilla and Aquila, my fellow workers in Christ Jesus, [4] who have risked their own necks for my life, to whom not only I am thankful, but also all the churches of the Gentiles; [5] and *greet* the church that is in their house. Greet my much-loved Epaenetus, who is the first fruits from Achaia for Christ.

**6.** Greet Miriam, who has toiled much for us.

**7.** Greet Andronicus and Junias, my relatives and fellow captives, who are highly regarded among the apostles, who also were in Christ before me.

**8.** Greet Amplias, my much-loved *one* in the Lord.

**9.** Greet Urbanus, our fellow worker in Christ, and my much-loved Stachys.

**10.** Greet Apelles, an approved *one* in Christ. Greet those *who are* in the family of Aristobulus.

**11.** Greet Herodian, my fellow countryman. Greet those *who are* in the family of Narcissus, who are in the Lord.

**12.** Greet Tryphena and Tryphosa, who have toiled in the Lord. Greet the much-loved Persis, who toiled a lot in the Lord.

**13.** Greet Rufus, a chosen *one* in the Lord, and *greet* his mother and mine.

**14.** Greet Asyncritus, Phlegon, Hermas, Patrobas, Hermes, and the brothers *who are* with them.

**15.** Greet Philologus and Julia, Nereus and his sister, and Olympas, and all the saints *who are* with them.

**16.** Greet one another with a holy kiss. The churches of Christ greet you.

## Beware of Those Who Divide

**17.** But I urge you, brothers, to take note of those who cause divisions and snares contrary to the doctrine that you have learned, and avoid them. [8] For such people do not serve our Lord Jesus Christ, but instead their own belly, and so with smooth talk and flattery they deceive the hearts of the unsuspecting. [19] For *the report of* your obedience has reached to all. So I rejoice over you, but I want you to be wise regarding what is good and innocent regarding what is evil. [20] Now the God of peace shall crush Satan beneath your feet soon. The grace of our Lord Jesus Christ *be* with you.

## Postscript with Greetings from Others

**21.** Timothy, my fellow worker, greets you, and *so do* Lucius and Jason and Sosipater, my fellow countrymen.

**22.** I, Tertius, who wrote this epistle in the Lord, greet you.

**23.** Gaius, my host and *the host* of the whole church, greets you. Erastus, the city treasurer, greets you, and *so does* Quartus, a brother.

**24.** The grace of our Lord Jesus Christ *be* with you all. Amen.

# Scripture Index

# Subject Index

# BOOKS BY ZANE HODGES

- *Absolutely Free (2nd ed.)*
- *The Atonement and Other Writings*
- *The Epistle of James*
- *The Epistles of John*
- *Faith in His Name: Listening to the Gospel of John*
- *First Peter: The Salvation of the Soul*
- *A Free Grace Primer*
- *Grace in Eclipse*
- *The Gospel Under Siege*
- *Harmony with God*
- *The Hungry Inherit*
- *Jesus, God's Prophet*
- *Power to Make War*
- *Power to Stand: An Exposition of Jude*
- *Romans: Deliverance from Wrath*
- *Second Peter: Shunning Error in Light of the Savior's Soon Return*
- *Six Secrets of the Christian Life (Second Edition)*
- *Spiritual Lessons from the Life of David*

You can purchase these
and other books from:

## GRACE EVANGELICAL SOCIETY

FAITHALONE.ORG
GES@FAITHALONE.ORG
940-270-8827

Made in United States
Troutdale, OR
02/18/2025

29078254R00276